The publisher gratefully acknowledges the generous contribution to this book provided by the Classical Literature Endowment Fund of the University of California Press Foundation, which is supported by a major gift from Joan Palevsky.

SCENTING SALVATION

THE TRANSFORMATION
OF THE CLASSICAL HERITAGE

Peter Brown, General Editor

SCENTING SALVATION

Ancient Christianity
and the Olfactory Imagination

Susan Ashbrook Harvey

University of California Press   Berkeley Los Angeles London

University of California Press, one of the most
distinguished university presses in the United
States, enriches lives around the world by advanc-
ing scholarship in the humanities, social sciences,
and natural sciences. Its activities are supported by
the UC Press Foundation and by philanthropic
contributions from individuals and institutions.
For more information, visit www.ucpress.edu.

University of California Press
Berkeley and Los Angeles, California

University of California Press, Ltd.
London, England

Library of Congress Cataloging-in-Publication Data

Harvey, Susan Ashbrook.
    Scenting salvation: ancient Christianity and
the olfactory imagination / Susan Ashbrook
Harvey.
        p.   cm.
    Includes bibliographical references and index.
    ISBN—10 0–520–24147–9 (hardcover : alk.
    paper), ISBN—13 97–0–520–24147–3
    (hardcover : alk. paper)
    1. Smell—Religious aspects—Christianity—
History.   2. Senses and sensation—Religious
aspects—Christianity—History.   3. Odors.
4. Worship.   5. Sacrifice.   I. Title.   II. Series.

BT741.3.H37   2006
248.2—dc22   2005013451

Manufactured in the United States of America
13   12   11   10   09   08   07   06   05
10   9   8   7   6   5   4   3   2   1

This book is printed on New Leaf EcoBook 60,
containing 60% post-consumer waste, processed
chlorine free; 30% de-inked recycled fiber, elemental chlorine free; and 10% FSC-certified virgin
fiber, totally chlorine free. EcoBook 60 is acid-free
and meets the minimum requirements of
ANSI/ASTM D5634–01 (Permanence of Paper).

For *George Every*
1909–2003

Those who are wise shall shine like the brightness
of the sky, and those who lead many to righteousness,
like the stars forever and ever.

Daniel 12.3

CONTENTS

ACKNOWLEDGMENTS

In May 1983, at a Dumbarton Oaks symposium on Byzantine medicine, Gary Vikan challenged me to fit the prominent role of incense devotion in the Byzantine stylite cults into my work on these pillar saints. Intrigued, I began to collect citations as I came across them, but other obligations commanded my attention. In the fall of 1991, I finally turned to the question in earnest. I found myself immediately disoriented. Whatever assumptions I had brought about incense—notions of sacrifice, or of transforming matter into spirit—were clearly wrong, off-target, secondary, or of little help in understanding the different kinds of evidence, both material and literary. What struck me instead was the issue of smell itself. Until I could get at that, there seemed little I could do with incense and pillar saints, or any other aspect of late antique incense practice. I had occasion to discuss this puzzle with Peter Brown that fall, who assured me that the project was worth a book, not an article. My debt to these two scholars is immense. Not only did they each, at different times, set this project in motion, but both have continued with unflagging support to encourage me through the tangled route to its completion.

Generous fellowships from the National Endowment for the Humanities and the George A. and Eliza Gardner Howard Foundation allowed me to spend the 1993–94 and 1994–95 academic years undertaking substantial research for this book. In different years, Brown University kindly enabled me to engage the help of several excellent undergraduate and graduate research assistants: Michael Foat, Stephanie Downey, Aaron Weiss, Megan Rooney, and Alex Myers all worked on specific parts of the manuscript with me, and to all I am grateful. An academic leave in 2000–2001 allowed me to complete the bulk of the writing. In the spring of 2001, Samuel Rubenson kindly invited me to spend a week in the peerless hospitality of the Faculty of Theology at Lund University in Sweden. It was a critical time in my writing, and I remain indebted to everyone involved for a week of immeasurably rich scholarly discussion (and astonishing food!).

Brown University has been a marvelous place to undertake this project. My colleagues in the Department of Religious Studies, as well as elsewhere in the university community—above all in the Ancient Studies and Medieval Studies programs—have been unfailingly generous with their own knowledge, encouraging and enthusiastic about the book, and ever supportive during my (many) times of doubt. Colleagues in Brown's ongoing Seminar in the Culture and Religion of the Ancient Mediterranean and in Medieval Circle have read and listened to numerous bits and pieces of the book, always with constructive feedback and suggestions. I am grateful especially to Shaye Cohen (now at Harvard), Ross Kraemer, Saul Olyan, Jock Reeder, Barney Twiss (now at Florida State), Muhammad Qasim Zaman, John Bodel, Mary-Louise Gill, David Konstan, William Monroe, and Joseph Pucci. James McIlwain, from Neurology and Medieval Studies, and Rachel Herz, in Psychology, guided me with invaluable insight through scientific material both ancient and modern. In a league all his own, and to a degree I cannot name, Stan Stowers worked with me tirelessly not only on the seemingly endless array of knots and puzzles, but even more crucially, on how to think about and conceptualize the issues in the broadest sense.

A project of so many years gains more debts along the way than one can properly acknowledge. Many people have sent me interesting olfactory passages they have come across, or have helped when I have encountered textual problems or questions outside my own expertise (and in a book like this one, every chapter seemed to raise the specter of the latter). I have especially appreciated the help of: Joseph Amar, Gary Anderson, Jeffrey Anderson, John Behr, Peter Bouteneff, Sebastian Brock, Elizabeth Clark, Nicholas Constas, Brian Daley, John Fitzgerald, Elliott Ginsburg, James Goehring, Alexander Golitzin, Sidney Griffith, Susan Holman, Thomas Hopko, Derek Krueger, Thomas Mathews, Bernadette McNary-Zak, Paul Meyendorff, Patricia Cox Miller, Eugene Rogers, Philip Rousseau, Leigh Schmidt, Alice-Mary Talbot, Stephen Thompson, Arthur Urbano, Lucas Van Rompay, and Frances Young.

I am grateful to my fellow scholars of olfactory history, Béatrice Caseau and Constance Classen, who have graciously shared their work with me as well as their love for this oddly compelling subject. Béatrice, in particular, has been an inspiration at every point. I must include Georgia Frank here, as well, who with her explorations of sight and visuality has been my constant companion in the world of the ancient senses for many years now. Sarah Bassett, Flora Keshgegian, and Constance Furey each with their particular expertise and wisdom helped me with the writing and completion of the manuscript. The bonds of writing partners carry a devotion all their own, and I am profoundly thankful to all three.

Peter Brown has given not only support, but also concrete help, at every stage of this project. He was the first person to read the original manuscript in draft, and has once again welcomed me into the gracious community of his series, The Transformation of the Classical Heritage. At the University of California Press, I have profited deeply from not one, but several superb editors: Mary Lamprech guided me early on, with her trademark clarity, in conceiving and defining the project as a book; Kate Toll bore the burden of midwifery with elegant patience, wit, and incisive wisdom; Laura Cerruti and Cynthia Fulton have carried the final tasks with thoughtful and cheerful efficiency. I thank them all.

In all these instances, shortcomings and stubbornness remain my own responsibility.

Once again, my family has been the source and center enabling me to see this through. My father, James Ashbrook, did not live to see the book finally written, but some of the richest, most satisfying conversations of our life together took place around it. The inspiration of his own scholarship and theological reflection are always with me. My mother, Patricia Ashbrook, has somehow taken up his role while never diminishing the gift of her own singular wisdom. No one has suffered through the hard drudgery of the work, nor shared my profound joys, to the extent of my husband Jim and our daughter Julia Claire. They remain my rock, my refuge, and my firm foundation.

I met George Every in the fall of 1975. I was a new graduate student in the Center for Byzantine Studies at the University of Birmingham, England. George was recently retired from his long career teaching at Kelham College, and newly resident at Oscott College nearby. For the next twenty-eight years, until his death on September 2, 2003, at the age of ninety-four, George played a unique role in my life: teacher, mentor, spiritual guide, *starets*. I am glad that he was able to read this book in draft, and to know its dedication to his incomparable spirit. It seems a paltry offering in return for the grace of his friendship over so many years. Yet, it suits him. No one brought a more delicious sense of zest and adventure to the study of religion and history than George. Memory eternal, beloved teacher!

Portions of this book have appeared in earlier form as articles in various places. I gratefully acknowledge permission from the publishers to reproduce these materials as follows:

Parts of chapters 2, 3, and 6 appeared in "St. Ephrem on the Scent of Salvation," *Journal of Theological Studies*, n.s., 49 (1998): 109–28.

A portion of chapter 2 appeared as "Incense Offerings in the Syriac *Transitus Mariae*: Ritual and Knowledge in Ancient Christianity," in *The Early Church in its Context: Essays in Honor of Everett Ferguson*, edited by Abraham J. Malherbe, Frederick W. Norris, and James W. Thompson (Leiden: Brill, 1998), pp. 175–91.

Part of chapter 3 appeared as "Why the Perfume Mattered: The Sinful Woman in Syriac Exegetical Tradition," in *In Dominico Eloquio / In Lordly Eloquence: Essays on Patristic Exegesis in Honor of Robert Louis Wilken*, edited by Paul M. Blowers, Angela Russell Christman, David G. Hunter, and Robin Darling Young (Grand Rapids, MI: Eerdmans, 2002), pp. 69–89.

Portions of chapter 4 appeared as "Olfactory Knowing: Signs of Smell in the *Lives of Simeon Stylites*," in *After Bardaisan: Studies on Continuity and Change in Syriac Christianity in Honour of Han J. W. Drijvers*, edited by G. J. Reinink and A. C. Klugkist, OLA 89 (Leuven: Peeters Press, 1999), pp. 23–34.

Part of chapter 5 appeared as "On Holy Stench: When the Odor of Sanctity Sickens," *Studia Patristica* 35, edited by M. F. Wiles and E. J. Yarnold (Leuven: Peeters Press, 2001), pp. 90–101.

For biblical quotations, I have followed the Revised Standard Version, unless otherwise noted. Absolute consistency in transliterations has been impossible to maintain. In general, I have used the most familiar forms of names and terms, if such forms exist, or the simplest methods of transliterating phonetically. Specialists will not be pleased, no doubt, but I hope this will help others for whom the worlds of Greek and Syriac are further afield.

ABBREVIATIONS

AAA   Acta Apostolorum Apocrypha

AB   *Analecta Bollandiana*

ACO   *Acta Conciliorum Oecumenicorum*, ed. E. Schwartz. Berlin: de Gruyter, 1924–40. New ed. J. Staub, 1971.

ACW   Ancient Christian Writers

AJA   *American Journal of Archaeology*

AMS   *Acta Martyrum et Sanctorum*, ed. P. Bedjan. 7 vols. Paris/Leipzig: Otto Harrassowitz, 1890–97. Repr. Hildesheim: Georg Olms, 1968.

ANF   Ante-Nicene Fathers

ANL   Ante-Nicene Library

ANRW   *Aufstieg und Niedergang der römischen Welt*

BJRL   *Bulletin of the John Rylands Library*

BMGS   *Byzantine and Modern Greek Studies*

BSAC   *Bulletin de la Société d'Archéologie Copte*

CA   *Cahiers Archéologiques*

CCR   *Coptic Church Review*

CCSA   Corpus Christianorum, Series Apocrypha

CCSL   Corpus Christianorum, Series Latina

CPG	*Clavis Patrum Graecorum*. Ed. M. Geerard. Turnhout: Brepols, 1974–87. 5 Vols.
CSCO	Corpus Scriptorum Christianorum Orientalium
	Scrip. Aeth. Scriptores Aethiopici
	Scrip. Cop. Scriptores Coptici
	Scrip. Syr. Scriptores Syri
	Sub. Subsidia
CSEL	Corpus Scriptorum Ecclesiasticorum Latinorum
DOP	*Dumbarton Oaks Papers*
ECR	*Eastern Churches Review*
FC	Fathers of the Church
GCS	Griechischen christlichen Schriftsteller
HE	*Historia Ecclesiastica*
HR/RH	*Historical Reflections/ Réflexions Historiques*
HTR	*Harvard Theological Review*
JAAR	*Journal of the American Academy of Religion*
JAOS	*Journal of the American Oriental Society*
JCSSS	*Journal of the Canadian Society for Syriac Studies*
JEA	*Journal of Egyptian Archaeology*
JECS	*Journal of Early Christian Studies*
JHS	*Journal of Hellenic Studies*
JR	*Journal of Religion*
JRS	*Journal of Roman Studies*
JSJ	*Journal for the Study of Judaism*
JSL	*Journal of Sacred Literature*
JSNT	*Journal for the Study of the New Testament*
JSOT	*Journal for the Study of the Old Testament*
JSSS	*Journal of Semitic Studies Supplement*
JTS	*Journal of Theological Studies*

LCC	Library of Christian Classics
LCL	Loeb Classical Library
LXX	the Septuagint (to indicate a variant numbering or reading from the standardized biblical versions)
MFC	Message of the Fathers of the Church
MGH	Monumenta Germaniae Historica
	AA Auctores Antiquissimi
	Ep Epistolae
	SRM Scriptores rerum merovingicarum
MPER	Mitteilung Papyrussammlung Erzherzog Rainer
NPNF	Select Library of Nicene and Post-Nicene Fathers
NT	Novum Testamentum
OC	Oriens Christianus
OCA	Orientalia Christiana Analecta
OCP	Orientalia Christiana Periodica
OLA	Orientalia Lovaniensia Analecta
OS	Orientalia Suecana
PETSE	Papers of the Estonian Theological School in Exile
PG	J. P. Migne, Patrologia Graeca
PL	J. P. Migne, Patrologia Latina.
PO	Patrologia Orientalis
PS	Patrologia Syriaca
PTS	Patristische Texte und Studien
RAM	Revue d'Ascétique et de Mystique
RB	Revue Biblique
REB	Revue des Études Byzantines
RHR	Revue de l'Histoire des Religions
RQ	Revue de Qumran
RSR	Revue des Sciences Religieuses

SC	Sources Chrétiennes
SCH	Studies in Church History
SEERI	St. Ephrem Ecumenical Research Institute
SH	Subsidia Hagiographica
SM	*Studia Monastica*
SMAP	Studies in Mediterranean Archaeology Pocket Book
SNTS	Society for New Testament Studies
SP	*Studia Patristica*
SPCK	Society for the Promotion of Christian Knowledge
SSS	Studies Supplementary to *Sobornost*
SVC	Supplements to *Vigiliae Christianae*
SVT	Supplements to *Vetus Testamentum*
SVTQ	St. Vladimir's *Theological Quarterly*
TH	*Théologique Historique*
TS	*Theological Studies*
TU	Texte und Untersuchungen
VC	*Vigiliae Christianae*
VT	*Vetus Testamentum*

A certain perception takes place in the brain,
prompted by the bodily senses, which is then
transmitted to the faculties of discernment, and
adds to the treasury of knowledge something that
was not there before. The eloquent Gregory says
that the mind which is determined to ignore
corporeal things will find itself weakened and
frustrated.

John of Damascus, *On the Divine Languages* 1.11 [1]

The humble one approaches the beasts of prey and
as soon as their eye rests on him, their wildness is
tamed and they come to him and accompany him
as their master, wagging their tails and licking his
hands and his feet. For they smell from him the
smell which spread from Adam before his transgression, when the beasts gathered near him and
he gave them names, in Paradise—the smell which
was taken from us and given back to us anew by
Christ through His advent, which made the smell
of the human race sweet.

Isaac the Syrian, *Homily* 82. [2]

Christianity emerged in a world where smells mattered. They mattered for
what they did. They mattered for what they meant. Smells affected what or
whom they touched, rendering the encounter attractive, repulsive, soothing or
dangerous. Smells revealed things about the object, person, or place from
which they wafted. Smells mattered because they were invisible, because they
were transitory, because they were mobile, because they lingered, because of
their potency to change substance or experience or meaning. Throughout the
cultures of the ancient Mediterranean regions, a common understanding prevailed that sensory experiences carried effective power for good and for ill in
physical, social, and political terms; further, that sensory experiences carried
cosmological significance, ordering human life within the cosmos. The place of
smell in these cultures demonstrated just such an understanding.

Ancient Christians shared in broad traditions regarding olfactory sensibilities, indications, and practices. From one end of the Mediterranean to the other as far as ancient memory stretched, good smells were associated with all that was "good" in life and beyond: good food, good health, good relationships, incorruptibility, immortality, divine presence, divine favor. In turn, bad smells indicated the reverse: ill health, decay, disorder, disfavor, mortality, evil inclination, destruction. Furthermore, there was general agreement across Mediterranean peoples as to what constituted good and bad smells, enabling the proliferation of olfactory practices that displayed and expressed these associations as cultural codes. These codes were not based on symbolism as a disembodied language, but on the concrete view that smells participated in effecting the processes they represented. Odors could cleanse, purify, ward off, or heal; they could contaminate, pollute, endanger. Medical science, mythology, social systems, and ritual practices converged to sustain this olfactory orientation across the Mediterranean world.

To the ancient mind, then, odors fair and foul could order and classify human relations in the social or political spheres, as well as human-divine interaction. Such an orientation toward smells was gained through cultural habits. Christians utilized those habits, drawing upon them as instruments by which to construct experiences, practices, and meanings that would yield a distinctly Christian worldview and identity in the midst of the huge and variegated population that interacted in the Mediterranean regions. By holding up the familiar, by articulating and demarcating its possibilities, Christians could realign patterns of the common olfactory legacy and reconfigure their consequences for social meaning.

Earliest Christianity was characterized by an austerity in its religious practices, both in ritual and in devotional piety, in keeping with its general alienation from worldly (non-Christian) order. With its legalization and subsequent shift to political and social domination in the Roman Empire over the course of the fourth century, Christianity also came to demonstrate a changed relationship to its physical context. A dramatic elaboration of Christian practices accompanied this change, with a striking intensification of sensory engagement. Developments in the uses and meanings of smells were part of the process. By the fifth century, a lavishly olfactory piety attended Christianity in its expressions, ritual practices, and devotional experiences. To name but a few examples: incense, almost uniformly condemned in Christian writings prior to the late fourth century, now drenched every form of Christian ceremonial, both private and public; scented oils gained sacramental usage; perfumed unctions were liberally applied in paraliturgical rites. In ritual activities, homiletic literature, hymnography, hagiography, historiographical texts, and disciplinary manuals, smells were often stressed. For the late antique Christian, odors served to effect changes in moral condition, to discipline the body towards a more perfectly fashioned existence, to instruct on the qualities and consequences of human and divine natures, to classify and order human-divine relation and interaction in explicitly Christian terms.

This book is a study of how Christianity participated in the ancient uses of and attitudes towards smells. Above all, it is a study of how Christians took note of their cultural inheritance, granted it deliberate attention, engaged and changed it for their own purposes. My concern is with the Christian exploration of the ancient olfactory imagination. I will argue that olfactory practices and their development within Christian ritual contexts affected how Christians constructed the experience of smell even at the most mundane level in their daily habits. The results were a distinctive religious epistemology which, in turn, yielded a particular human identity. That is, I will argue that Christians used olfactory experience to formulate religious knowledge: to posit knowledge of the divine and, consequently, knowledge about the human. The two quotations at the beginning of this introduction are statements of this understanding. John of Damascus reminded his readers that sensory experiences provided knowledge which eluded the rational intellect alone and could not be gained in any other way. Isaac the Syrian evoked the Christian goal: the humble one—that person whose knowledge of God had engendered the life of perfect devotion—was one who had recovered the identity of humanity in its original, prelapsarian condition, an identity made known by its smell. How could olfactory experience be construed in revelatory terms? What specifically could it convey? How and what could be known through smell?

The Christian use of olfactory experience for purposes of religious epistemology was one strategy in the larger process of Christianization that marked the whole of late antique Roman history. As such, this study looks at one strand of a much larger tapestry. I make no claim that smells were more important for Christians than for other religious groups of the ancient Mediterranean. Rather, I will argue for the distinctive ways by which Christians utilized olfactory practices and their significations in order to construct a particular identity. Again, I make no claim that smell was more important than other senses in the ancient Christian reckoning, for Christians shared the perspective of their broader culture that sight and sound were the most important experiences of the human sensorium. Rather, I seek to redress an imbalance. Modern scholars, like their ancient counterparts, have tended to privilege the visual in their treatment of ancient Christianity (notably as culminating in the eastern Christian piety of icons), and have utilized the imagery of sight and hearing as dominant themes for analyzing the history of western Christianity.[3] Recent discussions of "embodiment" and of religion as an "embodied" activity have shown a marked interest in expanding our understanding of the role of the senses.[4] For the study of antiquity, an exploration of the "lesser" senses is required if we are to grasp more fully how the ancients understood the body as a whole body, and bodily experience as a necessary component of religion, and indeed, of human life. I choose to focus on smell as a category of religious experience in order to expand our understanding of ancient Christian piety as practices that carried cultural meanings available for epistemological purposes.

When we look at primary sources in terms of sensory experience, a wealth of material emerges that is significant for epistemology and identity both, but which has not received adequate scholarly attention. These materials point towards variegated practices of the Christian community, and not only to explications by theologians or spokespersons who seized the roles of interpreters and teachers. Intellectual, philosophically informed discussion was one aspect of what religious epistemology required in the ancient understanding. But we can learn as much, and sometimes more, by considering the sensory imagery that laced hymnography, or that punctuated hagiographical narratives. Such imagery will have been more commonly encountered than, for example, the highly refined medical (and therefore philosophically cultivated) expositions of Aristotle or Theophrastus or Galen or Nemesius of Emesa.

My exploration of olfactory experience in ancient Christianity has been influenced by several developments in current scholarship. First is the reassessment of early Christian asceticism that has taken place in recent years, in concert with interest in the body as a primary topic for cultural study.[5] This reassessment has cast vivid light on the importance of the physical body in the early Christian world. Much of this scholarship has presented asceticism as a practice involving the deliberate, constructive use of the body by ancient Christians with profound social and political consequences.[6] Nonetheless, there remains a tendency to interpret early Christian asceticism as a "world-renouncing" behavior, in a religion characterized as fundamentally hostile to the body and to physical experience.[7] The study I offer here seriously challenges that lingering tendency. It does so first by bringing into consideration the importance many ascetic texts gave to sensory experience in its ritualistic and epistemological possibilities. But furthermore, current interest in the body generally stands in the context of cultural debates about sexuality, defined at the most basic level in terms of procreative sexual activity and then further with respect to power and relation. The study of sense perception allows consideration of the body, its cultural and social locations, experiences, roles, and functions from a different perspective. This difference in vantage point opens fresh encounters with our ancient subjects, and reveals aspects of their world we have not previously taken into account but which, for the ancients, were clearly essential to their habits of activity and thought.

To add richer texture to the picture, I have found that Syriac Christianity—often cited as generating the most extreme of late antique ascetic movements—also provides some of the most sophisticated olfactory material of that time period.[8] This is true both in terms of preferred literary imagery, and in the extant evidence for the expansion of olfactory uses in Christian ritual (developments in the use of incense, or of holy chrism, for example). Such sensory—and specifically olfactory—emphasis in practice and in rhetoric demands special consideration when its occurrence coincides with ascetic practices of particular severity, or else we are missing crucial aspects of the ancient understanding of ascetic activity. By adding close consideration of Syriac evidence to the more familiar material of Greek and Latin writers, I hope to deepen our knowledge of the cosmopolitan culture of the later Roman Empire and of the diverse traditions that contributed to the Christianity of the time.

A further impetus to my study is that scholarship on early Christian asceticism has often obscured, or left aside, the fundamental religious context of the liturgical community as that in which Christian piety was molded. Yet in the most basic sense, liturgy provided the terms by which ancient Christian writers negotiated the body. Liturgy, like ascetic practice, was a means by which the body was reformed and remade. The senses no less than bodily desires were disciplined and refashioned in the process of the liturgy's movement and over the course of the liturgical cycle. An adequate treatment of early Christian asceticism requires an understanding of its liturgical context as the prerequisite for and continuing base of the ascetic vocation. Liturgy framed the Christian perception of bodily condition, discipline, and transformation.[9] The study of olfactory experience moves this context into the foreground, recasting the contours of discussion to include ancient views of the body not apparent when asceticism is studied in counterpoint to sexuality. The uses and meanings of scents in sacred ritual, their interpretation in mystagogical commentaries, and the analysis of sense perception by ancient theologians for purposes of religious epistemology are areas of inquiry that conjoin liturgy, asceticism, and theology as mutually inclusive domains of experience—as they were for the ancient Christian participant.

From another vantage point, the growing literature on the anthropology and history of the senses demands an application to early Christian materials. Recent studies on the anthropology of smell have argued that de-emphasis or devaluation of olfactory experience is a trait peculiar to the modern west and its specific intellectual traditions.[10] Constance Classen, David Howes, and Anthony Synnott have claimed further that lack of attention to olfaction as a cultural experience impoverishes our ability to understand the richly textured methods by which cultures express the nature and meaning of order and relation in their communities as well as their cosmologies.[11] I have found their work especially helpful in suggesting models by which to approach cultural understandings of sense perception generally, and smell in particular. The groundbreaking historical work by Marcel Detienne in *The Gardens of Adonis: Spices in Greek Mythology*,[12] and Alain Corbin in *The Foul and the Fragrant: Odor and the French Social Imagination* demonstrated how much can be gained when olfactory experience is pursued as a category of socio-cultural analysis (in their respective instances, for classical Greece and for modern France).[13] Jean-Pierre Albert's *Odeurs de Sainteté: La mythologie chrétienne des aromates* has applied their models to the Christian imagination of medieval Europe.[14] More recently, the illuminating dissertation and subsequent articles by Béatrice Caseau reconstruct daily life in late antiquity according to the uses and roles of smells.[15] Caseau's research is a tour de force of historical investigation that continues the work Saara Lilja undertook with classical poetry, but with a far more sophisticated approach to religious activity.[16] Caseau has laid out the cultural spectrum of odors, their uses and meanings, that confronted Christians in their early centuries; and she has traced the ways in which Christians came to appropriate these in both religious and profane contexts. Her use of material evidence is especially helpful for historians as she gives considerable attention to the traffic in spices, the production of incense and perfumes, recipes for different concoctions, and above all medical and hygienic uses of smells. Béatrice Caseau's work stands in relation to the present study as a history of practices in relation to a study of discourse. Her focus on the concrete *realia* of ancient olfactory practices enables a focus like mine on the religious uses of cultural imagination through ritual and disciplinary (ascetic) activity.

With these methodological considerations underlying my study, then, I have organized the material as follows.

Chapter 1 surveys the olfactory culture into which Christianity emerged, including Greco-Roman and Jewish perspectives. It presents Christianity's early austerity in its olfactory piety, as well as its formative explorations of the religious dimensions of smells. In particular, the biblical tropes—both from the canonical texts and from their extracanonical elaborations—are presented as providing the literary paradigms most influential for the outworking of a Christian olfactory understanding. Two basic paradigms governed the development of a Christian olfactory culture: incense as the marker of sacrifice, the process of human-divine interaction; and perfume as the marker of divine presence, signifying the condition of blessing or grace.

Chapter 2 charts the elaboration of Christian ritual in the post-Constantinian era of the fourth and fifth centuries, considering how Christian rituals remade and redefined the human body, sustained its new identity, and provided guidance for individual and social conduct in ritually defined terms. Consistently, I argue, fragrances, their uses and reception, were fundamental to the construction and maintenance of these perspectives. These ritual developments took place in the context of a dramatically changed political setting for Christianity, and were accompanied by a striking reorientation to the natural world and its physical encounter through bodily experience. Liturgical hymnography, catechetical homilies, civic sermons, and hagiography all illustrate the multiple ways by which the lay Christian population was taught to experience the world through the body explicitly as a place of human-divine encounter and relation. The lavish proliferation of incense usage and holy oils that characterized liturgical and devotional developments during this period contributed distinct habits of practices and perceptions, enabling a changed Christian sensorium to be established.

Chapter 3 examines the emergence of a Christian consensus that the body of the Christian in its received experiences and enacted responses yielded distinct knowledge of God. Ancient medical and philosophical traditions provided sophisticated intellectual tools for the analysis of sense perception and its role in epistemology. Christian thinkers engaged those traditions and utilized them in conjunction with biblical and theological resources to seek nuanced and critical understandings of the manner by which sensory experience contributed to a Christian knowledge of the world, the human person, and divinity. The instructive capacity of smell was crucial to this understanding, due to the distinctive qualities of olfactory experience. Invisible, silent, yet tangibly felt, smells were acutely effective in conveying divine presence or absence, demonic activity, or moral condition. Uncontainable, smells were transgressive in movement, crossing human and divine domains as intersecting paths of interaction. Smells provided concrete encounters that appeared to defy articulation or form, yet necessitated a physically informed mode of understanding. Christian intellectuals utilized olfactory experience to explore religious epistemology through practical knowledge and scientific expertise; or as analogies, metaphors, or illustrations from nature. Above all, they engaged olfaction as a bodily sensation that was intrinsically revelatory of identity, moral condition, and divine relation. Framed by such a sophisticated intellectual context, Christian preachers and hymnographers could employ concise yet highly effective patterns of olfactory imagery in the instruction of their congregations.

Chapter 4 considers how an ascetic discourse extended the ritual process for Christianity, beyond the ecclesiastical structures of institutional practices into the body of the individual believer in its social and political locations. I argue that Christian leaders used an ascetic rhetoric to designate sensory contexts:

where catechetical and liturgical instruction had encouraged sensory engagement within the liturgical or devotional setting, homilists would also, in turn, admonish their congregations about the grave moral dangers of sensory pleasures outside those ritually defined boundaries. Ascetic instruction was used both for the lay congregation and in monastic communities to train the Christian not only in the proper use of the senses, but also in the appropriate location of their sensory experiences. That is, the body of the ascetically trained Christian was rhetorically and ritually positioned so that sensory experiences engaged their liturgical counterparts, no matter where the individual was. The emergence of the "spiritual senses" as a strategy for biblical interpretation developed, in the context of this larger ascetic discourse, to define bodily experience in terms that rendered it inclusive of divine as well as human or natural encounter. Liturgy provided the practices and images used to frame the ascetic's activities, allowing even the most physically isolated or severe forms of ascetic discipline to be ritually connected to the liturgical life of the larger ecclesiastical community. Olfactory piety and imagery were again the most consistent vehicles for this reorientation of Christian sensory experience.

To illustrate the intersections of ascetic discipline, devotional piety, and liturgical community, I take the case of the early stylite saints Simeon the Elder and Simeon the Younger, two saints whose cults were characterized by extensive incense practices. The hagiographical depictions of these two saints exhibit strong liturgical patterns as their ordering frames. Incense piety is the clearest marker for this orientation, and hagiographical texts that highlight incense practices tend also to emphasize olfactory experience in broader terms (the smells of wounds, illnesses, relics, ointments, decay, perfumes, heavenly visitations). The hagiographies for these two saints utilize such olfactory references to implicate the body of the witness (the one who heard or read the story) as deeply as the body of the saint itself as a locus for change and redefinition (the experience of the body as redeemed).

Chapter 5 addresses the situation of grave religious tension created by the prescribed (and described) ascetic practices of late antique Christianity. More often than not, these generated odors that seemed to violate not only the inherited system of olfactory codes, but even that constructed through Christian ritual and teaching. The complexities of ancient Christian olfactory culture stand out most clearly in the context of asceticism. How, indeed, was the Christian to understand stench? Although the term "odor of sanctity" captures the ambivalence of bodily smells in relation to holiness, late antique Christians were profoundly dismayed in those instances where foul smells were deliberately employed in devotional practices or offensively yielded through them. I consider how and why foul odors were normatively used in Christian discourse to express moral condition; the stark challenge to such moral ordering that holy stench represented; and the singular articulation of the human moral dilemma it offered, when experienced in the instances of saints who died of illness.

Chapter 6 turns to the telos of Christian knowing. The problem of holy stench in late antique Christian texts leads invariably to the question of eschatology, the subject which underlies the entire liturgical—and conceptual—framework of ancient Christianity. Would the resurrected body of the life to come be a sensorily active one, and if so, why? The place of olfactory experience in ancient Christian anticipation of the resurrected life provides a fitting discussion by which to draw together the social, ritual, contemplative, and literary aspects of this study.

> Religious symbols . . . reek of meaning.
>
> Clifford Geertz[1]

A Martyr's Scent

Around the year 155 A.D., the elderly bishop Polycarp was martyred in the city of Smyrna on charges of refusal to sacrifice to the Roman gods. Christian witnesses to Polycarp's execution wrote a letter reporting the event to their neighboring church in the city of Philomelium in Phrygia. But they addressed their letter further to "the holy Church in every place;" it quickly circulated throughout the Christian communities of the Roman Empire and beyond. By their epistle the Christians of Smyrna intended to render account of the hardships they had suffered in persecution, culminating in the death of their renowned and beloved leader. They also needed to make sense of his death, for themselves and for Christians everywhere.

Accordingly, the letter abounds with allusions to the rich literary traditions surrounding the classical concept of the "noble death,"[2] amply demonstrated with descriptions of Polycarp's serenity, steadfastness under torture, and calm acceptance of execution. More importantly, the writers declared that Polycarp had chosen his death on behalf of all believers and not simply for his own salvation. Overt parallels were drawn between Polycarp's final days and the passion narratives of Jesus of Nazareth. Such presentation depicts Polycarp's death in unequivocal terms as a true martyrdom honorable to divine as well as human eyes.

A further interpretive strategy of the letter was the Smyrneans' use of familiar sensory impressions to articulate what had taken place. The witnesses told of Polycarp's arrest, his brief trial, and his execution in the public stadium of the city in the presence of the gathered populace. Then they described their own experience of Polycarp's martyrdom:

> . . . the men in charge of the fire started to light it. A great flame blazed up and those of us to whom it was given to see beheld a miracle. And we have been preserved to recount the story to others. For the flames, bellying out like a ship's sail in the wind, formed into the shape of a vault and thus surrounded the martyr's body as with a wall. And he was within it not as burning flesh but rather as bread being baked, or like gold and silver being purified in a smelting furnace. And from it we perceived such a delightful fragrance as though it were smoking incense or some other costly perfume.
>
> At last when these vicious men realized that his body could not be consumed by the fire they ordered a *confector* to go up and plunge a dagger into the body. When he did this there came out such a quantity of blood that the flames were extinguished.[3]

The experience these Christian witnesses claimed was one in which their senses redefined the event. The fire they saw enshrined rather than destroyed their bishop. The air they breathed billowed with the aroma of baking bread—the comforting promise of daily sustenance, and for Christians the center of (sacrificial) fellowship in the name of Christ. Moreover, the fire seemed not to destroy Polycarp's body, but rather to purify it as in a crucible, until the air no longer carried the stench of burning flesh, but instead a fragrance as sweet as frankincense, the precious savor of sacrifice pleasing to God. The dove recalled the presence of the Holy Spirit at Christ's baptism (Mk 1:10; Mt 3:16; Lk 3:22), and blood pouring from the martyr's side recalled Christ's own crucifixion (Jn 19:34). Visuality framed this scene, starting with fire and ending with blood. But olfactory experience marked its meaning, as the smells of bread and frankincense signalled the supreme moment of Christian offering ("This is my body . . . broken for you"). With a few, deft, sensory images—a glimpse, a fragrance, a texture—Polycarp's followers rendered a deeply traumatic event into a theological teaching that would become foundational for the emerging Christian identity. Their bishop's death was neither meaningless nor a defeat. Rather, it had been a pure and holy sacrifice acceptable to God. Like the death of Jesus Christ to which it conformed in style and manner, it heralded the promise of salvation, eternal life, for all believers.

Of all the imagery that laced the Smyrneans' letter, that of frankincense carried particular poignancy because of its universal association with sacrificial offering.[4] In the religious systems of the ancient Mediterranean world, sacrifice was the central component of community order and identity. In its most basic sense, sacrifice was a relational activity. The ritual processes of sacrifice established and maintained the relationships that bound the human order to the divine one. Moreover, through ritual roles, functions, and sequenced actions, sacrifice articulated the ties that constituted the human social order. It demarcated distinctions and connections within the local community, and of the local community in relation to larger political and ethnic structures. Sacrifice maintained an ordered cosmos, inclusive of human and divine domains.[5]

From the simple to the complex, Mediterranean sacrificial practices could be—and in ancient texts almost always were—characterized by the smells they generated. Incense was burned along the route the ritual procession would follow, and at the location where the rite was held. Flowers, wreaths, and perfumes adorned altars, cult statues, sacrificial victims, ritual leaders, ritual garments, and participants. Libations added the scent of (perfumed) wine. On the occasions of animal sacrifice, the smell of blood and roasting or boiling meat deepened the multiple aromas.[6] Because fire was a frequent component, these smells were associated further with their accompanying smoke. In the smoke, the combined smells of the ritual process could be seen to pass, literally, from earth to heaven. Lucian described animal sacrifice in just such terms, as olfactorily visual: "A godly steam, and fit for godly nostrils, rises heavenwards, and drifts to each quarter of the sky."[7]

The "scent" of sacrifice was thus diverse, comprised of the offering and all that attended and adorned the sequence of ritual actions. It might be as simple as frankincense alone; it might carry the grand fragrances of extravagant ceremony.[8] But to the ancients—whether Greek, Roman, Egyptian, Syrian, Jew—the savor of sacrifice required "beauty" if it was to be worthy, or even appropriate, for the deity to whom it was offered. Fragrance was itself an attribute of divinity, and of everything characterizing the divine. Gods and goddesses could be recognized by the perfumed scent they wafted; their divine abodes were redolent with sweet scents.[9] Rich flora and fauna adorned the places dear to them in the natural world,[10] and the marvelous utopias of legend where the inhabitants dwelt always in the gods' favor.[11] Those humans whose lives demonstrated exceptional blessing themselves exhaled a wondrous scent, near to the divine as they were.[12] Altars, devotees, and sacrificers bedecked with flowers were known to be especially cherished by the gods.[13] The stench of wounds or illness—marks of human mortality—could invalidate religious activities: in Greek myth, Philoctetes had been exiled on the island of Lemnos when Odysseus and his men feared the stink from his wound would pollute their sacrifices.[14]

Incense was not necessarily the only offering, nor the most important or powerful one, but it was a general accompaniment to sacrificial rituals of all kinds.

Its scent was a marker of the occasion, and in any context "incense" could be a term equivalent to "sacrifice." Unlike animal sacrifice, which provided meat for the priests and community to eat, incense offerings left no usable product. Hence incense was the quintessential example of the whole burnt offering, the holocaust—a cheaper, simpler alternative to animal holocaust, and one that effectively represented the sacrificial process in larger terms. In Roman times especially, it gained exalted status for just this reason. Eunapius described the "poor and humble" house of the philosopher Julian of Cappadocia as so fragrant with incense that it resembled "a holy temple."[15] Apollonius of Tyana offered only frankincense, but could tell from the path of the smoke and the qualities of the fire as it burned that his prayer was accepted.[16] Plutarch spoke with admiration of the Egyptian practice of offering incense three times daily to the sun: resin in the morning, myrrh at noon, and a compound of sixteen spices at evening. The last, he noted, was "not put together haphazardly, but whenever the unguent-makers are mixing these ingredients, sacred writings are read out to them."[17]

The burning of incense was understood to be transformative rather than destructive. It changed the ordinary matter of resin or gum into exquisite fragrance, a substance intangible yet perceptible both by scent and by sight of the fragrant smoke. Altered or "purified" by burning, incense travelled heavenward: a physical image of ascent that mirrored both polytheistic and Jewish cosmologies. The image of prayer rising up like incense to the deity was common across religious traditions. Christians themselves cited Psalm 141:2 (LXX 140.2) on innumerable occasions: "Let my prayer be counted as incense before thee, / and the lifting up of my hands as an evening sacrifice!" At the same time, sacrificial incense was not only itself a transformed substance. It had the capacity to transform the human worshipper who offered it, or even encountered it, into a state of exceptional piety. Its lingering scents attuned the mind to devotion and adoration both before and long after the act of sacrifice had taken place. Thus the extraordinary beauty of the temple to the Syrian Goddess in Phoenician Hierapolis was measured by its fragrance: a fragrance that marked the faithful indelibly thereafter:

> An ambrosial fragrance comes [from that temple], such as they say comes from the land of Arabia. And as you approach even from a distance it sends forth a scent that is very pleasant. And as you depart, it does not leave you. Your clothes retain the scent for a long time, and you remember it forever.[18]

Incense carried similar significations in the various religions of the ancient Mediterranean.[19] Christians, however, took scripture as their conceptual guide.

They drew their imagery from the elaborate traditions of ancient Judaism where the smells of burnt sacrifice were remembered as part of their earliest cultic activities, and textually represented in such terms.[20] Cain and Abel had made the first burnt offerings, Abel's acceptable to God and Cain's not (Gen 4:3–5). When Noah offered sacrifice "of every clean animal and every clean bird" after the flood subsided, "the Lord smelled the pleasing odor" and granted divine blessing in return (Gen 8:20–9:1). Incense offerings were prominent in the cultic system institutionalized in the First Temple.[21] In the Second Temple period, the prescriptions of Exodus 30, Leviticus 2 and 16 were taken as programmatic and upheld as the ideal in any depiction of proper Jewish worship thereafter.[22] Jews used these passages as their guides, whether opposing the Jerusalem Temple cult, as did the Qumran communities on the grounds that the priestly line was corrupt; or, after the destruction of the Temple in 70 C.E., when envisioning its reestablishment at some future time.[23] These same passages would also prove foundational for Christian incense imagery, and later, for Christian incense practices.

In their representations of the ideal temple and its ideal use, the biblical texts set incense among a complex of fragrances that served to demarcate sacred space, sacred action, and sacred identity. Exodus 30 gave instructions for building the incense altar, which was to be made of the odoriferous acacia wood. Set in place before the veil of the ark of the covenant, the altar was to be used for incense offerings only; other burnt offerings, or cereal offerings, or libations, were to be performed elsewhere. Incense was to be burned by the priest twice daily, at morning and evening, as "a perpetual incense before the Lord throughout your generations" (Ex 30:8). Instructions follow for making the holy oil with which to anoint the tabernacle, the ark of the covenant, the ritual furniture and implements, and the incense altar, as well as the priests. It should be composed of liquid myrrh, cinnamon, aromatic cane, cassia, and olive oil, "blended as by the perfumer" (Ex 30:25). In turn, the holy incense was to be composed of sweet spices in equal parts: stacte, onycha, galbanum, frankincense, and salt. Both the holy oil and the holy incense were to be utterly exclusive in their usage: "This shall be my holy anointing oil [God commands]. . . . It shall not be poured upon the bodies of ordinary men, and you shall make no other like it in composition. . . . [This incense] you shall not make for yourselves; it shall be for you holy to the Lord. Whoever makes any like it to use as perfume shall be cut off from his people."[24] It was this holy incense of which the high priest was to take two handfuls, "beaten small," to offer once a year at the mercy seat on the Day of Atonement, that its clouds might protect him in the presence of God.[25]

In whatever forms these prescriptions were enacted, holy oil and holy incense gave unique fragrance to the Temple and its rituals. Other fragrances heightened the sensory quality of cultic activity. Cereal and bread offerings were spiced with frankincense.[26] Lamps scented the air with their oil; the cleansing rituals mandated for the Temple area, the priests, and their garments would also have contributed distinctive smells. While animal slaughter and cooking meat are often thought to be the primary odors of sacrifice, Jewish tradition—like that of their Greek and Roman neighbors—set its sacrifices in the midst of air already dense with complex and pungent ritual aromas.

Although we may rightly expect that there was diversity in practice, the ideal paradigm formulated during the Second Temple period restricted burnt sacrifices, including incense, to the Jerusalem Temple. The role of sacred smells in Jewish ritual practices performed in other locations is not entirely clear. Spices were set out for the Sabbath observance, but there is no evidence that they were burned as an incense offering.[27] Archaeological evidence from synagogues of the Roman period may indicate incense use despite the Temple restriction. Whether or not certain implements found in excavations were incense shovels or burners, and whether or not they were employed as such as part of sacred rituals, remain contested questions.[28] Since, as we will see, the burning of incense was also a standard means of cleaning buildings, the presence of implements for that purpose need not indicate more than hygienic usage—which, in a special building, could well have been conducted with special utensils even when not part of sacred ritual. Nonetheless, the centralization of the priestly cultic system during the Second Temple period meant that the destruction of the Jerusalem Temple in 70 C.E. forced dramatic changes in Jewish ritual practices. While certain rituals were eventually relocated to the synagogues, the sacrificial system as a cultic one was not reconstituted in another form. Other activities emerged in Jewish practice as sacrificial in nature. But Jews did not cease to understand themselves as belonging to a religion that practiced Temple sacrifice involving burnt offerings. Instead, burnt sacrifice was understood to be suspended until such time as the Temple would again be built and consecrated. In the meantime, holy tradition upheld the memory of the richly scented Temple: ". . . from Jericho they could smell the smell at the compounding of the incense. R. Eleazar b. Diglai said: My father's house kept goats in the mountain of Machwar, and they used to sneeze from the smell of the compounding of the incense."[29]

Within the ideal put forward in Exodus 30 and Leviticus 16, incense as a component of Jewish sacrificial ritual is shown to have had certain characteristics. Most often (but not always), it was an accompaniment to the sacrificial system and not a central focus. Varieties of offerings were mandated in the Torah: incense, libations, grains, birds, animals. Varieties of functions were identified for those sacrifices: they expiated sins, propitiated blessings, offered thanks, offered praise, marked covenants, defined identity and location. Overall, however, animal sacrifice held a certain primacy. Blood—its shedding, collection, sprinkling, and pouring—was a major concern.[30] Animal sacrifice allowed for offerings shared between God and God's people, when certain portions were burned and others cooked for consumption by the priests or the community.[31] For ancient Israel, its most potent form was the holocaust, or whole burnt offering: that offering wholly destroyed and thereby wholly given to God. In biblical texts, incense offerings were often contributions to sacrifice, rather than its constituent element.

Even so, incense appears to have been uniquely significant in function. Biblical texts apart from those related to the Temple cult refer to incense as a sweet savor pleasing to God. Within the cultic system proper, the Jerusalem Temple itself could not operate as required without it. Incense offerings demarcated temple space as sacred, yielding fragrance unique to the God whose temple it was; incense offerings enshielded and protected its priests at its most sacred ritual, the annual Day of Atonement. The mere scent of incense could image the cultic tradition as a whole.

Alone of the ancient Mediterranean religions, early Christianity followed the customs neither of animal sacrifice nor of incense offerings. These omissions of practice are striking because both were integral to Jewish Temple cult as well as to the many pagan cults of the Mediterranean world out of which Christianity emerged. Yet Christians assumed themselves to be, and presented themselves as, a sacrificing people. Biblical literature provided them a ready means to do so. Clement of Alexandria could give a "spiritual" reading of a biblical text, interpreting it in ethical rather than literal terms, and his reading assumes an audience already familiar with such modes of interpretation: "If anyone object that the great High Priest, the Lord, offers up to God incense of sweet odor, let this not be understood as the sacrifice and good odor of incense, but as the acceptable gift of love, a spiritual fragrance on the altar, that the Lord offers up."[32] Again, Origen could offer a "symbolic" reading, likening the composition of holy incense in Leviticus 24:7 to the diverse virtues that, when compounded together, constitute pure prayer. The relationship was typological. Certainly, he admonished, God had not commanded such elaborate instructions simply to encourage the international spice trade:

> The type of incense symbolizes prayer. . . . For do not think that the omnipotent
> God commanded this and consecrated this in the Law that incense be brought
> from Arabia. But this is the incense that God seeks to be offered by human
> beings to him, from which he receives a "pleasing odor," prayers from a pure
> heart and good conscience in which God truly receives a pleasing warmth.[33]

Yet Christians had no reason to think of themselves as other than a sacrificing people. Jesus and his followers had been active participants in the Jerusalem Temple cult. Jewish biblical traditions provided ample means for interpreting the death of Jesus in sacrificial terms, and allusions to the Psalms or the Prophets that carried such sense were sprinkled through gospel accounts, particularly in the passion narratives.[34] Epistolary admonitions drew on the same motifs, as in Ephesians 5:2: "And walk in love, as Christ loved us and gave himself up for us, a fragrant offering and sacrifice to God." The Letter to the Hebrews directly negotiated the sacrificial heritage of Judaism when it relocated Temple cult into the person and action of Jesus Christ, sacrifice and sacrificer.[35] Revelation 5:8 and 8:3–5 presented incense offerings as continual in the heavenly sanctuary.

The apostle Paul filled his letters with allusions to the Temple practices that he himself observed along with others of the apostolic community, prior to the Temple's destruction in 70 C.E.[36] Thus he described the gifts the Philippians sent to him as "a fragrant offering, a sacrifice acceptable and pleasing to God."[37] So, too, did he describe the consequences of his work: "Even if I am to be poured as a libation upon the sacrificial offering of your faith, I am glad and rejoice with you all."[38] In one particularly trenchant passage, Paul used the olfactory dimensions of sacrifice to indicate the critical epistemological qualities carried by the experience of smell. In 2 Corinthians 2:14–16 he wrote:

> But thanks be to God, who in Christ always leads us in triumph, and through us spreads the fragrance (osmen) of the knowledge of him everywhere. For we are the aroma (euodia) of Christ to God among those who are being saved and among those who are perishing, to one a fragrance (osme) from death to death, to the other a fragrance (osme) from life to life.

Scholars have long debated Paul's use of imagery in this passage, and the degree to which its sacrificial language drew more strongly from Jewish or pagan practices.[39] Some have wished to see it as evidence for distinctive ritual anointings in the earliest Christian communities, although there is little evidence to support such a view.[40] Rather, in literary terms, Paul engages a number of topoi familiar from both biblical and philosophical traditions: the notion that divine Wisdom gives forth a fragrance, or that virtue itself yields fragrance;[41] that divine knowledge yields moral transformation in the one who receives it, and so, too, that the wise person's speech or character has a transformative impact on his or her followers; the belief that inhaling the breath of a divinity, or of a wise person, can instill wisdom or virtue.[42] These were the same topoi to be used, for example, when Ignatius of Antioch instructed the Ephesians, "For this reason did the Lord receive ointment on his head (Mt 26:6–7) that he might breathe immortality on the Church. Be not anointed with the evil odor of the doctrine of the prince of this world."[43] These motifs will appear often in the course of this book, and I will consider their resonances in different contexts in due course.

At this point, however, it is worth noting how Paul's imagery in 2 Corinthians 2:14–16 engaged the simple processes of olfactory encounter to represent the progression of divine revelation in human history.[44] Here Paul takes the essential action of sacrifice, the forging of relationship through an offering; that action he characterizes by its resulting smell. The smell is a "good odor" (*euodia*) because it is yielded by the action that binds Christ to God. By this "good odor" alone, one can recognize God—have "knowledge of him"—even in the absence of any visible or explicit presence. Further, as with any smell, this "good odor" travels afar ("everywhere"), spreading its signification ("knowledge of him") as it goes. The apostles are the bodied enactment of this olfactory process, for they travel abroad spreading the gospel of Christ's sacrifice in exactly the same way that the aroma of a sacrifice wafts far beyond altar or temple precinct, invisibly yet tangibly encountered. But Paul does more with these images, using a further, crucial aspect of olfactory experience to express the difficulties of the apostolic effort: smells are ambiguous in their effects. Perception of a smell, reception of its qualities, will not be uniformly experienced. A sweet odor to one person will be malodorous to another. To some people, then, the "aroma of Christ" will seem foul, a perception that proves the falsity of their understanding and will lead therefore "from death to death." To others, this aroma will be experienced as truly "good": already open to God's initiative, these people will be led "from life to life." Paul's statement here identifies the importance of Christ's relationship to God, the revelatory quality of that relationship, and the nature of apostolic activity, all by invoking fundamental aspects of ancient olfactory experience—its indication of relationship (sacrifice), its capacity to convey knowledge, and its ambiguous effect upon those receiving it. As we will see, this text more than any other scriptural passage provided the ancient Christian paradigms for considering the experience of smell.

The New Testament rhetoric of sacrifice was formulated in a context actively engaged in Jewish sacrificial traditions. When the Temple was destroyed, there was no immediate conviction of change to the nature of the Jewish ritual activities, but rather the suspension of cultic practices until such time as the Temple would be reconstituted. As Christians and Jews clarified and hardened their separate religious identities, Christians already had a biblical inheritance in which the sacrificial language and imagery of the Hebrew Bible were recast for their use through the writings of the earliest Christian communities. As in the Letter to the Hebrews, Christians could—and did—see traditional sacrificial practices, whether Jewish or pagan, to be superseded by the actions of Christ. Paul's letters gave Christians models for seeing their biblical inheritance embodied in their own activities on behalf of the gospel message. Sacrifice was one theme used to characterize the communion ritual of bread and wine that Christians celebrated, and by the third century had become its dominant motif. The flexibility and variety of sacrificial imagery available to early Christian writers is as evident as it is pervasive in the extant texts, demonstrating that sacrificial motifs could allow for wide variations in application. Christians understood themselves to belong to a religion in which sacrifice was a central activity.

Most poignantly, sacrifice was the obvious language by which to eulogize those Christians who died in persecution, as in the case of Polycarp. Paul had used it for himself; so, too, did Ignatius of Antioch employ its imagery for his own pending death in the letters he wrote en route to his trial and death in Rome.[45] Provoked by capricious circumstance and at the whim of local governor or imperial decree, persecution was a sporadic but always terrifying threat for Christian communities of the Roman Empire prior to their legalization in 312/3 by the emperor Constantine.[46] Outbreaks brought the arrest and torture of Christians, and sometimes their execution. The order to participate in sacrificial rites was the usual test to which accused Christians were put. As early as Pliny's limited execution of Christians in Bithynia around the year 112, the refusal to offer incense to the Roman gods was a criterion for condemnation.[47] Apostates who succumbed to threats or torture became known as "incense-burners" (turificati).[48]

The death of Jesus at the hands of Roman officials and the martyrdoms of Christians that followed were events that lent dramatic force to the rhetoric of sacrifice that Christians employed as the religion began to form its own distinctive identity and practices. Such rhetoric was concise in expression and effective in its significance: Polycarp was one of many whose deaths were said to have scented the air with a "sweet savor pleasing to God." To represent the martyr as the incense offering was not only to appropriate an ancient religious practice, but further to make the symbolic reading a starkly physical one.

While there was neither occasion nor means by which early Christians could have arrived at consensus on the issue, abstinence from incense offerings in their own rituals seems to have marked the first three centuries of Christian worship. Not until long after their legalization in the fourth century did Christians begin to burn incense in their liturgical gatherings and private devotional practices. The abstention is notable not only for its singularity in Mediterranean religious practice, but further in light of the lavish incense piety that late antique Christianity would subsequently develop. Yet from the view of discourse, at least, there was no discontinuity in Christian rituals whether incense was used or not. The language by which Christians characterized themselves and their religious practices across these first centuries was consistently one that used the rhetoric of sacrifice—and often the imagery of incense—to express identity and meaning.[49] Commenting on Malachi 1:11, "For from the rising of the sun to its setting my name is great among the nations, and in every place incense is offered to my name, and a pure offering," Irenaeus wrote:

> The oblation of the church, therefore, which the Lord commanded to be offered throughout the world, has been accounted by God a pure sacrifice and is acceptable to Him. . . . And the class of oblations in general has not been done away with, for there were oblations then, and there are oblations now; there were sacrifices among the People, there are sacrifices in the church. Rather, the kind alone has been changed.[50]

Christians were indeed a sacrificing people. The aroma of bread adorned their altars; the odor of burning flesh accompanied their martyrs. Christians used these smells to explain their actions and interpret the events they experienced; they articulated them specifically as the smells of sacrifice. What could be accomplished through such a sensibility?

Sacrifice: The Aroma of Relation

When Polycarp stood in the stadium of Smyrna, the presiding Roman officials accused him of "atheism." His refusal to participate in the traditional sacrifices meant exactly that in Greco-Roman culture, not because it was wrong to criticize sacrifice as a religious practice but because Polycarp failed to render due honor to the gods.[51] The polytheism of the Roman Empire was for the most part a flexible system; local cults and practices could generally be accommodated into its framework. Imperial religious policy was built upon practices that required the mutual respect for and veneration of local deities, as a reciprocal action between Rome and other cities of the Empire. In Rome itself, the Palatine Hill received numerous shrines and altars for the divinities of the Empire's peoples. In turn, provincial cities and towns performed rites to the genius (guardian spirit) of Rome, to Rome's gods, and on behalf of the emperor.[52] Jews carried a legal exemption from participation in sacrifice because the Empire recognized them as a sacrificing people in their Temple cult, and because of the antiquity of their religious traditions. Jews were legally bound to pray for and offer sacrifice on behalf of the emperor and Empire, a distinction in practice they could accept. Christians were not part of that exemption, and as animosity grew between Christians and Jews their bitter opposition towards each other disallowed the possibility of Christians' being accorded that honor. Whatever other circumstances contributed to the persecution of Christians in specific instances, in Roman eyes a serious matter was their blunt impiety with respect to traditional religious practices.[53] At the trial of the Scillitan martyrs in 180, the proconsul Saturninus admonished the Christians at the hearing, "We too are a religious people. . . . If you begin to malign our sacred rites, I shall not listen to you."[54]

That sacrifice marked the relation between humanity and divinity was a generally unquestioned assumption in antiquity. But what was the nature of that relationship, and what was the appropriate means of marking it? Ancient religions were not uncritical of their own practices. Christianity emerged in an era when Jewish thinkers as well as Greco-Roman philosophers had written at length on the subject. Under the pervasive influence of Hellenistic philosophy, there was common agreement that by nature divinity could not require sacrifice out of any need, since the divine was wholly self-sufficient. Material offerings—food, wine, spices, temples and their ornamentation—were superfluous as far as the gods were concerned. Yet when offered with the proper moral disposition, traditional sacrifices could provide disciplinary or didactic activities for the human community; sacrifices could work to foster greater human virtue—their "requirement" by the gods was for our sake, not that of the divine. Instead, what mattered was to offer a pure heart, a virtuous life. External rituals were meaningful only in their capacity to indicate the genuine offering of the self. Spiritual sacrifice, the *logike thusia*, was a theme that flourished abundantly in pagan, Jewish, and Christian writings of the Roman Empire.[55]

Such discussions included the argument that bloodless sacrifice was morally superior to that of animal slaughter, and served to raise the significance of incense as an accoutrement of religious ritual.[56] The Jewish philosopher and exegete Philo of Alexandria captured the significance of what incense could represent:

> Even the least morcel of incense offered by a man of religion is more precious in the sight of God than thousands of cattle sacrificed by men of little worth. For as gold is better than casual stones and all in the inner shrine more sacred than what stands outside, so and in the same measure is the thankoffering of incense superior to that of the blood of beasts. And therefore the altar of incense receives special honor. . . . The symbolical meaning is just this and nothing else: that what is precious in the sight of God is not the number of victims immolated but the true purity of a rational spirit in him who makes the sacrifice.[57]

Two aspects of Philo's statement are noteworthy. First, he argues that expense or ostentatious ceremony were illusory qualities of religious ritual, for they were mere external components. As such they were deceptive coverings of the heart of the matter, the disposition of the one who sought to approach God. Secondly, then, the purity of that disposition would be the effective—and the only effective— offering to God. Incense could best represent such an offering: it could be simple (frankincense alone, with no other spices), inexpensive, and burned without elaborate trappings. Its primary trait was its scent. Elsewhere Philo scorned the "wearisome labors" of the one who made protracted ritual purifications, followed by profligate adornment of a temple, culminating in a vast bloodbath of victims for the altar. Cultic ritual was no substitute for holiness, nor was God interested in bribery or flattery. Philo exhorted, "Authentic worship is that of a soul bringing the plain truth as its only sacrifice; counterfeit are all exhibitions made by means of external abundance."[58] It was a position shared by the sectarian communities of the Dead Sea Scrolls, whose objections to Temple sacrifice were based on their belief that the priesthood of their present age was corrupt: "And prayer rightly offered shall be as an acceptable fragrance of righteousness, and perfection of way as a delectable free-will offering."[59]

The same sentiments were commonplace among Greek and Roman thinkers, even from otherwise divergent philosophical schools. The Epicurean philosopher Lucretius excoriated the trappings of religious ritual:

It is no piety to show oneself often with covered head, turning towards a stone and approaching every altar, none to fall prostrate upon the ground and to spread open the palms before shrines of the gods, none to sprinkle altars with the blood of beasts in showers and to link vow to vow; but rather to be able to survey all things with mind at peace.[60]

In his treatise On Abstinence, Porphyry, a third century C.E. Neoplatonist, had cited Theophrastus, disciple and successor of Aristotle, in support of the argument that animal sacrifice marked the decline of human civilization.[61] Its appearance in human history was late, Porphryry argued, and due to the accident of famine.[62] Even incense was not original to religious practice, emerging only after civilization had become complex and desirous of elaborate needs; as incense was an intricate compound of spices, so had it seemed an appropriate offering in such circumstances. Instead, the first offering had been the simplest available—the burning of grass, since by Porphyry's reckoning grass was the first and simplest plant to appear on earth.[63] Again citing Theophrastus as his authority, Porphyry admonished that it was not the expense or lavishness of sacrifice that mattered to the gods, but rather the disposition of the one who made the offering: "Hence the sacrifice which is attended with a small expense is pleasing to the Gods, and divinity looks more to the disposition and manners of those that sacrifice, than to the multitude of things which are sacrificed."[64]

Thus when Christians sought to discredit the sacrifices of others, resources were easily at hand. The Hebrew Bible abounded with critiques of the Temple cult; God's rejection of sacrifice was a consistent theme in the prophets and in Psalms.[65] Such passages stood side by side with Temple practice in Jewish tradition, not as a call to abandon sacrifice and sacrificial practices but rather to prevent the view that such practices were a mechanical process to appease God. Instead, the life of the community must accord with God's command; the prescriptions for sacrifice were inextricably bound to ethical precepts. Christians were fond of quoting Psalm 51:17 (LXX 50:17), "The sacrifice acceptable to God is a broken spirit; a broken and contrite heart, O God, thou wilt not despise." In the Hebrew Bible such statements presumed that a "right spirit" could in fact offer sacrifices pleasing to God, and that these were best expressed through the processes of the Temple system performed with the proper disposition. In the hands of Jewish critics, whether philosophical or sectarian, that view was reiterated often in early Christian times. But when Christian writers utilized these statements, they did so as part of a supersessionist view that saw Temple tradition wholly replaced by the work of Christ, and now fulfilled in the ritual gatherings of Christians.[66] Origen, for one, would write, "our altars are the mind of each righteous man, from which true and intelligible incense with a sweet savor is sent up, prayers from a pure conscience."[67] Such usage allowed Christians to draw on the shared cultural codes by which olfactory experience marked a moral cosmology as much as it marked religious ceremony. Hence Origen again: "What better gift can a rational being send up to God than the fragrant word of prayer, when it is offered from a conscience untainted with the foul smell of sin?"[68]

In like manner, when Clement of Alexandria attacked Greek sacrificial practices, he did so by quoting at length from the critiques that peppered Greek comedies. These had openly mocked the Greek custom of burning the inedible portions of an animal for the offering to the gods, while cooking the edible parts for the community feast that followed the sacrifice. Was this "sacrifice," and if so, for whose benefit?[69] Clement satirized the implications of Greek ritual both in terms of performance (should not the cooks be deified? And the stoves be understood as altars?), and in terms of what such an offering must mean about the nature of the gods (if they have no need for nourishment, how and in what way was the smoke useful for them? Do the gods breathe?). Scorning these caricatures as silliness, he replied to his own questions:

> But if the Deity, being by nature exempt from all need, rejoices to be honoured, we have good reason for honouring God by prayer, and for sending up most rightly this sacrifice, the best and holiest of sacrifices when joined with

righteousness. . . . For the Church's sacrifice is indeed speech rising, like incense, from holy souls, while every thought of the heart is laid open to God along with the sacrifice.[70]

Early in the fourth century, Arnobius of Sicca provided a detailed denunciation of incense and wine offerings in pagan rituals, drawing from the whole spectrum of the critique tradition. How could pagans account for the relatively late emergence of such offerings in human history: had the ancients lived in unbroken sin because they had not known these practices? Incense and wine libations implied an anthropomorphism that delimited and degraded the nature of divinity: Do the gods have noses through which they breathe? Can they feel thirst? How exactly could burning incense render honor to the gods— "we are not asking about your point of view but about that of the gods . . . how great is that honor or just what does it consist of, made as it is from the sweat of wood and manufactured from the resin of a tree? . . . Does this, then, honor and magnify those dignities on high?" Wine was poured on the burning incense coals to intensify the sweet fragrance, but to what end: "What, indeed, has a god to do with wine, or what or how great is the power that goes with its essence that, when it is poured out, his sublimity is enhanced, and his authority is supposed to be honored?" Most questionable of all, in Arnobius's view, was the dubious emphasis on olfactory experience by which these offerings were justified. On what basis could people think that odors pleasing to their noses should also be pleasing to deities? "May it not be possible that what brings pleasure to you, may seem to them on the other hand harsh and disagreeable?" And since deities are of diverse natures amongst themselves, how could we suppose they all should have the same likes and dislikes? Finally, what possible effect could "reeking fumes" have on beings who are by nature incorporeal, and thus incapable of sensation or physical relation? Surely these practices prevailed by custom rather than rational examination of truth; as he saw it, the entire enterprise was preposterous.[71] Around the same time, Eusebius of Caesarea also drew on the tradition of using pagan self-criticism to support Christian claims. He cited Porphyry for the view that material offerings were wholly superfluous, if not impure, when approaching the divine.[72]

Often such critiques—pagan, Jewish, or Christian—depicted sacrificial ceremonies in lurid caricature, relying on the variegated olfactory elements that the different components of the rituals would yield to evoke scenes of ridiculous and ineffectual excess.[73] The results were presented as literally suffocating for the participants, who were as likely to choke as to hallucinate from the fumes, according to Tertullian.[74] Indeed, Tertullian commented, while it seemed that some cults worked best through the agency of blood, and others through the agency of odors, the burning of incense was the original and apparently still the most popular form of servicing both divine types; hence the necessity of incense merchants in the marketplace, "For idolatry can more easily do without an idol than without the wares of the incense-dealer."[75]

One such passage appears in the Christian portion of the Sibylline Oracles, but could have been written in Christian, Jewish, or pagan circles. Despite its derogatory stance, it gives account of the intensive sensory—and especially olfactory—qualities of traditional Mediterranean practices:

Having a remembrance of joy in worship,
We walk the paths of piety and truth.
We are never allowed to approach the sanctuaries of temples
Nor to pour libations to statues nor to honor them with prayers,
Nor with delightful scents of flowers nor with gleams
Of lamps, nor even to embellish them with offerings,
Nor with breaths of incense sending up a flame on altars,
Nor with libations from the sacrifice of bulls, rejoicing in gore, to send blood
    from the slaughter of sheep as propitiatory offerings for earthly penalty;
Nor to defile the light of the sky with smoke from burnt offerings,
And polluted breezes from a fire that burns flesh.
But rejoicing with holy minds and glad spirit,
Abundant love and hands that bring good gifts
With gracious psalms and songs appropriate to God,
We are bidden to sing your praises as imperishable and pure from all deceit,
God, wise begetter of all.[76]

Christians drew on these discussions for their own purposes. Sacrificial critiques allowed Christian apologists to justify Christian ritual practice with its culturally discordant lack of animal or incense offerings, and to claim philosophical superiority in the process. The argument about the self-sufficiency of the divine explained Christian abstention from traditional sacrifice, an abstention which had come about by happenstance rather than conscious choice, as already noted. Still, as the philosophical critique of sacrifice pervaded religious writings, Christians used it to render their practices deliberate and distinct. Irenaeus wrote, "God did not seek sacrifices and holocausts, but faith, and obedience, and righteousness."[77] Clement expressed this in more explicitly philosophical terms, "It is for this reason [the self-sufficiency of God] that we [Christians] fitly refrain from making any sacrifice to God, who has provided all things for all, being himself in need of nothing."[78] The position was argued most vehemently, and most effectively, with the assistance of olfactory imagery to signify what philosophers had identified as the intrinsic distortions of traditional sacrifice. Athenagoras explained,

> As to our [Christians'] not offering sacrifices: The Fashioner and Father of the universe has no need of blood, nor of the savor of fat, nor of the fragrance of flowers and incense. He is Himself the consummate fragrance, in need of nothing and self-sufficient. . . . What to me are whole-burnt-offerings of which God has no need? Indeed to offer sacrifices is necessary, but to offer an unbloody sacrifice, a spiritual worship (Rom 12:1)![79]

Clement joined philosophical and biblical proof-texts to explicate how Christian worship fulfilled scriptural requirements despite the absence of traditional sacrifices. First citing Theophrastus, he then interprets Exodus 30:25 on the composition of holy incense for the tabernacle:

> "It is not then expensive sacrifices that we should offer to God, but such sacrifices as are dear to him," [quoting Theophrastus as cited in Porphyry] viz. that composite incense of which the Law speaks [Ex 30:25], an incense compounded of many tongues and voices in the way of prayer, or rather which is being wrought into the unity of faith out of divers nations and dispositions by the divine bounty shown in the Covenants, and which is brought together in our songs of praise by purity of heart and righteous and upright living grounded in holy actions and righteous prayer.[80]

Clement explained the apparent austerity of Christian worship by applying sacrificial rhetoric to the ritual practices Christians did employ, and to the mode of life they pursued. The compound incense mandated by scripture was replicated in the prayer offered by the Christian community: just as holy incense was composed of various and fine spices, so, too, was the prayer of the church "compounded of many tongues and voices," "wrought into the unity of faith out of divers nations and dispositions." This united offering composed out of diversity was offered in ritual ("our songs of praise"), with proper disposition ("purity of heart"). It was offered further in the virtuous lives conducted by the faithful ("righteous and upright living grounded in holy actions and righteous prayer"). As Athenagoras said, sacrifice was necessary. Hence Clement presents the whole of Christian activity, collective or individual, as sacrifice. The same could be said for the functioning of the ecclesiastical community. It became commonplace for Christians to explain the choice of virginity as a sacrificial offering, for example.[81] Special roles within the church structure could also be identified in such terms, as when the *Apostolic Constitutions* enjoined, "Let the widows and orphans be esteemed as representing the altar of burnt-offering; and let the virgins be honored as representing the altar of incense, and the incense itself."[82] Traditional critiques of sacrificial practices allowed Christians to appropriate sacrificial rhetoric in the establishment of their own religious system.

Like Clement in the passage quoted above, Origen interpreted incense to represent aspects of the sacrificial process and the relationship it effected between the human community and its God. In his *Homilies on Leviticus*, Origen cites Leviticus 16:12 in this form, "And he will take up a censer filled with coals of fire from the altar that is before the Lord and he will fill his hands with finely composed incense." On this reading he comments:

> Indeed, our Lord did that more fully [than the high priest Aaron]. For he 'filled his hands with fine incense' about which it was written, 'Let my prayer be directed as incense in your sight.' [Ps 141 (LXX 140):2] Therefore, 'he filled his hands' with holy works which were done for the human race. But why does it say 'finely composed incense'? Because it is not one kind of work, but rather what is pleasing to God is made up of justice and piety, of chastity, of prudence and of all virtues of this sort.[83]

Like Clement, Origen interprets the offering of incense to mean prayer, and the composition of incense to be the compounded offering of good works. In the Levitical mandate, the incense is more precious because of the variety of its ingredients. So, too, is the offering of good works most pleasing to God when it is made up of many and diverse virtues. Origen's treatment of sacrifice, then, focuses on the actions that constitute the offering and its presentation to God. He uses the rhetoric of sacrifice to talk about what Christians should do with their bodies; he does not engage the sensory qualities that sacrificial rhetoric makes available. Hence his discussion of the whole burnt offering follows closely the model he presents for the incense offering. If the incense should be composed of diverse virtues and good works, the whole burnt offering is the giving of the whole self: "Each of us has in himself his whole burnt offering and he himself lights the altar of his whole burnt offering that it may always burn." The total embrace of Christianity is that offering: renunciation of the world, martyrdom, suffering, or asceticism. "[If I have done any of these] I have offered a whole burnt offering at the altar of God and myself become the priest of my offering."[84] From this offering, Origen declares, Christ will "fill his censer with coals" to offer a "pleasing odor" to God. The Christian offers the self as sacrifice; Christ the High Priest takes the choicest of sacrifices and in turn offers them again on the heavenly altar.

Blessed is he whose coals of his whole burnt offering [Christ] finds so living and so fiery that he may judge them worthy to be placed upon the 'altar of incense.' Blessed is he in whose heart he finds so subtle, so fine, and so spiritual an understanding and so composed with a diverse sweetness of virtues that he sees fit 'to fill his hands' from it and to offer to God the Father the pleasing odor of his understanding.[85]

Here Origen names the essential quality of sacrifice to be its offering, an action effected by burning. The burning binds the one offering to the One receiving. The image is vivid and, in Origen's hands, urgent. He links the Levitical mandates to the encounter with Christ on the road to Emmaus, an encounter realized when the apostles remembered "Did not our hearts burn within us?" (Lk 26:32) By burning was Christ revealed, and by burning is sacrifice made; the offering of the self must be a continual act of self-immolation: "Whence will you burn? . . . From where do you glow? Whence is the fire kindled in you?" Heaven forbid, Origen admonishes, that one should burn with the excitement of the circus, or with wrath, or with love of the flesh. "All this is an 'alien fire' and contrary to God."[86]

For Origen, then, sacrifice must be constituted of ethical actions as well as the "spiritual" element of "rational understanding" ("the fragrant word of prayer"). Spiritual sacrifice for him is in fact a concrete activity, an offering of the self that is expressed inwardly through the understanding and outwardly through the actions one performs. The activity of good works declares and displays a right relationship with God: it functions precisely as sacrifice. Hence it is fitting that Christ should take up such offerings to compose his holy incense.[87]

The olfactory dimensions of incense offerings were not in themselves significant in such discussions. Rather, what was important was how one component of sacrificial ritual, the scent of incense or the savor of burnt offering, could stand for the whole process of effecting a relationship between humanity and the divine. That process was discussed by Christians in its traditional representation (the biblical injunctions for the cultic system) and as redefined through the practices and conduct of the Christian community. Incense was an image that could be used to signify the activity of sacrifice, the elements that constituted that activity, or the relationship it denoted—a relationship maintained through the continual repetition of sacrifice as an offering. Most often in Christian critiques of traditional sacrifice, or Christian discussions of spiritual sacrifice, incense imagery was used in this way. Its olfactory qualities were not the point of consideration, although olfactory imagery was often used to evoke sacrificial meaning or signification. Instead, incense marked an activity, a process, and a relationship. For early Christian writers, incense offerings were important *as* offerings and not because they yielded a distinctive smell.

Daily Smells: Powers and Promises

For the social world in which Christianity existed, however, smells were extremely important. They were not byproducts of an object or action whose worth lay in some other of its qualities. Smells were effective agents in and of themselves, whether as qualities exuded or perceived or experienced. Origen acknowledged the situation when he continued his discussion of Christ as the Levitical High Priest who seeks to fill his hands with fine incense. To make sense of the passage in Leviticus and of his own reading of it, Origen had to treat the ingredients prescribed for holy incense.

> Therefore, our high priest, the Lord and Saviour, opens his hands and wants to receive from each one of us 'a finely composed incense.' We must inquire into the kinds of incense.
>
> We must seek 'frankincense' and not just any kind of frankincense but [that which is] clear. The high priest does not want to take something dark and sordid; he seeks something clear. But he also demands from you 'galbanum' whose nature is to chase away harmful serpents by the strength of its odor. He also seeks 'myrrh'; for he wants both our words and our deeds to be purified and cleansed. He also seeks 'onyx' [Ex 30:34], with which a certain animal is covered as by some shield and remains unharmed. So also he wants you to be protected 'with the shield of faith with which you may extinguish all the fiery darts of the evil one' [Eph 6:16]. Therefore, he wants all these to be set in order by you . . . [88]

On just such considerations did the Roman marketplace conduct its business. Aromatic products were essential for every aspect of daily life, as Origen's passage indicates. Available in different forms, grades, and potencies, aromatics were used as pesticides to ward off insects, rodents, and snakes; they were cleaning agents, used for objects, places, and persons; they were effective medications or strong poisons; they protected from illness. They sweetened the air of the household, adorned the person with rich scents, flavored foods and wines, anointed rulers, and dressed the bodies of the dead.[89] As ancient writers were not loathe to note, the smells of daily life were strong and thick: serious effort was required to render the person, the home, or the city agreeable.[90] Indeed, olfactory environment provided a measure for distinguishing social classes in the ancient world: the degree to which one could control that environment indicated levels of wealth, status, and power.[91] Athenaeus observed that gender, social class, and moral disposition were all marked by distinct smells.[92]

In the fourth century B.C.E., Theophrastus expressed his frustration that previous scientists and philosophers had failed to provide an adequate account of smell. "Odors (*osmai*)," he wrote, "are due to mixture (*ek mixeos*): for anything which is uncompounded has no smell, just as it has no taste: wherefore simple substances have no smell, such as water, air and fire."[93] The observation says much about what made olfactory experience compelling for Greco-Roman society. What Theophrastus understood to be causative—the mixing of substances, resulting in smells being emitted—in fact captures the olfactory qualities that intrigued Mediterranean cultures: their invisible complexity, their production by blending, their elusive presence. Clement's image of incense as the symbol for the prayer of the church, united out of diverse voices and peoples; or Origen's of incense denoting the compound of virtuous acts; even the witnesses to Polycarp's martyrdom who described both the aroma of baking bread and the sweet spice of frankincense—such images (or metaphors, or interpretations) relied on this cultural sensibility that mixture creates something unique from its constituent elements.

Further, as Theophrastus went on to explain, odors vary in strength, some "indistinct and insipid" and others of "distinct character." Yet they elude proper classification. The very process that produced smells—the mixing or encounter of substances—also yielded a protean result. Smell, he notes, is always ambiguous. While the experience is undeniable, its exact nature escapes any stable sense of order.

> But the various kinds of good or evil odour, although they exhibit considerable differences, have not received further distinguishing names, marking off one particular kind of sweetness or of bitterness from another: we speak of an odour as pungent, powerful, faint, sweet, or heavy, though some of these descriptions apply to evil-smelling things as well as to those which have a good odour.[94]

Despite, or rather because of, this elusive complexity, smells could map an ordered cosmology.[95] As Theophrastus charted them, smells conveyed an orientation underlying the basic pan-Mediterranean olfactory codes throughout antiquity:

> Putridity however is a general term, applied, one may say, to anything which is subject to decay: for anything which is decomposing has an evil odour . . . things that have been cooked, delicate things, and things which are least of an earthy nature have a good odour (odour being a matter of exhalation).[96]

The pattern of linking bad things with bad smells and good things with good smells was a common sensibility throughout the ancient world. Its associations are most easily demonstrated in the realm of myth, legend, and folklore, where this coding corresponds to the realms of mortality (wetness, coldness, decay, rot, illness, wounds, disintegration, death, destruction) and immortality (dryness, heat, preservation, vitality, health, bounty, beauty).[97] The pattern was reinforced, for example, by religious practices that utilized different smells, fair and foul, for ritual purposes; and justified by scientific analysis, as here by the observations of Theophrastus. Indeed, elsewhere Theophrastus would note that the "most excellent and fragrant" plants grow in sunny, hot climates; while nothing useful for perfumes can be grown in Europe (notoriously cold and wet in climate) except the iris flower.[98] Yet any consideration of how the ancients used smells for practical purposes quickly confronts the fact that this scheme is most often a muddied one. In the elusive ambiguity of smell—the trait that allowed the same descriptions for odors both pleasing and repulsive—lay its distinctive capabilities. Smell was potent because it defied control: it could not be confined in space any more than it could be classified into unequivocal categories.

Nor did anyone doubt the power of smell as an effective agent. Simply breathing bad air was known to be noxious to one's health.[99] Odors were critical indicators in medical diagnosis;[100] both foul and sweet-smelling substances were essential to cure the disordered female body.[101] Spiced wine mingled with frankincense could drive elephants mad, even if militarily trained;[102] wild beasts could be lulled to sleep with flower petals and aromatics.[103] Perfume was lethal to vultures, a bird that lived on putrid carrion, but could tame an entire flock of doves.[104] Panthers could emit a sweet scent by which to beguile their prey.[105] The ancient industry of aromatics was less an attempt to harness the powers of smells than to participate in their abundance.

In his treatise On Odors, Theophrastus discussed the different processes by which scents were made for use: aromatics were blended into spices or perfumes or incense in the form of powders, unguents, ointments, or liquids. Added to wine, perfume enhanced its taste; added to food, cooked or not, perfume spoiled the flavor, making it astringent and bitter. The composition and preparation of perfumes aimed entirely at making odors last; oil bases best preserved the scent (especially olive oil), and myrrh oil was the longest lasting. The scent of flowers was particularly short-lived. Perfumes could be compounded from various parts of a plant: flowers, leaves, twigs, roots, wood, fruit, and gum or resin. Different recipes had rules based on the character of the season, the time of gathering (whether before or after spices were in their prime), and the consideration that some spices needed time to ripen after being collected.

Proper containers were crucial in the matter of preserving fragrances. Periodically Theophrastus notes the medicinal and hygienic qualities of different spices, a topic he would treat extensively in his larger work, Enquiry into Plants.[106] In that work, he provides a "general list" of plants most often used in perfumes—and this well before the expansive spice trade of the Roman Empire: cassia, cinnamon, cardamon, spikenard, nairon, balsam, apalathos, storax, iris, narte, kostos, all-heal, saffone-crocus, myrrh, kyperion, gingergrass, sweet-flag, sweet marjoram, lotus, and dill. "Of these, it is the roots, bark, branches, wood, seeds, gum, or flowers which in different cases yield the perfume."[107]

It would be difficult to overstate the ancient love of aromatic products.[108] Centuries before Theophrastus wrote, the Egyptians had achieved great sophistication in the production of perfumes, scented cosmetics, unguents, and oils.[109] The ancient Near East accounted spices as treasure worthy of royalty.[110] Thus legend had it that spices were prominent among the gifts brought to King Solomon by the Queen of Sheba (1 Kgs 10:2); and the women who served King Ahasuerus of Persia spent twelve months perfuming themselves in preparation, "six months with oil of myrrh and six months with spices and ointments for women" (Est 2:12). Perfumes were the biblical means of deceit no less than of love.[111] Scholars have argued that the Aramaic terms behind the gospel story about the gifts of the Magi to the infant Jesus signified a third aromatic spice in addition to frankincense and myrrh, misidentified as "gold" in the Greek version recorded in Matthew 2:1–11.[112] Continuity in the plant species of the Greco-Roman world led to immense longevity in the medical and domestic use of plants.[113] Modern scholars have attempted to identify the plants named in ancient sources with those now known, and further, to replicate the perfumes or medicinal substances of various ancient cultures as well as their processes of production.[114] The results vary: as Theophrastus noted, fragrances are as fragile as they are powerful. There remain uncertainties, but clearly the practical uses, including medical ones, were sometimes well founded.

The spice trade that had laced the ancient Mediterranean world to the east through India to China, and to the south through the Arabian peninsula and well into east Africa, grew to mammoth proportions during the Roman Empire.[115] Its ramifications were already evident in the first century C.E. when Pliny the Elder composed his exhaustive Natural History.[116] Pliny describes more than sixty aromatics in detail, used for hygienic purposes, for medicines, for luxuries, for worship. Citron, for example, was especially good as a pesticide when storing garments; its medicinal value was great, and the Parthian nobles used its fruit pips to sweeten their breath.[117] The durability of the larger variety of cedar made it a choice (and appropriately fragrant) wood for statues of the gods.[118] Soaking books in citrus oil protected them from moths.[119] Wine kept better when stored in jars and cellars that were frequently fumigated with myrrh.[120] Papyrus flowers were used exclusively for wreaths to crown cult statues.[121] Storax could be burned to keep snakes away from perfume-producing trees.[122]

Two topics of concern to Pliny are particularly helpful for understanding the olfactory context of early Christianity: the perfume industry, and the incense market dominated by frankincense and myrrh. As so often in ancient olfactory culture, distinctions between perfume and incense according to criteria of secular or religious uses are difficult to sustain. Perfumes, which Pliny disdained as wasteful luxury, were everywhere present in ancient religious practices: cult statues and ceremonial wreaths were anointed with fine perfumes, cultic garments were specially scented, and fragrant waters were used in religious rites.[123] Spices were burned to clean and freshen household air. Myrrh was a primary ingredient in many medications and cleansing products, apart from its addition to sacrificial incense or its roles in burial rites. Frankincense was so closely identified with sacrificial rites that the term "incense" could denote this spice alone. But fumigations with frankincense were also among the common treatments for gynecological problems; and the gum was a staple for ophthalmological conditions.[124] Béatrice Caseau has argued persuasively that such practical use of odors was the key to their religious signification and usage.[125] However, the aesthetic qualities of fine scents that ancient Mediterranean cultures valued were also those that made them effective signifiers in religious practices. In both contexts, the salient qualities were beauty, transience, and invisibility (or incorporeality) in addition to their potency as agents. While scenting the body could be done simply—just as incense could be as simple as the fragrance of a single spice (or even the sweetness of grass alone, as Porphyry had argued)—perfumes, like incense, were more valued when complex. Compounds of multiple scents signified exceptional worth, not only in wealth but in effort: their redolence bespoke exotic ingredients obtained through difficult means and arduous transport, and elaborate processes of preparation.[126]

Pliny was appalled by the traffic in luxuries, among which perfume was "the very climax of luxury and the most important example."[127] According to him, the invention of perfume had been the product of human incontinence and greed: the Persians had started it all (decadent race!), and Alexander had introduced its pleasures to the Greeks and Romans.[128] In Pliny's eyes, it had become a ridiculous obsession: people used different perfumes for different parts of their bodies, even the soles of their feet ("how could it be noticed or give any pleasure from that part of the body?"); people sprinkled it on bathroom walls;

emperor and slave alike added it to bathtubs; military standards were anointed with it, and soldiers even used perfumed hair oil beneath their helmets.[129] "Good heavens! nowadays some people actually put scent in their drinks, and it is worth the bitter flavor for their body to enjoy the lavish scent both inside and outside."[130]

Disdainful as he was, Pliny nonetheless named the source of perfume's power: "The first thing to know about [perfumes] is that their importance changes, quite often their fame having passed away."[131] Indeed, perfumes were ephemeral in every sense.

> Perfumes serve the purpose of the most superfluous of all forms of luxury; for pearls and jewels do nevertheless pass to the wearer's heir, and clothes last for some time, but unguents lose their scent at once, and die in the very hour when they are used . . . and their cost is more than 400 denarii per pound! All that money is paid for a pleasure enjoyed by somebody else, for a person carrying scent about him does not smell it himself.[132]

Pliny complained bitterly that by the lowest possible reckoning, the spice trade in his day robbed the Empire of "a hundred million sesterces every year, that is the sum which our luxuries and our women cost us: for what fraction of these imports, I ask you, now goes to the gods or to the powers of the lower world?"[133]

In Pliny's eyes—and those of his society—the trade in frankincense and myrrh was as important as that of perfume, the more so because these two spices were as essential to health and hygiene as they were to the right practice of religion. The demand was such that two harvests a year were extracted for both frankincense and myrrh in the south Arabian peninsula. For both, elaborate rituals accompanied their cultivation, harvest, and transport. Of the Sabaei, the tribe that harvested the two, Pliny wrote that they used the wood of these spice trees for their cooking and in their homes, "so that the smoke and vapor of their towns and districts is just like that which rises from altars. In order therefore to remedy this smell they obtain storax in goat-skins and fumigate their houses with it."[134] Clearly, as Theophrastus had warned, smells sacred in one culture could be problematic in others. Pliny indicates a minimum of 1300–1700 tons of frankincense carried annually into the Roman Empire, in 7000–10,000 camel loads; while a minimum of 211 tons of myrrh, or 1184 camel-loads, entered annually. He estimated that the trade in frankincense and myrrh alone cost the Roman Empire at least 50 million sesterces per year.[135]

The trade in foreign spices would fluctuate and then drop dramatically after the fourth century. But it is worth keeping Pliny's figures in mind, as well as his observations and complaints. I have not lingered on Theophrastus and Pliny because they tell us all there is to know about the use of scents in the Greco-Roman world. Instead, I cite them at length because they represent the contours of the olfactory culture in which Christianity struggled to establish itself. That struggle is evident, in part, in the significance Christian writers of the second and third centuries attributed to their abstention from incense offerings or other ritual scents in their worship practices. But the challenges of daily life during the same period were more difficult. With religious meaning pervasive in every context—hinted in every scent—how could Christians establish their identity apart from their austere religious ceremonial?

Tertullian, for one, argued that Christian and pagan alike must recognize that aromatic products could be validly used without signalling pagan participation in either social or cultural terms. By this position he did not mean a notion of secularity, an understanding alien to antiquity. Rather, Tertullian insisted that Christians could use aromatics on terms appropriate to their own religious identity. As products from nature, aromatics were fruits of God's created order and therefore intended for human use and enjoyment. But the use determined the meaning. Flowers, or for that matter all fragrant substances,

> . . . are pure as being creatures of God and, to that extent, they are fit for common use. Yet it is the application of this use that makes all the difference. . . . if I find the odor of a place unpleasant, I burn some Arabian incense, but without the same ceremony, the same dress, and the same pomp with which it is done to idols.[136]

The razor's edge on which Tertullian stood lay precisely in the problematic territory of ceremony. On the one hand he stated flatly, "Of course we [Christians] do not buy incense."[137] By this he joined his fellow apologists in insisting that Christians abstained from incense in their worship and devotional activities. Yet where was the line drawn? For on the other hand, he mentions more than once the abundance of spices that attended Christian burial rites—indeed, that usage was his defense for the position that Christian practices did not harm the trade economy: "If the Arabians complain, let the people of Saba know that more of their wares and dearer ones are spent on burying Christians than on fumigating the gods."[138]

Tertullian labored to provide guidelines for Christian living that would recognize religious integrity at the most mundane level. "It is immaterial to me, if the same wares—I mean incense and the other exotic articles, which are a sacrifice to the idols—are also used by men as healing ointments and by us, moreover, for solace at a funeral."[139] Nonetheless, extreme vigilance of habit was required. Valid uses of aromatics must be carefully observed lest the Christian inadvertently approach pagan practices; rather, Christians must "avoid even from afar every breath of [idolatry] as if it were a pestilence."[140] To be sure, Christians could not isolate themselves altogether. Private festivals, then, could be celebrated in the familiar pattern even though this would mean abundant scents. In addition to the burial practices he cites elsewhere, he lists the gaining of the white toga, espousals, nuptials, and name-givings as ceremonial occasions at which "no danger can be noticed in the breath of idolatry which is mixed up with them."[141] These were occasions, Tertullian insisted, at which the participants rendered honor to the human person whose celebration it was, and not the divine. Hence one could be present since one would be merely an observer of the required sacrifices and not a participant in their performance. This position posed considerable difficulties for those Christians who were slaves, freedmen, or holders of civic offices, as Tertullian recognized. The painstaking care with which he demarcated what actions could and could not be acceptable for such persons graphically underscores the delicacy of the Christian position in Roman society.[142] Fourth-century church canons would also explicitly address this problem.[143]

Tertullian urged the recognition that among one's most treasured possessions, one should "count also the distinctive religious observances of your daily life."[144] Indeed, he argued that daily life was the reason that marriage between Christians and pagans should not take place. Constituted of numerous religious practices, daily life was a continual exercise of religious identity. One could not be a Christian wife to a pagan husband and fulfill either the duties of household management or the obligations of marital service without serious harm to one's faith. The feasts of paganism would clash with the fasting observances of Christianity; prayer requirements would have the wife at vigil when her husband expects to have her in bed; the Christian duty of visitation to the poor and sick would have her in neighborhoods offensive to her husband's moral code. Her every move would betray the deity to whom her life is dedicated: fasting before communion, making the sign of the cross over her bed or body, exsufflation to cast away demons (and since the pagan gods were held to be demons by Christians, such warding off of evil would be constant). In turn, her every sensory experience would implicate her in pagan practices. Tastes, sounds, and sights would not be extricable from their religious contexts. Most difficult to avoid would be the olfactory assaults. Incense offerings would burn in the house on the first of every month and at the new year; laurel wreaths and scented lamps would adorn the front door to celebrate the imperial cult. Mixed marriage was a series of sensory hazards, wherein the delectable odors (and sights, sounds, textures, and tastes) of false religion would tempt or deceive or taint the Christian partner at every turn. A Christian marriage, however, depends upon two spouses working together as partners in the common tasks of a life of faith. Together they pray, worship, fast, visit the sick and poor, suffer persecution, instruct one another, exhort one another, and sing the praise of God. They are "one in the way of life they follow, one in the religion they practice."[145] Tertullian makes no reference to the sensory aspects that would attend such a marriage. Thus he characterizes them: one type by sensory experience and the other by works.

But there was no escaping the world outside. What jobs could Christians hold without compromising their religious identity? Here, too, extreme care was needed, particularly in jobs at the marketplace. Tertullian insisted that there were certain professions Christians simply could not pursue without irrevocable harm to their religious integrity. Selling frankincense was one. For while Christians might insist that they themselves burned frankincense for no untoward reason (as Tertullian had noted, medicinal or hygienic use was valid), pagans would not, indeed could not, purchase frankincense without servicing their religion at the same time. How could a Christian seller of frankincense do what a Christian was required to do when encountering pagan sacrifices—spit upon the fumes, blow and spit upon the evil powers, exorcise himself—when it was his own supply of frankincense that fuelled the smoking altars?[146] Tertullian shared the view, attested by other writers of the era both pagan and Christian, that sacrificial smoke was never harmless. It might be ineffectual in any attempt to influence the divine, as all our writers have agreed, but it was the food upon which demons fed—the sustenance that kept demons alive. Origen reminded his audience in his *Exhortation to Martyrdom* that performing sacrifice was not an empty gesture or "a matter of indifference." Rather, sacrifice rendered the participants just as guilty as the demons themselves for the evils that would afflict the world, "since demons could not hold out without the rising smoke."[147]

Tertullian identifies the hazards posed to Christians in a non-Christian society. Like Aristides' *Apology* or the *Letter to Diognetus* earlier in the second century, Tertullian insisted that Christians were indistinguishable (most of the time) within the normal workings of society, save by the stringency of their ethical conduct.[148] But when he warns about the dangers of fumes or fragrances wafting from pagan rites—the dangers of what could be breathed in during the course of one's day—he touches a more basic difficulty. One could conduct oneself differently, even follow alternative practices, but one could not prevent sensory experience. Of this problem smell offered the best articulation, for while one could avert the eyes, block the ears, avoid touch or taste, one could not stop breathing. And breathing included olfactory encounter.

Clement of Alexandria was blunt on this point: the senses were problematic whether or not paganism was anywhere within reach. The true Christian (for Clement, the Christian "gnostic") must be focused on the unchanging realm of God. Physical experiences—more precisely, physical pleasures—could fix one's attention to the physical world, distracting the soul and turning it towards the ephemeral. Self-control was the only solution, and that meant control of the senses.

> Otherwise, we may reopen the doors of the soul without being aware of it, through the senses as through unfortified doors, to the very dissipation we had put to flight. . . . The man without self-control is easily led about by anything: eating, sleeping, social gatherings, as well as by his eyes and ears and stomach, and particularly to the point, by his sense of smell. Just as cattle are led by rings through their noses and by ropes, so, too, the self-indulgent are led by odors and perfumes and sweet scents rising from their wreaths.[149]

From this perspective, Christian activities were no less dangerous than pagan ones. Clement was deeply concerned, for example, that the Agape meals Christians celebrated should be simple affairs, and not an excuse for "sumptuous" feasting. For if the host served a meal "exhaling the odor of steaming meats and sauces . . . he desecrates [the Agape's] name by his drinking and self-indulgence and fragrant odors."[150] The Agape should be a repast of heavenly food, "a banquet of the Word." What could be worse than that love or charity, the "agape" proclaimed in 1 Corinthians 13:8–13, should be brought to naught "among all these dainty seasonings!" No, the food should be "plain and restrained," its serving in quantities appropriate for health; then there would be ample amounts left over to distribute among the poor, and the "feasting" would indeed have nurtured love.[151]

Clement was keenly aware that the physical world and its sensory pleasures had been created by God, intended for our good use and especially for our health. Total rejection of these experiences was the rejection of God's good will. The requirement, then, was to live with the gifts God had granted, appreciating but using them in such a way that the self was continually conforming towards its divine goal. From this perspective, Clement admonished, no situation was more challenging for the Christian than that of the dinner party. Good manners were not simply a socially expedient form of behavior: they were the best method of self-discipline in a situation where self-control was tested from every side.[152] Clement was not exaggerating: the Roman dinner party was a feast for every sense. Foods and wines would be judged by their spicing as much as by their flavors, varieties, and appearance; wine would be served in cups made of clay mixed with spices.[153] (On wines, Clement himself noted, "There is the Thasian wine, which is sweet-smelling; Lesbian wine, which is fragrant . . . and Italian wine that is redolent of flowers.")[154] Eating was accompanied by music and often dance from performers themselves as bedecked and adorned as the table: sights and sounds must be as delicious as the meal itself.[155] The good host would punctuate the courses with scented water for washing, perfumes to enrich the air and freshen the banqueters, fragrant wreaths to adorn the guests, and frankincense burning at the table altar.[156] As Clement emphasized, every detail of the occasion was marked by enticing smells: "the devil of gluttony leads by the nose."[157] The olfactory experience was the most difficult part of the situation for a guest to control, and the one quickest to lead astray. The art of good manners lay in moderate enjoyment of the goods without being driven to boorishness. One's behavior made clear the state of one's soul.

> Only a fool will hold his breath and gape at what is set before him at a public banquet, expressing his delight in words. But it is only a greater fool who will let his eyes become enslaved to these exotic delicacies, and allow self-control to be swept away, as it were, with the various dishes. Is it not utterly inane to keep leaning forward from one's couch, all but falling on one's nose into the dishes, as though, according to the common saying, one were leaning out from the nest of the couch to catch the escaping vapors with the nostrils?[158]

Clement writes at length about proper dinner manners: how to recline in seemly form, how to take bites of food and to chew with restrained dignity, how to drink wine, in what size sips (never gulps!) and what quantities, how to position the neck and head, how to shape the mouth into a demure and modest smile, how to belch without offense. Even in the midst of utter decadence, the Christian must radiate the serenity of one who is in no way disturbed by the tumult of sensory experiences that assaulted the diner at every moment. "We have been created, not to eat or drink, but to come to the knowledge of God."[159]

Clement's discussion of Christian comportment contains a fascinating account of the culinary trends of his day. When he turns to fragrances and perfumes, however, he faces a more daunting task. On the one hand, he can flatly state that sweet scents ("of wreaths, of perfumes") were not a necessity for Christians.[160] And he can follow this statement with an excursus on the right reading of the gospel story from Luke 7:36–50, on the Sinful Woman who came to anoint Christ's feet with fine ointment, washing them with her tears and wiping them with her hair. The excursus follows the model Clement had used in treating biblical texts on holy incense: the ointment symbolizes divine teachings and holy works, whose good odor is wafted abroad by Christ and the apostles (drawing on Paul's image from 2 Corinthians 2:14–16). Clement also plays with the word for "oil," *elaion*, as a symbol for mercy, *eleeo* (to have mercy), as a kind of divine pun. Throughout his discussion of perfumes, he returns time and again to the theme of spiritual sacrifice, calling for the "good odor" of holy works and the "spiritual fragrance" of love. "Men of our way of life should be redolent, not of perfume, but of perfection, and women should be fragrant with the odor of Christ, the royal chrism, not that of powders and perfumes."[161]

Yet Clement admits that Christians cannot abstain altogether from aromatic products, since these were known as necessary for hygiene and health. He points out that scented oils are good insecticides, and strengthen the disposition; they soften the skin, relax the muscles, and remove offensive body odors. Myrrh can be a stimulant for the weary, and effective in the treatment of catarrh, chills, and other dispositions. Rubbing the feet with a salve of warming or cooling oil helps with sinus congestion. But "there is all the difference in the world between rubbing oil on oneself and scenting oneself with it."[162] Of course, he chides, there are so many perfumes, available in such a variety of forms—oils, liquids, dry powders, ointments—that one could inadvertently be drawn into profligate use of them. And by the use to which one put scents, one's moral nature could be discerned. "There are women who always exude extreme vulgarity; they keep scenting and sprinkling their bed covers and their houses, and, in their daintiness, stop short only of making their chamberpots fragrant with myrrh."[163] Men, too, could find their noble characteristics emasculated by soft myrrh oil.[164]

Like Tertullian, Clement argues that everything depends on how the products are used. But in a more moderate view than Tertullian's, Clement advocates that there is a right use of perfumes for Christians—a right use that includes sensory pleasure as its justification.

> Yet let us not develop a fear of perfume, like vultures and scarabs who are said to die if anointed with the oil of roses. Let the women make use of a little of these perfumes, but not so much as to nauseate their husbands, for too much fragrance suggests a funeral, not married life. . . . Since we make no allowance for pleasure not connected with a necessity of life, surely let us also make distinctions here and choose only what is useful. There are perfumes that are neither soporific, nor erotic, suggestive neither of sexual relations nor of immodest harlotry, but wholesome and chaste, and refreshing to the mind that is tired and invigorating to the appetite.[165]

Here Clement shows the pragmatism as well as force of custom that worked against an advocacy for olfactory austerity: the protection against predators that perfume provided, and again the custom of (clearly lavish) aromatics in funeral practices. But he argues further a fine distinction between the dangers of erotic desire that heavy scents were thought to incite, and the healthful refreshment that sweet fragrance could bestow. In fact, he noted, God permitted fragrant oils as a relief from the harsh labor of human lives. The pleasure as well as the physical benefit was to be valued and appreciated, although it was pleasure for pragmatic purposes.[166]

In this view, Clement's is a rare voice among early Christian authors. But he does not push the distinctions too far and he is careful to delimit the boundaries of pleasure. Clement, like Tertullian, wrote extensively on the moral decadence of personal adornment, on the hazards of fleshly pleasures, on the lusts easily awakened by any sensory indulgence.[167] He, too, contributed to the rhetorical tradition, shared among the philosophical schools, that utilized sexuality and sexual activity as the trope for desire gone awry or, more fundamentally, lack of self-control.[168] The challenge he raises is his insistence that sensory experience is a good we have received from God, and its pleasures, rightly engaged, a gift divinely granted.

Tertullian joins Clement on this point when both expound the theme in their treatments of wreaths and crowns.[169] Woven of flowers and fragrant leaves, wreaths were a frequent adornment for places and persons in Roman society. They were a mark of honor or veneration, as well as an ornament of beauty. As already noted, they were set at doorways to mark religious festivals; they were awarded the victors in competitions, games, and military exploits; they were worn in civic and imperial ceremonial; they were worn on festive occasions, like banquets. Indeed, Tertullian complained, "the world places crowns upon brothels, latrines, bakeshops, elementary schools, and the very amphitheater; they crown, too, the place where the clothes are stripped from the slain gladiators, and the very biers of the dead."[170] The sheer frequency of wreaths, as well as their association with honor, belied the dangers they presented.

For both Clement and Tertullian, the problem with wreaths was that they distorted the right use of the senses. God had created flowers and fragrant plants for our benefit—for our health—and by their beauty, to be a reminder of the goodness of God's creation. But flowers or leaves could only serve these functions if they could be seen (for their beauty) and smelled (for their effects). When used in pagan rites, wreaths led Christians astray by their fragrance, which marked pagan and not Christian divinity. When used for personal adornment, the dangers were more insidious still. For the wearer could not partake of the benefits available by sight and smell: worn on the head, a wreath could not be seen or properly smelled except by others. Its effect, then, was no different from that of decorative perfume, distracting others with sensual delight and drawing undue attention to the wearer. The wearer thus violated the purpose for which God had made the flowers and given the senses with which to perceive them. Rather than turning one's attention to the Creator, wreaths turned one's attention to fleshly delights only. Clement stressed the essential good of flowers for health and medicine—benefits brought by the sensory impact of plants. Tertullian emphasized the importance of utilizing the senses as God created them to be used: to be filled with the beauty and goodness of creation. Both insisted that Christians should be ashamed of the frivolity of wreaths when considering the crown of thorns by which Christ had won their salvation; and Tertullian summoned the vision of the heavenly diadem that awaited the faithful Christian, of which the scriptures spoke (Rev 2:10, 6:2, 10:1).

In an interesting contrast, Tertullian here argued the significance of sense perception as a means of important religious knowledge. He stressed that God created the senses so that humanity could know and participate in the goodness of the created order as an indication of its Maker.[171] Clement, for his part, lists the medicinal qualities of the different flowers from which wreaths were made, and points out that these qualities are only therapeutic when the plants are properly used for that purpose.[172] His interests are consistently practical. Enjoyment of plants or flowers through their sensory effects was "useful" only insofar as it contributed to the awareness that God had created this world as a benefit for humanity.

Elsewhere, however, Clement discusses the right use of the senses as a means to discipline the self into continual awareness of God. Sensory awareness, properly directed, points beyond this world to its Maker. One should receive sensory experiences and utilize each one as a reminder of the divine; each sensory encounter then becomes first of all an acknowledgment of God, and thus a spiritual sacrifice of thanksgiving. Clement describes this process when answering the question of how the Christian gnostic can pray without ceasing:

> [The gnostic] is far from surrendering himself to the mob-government which tyrannizes over the theaters. . . . he repudiates both these spectacular pleasures and the other refinements of luxury, such as costly perfumes flattering the sense of smell, or combinations of meats and the attractions of various wines enticing the palate, or fragrant wreaths of a variety of flowers which enfeeble the soul through the sense. Enjoying all things soberly, he refers his enjoyment in every case to God as its author, whether it be of food or drink or ointment, and offers to the Giver first-fruits of the whole, using the speech which he has bestowed, to thank him both for the gift and for the use of it.[173]

Clement here highlights the role of olfaction both as an experience affective in its own right, and as an aspect necessarily attendant to the full experience of the other senses. In addition to its own impact on the person, he writes, smell enhances taste and intensifies beauty as experienced through sight or touch. Its perception, or received experience, allows the Christian to remain continually focused on God, for smell therefore affects its recipient even when the recipient does not indulge the other senses (by eating, for example, or touching, or looking). Tertullian had worried about the power of smell to endanger Christians by inadvertently exposing them to pagan practices through inhalation of sacrificial smoke or other fragrances with sacred meanings; simply breathing the smells implicated a person as participating in their offering. The pervasive presence of smell made it a carrier of continual danger. By the same means, Clement draws out the potential of smell to be a constant mode of discipline, an ever-present reminder of God.

These discussions by Tertullian and Clement are of great significance. They provide a rare, early glimpse of how Christian writers will begin to explore the nature and function of the senses in the post-Constantinian period. For here we have the consideration of how the experience of smell *in and of itself* might be important as a means of religious knowledge. In pre-Constantinian texts, as I have tried to show in this chapter, we most often see the body, its senses, and olfaction in particular, treated with respect to how they could be used to live a Christian life. While affirming God as Creator of all, Christians yet understood themselves to be living in a non-Christian world. In the early Christian view, the model Christ had offered was to use the body as the instrument through which to seek eternal life; its purpose was not to focus on this temporary, ephemeral world. The *Letter to Diognetus* had described Christians in these terms: "Their lot is cast 'in the flesh,' but they do not live 'after the flesh.' They pass their time upon the earth, but they have their citizenship in heaven."[174] Within this view, the instructions churches gave their members called them to live as simply as possible and to do good works as they waited quietly for a future life in God's kingdom. Such a life, as we have seen repeatedly in this chapter, should be sensorily austere lest sensory pleasures shackle one to this world. The body was important not for what the senses perceived, but for how one lived in it, for the actions by which one expressed one's faith: fasting, chastity, voluntary poverty, and service to others. As Methodius had exhorted, "whether we act virtuously or commit sin, it is through these our senses that our deeds, both good and evil, are strengthened." Therefore, he urged, "chastity" must be a condition of each of the senses, "causing holiness to shine forth from every one of them."[175]

In contrast to Tertullian and Clement, consider Origen once again on the right use of the senses. Origen, we have noted, viewed ethical action as the valid use of the body by the Christian, and as the proper means of offering sacrifice. His discussion of the "smells" of sacrifice was in fact a prescription for sacrificial relation brought into effect through bodily activity, with little attention to sensory aspects of that activity. So, too, in his *Homilies on Genesis*, Origen admonished his audience to "take up the circumcision worthy of the word of God in your ears and in your lips and in your heart and in the foreskin of your flesh and in all your members together."[176] Declaring that "circumcision" was a relationship with God rendered by a virtuous soul and ethical activity, Origen called further for the circumcision of each of the senses. For smell, this meant: "If someone acquires 'the good odor of Christ' and seeks 'a sweet odor' in works of mercy, his sense of smell is circumcised. But he who goes about 'anointed with the chief perfumes' must be said to be uncircumcised in his sense of smell."[177]

Further on, Origen offers a convoluted etymology by which he parses "Cetura," the name of Abraham's second wife (Gen 25:1–2), to mean *thymiama*, the Greek term he explains to signify "incense or a good odor." He continues his exegesis in kind:

> But let us see how someone becomes the 'good odor of Christ.' Sin is a foul affair. In fact, sinners are compared to pigs who wallow in sins as in foul dung. And David, as a repentant sinner, says: 'My sores have putrified and are abscessed.' [Ps 37(LXX 38).6]
>
> If there is, therefore, anyone of you in whom there is now no odor of sin, but an odor of justice, the sweetness of mercy, if anyone, by praying 'without ceasing' always offers incense to the Lord and says, 'Let my prayer be directed as incense in your sight, the lifting up of my hands as evening sacrifice,' this man has married Cetura.[178]

Other virtues that would indicate a Christian's "marriage to Cetura," Origen continues, are hospitality, care for the poor, patience, gentleness, and the like. These actions constitute the "sweet odor" of sacrifice that the story of Abraham's second marriage is meant to convey. Indeed, in his *Homilies on Leviticus* Origen advocates right usage of the senses in precisely these terms: the Christian must "restore these five [senses] to holy deeds and religious ministries." Further, Christians ought to add "five others which are the senses of the inner man," the "senses" which will allow the Christian to see, hear, taste, and touch God, and to "take that 'odor' about which the Apostle says, 'for we are the pleasing odor of Christ.'"[179] I will discuss Origen's notion of the interior senses more fully in chapter 4. What matters here is that in the *Homilies on Leviticus* Origen presents the "inner senses" as a condition of openness to God's teachings brought about by a "restoration" or correction of the physical senses, a correction instilled through ethical activity.

Recall the letter about Polycarp's martyrdom. There, the Smyrnean witnesses used their sensory experiences of the event to direct their attention away from this world, away from the earthly experience of suffering and injustice enacted before them. Instead, their senses turned them towards their relationship with the divine, a relationship recalled in the sacrificial scents of bread and frankincense. Subsequently, as hinted by Tertullian and Clement, Christians came increasingly to use their senses to direct their attention to this world as God's world. During the fourth century, the world from which early Christians had been alienated in bearing witness to their God would become the world that expressed that witness. After Christianity's legalization in 312/3, bodily experience and bodily engagement will become increasingly prominent in the behavior and discourse of late antique Christians over those of their earlier counterparts. In collective and individual worship, in public works and private piety, in civic, domestic, and monastic contexts, and in the texts that discuss all these, it will be not simply the actions one performs with one's body that matter, but further, the experiences received and known with the body that are valued. The body gained worth for Christians as a means for knowing God.

Dramatic changes in olfactory piety will mark and accompany this shift in Christian sensibility. The rest of this book treats those changes, how they happened and why they mattered. Before we can turn to late antique Christianity, however, one further consideration remains. In general, Christianity of the pre-Constantinian period can be characterized by its sensory austerity, whether in olfactory terms or otherwise. Its rituals and practices did not involve elaborate sensory engagement, and simplicity was encouraged in every context. Discussions bearing upon human physicality stressed bodily activity rather than sensory experience. But Tertullian and Clement raised the question of how sensory experience might be religiously significant in daily life, in the city, in the household, and in the natural world. For them, smells could point to God as Maker of this world, providing a knowledge of God's work and through that, perhaps, a knowledge of God's own self. Smells contained more than the eye could see. How might smells lead to God?

God's Perfume:
Imagined Glory and the Scent of Life

The letter reporting Polycarp's martyrdom had drawn on the smells of sacrifice to construct a particular understanding of what had taken place in that event. Other martyr accounts mention smells of an altogether different ilk. When a group of Christians were martyred in the Gallic cities of Lyons and Vienne in the year 177, their churches, too, wrote a letter about the tragedy that occurred. One of the martyrs, Attalus, was burned to death in an iron chair, the smoke filling the air with "sacrificial savor" as when Polycarp had died. However, when the Christian prisoners had entered the stadium to receive their execution by grievous torture, the witnesses reported this experience:

> [The Christians about to be martyred] went forth gladly; glory and great grace were mingled on their faces, so that they wore even their fetters as a becoming ornament, like a bride adorned with golden lace of many patterns, and they were perfumed with the sweet savor of Christ [2 Cor 2:15], so that some supposed that they had been anointed with worldly unguents.[180]

Here the witnesses saw their companions shining with joy, prepared to leave this world and enter God's Kingdom. The prospect transformed the martyrs, who bore a radiance fit for a wedding celebration rather than the funeral that would shortly take place. The image was apt since Christians received baptism as betrothal to Christ the Heavenly Bridegroom.[181] Death by martyrdom was the relocation of the believer from this world to the next, to that longed-for nuptial union in the heavenly bridal chamber. The witnesses turned attention to what awaited these martyrs beyond their suffering deaths by eliciting a sensation of that to which they were going. The smell of execution was rendered "sweet" by virtue of its meaning as Christian sacrifice to God. But here the "sweetness" denoted more than the action of offering and the relationship it signified; it exuded the beauty of where the martyrs soon would be. Those who watched presented this sensibility as tangible in its effect: heaven's beauty could not be seen in the horrid squalor of the stadium, but it could be sensed— inhaled—as surely as if the martyrs had been anointed with earthly perfume.

Christians, too, shared the Mediterranean perception that divinity was redolent with fragrance. The favorite text, shared by Jews and Christians, was Sirach 24.1–21, in which Wisdom describes how she came forth "from the mouth of God" to dwell throughout creation and take her place among the people of God. Rooted and flourishing like trees, God's Wisdom brought forth her fruits:

> Like cassia and camel's thorn I
>   gave forth the aroma of spices,
> and like choice myrrh I spread
>   a pleasant odor,
> like galbanum, onycha, and stacte,
>   and like the fragrance of
> frankincense in the tabernacle. (24.15)

So, too, the author exhorts, must the true devotee also conduct himself:

> Listen to me, O you holy sons,
>> and bud like a rose growing by
>> a stream of water;
> send forth fragrance like
>> frankincense,
>> and put forth blossoms like a lily.
> Scatter the fragrance, and sing a
>> hymn of praise;
>> bless the Lord for all his works. (39.13–14)

The "sweet fragrance of God"[182] was a scent that Christians knew, and they knew its source. For there was one context in which early Christians savored an intensity of sensory awareness and delight. It was not in this world, a place where sensation was transient and deceptively ambiguous, a place where the stench of tortured death might mean true beauty, or the pleasure of fine scents might mean the destruction of the unwitting soul. Instead, it was where God dwelt, or where God presided. Biblical literature presented early Christianity with another world to explore: a biblical world of immense imaginal proportions. For there was a counterpart to the learned exegesis of Jewish or Christian theologians and scholars. Biblical texts made available to the religious imagination a treasure store of characters, sagas, stories, and traditions. These were explored in the exuberant narrative literature that emerged among Jews and Christians alongside the core of sacred texts that would come to comprise the defined canons of these two religions. Such works fleshed out the skeletal stories, filled in the silences, and worked out the puzzles that abounded in biblical literature. Widely read and tremendously popular, extracanonical texts were a primary means of disseminating the foundational teachings of ancient Judaism and early Christianity in an accessible form. The second century B.C.E. through the fourth century C.E. was a period in which this literature flourished throughout the Mediterranean regions.[183]

It can be difficult to date these "apocryphal" or "pseudepigraphical" works with precision, and in instances based on the Hebrew Bible it is often difficult to establish whether a given text was originally Jewish or Christian. Often these works circulated widely amongst Christians and Jews alike, and in a variety of languages (Hebrew, Aramaic, Greek, and Latin for the older texts; Syriac, Coptic, and other languages of the Christian Orient as time went on). For early Christians, however, these works provided a narrative world wholly unlike that in which they lived. In stark contrast to the austerity of life and worship that dominated the rhetoric of early Christian sermons, treatises, and letters, extracanonical literature offered a feast for the sensory imagination. Thick with sensory descriptions, patently moral in the implications such descriptions carried, these texts allowed the ancient sensory imagination full rein as a means of religious instruction. From the wealth of examples, I take three to illustrate the profound richness of olfactory meaning, in particular, that informed the early Christian sensibility.

1 Enoch appears to have been written between the second century B.C.E. and the first century C.E., by numerous authors at different times. The text contains various eschatological themes, including Enoch's tour of heaven with the archangel Michael as his guide. The Tree of Life and others like it were among the wonders Enoch saw. In the midst of the seven mountains of northwest heaven, he tells us, there sat a throne "surrounded by fragrant trees." The sight alone was astonishingly beautiful, but the scents were overwhelming. Among the fragrant trees,

> . . . there was one tree such as I have never at all smelled; there was not a single one among those or other (trees) which is like it; among all the fragrances nothing could be so fragrant; its leaves, its flowers, and its wood would never wither forever; its fruit is beautiful and resembles the clustered fruits of a palm tree. At that moment I said, 'This is a beautiful tree, beautiful to view, with leaves so handsome, and blossoms (so) magnificent in appearance.[184]

To Enoch's wondering query, the archangel replied that this very mountain was the throne of God, on which God would sit when he descended to visit the earth with goodness. As for the tree of ineffable fragrance, it was forbidden that any human being should touch it before the Judgment Day when God would bring history to its conclusion. Then the tree would be given to "the righteous and the pious."

> And the elect will be presented with its fruit for life. [God] will plant it in the direction of the northeast, upon the holy place—in the direction of the house of the Lord, the Eternal King.
>
> > Then they shall be glad and rejoice in gladness,
> > and they shall enter into the holy (place);
> > its fragrance shall (penetrate) their bones,
> > long life will they live on earth,
> > Such as your fathers lived in their days.[185]

Trees of diverse scents filled Enoch's sight as well as his breath as he travelled through heaven. To the east he was brought near the Tree of Judgment, exuding "the smell of rubbish" despite an appearance like frankincense and myrrh (29.2).[186] Throughout the mountains, there wafted from the trees fragrances that seemed like mastic, cinnamon, nectar, sarara (a kind of balsam?), galbanum, aloe, almond, sweet scented fruits, nard, fragrant bark, cinnamon, and pepper (chs. 30–32). Arriving at last at the Garden of Righteousness, Enoch saw beyond these extraordinary trees many others, "their fragrance sweet, large ones, with much elegance and glorious." In their midst, one stood apart: "And the tree of wisdom, of which one eats and knows great wisdom, (was among them). It looked like the colors of the carob tree, its fruit like very beautiful grape clusters, and the fragrance of this tree travels and reaches afar." This tree, the archangel Raphael informed the prophet, was the tree of wisdom of which Adam and Eve had eaten, causing their expulsion from Eden.[187]

The lushness of this account is conveyed by its olfactory descriptions as much as by its visual imagery. Taste is implicated by the mention of fruits; some of the spices listed were common in cooking, also, but the lists ring more of perfumes, incense, and the aromatics of luxury than they do of culinary delights. The richness of texture defies touch, articulation, or even visual form: it is the scents that overwhelm the prophet, that pervade the celestial realm, and that will permeate the very bones of the righteous with life when the End Time brings the conclusion of temporal reality. Drawn from the descriptions of Eden in Genesis 1–2, the account embellishes a beauty far more sumptuous than had there been related, especially in the lengthy attention to fragrances. But the focus on the smells carries a critical association, for the fragrances of these trees will be the source of life at the end of time as Enoch sees it. The breath of life, once granted in Eden's glory, would be provided again and anew, with irresistible power and a sweet delight unimaginable in the limited world known in history. All this Enoch saw, smelled, sensed, and experienced on his celestial journey. The descriptions stand in vivid relief compared with the discussions of sensory experience we find in other early Christian texts. It is as if the capacity for sensory engagement had been funnelled into an otherworldly sensibility.

And yet the descriptions from 1 Enoch assume the reader will understand, because they rely on scents familiar and cherished in ancient culture. The first century C.E. versions of the Life of Adam and Eve resolve this paradox by presenting spices and aromatic plants as the one element in the inhabited world that had its direct source in Eden's splendor. Again, the text is one of multiple versions, circulated broadly among Jewish and Christian communities.[188] The story's context is Adam's final illness as he lies dying in suffering grief. His son Seth is certain Adam longs for the fruit of paradise; he begs his father to allow him to go in penitence and smeared with dung to beg for some of this fruit to soothe his father's pain. The stench of mortality in its sinful nature is at once counterposed to the delicious sweetness of the divine garden. But Adam exhorts Eve to go with Seth, with dust on their heads, to prostrate themselves in abasement and supplication in God's sight. "Perhaps he will have mercy and send his angel to the tree of his mercy, from which flows the oil of life, and will give you a little of it with which to anoint me, that I might have rest from these pains by which I am wasting away."[189] However, when Eve and Seth arrive at paradise and plead their cause, the archangel Michael comes to tell them on God's behalf that humanity cannot take from the oil of mercy until the Last Days. Instead, they are to return and stay with Adam as he dies. Yet Seth and Eve do not go back empty-handed, for they take with them aromatics spices, nard, crocus, calmine, and cinnamon.[190]

In the Greek version, the story continues as Adam has the family gather round his deathbed while Eve recounts the story of their Fall. In Eve's narrative, wherever and whenever God appears in Eden the garden suddenly blooms forth with plants and flowers in ever greater abundance; again, the sweet fragrance of the air of paradise denotes the gift of blossoming beauty, fecundity, and life. Eve recalls the horror as they received their sentence from God in the presence of the cherubim and prepared for their exile from the garden. In desperation, Adam had wept and besought the angels for mercy, "See, you are casting me out; I beg you, let me take fragrance from paradise, so that after I have gone out, I might bring an offering to God so that God will hear me." Adam's request is in fact religious. He does not request the fragrance of paradise to keep as a comfort, nor to heighten the nourishment they will seek from the meager sustenance of their lives outside of Eden. Adam requests Eden's scent so that he may approach God in the future with sacrificial offering, and the sweet aroma might incline God to a favorable response. The angels must beg God to grant this request, for the fragrances are not theirs to give. As Eve recalls the episode, God's compassion is wide: he grants the gift of spices to be both a means of nourishment and of sacrificial relation. "And God ordered Adam to come that he might take aromatic fragrances out of paradise for his sustenance. When the angels allowed him, he gathered both kinds [i.e., for sacrifice and for food]: crocus, nard, reed, cinnamon; and other seeds for his food." And so Adam and Eve left to make their home in the harsh earth beyond Eden's gate.[191]

Eve's narrative continues, portraying Adam's death and heaven's response. God himself came in his chariot with the cherubim to escort the body to its resting place in paradise, where it would await the general resurrection at the end of time. The celestial entourage is cloaked in the aromas of worship, befitting God's presence but also honoring the one who had died. The religious desires that had compelled Adam's request for spices are here justified, for in this scene the scents of worship, honor, adoration, and life swirl and entwine in billowing waves. Eve describes it, "I myself saw golden censers and three bowls, and behold, all the angels with frankincense and the censers and the bowls came to the altar and breathed on them, and the fumes of the incense hid the sky."[192] When the body had been properly prepared, the angels gathered in their ranks with censers and trumpets, mounting up with God upon and above the winds, carrying Adam's body into paradise. "And they came into paradise and all the plants of paradise were stirred, so that all those born of Adam became drowsy from the fragrance."[193] Laying the body to rest, God commanded Michael, Gabriel, Uriel and Raphael to enshroud it and pour over it "oil from the oil of fragrance." In a final act of mercy, "God sent seven angels into paradise and they brought many fragrances and set them in the earth."[194] The scents of the occasion were dizzyingly multifold, as Eve's narrative had indicated. So rich were the fragrances of paradise's garden that mortals could not endure them undiluted; Adam's family was lulled by the intensity of the scents. God honored and mourned his first created by anointing him with perfumed oil of the very fragrance itself. And God's compassion abounded further, to the granting of spices to the world.

If 1 *Enoch* identified the singular power and beauty of heaven by its distinctive fragrances, the *Life of Adam and Eve* went further. Here the scents of paradise are combined from its natural beauty (blossoming plants and flowers) and the actions that joined its inhabitants in their relationships. Incense was the vehicle of heavenly worship, just as it was definitive for human access to God; it offered glory, it indicated sacrifice (or the relationship of human to divine), it bestowed honor. Oil from the fragrances of paradise—from its trees, from its air—could soothe illness, or adorn a mortal corpse with inexpressible beauty. By granting spices to the earthly world, God expressed surpassing mercy: in their earthly form, the spices of this world could yet give a portion of the unattainable beauty and comfort of paradise. As Adam had known, spices were the necessary means for the right human relationship to God, even as they were essential for mortal sustenance. In their fragrances, the spices of paradise joined heaven and earth, mortality and immortality, alienation and reconciliation, human and divine. This was a story that accounted for the unique significance of spices in religious usage and meaning, even as it diminished the importance (and beauty) of earthly life in comparison with that of heaven. The vehicle for expressing this complex of meanings—indeed, for comprehending the vicissitudes of humanity's relation to God—was above all the experience of smell. In this story, olfactory encounter exceeded all that the other senses could convey; it exceeded what the mind could grasp. Where 1 *Enoch* used olfactory sensation to indicate its scenes of culminating glory, the

Life of Adam and Eve uses it to reconsider the whole panorama that constitutes the created order as it functions in its fallen state. The sensory intensity of these texts, and above all their olfactory richness, have no counterpart in other Christian literature of the pre-Constantinian era.

Following the model articulated in the Life of Adam and Eve, when early Christian writers wished to evoke divine presence in concrete terms they did so with olfactory imagery. Here the invisible and uncontainable qualities of smells made such imagery especially effective. Unseen yet perceived, smells travelled and permeated the consciousness, transgressing whatever boundaries might be set to restrict their course. How appropriate, then, to imagine them crossing the divide between heaven and earth, carrying a whiff of paradisiacal beauty, elusive yet lingering in the encounter they caused. Odors could transgress the chasm that separated the fallen order from God; they could elicit an unworldly sensation of beauty. The Christian witnesses at Lyons and Vienne described the sweet savor of Christ exuded by the martyrs as surely as if they had been anointed with earthly perfume. In so doing, they evoked a sense of the place where the martyrs would soon be with God, its fragrance already spilling over into this world in honor of their glorious witness. This exact sensation was expressed by the Carthaginian martyr Saturus, when he described experiencing a vision in which he and his fellow martyrs entered heaven. There, "All of us were sustained by a most delicious odor that seemed to satisfy us"—the fragrance was beauty and food both, as it had been in the Life of Adam and Eve.[195] In like manner, Syriac tradition speaks of the Holy Spirit's arrival at the baptismal water of the Jordan as marked by sweet aroma, and Pentecost, too, as characterized by a drenching sweet scent; the powerful and unearthly beauty of the fragrance indicated divine presence in either instance.[196] In the Odes of Solomon, the ecstasy the Odist experiences in worship results in a similar sensation, "My eyes were enlightened, / And my face received the dew; / And my breath was refreshed / By the pleasant fragrance of the Lord."[197]

Within this perspective, whatever was truly beautiful in the sensations of this world came in fact from beyond it, while the beauty of the created world was pale by comparison, if not altogether false. The tale of Joseph and Aseneth represents the contours of this piety when the biblical imagination located its stories in the human realm rather than in heaven.[198] Before meeting the mysterious Hebrew Joseph, Aseneth, a young pagan virgin, delights in the beauty of her home, its trees dripping with delicious fruits, its paving stones scented with perfume, and every luxury hers. But Joseph disdains her life, declaring her "anointed with the ointment of perdition," while he himself was "anointed with the blessed ointment of incorruptibility."[199] Chastened and pierced with compunction, Aseneth secludes herself in bitter penitence, seeking to purify her soul until it might be worthy of acceptance by Joseph's God. After eight days of fasting, mourning, and keeping vigil in sackcloth and ashes, Aseneth prays a long and fervent confession to the Lord. In response a heavenly messenger appears, promising Aseneth that she will be made new, nourished with the bread of life and cup of immortality, and "anointed with the ointment of incorruptibility."

Aseneth begs the messenger to accept her hospitality, offering food and good wine "whose perfume wafts unto heaven." But the messenger orders Aseneth to bring him a honeycomb that has miraculously appeared in her chamber, "white as snow, and full of honey, and its fragrance was like the scent of life." Aseneth is puzzled and confused, asking, "Might it not have come from your mouth, since its fragrance is like the fragrance of perfume?" In compassion and blessing, the messenger explains that it is for her to eat, "For this honey the bees of the paradise of delight have made, and the angels of God eat of it, and all who eat of it shall not die for eternity." After placing a piece of the honeycomb in each of their mouths, the messenger burns the rest. The comb is consumed, exuding a sweet odor.[200] Shortly thereafter Aseneth emerges from her chamber, transformed and radiant, worthy of her holy bridegroom Joseph.

Here the true fragrances of beauty are those of worship offered to God as sacrifice (the wine whose odor wafts heavenward), or those out of heaven itself (the messenger, the honeycomb). A life of pure devotion to God renders one redolent with the ointment of incorruptibility; the honeycomb perfumes the air with the "scent of life." In Joseph's initial rejection of Aseneth, it would seem that every earthly beauty is nothing but perdition, of which Aseneth herself reeks; in her penitence she must rid herself of her adornments, her luxurious food, her offerings and libations for her gods. Beauty—life itself—is brought from heaven, its scent travelling from that realm to the earthly one. It wafts from the messenger, from his words, from his gifts. It heralds a life incorruptible, and Aseneth, too, soon exudes its blessing.

Whatever was near to God, whatever was sent or given by God—these were known by their wondrous smells, exquisite fragrances that bestowed life upon all they touched. From God had come such a breath of life. Adam had breathed it. In the early Christian understanding, its scent tinged the created order, renewed each time God caused the separation of earth and heaven to be breached. The stench of mortality, of sin, of decadence or suffering filled the air as humanity inhabited life apart from God. Yet that stench could be penetrated and overpowered by the scent of life that wafted from heaven, or poured forth from God's mouth. This scenario pervades apocryphal and pseudepigraphical literature, as consistently as reticence and austerity regarding the senses characterize early Christian writings. They are compatible views: both insist the wealth of sensory experience lies in what can be experienced of God. In the earthly world and in the earthly life, early Christians claimed, that wealth could be encountered only faintly. Nonetheless, its experience was real, for it could be sensed and thereby known.

The biblical imagination of early Christianity thus shared fully in the olfactory codes of the ancient Mediterranean world. Smells could be deceptive, misleading, dangerous; they could be revelatory, therapeutic, and true. They were essential and basic in religious practices because they indicated what was most essential and basic in human experience: life itself. Hence the association of "good things" with "good smells" and "bad things" with "bad smells" mapped a cosmology that ordered human life and experience in relation to a divine realm perceived as ultimately beneficent (and fragrant). This cosmology yet allowed for immense flexibility and ambiguity, vividly conveyed in the elusive and protean qualities that smells carried or provoked.

The smells that marked ancient Mediterranean religious practices represented and upheld this cosmology, a representation Christians would come to appropriate in their own ritual developments in the course of late antiquity. Indeed, it was because Christians both understood and identified with the intersection between religious ritual and cultural imagination that they could Christianize one of the more haunting ancient myths of the Mediterranean world, that of the phoenix.[201] Once every five hundred or one thousand years, so the story went, the phoenix prepared for its death by building its own funeral bier out of an extraordinary blend of spices: cinnamon, amomum, balsam, cassia, acanthus, frankincense, spikenard, and myrrh, as one version told it.[202] Writers of the Roman Empire added the epilogue that the phoenix then regenerated from its own ashes, and Christians were quick to find here a paradigm, and even a proof-text, for the crucifixion and resurrection of Christ.[203] The crux of the story, of course, were the spices the phoenix chose, for even its shortest telling identified these as frankincense and myrrh, the two spices that encapsuled the entire spectrum of ancient Mediterranean sacrifice. Nature and culture, ritual and myth, life and death—all were held together in the tale of the phoenix, whether in its pre-Christian versions or in its Christian form. To Christian ears this was not only because these were the spices of sacrifice and perfume; it was so because these were the scents that grew in paradise, that God had granted to Adam as a comfort in his fallen mortality, and that heavenly messengers might continue to bestow upon the blessed. Whether in biblical or mythical imagination, whether in Roman or Christian culture, incense and perfume provided the paradigms for human-divine relations.

Pre-Constantinian Christianity existed precariously in a hostile world. Yet it shared fundamental sensibilities with that world. To balance the tension, early

Christian writers most often relegated positive exploration of sensory experience to the realm of religious imagination. The place where the senses could be filled with God's presence was a place located elsewhere than the world in which Christians lived. This historical situation would change. When it did, in the course of the fourth century, Christians would find themselves reorienting their senses to a changed world order. Once again, smells and their meanings would prove crucial guides to mark the course.

The ancient things have passed away,
    And Christ, the son of Mary, brings to light all
    things new.
[O Adam,] Catch the scent of this fresh smell, and
    at once burst into new life.

Romanos, On the Nativity (2)[1]

A New Place

Although scholars rightly stress the continuity between pre- and post-Constantinian Christianity,[2] there is no question that the fourth century marks a huge turning point for Christianity's history. At the time of its legalization in 313 C.E., Christianity represented a tiny minority of the Empire's population. Nonetheless, the legislation passed by the Emperor Theodosius I during the 380s and 390s not only declared Christianity the state religion, but forbade the public practice of any other religion except Judaism.[3] In between these poles of legal identity, Christianity enjoyed the substantial benefits of imperial favor under successive regimes and attained increasing political, social, and economic status within the Roman Empire.[4] Much of Christianity's success in this process lay in its capacity to absorb and appropriate older traditions, or to rearticulate traditional themes and patterns within its own modes of discourse.[5]

Once legalized, Christianity could be publicly practiced and displayed. It could—and did—turn its attention to clarifying and standardizing its institutional identity, its normative teachings, its devotional practices and ritual activities. The process was tumultuous, to be sure: violence characterized the conflicts internal to Christianity as much as its external relations with other religions.[6] But over the course of the fourth century, a changed sensibility came to dominate Christian expression in its various forms. As Christianity laid increasing claim to social and political power, the church also showed increasing empha-sis on claiming the physical world as a realm of positive spiritual encounter through the engagement of physical experience. In this changed situation, the sensory qualities of Christian piety bloomed. The Christian's religious experi-ence in ritual, art, and devotional piety, previously austere in their sensory aspects, became in the post-Constantinian era a feast for the physical senses.[7]

The fourth century brought the emergence of pilgrimage, relics, and the cult of saints; the flowering of church art and architecture on a monumental scale; and the enrichment of liturgy, in which the grandeur of imperial court cere-mony and biblical temple imagery were transposed into the ecclesial setting. Christian ritual added the visual power of pageantry, the tactile richness of pro-cession and prostration to the sound of choirs and the taste of the Eucharist. The fourth century also brought the emergence of monasticism with a grow-ing severity of ascetic discipline. At every turn, Christianity encouraged and engaged a tangible, palpable piety physically experienced and expressed.

By the fifth century all these areas of religious endeavor were marked by generous olfactory practices. Gradually prayers, private and public, then the liturgy itself and every occasion of Christian ceremony became drenched in the fragrance of incense. The aroma once faintly sensed by Christian witnesses to Polycarp's execution now adorned every Christian home, shrine, tomb, church, pilgrimage site, or monastic cell. Alongside the proliferation of Christian incense usages came an equally notable expansion in the use of perfumed holy oils, a use expanded within Christian sacred rituals as well as in the paralitur-gical activities that comprised pilgrimage, the veneration of relics, and the cult of saints whether living or dead. These changes in olfactory piety were not insti-tuted by any kind of official fiat, but rather accrued over time. Archaeological finds, documentary and literary evidence all demonstrate dramatic increases in Christian uses of incense and holy oils during late antiquity, to the point of obliterating the memory of earlier obstinacy in opposition to such ritual adornments. Catechetical lectures and liturgical handbooks of the same period sought to articulate Christian significations to these forms of piety. For they were not new or unfamiliar religious practices; Christians used incense and holy oils in ways deeply familiar to ancient Mediterranean traditions. But they chose to employ such practices, where formerly they had eschewed them, specifically to articulate Christian identity and to serve the tasks Christian ritu-als were designed to accomplish.

This turn in sensory appreciation was not a change in Christian belief about the created order or the nature of the physical world. In part it accompanied Christianity's rise to power and concomitant investment in the world in which it operated. But it also stemmed from the penetrating influence of theological discussions. Earlier apologists and theologians had stressed the physical reality of Christ's crucifixion and resurrection in opposition to docetic views that denied it; and they proclaimed the goodness of God's creation in opposition to dualist teachings that disallowed positive value or salvific worth to the body or the physical domain. The trinitarian and Christological controversies of the fourth and fifth centuries continued the trajectory with the teaching that at the incarnation the divine itself had entered into matter, sanctifying and renewing the whole of material existence. The elaboration of Christian piety in sensory terms was a further expression of this view. Within a century of Constantine's death, these changes in sensibility were everywhere evident. Christians lived in the world as in a new place.

A Revelatory World

Christian apologists had stressed the importance of affirming God as the Creator whose creation was manifestly good. This position was essential to their claim that the Christian God was to be identified with the God of Genesis, who had declared the goodness of his creation at the moment of its making. Occasionally early Christian writers would comment further that as God's creation, the physical world in its beauty pointed to its Maker. This was a sentiment amply expressed in the Psalms, and voiced in early Christian hymns.[8] Hence, as Clement and Tertullian had urged, physical experience could lead a Christian to reflect on God's work and through that reflection, on the nature of God himself.[9]

In the fourth century, Christian writers seized upon this theme with delight. In hymns and homilies they extolled God as one whose every divine action revealed him and made him known. Ontologically, Creator and creation were separated by a vast, unbreachable gap. Yet as God's handiwork, the created universe had an endless capacity to reveal its Maker. Through that revelation, one could learn something of the divine nature itself. "The world," wrote Basil of Caesarea, "is a work of art." What then might we say of its Maker?

> Let us glorify the Master Craftsman for all that has been done wisely and skill-fully; and from the beauty of the visible things let us form an idea of Him who is more than beautiful; and from the greatness of [what is perceptible and circumscribed] let us conceive of Him who is infinite and immense and who surpasses all understanding in the plenitude of His power.[10]

Indeed, Basil's brother, Gregory of Nyssa, wrote that this was the reason why humanity had been created at the end of the six days of creation:

[God] thus manifests man in the world [last of creation] to be the beholder of some of the wonders therein, and the lord of others; that by his enjoyment he might have knowledge of the Giver, and by the beauty and majesty of the things he saw might trace out that power of the Maker which is beyond language and speech.[11]

But creation was not simply God's workmanship. Ephrem the Syrian pointed out that as God's work it was also indelibly engraved by his touch:

> In every place, if you look, His symbol is there,
> and when you read, you will find His types.
> For by Him were created all creatures,
> and He engraved His symbols upon His possessions.
> When He created the world,
> He gazed at it and adorned it with His images.
> Streams of His symbols opened, flowed and poured forth
> His symbols on His members.[12]

Thus nature no less than Scripture revealed and declared God's truth.[13] Ephrem spoke of the Old and New Testaments and nature as three harps on which the Church played the music of Christ, all proclaiming the same God in perfect harmony.[14] Marked by the signs of its maker, the natural world was stamped as if with an artist's imprint.[15] Accordingly, Ephrem wrote, nature, too, participated in God's salvific action for creation by conceiving and bearing God's purpose as Mary did at the incarnation:

> The creation conceived His symbols; Mary conceived His limbs.
> Therefore many wombs brought forth the Only-begotten.
> The belly brought Him forth by travail, and the creation also brought Him forth
>   by symbols.[16]

As Ephrem explained, one such symbol was the cross, which nature displayed among the forms and actions of its plants and creatures in myriad ways. Moreover, nature functioned physiologically by processes which required the cross as their configuration; a bird could not fly if its wings were not outstretched in the sign of the cross.[17] Basil similarly exhorted, "I want the marvel of creation to gain such complete acceptance from you that, wherever you may be found and whatever kind of plants you may chance upon, you may receive a clear reminder of the Creator."[18]

Still, it was not enough that nature should reveal. Humanity must receive this revelation, read nature as it read scripture, hear its song as it heard the harp of David. In Ephrem's understanding, humanity's alienation resulting from the Fall had led to a weariness in nature, an exhaustion born of the discouraging effort to make known a revelation obscured by humanity's sinful state.[19] Christ's incarnation renewed the sanctification of the natural world even as it redeemed the human body. Prudentius wrote a hymn for Christmas Day that offered a similar sense, linking the nativity celebration with winter's turn towards spring. Where Basil had drawn on the majestic rhetoric of Stoic cosmology to expound his sermons on the *Hexaemeron*, Prudentius sounded the lush strains of Latin bucolic poetry and especially Vergil's *Eclogues*. The hymn resonates with the olfactory changes in liturgical practice, for Prudentius stresses the sweet scents that heralded the earth's renewal:

[O Mary], thy Infant's feeble cry proclaimed
The springtime of the universe;
The world reborn then cast aside
The gloom of winter's lethargy.

The earth, I think, with lavish hand
enameled every field with flowers,
And even Syrtis' desert sands
Were sweet with nectar and with nard.
. . .
Now from the rocks sweet honey flows
Now fragrant liquor is distilled
From shrivelled trunks of aged oaks,
And tamarisks yield ambrosial balms.[20]

For Ephrem, this sanctification specifically included the capacity to reflect and encounter the divine within the physical world. Through baptism, the believer entered into the renewed condition of the created order, acquiring "new senses" by which to experience it.[21] The sanctified human body could then receive knowledge of God through its own sensory experiences, could know something of God through its own physicality. In turn, the natural world revealed knowledge of God to those capable of perceiving it through bodily awareness. Thus Ephrem wrote that it was the whole person of the believer, body as well as soul, in which God delighted to dwell: "Your bride is the soul, the body Your bridal chamber / Your guests are the senses with the thoughts."[22] Moreover, it pleased God to provide a world for the believer to experience that

would celebrate the grandeur of God's physical creation, as fitting complement—and as foretaste—to the celestial glory:

> Let us see those things [God] does for us every day!
> How many tastes for the mouth! How many beauties for the eye!
> How many melodies for the ear! How many scents for the nostrils!
> Who is sufficient in comparison to the goodness of these little things?[23]

Cyril of Jerusalem contributed to this picture in his *Catechetical Homilies*, when
he stressed the marvel of the human body as God's workmanship.[24] "Let no one
tell you that this body of ours is a stranger to God," he exhorted, lambasting
those ("heretics") who would insist that the body either could not be saved, or
itself was the obstacle to salvation.[25] Consider, he urged, how each of the senses
was perfectly formed to receive its appropriate experience and enact its proper
task; how skillfully the organs and body parts were woven together, how intricate their design, how fittingly they performed their work. By stressing the
unique worth of each of the five senses, Cyril reminded his listeners that God's
actions were always purposeful. The care with which the human sensorium was
designed was not gratuitous. In a later homily Cyril returned to the theme of the
body's essential role in the salvation process, urging that "nothing is done without the body. We blaspheme by the mouth, and with the mouth we pray. We
commit fornication through the body, and through the body we preserve our
purity. We rob by the hand, by the hand we give alms, and so forth. . . . We must
render account to God of everything we have done through the body."[26]

Within this view, the incarnation set in motion a sanctifying process which the
Christian, once baptized, could experience at every moment of every day. The
process was ongoing, reinforced and sustained through the church's liturgical celebration of the Eucharist. Just as Christ entered the created order at his birth, so,
too, Ephrem wrote, he entered into every person who consumed his holy bread:
"The priests of the churches grasp You in their hands / the Bread of Life that came
down and was mingled with the senses."[27] Sanctified, the body received revelation
from within and without: as the divine was "mingled with the senses," the senses
could then perceive the divine in the world they experienced. Through this process
of sanctification, the liturgy taught not only *how* to experience God with the body,
but further, *what* to experience. Again, Ephrem exhorted his congregation,

> [Christ's] body was newly mixed with our bodies,
> and His pure blood has been poured out into our veins,
> and His voice into our ears, and His brightness into our eyes.
> All of Him has been mixed with all of us by His compassion.[28]

As Ephrem here recalled, the faithful consumed body and blood, bread and wine; received the Word through the scripture readings, beheld divine glory in the worship service. Christ filled the faithful, their bodies, their senses. Just as baptism caused the body to acquire new senses in its rebirth, so, too, the liturgy ritually transformed human condition and location, bringing the faithful to stand, redeemed, in the presence of God. With every sense, they encountered God's presence and God's work. The paradigm was Mary's transformation at the moment when she conceived Christ:

> Although He was begotten, indeed He was in you [Mary]
> so that entirely gazing out from your members
> was His brightness, and upon your beauty was spread
> His love, and upon all of you He was stretched out.
> You wove a garment for Him, but His glory extended
> over all your senses.[29]

It was a grand vision, to be sure; but it was not the whole story. For if the body was the means by which to experience and know one's Maker in every right way, it was also the means to experience and know every wrong element of the human condition—as Cyril of Jerusalem had reminded his catechumens. The true Christian devoted the whole self, body and soul, to God. Yet the consistent human experience was that of a divided self: the soul was willing, the flesh was weak. Even when the soul was steadfast, the body sickened and died. Mortality was the punishment for Adam and Eve's disobedience against God, and therefore a moral condition more than a physical trait. The physical consequences of mortality—sickness, bodily decay, and disintegration—were the direct results of that sin, and hence always the indication of sin's presence. Once again, smells marked the meaning. To be mortal was to reek of sin; rottenness and putrefaction were mortality's nature, revolting stink its unmistakable mark. Wherever such physical sensations were encountered, they announced Satan's continuing presence.

The oneness of the believer had been God's intention, as Christian writers consistently repeated.[30] Cyril of Jerusalem pointed out that if the body were the source of sin, then corpses would sin; hence "the body of itself does not sin, but the soul through the body. The body is the soul's instrument, its cloak and garment."[31] Ephrem, in turn, addressed God from the midst of this tragic division:

> You had joined [body and soul] together in love, but they parted and separated
>   in pain. . . .
> Body and soul go to court to see which caused the other to sin;
> but the wrong belongs to both, for free will belongs to both.[32]

The body was at fault, but was not in itself the cause of the fallen condition. Rather, its state revealed (or expressed) the soul or the inward disposition of the heart. What the sacraments of baptism and Eucharist accomplished, then, was the restoration of oneness of being—and with it, appropriate sensory experience. Augustine described God's call to humanity and his own response in terms that engaged the whole bodily sensorium:

> You [O Lord] called and cried aloud and shattered my deafness. You were radiant and resplendent, you put to flight my blindness. You were fragrant and I drew in my breath and now pant after you. I tasted you, and I feel but hunger and thirst for you. You touched me, and I am set on fire to attain the peace which is yours.[33]

Late antique Christian writers often employed olfactory imagery to capture the essence of human-divine encounter. In Ephrem's hymns, for example, eating and smelling were closely related experiences; so, too, were the concepts, Bread of Life and Fragrance of Life.[34] When eaten as the Bread of Life, Christ pervaded the whole of the believer's being. But Christ was also inhaled as the Fragrance of Life, and as such again penetrated throughout the believer. Ephrem titled Christ the "Glorious Lily,"[35] the "Treasure of Perfumes" round whom the faithful gathered, "that they might inhale and be sated, and that the power of [Christ's] deeds / might permeate their senses."[36] Through the act of breathing—the life force itself—Ephrem insisted, Christ's presence saturated the believer. Interestingly, it was fragrance rather than breath that Ephrem highlighted again and again; his olfactory imagery was about encounter, not animation. The breath of life that Adam received at creation animated his lifeless body. The fragrance of Christ inhaled by the believer indicated by its smell the action of human-divine encounter through sensory experience.[37]

Throughout Ephrem's hymns, as we would expect, fragrances of extraordinary beauty reveal divine presence. Yet Ephrem's primary interest was not fragrance as an attribute of the divine. Rather, Ephrem emphasized the experience of smell as a means by which the believer encountered the divine, knew the divine to be present and active in the affairs of the created order, and learned God's favor or disfavor. Hence Ephrem described the first Pentecost as a moment at which God made known the elect condition of Christ's disciples, filling them with holy power through the Spirit. In Ephrem's telling, both the revelation and the empowerment were activated by the scent that overtook the occasion:

> When the blessed Apostles
>   were gathered together
> the place shook
>   and the scent of Paradise

having recognized its home
    poured forth its perfumes . . . [38]

Again, Ephrem could refer to Jacob, Bishop of Nisibis, as one who had the "fragrance of [divine] truth" preserved in him.[39] Ephrem thus presented fragrance as a vehicle for recognizing divine blessing, for receiving revelation, and for manifesting it in turn, as the Apostles at Pentecost[40] or Jacob of Nisibis made known God's purpose through the sacred scent they gave forth. The pan-Mediterranean olfactory codes that Christians shared came in late antiquity to be constantly employed by Christian writers. When texts declared that the air filled with perfume as Constantine's mother Helena dug up the True Cross in Jerusalem,[41] or that Melania the Younger and her husband Pinian prayed to be relieved of the burdens of secular life and suddenly found themselves engulfed in "heavenly perfume," announcing divine acceptance of their vows,[42] such descriptions marked divine participation in the events at hand. The same sensibility marks reports of sweet fragrance at the orthodox rededication of a church formerly used by heretics, at the death of a holy man or woman, or at the presence of holy relics.[43] In like manner, literary accounts report that visions of hell were accompanied by "much ill odor and a hateful vapor,"[44] exorcised demons made their departures wreathed in stench,[45] and heretics could be revealed as such simply by the foul smell they emitted.[46]

Scholars of Christian tradition have often highlighted sight and sound as primary modes of Christian revelation, through the well-known images of Christ as Light and Christ as Word.[47] However, as the present discussion makes clear, ancient Christians could utilize sensory awareness and sense perception in fuller terms. Basil sounded the appropriate word of caution: "Truly it is not possible to attain a worthy view of the God of the universe from these things, but to be led on by them, as also by each of the tiniest of plants and animals to some slight and faint impression of Him."[48] Through smell, it seemed to these writers, human and divine could meet—not face to face as distinct realities, but intermingled in a communion of being. Olfactory experience could mirror sacramental reality: to smell God was to know God as a transcendent yet transforming presence, a presence actively known through bodily experience.

Participatory Knowing: Ritual Scents and Devotional Uses

Olfactory experience could be revelatory of the divine. So, too, could humanity acknowledge its fallen and redeemed conditions to the divine through the smells by which worship was practiced or holy encounter sought. Late antique

Christian writers interpreted sensory experiences according to their correlates in religious ritual, and especially the liturgy, where physical sensations were ordered and explicated for the worshipping community. These writers presupposed that believers understood how smells carried religious meanings according to the paradigmatic odors of sacred ritual. In the post-Constantinian era, holy oil and incense received careful pedagogical treatment by Christian homilists, at the same time that they became central components of Christian ritual activity. The ritual context was itself a didactic medium in which to learn sensory meanings. Properly instructed through ecclesial word and deed, believers could then extend the religious uses of scents by adding them to domestic or paraliturgical devotional activities and by associating mundane smells with their ritual counterparts. By such actions the orientation of the liturgical context prevailed far beyond the physical confines of church sanctuary and official ceremony, profoundly linking the events and activities of daily life to the salvation drama enacted within the liturgy itself.[49]

Holy Oil

Unlike incense, holy oil had been used by Christians continuously from their beginnings. However, the evidence for earliest Christian use is scanty and unclear.[50] In the canonical gospels, Jesus was anointed with perfumed ointment on his feet by the Sinful Woman, on his head by Mary of Bethany, and at his burial. In general, patristic writers saw the Sinful Woman's anointing as an honorific act, following the ancient custom of using perfumed ointment to show respect and veneration for a notable person.[51] The anointing of his head was interpreted to be a prophetic act signalling his death to come, and the burial occasion to follow the traditional preparations of a dead body for the tomb. Only two New Testament passages explicitly mention anointing the faithful: Mark 6:13 and James 5:14–15. Both texts refer to the anointing of the sick—in the Markan passage by the apostles (not by Christ), and in the epistle by the presbyters. Both passages use the term *aleipho*, to anoint or pour out, the same term used in the instances of Jesus' anointment. Other New Testament texts use the verb *chrio* and its derivative noun *chrisma*, the root for the verbal adjective *christos*, the Anointed One. These passages (for example, Luke 4:18, Acts 10:38, 1 John 2:20, 27) are more complicated, for it is never clear that an actual anointing takes place. Instead, these are cases where the writers refer to anointing with the Holy Spirit or the pouring out of the Spirit. These instances resonate with Hebrew uses for the word *mashah* (from which the term *meshiah*, Messiah, the Anointed) and carry strong associations from the Hebrew Bible. Most important for early Christians were the ideas of priesthood, kingship, and prophecy as offices of sacred activity conferred through an anointing with holy oil. Early Christians applied these concepts to the figure of Christ, as well as to themselves as his followers.

Missing from the New Testament is any unambiguous reference to the use of holy oil in the baptismal ceremony. In the second and third centuries, Christian writers and church orders sometimes refer to baptismal anointing. At the same time, they present a variety of ritual sequences for baptism with anointment sometimes preceding and sometimes following immersion in water.[52] In the case of church orders, such as the *Didache* or the *Apostolic Tradition* of Hippolytus, it is difficult to establish to what degree—if any—these orders were in use, or whether they simply represented someone's concept of ideal ecclesiastical arrangements. Where we can be certain of the description of an actual rite, as in Tertullian's treatise "On Baptism," the difficulty lies in assessing whether this describes local custom or (less likely) a more widespread practice.[53]

In these early sources, attention was rarely paid to the olfactory aspects of ritual anointing—a pattern similar to that for early Christian discussions of incense. The notion of scent was intrinsic to the two Greek terms used for holy oil, *chrisma* and *myron*. The latter in particular signified perfumed ointment, but explicit comments on the fragrance of holy oil are unusual. Instead, the texts highlight the oil as a significant substance, indicating its ritual identification (its consecration, or its identification as a "blessed" substance), and prescribing its ritual application. In the *Apostolic Tradition*, for example, oil is blessed immediately after the Eucharist.[54] The prayer cited recalls oil as the medium through which Old Testament kings, priests, and prophets received their offices, and refers also to oil as an agent of strength and health, its traditional medicinal use. What is not specified is whether the oil receiving this blessing was to be used in the baptismal ritual recounted later in the text, or whether it was blessed for the anointing of the sick, as the reference to "strength and health" might indicate. However, in the baptismal portion of this text, two different holy oils are required for the initiation rite, the Oil of Exorcism and the Oil of Thanksgiving.[55] The former was used to anoint the candidate immediately after the renunciation of Satan as part of the exorcism in preparation for baptism.[56] Following immersion, the initiate was anointed with the Oil of Thanksgiving. After putting on the new baptismal garments, the initiate received a further anointing on the forehead to give the "seal" (*sphragis*) of the Holy Spirit.[57] Tertullian mentions only one anointing, given after the immersion and over the whole body. He explains it with two biblical citations: the Old Testament type of Aaron's anointing by Moses to signify his priesthood (Ex 29:7; Ps 133:2 [LXX 132:2]), which Tertullian terms the "carnal" model, and Christ's anointment with the Holy Spirit (Lk 4:18; Acts 10:38), which he calls the "spiritual" model.[58]

A handful of second- and third-century texts offer a more heightened appreciation for the role of the oil and the contributing aspect of its scent. In the *Gospel of Philip*, holy oil is a major theme.[59] Baptism is said to require two elements, water and chrism. However, the text offers further comment at a later point: "Chrism has more authority than baptism. For because of chrism we are called Christians, not because of baptism. And the Anointed (Christ) was named for chrism, for the father anointed the son, and the son anointed the apostles, and the apostles anointed us."[60] Elsewhere the text refers to the "fragrance of spiritual love" that accompanies the anointed, engulfing even the unbaptized who may "still remain within their fragrance" after the anointed have departed.[61] Here holy oil was both agent and indicator. It was the means by which relation was established first within the divine realm and then between the divine and human realms; it was the medium for initiation and for the reception of a new identity as Christians—an identity made known to others by the fragrance they exuded because of their anointment.[62] In the *Acts of Thomas*, it appears that oil rather than water is the essential ingredient for initiation: in ch. 27 oil alone accomplishes the baptism, and the prayer spoken over the oil parallels the prayer offered over the Eucharist in ch. 51.[63] Indeed, at an early incident in the narrative, Thomas uses scented oil in a fashion that not only distinguishes his identity as holy, but that further recalls baptismal anointing as a ritual that remakes the body and its senses. At the wedding feast of King Gundaphorus's daughter, the celebratory feast was followed by offering the guests wreaths of flowers and perfume with which to adorn themselves:

> And when they had dined and drunk, and crowns and scented oils were brought, each one took of the oil and anointed his face, another his chin (his beard), another again other parts of his body; but the apostle [Thomas] anointed the crown of his head and smeared a little upon his nostrils, dropped some also into his ears, touched his teeth with it, and carefully anointed the parts about his heart; and the crown that was brought to him, woven of myrtle and other flowers, he took up and set upon his head.[64]

The Coptic version of the *Didache* added a prayer for the consecration of myron in chapter 10, in a work that otherwise mentions no anointings or use of any sacred scents.[65] Once again, it is not clear whether this myron was intended for baptismal use, or for anointing the sick.[66] The Coptic ointment prayer seems to be the source for the prayer prescribed for baptismal ointment in the fourth-century Syrian *Apostolic Constitutions*, where the blessing was explicitly given for "the fragrance of the myron."[67] Here the text specified that the fragrance marked the presence of the Holy Spirit, and therefore the transformation of the believer that the ritual effected. These texts raise epistemological themes that would become important in post-Constantinian Christian literature as holy oils received more extended discussion: the oil's ritual capacities were linked to its ability to impart knowledge, both of divine presence or participation and of changed human condition or identity.

Clearly, holy oil had become a common component of Christian initiation well before the fourth century, although its usage and stated significance varied to a great degree. In the fourth century, the larger effort to unify Christian practices resulted in a basic standardization of baptismal patterns clustered around major sees. These patterns were explicated in the four sets of catechetical lectures that survive from the era in the works of Cyril of Jerusalem, Ambrose of Milan, Theodore of Mopsuestia, and John Chrysostom.[68] Yet there continued to be differences in the number of baptismal anointings within the ritual, their locations within the sequence of the ceremony, and their locations on the initiate's body. Although some places may have had an original single anointing, two or three in the course of the ceremony became the general practice. Anointing preceded or followed immersion in water, or was performed in both contexts, although eventually at least one anointing (sometimes two) before and one after immersion became the rule. Depending on the particular segment of the ceremony, an initiate would be anointed on the forehead, over the whole body, or on the sense organs. Hygienic and medicinal customs influenced the elaboration of baptismal anointings. The Greco-Roman custom of anointing the body prior to bathing probably contributed to the spread of a pre-immersion anointing of the whole body. The frequent use of ointments for various medical problems (skin disease, sores, wounds, headaches, congestion) contributed to the imagery of holy oil as a healing balm, Christ as the Good Physician, and to baptism as a healing of the wounded human nature. The same associations influenced the increasingly ritualized practices of anointing the sick.[69]

Much scholarship has been devoted to analyzing the differences in ritual procedure and ecclesiastical interpretation, but a comprehensive overview on baptismal practice need not concern us here.[70] Rather, a sampling of late antique sources can indicate the wealth of imagery, associations, and resonances made available to ancient Christians through their use of holy oil first as a medium of initiation and subsequently in other ritual contexts.

Often the pre-immersion anointings are described as exorcistic and apotropaic in purpose. The oil shielded the body so that demonic forces were warded off or dispelled as by "a fierce fire," in Cyril of Jerusalem's terms.[71] Chrysostom explained that the body was anointed just prior to immersion, "so that all your limbs may be fortified and unconquered by the darts which the

Adversary aims at you."[72] Theodore of Mopsuestia instructed that the anointing of the forehead set a mark that could be seen by demons from far off, averting their approach.[73] Gregory of Nazianzus insisted this protection was one of the most important aspects of the baptismal process, and urged his congregation to invoke its power against demons on a daily basis.[74] Ambrose compared this anointing to the rubbing down of athletes with oil prior to their wrestling matches.[75] An anonymous Syriac commentary adds to the same image, "a man who enters the contest of a fight is anointed with oil so that the hands of the person fighting with him may slip off from him. Oil is the invincible armor against demons."[76]

The anointing of the forehead was also the granting of the "seal" or "sign." Theodore likens it to the brand of ownership that marked a sheep, or to the tattoo worn by an imperial soldier.[77] While Syriac texts seem to have made a distinction between "sign" or "mark" (rushma) and "seal" (hatma), the Greek term "sphragis" probably covered both senses.[78] Syriac authors referred to baptismal anointing also with the term "imprint" or "incise" (Syr. tba'), and the anointing was likened to the Jewish rite of circumcision, the oil cutting (Syr. gzar) like the sword.[79]

None of this imagery engaged holy oil through its smell. Rather, the images arise from the oil as an applied substance, or from the ritual application as a process. Where Chrysostom had described the pre-immersion anointing of the whole body as the putting on of armor, Theodore called it the sign of the garment of immortality in which baptism would clothe the initiate. Oil makes this symbol, Theodore says, because clothes only touch part of the body and only on the exterior; oil, by contrast, penetrates the entire person just as "all our nature will put on immortality at the time of the resurrection, and all that is seen in us, whether internal or external, will undoubtedly be changed into incorruptibility according to the working of the Holy Spirit which shall then be with us."[80] The anointing of the whole body also fit easily with the imagery ubiquitous in the eastern texts of baptism as a new birth, or the putting on of a new body.[81] Olfactory imagery was not always relevant to such metaphors.

But the lacunae may have a simpler explanation. A further ritual distinction existed between the oils used for pre- and post-baptismal anointings, as had already been the case in the Apostolic Tradition. The oil used for the catechumens was generally plain olive oil, while the post-baptismal anointings (or, in Chrysostom, the second pre-immersion anointing) were done with perfumed myron. The addition of the use of myron as a scented oil happened more slowly in some regions than others—East Syriac tradition seems never to have taken on the practice at all—but gradually became the general custom. By this contrast alone, the role of scent in the ritual process was brought to the foreground.[82]

Baptismal candidates were prepared for the olfactory shift from unscented to scented oil in those cases where an anointing of the senses was practiced, a different type of anointment than that connected with ownership or protection. The forehead was anointed first, then the sense organs, specifically the ears and nostrils. Both Ambrose and Cyril of Jerusalem discuss this sequence as a process of opening or attuning the senses towards the divine—what Ephrem meant when he spoke of the baptized gaining "new senses."[83] The anointing of the nostrils was a prominent moment in this ritual segment, further distinguished when the participants then smelled a differently scented oil. Ambrose and Cyril underscored the olfactory significance by citing the "good odor of Christ" from 2 Corinthians 2:15. Ambrose explained that the nostrils warranted the exceptional attention, "[i]n order that you may receive the good odor of eternal piety . . . and that there may be in you the full fragrance of faith and devotion."[84] Cyril dwelt on the very moment of smelling the myron, "that, scenting the divine oil, you may say, 'We are the incense offered by Christ to God.'"[85]

The composition of the myron also warranted reflection. Chrysostom commented, "The chrism is a mixture of olive oil and unguent; the unguent is for the bride, the oil is for the athlete."[86] In Syriac tradition, it became common to present the twofold composition of the myron (olive oil and balsam) as representing the two natures of Christ. Ps.-Dionysius the Areopagite viewed the combination of scents composing the myron as essential to its epistemological power, and not only to its ritual function. The baptismal anointing gave "a sweet odor to the one being initiated," he noted, as it joined the initiate to the Holy Spirit. Yet the work of the "sweetening" happened internally to the newly baptized, and did not rest on the body as an external symbol.[87] Thus, he wrote, the rich mixture of fragrances in the myron was appropriate for the diverse congregation that would perceive the myron's smell: "the participants receive these fragrances, but they do so in proportion to their capacity to have a share of this fragrance. . . . So it is that the composition of the ointment is symbolic, giving a form to what is without form."[88] We will consider Dionysius's extensive reflections on the myron further below. However, his insight here is helpful: the olfactory experience of the baptismal ointment captured exactly the encounter of the ritual. The myron's fragrance granted perceptible yet invisible form to a transformation (new birth) and an encounter (the human with the divine) that could not be seen. Moreover, baptism/salvation was available to anyone who sought it; intelligence, philosophical training, or contemplative wisdom were not necessary prerequisites, although in a system such as Dionysius's such attributes were essential for any deep understanding of religious activity or pursuit of the divine. How appropriate, then, that a perfumed substance should be the medium for this human-divine relation: not only invisible, but also uncontainable, its odor spread, received by anyone in its path. Yet those with the proper disposition and training would find within the fragrance a greater wealth of meaning. To each person, Dionysius wrote, the perfume of the myron poured out its riches in a degree appropriate to that one's capacity for understanding.[89]

Cyril of Jerusalem's *Catechetical Homilies* gave sustained attention to the fragrances of the baptismal ceremony and the olfactory experiences that resulted from their encounter. Indeed, the opening statement of his *Procatechesis* (introductory lecture) was a vivid evocation of the ritual odors and imaginal smells his audience would encounter in the course of their baptism:

> Already, my dear candidates for Enlightenment, scents of Paradise are wafted towards you, already you are culling mystic blossoms for the weaving of heavenly garlands; already the fragrance of the Holy Spirit has blown about you . . . You have walked in procession with the tapers of brides in your hands and the desire of heavenly citizenship in your hearts.[90]

With striking economy, these olfactory images allowed Cyril to present a variety of themes: baptism as a marriage between the believer and Christ, the Heavenly Bridegroom; the church as the earthly entrance to the heavenly paradise; and the presence of the Holy Spirit. All were images conveyed by the fragrances that accompanied the baptismal ritual and the eucharistic liturgy that followed it. The smells provided olfactory cues by which the participants could understand different aspects of the ritual. In Lectures 13 and 14, Cyril dwelt on gardens, flowers, and spices as he carefully interwove passages from the Song of Songs with the passion narratives of the gospels. Thus he presented the suffering, death, and burial of Christ through the bridal imagery of the Song, conjoining marriage and sacrifice, baptism and Eucharist.[91]

Ritual scents enabled a mingling of these rites, so that olfactory sensation blurred the distinctions between them as ritual events. These same scents evoked the mingling of human and divine worlds. Ritual substances bridged across the divide, transferring qualities from the divine to the human as seamlessly as odors are transferred and absorbed by mere proximity. Cyril devoted an entire lecture to the baptismal myron, in which he expounded precisely this point.[92] When Christ was baptized in the Jordan, Cyril explained, he imparted "the fragrance of His Godhead" to the waters. As he came up from the river, he was anointed "not by men with material oil or balsam," but by God with the "mystical oil of gladness, that is, with the Holy Spirit." Through baptism by water and oil, then, believers are made "Christs," "anointed ones," becoming "partakers and fellows of Christ" as they are imbued with divine presence—a presence recalled through its lingering fragrance. "Beware of supposing that this ointment is mere ointment," Cyril admonished:

> Just as after the invocation of the Holy Spirit the eucharistic bread is no longer ordinary bread, but the Body of Christ, so this holy oil, in conjunction with the invocation, is no longer simple or common oil, but becomes the gracious gift of Christ and the Holy Spirit, producing the advent of the deity. With this ointment your forehead and sense organs have been sacramentally anointed, in such wise that while your body is anointed with the visible oil, your soul is sanctified by the holy, quickening Spirit.[93]

Cyril urged his congregation to "keep this chrism unsullied" and to progress in works of faith.[94] In similar manner, Chrysostom spoke of sin in his catechetical homilies as "not only heavy but ill-smelling," an image rendered more vivid by its immediate context in contrast to the perfumed myron of the baptismal ceremony. Addressing both catechumens and those already baptized, Chrysostom exhorted them to "keep the bloom of their luster," to preserve the purity of their sacramental identities, lest sin (advertent or not) cause them to be suddenly covered with "a great disgrace, a heavy burden, and a foul stench."[95] The scent of the myron marked the efficacy of the ritual, but scent could also be temporary—just as the redeemed state could be lost through recourse to a sinful life. Christians must "drain off the stench and set forth the unguent of the Spirit."[96]

In a pattern similar to that for incense, late antique Christianity showed an enhanced interest in holy oil specifically as an odoriferous substance: a ritual element in which the olfactory aspect was seen to be crucial to its ritual efficacy and to its religious significations. For late antiquity also brought the development of more elaborately scented holy oils. Unadorned olive oil seems to have sufficed for some ritual uses including baptism even into the fourth century, or olive oil with the addition of a single spice, such as balsam. Ephrem the Syrian wrote a series of hymns on holy oil in which he explored multiple images for baptismal anointing as well as the anointing of the sick.[97] In these hymns he makes little reference to smells, perhaps because in the fourth century the Syrians generally used unscented olive oil for their ritual needs. He mentions that oil could be mixed with many spices to constitute different medicines,[98] and when he cites Christ's anointing by the Sinful Woman he attributes exceptional power to the scent wafting from her ointment: the power to distinguish concealed identities, a prophetic capacity just as her action was a prophetic deed.[99] Rather than exploring the olfactory effects of oil at any length, however, he dwells instead on its practical uses, lyrically lacing its mundane abilities to the effects of its ritual uses as symbol for and instrument of Christ and the Holy Spirit. By contrast, John Chrysostom urged the Christians of Antioch to lavishly anoint their whole bodies with holy oil from the tomb of the martyrs, for moral as well as physical benefit: "for through its pleasant smell the oil reminds you of the martyrs' contests, and bridles and restrains all wantonness in considerable patience, and overcomes the diseases of the soul."[100]

But richer perfumes began to characterize the myron of late antique ecclesiastical use. Exegetes and homilists took interest in the spices that scripture identified for anointing priests, healing the sick, anointing the dead, or perfuming the betrothed (the Song of Songs being especially important in this regard). These spices gained value for the biblical associations they evoked and contributed to oils employed for sacred uses. In the Byzantine era, as many as fifty-two spices were used in the oil consecrated by the Patriarch of Constantinople.[101] As its perfumed quality gained importance, holy oil became as prominent as incense in the construction and maintenance of an olfactory piety for late antique Christianity. Accordingly, Paulinus of Nola described the baptism of the nobleman Baebianus:

> After the bishop then completed the holy ritual in due sequence, Baebianus tasted God's sacrament and smelled sweetly with the chrism, and expressed his wonder at the marvellous majesty of the rite. But what was the fragrance, he asked, which he felt slipping into his heart, healing with sweet nectar his inner parts? Then his attentive wife informed him that the ointment breathed forth life springing from Christ's name.[102]

For ancient Christians, as we saw in chapter 1, incense took its base meaning from its identification with sacrifice. Incense served as a medium for human initiative towards the divine, and its fragrance marked the process of human-divine encounter. Holy oil, by contrast, represented divine initiative towards the human. Christian writers sometimes emphasized its tactile quality as a substance rubbed into the skin and thereby absorbed into the person. When authors stressed its scent, however, its perfume was seen to mark divine presence. The oil allowed that presence to penetrate the person anointed, who became redolent with divine scent: the perfumed condition signified a state of grace in which the divine was mingled intimately with the human person. Once again smell was the effective signifier, for the perfume announced a presence that was tangibly perceived while remaining invisible, silent, and incorporeal. Where incense marked the activity of human-divine encounter as a process, perfumed ointment signified the state of being within that encounter.

The divine was present in the scent, and in the person who carried its fragrance. In his Oration 40, "On Holy Baptism," Gregory of Nazianzus urged that baptism be the occasion for the purification of the senses. As he called for the cleansing of sight, hearing, touch, and taste, Gregory paused on smell: "Let us be healed also in smell, that we . . . may smell the Ointment that was poured out for us, spiritually receiving it; and [that we may be] so formed and transformed by it, that from us too a sweet odor may be smelled."[103]

Incense

The fourth-century evidence for the gradual incorporation of incense practices into Christian usage is tantalizing; not until the fifth century do we find incense explicitly and commonly included as part of the Christian liturgy. Instead, the fourth century indicates increasing incense use by Christians as their activities took on greater public emphasis, and as their occasions of public ceremony commanded a pronounced grandeur and majesty. There are references to Christians using incense in the burial processions for the funerals of important figures, as in the instance of the bishop Peter of Alexandria, a usage traditional in ancient Mediterranean burial practices and also traditional as an honorific offering for notable persons.[104] Other Christian processions involved the use of incense in the same way: the transference of relics from one city to another; memorial prayers at tombs or shrines; public ceremonies involving ecclesiastical leaders (the visitation of a bishop, or the consecration of a church), or ecclesiastical participation in civic events celebrating imperial or other government occasions.[105] It would be difficult to distinguish these uses from devotional prayer offerings, although the basic principle would have been honorific—the use of incense to perfume the air as a marker that the person or occasion was of exceptional importance or worth. But the ritual actions as well as their associations would have been similar to the point where separating Christian liturgical celebration from other Christian ceremony became moot. Indeed, on some occasions Christians of the fourth century clearly misunderstood the implications of incense use as a public religious signifier, with confusion—even tragedy—as a result when onlookers took their actions as pagan devotions.[106]

As Christian worship took an increasingly visible role in urban settings, processions became dominant segments of the liturgical cycle.[107] The development of the stational liturgy was a major feature of late antique Christianity: these were liturgical celebrations conducted in cities, by bishops, incorporating various locations and church buildings.[108] Processions brought the celebrants into the church followed by the congregation; processions brought the emperor into the church; processions brought the eucharistic gifts: all were actions that took people or sacred objects from somewhere outside the church building and brought them inside, into the nave, into the sanctuary, or onto the altar. The drama of liturgy as a processional event influenced church architecture as well as itself being encouraged by architectural developments in post-Constantinian church building. The processional emphasis also had a profound impact on the urban face of late antique Christianity. As Christian processions wound through city streets, urban spaces that had once been filled by pagan rituals were filled instead with the sights and sounds of Christian celebrations, and increasingly, the scents. Following deeply ingrained cultural habit, Christian processions—like any others of the ancient Mediterranean—were adorned with lighted candles of scented wax and fragrant censers to mark the solemnity, honor, celebration, or importance of the occasion; the perfume of holy oils would also have been apparent.[109] Christian worship was no longer confined to the enclosed spaces of church buildings, homes, or designated burial sites. By processions, Christians laid claim to the geography of late antique municipalities, small or great; their scent would linger long after the spectacle had passed by.[110]

The addition of incense to the eucharistic liturgy proper is difficult to track. The Book of Pontiffs records the Emperor Constantine's gift of censers to the church at Rome: were these for fumigatory use, to keep the sanctuary clean and appropriately fragrant, or were they to be used for the burning of incense as part of the liturgical ceremony?[111] Scholars such as Béatrice Caseau and Stephen Gero have raised similar questions about accepting the Apologists' claim of a total ban on Christian incense use prior to Christianity's legalization: since public meeting spaces were regularly cleaned and scented by fumigations using incense, it is difficult to see how there would not have been ambiguities in Christian custom.[112] Eusebius of Caesarea's account of the dedication of the Church at Tyre in 312 is a good example of the problematic evidence.[113] The historian stressed the grandeur of spectacle and glory of pomp that characterized the occasion, and recounted a dedication speech abounding in olfactory imagery—including a magnificent rhetorical portrait of Christ, "the great High-Priest of the universe," receiving "with joyful countenance and upturned hands the sweet-smelling incense from all, and the bloodless and immaterial sacrifices offered in prayer," to offer them in turn to God.[114] Did Eusebius mean that incense accompanied the ceremony as part of the "pomp"—and, if so, what was its place in the ritual? Or did he intend "incense" to be a metaphor for the prayers offered? Again, Ambrose of Milan referred to the evening prayer office as "the hour of incense;" did this statement refer to the burning of incense at vespers, or simply recall the Old Testament citations Christians used to structure that service, such as Exodus 30:7–8 or Psalms 141 (LXX 140):2?[115]

The pilgrim Egeria recorded the use of incense in Jerusalem circa 381, in the Resurrection matins service on Sunday mornings, where it was part of the liturgical drama of the myrrh-bearing women at the tomb.[116] It is not clear what purpose the incense served in this rite, but hers is the only mention of liturgical use of which we can be certain at this early date.

Most of the earliest evidence for Christian use of incense whether for private or liturgical prayer ritual is Syrian. Ephrem Syrus in his *Hymns on Nisibis*, written before 363, refers to Bishop Abraham of Nisibis using incense, although he does not tell us whether the context was liturgical or in private prayer practice.[117] Around the same time, in the 370s, censers were used continually in Edessa at the tomb of the Edessan Martyrs and Julian Saba as a prayer offering.[118] The late fourth-century *Apostolic Constitutions*, of Syrian provenance, refer in canon 3 to incense at the altar.[119] In the first years of the fifth century, Simeon the Stylite as a young boy gathered storax to burn as incense while tending his father's sheep, in his first practice of prayer (although shepherds used storax to ward off snakes, rodents, or other predators from their flocks: was this custom a factor in Simeon's practice?). In time, after his unsuccessful years as a coenobitic monk, Simeon would live as a recluse in a small hut with an altar and a censer on it.[120] His contemporary (and biographer) Theodoret of Cyrrhus refers to the liturgical use of incense,[121] and so the witnesses begin to grow. By the late fifth century, incense was a staple of Christian prayer practice, public and private, wherever the church was found.

Modern historians of Christian worship have paid scant attention to the introduction of incense into the liturgical cycle or to its impact on devotional piety. Instead, abstract generalizations have been used to characterize its functions: incense was "mimetic" at the Resurrection Matins on Sundays in Jerusalem, imaging the myrrh-bearing women at the tomb; "fumigatory" and "exorcistic" at the beginning of a liturgy; "honorific" at the reading of the Gospel and at the Great Entrance; "intercessory" at matins; "propitiatory" and "penitential" at vespers.[122] These terms are descriptive with reference to larger sacrificial traditions of the ancient Mediterranean: they denote the manner by which ancient sacrificial ritual constituted and maintained relationships, ordering the power structures between the human and divine realms, and within the human community itself.[123] But, as we will see, late antique Christian piety deflected the signification of incense away from its sacrificial function to an epistemological one, wherein the relation between sense perception and religious knowledge became the primary focus. That is, incense became important for its role in the development of smell as a category of religious experience, significant for what it revealed, as distinct from what it established or reinforced, about the nature of human-divine relation.

The addition of incense to Christian worship affected Christian olfactory imagery because ritual use and context underscored the sense of smell as religiously important, granting it sacred connotations in living settings and current Christian practices. The addition enabled a far richer exploration of olfactory symbolism, allowing greater nuance in writers' treatment of its possibilities. Ephrem the Syrian's writings are a major landmark in this process of ritual change: he provides some of the earliest references to Christian incense usage, and he does so with an awareness of the distinct contribution the experience of smell could make to religious knowledge.

Writing in a time of such immense change, Ephrem must take care to distinguish the incense offerings of what he understood to be "true" religion—Christianity, and the Judaism that formed its antecedent—from those of "false" religions still active in the cities and villages of his day. To this end, Ephrem refers positively to biblical stories where Jewish cult practices involving incense offerings provided types for Christian worship. In his hymns, the incense offered by ancient Israelites smelled sweet when it signified proper human-divine relations: appropriate reverence and honor to God, or prayer offered with fitting humility.[124] In his view, these offerings anticipated the human-divine relationship Christianity would bring to maturity with God through Christ. There is a sense of fulfilled tradition when Ephrem praises the incense offered by his bishop, Abraham of Nisibis, in propitiatory prayer. Ephrem exhorts Abraham, "May your fasting be a defense for our land, your prayer a shield for our city! / May your incense acquire reconciliation! Blessed is He who has hallowed your offerings."[125] Although it is not clear from Ephrem's verse whether incense was part of Abraham's private devotions or public liturgical celebration, Ephrem assumes the incense to be an efficacious accompaniment to Abraham's prayers.

By contrast, Ephrem's references to the incense offerings of pagan worship are wholly negative. For Ephrem, pagan worship was fundamentally false and therefore its sacrifices—and its incense offerings—were by nature foul, "gloomy" in their vapor and "loathsome" in their odor.[126] Sweet fragrance, like truth itself, was possible only where Christ was present, the sweetness marking his divine participation in the offering.

> Blessed is the one who sends up his sacrifices in Your hand
> and the smell of whose incense is sweetened by You.
> [O, You who are] Purifying Sprinkling, Pardoning Hyssop!
> Who pardons all their sins in a baptism of water!
> All the sprinklings of the Levites are unable
> to pardon one people with their weak hyssops.

Blessed are the peoples [whose] hyssop was the Merciful One,
Who purified them with mercy. . . .
Blessed is the One whose intercession became a censer and was offered by You
to Your Father![127]

As the final verse indicates, Christ's offering was fragrant because he was both sacrificed and sacrificer.[128] True worship smelled sweet, in Ephrem's view, because Christ offered it eternally as the High Priest performing the perfect sacrifice. Because he was also the sacrifice offered, Christ was himself the odor scenting the fragrance of worship. Ephrem imaged the death of Christ as the true sacrificial incense offering, which Christians were called to imitate at the very least by the nature and quality of their love:

Come, let us make our love a great, common censer. Let us offer up our songs and prayers like incense to the One Who made His cross a censer to the Divinity, and offered His blood on behalf of us all.[129]

The introduction of incense into Christian ritual after more than three hundred years of exclusion carried both the inheritance of traditional meanings, including the sacrificial symbolism that had been deeply embedded in early Christian writings, as well as fresh nuances sprung from Christianity's own developments. With the turn of the fifth century, Christian writers regularly describe incense usage as part of an olfactory dialogue in which human and divine each approached the other through scent. The faithful offered incense; in response, God was understood to pour forth the powerful aroma of divinity, the rich perfume that Ephrem named the Fragrance of Life, signifying holy presence and blessing upon the faithful, a community in right relation with their Creator.

Yet late antique Christian writers came quickly to deflect the religious signification of incense offerings away from sacrificial imagery and towards epistemology. The fragrance itself became important, apart from the action of offering. The smell of incense signified a relationship of order established by sacrifice, but its greater worth lay in the knowledge of God it conveyed. An early indication of this shift in ritual understanding can be seen in the *Hymns on Julian Saba*, the first four of which were probably written by Ephrem.[130] As so often, one cannot be certain whether Ephrem speaks here metaphorically or literally. However, the first and fourth hymns seem to refer to a censer burning at Julian's tomb.[131] When Ephrem describes the censer he is not concerned with incense as an honorific sacrifice, although that would be the tradition for funerary offerings. Rather, his focus is the revelation carried by the incense fragrance as it wafts near and far:

> Who needs to ask about you [Julian],
> for lo! your ascetic practices are like heralds in creation.
> A great censer is in our land,
> whose strong perfume is with those nearby
> and whose lovely fragrance is with those far off
>   who have heard the news of him.[132]

Julian's tomb in Edessa had become a pilgrimage site, Ephrem writes, from which the censer sends forth news of the saint and the God to whom his holy life bore witness:

> Rich is the incense from [Julian's] censer,
> Its fragrance billows and wafts to every place.
> How much indeed would our land give thanks that it is worthy,
> for behold, in it is laid a treasure of sweet spices,
> whose fragrance goes out to people that they might come to it.[133]

The incense burning at Julian's tomb proclaims, teaches, and summons all who breathe its sweetness.[134]

By placing emphasis on what the believer could learn from the olfactory aspect of ritual piety—what the smell of the incense offering could teach—Ephrem points to a human-divine relationship that worked as one of communion at every level. Knowledge of God was instilled in the believer who inhaled the scent of worship; it mingled and penetrated throughout the believer's being, imparted through participation in the ritual structure itself. The fragrance of incense was a symbol of divine-human encounter, a symbol that became the vehicle for its own realization.

Ephrem presents incense as a primary attribute of worship, a fragrance that expresses true or false relation (true or false worship/sacrifice) by the quality of its smell, but which also conveys divine presence and imparts knowledge about the divine. Clearly, scent which can communicate between the divine and human realms must consist of more than an incense offering made by human hands. Human offering as the imitation of Christ's priestly offering implicates Christ's participation in the action. But the mimetic qualities of Christian worship go further. By himself becoming offering as well as priest, sacrifice as well as sacrificer, Christ participates in every Christian offering as the substance offered: it is the scent of Christ that mingles in the fragrance of the incense rising. We see this understanding when Ephrem likens incense offerings to the deaths of the martyrs and to the death of Christ:

Incenses are, like the martyrs, cast into the fire.
Their scents rise up like their good Lord
Who by means of His death breathed out the fragrance of His life.[135]

Here is the exact bridge between sacrifice and knowledge, between Bread of Life and Fragrance of Life. To the ancients, incense was a fitting accompaniment for sacrifice because it imaged the sacrificial act. When Christ offered himself in perfect sacrifice, however, the aroma released in the offering was the "fragrance of His life". Just as the faithful consumed the Eucharist, "the Medicine of Life" (as it was called in Syriac tradition) so, too, did they smell the holy scent of incense and find in it that divine force altered human life. In an olfactory image (or icon) of the resurrection, what should have been the smell of destruction in fact became the smell of new life. Thus Ephrem indicates the paradox of Lenten penitential rites: "In the sackcloth of [the fast] is hidden the garment of glory / and from its ash wafts the Fragrance of Life."[136] More poignant still, Ephrem writes that Death itself feared the blood of Christ, because in it was hidden the Fragrance of Life.[137] Christian sacred ritual not only mediated the human-divine relationship, it also instructed the faithful about divine action and intention through their sensory participation in the ritual process. Religious understanding deepened as participants experienced and attended to the odors of worship.

In many respects, Ephrem's ruminations on the religious signification of smell accord with earlier Christian writings that used incense as a literary image through which to explore the process of human-divine interaction, as discussed in chapter 1. However, his earlier counterparts had used such imagery in a context where Christians were attempting to differentiate themselves from their pagan contemporaries, and relied on differences in religious ritual to be a major aspect of that effort. When they spoke of prayer or good works as "sweet-smelling sacrifices" pleasing to God, they applied cultic language to daily life without having close counterparts to the image in Christian ritual. By contrast, Ephrem wrote in a situation where Christians were cultivating an enhanced olfactory piety, as their usage of scented holy oils and incense expanded. For him and other late antique writers, the use of incense rhetoric intersected with current Christian practices in terms that identified individual actions with the collective worship of the church in ever more concrete terms.

It was a time of overlapping sensibilities, of the earlier model and the changing situation. Basil of Caesarea referred to psalmody as the offering of a sweet spiritual incense to God; good works continued to be characterized as a fragrant sacrifice pleasing to God.[138] Augustine of Hippo described the Lord's Prayer as "the daily incense . . . offered to God on the altar of the heart;" elsewhere he characterized the prayers offered together by Christian friends as incense ascending from the censers of their hearts toward God who "delights in the odor of [his] holy temple."[139] Ephrem could describe any occasion of individual piety or prayer as if he were describing a liturgy. When Jonah was trapped in the belly of the whale, "A pure temple the fish became for [Jonah], / and the mouth of Jonah [became] a censer. / The smell of incense rose up from with the abyss / to the High one."[140] Or again, Adam's life in paradise before the Fall:

> Like a priest
>   with fragrant incense
> Adam's keeping of the commandment
>   was to be his censer
> then he might enter before the Hidden One
>   into that hidden Tabernacle.[141]

As such imagery was used in the context of proliferating incense piety, it blurred the distinction between the mundane and the liturgical. Christian life was presented as liturgy. Incense imagery was enough to summon the identification. Hence the sixth-century bishop John of Ephesus praised the honest traders Elijah and Theodore of Amida, whose holy vocation was to run their business fairly: "the labor carried on without deceit or extortion or lying rose up like the smoke of incense at all times from the devout men to Him who knows all. . . . and His blessing rested on all they did."[142]

The introduction of incense into Christian sacred ritual was one aspect of a rich and complex multiplication of olfactory symbols in the Christian discourse of late antiquity. In the context of devotional piety, however, incense appears to have been the most consistent accompaniment of religious experience. It was incense that transformed events or encounters, wherever or whatever the circumstances, so that they carried liturgical meaning—a situation demonstrated by incense practices, but also by the frequency of incense use as a literary topos for marking exceptional devotion.[143] Most often the liturgical quality was in the sense of human approach towards the divine, frequently supplicatory, or the promise of divine response to human need. Such was the case when incense was burned at the vigil for a dying ascetic, or to mark the death of a saint;[144] or when villages burned incense while marching in procession to seek divine intervention from a holy man or through collective prayer in cases of illness or natural disaster.[145] Incense accompanied the prayers of the true ascetic;[146] incense gave miraculous power to the prayers of a saintly bishop.[147] Incense caused the mute to speak.[148] In this way, too, the expansion of a liturgical incense piety would have appeared seamlessly inclusive of the incense regularly used as an accompaniment to spells, charms, or other magical practices—actions commonly undertaken by ancient people (including Christians) to ward off illness, heal the sick, effect fertility, prevent miscarriage, fend off demons, harm one's enemies, or elicit love.[149] The use of incense in such ritual activities—referred to as "magic" by modern scholars, and occasionally by ancient commentators—is difficult to distinguish from its presence in the supplicatory prayers of private devotional practice. Indeed, the distinction between "magic" and "religion," a hotly contested topic in current scholarship, would be irrelevant as far as the ritual function of incense use was concerned.[150]

Experiences gained identification with the salvific process of Christian sacred ritual when incense was employed, or simply when writers utilized incense imagery or described incense piety in their narratives.[151] Incense granted not only religious significance but also religious power in the social (and sometimes political) domain, as when women burning incense led the victory procession following the deposition of Nestorius at the Council of Ephesus in 431.[152] It was incense above all other religiously implicating smells that announced the content of human-divine relation in a given situation. The capacity of incense to function as a fundamental carrier of religious meaning in late antique culture depended not only on its own complex of ritual meanings, but also on its ability to absorb the roles and meanings of other sacred scents. In devotional practice, incense usage was a kind of shorthand—an abbreviated expression of the larger mediating structures and processes by which Christianity ordered the cosmologies and lives of its adherents.

Participatory Knowing: Scents and Sense

Late antique Christians delighted in the beauty of a created order they understood to be revelatory of its Maker. It was a beauty available to them because their senses had been opened to its presence, and trained to perceive its teaching. Baptism fashioned the body anew; liturgy guided its experience.[153] When late antique Christians described the liturgical celebrations in which they participated, they did so with wonder and appreciation for more than the spectacle they witnessed. Liturgy, in their telling, was a thickly textured sensory weaving, an experience as Ephrem had said that "filled the senses." When the pilgrim Egeria reported the liturgical customs of Jerusalem, she emphasized the abundant use of lights: candles, torches, large glass lamps, candelabras. The quality of light was heightened on feast days, she reported, by the festal decorations of the churches: silk hangings and curtains trimmed with gold stripes, sacred vessels of gold set with gems and precious stones, all brought together in buildings lavishly adorned with shining marble, glittering mosaics, and gold ornaments.[154] Other late antique Christians expressly noted that the light of worship was a fragrant one, filling the space of Christian ritual with scents that carried the devotional actions beyond what could be seen. A hymn by Prudentius, "On the Lighting of the Lamp" for evening prayer, captures the mingling of the senses elicited by the objects of ritual adornment. Calling on Christ who fashioned stars and moon to ease the dark of night, Prudentius exhorted the faithful to set their hope upon their Lord:

This we nourish in lamps dripping with dewy oil,
Or dry torches are lit from the celestial fire;
We make candles with wicks dipped in the flowers' wax,
From which honey was pressed, hidden in yellow combs.

Bright the glimmering flame, whether a hollow urn
Feeds the oil to the wick thirsting for nutriment,
Or the resin of pine burns on the flaring torch,
Or coarse fiber of flax drinks up the waxen round;

Warm nectar from the crown, burning with lively flame,
Tears, sweet smelling, distils, flowing down drop by drop,
For the force of the heat causes the molten wax
To descend in a shower shed from the taper's point.
. . .
This light deign to receive which, I, Thy servant bring,
Light imbued with the oil, chrism of holy peace.

Take it, Father Most High, through Thine Anointed Son,
Christ, Thy Splendor revealed, Lord of the universe,
Sole-begotten by Thee, breathing the Paraclete,
Loving Spirit of Truth, from Thy paternal heart.[155]

Prudentius's verses did more than attune the congregation to the sensations that accompanied their prayers by candlelight. Through the sensorium of liturgical devotion, Prudentius evoked the natural landscape from which the scented wax was taken—the bucolic sweetness of bees, flowers, hives, and honeycomb—and dwelt at length on the cosmos as one ordered by alternating days and nights, through the vibrant cycle of seasons, directed by Christ the

Author of Light. Just as late antique Christians drew on the beauty and harmony of the natural world to instruct the faithful about the nature of divinity (seeing the natural world as revelatory), Prudentius also used the physical experience of ritual acts—lighting candles for evening prayer—to bring the worshipper into intimate relation with the created world, and through that to approach their Creator. Here the separate space of the church sanctuary becomes inclusive of the natural landscape that surrounds it, again blurring the boundaries between the sacred and the mundane.[156]

Attunement to ritual scents other than incense allowed liturgical celebration to convey multiform meanings through smells that signified other foundational bonds than that of the sacrifice. The use of aromatics in funeral rites—already problematic for Tertullian and Clement of Alexandria—in the fourth century still posed a threat to Christian leaders like Gregory of Nazianzus or John Chrysostom, who feared Christians were mistaking a traditional ("pagan") custom for a Christian practice.[157] Yet the role of spices in burial could only contribute to the emerging olfactory piety of Christians; the addition of incense to Christian funerals further enhanced the identification.[158] The associations between fragrance and marriage were perhaps an even more notable case. Just as Cyril and Ambrose had used the aromatic rites of baptism to evoke nuptial as well as eucharistic associations, the scents of perfumed wax, fragrant oils, flowers, and spices that adorned the Christian sanctuaries of late antiquity enhanced the pervasive bridal imagery of Christian teaching that Christ the Heavenly Bridegroom was betrothed to each individual believer and to the collective Church as bride. When late antique Syriac redactors recast the third-century *Acts of Judas Thomas* to better reflect orthodox theological themes, they reworked the famed Hymn of the Bride to celebrate the church in the glory of its ritual adornments:

> My church is the daughter of light,
> the splendor of kings is hers.
> Charming and winsome is her aspect,
> fair and adorned with every good work.
> Her garments are like unto flowers,
> the smell thereof is fragrant and pleasant.
> On her head dwells the King,
> and He feeds those who dwell with Him beneath.
> . . .
> Her bridal chamber is lighted up,
> and full of sweet odor of salvation.
> A censer is ready in its midst,
> love and belief and hope,
> gladdening all.[159]

The enrichment of Christian liturgy could allow the intermingling of the ritual and natural worlds; it could be used—by homilists, theologians, hymnographers, artists, and architects—to instruct the faithful on the use of the senses and bodily experience as tools to keep the believer constantly oriented toward the divine. Ephrem praised the church precisely for the sensory richness of its worship.[160] As Basil of Caesarea expressed it, "If the court of the sanctuary is so beautiful, and the vestibule of the temple is so august and magnificent, dazzling the eyes of our soul with its surpassing beauty, what must be the holy of holies?"[161] Worship declared the splendor of God's majesty, and participants perceived, felt, and experienced that splendor with all of their senses, attuned now to a sensory understanding that connected the ritual and natural worlds. Gregory of Nyssa sounded a more sobering note when he reminded the faithful that the use of imagery to convey the sacred—as in the richness of liturgical experience—served a noble purpose, but always fell short of the truth: "The beauty grasped is great; but infinitely greater is the beauty of which we get a glimpse from the appearances."[162]

But this enrichment also obscured the distinction in ritual activity that early Christians had used to maintain an identity separate from the other religions around them. Jerome had to defend the elaboration of Christian piety from those who charged it was nothing other than pagan idolatry. He upheld the veneration of relics by kiss and touch, the beautifully worked reliquaries in which they were kept, the use of scented candles, the celebrations at martyrs' shrines, all as devotional practices that served the faithful and did not detract from the distinctiveness of their Christian identity. Christ had not refused the perfumed ointment of the Sinful Woman, Jerome admonished, nor did the martyrs require candlelight; but through these the faithful could express their devotion. "In the one case [paganism] respect was paid to the idols and therefore the ceremony is to be abhorred; in the other [Christianity] the martyrs are venerated, and the same ceremony is therefore to be allowed."[163] The inaugural hymn for the church of Hagia Sophia in Edessa extolled the contrast between the "odor of sweetness" that attended the liturgy celebrated there, and the "reeking smoke" of pre-Christian (and therefore false) sacrifice; yet the splendor of the occasion would scarcely have lacked olfactory intensity (with much accompanying smoke).[164] Jacob of Serug described the baptism of Christ in the Jordan as a betrothal feast in which Christ the Bridegroom prepared the "Church of the Nations," the gentiles, to be his bride. As Jacob told the story, Christ used the waters he himself had sanctified to wash "[the Church's] beauty that was altered by the incense of idols;" and because "that smell of the holocausts sacrificed was concentrated in her," he cleansed her, "to make her body fragrant."[165] Yet the churches in which Jacob preached would have themselves been filled with the sacrificial perfume of Christian incense offerings.

Paulinus of Nola extolled the beauty of Christian celebrations at the shrine of St. Felix. The saint's holy bones lay in a "fragrant tomb," its threshold hung with shining linens, its altar "crowned with crowds . . . of fragrant lamps;" the crowds of devotees sounded forth their hymns of praise while strewing the roads with flower blossoms and adorning the shrine with garlands as the countryside, too, lay ripe with blooming promise.[166] Paulinus's poems are an eloquent example of the continuity between ancient local custom and the fashioning of Christian practice.[167] For while Paulinus was careful to distinguish Christian celebrations from those of native religious occasions in the Italian province, the accoutrements and gestures of ritual celebration were recognizably the same—including the lavish olfactory ornamentation in the use of flowers, scented oils, and ritual fragrances so often praised by Paulinus.[168] Prudentius, too, applauded the generous gifts of flowers and perfumes with which the crowds bedecked the shrines and tombs of saints and martyrs.[169] Such practices might be termed "ritual habits;" these were the actions by which peoples of the ancient Mediterranean world expressed identity, need, and order.[170] The early sixth-century Syriac chronicler Joshua the Stylite recorded two public celebrations in the year 497/8 among the citizens of Edessa, involving festive processions with abundant incense, candles, and song.[171] The first was the citywide celebration of an annual "pagan" festival, for which the Edessans suffered divine punishment in that year. The second, in the same year, instituted a new annual Christian festival to commemorate a special remission of taxes.

The charge that such a physically ornamented piety turned Christian worship into pagan idolatry would again be raised by the Iconoclasts, in the eighth century. While the focus of debate at that time was the practice of icon veneration, the defense mounted by John of Damascus broadened the question to the role of the senses as a whole. John echoed Jerome's earlier point, "The practices you mention do not make our veneration of images loathsome, but those of the idolatrous Greeks [i.e., pagans]. It is not necessary, on account of pagan abuse, to abolish pious practice."[172] John argued that icons were not different from other ritual objects, and further advocated the importance of a sensorily engaged liturgical celebration. He insisted on the pedagogical validity of what devotional sensory experiences taught the participants about divine nature and divine activity. Christ himself had approached humankind through corporeality in the incarnation, making the material world the medium of his saving work; to deny the importance of the material aspects of worship was also to deny what God had done through and in the incarnate Lord. Through the body Christ had come to us; through the body we, too, could and should approach him.

> If you say that God ought only to be apprehended spiritually, then take away everything bodily, the lights, the fragrant incense, even vocal prayer, the divine mysteries themselves that are celebrated with matter, the bread, the wine, the oil of chrismation, the form of the cross. For these are all material: the cross, the sponge, the reed, the lance that pierced the life-bearing side.[173]

The practices of an enriched Christian piety, then, engaged the senses because God's salvation had been brought about through the physical, material world. Again liturgy was a pedagogical tool, for John pointed out that the church taught devotional practices explicitly as a means for instruction about God. Teaching that objects used in worship must be treated reverently and with respect, the church at the same time taught that worship belonged only to the God in whose honor such objects were used: the Bible, of course, but also "patens and chalices, thuribles, lamps and tables: all these are to be reverenced."[174]

Christian piety was enhanced by the use of such ritual adornments, but that use also heightened the significance of the objects themselves. Their treatment served to establish and maintain the sacrality of the ritual space they helped to constitute. The west Syrian *Synodicon*, for example, contains canons instructing that the altar should be washed with scented water; further, what cleansing process was appropriate for the vessels in which the holy myron was kept, if they became rancid or malodorous; and further, the handling of the myron.[175] Incense filled a sanctuary or shrine with fragrance appropriate for worship, but the scents used to cleanse and perfume the ritual setting were themselves an essential contribution to its distinctive space. Scents served to demarcate space, objects, and actions through which human-divine relation was negotiated in the liturgy. If incense and holy oils were the most important ritual fragrances in late antique Christian worship, the qualities that made their contribution effective were extended beyond their specific use to broader aspects of worship by the use of other aromatics in the context of pietistic expression.

In early Christian legend, beautiful fragrances were the mark of God's heavenly kingdom; spices were a gift brought from paradise to Adam and Eve in their fallen state, to provide them comfort and solace.[176] This sensibility pervades late antique descriptions of religious scents: they were beautiful because their fragrances were not from earthly sources alone.[177] The ritual context of the liturgy established a space in which the divine and human domains mingled; the air was a permeable divide between them, a porous veil separating and bridging the seen and the unseen. Ambrose summoned his congregation to attend the liturgy and "enjoy the good odor of eternal life, which has been breathed upon you by the grace of the sacraments."[178] The scents of worship heralded the life-giving breath of the Holy Spirit whose presence caused the ritual to accomplish its purpose: "His coming is gentle, the perception of Him fragrant, His yoke light; rays of light and knowledge shine forth before His coming."[179]

Diverse scents mingled in Christian rituals, marking actions and presences human and divine. Scents blurred the boundaries between ritual and natural space, between liturgical and mundane practice, between human and divine domains. A heightened olfactory awareness characterizes much of late antique literature, expressed in anecdotes that demonstrate how distinct functions, actors, and locations were conceptually joined through olfactory imagery that played across these contrasting demarcations. Often, such anecdotes intersect the basic significations of ointment (presence) and incense (sacrifice), as when Gregory of Tours reported the miraculous rescue of a ship caught in a terrible storm. The people on board prayed fervently, and as they did: "While this was happening, suddenly a very sweet fragrance like balsam covered the boat, and as if someone had gone around with a censer, the fragrance of incense was overpowering. At the approach of this fragrance the savagely violent winds stopped."[180] In this instance, the efficacy of the prayer offering was marked by the divinely supplied odor of incense; an odor which acted like the perfume of divine presence by stilling the storm.

Such intersection was also the way writers characterized the devotional practices of pilgrimage. The sixth-century Piacenza Pilgrim kept a diary of his travels through the Holy Land, recording in some detail the rituals performed at the various sites he visited. Incense offerings and requests for blessed holy oil are frequently mentioned in his account, which notes further that incense was sometimes used during incubation of the sick at shrines to induce visions, and that holy oil could sometimes smell like sulphur.[181] On occasion, the qualities of oil and incense were conjoined, as in his report of what happened at the blessing of the Jordan River on Epiphany:

All the shipowners of Alexandria have men there that day with great jars of spices and balsam, and as soon as the river has been blessed, before the baptism starts, they pour them out into the water, and draw out holy water. This water they use for sprinkling their ships when they are about to set sail.[182]

Paulinus of Nola wrote at length about suppliants who came to the tomb of St. Felix, seeking cures for illness. Relics in Paulinus's poems (as in most Christian descriptions) always shed forth a "fragrance pleasing to Christ," recalling the sacrificial imagery of martyr accounts.[183] To the fragrance of the saint's tomb, pilgrims added that of perfumed ointment. This they would pour into a hole in the top of the reliquary that held the saint's bones, catching it again as it flowed through a hole in the bottom, now blessed by the martyr's touch and potent as a healing substance.[184] In Paulinus's description, the powerful scent was not yielded by the expensive unguents brought for blessing, but imparted into them by the odor of sanctity exuding from the bones, "a healing breath and a hidden fragrance, conferring a sacramental quality on the pouring vessels."[185] The fragrance of the saint was the mark of divine grace which the faithful could now receive through the blessed oil—just as had happened in baptismal anointing.[186] When Evagrius Scholasticus described the scent wafting from the relics of St. Euphemia, "such as no perfumer would create, but it is strange and extraordinary, presenting through itself the power of its origins," he claimed further that it was perceived without distinction by believers and unbelievers alike, being "sent forth for all equally."[187]

Whether for incense or holy oil, the beauty of religious scent was held to be efficacious, powerful, and true because its source lay in the fragrance of divinity itself, the center and destination of worship. Paulinus encapsuled the olfactory piety of late antique Christians when he titled Christ the "Flower of God," the one who "cleans the enfeebling foulness from our sluggish bodies and renews the dispositions of our minds."[188] Just so, Paulinus admonished his congregation, "We must eagerly hasten to [Christ's] fragrant perfume, so that the smell of death may flee far from us."[189] By the power of this one scent, the effects of all other scents were set in order. The stench of death was undone.

Excursus: Incense Offerings in the Syriac *Transitus Mariae*

Scholars have long recognized that hagiography and sacred legends contain a wealth of historical material related to incense practices.[190] Especially from the perspective of private devotional use, sacred narratives offer numerous descriptions of when and how people employed incense for religious purposes apart from the ecclesial setting of the eucharistic liturgy or the monastic offices. Such narratives also contain eloquent testimony to the variety of meanings incense carried for the larger Christian community, articulated in terms distinct from those of ritual commentaries or homiletic discourse. In story, the fluid interactions between types and functions of sacred odors were fully explored. From this context we may gain some measure of the development of Christian incense usage as it became normative, and what impact this usage had on Christian sensibility. We may further assess the fervor, both learned and popular, which accompanied the rapid burgeoning of Christian incense practices, as a "piety of fragrance" became prominent in the course of late antique Christianity. Literary incense imagery, especially in the variegated patterns of meaning found in hagiographical or legendary narrative, offered an effective instrument for this burgeoning. The Syriac recensions of the *Transitus Mariae* narratives provide a striking case in point.

The story of the death or "falling asleep" (*dormitio, koimesis*) and assumption of the Virgin Mary is told in the apocryphal account known as the *Transitus Mariae*.[191] Ancient versions of the *Transitus* (= "passing") survive in Greek, Latin, Syriac, Coptic, Arabic, Armenian, Georgian, and Ethiopic; the Old Irish, too, seems to preserve archaic elements.[192] As a full narrative, however, the earliest extant form of the story survives in Syriac, in a wealthy tangle of manuscripts. The oldest recension of the Syriac *Dormition*—so-called because its account of the Assumption, or Mary's removal to heaven after her death, is minimal and lacks the elaborate afterlife described in other versions—was published by William Wright in 1865 and most likely dates to the late fifth century.[193] Two sixth-century Syriac expansions of the text also survive, the first, a *History of the Virgin Mary in Six Books*, again edited by Wright in 1865,[194] and a second *History of the Virgin Mary in Five Books* edited by Agnes Smith Lewis in 1902.[195]

Because the Syriac manuscript tradition for the *Transitus Mariae* is both ancient and abundant, it has received considerable attention by scholars of Marian doctrine and devotion.[196] However, these three recensions carry an historical witness quite apart from questions of Mariology: they chart, in vivid terms, the changing role of olfactory experience in late antique Christianity.[197] The Christian piety of fragrance came into prominence during the century spanned by these three recensions. Indeed, the developing text of the Syriac *Transitus* shifts its story from one with an occasional olfactory image, to one displaying a densely textured sensory piety in which the use and perception of odors predominates. The early Syriac *Dormition* (late fifth century) has seven instances of holy fragrance;[198] the subsequent *History in Six Books* has fifteen; the later sixth-century *History in Five Books* has forty-two.[199] The developing Syriac *Transitus* tradition thus offers a distinct charting of a Christian devotional piety in transition. Tracing the fragrance motif in these three recensions casts the changes into sharp relief.[200]

The fifth-century Syriac *Dormition* grants a minor role to fragrance, but one in which we see the contours of incense piety that emerged during that century as its usage became normative. Fragrance occurs in this text from two perspectives: the incense offered on human initiative to the divine, and the perfume offered on divine initiative to the created order. In this earliest recension, a movement to and from the human and divine persons is at work through sacred odors.

From the human side of the story, incense is used and identified with prayer; on every occasion but one, the prayer is supplicatory. The incense offering marks both special urgency in the nature of the prayer, and unusual efficacy in the prayer's power to elicit divine response. Prayer with incense is thus a heightened form of supplicatory speech. Such is the sense when Mary takes a thurible and incense to pray at the tomb of Christ, that her trials with her Jewish persecutors be brought to an end and her death be soon;[201] again when she prays with a censer burning beside her during the continuation of her ordeals;[202] and again when an invalid prays to Mary while burning incense, for healing by intercession.[203] In each case, the burning incense offers the physical evidence of the prayer's journey heavenward. More than a physical image, however, incense plays a mediatory role: it is the means by which prayer reaches its destination and it initiates the response hoped for. Mary offers incense with her prayer and "the moment that her prayer had gone up to heaven, the angel of the Lord came down to her."[204] The invalid is healed at the moment he offers incense with his prayer to Mary.[205] Incense offered with prayer provides a salvific bridge between suppliant and savior.

In these instances, the use of incense is noted but the fragrance of incense is not. We might then understand the role of burning to be the key element of the action, transfiguring substance from material to immaterial nature. However, this Dormition highlights fragrance in two other episodes where smell is critical to the meaning of the event; these, in turn, reflect back on the episodes of incense offering. First is Mary's reminiscence of the Annunciation. After Gabriel's prophetic greeting, Mary had realized her conception by the Holy Spirit like this: "a sweet odor was diffused through the whole house; and the foundations of the house too sent forth waves of odors through the whole quarter." Her immediate response: "And I arose, and set forth incense, and fell on my face, and glorified the name of the grace of my Lord."[206] Spoken words are not the important language in this olfactory dialogue, nor does fragrance function as a metaphor for prayer. In this account, divine presence is activated by and cognitively known through heavenly fragrance. Mary replies with an incense offering that does more than render honor to her Lord, as her humble position would dictate. Fragrance here is the means by which grace is present, and the means by which it is actively received and thereby effective. Fragrance accomplishes divine will in the realization of Mary's conception, and again as the mechanism for Mary's acquiescence to a divine economy that will be played out in the physical realm. The scents that compose this dialogue are powerful as sacred agents because of their functional meaning in the encounter of human and divine, orchestrated in the text according to the familiar patterns of prayer ritual.

The second incident occurs at the end of the Dormition, when Mary's glorified body is transported to paradise in the midst of a celestial liturgy. We are told, "And a pleasant and sweet odor went forth from the highest heavens of [the Lord's] glory to all parts of creation."[207] Again, divine action is made known through fragrance. The reader is reminded that smells in this text are sweet because their meaning exceeds the natural course of human experience. To initiate fragrance by offering incense or to smell God's pleasure by breathing divine perfume was to participate in a heavenly order through the earthly gateway of human perception. That heavenly order was known through the revelation of history and scripture, and it was accessible to human experience through Christian sacred ritual. The smells in this text are identified as the smells offered and received in the liturgy. Their meanings are defined by that ritual process as it first allows the human person, enveloped in fragrance, to approach the divine; then to be sanctified by divine grace, known by the fragrant presence of the Holy Spirit; and then to experience the sweet aroma of divine glory. Smell is a minor element in the overall narrative of this first recension, but it works as the language of divine encounter at the most decisive points of the story.

The second recension of the Syriac Transitus, the sixth-century History in Six Books, elaborates this earlier Dormition with a liturgical imagery to frame and drive the narrative. The story's setting is now a liturgy: the text opens with the entire Christian community summoned to join the ranks of heavenly hosts standing in worship before the glory of the Trinity. Its purpose is now ecclesial: the story records how the monks of Mt. Sinai discovered the ancient books of the Dormition and Assumption, written for the purpose of instituting three Marian feasts into the church calendar—precursors of, but not related to, the six Marian feasts that came to be set in Byzantine tradition.[208] Finally, the conclusion incorporates a lengthy tour of heaven and hell, and a Marian apocalypse. Mary now has an afterlife of doctrinal as well as devotional significance.

In keeping with the liturgical elaboration of this text, the narrative occurrences of fragrance have doubled over the earlier Dormition. However, the instances are more strictly formulaic and the Annunciation is no longer an olfactory event.[209] Incense accompanies twelve occasions of prayer—not many, given the number of prayers offered in this text. It is burned honorifically to glorify God and in supplication to beg divine intervention. Its ritual function has not changed from the earlier recension, but its narrative telling is enhanced through word redundancy: for example, "My Lady Mary said to John, 'Set forth the censer of incense and pray.' And Mar John set forth the censer of incense and prayed . . . ".[210] In this fashion, incense is offered by priests in the worshipping congregation past,[211] present,[212] and future.[213] It is offered by Mary,[214] the apostles,[215] and the ranks of the prophets in heaven.[216] Thus incense is offered by the individual, corporate, and celestial bodies of the church. In turn, smells mark the geography of the cosmos: here the air of paradise is suffused with sweet perfume even as hell exudes stench.[217] The relatively minor narrative shift in the quantity of holy odors marks a qualitative turn in sensibility. In this text (as in the larger culture) olfactory codes define the sanctified community of the faithful internally to one another and externally to creation as a whole. Holy smells restructure the meaning of historical time in relation to eternity, and they demarcate sacred from profane, salvation from damnation, and redeemed creation from the fallen order.

The turn in religious sensibility comes full force in the sixth-century *History in Five Books*, significantly related to both previous recensions.[218] Scholars have generally ignored this recension of the *Transitus* on the grounds that it represents a later and "more corrupt" form of the story, by which apparently is meant the still further liturgical expansion of the narrative. Agnes Smith Lewis's 1902 edition has also suffered neglect because of how she chose to reconstruct the badly damaged text, filling in lacunae from two other manuscripts (one probably later, and therefore, in the eyes of some scholars, less reliable), and printing the edition such that the original and reconstructed portions are not easily distinguished.[219] Yet this text preserves important information related to the celebration of the Dormition feast not found elsewhere.[220] And it is this text that most fully exploits fragrance as a motif and as a device; the reconstructed portions are entirely consistent with this development. One could say we have evidence here that the process of olfactory symbolization continued to play itself out.

In this third recension, the story is told within an ever more complex liturgical frame. The narrative opens with an invocation that the Trinity should bless the worshipping ranks of created order above and below, past and present, arrayed in their full ritual splendor and performing their ritual roles with glory. Later in the story this massive congregation reappears to attend Mary's deathbed with an elaborate service lasting five days and five nights. The three Marian feasts, tied as before to the agrarian cycle, are mandated with extensive liturgical instructions. The celestial liturgy when Mary arrives in paradise is yet more sumptuous still.

In this text, prayer is generally offered with lavish incense, especially when performed by Mary and the apostles; divine response is most often in the form of heavenly perfume sent forth in exuberant waves. The paths of sacred smells are closely noted: how the incense moves from the censer heavenward through all the celestial regions, and how the divine perfume pours earthward throughout all the world.[221] Fragrance—not the sacrificial offering, not the burning—is now the focus of religious experience, and it is a focus of great might. In this text the Jews make three attempts to murder Mary. The first time, "the odor of the faith that proceeded from [Mary] the Blessed One smote them, and their minds were troubled";[222] thus the incident came to naught. Twice more, while Mary lay on her deathbed, attempts were made—both foiled by angelic hosts drenching the air with their perfume.[223] In this text, not only does paradise throb with sweet scent even as hell reeks of stench, but the celestial liturgy in celebration of Mary's arrival in heaven causes such a commotion that "the bones of the just which were imprisoned within the earth, moved, and a sweet odor was wafted through all the corners of the world."[224]

So much incense is burned and so much heavenly perfume poured out in this text that we cannot be surprised when the "odor" of Mary's faith paralyzes a lynch mob; nor indeed, when the apostles' tears at her death turn the dust of the ground to clay and "that clay caused a scent of perfume to exude and the apostles were gladdened by it."[225] How is the reader to distinguish between a piety now practiced through the medium of incense use, and the belief that knowledge of divine will is to be perceived and identified through the experience of holy fragrance? How could one distinguish the aroma of human worship from the scent of divine presence?[226]

The Syriac tradition of the *Transitus*, more than any other of the surviving versions, provides this focused development of the holy fragrance motif, in keeping with other patterns of Syrian Christianity. The incense aspect of olfactory symbolism was particularly vivid in the Syrian Orient. Christian liturgical use of incense apparently emerged first and then most prominently in the Syrian Orient.[227] As a motif within asceticism, it is the Syrian tradition that poignantly embodies incense in the holy person's ascetic praxis: the stylite on the pillar is the incense on the altar;[228] the ascetic naked in the wilderness is the ecclesial body in microcosm, the body serving as sanctuary, the mind as altar, tears as the incense on that altar.[229] In Syrian tradition, incense had an early and influential role in the sensorium of Christian piety. Here we see its influence at work, in a manner that illuminates the larger Christian perspective.

These three recensions of the Syriac *Transitus Mariae*, closely interrelated as texts, tell the same story of Mary's "passing." A relatively late addition to the body of Christian apocryphal legends, the story presents the salvation drama of the gospels as it will be brought to fulfillment for the human race, in terms that affirm the institutional and doctrinal positions of the post-Nicene church. The story defines Mary's relationship to the apostolic ecclesiastical structure by the gathering of the apostles for her death, and to the charismatic roots of the church with the inclusion of Paul among them. In accordance with the Christological concerns of the late fourth and fifth centuries, the story affirms her participation in salvation history as the place where human and divine met in the singular reality of the incarnation. Her transport to heaven is the promise which the resurrection bestowed on all believers, here foretold as a glimpse of what awaits the faithful. In this story, the essential boundaries that circumscribe the realms of the human and the divine are literally "passed over," to remake Mary's condition and location in the cosmos, bringing her to the very heart of God's domain. This chronicle holds the whole story of the church in its narrative.

Across the three earliest Syriac recensions, this same story is told with increasing reliance on the making and experiencing of smells to convey its purpose. As with any writing of this type—anonymous, apocryphal—a number of agendas are at work. Some are overtly tied to political issues, here most prominently the intense Christological debates, in which devotion to the Virgin Mary played a major role.[230] Some are more inchoate, operating at a less conscious level (for writer or reader) even while tapping into important currents of cultural change. The role of smell across these three texts indicates such an agenda, in which there is a growing awareness of the potency of sensory experience to carry and to clarify religious meaning. A general stress on the senses may be behind this, but the texts demonstrate appreciation for what can be distinctively conveyed through olfactory encounters. The increasing presence of olfactory imagery in the texts matches the growth of incense piety in public and private prayer, and responds to it. The common religious life in which the story was received naturally provided the terms of worship or devotion that would clothe its literary form. But it was the imaginative context of story that would explore the activity of incense offering for the possibilities of its spiritual meanings.

Hence the shift we have noted in these texts from incense as a sacrificial offering, with burning as its key element, to incense as a dialogic device providing an olfactory language that served to bridge the human and divine spheres. Fragrance itself becomes the source and locus of power. This shift draws on the familiar notion of divine presence known and interpreted through fragrance. The pan-Mediterranean association of divinity and heavenly worlds with sweet scents has been a frequent backdrop to our study. Here, however, that concept is employed not as a static attribute of the divine but as a dynamic quality that actively engages human experience. The divine smells sweet, and the course of human lives alters as a result. Fragrance is not a descriptive aspect of the holy, but rather an active agent of divine presence.

The *Transitus* is the story of Mary's (and humanity's) passing across the boundaries of the old dispensation into the new, and it is precisely the transgressive qualities of smell that make it an effective carrier of this message. In the story, smell can be the medium of revelation and agency that operates apart from the more clearly identified experiences of hearing (Christ as Word; the revelation of scripture) and sight (Christ as Light; the revelation of history). First at her conception by the Holy Spirit and then at her death, Mary passes over boundaries no person has crossed before her. The boundaries between human and divine are redrawn to be mutually inclusive. Fragrance becomes a fitting icon for Mary's salvific activity, enacted for the whole human race. Thus her image is enshrined for Byzantine tradition in the Akathist verses composed in the tenth century by Joseph the Hymnographer, chanted still in Orthodox Lenten services:

Hail [Mary], from whom alone there springs the unfading Rose; hail, for thou hast borne the sweetly-smelling Apple. Hail, maiden unwedded, nosegay of the only King and preservation of the world.

Hail, Lady, treasure-house of purity, raising us from our fall; hail, lily whose sweet scent is known to all the faithful; hail, fragrant incense and precious oil of myrrh.[231]

The Syriac *Transitus Mariae* tradition contextualizes its smells within the church as a structured worshipping community. The narrative is one in which liturgies are celebrated on earth and in heaven, and various ranks of holy offices are represented by the identified characters. Mary's own role as the story's center of meaning has a certain paradoxical quality in relation to the ecclesiology of the broader narrative. It is her use of incense in prayer and her experience of divine odors that mark all religious significations of smell in the texts. Yet there can be no confusion as to her place in the ecclesiastical order, for she is a woman. Her lay status is not overridden by the authority of her sanctity, despite her unique role in the salvation drama. However exalted the language of Marian devotion in late antiquity, it never conflicted with the authority determined by the church's hierarchical structure. From the perspective of Mary as a layperson, therefore, it is noteworthy that smell in the Syriac *Transitus* texts grants an active quality of religious authority to Mary's devotional practices. Her interaction with the divine (the archangel Gabriel, the Holy Spirit, Christ in Glory, the heavenly hosts) is direct, albeit mediated by ritual structure. Her engagement with these divine persons is enacted in a highly formalized manner according to the ritual patterns dictated by the church's daily prayer offices and the eucharistic liturgy. But in the story, her character is the one who initiates this interaction, responds to divine summons, directs the apostles in prayer, and is effective as intercessory mediator for other suppliants—all actions demonstrating her religious authority, and all conducted by means of odors.[232] Smell invisibly yet tangibly links the rituals of lay individuals to the collective rituals of the church body, within its authoritative framework—a framework it serves both to establish and to maintain.

Behold, the smell of my son
   is as the smell of a plentiful field which the
   Lord has blessed.

Genesis 27:27

Late antique Christianity cultivated a piety that was both sensorily rich and sensorily self-aware. Liturgical developments, paraliturgical rituals, and the activities of personal piety (whether in domestic or monastic contexts) all served to engage participants in practices that included sensory experience as an essential component. Both through ritual practice and through related instruction (homilies, hymns, or other forms of didactic discourse), Christians granted value to the senses as channels through which believers could approach and encounter the divine. But more was at stake than engagement of the senses in the process of human-divine interaction. A consensus was apparent that the body of the Christian in its received experiences and enacted responses yielded distinct knowledge of God. The instructive capacity of smell was crucial to this understanding, due to the qualities of olfactory experience that caused it to differ in its results from what might be gained through the other senses.

Thus far we have considered how scents were ritually employed in the ancient world to structure the process and condition of human-divine relation. Furthermore, we have seen how Christian writers drew attention to olfactory experience for its religious value as an epistemological tool. In this chapter I will argue that amidst the variety of significations late antique Christians granted olfactory experience, its most important contribution was seen to lie in its capacity to reveal identity. Smells were concretely evident when sights, sounds, and tastes were not; olfactory experience was tangibly perceived, although it did not involve the body's limbs as did touch. These qualities made smell a singularly effective means of discerning divine presence or absence, demonic activity, or moral condition. Such significations expressed the cosmological orientation of the ancient Mediterranean world, whereby olfactory codes served to structure human experience in relation to divine order. These codes operated by signifying identity within a cosmos understood to be morally constructed: "good" identity (God, Christ, the Holy Spirit, angels, saints, virtuous believers) smelled "good," as did the places associated with it (paradise or heaven); "bad" identity and its locations smelled "bad" (Satan, demons, hell, heretics, sinful people). Moral ambiguity—the uncertainties of human experience—yielded ambivalent olfactory cues, as we will see in chapter 5. Whether in clear or murky circumstances, however, ancient Christians used smells to ascertain, probe, and explicate identities within both the human and divine domains: olfaction provided knowledge—essential knowledge—to which there was no other means of access.

Two basic knowledge "systems" (for lack of a better term) were available to ancient Christians for approaching olfaction epistemologically. The first was what we have been considering thus far, in chapters 1 and 2: a system of cultural habit—the instincts, associations, and traditions through which cultural codes were constructed and by which societies granted sensory experience qualitative meanings. The second was through science, comprised of the knowledge acquired through philosophy, medicine, and other modes of scientific inquiry. These two systems of knowledge co-existed at times with considerable tension between them.[1] Clement of Alexandria was a case in point, as he attempted to negotiate a Christian response to the prevalent use of perfumes, substances he recognized to be medicinally useful even while morally dangerous; these traits he had to reconcile with sensory experiences he understood to be important reminders of God's good work as loving Creator. In late antiquity, Christians laid claim not only to the physical world in which they lived (as we saw in chapter 2), but further to the modes of knowledge available within it. Precisely what, then, did Christians claim to know through smell, and how did they know it?

Sense Perception in the Ancient Mind

Sense perception as an area of scientific inquiry had vexed the minds of Greek philosophers and medical experts as early as the pre-Socratics and their Hippocratic counterparts. Questions about the senses were part of the investigation of the human person as a physical, cognitive, and moral entity. In some schools of thought, the senses represented the bridge between the body and its soul—with "soul" serving as a collective term to denote the life principle, rational mind, and emotive faculties that made a body a living, thinking person. Other times the senses were treated as that faculty through which the human person (body and soul) was joined to the physical cosmos. Debates, research, and speculation continued throughout the Greco-Roman world right through the late antique period, as ancient scientists puzzled over a fundamental set of problems: what was the purpose of the senses? how did they work? what comprised the experience of perception? how could the different senses be accounted for? could the senses contradict one another? did they convey true knowledge, and if so, what kind of knowledge was it? Was the relation between subject and object simply a mechanical one, or did sense perception effect a cognitive change in the perceiver?

Ancient thinkers often compared sense perception in animals with that in humans; in the case of Aristotle, for one, such comparative study was extensive in scope.[2] Ancient scientists admired animals for their instinctive cleverness, and the theme of animal "wisdom" was a favorite motif in philosophical discussions, especially those of the Stoic tradition with its stress on the beneficent order of nature and the cosmos.[3] But the comparisons were also stylized in presentation. Their ideological agenda lay in establishing clear boundaries between "animal" and "human" natures, to uphold a hierarchy of natural order in which the human person stood at the pinnacle. Ancient authors might stress the superiority of the sensory faculties in certain animals as compared with their human counterparts—for example, that the human capacity for smell was considerably weaker than that of other animals.[4] But the point was to demonstrate that the intelligence of animals was effectively limited to their sensory cognition, whereas humans added rational thinking to knowledge gained through the senses.

As philosophers saw it, humans and animals alike required the senses in order to navigate the world and survive; but humans alone could think beyond the sensible world to other modes of understanding. Sensory knowledge by itself was limited in content to the sensible domain, its usefulness immediate and pragmatic, applicable to physical survival but not to a higher truth. Humans could compensate for weak sensory capabilities (for example, olfaction in general or specific instances like blindness) and also exceed the limitations of sense perception by their ability to utilize sensory knowledge through the sophistication of the rational mind. Sensory experience could then be used to greater ends, be they social, intellectual, or moral.

Ancient theories of perception understood the senses to be basically tactile in orientation: to involve some kind of direct contact between the sensing subject and the object being sensed.[5] In Platonic and Stoic physics, a ray extending outward from the eye encountered the object of vision. In the atomistic tradition, particles streamed continuously from objects into the atmosphere to strike the subject's eye or ear or nose. All agreed that taste and touch both operated by tactile engagement with their object. Perception might (or might not) take place through an elemental intermediary—transmitted by air, water, or fire. But sense perception was commonly understood to be an experience of physical encounter, in a universe the ancients believed tobe physical, or material, even in its incorporeal aspects.[6] Thus experience of the divine as described by ancient writers was traditionally rendered in sensory terms, even when the divine being was represented as incorporeal: divinities "appeared" in visions or in sightings; deities "spoke" in disembodied voices, or through oracles or signs; odors signalled divine presence (favorable or dangerous). Some thinkers, like Plato or (much later) Plotinus, saw the senses as limited to the experience of sensible things.[7] By contrast, for the Epicureans the senses were the source of all knowledge: as Lucretius stated, "You will find that it is from the senses in the first instance that the concept of truth has come, and that the senses cannot be refuted."[8] But in the ancient understanding, the cosmos itself was a material order, inclusive of all nature—and of divine and human beings and domains. Corporeality and incorporeality were both forms of material existence.[9] In such a cosmology, sense perception could not be considered inconsequential, even if its scope of operation was held to be limited.

Different schools of thought argued over which was the active or dominant aspect of sensory experience and which the passive, reflexive one: subject, object, or medium of transmission. They argued further over the kind of knowledge sense perception conveyed. Aristotle's student and successor Theophrastus was dismayed at what he held to be the flawed and inadequate analyses of sense perception offered by those philosophers who preceded his own efforts.[10] In his treatise, On the Senses, extant only in fragments, Theophrastus divided previous investigators into two basic camps: those (like the atomists) who accounted for sensory experience through similarity in nature, when, through a process of effluence, like was borne towards like; and those (whose model Aristotle would develop) who saw sensation as a process of alteration in which opposites rather than likes affected each other. In this work, Theophrastus critiqued the theories of Parmenides, Empedocles, Plato, Anaxagoras, Heraclitus, Clidemus, Diogenes, and Democritus; even Aristotle's views were deemed wanting, though by implication rather than explicit discussion.[11] Theophrastus insisted that sensory experience yielded genuine knowledge of a world infinitely varied in the diversity of its life forms. Objects of perception and their sensible qualities existed independently of the sensory process. Theophrastus admitted that sense perception was to some extent unstable: it was biased by the subjectivity of the one perceiving, and prone to error or illusion. Yet he held up the senses as essential and trustworthy guides through which to examine the cosmos. Aristotle had valued the senses for their role in the empirical generation of knowledge about a universe he understood to be rigidly ordered in function and purpose, culminating in the overarching notion of final causality. For Theophrastus, the senses revealed a cosmos of such complexity that final causality could not account for it.[12]

During the Hellenistic era, in keeping with dramatic changes in medical science, philosophers shared Theophrastus's dissatisfaction and lifted sense perception to an area of primary concern.[13] Though disagreeing profoundly in their epistemological teachings, both Stoics and Epicureans saw the senses as the source of all knowledge, indeed the only source that could be had. Both schools struggled to account for sensory illusions, false impressions, and disparity between sense experiences. These schools of thought located the processing of sensory information in different parts of the human person. For the Stoics, sense organs received impressions of what they encountered and carried information to the *hegemonikon*, or governing principle of the mind, which then had to assent to the sense impression to complete the process of perception. For the Epicureans, sense organs were themselves the processors of their experiences, in such a way that every perception held the measure of its validity and accuracy. Yet for both, the senses were foundational for any discussion of knowledge or truth.[14]

Consideration of smell as a discrete category of sensory experience took place within these overall trajectories. In the *Timaeus*, Plato had discussed smell in the very terms Theophrastus would later find so unhelpful.[15] Plato here understood the human faculty of smell to lack any definite pattern; smells themselves, "half-formed things," he saw as indefinite to such a degree that they could not be classified by names or types, but only according to whether they were pleasant or unpleasant. Nonetheless, Plato posited two attributes of smell that offer interesting correlation to its cultural significance in the ancient Mediterranean world. First, he claimed that smells occurred when substances were in the process of changing their state through liquification, decomposition, dissolution, or evaporation. Their source was the condition of instability, cast by Plato in terms that left no question as to its inferior and even frightening aspects. Second, whether in pleasant or unpleasant form, smells affected the body to an extreme degree, either doing it great violence or restoring it to its "natural condition." Thus Plato identified smells as powerful agents, but also as powerfully indistinct, operating in some fashion without clear pattern or classification.[16]

Aristotle followed Plato's paradigm in its general aspects, stressing the difficulty of analyzing smell and its objects because humans have an "inferior" sense of smell and a resulting lack of ability to discriminate odors accurately.[17] However, Aristotle also suggested possible ways of categorizing smells according to analogies with taste, and he was expressly interested in the physiological process of smell both in humans and in animals.[18] His successor Theophrastus, as seen above and in chapter 1, was particularly vexed about the question of olfactory categories.[19] Theophrastus was less concerned with olfaction as a sensory process than with smells, their types, and the conditions or circumstances by which they were generated. Later theorists, including the great Roman doctor Galen, cited Aristotle and Theophrastus together as authorities whose discussions of sense perception in general and smell in particular could be taken as definitive.[20]

Because knowledge in antiquity was a moral enterprise, the senses and their experiences could be ranked in value. Plato began a seemingly intractable tradition when he declared sight to be the worthiest and most important sense: through sight, he taught, we have observed the universe. In the process of that observation we have by necessity invented numbers, gained the understanding of time, inquired into metaphysics, and learned philosophy.[21] Aristotle mused that while sight conveyed the largest amount of information and offered the greatest aesthetic value through its capacity to apprehend beauty, yet hearing was of great ethical import because it was the means by which to encounter language, persuasion, and reasoning.[22] Touch and taste, agreed to be the lowest of the senses because they were common to the most lowly of creatures, were nonetheless seen as essential for survival.[23]

There was disagreement as to where smell belonged in this scheme: some placed smell with the "lower" senses, others saw it as more kindred to sight and hearing in the worth of its experience. Galen viewed smell as a superior sense because he thought the nostrils were directly linked to the brain, allowing unmediated information to be processed at once without the need for an intervening sensory nerve.[24] Cicero provided a Stoic version of how the human body exemplified the ordered cosmos, with the senses in a privileged location and olfaction placed for optimum function:

> Human beings are sprung from the earth not as natives and dwellers there, but to survey the heavenly realm above, an insight granted to no other species of living creatures. Our senses have been created and located in the citadel, so to say, of our heads, for necessary purposes; they identify and give notice of external objects. The eyes are our watchmen, and so they occupy the highest vantage-point . . . Again, the nostrils are both aptly set high because every smell is borne upwards, and with good reason they are aligned with the mouth, because they have an important role in discriminating food and drink.[25]

Lucretius, perhaps the most eloquent of the Epicureans, explained perception as the encounter with the fine particles that emanate from all things: "So true it is that from all things there is a different something which passes off in a flow, and disperses in every direction around; there is no delay, no rest to interrupt the flow, since we constantly feel it, and we can at all times see all these, smell them, and perceive the sound."[26] The particles that were bent, or crooked, in certain distinctive shapes were those that caused perceptible smells.[27] Lucretius understood smells to be of weaker impact than sights or sounds, and, it would seem, somehow also less admirable:

> For [smell] moves slowly in coming, and is ready gradually to die away first, being dispersed abroad into the breezes of the air: first because it is emitted with difficulty from the depths of each thing. . .again it may be seen that smell is made of larger elements than voice. . .A further reason is that smell is evidently composed of larger atoms than sound . . .Wherefore also you will see that it is not so easy to trace out in what part the scent is situated; for the blow grows cold in its leisurely course through the air and does not run in hot to the sense with news of the object.[28]

Lucretius dismissed smell as physically—and apparently, morally—inefficient, inconsequential, and inept. If harsher in judgment than other commentators on the senses, Lucretius's appraisal was not discordant with the overall picture, which ranked smell as decidedly less important than sight or hearing, and of marginal significance beyond its role of identifying amenable or adverse substances. Conscious consideration of olfaction, then, tended to result in the relegation of smell to relative insignificance, albeit recognizing the usefulness of smells for certain practical points of knowledge.[29] Such considerations and conclusions stand in tension with the prominent role smells played throughout the ancient Mediterranean sphere in cultural and social fields of meaning. Christian thinkers would present a similar paradox, informed by their particular contexts of discussion.

Christian Senses in a Christian World

The Common Era added another set of voices to discussion of the senses: those of Christian thinkers. Christian intellectuals from their earliest writings had made use of the accomplishments of philosophy and classical learning in their efforts to articulate a distinct identity for their community of believers. The New Testament letters of Paul had already set this course.[30] In chapter 1, I considered this situation in terms of how Christian leaders guided their flocks through the challenges of daily life in a non-Christian society. But Christian intellectuals also faced the task of reconciling the legacies of philosophy and science—legacies they had imbibed deeply in their own education and intellectual training—with biblical traditions and theological problems that did not necessarily share the same presuppositions. Was there an unbreachable gap between knowledge granted by divine revelation and knowledge available through classical modes of empirical inquiry? Despite Tertullian's famous challenge, "What has Athens to do with Jerusalem?"[31] early Christians argued that if their God was the creator and ruler of all, as they believed, then science could only support their beliefs. Knowledge of the world and of the human person in it could serve to demonstrate the extent of God's provident workmanship as displayed in the created order. Bishop Theophilus of Antioch late in the second century would insist on this view in his apology *Ad Autolycum*, quoting extensively from Genesis and the Psalms.[32]

Attention to the physiology of sense perception was part of ancient Christianity's response to this larger challenge. In the early church, discussion of the senses often took place in the context of debates about the corporeal and physical reality of the incarnate Christ, or about creation *ex nihilo*. Both positions were immediately problematic to the intelligentsia of the Greco-Roman world. Quite apart from arguments about whether or not the physical world was intrinsically evil, these positions were at odds with current views of the necessary qualities of "nature"—in which, for example, corruptibility and incorruptibility were mutually exclusive categories that could not be altered or mixed; and views which held matter to be by nature eternal, subject to its own requisite laws, and to that degree unable to be altered by divine whim. These points were strongly argued by the pagan critic Celsus, whose late second-century work, *On True Doctrine*, provided the first sustained examination of Christianity by an outsider.[33] How could a divine power (God) violate the laws of nature to create a physical realm without any matter to start with? How could Christian claims that Jesus was divine yet incarnate as a human person be evaluated scientifically? What was the worth, and what the relative truth-value, of biblical miracles based on sensory experience?[34]

In his monumental reply *Against Celsus*, Origen sought to defend a Christian position that would acknowledge the physical world and physical experience within it as wholly God's work, yet also protect the absolute "otherness" of God. Like other early Christian writers (especially Clement of Alexandria and Tertullian), Origen insisted that Christians must utilize the physical world and knowledge gained through sensory experience in order to seek God, whose reality and nature exceeded the realm of the senses.[35] Sense perception was necessary for the demands of life in a physical world, and God had created the human body accordingly. But neither the body nor the physical world could chart the whole of what could be known:

> Anyone interested should realize that we need a body for various purposes because we are in a material place, and so it needs to be of the same character as that of the nature of the material place, whatever that may be. . . . But in order to know God we need no body at all. The knowledge of God is not derived from the eye of the body, but from the mind which sees that which is in the image of the Creator and by divine providence has received the power to know God.[36]

Origen represented a version of Platonic tradition (much though he disliked Plato) that held to a rigid distinction between knowledge from the senses, which was necessarily limited, and knowledge from the intellect, which could far surpass the confines of a finite, physical existence. His views were shared by some intellectuals, Christian and non-Christian, who like him sought the solution in an alternative set of "spiritual" senses that would allow one to seek a knowledge distinct from and superior to that of physical nature. We will turn to the spiritual senses in chapter 4, but before we can assess what that tradition might represent, we must consider how late antique Christians analyzed and evaluated the physical senses, including smell.

Origen's view is that most often cited—or even assumed—in scholarly treatments of ancient Christianity. It is often illustrated, for example, by an author such as Augustine of Hippo, who shared Origen's Platonic inclinations in setting up soul (mind, for Augustine) and body in a hierarchical dualism that privileged the former dramatically over the latter. Yet we must be careful in how we read discussions of the senses, for an author may present one kind of view in philosophical discussion and another through the literary use of sensory imagery and allusion in broader writings. Augustine's treatment of the senses is in fact ambiguous, in part as a result of the conflicting vocabularies on which he drew: the intrinsic dualism from his deep immersion in the middle Platonism of Plotinus and the Neoplatonic foundations of Ambrose of Milan's preaching did not readily cohere with the biblical rhetoric that exclaimed on human-divine relation through the wonders of the created universe. In a lengthy discussion on the senses in his treatise on *The Trinity*, Augustine argues for two types of knowledge, that which the mind knows through the senses of the body, and that which is known through the mind itself; these he represents through the imagery of the "eye of the body" and the "eye of the mind." The bodily senses, he notes, generally present knowledge that is wrong, distorted, deceptive, or the product of dreams, illusions, or insanity. They present unstable unknowledge. By contrast, the eye of the mind can search out stable, certain, unchanging truth. Even while acknowledging that the bodily senses have something to offer by their perception of God's creation, he yet discounts their significance even in that capacity. Genuinely unenthusiastic about what the senses might offer the believer, Augustine claims it is sufficient for him to take the example of only one sense, that of sight, for sustained analysis on the question of epistemology.[37] For such a thinker, it would appear that olfactory experience or the possible significations of smells should scarcely warrant comment.

Indeed, by his own admission Augustine had little interest in smells of any kind,[38] and his understanding of olfaction as a physiological process was unsophisticated in comparison with other ancient philosophers, medical writers, or Christian intellectuals.[39] Because of these limitations, however, Augustine's views are pertinent to an appreciation of the ways in which olfactory experience had wound itself inextricably into the religious sensibilities of the late antique Christian mind. Examples from the *Confessions* make the point.[40]

In the *Confessions* Augustine presented his turbulent quest for Christian truth through an extended narrative trope, casting the body and its sensory experiences as primary obstacles against which his will had to contend before he could find the rest and peace of faithful devotion to God. He used olfactory metaphors to add texture to the trope. Describing his student years, for example, he commented, "I rolled in the dung [of Babylon] as if rolling in spices and precious ointments."[41] The olfactory imagery elicits moral judgments of decadence, sin, and wanton, undisciplined self-indulgence, with allusions that parody the imagery of the Song of Songs to demonstrate the extent of his own self-deception. In another instance, Augustine recalls the intense desire for God that his Neoplatonic studies awakened in him. Reflecting on his inability at the time to pursue that desire with wholehearted commitment, Augustine summons the capacity of smell to strike the consciousness with tangible force, to herald the promise of its source—a source as yet unperceived—and to linger in the memory: "I did not possess the strength to keep my vision fixed. . . . I carried with me only a loving memory and a desire for that of which I had the aroma but which I had not yet the capacity to eat."[42]

Repeatedly in the *Confessions* Augustine attempts to offer a positive valuation of the senses, yet each time he presents them as inherently limited and limiting in the knowledge they may provide.[43] At best, he sees the senses as well ordered when they are properly disciplined, insofar as they are God's deliberate handiwork. Still, they are but a way station to be passed in pursuit of the highest truth. At Ostia, in the vision he shared with his mother Monica, "The conversation led us towards the conclusion that the pleasure of the bodily senses, however delightful in the radiant light of this physical world, is seen by comparison with the life of eternity to be not even worth considering."[44]

Nonetheless, Augustine offers a poignant comparison between the experience of the physical world and his encounter with God. In book 4, when he recalls the devastating blow of the death of his unnamed friend when they were young men, he speaks of the emptiness of sensory experience in grief: "There was no rest in pleasant groves, nor in games or songs, nor in sweet-scented places, nor in exquisite feasts, nor in the pleasures of the bedroom and bed, nor finally, in books and poetry."[45] The antithesis to this emptiness is presented in book 10, where Augustine struggles to find a language to fit his experience of God:

> But when I love you, [O Lord,] what do I love? It is not a physical beauty nor temporal glory nor the brightness of light dear to earthly eyes, nor the sweet melodies of all kinds of songs, nor the gentle odors of flowers and ointments and perfumes, nor manna or honey, nor limbs welcoming the embraces of the flesh; it is not these I love when I love my God. Yet there is a light I love, and a food, and a kind of embrace of my inner man, where my soul is floodlit by light which space cannot contain, where there is sound that time cannot seize, where there is a perfume which no breeze disperses, where there is a taste for food no amount of eating can lessen, and where there is a bond of union that no satiety can part. That is what I love when I love my God.[46]

The language here, with its evocation of the "inner man," sets the passage within the tradition of the "spiritual," or interior, senses, to which we will return in chapter 4. But should this passage be bracketed into such a concrete bodily dualism, in which physical experience, its processes, its modes of perception and sensory awareness are entirely disconnected from the mind's experience of God (as Augustine calls it)? Is there not something far more nuanced here, in which sensory experience both frames and informs the human-divine encounter Augustine seeks to capture? In another depiction of the experience of God in *Confessions* book 10, Augustine requires the reader to summon all the senses in all their power, and (as argued in chapter 2), in terms that recall the full splendor of liturgical celebration as that context in which the Christian's faith is wholly expressed:

> [O Lord,] you called and cried aloud and shattered my deafness. You were radiant and resplendent, you put to flight my blindness. You were fragrant, and I drew in my breath and now pant after you. I tasted you, and I feel but hunger and thirst for you. You touched me, and I am set on fire to attain the peace which is yours.[47]

Here, surely, is human experience that requires the body even as it exceeds the body's limitations. And for this, even in Augustine's hands, the five senses—including smell—are necessary. They are necessary for the qualities of experience they make possible, for the varied means of reception they open, for the diversity of engagement and interaction they make available to the human person. To capture most fully what Augustine wants to express, he cannot, in the end, eliminate the senses, each with its own contribution to the process of knowing God. If nothing more, these passages must be taken as moments that show the impress of a liturgical context and devotional piety that relied on sensory engagement for the formation of a Christian epistemology.

However, Origen and Augustine were not the only voices of late antiquity. There were other Christian responses to the questions raised by science in relation to Christian teaching, voices that were both more common and more accessible to a broader range of Christian discussion. In fact, the amount of attention given to philosophically informed or scientific consideration of the senses in late antique Christian writing is sharply notable in contrast to that of the pre-Constantinian works.

In a series of fourth- and early fifth-century texts—for the most part contemporaneous with Augustine's career—Christian intellectuals drew upon the science of the human body as it was presented in the academies of their day to demonstrate the intrinsic goodness, beauty, and foresight of God's work as Creator. Their inheritance in this endeavor included the perennial problem of the relation between the incorporeal soul and the instruments of physical sensation contained in a corporeal body; the Platonic understanding of the soul as pre-existent and impassible; the Peripatetic teaching, exemplified by Aristotle and Theophrastus, that there was no perception unmediated by a body; the Epicurean and Stoic insistence on the sensory foundation of all true knowledge; and the question of whether or not some form of atomism operated in the physical domain and activated sensory experience. The eclectic results that could come of such varied traditions were already apparent in the writings of medical experts like Galen.[48] That educated Christians, too, should attempt to reconcile such a smorgasbord of views was no surprise, for the enterprise might be expected of any intellectual of the time.[49]

Hence we find treatises by Lactantius, Gregory of Nyssa, Theodoret of Cyrrhus, and (in most sophisticated form) Nemesius of Emesa, all taking a detailed consideration of the human body, its construction and physiological functioning, as a platform through which to praise the wondrous providence of God.[50] To some extent, these form a continuum with earlier Christian writings, especially as seen in the work of Clement of Alexandria, where a learned medical understanding was also apparent—an indication of the traditional place of such study in classical education.[51] The difference lies in the changed perspective of late antique Christian literature, with its exuberant celebration of the created world as the magnificent expression of its Maker.[52] These treatises share the perspective of Christian leaders addressing a more general audience during the same era. Cyril of Jerusalem's discussion of the human body in his *Catechetical Homilies* presents a similar if simplified exaltation of the wonders of human anatomy; Basil of Caesarea's *Homilies on the Hexaemeron* presume such an understanding in his explication of the marvels of the natural order. Indeed, Gregory composed "On the Making of Man" to complete this unfinished series of Basil's sermons.

These treatises all show a marked appreciation for sense perception as a valued means by which created beings could obtain knowledge of their Creator. In the human person, they instructed, sensory knowledge serves the intellect to guide the mind towards a fuller understanding of God's works and God's nature. Hence, Lactantius explains, the senses are located in the head, the highest part of the body, so that they can quickly administer their experiences to the brain.[53] The greater such understanding, the stronger one's devotion to God will be. Knowledge in the widest sense serves to deepen the human-divine bond, for it brings a more profound understanding not only of the greatness of creation as a work, but, further, of God's extraordinary love for humanity in providing such a world. Nemesius chastised those who downplayed the importance of the body by seeing it as a mere instrument of the soul. "Man's being is on the boundary between the intelligible order and the phenomenal order," he wrote.[54] Located thus, humanity stood as the unique point of connection between the two domains. Commenting on the creation story in Genesis, Nemesius admonished,

> God created both an intelligible and a phenomenal order, and required some one creature to link these two together, in such wise that the entire universe should form one agreeable unity unbroken by internal incoherences. For this reason, then, man was made a living creature such as should combine together the intelligible and phenomenal nature.[55]

The senses, then, did not merely navigate the physical world; they joined it to the whole of God's work, providing a fit and proper fullness to knowledge thereof. Gregory of Nyssa explained that the particular parts of the body were formed for three reasons: to give life, to make that life good, and to allow life to continue through propagation. The brain, heart, and liver were organs necessary for life. The senses were the organs that made life good. The procreative organs allowed a future, by ensuring a succession of descendants. The senses were a kind of extra blessing, allowing humanity to enjoy the world but not strictly necessary for survival since even if one or more was lacking, a person could nonetheless live. But, "without these forms of activity [i.e., the senses], it is impossible to enjoy participation in the pleasures of life." The senses, therefore, were made that we might experience the goodness and beauty of God's creation.[56]

Moreover, as Theodoret pointed out, the variety of the senses made them all the more valuable. For "all these [body] parts we have mentioned, as well as those we have passed over in silence, contribute to the perfection of the one body. Although each is entrusted with its proper function, it contributes to the good of the whole." All the more reason that we must be grateful to God in his wisdom, for when the eye sees or the ear hears or the mouth tastes or the nose smells, none of these parts is alone in the enjoyment or benefit of what it experiences; rather, God made "what is proper to each to the advantage of all."[57] In fact, Nemesius argued, one might think that because there were four elements (earth, air, fire, and water), there should also be four senses—each one appropriate to perceiving each of the elements in kind. But smells do not easily conform to this model, for "vapors and the whole range of scents" are by nature intermediate between air and water. "Therefore, a fifth sense, that of smell, has been invented by Nature for this reason, that nothing capable of being known should evade our perception."[58]

Hence the sense of smell had an essential (if not primary) role within the body's harmonious constitution. Lactantius noted that the nose has a beautiful construction, usefully placed so as to protect the eyes, and efficient in its threefold operation of breathing, smelling, and expelling unnecessary mucus.[59] Theodoret praised its efficiency in processing odors, taking in the pleasant while repelling the unpleasant, and fashioned in such a way as to both protect and assist the brain.[60] Nemesius, the most learned of ancient Christian medical commentators, opined that smell was useful for its ability to discern objects in which the humors were rightly balanced (fragrant), those of average constitution (indifferent odor), and those of inferior or unsatisfactory constitution (offensive odor). He noted that smells like sounds could be perceived from all directions; further, that smell, sight, and hearing could convey the purest pleasures since these senses could operate from a distance, not requiring actual contact with their object in order to take in its pleasures, as did taste and touch.[61]

In these and other patristic treatises containing detailed discussion of anatomy or physiology, Christians did not add anything original to the medical knowledge of their time. Instead, they utilized existing conventions to serve their theological agenda: to demonstrate a good and provident God, to extol the wonders of creation as God's work, to use the human person as a prime example thereof. The content and rhetorical devices in these instances do not differ from those in similar discussions by contemporary non-Christians. Praise for the benevolent order of the cosmos or discussion of "the nature of things" had been long-standing themes in classical philosophy since Plato's *Timaeus*, their appropriate treatments included in the curricula of grammar and rhetorical schools.[62] One need not have been highly trained in medical science to draw on its rhetoric for purposes of moral, or theological, exposition (although Nemesius, at least, clearly was). Perhaps because the theme was a conventional one with set tropes, these texts are notably free of the distrust and admonitions against the senses that so often characterize Christian preaching of this period. Instead, these treatises by Lactantius, Gregory, Theodoret, and Nemesius seem to follow a model of rhetorical tradition, in which the cosmos and humanity's place in it are praised for their intrinsic moral order, goodness, and aesthetic beauty. This was a fitting theme in an era that raised the significance of incarnation theology as Christians came increasingly to the fore in every area of social and political leadership within the Roman Empire. It resonates with oratorical suasion, with ceremony, with ritual splendor. It was, in fact, a fitting theme for a Christianity concerned with locating itself in the public arena.

Denouncement of sensory experience as a source of moral decadence, or ascetic exhortation to free the soul from the confines of the senses to enable more perfect contemplation of God, were discursive themes often heard in late antique homiletic and monastic literature. Scholars have sometimes presented such treatments as if they were the primary, or even the sole, attitude towards the senses or bodily experience in the ancient church.[63] But the changes in Christian practices, rituals, and devotional piety that characterized late antiquity require a more nuanced understanding. As we will see, representations of the senses as morally detrimental had a particular place in the worldview of late antique Christianity. But so, too, did the positive assessment found where the stress lay on creation as God's handiwork, and the human person—body and soul—as its culmination.

Despite the occasionally lavish praise for the body's wondrous workings, no ancient author would have claimed sensory knowledge to be sufficient in relation to God. Even while extolling the unique contribution each of the five senses made to the composite knowledge available to the human mind, Lactantius, Gregory, Theodoret, and Nemesius all presented sensory knowledge as of practical, and therefore limited, value. Sense perception could provide plentiful information about the qualities of the physical world; to that extent, it revealed something about the God who made it. The senses were witnesses to God's work. They made known its manifold nature. Through this activity they could, and should, lead the believer to look beyond the confines of the physical world. Precisely because the senses provided knowledge of a bounded kind, they offered a fundamental teaching about the incomprehensibility—the "unboundedness"—of God. These sentiments were pervasive in ancient Christian literature. As Basil of Caesarea repeatedly stressed, sensory knowledge was a partial knowledge, but nonetheless true in what it could offer. So, too, he admonished, was human knowledge of God partial yet true: one could know God's attributes and actions, but not God's substance (*ousia*).[64] Gregory of Nazianzus exhorted that creation itself, by virtue of being God's work, exceeded the limits of what the senses could grasp or the mind, through and beyond them, could understand. Instead of finding God in the visible world, "every thinking being . . . [must discover] God through the beauty and order of things seen, using sight as a guide to what transcends sight without losing God through the grandeur of what it sees."[65]

Late antique Christian intellectuals drew on the traditions of philosophy and science to provide an adequate appreciation for the natural world as God's work. The effort required them to discuss the nature of sense perception, its contributions and limitations as a source of human knowledge. Their assessment from this perspective was necessarily positive, lest they imply that God had created any part of his creation without purpose or benefit. But the epistemological approach based on the ancient system of scientific inquiry allowed Christian thinkers a further boon: olfaction as a basic human experience could provide instructive theological metaphors through which to teach about God and the nature of divine identity. From the conventions of philosophical and scientific discourse, Christian thinkers drew a series of striking olfactory models for just that purpose.

Olfactory Analogies as Theological Tools

When John Chrysostom preached on 2 Corinthians, he lingered on the text of 2 Corinthians 2:14–16, the oft-cited Pauline passage that interwove a complex of sacrificial and perfume imagery.[66] It was in fact the olfactory language that held his attention, for reasons that resonated all the way back to Plato's *Timaeus* and its unhappily vague treatment of smell. For Plato and the sensory commentators who followed him, as we noted above, the experience of smell was disturbingly cryptic, difficult to control because smells eluded distinct formation or clear classification.[67] For Chrysostom, however, these were the qualities that rendered Paul's language appropriate. Commenting on verse fourteen, "But thanks be to God, who in Christ always leads us in triumph, and through us spreads the fragrance of the knowledge of him everywhere," Chrysostom expounded, "[Paul] did not say, 'the knowledge;' but 'the fragrance of the knowledge;' for such is the nature of the present knowledge, not very clear nor uncovered." It was precisely the discernible yet elusive character of smell that Chrysostom held up as analogous to human knowledge of God.

> Now the one who perceives the fragrance knows that there is ointment lying somewhere; but of what nature it is he does not yet know, unless he happens before to have seen it. So also we. That God is, we know, but what in substance we know not yet. We are then, as it were, a royal censer, breathing whithersoever we go of the heavenly ointment and spiritual sweet fragrance.[68]

Perceiving a smell, one knows that it has a source: but the source need not be visible or even near, as the ancient commentators had noted. Indelibly expressive of its source, a scent yet operated apart from it. An odor thus revealed something even as it concealed it. So, too, instructed Chrysostom, did the Christian inform the world, still largely non-Christian, about God: spreading a sense of God through the witness of their lives and teaching (he in fact goes on to refer to the martyrs), they themselves could not offer more, for human knowledge of God was necessarily incomplete. Certain experience, of a source whose substance remained uncertain; distinct knowledge, of an indistinct source: such was the Christian witness to a God who defied the limits of human comprehension. Such was the fragrance from a perfume, proximate yet unseen.

Chrysostom continued to verses fifteen and sixteen, "For we are the aroma of Christ to God among those who are being saved and among those who are perishing, to one a fragrance from death to death, to the other a fragrance from life to life." Consider, Chrysostom reflected, the ambiguous power of smells. They were medicine and poison; they could heal or destroy. God's fragrance was surely sweet, and surely as unchanging as God's nature. But it was manifested in the world, through the presence of Christians, among believers and non-believers, among those who would heed its scent and those who would not. The fragrance of God remained the same. It was the disposition of the recipient that determined how the scent would work. So, too, Chrysostom reminded his audience, light was still light even when it blinded the weak, and honey was still sweet even when it tasted bitter to those with disease. Christians were the "aroma of Christ to God" on two accounts, through the sacrificial act of their own martyrdoms and through their accompaniment of (or witness to) Christ's death on the cross, just as incense accompanied traditional sacrifices. From either view, Chrysostom admonished, Christians were this aroma among the saved and the damned.

> For this sweet fragrance some so receive that they are saved, others so that they perish. So that should any one be lost, the fault is from himself: for both ointment

is said to suffocate swine, and light (as I before observed,) to blind the weak. And such is the nature of good things; they not only correct what is akin to them, but also destroy the opposite.[69]

Chrysostom explicated the Pauline passage in terms that echoed two frequent observations among the ancient medical discussions: the cryptic perception of odor (tangible yet invisible, derived from a source yet distinct from it), and the odor's effect upon the one perceiving it (an effect determined by the perceiver's disposition). In Chrysostom's exegesis, the first quality revealed something of God; the second, something of the human person. Both revelations pertained to the truth of each of the two identities. Both identities without the olfactory encounter were not necessarily evident (God was invisible, and the person who seemed virtuous might or might not be truly so). The Pauline passage in Chrysostom's exposition gained graphic theological clarity simply by considering fundamental qualities of olfactory experience.

The relation between scent and source also lent itself to Trinitarian problems. Church leaders struggled to expound the relationship between Father, Son, and Holy Spirit: to account for particularity and unity within the Godhead, to safeguard equality among the divine persons, and to present a dynamic mutuality of existence and activity between them. Analogies from light—the sun, its rays, and heat; the light of one torch lit from another—had been freely drawn since the second century, memorably presented by Justin Martyr and Tertullian, and enshrined in the Nicene Creed at the ecumenical council of 325.[70] Gregory of Nyssa found it fruitful to expand the visual and tactile models of light by adding analogies from odors. In his treatise, *Against Eunomius*, Gregory argued for the consubstantiality of God the Father and God the Son (that the two divine persons were of the same divine essence [*ousia*]); and that the Son was co-eternal with the Father (that divine generation did not imply a hierarchy with the Son as a later and lesser divine being than the Father). To make the point, he discussed the different types of generation known from the natural world. Generation caused by effluence, he argued, offered fitting analogy.

> [Other types of generation] again are by material efflux. In these the original remains as it was before, and that which flows from it is contemplated by itself, as in the case of the sun and its beam, or the lamp and its radiance, or of scents and ointments, and the quality given off from them. For these, while remaining undiminished in themselves, have each accompanying them the special and peculiar effect which they naturally produce, as the sun his ray, the lamp its brightness, and perfumes the fragrance which they engender in the air.[71]

Scripture made use of this type of generation by material effluence, Gregory continued, when it spoke of the Son as "the brightness of the glory" (Heb 1:3), or "the scent of ointment" (Song 1:3), or "the breath of God" (Wis 7:25). The analogy was a model applicable both for the concept of consubstantiality and for that of eternal coexistence:

> We must understand by the significance of this expression, an existence at once derived from and subsisting with the Father. For neither is the figure of breath intended to convey to us the notion of dispersion into the air from the material from which it is formed, nor is the figure of fragrance designed to express the passing off of the quality of the ointment into the air, nor the figure of effulgence the efflux which takes place by means of the rays from the body of the sun: but as has been said in all cases, by such a mode of generation is indicated this alone, that the Son is of the Father and is conceived along with Him, no interval intervening between the Father and Him who is of the Father.[72]

The use of odor and source as an analogy for Father and Son had been employed some decades earlier by Eusebius of Caesarea, though in less developed form.[73] Such usage rested on the philosophical and scientific traditions that had highlighted the distinct qualities of sense perception and of olfaction in particular: the singularity that could at times characterize the perceptual encounter of each of the senses, and that enabled smell to function without other sensory assistance (that one could smell what was invisible, silent, and incorporeal); further, the physiological nature of the object that caused it to yield its scent, or, in the case of the sun, its light or warmth. The fruitfulness of this model for discussion of divinity had not been lost in philosophical circles. Plotinus had used it to explain how the One, by nature unmoved and unmoving, could be the source of what comes into being in time. The passage is instructive for its indication that patristic use of this analogy was part of broader intellectual discussions in late ancient culture. Plotinus begins with the analogy of light from the sun, which radiates from and surrounds the sun without the sun's itself changing.

> All things which exist, as long as they remain in being, necessarily produce from their own substances, in dependence on their present power, a surrounding reality directed to what is outside them, a kind of image of the archetypes from which it was produced: fire produces the heat which comes from it; snow does not only keep its cold inside itself. Perfumed things show this particularly clearly. As long as they exist, something is diffused from themselves around them, and what is near them enjoys their existence.[74]

The manner in which odors demonstrated this intimacy of relation and separation was especially apt. As Lactantius had noted, "the taking in of an odor causes no loss whatever of the matter of the odor."[75] Insofar as scientific inquiry had sought to explain both olfaction and its object—both the experience of smell, and smells themselves—the olfactory analogy provided nuanced material for consideration. It spoke to the experience of encounter; it offered ways to image the source of what was encountered; it accounted for perception and source in a dynamic relationship that protected the inviolability and incomprehensibility of the source itself. One of the most striking applications of the scientific olfactory model, roughly contemporaneous with Plotinus, is found in the Valentinian *Gospel of Truth*. The passage uses the physiology of olfactory generation to describe how God the Father fills the Elect (his children) with his presence.

> For the father's children are themselves his fragrance, for they are from the loveliness of his face. Therefore the father loves his fragrance and manifests it everywhere. And when it mingles with matter it imparts his fragrance to the light, and by his silence he makes it superior in every way to every sound. For it is not the ears that smell the fragrance, rather it is the spirit that possesses the faculty of smell and draws the fragrance towards itself for itself and sinks down into the father's fragrance; thus it nourishes it and takes it to what it emanated from, the original cold fragrance. And it is a soul-endowed modeled form, being like a cold liquid that has sunk into some loose earth; and those who see it suppose that (only) earth is there. Afterward, it reevaporates when a gust (of wind) draws it off and it becomes warm. Cold fragrances, then, result from division. For this reason, faith came and did away with division, and it brought the warm fullness of love . . .[76]

The analogy was substantive, yet—again the essence of olfaction—elusive. These characteristics were amply explored by that most subtle of theologians, Cyril of Alexandria, in discussions about the Holy Spirit and aspects of Christology.[77] Fragrance and its source provided him analogies for consubstantiality, incarnation, and hypostatic union within the Godhead, as well as for the way the human person could have knowledge of or participation in the divine while still preserving the complete distinction between divine and human natures. The olfactory analogies he used were the same ones employed by John Chrysostom and Gregory of Nyssa, applied to further points of theological debate. Again, his use echoes philosophical and medical considerations of olfaction and odors. John of Damascus would later summarize such imagery as being that which creation provided to make visible the invisible things of God. By means of these sensory images, he explained, the Christian would be reminded, for example, of the Trinity: "we use the images of the sun, the light, and burning rays; or a running fountain; or an overflowing river; or the mind, speech and spirit within us; or a rose tree, a flower, and a sweet fragrance."[78]

A further set of analogies took up smell as encountered through perfumed oil/ointment. These appear most often with several frequently cited biblical citations: Psalms 45 [44]:7–8 ("Therefore God, your God, has anointed you / with the oil of gladness above your fellows; your robes are all fragrant with myrrh and aloes and cassia"); Psalms 133 [132]:2 ("the precious oil upon the head / running down upon the beard, / upon the beard of Aaron")—both referring to the perfumed holy oil used to anoint the high priests of Israel;[79] and Song 1:3 ("Your anointing oils are fragrant, / your name is oil poured out; / therefore the maidens love you").[80] The verses from Psalms were often invoked by Christian authors in relation to holy oil, whether for baptism or for other uses. The citation from the Song of Songs was routinely applied to Christ; along with Psalms 141 [140]:2 and 2 Corinthians 2:14–16, it was a favorite verse of patristic authors east and west, and tremendously influential in the discourse of olfactory piety.

Analogies involving these verses appear throughout patristic literature, and place the focus on fragrance as encountered in oil or ointment. This specificity of source and location distinguishes such analogies from those considered above, where invisibility or uncertainty of the odor's source was crucial to the figure's meaning. Furthermore, these analogies deliberately highlight the medium through which the scent is carried: the substance of oil or ointment is essential for the olfactory image being invoked. In the image of perfumed oil, smell is enhanced by touch to add dimensions of quantity, texture, and transferability.

Ambrose of Milan drew repeatedly on the image of perfumed oil in his treatise, The Holy Spirit, at different points applying the image and its biblical verses to the Holy Spirit or to Christ.[81] In chapter nine, he has an extended discussion of the Spirit as the oil with which Christ was anointed by God at the baptism in the Jordan.[82] Ambrose begins by reminding his audience that perfumed oil is a composite substance, whose scent is generated by the various ingredients it combines: "And well is [the Spirit] ointment, because He is called the oil of gladness, the joining together of many graces giving forth fragrance."[83] A series of biblical citations follows, to justify the title Oil of Gladness for the Spirit and to demonstrate that this indeed was the oil with which Christ had been anointed. Ambrose then uses this identity as "oil" to argue the full divinity of the Spirit within the Trinity. Where Gregory of Nyssa had used scent and source to present a concept of generation that would uphold Father and Son as consubstantial and co-eternal, Ambrose uses the chemical characteristics of oil (which he has already defined as "fragrant") to argue the Spirit's uncreated nature as the Third Person of the Godhead.

> And well did [the Psalmist] say oil of gladness, lest you might think [the Spirit] a creature, for the nature of the oil is such that it by no means mingles with the moisture of another nature. . . . So since he wastes his time who wishes to mingle oil with moister material, because, since the nature of oil is lighter than others, while other materials settle, it rises and is separated, how do those meanest of hucksters think that the oil of gladness can be fraudulently mingled with other creatures, when surely corporeal things cannot be mixed with the incorporeal, nor created things with the uncreated?[84]

Ambrose uses the trait of oil's viscosity as an image for the fundamentally incompatible (literally, unmixable) material of created (e.g., human) and uncreated (divine) natures. Viscosity leads him to the image of oil as medicine. The oil with which Christ was anointed, Ambrose insists, could not have been a "customary or common oil" such as either "refreshed wounds or relieved fever". It needed to be a life-giving medicine for a world afflicted by mortality, powerful enough to "destroy the stench of sorrowful death."[85] Although he does not present the elision from oil to medicine in olfactory terms, Ambrose's ancient audience knew that it was spices, herbs, and their smells that made healing balms medicinally effective. Viscosity prevented oil from mixing with other types of liquids; but the same trait made it suitable for absorbing and transferring the aromatic substances that healed wounds or sores, or regulated the temperature of bodily humors. Ambrose does not have to mention the scents of medicinal oils, for his audience could not have imagined medicine without its odor (fair or foul, depending on the need)—an odor again yielded, as in perfume, from a composition of ingredients. As we saw in chapter 2, baptismal anointment was often treated as a medically therapeutic act—like the Eucharist, undertaken "for the healing of soul and body." The oil used necessarily carried healing properties whether or not it was the same as that consecrated for anointing the sick, by virtue of its aromatic ingredients. "Oil" could be used as a medical image for theological instruction; but to indicate therapeutic value the image had to include the notion of scent even when no olfactory qualifiers were attached to it. When Ambrose spoke of the Holy Spirit as an oil that could heal mortality, the trope evoked an olfactory sensibility.

In Gregory of Nyssa's treatise, On the Holy Spirit, he, too, used the image of oil to discuss Christ's anointment with the Spirit, but in his case the issue was the Spirit's relation to the Son as full Persons of the one Godhead.[86] Gregory also found the viscosity of oil a fruitful analogy, but this time for its tactility, the manner of oil's absorption by the skin.

> . . . the thought of "unction" conveys the hidden meaning that there is no interval of separation between the Son and the Holy Spirit. For as between the body's surface and the liquid of the oil nothing intervening can be detected, either in reason or in perception, so inseparable is the union of the Spirit with the Son; and the result is that whosoever is to touch the Son by faith must needs first encounter the oil in the very act of touching; there is not a part of him devoid of the Holy Spirit. Therefore belief in the Lordship of the Son arises in those who entertain it, by means of the Holy Ghost; on all sides the Holy Ghost is met by those who by faith approach the Son.[87]

Although the passage is clearly discussing the anointing of Christ, scholars have debated whether or not Gregory is also alluding to baptismal anointment. If so, the text would provide evidence about the baptismal practices followed in fourth-century Cappadocia.[88] However, the passage does not require exact correlation to baptismal practice for the audience to grasp its meaning. The description of oil's penetration into skin such that no interval "either in reason or in perception" can be discerned, offers a vivid analogy to the biblical image of Christ's anointment with the Spirit. They remain separate "things," but so intimately connected that no separation can be detected; moreover, they are so interconnected that one cannot encounter one without encountering the other at the same moment. When scholars wonder how the late antique populace could grapple with the complexities of patristic theology, they are forgetting the use of such analogies or metaphors to present orthodox teaching to the larger community in accessible terms.

But I would also stress that Gregory's analogy is a functionally olfactory one, although the passage does not identify the model by its scent. Because the discussion explores Christ's divine anointment with the Holy Spirit, and because that image itself conflates the Old Testament passages of priestly anointment with fragrant holy oil, the consideration of ointment in the analogy necessarily includes the ritual ointment's perfume. The sense would link with the pervasive image of the Holy Spirit as an invisible but perceptible fragrance: for when scented oil has been absorbed into the skin it is the fragrance that is most immediately apparent. It was this quality that Cyril of Jerusalem had discussed in his catechetical lectures, when he noted that the baptized congregants would exude the perfume of the holy oil, signalling also that they were now filled with the Spirit, while the unbaptized were anointed with unscented oil. Oil's capacity for absorption was a trait primarily known through touch; but its fragrance marked the action.

Gregory's passage need not have referred to the actual baptismal practices of his audience for its meaning to carry olfactory sense. All of the analogies we have considered in this section are noteworthy for how they employ the common themes of olfaction as considered through scientific inquiry and empirical experience. Their meaning is based on the common understanding that was part of medical and philosophical investigations, and grounded in how smells were generated, encountered, experienced, and effective in the course of mundane life. However, although these analogies were based on physical experience, their use in theological discussion also set them within the domain of religious, and hence ritual, meaning. Any mention of perfumed oil or ointment used in relation to the divine in theological discussion echoed also with its correlate of holy oil in Christian ritual practice. The appearance and exploration of olfactory analogies, images, or metaphors in late antique theological texts coincide with the proliferation of olfactory practices in Christian worship and devotion. These developments are not so much causally related—for no deliberate decision regarding the sensory changes in Christian piety or theological discourse of the fourth and fifth centuries can be located—but they are rather mutually inclusive expressions of the same shift in physical sensibility that marked late antique as distinct from earlier Christianity.

The post-Constantinian increase in olfactory rhetoric was part and parcel of the proliferation of olfactory piety: the rhetoric and piety both testify to Christianity's changed orientation towards the physical world in which it was located. As Christians gained political and social power in the world around them, the world gained positive valuation among Christians as their context for encountering, knowing, and living in relationship with the divine. Physical or sensory experiences in the world exuded theological implications for the Christian thinker who sought to reconcile science and philosophy with the Bible. Furthermore, the Christian thinker's task was to articulate a set of beliefs that could integrate history and practices with a biblical literature that provided the imagistic resources through which Christians saw their place in the cosmos as God's ordered intention. This situation is sharply evident when olfactory analogies appear in theological treatises, bringing together biblical references and the rhetoric of scientific observation.

Christian intellectuals also made use of perfume imagery through play upon its sweet fragrance apart from its mediating substance (of oil or ointment). Ambrose of Milan often drew upon the Song of Songs in his discussions of Christ. In his treatise, *The Holy Spirit*, he takes Song 1:3 first as a verse uttered about the Spirit, but then speaking of Christ the eternal Son and Christ in history.

For the name of the Son also is poured forth. . . . For just as ointment inclosed in a vase keeps in its odor, which odor is held back as long as it is in the narrow confines of the vase, although it cannot reach many, yet it preserves its strength, but when the ointment has been poured forth, it is diffused far and wide; so, too, the name of Christ before His coming among the people of Israel, was inclosed in the minds of the Jews as in a vase. . . . But after by His coming He had shone throughout all the world, He spread that divine name of His throughout every creature. . . . Therefore, the pouring out of [Christ's] name signifies a kind of abundant exuberance of graces, and a plenitude of heavenly blessings, for whatever is poured forth flows forth from abundance.[89]

Ambrose here draws on different practical aspects of perfume: the containment and preservation of its scent in closed jars, its powerful strength of fragrance when released, and again its composite nature as the source of its abundant scent. These provide him instructive analogies by which to present the salvation drama as told in biblical history: before the incarnation, Christ was enclosed in "the mind of the Jews" (in their scriptures, in prophecy, in the divine presence among them) as perfume in a stoppered bottle, his scent restricted to their small number. With the incarnation Christ poured into human history as perfume from the bottle, his scent—his name—no longer confined but spread throughout the world in "abundant exuberance." The image of perfume poured out evokes richness, beauty, generosity, unrestricted celebration.

Later, Ambrose returns to the Song for its floral imagery, again to instruct on the work of Christ. The passage, remarkable for its depiction of beauty increased by violence, is worth citing at length.

Christ is the flower of Mary, who sprouted forth from a virginal womb to spread the good odor of faith throughout the whole world, as he himself said: 'I am the flower of the field, and the lily of the valley.' (Song 2:1)

The flower, even when cut, keeps its odor, and when bruised increases it, and when torn does not lose it; so, too, the Lord Jesus on that gibbet of the cross neither failed when bruised, nor fainted when torn; and when cut by the pricking of the lance, made more beautiful by the sacred color of the outpoured blood, He grew young again, Himself not knowing how to die and exhaling among the dead the gift of eternal life.

A good rod, as some think, is the flesh of the Lord which raised itself from the root of the earth to the regions above and carried about the world the sweet-smelling fruits of the holy religion, the mysteries of the divine generation, and pouring out grace upon the altars of heaven.[90]

In this instance, Ambrose takes the techniques of extracting floral fragrance as a model for the story of Christ's birth, life, death, and resurrection. The life cycle of the flower becomes the analogy. A flower's beauty is known when it blooms and sheds forth its scent; the scent is extracted for perfume by different methods which safeguard and even intensify it, but require the flower's complete destruction in the process.[91] So, too, the "good odor" of Christ—an image surely alluding to 2 Corinthians 2:14–16 as well—was spread openly with the incarnation; collected and intensified by the passion and death; and dispersed, now as the fragrant breath of life, throughout the world in the sweet scents of religious practice, theology, and worship.

Chrysostom had used the image from 2 Corinthians 2:14 of "the fragrance of the knowledge of God" to denote humanity's necessarily incomplete understanding of the divine: we know the fragrance, not its source; the scent carries a suggestion, a partial revelation, a mark of presence not fully known. Other theologians used the relationship of fragrance and source as analogous to that between the three Persons of the undivided Trinity, or to account for different aspects of it. In each instance, the fragrance is part of a much more complicated whole, from which it may operate with some independence but without which it could not exist. Ambrose, with the depiction drawn from perfume production, evokes also the echo of sacrificial scents. For both perfume and sacrifice, the perfection of the fragrance is released only through the annihilation of the source: like gold purified of dross, the scent is the purified matter that survives (at least briefly) when flower or resin have been destroyed. In these contexts scent is the perfected transformation of the whole, the continuing and present reminder, or revelation, of a source wholly changed in the process of its being made known—as if, once yielded, the scent reveals a source far different from that first seen.

Most often, however, theological play with the language of perfume and sweet scents had its origin in the Song of Songs, an incomparably influential text for Christian writers. The rich sensory images of its love story were dominated by references to spices, flowers, fruits, perfumes, unguents, and delight in every delicious scent. Ancient Christian commentators almost uniformly presumed the identity of the Beloved to be Christ or the Holy Spirit, and that of the Bride to be the church or the individual believer; Jewish thinkers similarly interpreted the Song to address God's relationship with Israel.[92] The Song hovered close by all discussion of divine love, of human-divine relation, of Christ as Heavenly Bridegroom, of the church or the believer as Bride, of baptism as marriage. It was not only direct exegesis of the Song that elicited this reading of its content, presuming its subject to be the love between God and humanity in its various forms. Any treatment of Christ or the Holy Spirit in ancient Christian writings could include allusions to the Song's lush olfactory imagery. Divine presence, divine nature, divine love, divine action in history; the impact of such divine traits or attributes on the human person, how the human person experienced them or responded in turn—all were presented with and through the Song's language of perfume.[93] The exegesis of the Song of Songs in ancient Christianity is a topic in its own right.[94] What I wish to highlight here is that the Song's perfume imagery could be used for olfactory analogies in the same mode of philosophical and scientific discourse that we have been considering. Ambrose's passage on Song 2:1 and the methods of perfume production is a prime example.

Elsewhere, however, Ambrose followed the more common route of taking the Song's perfumes as images for the love between Christ and the church.[95] In an address to a group of newly baptized Christians, he likened their reception of baptismal anointment to the response of the maidens in Song 1:2–3 to the Beloved's perfume, "How many souls renewed today have loved Thee Lord Jesus, saying: 'Draw us after thee; let us run to the odor of thy garments,' that they may drink in the odor of the Resurrection."[96] The image here is not an analogy used to convey a difficult point of theological debate. Instead, Ambrose engages the traditional identification of divinity by sweet scent, further enhanced by Christ's promise of resurrection for those who would follow him—a promise here imaged by the suggestion of its fragrance, a hint of the breath of life. When Christians shared the ancient association of divinity with perfumed odor, they participated in a system of knowledge based in cultural habit rather than science or philosophy. For late antique Christian writers, this system instilled in believers the means to express human experience of the divine, and further, contributed in distinctive ways to human knowledge about the divine. In late antiquity, moreover, this orientation was continued in a context of Christian practices that now ritually supported it through the proliferation of olfactory piety. The expanded use of ritual scents contributed to the cultural habits by which Christians might think about or articulate divine identity and human identity in relation to it.

Revelatory Scents: Olfaction and Identity

Theophrastus had asserted that everything that had a smell had its own, distinctive smell. Further, he argued that every smell belonging to a living thing conveyed not only identity, but also condition and circumstance.[97] The cultural correlate to this position was the tradition of interpreting smells as indicators of identity, nature, character, and moral state. This perspective explained why smells could function diagnostically: they indicated the essence of something by revealing its aspects or attributes. The model was pervasive in late antique Christian writings. Basil of Caesarea and Gregory of Nyssa mention the common medical practice of diagnosing illness by smelling the patient's breath,.a practice Galen had encouraged.[98] The breath's odor would indicate the balance of humors in the sick person's body, as well as other marks by which the illness could be properly identified. Similarly, Syriac astrologers could predict whether a person would exude a pleasant or unpleasant smell based on the month of birth.[99] The cultural assumption was that fate was determinative of the circumstances in which one conducted one's life; one's smell could reveal whether those given conditions were favorable or unfavorable for prosperity and good fortune.

The monk Hilarion was able to diagnose moral condition from personal odors: "The old man had extraordinary grace to know from the odor of the body, the clothing, and the things that anyone had touched what devil or what vice had predominance over him."[100] Indeed, smells made known one's manner of life. When Mary, the niece of the holy man Abraham of Qidun, fell into perdition and fled to a brothel, Abraham went to her rescue disguised as a soldier; the young niece recognized him by "the smell of asceticism that issued from the blessed man's body."[101] When the Syriac saint Malkha fled from his family to become a monk, his mother and sister thought he had returned when they recognized his smell in clothing he had given away.[102] Indicative of one's own person and state, one's smell could transfer one's moral characteristics to others. Gregory the Great adapted a familiar topos from epistolary convention, combining it with 2 Corinthians 2:15, when writing to a friend he dearly missed:

> And we, as often as we hear anything of good people, draw in as it were through our nostrils a breath of sweetness. And when Paul the Apostle said, 'We are a good odor of Christ unto God,' it is plainly given to be understood that he exhibited himself as a savor indeed to the present, but as an odor to the absent. We therefore, while we cannot be nourished by the savor of your presence, are so by the odor of your absence.[103]

It was a sensibility that endured. In the eighth century, Syrian villagers who converted from Christianity to Islam were recognized as apostates because of their odor:

> But they [the converts to Islam] grew different from the faithful people in both person and name; in person, because their once happy personal appearance became repugnant, in such a way that they were recognised by the intelligent

ones through their persons, odor, and the look of their eyes. . . . instead of a sweet odor of the holy myron a stinking and fetid smell emanated from them.[104]

The correspondence of personal odor with moral condition pervaded biblical interpretation in the same fashion. Ephrem Syrus used scents to contrast types of marital relations from Genesis with that of the Virgin Mary at the incarnation. Tamar had deceived her father-in-law, Judah (Gen 38:13–26), while Joseph had maintained virtuous fortitude (Gen 39:41–45): "Tamar reeked of the smell of her father-in-law, / for she had stolen perfumes. Not even the slightest scent / of Joseph wafted from the garments of his bride." But because Mary conceived Christ, the Glorious Lily and Treasure of Perfumes, there was no need of sexual intercourse, "of the flower or its fragrance."[105] The smells in such texts did not function literarily as analogy or metaphor. Rather, the uniqueness of personal odor expressed what was most profoundly intrinsic: the essence of character, the moral self as true self. An anonymous Syriac verse homily told the story of Abraham and the sacrifice of Isaac from Genesis 22 through the imagined view of Sarah's perspective. Believing her only son to have died in innocence, Sarah grieves with poignant lament, wishing she could fly like an eagle to see the place of his binding and his ashes, "and bring back a little of his blood, to be comforted by its smell."[106]

Personal odors conveyed identity and revealed the individual's moral condition. They could not be disguised, either by intention or design: "Do not," Paulinus exhorted, "wander abroad with perfumed clothes and hair seeking recognition from men's nostrils wherever you pass."[107] One's odor expressed one's nature, the truth of one's self. To smell that odor was to gain the knowledge it contained. In the Acts of John, the apostle John banishes an evil spirit with an exorcism formula commanding, "Be removed, then, from those who hope in the Lord; from their thoughts, from their minds, from their souls, from their bodies, from their action, from their life, their behaviour, their way of life, their practice, their counsel, from their resurrection to God, from their fragrance in which you can have no share. . ."[108] The ancient Mediterranean belief that divine presence was made known through sweet fragrance was another variation on this theme. Late antique Christian writers drew on the topoi of divine fragrances, as we have already seen, to signify divine presence and participation in human affairs, in sacred ritual, and in human history. But they also employed these conventions for epistemological use, to explore and convey knowledge about God.

That such usage was never simply metaphor or analogy was clear from discussions about the incarnation. The notion of God become human lifted the role of sense perception in knowing God to intense significance: the senses perceived God through his handiwork in the natural world, yes. But in the incarnate Christ, the senses had perceived God himself; God had chosen to reveal himself according to the human capacity for knowledge gained sensorily as well as through the mind's understanding. When Ephrem recalled the story of Jesus' rejection by the people of Nazareth in Luke 4:28–30, he exclaimed about this very paradox: "They spoke ill of our Lord because of His body and thought that He was not God. . . . yet it was because of His body—the body that they experienced as passing among them—that they recognized that He is God."[109] From the nativity to the resurrection, God had become known to humankind in and through the senses. The *Gospel of Truth* had caught the significance of this direct sensory engagement: "Acquaintance from the father and the appearance of his son gave [the people] a means to comprehend. For when they saw and heard him, he let them taste and smell of himself and touch the beloved son."[110] While the immediacy of that encounter was confined to the historical moment of the gospel story, its power was seen to continue to permeate every sensory encounter revelatory of the divine. Ephrem had lambasted the heretical Bardaisanites, among other charges, for reducing God to nothing more than divine fragrance—mere perfume or smoke that could be dissipated but had no greater reality.[111] To the true believer, the fragrance of God heralded that divinity which could only (as John Chrysostom had said) be partially realized—but the whole was there.

The notion worked as a powerful aid in devotional piety, especially when seeking an affective impact on the believer. In an anonymous Syriac hymn, the hymn writer presents a kind of meditation on the Christ child, newborn and cradled in the Virgin Mary's lap. Repeatedly, it is the baby's scent on which he dwells. Even while stressing Christ's humanity, the hymn thus proclaims his divinity:

> The sight of You delights, Your smell is sweet, Your mouth is holy. . . .
> How sweet is Your breath, how lovely Your baby state.
> . . .
> Your eyes are merry with delight at all who kiss You,
> Your lips distil the fragrance of life,
> While balsam flows from Your fingertips.
> Your eyes are lovely
> As they gaze on Your mother
> . . .
> Who can set eyes on You and not breathe in Your fragrance?
> Even Your dribble causes onlookers to wonder,
> And Your manifest form amazes rational beings.
> Your tiny hands are clasped,
> Your feet are kicking,

How lovely You are in every way.
Even Your mouth's murmur tells of Your Father.
How gorgeous is Your beauty, how sweet [Your] smell –
Your mouth is very honey,
O infant God![112]

This "sensibility" of God—the availability of God to the human senses—came increasingly to be stressed in late antique Christian aesthetics. The emergence of icon piety at this point in time was no accident.[113] In literary expression, late antique Christian writers routinely used fragrance to identify divine characters in the stories they told. An angel's arrival would be apparent first by a heavenly scent "seeping down from the sky and into the nostrils;" his departure would "lend fragrance to the air from afar with his holy scent."[114] Legends proclaimed that divine perfume had poured from the cave where Jesus was born; that the scent of the Magi's spice offering filled all the towns through which the three Persians passed; that the odor of the Christ child's clothing had healed a blind child.[115] Monks visiting the shrine on Mt. Sinai, marking the place where Moses had received the Law, described it as redolent with celestial perfume.[116]

Such instances had their counterparts in personal recollections. Augustine remembered how his mother, Monica, "used to say that, by a certain smell indescribable in words, she could often tell the difference between [God's] revelation and her own soul dreaming."[117] Cyril of Scythopolis told how his work as hagiographer began when the two saints Sabas and Euthymius appeared to him in a vision and placed on his tongue a substance with the texture of oil, a taste sweeter than honey, and an ineffable fragrance that lingered in his mouth and gave him the strength to begin his writing.[118] There was a pervasive expectation that the Holy Spirit would be present to the praying Christian with purity of heart, a presence known by its fragrance; so John Cassian: "we are often suddenly filled in these visitations with odors that go beyond the sweetness of human making, such that a mind which has been relaxed by this delightful sensation is seized with a certain spiritual ecstasy and forgets that it is dwelling in the flesh."[119] The Egyptian monk Ammonas wrote to his monastic brethren that upon those whose hearts were perfectly cleansed in preparation, the Holy Spirit would not cease to pour fragrance and sweetness.[120]

But there was expectation, too, that divine fragrance would work upon and change the one perceiving it. Smells penetrate and permeate what they encounter; they are transferred by contact, attaching their odor—and the knowledge it carries—to whatever and whomever they touch. This was true of smells generated in the physical realm, as the ancients often noted. How much more so, then, must it be true of divine smells. Paulinus praised the new ascetics in Nola and among them Eunomia, a young virgin devoted to Christ from her childhood. Upon her, Christ had early sprinkled "the perfume of his name. Accordingly, the tresses of her soul [were] steeped in it, and the chaste head of her mind anointed with it, and so her breath [had] the holy scent of her heavenly bridegroom."[121] The Syriac version of the *Life of Antony* spoke of reptiles finding the saint when he was enclosed in the abandoned fortress because his smell was "not of human beings."[122] Indeed, frenzied dogs could be stilled by St. Ioannikios's sweet scent.[123]

The transference of holy scent from divine presence to the chosen person took place within an olfactory dialogue. Personal odor revealed the inner disposition (moral nature) of the chosen one, above and beyond any devotional act that person performed; that odor was then transformed by the divine fragrance poured forth in response, leaving the chosen one redolent with a grace that could be smelled by others. An anonymous Syriac hymn wrongly attributed to Ephrem describes the exchange in the case of the biblical prophet and king, David, when he was anointed with ritual holy oil. The anointing gave him an odor pleasing to the Holy Spirit because it was rightly performed, but the "odor of his heart" was the more pleasing offering. In response the Spirit dwelt in him, granting his heart fragrant blessing:

> At David's anointing, my brothers, there came down the Spirit who gave scent
> to his heart; for the scent of David's heart pleased him, just as the scent of the oil;
> the Spirit dwelt in him and sang in him.[124]

Divine visitation might fill persons with holy fragrance beyond that of their own dispositions. Yet holy fragrance was as transitory as any scent: it could not be preserved in a faulty container. "Into hearts that are pure the Spirit enters," Prudentius wrote; but the consecrated heart that grew defiled with the "murky vapors" and "black corruption" of fiery passions forced grace to depart.[125] One might pray to receive divine fragrance, as when Abo the Perfumer prepared for his martyrdom at the hands of Saracens, petitioning Christ that he be filled "with the imperishable perfume" of divine love.[126] But the perception of divine fragrance was itself an act caused by grace, no less than exuding its scent.

Late antique Christian writers presented the encounter with divine fragrance as revelatory of the one whose scent poured forth, and of the one who was able to perceive it. Such encounter was also shown to be transformative of the human subject, who might well be found to breathe forth a holy scent as a result. Christian authors hence presented faith itself as a process in which olfactory experience might mark stages on the way towards the life of true devotion. Such, for example, was the impact described by Severus of Minorca in his *Letter* on the Conversion of the Jews.[127] The mass conversion in Minorca that Severus recorded was punctuated, by his account, with divine signs and portents that contributed to the heightened emotional state of the community. Among these were recurrences of mysterious, sweet-tasting, fragrant substances that appeared like hail or rainwater; and the sudden filling of the church "with such a marvelous and truly heavenly odor that nearly all the brethren sensed the presence of the Holy Spirit, which we had also sensed sometimes in the past, but only a few among us."[128] By the fragrance was the nature of the presence known.

The fragrance of divine identity did more than bestow the mark of grace upon the faithful believer who perceived it. It was itself the carrier of what was intrinsic to the divine: the power to give life. The "fragrance of life," a phrase pregnant with meaning in this late antique context,[129] was not a didactic figure of speech used to instruct the faithful. It was the expression of how God's creative force worked in the universe. Romanos the Melodist put the image to work in his second Hymn on the Nativity (Nativity 2).[130] The hymn tells the story of how Adam and Eve, asleep in Hades, awake at the birth of Christ, the event that begins the process of their redemption into new and everlasting life. Eve is the first to perceive that all things have changed. As she had once heard the voice of the serpent in deceit, now she hears the voice of Mary singing to the newborn Christ child. She summons her husband, who fears to trust his ears that had formerly deceived him. The story moves from auditory to olfactory knowing: exhorting Adam not to fear his hearing—which had once led him astray through her words—Eve calls him to smell what is happening.

> Be fully reassured, my husband, by the words of your wife;
>   For you will not find me again giving you bitter advice.
> The ancient things have passed away,
>   And Christ, the son of Mary, brings to light all things new.
> Catch the scent of this fresh smell, and at once burst into new life.
> Stand erect like an ear of corn, for spring has overtaken you.
> Jesus Christ breathes forth a fresh breeze.[131]

Adam takes note, and it is indeed his sense of smell that alerts him to the incomprehensible change that has begun. He smells beauty, paradise, the Tree of Life, life itself:

> I recognize, wife, the spring, and I sense the luxury
>   which we enjoyed in the past; for indeed I see
> A new, another paradise, the virgin,
>   Bearing in her arms the tree of life itself, which once

The cherubim kept sacred, kept me from touching.
    And I, watching the untouched tree grow,
Am aware, wife, of a new breath—bringing life
    to me, who was formerly dust and lifeless clay,
Making me come alive. And now, strengthened by this fragrance,
    I advance to her who causes the fruit of our life to grow,
    Mary, full of grace.[132]

Thus to smell God was to smell life as it would be fulfilled in immortality, what Ambrose had called "the odor of the resurrection." It was a smell that could be known in this present world by the one who lived in devotion to God. As Isaac the Syrian said, "Thus the one who lives with love in this creation smells life from God. He breathes here of the air of resurrection. In this air the righteous will delight at the resurrection."[133]

While this scent of life was a smell of beauty to the faithful, it was a smell whose scent was powerful and therefore terrifying to the forces of death, just as the Pauline passage of 2 Corinthians 2:16 had warned. It was a smell that not only identified its divine source but also did God's work in the act of granting life. In his hymns, Ephrem portrayed the final work of Christ in pungent terms. Adam was the one who "became leprous and repulsive / because the serpent had breathed on him;" hence "the Garden cast him from its midst."[134] Fragrant Eden could not tolerate the stench of mortality. But neither could Death endure the odor of life breathed forth from the crucified Lord, an odor that struck Death with terror when he approached the cross to smell Christ's blood.[135] It was this odor that raised the dead when Christ descended to Sheol.[136]

Instead of death which has breathed the fragrance of mortality
    upon all,
The Living Fragrance who gives life to all breathes forth
    in Sheol.
From His life the dead breathe new life,
    for death dies within them.[137]

Elsewhere Ephrem linked the concepts of inhaling and consuming, of fragrance and food. At times he switched his framing of Christ's descent to Hades from olfactory to alimentary imagery, from Christ as the Fragrance of Life to Christ as the Bread of Life. When Sheol could not bear the presence of Christ within its midst, it vomited him forth and all the faithful dead with him.[138] Because Christians consume Christ's body and blood, wrote Ephrem, they too will be intolerable for Death. As we noted above, consuming the Eucharist mingles the being of Christ throughout the being of the believer: "All of Him has been mixed into all of us."[139] Consequently, "For this reason, You mixed Your blood, which repelled death and terrified it, in the bodies of Your worshippers, so that the mouths of [dead idols] who consume them would be repelled by their life."[140] The presence of Christ within the believer—the result of consuming the Eucharist—will be salvific in a cosmic sense: all creation will be healed and saved. But Ephrem implies that until the final triumph of God's Kingdom, the force of divinity within the believer is also specifically apotropaic in the place where the dead repose.

At least on this point, Ephrem's successors seem both to conflate the layers of Ephrem's imagery on the Fragrance of Life, and to narrow its sense to a sharply honed apotropaic force exerted by the odor the faithful breathed forth—the odor they acquired by Christ's presence within them. In the *Epiphany Hymns*, written from Ephrem's school and very near to his theology, the baptismal anointing is "an odor loathsome to Satan, [but] to God its perfume is sweet."[141] Subsequently, Jacob of Serug finds the scent from the Eucharist to be all-conquering and abominable to the forces of death. The oblation offered in memorial services yields a scent that sustains the dead like food while they await the final resurrection:

> To the Fragrance of Life pouring forth from the great sacrifice,
> all the souls gather and come to receive pardon.
> And from the resurrection which caused the body of the Son of God to rise
> every day the dead breathe in life and receive mercy from it.[142]

Where Ephrem had portrayed the harrowing of hell in alimentary terms (Sheol vomiting Christ out), Jacob presents an olfactory version of the apotropaic powers gained from consuming the Eucharist: "May the fire [of Gehenna] stand awed before my members, when the odor of Your body and pure blood, mixed in me, strikes forth."[143] The image is preserved almost verbatim in an early medieval burial hymn still used in the funeral rite of the Maronite church: "I consumed Your holy body so that the flames would not consume me . . . For the flames will flee from my path as the fragrance of Your holy body and blood emanates from me."[144]

In this context of cosmic warfare between mortality and immortality, the Fragrance of Life is a weapon to preserve the faithful from the destruction of death. Residing within the believer's body, Christ's odor is a hardened armor, protecting but not changing or teaching the faithful who receive its power. These apotropaic passages appear to be derived from Ephrem's images of scent and salvation, albeit impoverished renderings thereof.[145] The believer gains protection from the forces of death as an interim condition. Emphasis on the apotropaic effect of divine odor represents a model of human-divine relation simplified from that which Ephrem and other late antique Christian writers sought to nurture. Here, the breach separating Creator and created order remains absolute. The odor of Christ resides in the believer who has consumed the Eucharist, a power that remains separate from the being and condition of his partakers even while mingled within them. Ever vulnerable to the powers of destruction, the believer is shielded more than transformed. Right relation with God places the believer in a privileged location of shelter as the forces and powers of the cosmos are reordered to be subservient to divine will. This, too, is a salvific model, but one that allows little human participation in the event of redemption. The believer is essentially the passive recipient of divine help, rather than the active participant in its process. Yet there remains an awareness that the air one breathed could carry the promise and power of salvation, the fragrance of life itself. Odor identified the nature and state of its source.

Remembering Knowledge:
Liturgical Commentaries

The post-Constantinian era brought tremendous change in Christian rituals and devotional practices. Often these changes occurred over time without direct guidance from leaders or councils, but rather as shifts in local or common practice that were explicated subsequently through official channels (conciliar statements or canons, episcopal instruction, imperial decree). The catechetical homilies of the fourth century were a response to this situation, providing congregations with careful exposition of liturgical rites and offering instruction on the actions, gestures, and spoken formulae of ecclesiastical rites. These were especially useful in an era that brought a huge influx of population into the churches, and when adult baptism was the normal practice. After the fourth century, as infant baptism became more common, the great catechetical sermons of Cyril of Jerusalem, John Chrysostom, Theodore of Mopsuestia, and Ambrose of Milan circulated widely in numerous copies, ensuring a continuing instruction of the lay population.

At the end of the fifth century, however, a new form of liturgical instruction began to appear, directed to a different audience and with a different intention. These were the liturgical commentaries properly speaking. They were addressed not to a catechumenate of recent converts, nor to a lay populace in need of teaching. Instead, they targeted those who had already received instruction in the faith: monastics especially (who sometimes felt they were not required to participate in the standard activities of Christian sacramental life), or clergy and bishops. Their purpose was to provide more advanced teachings on liturgical practices, and to summarize interpretive traditions of the church.[146] In their Byzantine and Syriac forms, they self-consciously develop the themes of the earlier catechetical sermons.

Liturgical commentaries have something in common with biblical commentaries, for they approach the liturgy as a performance that can be read as one would read a biblical text, through established exegetical and hermeneutical strategies. They see liturgy like scripture: as a form of divine revelation whose every moment contains levels of meaning, each level able to convey some essential portion of divine truth to the faithful. Because they offer a self-consciously considered exposition of sacred ritual intended for an audience of ritual specialists (that is, monastics and clerics), I would suggest that we might also read them as texts primarily concerned with epistemology. In their attention to details of gesture and movement, of objects and garments, sequences, order, spaces, and form, these commentaries bring together the ritual memory of Christians, in terms that evoke both systems of knowledge this chapter has explored—that of intellectual training passed on through philosophical and scientific traditions, and that of cultural habit. The explications they provide would not have been self-evident to a practitioner of another religion who might have accidentally wandered into a Christian liturgy with no prior preparation. Moreover, their instruction would only have been as familiar to the Christian congregation as clergy or monastics had taken the opportunity to make it known.

What did the different priestly vestments signify? What was the purpose or meaning of the liturgical fans? Why was incense burned at certain points of the service? Why was incense carried through the nave? Why were the gospel books brought out to the congregation and then carried to the altar? A wealth of description and explanation on such details survive in these commentaries, granting conscious intention to each. As with any literature of this type, we should be careful not to take these texts as representative of "standard opinion," nor as widely read. But they do offer insight into important traditions of ritual knowledge—of religious epistemology as codified in the liturgical practices of their time. As literature that developed well after the ritual and devotional changes begun in the fourth century, they provide reflection on the kind of knowledge these practices made available to Christians. Accordingly, they have important contributions on the olfactory practices that came to punctuate late antique Christian worship. For incense and myron, at least, the Byzantine and Syriac traditions continue to show a markedly greater emphasis and appreciation than what develops in western practices during the same period.[147] It is from these commentaries, then, that I take notable highlights by which to consider the issues of the present chapter.

In a formal sense, we can mark the emergence of the eastern liturgical commentaries around the year 500 with the works of the unknown author who referred to himself as Dionysius the Areopagite.[148] Scholars have long struggled with Dionysius, puzzling in particular over the matter of his evident debt to Neoplatonism and the charge that his writings verge on being nearly "Christless."[149] The setting of Neoplatonism in direct opposition to a Christian notion of revelation by modern scholars has unfortunately dominated discussion of this author, and indeed has led to considerable distortion of his content.[150] More recently, as scholars have established the late antique Syrian Orient as Dionysius's milieu, there has come a welcome effort to set his writings within the distinctive ascetic and liturgical contexts warranted by that location. What is emerging is a liturgically grounded, profoundly Christocentric reading of this author, in which Platonic influence is overshadowed by—or at the least, contextualized within—an embodied and enacted liturgical piety.[151] For our purposes, I wish to note two emphases in Dionysius's writings that are often overlooked by others, but which stand out in the context of the changing post-Constantinian orientation to the physical world: his insistence on the significance of sensory experience as an epistemological tool, and the extraordinary prominence he gives to the olfactory aspects of liturgical practices. Both raise intriguing questions if one is committed to reading "Platonism" in rigid terms.

In the *Celestial Hierarchy*, Dionysius states bluntly that humans require sensory experience for their understanding of God and of the divine realm. By this he does not mean that the physical, sensory realm stands in analogous relation to heaven. He does not posit a baldly symbolic correlation, in which the physical components of worship are set forth as images of a "higher" reality. Instead, he argues that the liturgical setting guides (or trains) the senses so that they lead the believer to experience realities beyond the immediacy of the concrete situation. The immediate setting opens the senses, allowing them to bind the mundane, sensory experience of the worshipper to the celestial domain in which it must ultimately take place.

> For it is quite impossible that we humans should, in any immaterial way, rise up to imitate and to contemplate the heavenly hierarchies without the aid of those material means capable of guiding us as our nature requires. Hence, any thinking person realizes that the appearances of beauty are signs of an invisible loveliness. The beautiful odors which strike the senses are representations of a conceptual diffusion. Material lights are images of the outpouring of an immaterial gift of life.[152]

The liturgy conducted here, in the visible, corporeal, and odoriferous reality, is an icon of its celestial counterpart: it opens beyond itself at the same time that it participates in the prototype it images, a participation that provides the essential reality of its own activity. The church's liturgy thus stands in iconic relation both to the interior actions of the individual believer's soul at worship, and to the celestial reality which is itself a liturgy. The material symbol or image does not "stand for" a divine counterpart; it is rather "theophoros," God-bearing, that which conveys the divine. "Everything can be a help in contemplation . . . even those forms drawn from the lowliest matter" because worship is the activity of the human-divine relationship.[153] It is so for Dionysius in three simultaneous, coexistent "liturgies," or "churches": that of the interior person, the soul (called elsewhere in Syriac tradition the "little church"); that of the exterior, visible, and earthly church; and that of the celestial, heavenly church.[154] So complete is the coordination of these realms of activity that sensory experience within the liturgy is necessarily, and always, iconic: it is experience that is by nature incarnational, as the divine is present in and through it.[155] For this reason, Dionysius says, theologians may use sensory imagery and sensory experience within the liturgy "not only to make known the ranks of heaven but also to reveal something of God himself." They might use "the most exalted imagery, calling God for instance sun of righteousness;" or they might, surprisingly but not inappropriately, use images "of the lowliest kind, such as sweet smelling ointment."[156] There are different domains of reality, and there are different capacities for receiving and understanding religious truth. Each level of knowledge is worthwhile, as each can serve to bind the believer through the liturgy to the divine. This is in fact the liturgy's purpose. From this perspective, no element of liturgy is gratuitous or insignificant in itself. Form and function are as important as the divine presence they signify, and the senses are essential to their realization. In the above quotation, Dionysius highlights not only the fragrant scents of worship, but their characteristic movement of diffusion—the qualities by which smells work are not less meaningful than their beauty.

In his *Ecclesiastical Hierarchy*, Dionysius provides a commentary on the various rites and offices of the church. These, like the scriptures themselves, are gifts to us from the divine that are ours in the form of "sacred symbols."[157] Whether through scripture or rite, perceptible images and perceptible experiences are used to bestow religious knowledge; "sacred symbols are actually the perceptible tokens of the conceptual things" that lead to the understanding of divine reality. Every perceptible aspect is heavy with meaning. In baptism, anointment with holy oil gives the initiate a sweet scent, but the joining to the Holy Spirit that it marks is "not something [ultimately] describable . . . for it is in the domain of the mind that [this outpouring] does its work of sweetening and of making perfect."[158] In preparation for the eucharistic liturgy, the priest censes the altar and then, walking through the nave, censes the entire church prior to the liturgy's commencement. The actions and their olfactory impress mimic and enact the transfusion of divine presence into the world, a presence that in no way diminishes the divine being in its eternal essence:

> We must look attentively upon the beauty which gives [the image] so divine a form and we must turn a reverent glance to the double movement of the hierarch when he goes first from the divine altar to the far edges of the sacred place spreading the fragrance and then returns to the altar. For the blessed divinity, which transcends all being, while proceeding gradually outward because of goodness to commune with those who partake of him, never actually departs from his essential stability and immobility.[159]

In Book 4, Dionysius presents a third rite, "belonging to the same order" as baptism and Eucharist, the sacrament of the holy myron.[160] The section is arresting in part because it describes a ritual—the blessing of the holy oil—not mentioned in the earlier catechetical homilies that survive in Greek or Latin, but rather finding its counterpart in Syriac texts of the sixth century and thereafter. But more unsettling is its olfactory emphasis in a work that otherwise seems to privilege the practices and imagery of visual piety (as one would expect in a Platonic system). Dionysius describes the rite as one that sets the myron in a literal and ritual space of singular power. After dismissing the "imperfect orders" (the laity as well as the unbaptized), the bishop censes the inner sanctuary of the church while the attendant clergy chant psalms and read from the scriptures. Then the bishop takes the myron, "covered by a dozen sacred veils," and sets it on the altar. Unlike baptism or eucharistic liturgy, no processions enter or leave the larger area of the church nave; the consecration is confined to the clergy, within the (separated) sanctuary, at the holiest of holy loci. On the altar, the myron is blessed. There it remains, for use "in the holy sacraments of sanctification for almost all of the hierarchy's rites of consecration."[161]

Dionysius follows this summary description with a discussion of the ritual's meaning, dwelling at length on olfactory experience as revelatory of divine truth and as vehicle of religious knowledge, in a treatment unparalleled in previous works of liturgical instruction. Even the handling of the ointment is pregnant with sense:

> It shows us that divine men cover in secret the fragrance of that sanctity within their minds. For God himself has forbidden that sacred men, in some wish for

glory, should vainly scatter abroad the beauty and fragrance of their virtuous striving for resemblance to the hidden God. These divine beauties are concealed. Their fragrance is something beyond any effort of the understanding.[162]

Among the most perfect—the true clergy and hierarchs of the church, the monastics, the saints—sanctity resides within, concealed by an external, mundane appearance, invisible. Yet it is perceptible, a "fragrant, secret beauty," "an exact likeness of God" (4.3.1). The holy person is as the rite itself: disguised by a "fine exterior appearance," by "splendid and sacred ceremony" (4.3.2). Perfected believer and sacrament are together "truly divine images of that infinitely divine fragrance" which is God's own being (4.3.1). Beyond the exterior veil, Dionysius exhorts, lies the reality.

> Let us see it for what it is, stripped of its veils, shiningly available in its blessed splendor, filling us abundantly with that fragrance which is apparent only to people of intelligence (i.e., the perfect). . . . For the ray of the most holy sacred things enlightens the men of God . . . it spreads its sweet fragrance into their mental reception openly. But this fragrance does not spread in a similar way to those [people] on a lowlier plane.[163]

The consecration of the myron, Dionysius explains, is a rite equal to the synaxis (eucharistic liturgy) "in dignity and effectiveness" (4.3.3). Its ritual components elicit the same experiences, perceptually and in understanding: the censing of the sanctuary serves, just as the censing of the nave in the synaxis, to mark God's outpouring even as he remains unchanged; God is everywhere perceptibly present, and nowhere visible. The parallels in ritual segments continue, enfolding the myron in actions that render it ritually like unto the eucharistic bread and wine. And indeed, as Dionysius moves through his levels of meaning, from this ecclesiological level of sense to the Christological one, he will end with the arresting image of the blessed myron being poured out to consecrate the very altar on which it is placed: the image, Dionysius exhorts, of Christ in his essential activity, "Jesus himself, our most divine altar . . . Jesus who consecrates himself for us."[164]

But the myron holds singular meaning beyond its ritual handling, and beyond the olfactory dimensions that attend or are emphasized by those actions. Dionysius expounds on the myron's constitution:

> The ointment is made up of a mixture of fragrant substances. It has within itself fragrances of rich quality. Now the participants receive these fragrances, but they do so in proportion to their capacity to have a share of this fragrance. In this way

we learn that the transcendent fragrance of the divine Jesus distributes its conceptual gifts over our own intellectual powers, filling them with a divine pleasure.

If there is a pleasurable scent, Dionysius explains, and if one has a healthy nose capable of distinguishing among odors, then one can receive through that healthy olfactory organ the great pleasure of that sweet scent. So, too, if no evil impulse distracts us, our powers of knowledge "can draw in the fragrance of the Deity and be filled with a sacred happiness and with God's nourishment." Hence "the composition of the ointment is symbolic, giving a form to what is without form." Jesus is the "rich source of the divine fragrances," pouring forth grace in "divine fragrances to delight the intelligence." The faithful will receive these scents, each to their own capacity and in proportion to their participation in the divine. The greater the holiness, and the higher the rank (angelic beings over human persons), "the greater the flood of fragrant odors since they are closer to the source."[165]

Dionysius's commentary on the consecration of holy oil draws, then, not only on the deeply familiar olfactory codes that functioned throughout the ancient Mediterranean sphere, but further on the empirical system of knowledge that underlay philosophical, scientific, and medical inquiry. In his exposition, the myron's scent matters because of the tangible delight it causes. Its sweetness is the appropriate adornment for a sacred setting and sacred ritual, marking off the place, its occupants (terrestrial and celestial), and their activities as separate from the mundane world and its occupations. The myron's fragrant beauty signifies the presence of the divine being that works through it, and the changed condition of the human person who partakes of it.

But the myron's smell is only one part of the olfactory work of this rite. For the physiological processes are equally—and perhaps even more so—critical to what is taking place. The myron is a composite substance, composed of multiple beautiful scents. Its fragrance is created by the mixture, and exuded from the ointment which is now its source. Unseen and unfelt, the fragrance fills its immediate space and then wafts far beyond, spreading even beyond the walls of the church itself. It is perceived by beings corporeal and incorporeal who have the capacity to receive its impress. Smelling it, they take it in to the extent of their olfactory capabilities, imbibing it within their innermost parts; its reception, in turn, affects their constitution, causing them to yield fragrant odor of their own. It is not enough, in Dionysius's commentary, to understand what the smell signifies; one must understand the physiology of olfaction, both what generates smells and what the perception of smells entails. Dionysius repeatedly stresses the ultimate goal of intellectual comprehension of the divine, yet his system begins with the body itself experiencing, through its sensory (olfactory) process, that which the believer must strive to know. Intellectual understanding is the cognitive reflection on that bodily experience, but the primacy of the sensing body renders its epistemological rewards available, to some extent at least, even to those who lack the higher inclination.

About a century later, in the course of the seventh century, Maximus Confessor produced a mystagogical commentary much indebted to Dionysius's *Celestial Hierarchy* and *Ecclesiastical Hierarchy*.[166] Relying on what had come before, however, Maximus does not provide much description of the actual rites nor details from the rubrics, rather taking the occasion to contemplate at length on the liturgy as source and demonstration of theological truth. Like his model Dionysius, Maximus is at pains to establish a profound correspondence between physical, perceptible experience and its intellectual, conceptual counterpart in the mind or soul, where alone can be had the highest knowledge of God.[167]

> For the whole spiritual world seems mystically imprinted on the whole sensible world in symbolic forms, for those who are capable of seeing this, and the whole sensible world is spiritually explained in the mind in the principles which it contains. In the spiritual world it is in principles; in the sensible world it is in figures.[168]

Maximus goes on to work out an elaborate—and eloquent—scheme of human person and cosmos in relation to one another as microcosm to macrocosm. The theme had ancient roots in Greek philosophy but was powerfully transferred by Maximus onto the forms, structures (architectural and institutional), and ritual practices of the human person, the church, and the order of the natural universe.[169] Yet Maximus treats the senses only in their total grouping, as "the senses," or through the example of sight.[170] It is for the reader to work out how Maximus would include olfaction *per se*, and the contrast to Dionysius is quite striking. In this Maximus heralds the decisive turn that Byzantine tradition takes towards visual piety, a focus that will take culminating form in the victory of icon devotion over iconoclasm in the ninth century.[171]

Nonetheless, the significance of the olfactory dimensions of liturgical experience were not lost to later Byzantine commentators, as indeed incense and myron continued their fundamental roles in Byzantine liturgical and devotional piety. We might chart their continuing contribution through two formulations. The first is from the eighth-century liturgical commentary of Germanus, Patriarch of Constantinople, writing in the same era as John of Damascus in his defense of icons.[172] Often described as achieving a great synthesis of the earlier liturgical and exegetical traditions, Germanus begins his commentary with the church itself—both the building and the people of God, the body of Christ. In this opening passage, he defines the church as the Bride of Christ, constructing this identification through olfactory allusions. As Bride, the church is cleansed through baptism, sprinkled with Christ's sacrificial blood, and sealed with the ointment of the Holy Spirit. A cascade of scriptural allusions emphasizes the complex construction of this identity: the fragrance of the lover's perfume poured forth and enticing, and the abundance of the ritual oil of the priestly calling.[173]

Subsequently, Germanus comments on the incense. Discussing the censing that follows the epistle reading, he expounds both Christological and Trinitarian interpretations: the censer is the humanity of Christ, the fire his divinity; the smoke "reveals the fragrance of the Holy Spirit which precedes."[174] But the incense in its censer also displays the divine economy, imaging the outworking of salvation in the course of human history and of each human believer:

> Again, the interior of the censer is understood as the [sanctified] womb of the [holy] virgin [and Theotokos] who bore the divine coal, Christ . . . All together, therefore, give forth the sweet-smelling fragrance. Or again, the interior of the censer points to the font of holy baptism, taking into itself the coal of divine fire, the sweetness of the operation of the Holy Spirit, which is the adoption of divine grace through faith, and exuding a good odor.[175]

Once more, at the procession of the Great Entrance, Germanus comments on the incense. He begins with the Holy Spirit, evoking the whole tradition of identification of the Spirit with sweet fragrance, known to the Christian within the liturgical context through the process and engagement of human-divine relation that sacrificial activity engendered. Nor could any evocation of sacrifice be made without allusion to Christological meaning.

> The Holy Spirit is seen spiritually in the fire, incense, smoke, and fragrant air: for the fire points to His divinity, and the fragrant smoke to His coming invisibly and filling us with good fragrance through the mystical, living, and unbloody services and sacrifice of burnt-offering. . . . [The incense] is also in imitation of the burial of Christ, when Joseph took down the body from the cross, wrapped it in clean linen, anointed it with spices and ointment.[176]

The epistemological concerns here are differently focused from those in the discussions of Dionysius. For Germanus the liturgical practices of anointment and incense are dynamic symbols that enact, quite literally, a living memory of the gospel story.[177] At the same time, they signify and bring to actualization a human-divine relationship dependent on doctrinal understandings of the nature of the Godhead in its three Persons. The historical significations of the symbols do not override this emphasis on liturgy as an experience through which the church as a whole, and the individual believer within it, gain knowledge of God, of Christ, of the Holy Spirit. That knowledge is gained experientially through bodily encounter with the components of the liturgy: its location, its sequences, its ritual objects and adornments, its gestures, its actions. This ritual knowledge is perfectly aligned with the knowledge revealed—again both historically and doctrinally—in scripture. Properly understood, each component must point to the whole meaning: the smells alone are able to convey all that is meant to transpire for the believer, both in affect and in understanding.

One last Byzantine example brings this tradition to sharp articulation as it was used to instruct the individual monk. In the tenth century, Symeon the New Theologian presented a discourse to his monastic readers that addressed the matter of liturgy through a discussion of "Feasts and Holy Communion."[178] The content of this, the Fourteenth Ethical Discourse, is strongly reminiscent of Dionysius's *Celestial Hierarchy*, both in interpretive method and in method of epistemological instruction.[179] Symeon here speaks to monks who are disdainful of the elaborate ceremonial of the liturgy, especially the adornments of lights, candles, incense, holy oil, and choral music. They clearly view these outward trappings of liturgy as turgid, pedantically belabored symbols of a religious truth that can only be distorted by such exterior expression. As monks, they seek God through a higher means: through the illumination of contemplation, through the interior practice of prayer. Symeon speaks passionately against such a view, insisting that corporate liturgical worship in its fullest ceremonial glory is not only appropriate for the person of faith, and not only worthy of God, but further—and most importantly—it is necessary for the believer who seeks true knowledge of God. "I indeed advise and encourage you to do these things [the use of lamps, candles, perfumes, incense, music], and to do them lavishly. Only, I want you to know the way you should do so. . . . What do the things you do in types and symbols really mean?"[180]

Symeon first provides simple symbolic correspondences: the lamps and candles should signify the illumined soul; the perfume of myron and incense is the dew of Mt. Hermon, or the oil running down Aaron's beard, or the sweet smell of the Holy Spirit, or the spiritual perfume by which the Spirit anoints the senses and makes everything fragrant. But these are more than simple correlations: through these symbolic meanings Symeon uses the sensory experiences of liturgy to provide knowledge about the divine. That this is profoundly (and not reductively) so is shown by the turn he then takes to instruct, through the components of liturgy, on the nature and identity of the human person. For only through knowledge of God can the Christian have knowledge of the human. Symeon makes the point most emphatically through his explication of liturgical scents, of incense and myron:

> For, if God has thus adorned what is soulless with fragrance and has glorified it, think how much more He will adorn you, if you choose, with the forms of the virtues and glorify you with the fragrance of the Holy Spirit—you, whom He made according to His own image and likeness. These aromatics, put together by human hands and perfuming your senses with the fragrance of scented oils, depict and, as it were, suggest your own creation by the art of their making. Because just as the perfumer's hands fashion the blended perfumes from different essences and the product is one essence out of many, so, too, did God's hands fashion you, who are cunningly composed and combined with the intelligible elements of the spiritual perfume, that is to say, with the gifts of the life-creating and all-efficacious Spirit. You, too, must give off the fragrance of His knowledge and wisdom, so that those who listen to the words of your teaching may smell His sweetness with the senses of the soul and be glad with spiritual joy.[181]

Symeon's teachings at this point strongly recall the *Ecclesiastical Hierarchy* of Dionysius, but in a pedagogical trajectory that brings to completion the task of knowing Dionysius had addressed. For the earlier writer had taken the cultural associations of scents as well as attention to their physiological properties and activities, and applied these aspects of smells and their perception to instruction on the nature of divinity. Symeon, taking the model to its next step, turns the same olfactory features back upon the human person, this time to illuminate by reflection what can be known and understood about humanity. It is a knowledge that assumes, and indeed requires, the prior instruction about God. For only through that knowledge can knowledge of the human self come, as Symeon expresses it. As Symeon explains, this is not only because the composition of physical fragrances provides a model by which to understand God's act of creating the human person. Furthermore, God has scented that which he has created: perfumed it with the Holy Spirit, given the breath of life as a fragrance of life, so that the human person in holiness pours forth, exudes, the scent of his Maker. And with a final allusion to 2 Corinthians 2:14–16, Symeon reminds that by giving forth the odor of the Creator, the believer is in fact spreading the fragrance of the knowledge of him wheresoever it might be known.

In like manner, two developments in Syrian Orthodox tradition are notable. First, over the course of the middle ages, west Syrian (that is, Syrian Orthodox) writers produced a series of discourses and commentaries on the consecration of the holy myron.[182] Until the thirteenth century, Syrian Orthodox bishops consecrated the myron on Holy Thursday (Thursday of the Passion Week). In contrast to the elaborate composition of Byzantine myron, they used only olive oil and balsam, in a combination often described as imaging the "composition" of Christ's human and divine natures, united in his incarnate Person.[183] For a time it appears these discourses were written to be delivered as homilies in the liturgy for Holy Thursday, the day of consecration, but after the eighth century this practice of presentation seems to have stopped. The earlier commentary by Dionysius the Areopagite was strongly influential, but not determinative for these writers.[184]

Late in the seventh century, the learned bishop Jacob of Edessa produced one of these discourses on the holy myron. Jacob begins with the Old Testament types, or symbols, by which scented oils provided foreshadowings of the divine revelation that would come to fulfillment with the incarnation of Christ and the writings of the New Testament.[185] The biblical examples Jacob cites are a gathering of texts that refer to ritual uses of holy oil, as well as to the bridal imagery of fine perfumes from the Song of Songs. But here, too, the myron as a fragrant oil is taken to be instructive as much for its empirical, scientifically recognizable qualities as for its allusive evocations of scriptural passages. For Jacob, anointment with perfumed oil provides an image for understanding the human-divine relation as it has been displayed in history: "Formerly [in Old Testament times], when the Bride saw the Bridegroom in symbol . . . she compared him to scented oil;" and so the Song of Songs used perfumes to describe the yearning felt by the faithful for God. Now that God is wholly revealed through the incarnate Lord, Jacob continues, the myron allows baptism to enact the joining of the believer to God through anointment with the Holy Spirit: "Here, however, the Church sees openly and clearly, with a pure face, God the Word. . . . She compares him to oil because he anointed and united with his eternal Godhead our temporal humanity."[186] Myron images further the incarnation by which God united himself with a human nature: "The 'oil' with which [Christ] was anointed is the human body which he united to himself; he described it as '[oil] of joy' because he voluntarily united it to his divinity in the hypostatic union and not as the result of compulsion."[187] But the myron's scent is also the mark of "divine knowledge of all sorts, and the variety of glorious understanding concerning [Christ], with which he makes fragrant all those who have shared in his glory".[188] As the spread of its sweet scent disperses far and wide, so does the myron pour forth teaching and knowledge of the whole of the divine dispensation.

Commenting also on the consecration rite, Jacob is careful to point out that the instructional capacity of the myron speaks to both the human and divine domains of sacred ritual: "on the one hand, [myron] is consecrated as is humanly befitting; on the other, it consecrates and perfects everything, as is divinely fitting" (12). The purity and fragrance of this myron images the holy teachings of the church, while other fragrances, albeit made for medicinal uses, can only image false teachings (13). In contrast to Dionysius, Jacob speaks in his description of the rite, not of twelve veils concealing the myron, but of twelve fans (or "wings"), flanked by twelve censers preceded by twelve lights (15–18). In an image particularly evocative for Syriac tradition, Jacob describes the effect of the incense: "In the twelve censers which give off a single fragrance is indicated the fact that, although [the oil] is single, yet it makes many fragrant, and it is with many in many parts."[189] Incense and holy oil, sacrifice and identity, thus conjoin their characteristics and their affective impact on those who perceive their fragrances, both those believers who participate in the rite and those who encounter its scent in the lingering aftermath.[190]

Syrian Orthodox tradition granted the myron particular importance by the continuation of commentaries devoted to its consecration and meaning. So, too, was incense strikingly valued by Syriac writers. Commencing in the seventh and eighth centuries, and flourishing particularly in the tenth and eleventh centuries, the Syrian Orthodox liturgy developed the prayers of the incense offering into a three-fold sequence: prayers said to introduce the incense offering (prumion, from the Greek proimion), prayers offered during the incense offering (sedre), and prayers that followed the incense offering ('etre). The process involved both a fusion of earlier prayers that had accompanied the morning and evening incense offerings for particular feast days or liturgical occasions; and their expansion and elaboration into this three-fold sequence.[191] It is an especially interesting development considering that the Syrian Orient was one of the earliest areas to have incorporated the public and devotional use of incense into Christian worship.[192] But further, as we will see in chapter 4, incense imagery played a foundational role in Syriac ascetic tradition throughout the late antique era. It may also be worth noting that here, as with the development of the myron commentaries, we have the legacies of a Christian tradition that took its medieval shape under Islamic domination, for the seventh-century Islamic conquests provided a political severance from the Byzantine empire to compound the theological divide that had already led, in the fifth and sixth centuries, to the formation of separate church hierarchies for the (dyophysite) Church of the East and the (miaphysite) Syrian Orthodox communities, as opposed to the Chalcedonian Orthodoxy insisted upon by the Byzantine Empire.[193]

The development of a three-fold prayer structure for the incense offering set that point of the liturgy into high relief. These prayers did not always specifically mention the incense, sometimes focusing instead on other imagery appropriate to the occasion as one of offering sacrifice, of penitential action, of offering praise and honor to God, of supplicating God's gracious mercy. But usually the incense was identified by name as the symbol and effective agent of the ritual moment, and with vivid didactic effect. It appears that the oldest association was with the offering of incense for the forgiveness of sins, and the biblical citations recall Aaron's incense offering in Numbers 16:46 on behalf of the people of Israel after they had rebelled against God. Hence the offering was also made with the petition for the purification from sin. The entire sequence moves from the opening doxology of the *prumion*, to the *sedro* (series, or list) recalling divine favors of the past and petitioning for forgiveness, to the *'etro* (literally the smoke or vapor of the incense) with its reference to the incense burned.[194] As both Joseph Amar and Jacob Thekeparampil have stressed, the prayers served well as a teaching medium through which to instruct the congregation on God's actions in history.[195] But as Thekeparampil has pointed out, these prayers are important for their presentation of Christ through the imagery of incense and its olfactory aspects; they present both a strong sacrificial theology, and one that takes self-conscious account of the sensory experience of incense, its odor and its effects on the perceiver.[196]

A number of these prayers use the symbolic, ritual, and sensory aspects of incense to present teachings about the nature of Christ and the meanings of his salvific actions. To do this, they draw together the sacrificial and perfume significations long familiar to Mediterranean cultures. At the same time, they explicitly identify what the believer should experience and thereby know about Christ as a result of what is smelled during and through the incense offering. By turns, the language is penitential and supplicatory, begging forgiveness of sins; it alludes to medical traditions, seeking healing (through smells) "for soul and body;" it presents moral psychology, citing the offering up of good deeds and virtuous conduct. The prayers dwell upon the scent of Christ's sacrificial death, and upon the sweet perfume of his love. In one *'etro* (prayer after the incense offering), the priest bestows on Christ a dazzling sequence of olfactory titles, and with them an elegantly forceful summary of salvation history as played out from creation until the present time.

God of holy fathers, Lord of heaven and earth, sweet odor (*riho basimo*) from which all the plants (*'eqore*) and sweet perfumes receive their fragrance, pleasant smoke of reconciliation (*'etro haniyo d-tar'uto*) that was offered for our sake to your heavenly Father, [O You, Christ] divine myron (*muron alohoyo*), spiritual perfume (*besmo metyad'ono*), concealed incense (*pirmo gnizo*), invisible odor (*riho kasyo*), and heavenly high priest, [he] who offered himself and who accepted himself. Also now, Lord, be pleased, and accept this smoke of incense that was offered to you by us at this hour, so that it may be for the tranquility and concord of your holy church, for the protection and progress of the good education of her children, for the peace, rest, and gladness of the peoples of the earth, for abundant harvests of the year, for temperate wind, for the bringing forth of the fruits of good works, and for the rest and good remembrance of those who preceded and slept in the orthodox faith, now.[197]

By this "incense Christology," as Thekeparampil calls it,[198] the ritual action of sacrifice—the process of human-divine relation—is mined for its epistemological capacities, through direct engagement of its olfactory content. The ritual moment instructs through its activity, its sequential gestures of burning the incense offering. But the words attending that activity instruct the congregation beyond the process thereby enacted. They explicate the nature of the divine with whom the relationship is sought, through the highlighting of the olfactory experience as a perception and as an encounter. There is a notable use here of the liturgy itself as an instructive medium, and not simply the homily as a discursive form within it, or the liturgical commentary as an external explication of it. Indeed, in Syriac tradition the liturgy had long provided the foundational teaching context of the church.[199] In the instance of the incense prayers, we have an example of liturgical pedagogy in which the bodily experience of sense perception within the ritual context was essential to the reception of the religious knowledge being conveyed. The pivotal experience was that of smell: smells generated and offered, perceived and inhaled; transferred, transformative, and finally exuded in turn. It was a knowledge available to all within reach of the wafting incense smoke.

Excursus: On the Sinful Woman in Syriac Tradition

The anonymous Sinful Woman who washed the feet of Christ with her tears, wiped them with her hair, and anointed them with perfumed ointment was a favorite theme of Syriac homilists and hymnographers of late antiquity.[200] While the treatment often blended elements from all three Synoptic versions of the story (Mk 14:3–9, Mt 26:6–13, Lk 7:36–50), it was the account in Luke 7, set at the house of Simon the Pharisee, which seemed most often to provide the homiletic material.[201] Syriac writers kept a distinction between this anonymous woman and Mary of Bethany who, in John 12:1–8, performs a similar act of anointment which Jesus declares a preparation for his burial; and further, did not confuse her with Mary Magdalene.[202] Rather, for Syriac writers the Sinful Woman with her alabaster flask of perfumed ointment merited her own attention and in her own right. Although the gospel incident was brief, providing no information about the woman except that "she was a woman of the city, who was a sinner" (Lk 7:37), Syriac homilists and hymnographers constructed an extensive narrative tradition about her, offering moral instruction by retelling the gospel episode as her story, and granting to her perfume a prominent and multivalent role in its meaning.

A Syriac verse homily, "On the Sinful Woman," wrongly attributed to Ephrem but probably written soon after his death, proved immensely influential in this regard for both Syriac and Greek writers, and eventually medieval Latin.[203] This homily retells the gospel story as a narrative drama about the Woman herself, shifting the scene to the events preceding and leading up to the meeting with Christ at Simon's house—events placed altogether outside the gospel text. The homily begins with the Woman hearing the news that Christ has come to dine with Simon. Immediately smitten with remorse, she laments her state with great anguish. Changing her clothes in an elaborate act of ritual repentance, she then takes her money and sets out for the Perfume Seller's shop. The change in her appearance as well as the lavish sum of gold she presents him as she orders his most precious scent cast the Perfumer into confused dismay. In consternation he addresses her:

> What is this appearance (schema) that you show today to your lovers, that you have stripped off wantonness and clothed yourself in humility? Before today when you came to me, your appearance was different than today's. You were clothed in fine raiment and carried little gold, and you sought (cheap) choice perfume to sweeten your wantonness. And now today, you have filthy garments and you carry much gold. I do not understand your change in how you are dressed. Either wear clothing like your perfume, or buy perfume like your clothing. For this perfume is neither fitting nor right for these clothes.[204]

The scene presents a marvelous confluence of visual and olfactory paradoxes. Previously, the Woman had dressed in sumptuous finery, yet worn cheap perfume. Now, clothed in the "sordid weeds of mourning" as Satan describes her soon after (sec. 6), devoid of jewelry, and barefoot, she asks of the Perfumer his most exquisite ointment. What to believe: sight or smell? In a fervent debate, the Woman convinces the Perfumer of her urgent need. With her alabaster jar now filled with the finest scent, she sets forth for Simon's house. Satan then appears in the guise of a former lover and attempts to dissuade her in a heated exchange. Failing to deter her course, Satan hastens to Simon's house where he seeks to prevent her entrance by rousing Simon against her. Again, the Woman will not be turned from her purpose. Finally, she obtains her entry and her goal, addressing Christ as she washes and anoints his feet. The episode is brought to an abrupt end with Christ offering praise and forgiveness to her, but reproach and the parable of the two debtors to Simon.

Syriac homilies and hymns will follow one of two patterns: they will focus either on the episode at Simon's house following Luke 7, or on the events prior to that incident as imaginatively constructed in the 'Ephremic' homily, "On the Sinful Woman." Other late antique homilies on the Sinful Woman show interest in the gospel incident, but without further narrative development. For example, John Chrysostom focuses on the account from Matthew 26 rather than Luke 7, so that the house is that of Simon the Leper and the criticism of the disciples is of the wasted money the ointment represents.[205] In a different pattern, a Coptic homily attributed to Chrysostom shares with Severus of Antioch, Homily 118, not only a focus on the Woman but also a philosophical discourse about the passions and an allegorical reading of the perfume as the virtues of the soul—an interpretation of perfumed ointments traditional to Greek patristic thought (as seen in chapter 1 for Clement of Alexandria and Origen) but not otherwise found in Syriac texts about the Sinful Woman.[206] Instead, Syriac writers on this episode develop the role of the Woman's perfume as an instrument of agency, an epistemological tool, and a sacramental indicator. This is a complex of functions that contrast markedly with the allegorical language of the soul and its virtues.

Ephrem treated the episode from Luke 7 at length in his Homily on Our Lord.[207] His central concern is the reality of Christ's divine nature, made known and accessible through the tangible humanity of his incarnate person. Ephrem approaches Christ by recalling the experiences through which various biblical figures encountered him, but his primary attention is on Simon the Pharisee, who repeatedly fails to understand the identity of his dinner guest. When the narrative focus turns to the Sinful Woman, it is her actions rather than a narrative character, or self, that Ephrem presents, in contrast to his portrait of Simon. The Woman's actions are shown to be important because they reveal Christ, Simon's dinner guest, not as the prophet Simon had thought, but rather as the Lord of Prophets, the Treasury of Healing present and at work in the very midst of Simon's earthly, worldly gathering. By her actions, the Woman confesses her Savior:

> Streaming tears immediately announced that they were being shed as in the
> presence of God. Plaintive kisses testified that they were coaxing the master of

the debt to tear up the bill. The precious oil of the sinful woman proclaimed that it was a "bribe" for her repentance. These were the medications the sinful woman offered her Physician, so that He could whiten the stains of her sins with her tears, and heal her wounds with her kisses, and make her bad name as sweet as the fragrance of her oil. This is the physician who heals a person with the medicine that that person brings to Him![208]

Ephrem delineates the separate elements of her homage—tears, kisses, precious oil—as distinct actions, granting to the Woman's behavior a ritual signification. While sequential usage of water (tears), veneration (kisses), and fine oil (anointment) would evoke strong liturgical associations for the audience, Ephrem insists that the Woman's actions superseded liturgical function because they were offered directly to God's divine self and not, as in ecclesiastical ritual, through the mediating structures of priestly efficacy: "that sinful woman . . . came to God, not to priests, to forgive her debts."[209]

For Jacob of Serug, the entire encounter must be seen as patterned into a eucharistic event.[210] In his homily, the Woman enters Simon's house carrying her perfume as its fragrance heralds her holy purpose. Just as a church sanctuary is perfumed with the mingled scents of incense and holy oil, so did the Woman transform the space of Simon's banquet from the mundane to the sacred by the aroma of perfume compounded with fervent intention: "With the fire of her love she kindled her tears like ointment / and the fragrance of her repentance was increasingly sweet."[211] Hence to the scent of ointment rendered holy by the very feet it would anoint, the Woman added the sacrificial odors of a love that burned so fiercely, she herself was transformed into the dual role of sacrificer and sacrificed.

Weeping was for her a pure censer, and she brought it with her,
and with groans she kindled it to smoke in the Holy of Holies.
She was for herself a priest who made petition for forgiveness,
and willingly with contrition she made sacrifice for reconciliation.[212]

In Jacob's rendering, the fluid meanings of ritual activity are fully explored. In the process of washing Christ's feet, the Woman's tears become the baptismal waters, consecrated with the chrism of the oil she had brought. As she herself washed and anointed Christ's feet, she entered into the "second womb of the Holy of Holies," finding herself baptised in the sea of Christ's love as he cleansed and purified her so that she might rise up pure and reborn.[213] Baptism and eucharistic sacrifice converge in Jacob's telling: "Before the great flood of holiness she offered herself / And He poured upon her waves of His love that she would be absolved by Him. / Her soul offered to the living fire the evilest body / and it kindled in the thicket of her soul and all of it was consumed."[214]

For Ephrem and Jacob, the perfumed ointment lends a liturgical air, quite literally, to the Woman's actions in her approach to and service of Christ. The ritual associations allow the Woman's actions to take on a collective significance, resonating with the liturgical rhythms of ecclesiastical life whether in a simple village setting or in the grand ceremonial of an urban cathedral. The specific ritual meanings drawn by our homilists lift the Woman's approach to Christ out of its unique situation as a gospel story. Instead, her actions are set into a narratively imposed ritual framework that assimilates them into the liturgical involvements of every believer, lay or ordained. She herself, priest and suppliant, prophet and penitent, fulfills multiple roles that comprise the orchestrated interactions of religious practice for the late antique Christian.

But what is the purpose of such a ritually oriented presentation of the Sinful Woman's story? Is it simply the commingling of biblical episode with liturgical structure, a frequent if important theme for patristic writers?[215] In the Homily on Our Lord, Ephrem had stressed that the Woman's actions were significant because of their confessional force, that is, because they indicated and made clear Christ's identity as God incarnate. Thus the Sinful Woman engaged Christ's human existence even while paying homage to, worshipping, and seeking redemption from his divine Person. From this perspective, the ritual elements of the Woman's actions are important for what they reveal—and their revelatory capacity sheds light on the entire episode, its characters, setting, and actions. Through her ritualized activity, Simon and the Woman are revealed as characters of false or true faith, and the dinner is shown to be not an occasion for the physical nourishment of the guests, but a sacramental gathering for the salvation of believers. For Ephrem, Jacob, and other Syriac writers highlighting the sacrificial elements of this story, the ritual qualities of the narrative sequence are held together by reference to the Woman's perfumed oil.[216] The sweet scent of spices allowed the homilists to invoke the sacrificial image of incense burning. Moreover, with the image of fragrance pervading the room as the Woman poured out her ointment, the vivid olfactory qualities of invisible yet tangible presence, of unseen yet physically experienced change, pervade the narrative as well, playing on the ancient Mediterranean topos of perfume as signifier of divine presence and transformation. By highlighting the Woman's perfumed ointment, our homilists bring into play an imagery of complex associations for ancient peoples that is concrete in its referents yet fluid in its evocations.

Perhaps the most original achievement in this group of homilies is the Greek kontakion by Romanos the Melodist, here strongly influenced by the

Syriac trends.[217] Clearly drawing from both the tradition of Ephrem and of the 'Ephremic' homily, "On the Sinful Woman," Romanos offers a telling of this story which utilizes olfactory experience as its primary frame of reference. Thus he opens his kontakion with the image of the Sinful Woman begging that Christ will "receive this perfume as pleader," and grant forgiveness "from the slime" of her deeds. In his telling, it is in fact the odor of Christ which first attracts the Woman:

> When she saw the words of Christ spreading everywhere like aromatic spice
> As they dispensed the breath of life to all the faithful,
> The harlot hated the bad odor of her deeds.[218]

By this concise opening scene, Romanos draws on the whole array of symbolic meanings that smell evoked for the ancient Mediterranean. Sin, mortality, and fallenness are indicated by stench; purity, divinity, and paradise are associated with sweet fragrance. In the "aroma" of Christ's words, the "fragrance of the knowledge of God" (2 Cor 2:15) spreads abroad, pervading the consciousness of those near and far; in this, fragrance and the experience of it provide an exact analogy for the human experience of the divine—invisible yet tangibly known, uncontainable and ever mobile, transgressive across any boundaries humans might set or see.

Buffetted thus by aromas of competing moral states, Romanos's Sinful Woman then agonizes through an internal dialogue, which brings her decision to seek her audience with Christ. Anticipating the liturgical pattern her approach will necessarily take, she explains the salvific purpose that brings Christ to Simon's house: "He sets up a table as an altar on which He is laid as a votive offering."[219]

The Woman's decision to go is also a decision to take perfume, which she celebrates with the announcement, "as I breathe, I renounce the slime of my deeds" (strophe 5). Here and elsewhere in the hymn, Romanos plays upon the verb emphuo, to breathe upon.[220] The verb alludes to the baptismal liturgy in which the candidates renounce Satan as the priest breathes upon them, and also to the passage in John 20:22 when Christ breathes upon the apostles, filling them with the Holy Spirit. Directly, in the following strophe (6), the Woman sets up a baptismal context:

> Therefore, I take the perfume and go forward.
>   I shall make the house of the Pharisee a baptistery,
> For there I shall be cleansed of my sin
>   and purified of my lawlessness.

I shall mix the bath with weeping, with oil and with perfume;
I shall cleanse myself and escape
from the slime of my deeds.[221]

In a whirlwind, the Woman storms through the Perfume Seller's shop, pur-
chasing his most expensive ointment. At Simon's house, she scandalizes the
Pharisee into heated exchange with Christ whose verbal chastisement upon the
obstinate host is swift and fierce. Absolving the Woman of her past, Christ
admonishes the other guests, "Behold the harlot whom you see; consider her
like the church / crying out: 'I breathe (emphuo) on the slime of my deeds.'"[222]
With this, his parting view of the Woman, Romanos conjoins the language of
exorcism and baptism, breath of life and rebirth, individual believer and ecclesiastical body.

Consider the olfactory sweep of Romanos's hymn: from the moral quality of
stench, through the evangelical experience of the "aroma" of Christ's words, to
the sacrificial altar, to the perfume of love, the anointing of baptismal waters,
the exsufflation of exorcism, the breath of life. All this Romanos conveys in the
smells which attend the Sinful Woman's imaginal thoughts and actions. By contrast, in Ephrem and Jacob's treatments the perfume was employed primarily as
an object to signify the important ritual qualities of the encounter between the
Sinful Woman and Christ. Here in Romanos's kontakion, the perfume matters
not only to demarcate religious ritual from social etiquette, but further as a
paedogogical tool to instruct the audience. By attending to the variant qualities
of olfactory experience as the homilist draws upon them, the audience is led to
a richer understanding of Christ, of the divine-human relationship, indeed of
the process of redemption—a process involving change both in one's inner
person and in one's external behavior.[223]

With this kontakion, then, we see the perfume carrying an epistemological
function, as the Woman learns of Christ, sees him, hears him, and also experiences him through an encounter that is physical—sensorily distinctive—as
well as intellectual and spiritual. In another anonymous Syriac homily, the epistemological function of the perfume is turned back onto the Woman herself in
relation to Christ. As she moves to anoint the feet of Christ,

The ointment which had made her body sweet she changed, and by the means
of Jesus' feet, she caused him to touch her soul and perfume it.
. . . the fragrance of her perfume was sweet, and the repentance she breathed
out in her thoughts was even more so, which, for Jesus, was sweeter than any
scent.[224]

In this homily, the Sinful Woman engaged her Savior and expressed her devotion through fragrance. So, too, for her character, the odor of her faith revealed her transformed condition, her cleansed spirit, and now chaste bodily expressions of love. In these homilies as a group, ritual provides the channel, and perfume the medium, by which the human-divine encounter takes place and through which its ramifications are known.

REDEEMING SCENTS

Ascetic Models

Even as it is not easy to tear out the scent from
lumps of frankincense, without its very nature
being destroyed: so it is not easy to draw out
mind and spirit from the whole body, without
the dissolution of all.

Lucretius, *On the Nature of Things*, 3.327–30[1]

Christian olfactory piety emerged and flourished at a particular moment in
Christian history. Its appearance marked a crucial turning point in the religion's
social and political location. From the Christian perspective, Christian triumph
in the Roman Empire brought with it an intensified significance for all things
physical. That intensity had both negative and positive articulations. Praise for
the majestic splendor of the natural world was matched by a rising severity in
asceticism and increasing valuation of celibacy as a Christian way of life. It is
important to see these trends as responses to the same situation: a heightened
importance of the physical realm. The Council of Nicea in 325 provided a theological framework in which to set this change, with its articulation of an
incarnation theology premised on the consubstantiality of the divine Persons.
There could be no question that Creator—Father, Son and Spirit—was ontologically severed from creation. Yet this incarnational stance dramatically
enhanced Christian emphasis on divine participation, and engagement, in the
created order. Late antique changes to Christian olfactory practices, and the
development of Christian epistemology inclusive of smell as an essential vehicle for Christian knowing, were events that marked the changing sensibilities.

Christianity inherited an ancient discourse familiar throughout the
Mediterranean world, in which the senses were deplored as sources of moral
danger. Identification of the senses with sexual licentiousness—"wanton
sensuality"—was a trope known in biblical literature, as in Greek and Roman

popular culture and intellectual traditions.[2] Christian thinkers made use of this tradition of moral psychology from their earliest writings; in late antiquity, they increased its tenor. Discussion of sexuality, of celibacy, of bodily discipline, of ascetic training—discussion of all such practices took on an indisputably shrill tone in late antique Christian texts. Recent scholarship has focused on this discourse about the senses in relation to the body, with strong attention to the surrounding medical and philosophical discussions.[3] Explorations of the prevalence and diversity of ascetic rhetoric and practice in the late antique period have focused consideration of asceticism in relation to the formation of the self.[4] Yet little attention has been given to the fundamental ritual contexts in which bodily practices were in fact being defined. Negative discourse about the senses became more shrill at the very moment that the deliberate engagement of sensory experience became prominent in Christian worship, devotional piety, domestic, civic, and monastic practices.[5] The coincidence of timing is no accident.

To some extent, these were competing discourses, serving different agendas within the late antique world, but responding to the same stimuli. The discourse of celibacy and self-mortification that utilized a rhetoric of sensory danger served a Christian identity and community defined against the prevailing political order. It undermined the possibility of complacency, even in a triumphant era. By contrast, the discourse of a sensorily engaged piety—the sensorium trained through the ritual practices of late antique Christianity in its daily activities—supported a public and imperial order that saw the Empire as God's earthly kingdom, albeit not without ambiguity or nuance. Political triumph did not alter the cosmic condition in which humanity lived, as Christianity defined it: a fallen condition, tragically impoverished from God's intention. But a discourse that imbued physical experience with positive religious valuation allowed a powerful reorientation to humanity's physicality. Increased attention to the importance of sensory experience prompted a fresh rhetoric of the body, in which the sensory body could contextualize the sexual body. Much scholarly attention has been paid to the rhetoric of sexuality and gender that emerged in late antiquity. But we must not forget the larger discourse on the body in which sexual discussion was set. That larger discourse presented the body as a sensing body, one for which its sensory experiences mattered profoundly in the formation and maintenance of the self, and as vehicles for religious knowledge: knowledge of God, and of the human person in relation to God. What, then, can the olfactory dimensions of late antique Christianity contribute to our understanding of Christian asceticism as it developed during this period?

The Smell of Danger:
Marking Sensory Contexts

The late antique growth of olfactory piety can appear discordant with the rise of asceticism that marked the same era. In the hands of Christian authors, asceticism—*askesis*, the practice of self-discipline or "training"—often presumed an anti-sensory rhetoric. Philosophical tradition had not necessarily bequeathed such an understanding. Where philosophers had been concerned about *enkrateia*, self-mastery, the senses could be described as morally neutral. What mattered was control of the passions, which in their responses to sensory stimuli might lead a person into irrational or irresponsible behavior. Sensory experience should not be allowed to prevail upon the rational or intellectual faculty of the mind. Marcus Aurelius, for example, could cite common smells of ancient life to illustrate how the rational person should feel indifferent to sensory stimuli, or might best respond to unpleasant sensations.

> Are you angry with the person whose arm-pits stink? Are you angry with the one whose mouth smells foul? What good will this anger do you? He has such a mouth, he has such arm-pits: it is necessary that such an emanation must come from such things—but the man has reason, it will be said, and he is able, if he takes pains, to discover wherein he offends—I wish you well of your discovery. Well, then, and you have reason: by your rational faculty stir up his rational faculty; show him his error, admonish him. For if he listens, you will cure him, and there is no need of anger. Neither tragic actor or whore.[6]

Self-mastery required discipline and self-regimentation, not necessarily the denigration of sensory experience.[7] As we saw in chapter 1, however, early Christian writers often warned against the pleasures of sensory experience, fearing that these endangered Christians by tying them to a world—a society and culture—defined and dominated by non-Christians. For authors such as Tertullian, Clement of Alexandria, or Origen, strict control of the senses most often was directed with a view to maintaining the clarity of distinct religious identities. Clement had warned his audience that the senses were the entrances through which temptations entered the soul; smell, he had admonished, was the most dangerous of all, for people were most easily led astray by following their nostrils.[8]

Fourth-century Christian writers echoed Clement's philosophical commonplace, but in a very different situation. The balance of political and social power was shifting, even if contemporaries could not be certain of Christianity's victory. Christian olfactory practices were increasingly common; incense and holy oil drew frequent comment from homilists and other spokespersons. When Christian leaders now admonished their audiences on the moral (and religious!) dangers of smell, it was not always clear what boundaries were at stake.

Sometimes a writer's position was determined by the occasion or even the literary genre of a given work. There were rhetorical conventions regarding discussion of the senses, and these differed depending on the situation and its literary form. When Basil of Caesarea extolled the glories of the natural world in his sermons on the Hexaemeron, for example, he praised the contribution of the senses to human awareness of God.[9] In his treatise defending classical education, however, Basil urged that attention always, and exclusively, be paid to care for the soul.[10] To do this, he admonished, one must despise the body thoroughly, "scorning the pleasures that arise through the senses," lest the senses distract the soul from its quest to seek knowledge of God in and through a life of virtue. Pleasant smells were a particular source of danger, in his view, but only by degree: "in a single word, the body in every part should be despised by everyone who does not care to be buried in its pleasures, as it were, in slime."[11]

Gregory of Nyssa had praised the senses for their capacity to make known the beauty of God's handiwork in his treatise *On the Making of Man*.[12] Elsewhere he chided the Christian congregation for taking delight in foods spiced with exotic flavorings from foreign lands, for "the loveliness of sight or smell or taste presents the senses with very transitory delight; except for the palate, there is no difference in the foods consumed, for nature changes all things equally into an evil smell."[13] Indeed, Gregory continued, the delight in sweet food was the means by which the serpent had beguiled Eve. From that small sensory indulgence, the floodgates of decadence sprang open:

> For having once crept from the necessary food towards delicacies, [the body] will proceed to what is pleasant to the eyes, seeking shining dishes and attractive servants. And so on to silver couches, soft divans, and transparent, gold-embroidered veils, magnificent chairs and tripods, washing vessels, mixing bowls, drinking horns, wine coolers and pitchers; water stoups, candlesticks, censers and similar things.[14]

As Clement of Alexandria had done, Gregory cited the well-known cliché that the senses were windows through which evil entered into the soul.[15] Yet the passage just quoted is an ironic description of luxury as morally reprehensible, for variations of all the mentioned objects were, by the time Gregory preached this sermon, becoming standard utensils and ornaments for liturgical celebration. Location and identified use differed, of course; in the sanctuary or shrine, for purposes of sacred ritual, the pleasures of sensory engagement served an altogether different end than they did in the context of a household. In the church, in the liturgy, the beauty of vestments, liturgical instruments, lamps, censers, linens, wine and bread, served as images of their heavenly counterparts in the celestial liturgy. At the very least, the earthly beauty of these sacred objects was meant to recall and remind the faithful of the One whose worship they served thus fittingly.

But the irony could not have been lost on Christian leaders, nor, for that matter, on their audiences. The harshness of anti-sensory rhetoric sometimes had to do with the simple insistence that the senses themselves—or the bodies receiving sensory experiences—could not distinguish one kind of pleasure from another without the most rigorous training. In his sermons on the Beatitudes, Gregory speaks of sensory experience as the nail that fixes the soul to the delights of the world in its material beauty, weighing the soul down inexorably just as heavy coverings weigh down shellfish or snails and hinder any easy movement on their part.[16] As liturgical splendor flourished, so, too, did an ecclesiastical discourse of sensory austerity. In the pre-Constantinian era, such a discourse served to differentiate Christian identity from a non-Christian world. In the post-Constantinian era, it was a summons to pay heed to where and how Christian prosperity was to be realized and what it properly signified.

From such a position, the degree to which ascetic exhortation colored late antique homiletics comes as no surprise. The monastic life was not alone in requiring conscientious training of the body through the disciplined reordering of sensory experience. The domestic life of the lay Christian required equal attention, equal training. Preaching on the proper way to raise children, John Chrysostom took up his topic with a striking image by which to think about the "success" of Christianity: "Like a wild beast swooping on a healthy, tender, and defenseless body, vainglory has fastened her foul teeth in her victim [the church] and injected poison and filled it with noisome stench."[17] Think of the child's soul as a city, Chrysostom exhorted. The body is the wall surrounding the city, and each of the senses a gate; "it is through these gates that thoughts are corrupted or rightly guided."[18] Each gate, then, must be guarded. Take the sense of smell, for instance:

This gate [the sense of smell] too admits much that is harmful if it be not kept barred—I mean fragrant scents and herbs. Nothing weakens, nothing relaxes the right tension of the soul as a pleasure in sweet odors. 'How then,' says some one, 'Must one take pleasure in filth?' That is not my meaning, but that one should not take pleasure either in the one or in the other. Let no one bring [the child] perfume, for, as soon as it penetrates to the brain, the whole body is relaxed.

Thereby pleasures are fanned into flame and greater schemes for their attainment. So bar this gate, for its function is to breathe the air, not to receive sweet odors.[19]

The sharpness of Chrysostom's admonitions here may contrast with the reasoned moderation of Clement of Alexandria's earlier advice about the medicinal uses of scents. But Clement himself could also speak very harshly about the dangers of smell when treating certain topics.[20] Again, the situation is critical to the moral force of the rhetoric, for Chrysostom addresses a congregation well-schooled in lavish ceremonial that included incense, both in the cathedral at Antioch and in civic celebrations at the shrines of the martyrs and saints.[21] The scents of liturgical activity were not gratuitous, as we noted in his catechetical homilies; nor did Chrysostom disdain olfactory experience as a useful theological tool in congregational instruction.[22] Rather, the Christian must discipline the body to take notice of sensory experience only within the confines of an ecclesiastically defined situation. In this way, Christian anti-sensory rhetoric sets the location of sensory pleasures outside the ritual context of devotional or liturgical practices, while heightening the importance of sensory awareness within those ecclesiastically controlled spaces.

Similarly, Ambrose of Milan, who had invited his catechumens to breathe deeply of sweet liturgical scents and be instructed thereby, could elsewhere present the senses as the Christian's most vulnerable point. In his sermon, "Flight from the World," he seems to present the mirror antithesis to the sensory sensitivity of his catechetical homilies. How, he asks, with so many bodily passions and so many worldly enticements, can one remain virtuous?

> The eye looks back and leads the mind's perception astray, the ear hears and turns one's attention away, a whiff of fragrance hinders thought, a kiss of the mouth introduces guilt, a touch kindles the fire of passion. . . . Indeed, Adam would not have come down from paradise unless he had been beguiled by pleasure.[23]

Ambrose ends this sermon with the exhortation that sensory experience and the knowledge it offers a person should only be considered instructive in early childhood; after that, body and world can only present the soul with the dangers of a "double inundation" of sensory experience and sensory knowledge.[24] The contrast to the close attention his catechetical homilies give to sensory experience within the liturgical setting is striking. Here, the barest trace of a scent threatens to sabotage the soul's entire discipline; to the catechumen in the liturgy, however, sweet scents guide the soul through the ritual processes and even through the revelatory capacities of the occasion.

As we might expect, Augustine was perhaps the most subtle in the dangers he thought the senses represented. The problem, he argued in the *Confessions*, was not only that of pleasure (and, in his view, the moral depravity it necessarily engendered). More ominously, the mind could trick the soul as to the reason and purpose for attending to sensory experience.

> [There is] another form of temptation, manifold in its dangers. Beside the lust of the flesh which inheres in the delight given by all pleasures of the senses . . . there exists in the soul, through the medium of the same bodily senses, a cupidity which does not take delight in carnal pleasure but in perceptions acquired through the flesh. It is a vain inquisitiveness dignified with the title of knowledge and science. . . . Pleasure pursues beautiful objects—what is agreeable to look at, to hear, to smell, to taste, to touch. But curiosity pursues the contraries of these delights with the motive of seeing what the experiences are like, not with a wish to undergo discomfort, but out of a lust for experimenting and knowing.[25]

The examples Augustine cites of this "lust for knowledge" are the crowds that gather round a mangled corpse, or the atrocities that take place in the city stadium to great public acclaim. Blood, sweat, wounds, death: even the odors of revulsion could lead a person hopelessly astray. The desire for knowledge itself was the most insidious temptation, Augustine claims, at any point that it was not focused on God. Sensory experiences could serve the faithful Christian only in the most rigid of circumstances: the ritual practices of Christian worship and devotion established and protected such conditions.

An ascetic rhetoric of sensory control thus permeated late antique homiletics and writing, even as Christian practices became more sensorily demanding—not only by their sensory complexity, but further, as we have seen in previous chapters, by the deliberate awareness of those sensory aspects that Christian preachers cultivated in their paedagogical roles. Physicality had gained the spotlight of Christian attention; its modes of experience were not to be left untended. Ascetic rhetoric provided means by which to grasp the volatile situation and reconfigure its structure.

The Fragrance of Virtue: Reordering Olfactory Experience

When Ambrose of Milan preached on the Old Testament patriarch Jacob as a model for the life of virtue, he employed a variety of olfactory commonplaces, biblical, philosophical, and cultural:

For of [Jacob] it is written, 'Behold, the smell of my son is as the smell of a plentiful field' (Gen 27:27). He had been made perfect in virtue's every flower and was fragrant with the grace of the holy blessing and of the happiness of heaven. He is indeed the field which the Lord has blessed. . . . in this field is the olive tree fruitful in the overflowing ointment of the peace of the Lord; in this field flourished the pomegranate trees (Song 8:2), that shelter many fruits. . . . And so Jacob was fragrant with the fragrance of such fruits. . . . Although the fragrance of the field is pleasant and sweet because it is a natural fragrance, still there breathed in the holy patriarch the fragrance of grace and virtue.[26]

Ambrose uses the philosophical trope of fragrance as a perfume composed of diverse virtues. He adds to the moral language of virtue the cultural coding of fragrance as indicative of divine presence, at once distinct from the mundane realm yet permeating and transforming it by infusing its sweet scent. The scent marked its source—the domain of heaven rather than earth; and it marked religious condition—Jacob as one uniquely blessed (or favored) by God. Mention of scent and ointment, and the allusion to the Song of Songs, tie the whole passage to a liturgical context with healing and bridal imagery. The passage thus conjoins an emphasis on ethical activity (the life of virtue) and religious ritual (the activity of human-divine relation); these activities combine to yield the "fragrance of virtue" that Jacob exuded from his person.

Ambrose used the method of "allegory" to read Genesis 27.27 so that it "speaks of other things" (allegoreo).[27] In the Genesis passage, the blind Isaac misidentifies his son by relying on touch and smell to inform him of what his eyes cannot see; hence Jacob steals Esau's blessing by deception. In Ambrose's hands, the passage speaks rather about the life of virtue which is favored by God. The "meaning" which Ambrose substitutes for that of the basic narrative sense, is one that relocates the text from its biblical place to the daily lives of his congregation. It is not a reading that disembodies his audience in any way. Instead, Ambrose relies on familiar philosophical and cultural olfactory codes to present his exegesis, presuming the habits by which olfactory sensations were commonly interpreted in the culture of his audience. Furthermore, he transplants the text into the domain of their daily activities, the social and religious practices through which they conduct their lives. The "fragrance of virtue" is a trope, then, that refers to the results of bodily actions, of life conducted in and through the body. Its olfactory cue—"fragrance"—also references concrete practices that are part of those daily actions (incense and holy oil: the scents of liturgical and devotional piety), and its positive connotation depends on the common code identifying sweet scent with divine presence. On another occasion, Ambrose likewise presented the expensive ointment with which the Sinful Woman had anointed Christ (Lk 7:36–50 and parallels): "Now they who bring good fragrances buy Christ, the incense with which the altars of a devoted heart are ablaze."[28]

The "fragrance of virtue" was a ubiquitous image in late antique Christian texts. As in this instance, its reference was generally to the results of moral and ethical conduct, in late antiquity almost invariably represented as ascetic activity; moreover, its resonance always and necessarily included the evocation of liturgical practice.[29] John Chrysostom would exhort his women parishioners to spurn the spices of India, Arabia, and Persia, "so costly and so useless." Why waste the money to provide scent for a body rotten within, "as if one should waste perfume upon dirt, or distill balms upon a brick"? Instead, he urged, there is "a precious ointment and a fragrance, with which you might anoint your soul . . . purchased not by gold, but by a virtuous will, and by faith unfeigned. Buy this perfume, the odor of which is able to fill the world." Indeed, it was such as could scent not only bodies, but whatever touched such bodies, casting out demons, and all vices. "This is a spice which is not the produce of the earth, but springs from virtue, which withers not, but blooms forever. . . . With this we are anointed at our Baptism, then we savor sweetly of it." But to keep its odor, John warned, one must enact the virtue it heralded: almsgiving, above all, was the best means both to acquire this scent and to keep it.[30]

In chapter 1, we discussed the positive valuation granted by early Christians to the body of the believer, particularly in its capacity to express human-divine relation through moral and ethical conduct. In late antiquity, the theme continues in a situation framed by a different liturgical sensibility. In the enhanced grandeur of Christian ceremonial, Christian leaders stressed the importance of the body for its expression of devotion to God through moral and ethical activity; they also praised the body as a vehicle for gaining religious knowledge.[31] Olfactory piety now demarcated liturgical practices. Liturgical instruction now highlighted the importance of sense perception in the human-divine relationship. In the liturgically charged atmosphere of late antique Christian discourse, the image "fragrance of virtue" served to reorder the meaning of ascetic practices. Where pre-Constantinian Christian asceticism most often served to demarcate the Christian community within its larger social context, in late antiquity the need was to locate ascetic practices (increasingly severe as they were) within the liturgical life of the church and within the liturgical body of the Christian.

Fragrance worked especially well in this role because it could carry sacrificial sense—the offering of good works, of prayer, of good teachings—while at the same time evoking the notion of identity, the perfumed scent of sanctity, divine presence, and grace. The "sweet smell" of virtuous conduct pervaded accounts of monastic life, with both religious meanings clearly intended.[32] The usage could easily be extended to the larger Christian community in any of its social patterns. Aphrahat the Persian Sage exhorted the Sons and Daughters of the Covenant, a consecrated order found in the Syrian Orient, "Let us be a sweet odor, that our fragrance may breathe forth all around."[33] Ephrem Syrus echoed the call to the whole congregation:

Our prayer has become like a hidden taste within our body,
but let it richly give forth the fragrance of our faith:
fragrance acts as a herald for the taste
in the case of that person who has acquired the furnace that tests all scents.[34]

Indeed, Ephrem presented the penitential activities of the Ninevites, converted by Jonah in the biblical account, as prototypical of the Christian ascetic life in these very terms:

[The Ninevites] made crowns of repentance.
. . .
They wove blossoms that did not fade.
Instead of flowers they wove an ascetic life.
Prayers they wove like lilies
That flourished in the flowing of tears.
Fasts they mingled with humiliation
And prayers by means of just deeds.
In ashes and sackcloth that made beauty fade
The crown of the saints rejoiced.[35]

In such terms, again, did the holy man Onnophrius command his disciple Paphnutius to take up the task of reporting the deeds of the desert ascetics to the larger world: "the Lord has appointed you to comfort the holy brothers who live in the desert, to proclaim their sweet fragrance among the brethren who worship God as a benefit to those who listen to you."[36] The multivalent sense of this ascetic "fragrance" is underscored in this text in an earlier passage where the saint instructs Paphnutius on what he must do when Onnophrius dies.

He also said to me, 'When you go to Egypt [= return from the desert to the inhabited world], proclaim my memory as fragrant incense to the brethren. Whoever makes an offering in my name and in memory of me, Jesus himself will bring him [into the feast] in the first hour of a thousand years.' But I said to him, 'If he is poor, he will not be able to make an offering in your name.' He said to me, 'Let him feed a poor brother in my name.' <I> said to <him>, 'If he is poor, he will not be able to feed him. . . . ' He said to me, 'Let him offer a little incense in my name.' But I said to him, 'If he is poor he will not be able to offer incense in your name on account of his poverty. Come, good father, let your grace rest upon us all . . . ' He said to me, 'Let him stand and say his prayers three times to God in my name and the Lord Jesus will bring him to the thousand years and he will receive an inheritance with all the saints.'[37]

This hagiographic account is especially rich as one that combines the olfactory image of spreading virtue by its report like fragrance, with the ritual uses of incense that would be familiar to the audience: offering incense as an honorific for a notable or venerated person, the related practice of burning incense as a memorial for the dead, the offering of good works as a sacrifice, and the offering of prayer as a sacrifice. The motif of fragrance/memorial/incense/ fame often appeared in hagiographies or homilies devoted to saints.[38] Paul of Tamma described the monk in his cell as the incense on the altar of God.[39] Theodoret of Cyrrhus ended his *Life of Macedonius* with the statement, "We, on bringing this narrative to an end, have reaped the fragrance that comes from narrating it."[40]

The topos of asceticism and fragrance easily shifted between referencing virtuous activity, and marking the special condition of grace apparent in the holy man or woman whose aura exuded the evidence of their virtuous, or blessed, state. Writers often used the image of blooming flowers to describe the diversity of virtues displayed in monastic communities.[41] John Cassian spoke of Abba Moses as one who "in the midst of those splendid flowers gave off a particularly sweet odor because of both his practical and contemplative virtue."[42] John Moschus titled his hagiographic collection the *Spiritual Meadow* for exactly this reason:

> In my opinion, the meadows in spring present a particularly delightful prospect. They display to the beholder a rich diversity of flowers which arrests him with its charm . . . the diversity and variety of innumerable flowers affords delights both to nostril and to eye on every side. Think of this present work in the same way. . . . I have plucked the finest flowers of the unknown meadow and worked them into a crown. . . . I have called this work *meadow* on account of the delight, the fragrance, and the benefit which it will afford those who come across it.[43]

When Symeon Salos spoke with his companion Deacon John, "he conversed with him so gracefully and with such compunction, that often perfume came from his mouth."[44] The fragrance of the holy person was not only perceived by those nearby, but could also permeate them if they held themselves in the right disposition. One anonymous homilist used the analogy to preface a sermon on the Holy Cross, begging the audience to attend to his teaching: "And let a man remember this: if he sends forth the good odor of one who has taken and rubbed on perfume, just as he does not cease being comforted himself, he also fills those who stand near with the good odor of that."[45]

The motif applied not only to the ascetic life of professed monks and nuns, but indeed, to the life of every faithful believer. Romanos the Melodist engaged it in his Kontakion on the Three Holy Children in the fiery furnace (Dan 3). Imprisoned in Babylon, the children pray to God with a hymn "as perfume blended of three essences." Babylon itself is described as a "sewer of idolatry . . . full of pagan sacrifices / and giving off an evil smell everywhere of transgressions." But the youths in their faithfulness "are like incense in the midst of slime." They call upon God to "breathe on us, Thy servants, / and on Thy true friend Daniel, / Who gives off fragrant odor and whom you love."[46] True identity, that of the innermost heart, is yet revealed and made known through its external manifestation—both in actions, and in the odor of one's nature.

Amidst the diversity of asceticism in late antiquity, two primary impulses guided the practices of Christian ascetics. One was the desire to use the body in a constructive sense—to remake the body, and with it the human person, body and soul, into the image of its redeemed state. The second, often guiding the expression of the first, was the Bible itself. Ancient Christians read scripture as an epic story culminating—and encapsuled—in the specific narrative of the gospels. The narrative purpose of scripture was summarized in the church's creeds, represented and reenacted in every Christian liturgy, and therefore able to be represented in any Christian body. Olfactory imagery was a primary means of linking biblical texts with liturgical actions and with ascetic practices; it enabled this entire scheme to be held together in a coherent whole.

An example was Ambrose of Milan's address, "Concerning Virgins," a text dominated by olfactory images and rhetoric.[47] "Concerning Virgins" refers repeatedly to scents and smells. In part this is because Ambrose draws often on the Song of Songs for a biblical base through which to present virginity as a mode of human-divine relationship. But bridal imagery is hardly his sole point, and olfactory images allow Ambrose to link from the Song to other biblical texts, all with the intent of unfolding an ever grander scale of meaning through which to present virginity. Olfactory imagery allows him to describe the process by which asceticism remakes the body (and the person), re-forming it and fashioning it anew as a body redeemed and worthy of the promise of incorruption. Taking two verses from the Song that praise the smell of the

Bridegroom, he writes of the two odors that are thus available to the Bride, the virgin who seeks Christ:

> See what progress thou settest forth, O Virgin. Thy first odor is above all spices (Song 1:3), which were used upon the burying of the Savior, and the fragrance arises from the mortified motions of the body, and the perishing of the delights of the members. Thy second odor, like the odor of Lebanon (Song 4:11), exhales the incorruption of the Lord's body, the flower of virginal chastity.[48]

The passage uses the bridal narrative of the Song interwoven with the passion narrative of the gospels, to portray what the practices of the ascetic virgin mean and what they accomplish: the death and burial of the old body, its decay and dissolution; and the sweet fragrance of immortality, revealed with Christ's resurrection and now emanating from the renewed body virginity brings forth. Later in the same work, Ambrose sets this intricate imagery into an explicit liturgical frame for its context. He addresses the virgins of his audience directly:

> [You, virgins,] whose souls I would without hesitation call altars, on which Christ is daily offered for the redemption of the body. For if the virgin's body be a temple of God, what is her soul, which, the ashes, as it were, of the body being shaken off, once more uncovered by the hand of the Eternal Priest, exhales the vapor of the divine fire. Blessed virgins, who emit a fragrance through divine grace as gardens do through flowers, temples through religion, altars through the priest.[49]

Here, then, the whole natural order and the whole civilized order (represented as a specifically religious order) find their meaningful structure through an ordering of scents. Allegorical reading thus allowed the figural language of biblical texts to remain vivid and compelling by enabling the application of biblical narratives or verses to the practices of Christian asceticism. This was true whether in the monastic community or in the city congregation. Often, the fragrances are the cue that the interpreter intends to place asceticism squarely within the liturgical life of the church. "Fragrance of virtue" was an effective image because its polysemantic force never lost its concrete sensibility even when lacing together multiple arenas of meaning—philosophical, ascetic, cultural, liturgical, epistemological. Evocations of these (vast) realms yet remained accessible to the most ordinary of ancient audiences when presented through the familiar experience of smell.[50]

Olfactory imagery pervaded the ascetic discourse of late antiquity. In most instances, it was not the dominant motif. In philosophical and scientific tradition, smell had not been ranked at equal importance with sight or hearing. It was held to be of intermediate, or low, worth—at best, useful in a limited way. This intellectual legacy interacted with a cultural sensibility steeped in a densely textured reliance on smells to order daily life. Hence we find smells present and operative as images or references in ancient Christian texts, but usually as undercurrents within a text's larger purpose. Yet these undercurrents gain significance when we recall the generous constancy of olfactory religious practices: what people *did* with smells reframes what they *said* about them. Olfactory images or references were made offhand, unintentionally, or with quite specific purposes in mind—any such instance can be illuminating.

However, olfactory imagery was most often what kept ascetic and contemplative literature tied to its context of the larger religious community. The late antique *Apocalypse of Paul* portrayed Christian renunciants—characterized as precursors of the monastic and ascetic practitioners to come—as revered by the angels and glorified before the throne of God, for the renunciants in their abstinence, fasts, and mourning held "in their hands the incense of their hearts."[51] As Christian liturgical practices blossomed in splendor, such imagery expressed concrete associations.

Ascetic discipline, self-mortification, and contemplative prayer were activities conducted in a larger arena of practices. At a basic level, olfactory imagery anchored those activities to the ritual life of the wider Christian community, by providing consistent referencing to incense and (holy) perfume. Gregory of Nyssa had warned that sensory experience "nailed" the soul to the material world in a detrimental and limiting way.[52] But olfactory imagery similarly "nailed" the practicing ascetic to the liturgical life of the church, thus framing ascetic activity, even at its most severe, by setting it definitively within the church's sacramental life.

The Spiritual Senses: Relocating Perception

Ancient Christians found numerous biblical models for experiencing a domain that lay beyond the physical senses, but to which the senses gave entry. In the narratives of Moses on Mt. Sinai, of Ezekiel's visions of the chariot or Isaiah's of the celestial altar, of the disciples at the Transfiguration of Christ on Mt. Tabor, and of the apostle Paul "caught up into Paradise," Christians read examples of holy men whose prayers had culminated in a direct encounter with the divine, during their mortal lifetimes and in their mortal bodies.[53] These encounters exceeded the confines of the natural, finite world and of the physical body within it, yet were bodily experienced and known by their recipients. The biblical accounts gave these narratives vivid sensory characteristics: the cloud and the pillar of fire; rustling wings; sapphire blue; burning tongs and sweet-tasting scroll; dazzling white; sights "that cannot be told." The Songs of Songs was a favorite example among both Christian and Jewish commentators, who seem not to have doubted that the Song's content was explicitly, or even solely, about human-divine relation—with God or Christ as the Bridegroom, and Israel or the Church or the individual believer as the Bride. Through the Song, sumptuous scents and fragrances appeared to mark every human encounter with the divine. In the Bible, divine revelation was made known to the faithful in experiences of a sensory nature, even as their content defied the contours of natural, physical experience. These texts both inspired and troubled late antique Christians: what did these frankly figural accounts mean?[54]

The language of the Bible thus contrasted with that of Greek and Roman philosophical tradition, which from the time of Plato had fostered a notion of the contemplative life as one that necessarily separated the experience of soul from body. The philosophical models for contemplative perfection were "out of body" experiences, literally "*ekstasis*" (standing outside oneself): Socrates in silent, unseeing meditation on the battlefield at Potidaea; Plotinus lifted out of his body in unitive encounter with the One.[55] Ancient Christians found a way to reconcile these contrasting languages of human-divine encounter in the notion of the "spiritual senses." These were envisioned as a set of senses parallel to the five physical senses but operating within the interior self and open to the perception of the divine realm beyond the physical one. Within Christian contemplative writings both east and west, the spiritual senses have had a long and rich history.[56]

While Origen may have been the first Christian to present a theory of the spiritual senses in any sustained sense, a distinction between the "inner" and "outer" person was already made by Paul in several of his New Testament letters.[57] Similar language is found in his contemporary, the Jewish philosopher Philo of Alexandria.[58] At roughly the same time that Origen was pursuing the idea of interior senses, it found a philosophical formulation also in the writings of Plotinus.[59] Platonic tradition had bequeathed a conception of the human person that distinguished body and soul—not always with clarity or consistency—in terms that opposed them in a dualism. Modern scholars, however, have often read Platonic dualism through the lens of modern understandings of dualism, rooted in the philosophical teachings of René Descartes. Cartesian dualism as we have inherited it posits a complete severance between body/matter/nature/the physical on the one hand; and soul/mind/nonmatter/the spiritual/the psychological on the other. Cartesian dualism has been a powerful principle in modern western intellectual history. But it cannot be transplanted back onto the ancient mind, where the opposition of "body" and "soul" was understood differently, and generally with a view to negotiating competing desires, appetites, or emotions in the self.[60]

For the ancients, as we have seen repeatedly in this study, divine and human domains overlapped in a material universe. The divine was experienced and made known in and through the physical realm, even while exceeding its every category and quality. Early Christians, who diverged from scientific tradition in their insistence on creation *ex nihilo*, posited an ontological distinction between Creator and created that was unbreachable from the human side, but which God himself repeatedly bridged in his desire to be known in relation to the human. Creation as a realm indelibly marked by its creator, humanity as a creation "in God's own image," and the incarnation and resurrection of Christ were Christian teachings that required the human person to be defined as one whose body could not be dismissed as insignificant, or excluded from the salvation process.[61] When we look at the spiritual senses as a major theme in late antique ascetic and devotional writings, we must be careful not to read a Cartesian model into their presentation.

The ascetic movement that dominated the landscape of late antique Christianity, and the ascetic rhetoric that was privileged in late antique Christian discourse, were both accompanied by an understanding that contemplative prayer was the highest pursuit of the Christian devotee. The notion of the spiritual senses was developed in monastic communities, devotional writings, and prayer manuals as part of the cultivation of a Christian ascetic practice of prayer. Scholars have sometimes presented this development as one that presumed an anti-sensory, anti-physical focus: prayer in which the soul was "freed" from the body. Indeed, Origen, Gregory of Nyssa, Ambrose of Milan, and Augustine all exhort that the spiritual senses can only be brought into use by a careful training of the self that requires the extinguishing, or even the destruction, of the "carnal" senses; each of them would insist that ultimately even the "spiritual senses" must be abandoned in the quest for God.[62]

But the very term "spiritual *senses*" should be a clue that ancient Christian teachings on contemplative prayer recognized the critical role of sensory experience in any human form of knowledge, including the understanding of God. There were two problems in this recognition: how to rightly interpret the figural language of the Bible, and how to reconcile the finite quality of sensory experience in the physical world with the infinite nature of the divine. The spiritual senses provided a way to answer both puzzles. In some writers, like Evagrius Ponticus and those who followed the system of noetic prayer he developed late in the fourth century, the spiritual senses receive scant attention, functioning at best only at an early stage of the contemplative's progress.[63] For others, discussion of the spiritual senses attended the effort to capture some hint of the intense experience of the divine that prayer might yield.[64] Ps.-Macarius had urged his fellow monks, "We ought to pray, not according to any bodily habit nor with a habit of loud noise nor out of a custom of silence or on bended knees. But we ought soberly to have an attentive mind, waiting expectantly on God until he comes and visits the soul by means of all its openings and its paths and senses."[65]

What was meant by the term "spiritual senses" in its practical use? How did the rhetoric of these senses function within the presentation of devotional activity, of prayer, and of human-divine relation? Did these interior "senses" perform an altogether different task from that of their physical counterparts? What was conveyed by the spiritual sense of smell? In different authors and different writings, these questions find various responses. But in broad strokes, the prevailing themes indicate that the rhetoric of the spiritual senses was one that recast the bodily experience of the contemplative, shifting it away from a location in the physical world in its finite existence, and placing it within the domain of divine presence. The actual content of spiritual sensory experience—how these senses functioned, what they perceived, and how the contemplative should process that knowledge—in fact seems to rely closely on a deep appreciation for physical sensory experience.

Here, too, attention to olfactory imagery provides us a fresh vantage point. Most of the time, wherever the spiritual sense of smell is invoked, it denotes a sacrificial context or sense, or signifies divine presence—the basic paradigms of incense and perfume we have seen repeatedly in this study. 2 Corinthians 2:14–16 is cited innumerable times as the exegetical key to understanding other biblical references to smell. As in the case of the "fragrance of virtue" motif in ascetic writings, such passages often link the interior activity of contemplative prayer to the larger liturgical context of the church as a whole. Furthermore, there is consistent attention to the quality of olfactory experience as an epistemological tool: the spiritual senses, too, were presented in terms of what they could contribute to knowledge of God.[66] In this regard, Origen and Gregory of Nyssa's discussions of the Song of Songs (in both cases, venues for the presentation of the spiritual senses) provide the most interesting examples of what olfaction contributed to the ancient Christian experience and knowledge of God. These two works thus merit specific attention.

In Origen's *Commentary on the Song of Songs*, the lavish scents of the biblical text are treated most often as indications of divine presence, divine identity, or divine grace. A moral reading is also given to the spices, which are thus shown to indicate virtues and good works.[67] But at certain points, Origen's consideration of the olfactory imagery requires sensitive attunement to the bodily experience of smell. At one point Origen combines two verses to give the reading,

"Thy name is an ointment emptied out. Therefore have the maidens loved Thee, have they drawn Thee. We will run after Thee into the fragrance of Thy ointments."[68] The Bride, he notes, is drawn to the Bridegroom at first only because of his fragrance, "under the compulsion of one single sense, the sense of smell alone." Despite the fragility of the sensation, the maidens yet run with her:

> This comes about, as we have seen, when as yet they have received only the scent of Him. What, do you think, will they do when the Word of God takes possession of their hearing, their sight, their touch, and their taste as well, and offers excellences from Himself that match each single sense according to its nature and capacity. . . . in this way he who has reached the peak of perfection and beatitude will be delighted by the Word of God in all his senses.[69]

Fragrance is once again shown to act as a herald for divine presence: to announce that which cannot be seen or heard or touched, but which is yet tangibly sensed. The encounter is sharply known: it prompts urgent, fervent response even when no other perceptual evidence validates the experience. Olfactory sensation is the entry into an encounter that will, in its wholeness, fill every sense beyond any imagining. Where Origen more often concerns himself with biblical intertextuality (cross-referencing texts), or with ethical activity, here he pauses to reflect on the nature of physiological experience as it can illumine the human-divine encounter. Olfaction sets in motion a sequence of reactions in the believer that turns the human-divine relationship away from alienation and towards intimate union: the scent of the Bridegroom's fragrance initiates first recognition, then longing, and then embracing of the divine. All this, as Origen marvels, from the sense of smell alone.

Elsewhere, Origen takes up the reading "My spikenard has yielded its (or His) odor."[70] Here Origen plays on the capacity of odors to transfer from one source to another, transgressing boundaries and permeating that which they encounter. Hence in this verse, Origen says, the spice of the Bride gains its scent only when it meets the Bridegroom: "in some marvelous way the spikenard, scentless so long as it was with the Bride, yielded its odor when it touched the Bridegroom's body; with the result, apparently, not that He has received something from it, but rather that the spikenard has received from Him." The transfer of scents will yield a new fragrance—a new identity—for the Bride. Following the variant reading, "My spikenard yielded His odor," Origen expounds the olfactory encounter in this way:

> this ointment of spikenard, with which the Bridegroom has been anointed, has acquired not the odor natural to the spikenard, but that of the Bridegroom

Himself; and that the nard has wafted His odor back to the Bride. She, in anointing the Bridegroom, has thus received as a gift the odor of His own ointment.[71]

So, too, Origen continues, did the Sinful Woman anoint the feet of Christ and wipe them with her hair, receiving back the fine ointment's fragrance now changed, "steeped in the character and virtue of His body." Through her hair she acquired "the odor not so much of the ointment as of the very Word of God, and what she has put on her own head is the fragrance of Christ, rather than that of the nard."[72] The entire discussion, first of the Song and then of the Sinful Woman, pivots on the unique mobility of smells, a mobility that crosses boundaries that otherwise cannot be breached—in this case, between human and divine natures. Infectious, scents attach to what they encounter, transferring their odor without diminishing the source. Origen uses olfactory experience here as more than an analogy for human-divine encounter. Rather, he engages it to encompass the entire dynamic through which the human person is transformed within the human-divine relationship.

Finally, Origen takes up smell in relation to free will. To do so he posits a notion reminiscent of Theophrastus, that every person emanates a distinct personal odor indicating moral character and condition. Commenting on the phrase, "the vines in flower have yielded their sweet smell" (Song 2:13a), he writes:

And I think it is not without reason that He says, 'their sweet smell,' and not a sweet smell: it was to show that there is in every soul a potential force and a freedom of the will, by means of which it has the power to do all things good. But this inborn good had been beguiled by the Fall, and perverted to sloth or wickedness: when it is amended by grace and restored by the teaching of the Word of God, then assuredly it yields that odor which God the Creator had originally implanted in it, but which the guilt of sin had taken away.[73]

Moreover, he writes, the angels and celestial powers are themselves the flowering vines that "impart to every soul her fragrant odor, and the grace which she received from her Creator at the first and now, after losing it, has again recovered. And with the sweetness of their celestial fragrance they drive away at last the stench of the mortality and corruption, that the soul has laid aside."[74] Odors sweet and foul have thus accompanied humanity from its perfect prelapsarian condition, through its Fall, and into its now changing state as it seeks to return to a redeemed status. These smells are powerful. They belong to the individual human person, and shift according to one's moral choices. The original human scent was sweet, implanted by God exactly so; and it will be again, as the heavenly beings assist the soul in its return to a graced condition.

The stench of mortality is transitory; the perfume of the resurrected state will endure. Through fluctuating smells, the history of salvation plays its course. The human person may follow the good odor intrinsic to personal identity or may choose to turn another way. But when it turns aright, fragrant help stands ready to impart strength and beauty to the redeemed soul. The force of Origen's reading depends on understanding the inextricable bond between self and odor that ancient culture recognized, and the volatility of that perception.

Gregory of Nyssa offers a certain contrast to Origen's perspective. Even more than Origen, Gregory represents an understanding of contemplative prayer that requires abandonment of any sensory experience at its highest levels.[75] In part, this difference rests on their respective agendas, for Origen was above all attempting to interpret scripture; while Gregory, standing on the firm foundation Origen had laid for those who followed, could move forward into contemplative prayer as a life predicated on what had already been established in the church. Gregory's was the era when monasticism had come to flourish throughout the Christian realm. Yet Gregory, too, presents his most exalted teachings on the contemplative life through the medium of biblical interpretation. Consequently, even in those discussions where Gregory admits to the utter inadequacy of language to present experience of the divine—those places where he insists on the totally apophatic nature of any encounter with God— he yet must engage sensory language for his purposes since that is what the biblical texts require.

Gregory's two greatest works on the contemplative life are his *Life of Moses* and the *Commentary on the Song of Songs*.[76] Each is governed by the figural language of the biblical narratives on which they focus: the *Life of Moses* is dominated by a rhetoric of visuality, of seeing, as Moses did on Sinai; the *Commentary on the Song of Songs*, of course, is steeped in olfactory imagery. Both Mariette Canevet and Verna Harrison have pointed out that Gregory's use of imagery cannot be dismissed as "mere" metaphor or analogy, nor simple counterbalance to the sophistication of his philosophical argumentation. Rather, it demonstrates his profound awareness of the limits of language however utilized—philosophically or poetically.[77] In the case of his *Commentary on the Song*, in fact, I would argue that Gregory's olfactory imagery highlights the limits of noetic experience. He seems to deliberately engage a bodily participation as essential to any genuine experience of God—and for Gregory, the dilemma is precisely that God can be experienced, although humanity lacks any adequate means for expressing or comprehending that which God is.[78]

Gregory has little to say about smells in his *Life of Moses*, beyond the standard references to incense as sacrifice, stench as sin, and the moral dangers of perfumes.[79] He states repeatedly that sensory knowledge is finite while God is infinite; thus the senses can neither contemplate God nor comprehend Him.[80] Instead, the true vision of God is the ceaseless desire to see more, to comprehend more, to contemplate more of God, and never to be satisfied by what one has seen.[81] In his *Commentary on the Song*, however, Gregory does not avoid the challenge of this text in its insistent evocation of sensory experience, and particularly of scents and fragrances. Like Origen, Gregory most often uses the trope of the "fragrance of virtue," discussing at length and repeatedly the various perfumes as compounded of virtues, and using 2 Corinthians 2:14–16 to connect these passages with the "good odor of Christ." But in several places, Gregory's exegesis requires attunement to the salient qualities of physical olfactory experience and even habits in order to grasp his instruction on the divine. In such instances, he seems to rely on what the body can know through smell in order to capture what eludes the mind in understanding.

For instance, in one discussion of the perfumes of the Song, Gregory invokes the lingering, extensive quality of scent. Far from its source, scent can be recognized even when faint. The experience is one we realize to be a partial encounter, but it can nonetheless be of penetrating beauty. Gregory applies this quality to the perfume of divine presence.

> Whatever name we may adopt to signify the perfume of divinity, it is not the perfume itself which we signify by our expressions; rather, we reveal just the slightest trace of the divine odor by means of our theological terms. As in the case of jars from which perfume has been poured out, the perfume's own nature is not known. But from the slight traces left from the vapors in the jar we get some idea about the perfume that has been emptied out. Hence, we learn that the perfume of divinity, whatever it is in its essence, transcends every name. However, the wonders visible in the universe give material for the theological terms by which we call God wise, powerful, good. . . . All these give some indication of the divine perfume's quality. Creation retains some traces of this divine perfume through its visible wonders as in the example of a perfume jar.[82]

Indeed, Gregory goes on, smell is the first way that we encounter divinity. As the Bride draws near to her Bridegroom, "before her spouse's beauty appears, with the sense of smell she touches the one she seeks." She recognizes him first by his scent, and then discerns that her own fragrance has been changed by his. The "good odor" of the Bridegroom is unique, uniquely composed, and uniquely available to the person who has "purified" senses. From this experience, Gregory says, the whole of God's work and presence in the created order becomes clear: "We think that the Word teaches us here about his essence underlying the order and structure of creation: it is inaccessible, intangible, and incomprehensible. Instead of the Word we have in us this compounded fragrance from the perfection of the virtues."[83]

Gregory turns to the transformative capacity of smells, a quality dependent upon their volatile affective power. Bringing 2 Corinthians 2:14–16 to bear upon the image of the Bridegroom's perfume, Gregory describes the apostle Paul as one who imitated the Bridegroom by his virtues and "depicted by his fragrance the unapproachable beauty." Rendering himself by this means into the "good odor of Christ," Paul then "gave himself to others as incense . . . a fragrance bringing either life or death." Consider, Gregory adds, the effect of perfume on beetles and doves. A dove is strengthened by inhaling the scent, while the beetle dies from the same experience.

> Thus it was with that divine incense, the great Paul, who resembled the dove. Titus, Silvanus, and Timothy all partook of the fragrance of Paul's perfume and progressed in every deed with Paul their example. On the other hand, if a person was like Demas (2 Tim 4:10), or Alexander (2 Tim 4:14), or Hermogenes (2 Tim 1:15) and did not bear the incense of temperance, he was banished like the beetle by the perfume's good fragrance.[84]

Gregory uses perfume as an image for the transformative impact of the divine on the human. He uses perfume imagery in this mode also to invoke the sacrament of baptism for the individual, and the whole body of the church in the world. He thereby uses the biblical imagery to link soteriology and ecclesiology to his real purpose, the human encounter with the divine. No experience of God, then, is to be separated from the liturgical and ecclesial life of the believer.

Yet Gregory's model for knowing the encounter with God remains, in the *Commentary on the Song*, the individual body and its physiological functions. Discussing the "sachet of myrrh" that lies between the Bride's breasts (Song 1:13), Gregory remarks on the habit of women to adorn themselves with perfumes hidden in their garments, so that their companions or husbands will be attracted by the fragrance of their clothing and by the scent that their bodies acquire through it. The physiological process that activates and transfers the fragrance is the same as that which attends the desire for God that lies in the believer's heart.

> . . . the heart is said to be a source of warmth from which the body's heat is distributed through the arteries. The body's members are thereby heated, animated, and nourished by the heart's fire. Therefore, the bride has received the good odor of Christ in the governing part of the soul and has made her own

heart a kind of sachet for such incense. And so she makes all her actions, like parts of the body, seethe with the breath from her heart so that no iniquity can cool her love for God in any member of her body. . . . Observe how much the bride has grown when in her own nard she recognizes the good fragrance of her spouse. She has made of him sweet myrrh and received this perfume in the sachet of her heart.[85]

The image of divine presence as fragrance also provides Gregory a vivid means to describe how and why Christ reveals himself to each individual according to that one's capacity for understanding (a frequent trope in such discussions). Like fruit on a vine, Christ is seen in different forms, changing with time: "now budding, now blossoming, now mature, now ripe and finally as wine." Although the scent changes with the fruit's condition in time, the function of the scent remains constant: it marks the presence of grace, and heralds a fuller beauty to come. The blossom's scent, Gregory says, gives the promise of hope.

Meanwhile [the fruit] does not lack any delight, for it gladdens our sense of smell instead of our taste with its expectation of the future; by its fragrance of hope it sweetens the soul's senses. A faith firm in a grace we hope for becomes a delight for us who wait in patience.[86]

Throughout his Commentary on the Song, Gregory comments on the special olfactory qualities of the different flora, fauna, and spices mentioned in the text. Cypress wood has a pleasant smell, but is also useful in artwork because its scent prevents decay.[87] Lilies delight two senses, sight and smell, but apples give joy to three since they also give joy to taste.[88] Myrrh is appropriate to anoint the dead, but frankincense is solely consecrated to God.[89] Saffron conceals more beautiful flowers within the cloudy petals of its exterior blossoms; these hidden flowers are richer in color, scent, and medicinal properties. Cinnamon is a spice of exceptional power, able to instantly cool boiling water, cleanse corrupt matter, or even force a sleeping person to prophesy.[90] For each plant, Gregory provides an allegory to apply its special qualities to the soul; and each spice he presents in turn to mark the successively higher ascent of the Bride in her quest for the Bridegroom. At the end of his commentary, Gregory repeats his admonition that in its highest ascent towards God the soul must cast off any sensory awareness.[91] Yet Gregory's work to interpret the Song of Songs surely tests the limits of allegory as a reading strategy. Ethical models for the "fragrance of virtue" adorn its every page, it is true. Nonetheless, peppered with the cultural commonplaces and practical wisdom on which olfactory uses were based in late Roman society, and sprinkled with medically informed observations on physiology, Gregory's commentary succeeds in abstracting the noetic process of contemplation while yet remaining firmly grounded in the sensory activity of the body. Gregory's *Commentary on the Song* is a *locus classicus* for discussion of the spiritual senses. Yet it cannot be read without constant reference to bodily sensation and experience. In this, it remains faithful to the biblical text on which it rests.

When the spiritual senses took root in eastern monastic tradition, however, they did so as more than a method of scriptural exegesis. In monastic and hagiographic writings, the line separating physical and spiritual sensory activity blurs. The reader must see that the measure of a saint lies not in the ability to obliterate one set of senses and cultivate another. Rather, the saint is one who succeeds in forging the physical senses into spiritual ones: to discern through bodily sensory experience truths and revelations made known by divine grace and offered to the purified, properly trained senses of the holy man or woman. St. Euthymius maintained vigilance regarding the state of his soul by keeping active the "eye of his soul."[92] In time this disciplinary habit grew into a charism by which his senses attuned him to the moral situations of others. Euthymius's hagiographer, Cyril of Scythopolis, presents this as a charism of "second sight," through which God granted the saint the power to discern, "from seeing the appearance of the body," the movement of a person's soul and its inner turmoil.[93] But Euthymius could also discern which demon afflicted a monk, or which temptations or impure thoughts, simply by the smell of the person.[94] Moreover, when he was in the liturgy itself, Euthymius often saw angels concelebrating with him.[95] His senses took in the divine as well as human realities in which he stood.

John Climacus, whose career spanned the late sixth and early seventh centuries, presented the same sensibility in his instruction to monks known as *The Ladder of Divine Ascent*. Discernment, John writes, can be a matter of olfactory awareness. Monks would do well to remember that the Lord rejoices in "the purity and cleanliness of our bodies," while demons delight in "the foul smell" of fornication and bodily defilement.[96] But one can be deceived. A monk might think, for example, that he senses "the full fragrance of myrrh" within himself during prayer, the unmistakable mark of divine presence. If his response involves the slightest stir of pride, however, then his gain is utterly lost; indeed, the "stench of pride" could linger long in the nostrils.[97] Attunement to the spiritual meaning of odors must furthermore be directed both towards oneself and to others:

> Everyone with a healthy sense of smell can detect hidden perfumes, and a pure soul can quickly recognize in others the sheer fragrance of goodness that he

himself has received from God. And indeed he can also recognize—as others cannot—the foul odor from which he himself has been liberated.[98]

What one finds in monastic and ascetical literature, in fact, is a certain slippage between the notion of the spiritual senses, and the more common cultural associations of divine presence or states of grace known through sweet odors. Olfactory devotional practices (the use of incense in prayer, the use of holy oil for healing or blessings) combined with the explosion of the cult of saints, the veneration of relics, and pilgrimage piety, to yield experiences described in terms that render the distinction between physical and spiritual senses moot. In this context, the sweet scent of relics takes on additional meaning. Consider again John Climacus, describing the experience of his community when they performed the burial rites for the priest monk Menas, who died after living fifty-nine years in the monastery.

> Three days after the death of this saintly monk, when we had finished with the customary rites, the place where he lay was suddenly filled with a great fragrance. We were allowed by the superior to open the coffin in which he lay, and when this was done we had sight of what seemed like two streams of myrrh flowing from his venerable feet. The teacher said to all of us, 'Look, the sweat of his labors has been offered up as myrrh to God, and has been truly accepted.'[99]

In the sixth century, Byzantine monastic sources and hagiography begin to report the miracles of myrrh-gushing relics or icons, phenomena which continue to characterize the devotional experiences of Orthodox Christians to this day.[100] Byzantine monastic and contemplative writings have often been characterized by an emphasis on the spiritual senses culminating in a pure sense of sight, when the holy person sees the Uncreated Light, that form by which Christ made himself known to his disciples on Mt. Tabor.[101] Yet it was Byzantine monasticism that actively cultivated and sustained a contemplative culture steeped in olfactory practices, olfactory miracles, and the ascetic goal of "purified" or "spiritual" senses by which to integrate these experiences into the life of prayer.[102] Attention to the smells through which devotion was expressed, and by which the holy was experienced, reminds us that eastern ascetic traditions genuinely included a profoundly embodied and sensorily aware orientation. The notion of spiritual senses perhaps began in response to an exegetical need. But it developed further within eastern monastic traditions inclusive of practices and perceptions that required an intentional sensory base. Instead of separate sets of senses, the goal was the transformation of the physical senses into vehicles through which bodily sensation conveyed experience and knowledge of the divine.[103]

Ascetic Practice and Embodied Liturgy

In chapter 1, we considered how early Christians used sacrificial language and biblical imagery to present their devotional practices and daily activities in terms that established a distinct identity for Christians as a community of believers. Olfactory imagery of incense or perfume was a primary vehicle in this strategy of representation. In late antiquity such discourse continued, enhanced by the proliferation of Christian ritual practices that deliberately employed olfactory elements. The "Christian meaning" of smells came to rest not only on the traditional language of ancient Mediterranean cultic activities, but also on their current ritual associations and indeed, on the particular resonances their ritual uses carried within a Christian frame of reference.

In the present chapter, I have argued that olfactory discussions in late antique ascetic writings functioned to redefine the sensory contexts in which the Christian acted, to reorder the qualities of sensory experience, and to relocate the processes of sensory encounter. In each case, the olfactory cues tuned the audience in to an overarching framework that was, invariably, liturgical. Liturgy was the context in which every Christian act, practice, or perception was to be understood. Olfactory imagery was most often the marker that signified this orientation. But liturgy itself was held to be the enactment of biblical revelation: the Bible provided the forms, images, models, teachings, and stories by which Christians accounted for the details of liturgical activity (even when those details were of Greek or Roman source). Olfactory imagery, then, functioned in late antique Christianity to integrate ascetic practice into the liturgical life of the church, specifically as that practice enacted Christianity's biblical imagination. Olfactory rhetoric held together asceticism, liturgy, and biblical exegesis, joining the practices of individuals into the ritual world of the ecclesial community.

Early Christianity was marked by asceticism from its inception. But in the fourth century that inclination took a dramatic turn in importance. Monasticism as a separate place and mode of existence emerged over the course of that century, and with it an impulse towards more stringent ascetic practices. At the same time, asceticism continued to be fostered outside the monastic context, as Christians in every social location were urged through homilies and episcopal pronouncements to pursue ascetic ideals. Late antique Christian asceticism, however, was informed by biblical traditions expressed through the dramatic changes in liturgical practice that emerged in the post-Constantinian era—and I mean here "liturgy" understood in the broadest sense, inclusive of devotional activities undertaken individually or collectively, in public or private, in domestic, civic, or monastic space. Without question, the impact of this changed liturgical context on ascetic understanding was profound.

Nowhere is the impact clearer than in the case of Syriac Christianity, where ascetic devotion was the hallmark of Christian identity from its earliest presence, and where asceticism was arguably pursued in its most extreme forms during the late antique period.[104] Indeed, the stylite on his pillar or the grazer naked in the wilderness were perhaps the most notorious examples of late antique ascetic zeal (to both the ancient and modern minds).[105] Syriac ascetic tradition interacted with and influenced other currents in the late ancient Christian world, yet its expressions remained distinct.[106] One of the most striking features of Syriac Christianity was its early attraction to olfactory piety: most of the earliest references to the Christian use of incense are of Syrian provenance, and from the fourth century onwards Syriac writers lavished attention on incense and holy oils. Most intriguing, however, is the degree to which olfactory imagery and piety characterized the presentation of Syrian asceticism in both prescriptive and descriptive texts of the late antique era and well into the middle ages. In fact, Syrian asceticism might be characterized as the individual bodily enactment of the collective liturgical process as it was conducted in ancient Syriac churches; such, at least, is the sense of the olfactory imagery one finds in the ascetical literature.

The Syrians were not alone in depicting the body as an architectural space in which the human-divine relationship was enacted. Two literary topoi were already commonplace. One was the trope of the self as a house which must be rendered fitting for a king—that is, God—to come and dwell in. Philo had explored this image at length, considering in turn what would be necessary to make the house suitably dignified, worthy, beautiful, fitting, and strong for its Royal Visitor.[107] This was a beloved image among late antique ascetic writers.[108] The other, often joined to the first, was an image discussed in chapter 1, of the soul's interior sanctuary with prayer the offering upon the heart's altar.[109] Origen, for example, had expounded this image in his Homily 9 On Exodus: the true believer must construct a tabernacle, a sanctuary, for God in the body as in the church, adorned with virtues as with sumptuous ornaments. Sacrifices of prayer must be offered, especially upon the altar of the innermost heart.[110] Certainly, the image of self or heart as censer is as frequent in late antique writings as in early Christian texts, forming a staple image of ascetical literature, most often with reference to 1 Corinthians 6:19, the teaching of the body as a temple of the Holy Spirit.

Aphrahat and Ephrem the Syrian, the two foundational Syriac writers of the fourth century, both set these images to good use in exhorting the faithful to live an ascetic life in pursuit of pure devotion. Aphrahat's Demonstration 1, "On Faith," begins with a lengthy treatment of the image of the faithful soul as a building constructed with Christ as the cornerstone; and if constructed rightly,

then also the dwelling place of Christ the King.[111] Ephrem renders this image
in terms that provide a glimpse of late antique housework:

> Let us become builders of our minds
>   into temples fitting for God.
> When the master dwells in your house
>   honor comes to your doorstep.
> How much more, then, will your gate be exalted
>   if God dwells in you.
> Be for Him temple and priest
>   and serve Him inside your temple.
> Just as He is for your sake
>   priest and sacrifice and libation,
> you be for His sake
>   temple and priest and offering.
> For your mind to become a temple,
>   do not leave filth in it.
> Do not leave in the house of God
>   anything hateful to God.
> Let the house of God be adorned
>   with whatever is proper for God.
> But if there is passion there
>   harlotry will dwell there.
> And if there is anger there
>   smoke will rise up there.
> Expel wrath from there
>   and envy, whose smell is abhorrent.
> Bring in and set love there,
>   a censer full of fragrance.
> Sweep and cast out dung from there,
>   hateful company and habits.
> Scatter in it good doings
>   like flowers and like blossoms.
> And instead of rose or lilies,
>   adorn it with prayers.[112]

In the sixth century, Jacob of Serug would present a more elaborate version
of this theme to describe the Virgin Mary's preparations for her conception by
the Holy Spirit. Jacob's implication is that all Christians must subject themselves to a similarly thorough cleaning job, if they are to be worthy of Christ's
presence within them. In a homily on the Nativity, Jacob portrays Mary receiving the archangel Gabriel's announcement of her pending impregnation.

At once Mary undertakes the cleansing and beautifying of both her inner and outer self, to render her entire being fitting for the indwelling of the Son. In Jacob's lyrical telling, housekeeping transforms into church cleaning, and the cleansing properties of aromatics elide into the ritual preparations of liturgical offering.

> She gathered and removed all [improper] reckonings from her mind.
> She sprinkled her pure temple with love before the Holy One.
> She swept her house with the holiness that was within her,
> and she embellished its inner walls with all kinds (of acts) of reverence.
> Again in it she set in order the good signets of perfection.
> She replenished it with blossoms of all manners of modesty.
> She levelled its land [Mk 1:3] with the choice implements of virginity.
> She hung up ornaments, crowns of praises of watchful care.
> She took up and laced together veils out of chastity;
> She spread out and stretched out spacious garments of watchfulness.
> She poured out as oil, good deeds in her lamp [Mt 25:1–13]
> and her great flame has been inflamed in the temple of her body.
> She burned the fragrance of her prayers warmly
> so that the pure fire of her faith should serve as incense.
> She threw, as sweet spices, the sounds of praise into the fire of her love,
> and from her thanksgiving breathed the fragrance of choice incense.
> . . .
> And while the house was made radiant by these things in a holy manner,
> the Son of the King entered and dwelt in the shrine of virginity.[113]

The correlation between individual and collective prayer, interior sanctuary and actual church building, raised the link between the earthly liturgy offered by the church and the celestial liturgy served unceasingly by the angels. In the hands of monastic writers in particular, this link was more than a correlation: the church's liturgy was meant to be the living image, the iconic representation, of that performed by the heavenly hosts. At the turn of the fifth century, an anonymous Syriac author brought together this iconic image with that of the body's interior liturgy, to present to an ascetic audience a lucid explication of the liturgy as a threefold enactment, taking place in heaven, in the church, and in the ascetic true believer's heart. The passage, from *The Book of Steps, Discourse* 12, is often cited by scholars because of the clarity with which it captures the impulse of Syrian asceticism.

> Let us pray with our body as well as with our heart, just as Jesus blessed and
> prayed in body and in spirit; and so too did the apostles and prophets pray. . . .

By starting from these visible things, and provided our bodies become temples and our hearts altars, we might find ourselves in their heavenly counterparts which cannot be seen by eyes of the flesh, migrating there and entering in while we are still in this visible church with its priesthood and its ministry acting as fair examples for all those who imitate there the vigils, fasting and endurance of our Lord and of those who have preached him. Let us both do and teach this; then, once we have attained to humility and have shown honor to everyone, great and small, the heavenly church and the spiritual altar will be revealed to us, and on the altar we shall make a sacrifice of thanksgiving in the prayer of our hearts and in the supplication of our bodies, believing all the time in this visible altar, and assured in this priesthood ministering there. . . . As for the church in heaven, all that is good takes its beginning from there. . . . After its likeness the church on earth came into being, along with its priests and its altar; according to the pattern of its ministry the body ministers outwardly, while the heart acts as priest inwardly. Those who are diligent in this visible church become like that heavenly church as they follow after it.[114]

The prayer of the individual's heart, a favorite theme in Syriac writings, was hence seen to be offered as sacrifice within the body as a sacred temple.[115] In the ascetic whose bodily discipline displayed that interior disposition, that prayer became expressive of the full liturgical process. The intimate relationship between celestial, earthly, and personal liturgy involved a mutual participation that gave the ascetic's activity its viability and gave the church's sacraments their transformative power. This understanding was poignantly stated in an anonymous fifth-century Syriac verse homily, "On Hermits and Desert Dwellers."[116] The homily is written in praise of the wandering Syriac ascetics called "grazers" (boskoi) in Greek. The Greek historian Evagrius Scholasticus had described these holy men and women as fulfilling the New Testament image of those who suffered righteously for the faith, "wandering over deserts and mountains, and in dens and caves of the earth" (Heb 11:38).[117] But in Syriac tradition, multiple biblical models underlay this mode of ascetic discipline: Elijah and John the Baptist living in the wilderness; the temptation of Christ that took place in the desert.[118] It was sometimes seen as a penitential model, imitating the punishment of King Nebuchadnezzar in his madness, eating grass and having "his hair long like eagles' feathers and his nails like birds' claws" (Dan 4:33).[119] Or again, an anticipation of the return to Eden, to the life of Adam and Eve before the fall, a life among the animals and with creation in harmony.[120] All these resonances and more underlie the idealized portrayal seen in the homily, "On Hermits and Desert Dwellers." But liturgy stands at the center, providing image and structure to articulate the haunting sense of this ascetic vocation.

Their bodies are temples of the Spirit, their minds are churches;
their prayer is pure incense, and their tears are fragrant smoke.
Their groaning is like the oblation; their psalmody [like] joyous melodies.
Their sighs are pearls, and their modesty is like beryl.
When their tears stream down, they banish harm from the earth;
and when their petition is raised, it fills the world with assistance. . . .
They stay very late at service,[121] and they rise early for service.
The whole day and night, their occupation is the service.
Instead of incense, which they do not have, their purity is reconciliation.
And instead of a church building, they becomes temples of the Holy Spirit.
Instead of altars, [they have] their minds. And as oblations, their prayers
are offered to the Godhead, pleasing him at all times.
The wilderness that everyone fears has become a great place of refuge for them,
where assistance flows from their bones to all creation.[122]

The final line here refers to the relics their bones became when one of the wanderers died. Elsewhere in the homily, these unknown relics—concealed by the anonymity of the wilderness—are said to be guarded as treasure by the angels themselves.[123] Thus the wandering ascetics were shown to embody the liturgical life of the church, and to have their liturgical offering received and venerated by the heavenly church community. Once again, incense imagery holds the pattern together. The transposing of ritual beauty onto the description of these harsh lives jolts the modern ear. But the imagery served emphatically to draw this stark anchoretic vocation directly into the center of the ecclesial community and its ritual expressions. It caused diverse practices to intersect. That such a view was more than the homilist's rhetoric is apparent from the case of the stylite saints. There, we find incense practices used to characterize the ascetic work of the saint and the devotions of the laity in relation to them; incense, moreover, seems to have provided a foundational understanding for the stylite's vocation. In this instance, the interaction between olfactory piety and olfactory rhetoric is brought into sharp relief.

The Stylite's Model

Scholars have long noted the prominence of incense piety in the hagiographies and cultic devotion related to the early Byzantine stylites. Both literary and material evidence supports this view. The Syriac Life of Simeon the Stylite the Elder contains one of our earliest references to Christian incense offerings, in its poignant description of Simeon as a young shepherd watching his flocks and gathering storax to burn in reverent offering to God.[124] This Syriac Life and the Greek Life of Simeon by the monk Antonios provide elaborate descriptions of the stylite's death and funeral in 459 as events characterized almost exclusively by the incense offerings of the stylite's disciples, the crowds of faithful, and the officials in attendance.[125] The Greek *Life of Daniel the Stylite* (d. 493), Simeon's immediate successor, records Daniel's command to his disciples that incense be offered continuously as the hour of his own death approached.[126] The Greek *Life of Simeon the Stylite the Younger* (d. 592) appears to contain more references to incense use, both for individual intercessory prayers and in liturgical settings, than any other hagiography known to us.[127]

Archaeological evidence is equally striking. Elaborate monastic and pilgrim complexes grew up around the two Simeons during their careers, and these remained active pilgrimage centers long after the saints had died: Qal'at Sim'an at the pillar of Simeon the Elder outside Aleppo, and the monastery at the pillar of Simeon the Younger on the Wondrous Mountain outside Antakya (Antioch).[128] Both sites have yielded clay pilgrim tokens imprinted with the image of their respective stylites. The enormous number of tokens carrying the image of Simeon the Younger, in particular, is notable for the place of censers in the iconography of the image. Generally, the imprint shows the stylite on his pillar and another figure (disciple or pilgrim) approaching him on a ladder, swinging a censer. The material finds related to Simeon the Younger's cult have been analyzed in relation to his hagiography to produce information about the role of incense use in the private devotional prayer practices associated with this saint's veneration.[129] It is clear that the offering of incense in intercessory prayer to Simeon's image was seen by the faithful as a means for ritually connecting the saint on his pillar with one's own supplication, wherever one might be; further, that the incense provided the channel by which the prayer was sent to God through the saint, and by which divine response was channelled back through the saint to the suppliant. The Simeon tokens assume a common incense piety, even as they prescribe its application to this particular cult.[130]

This historical evidence helps to document the emergence and flowering of incense piety in the Christian east, especially as an important aspect of intercessory prayer, individual and corporate, and most acutely in relation to the cult of saints. Incense offerings were associated with gaining access to the saint's holy powers to heal or to rescue. Here, too, the transgressive quality of olfactory experience was crucial, as the aroma of incense wafted across whatever stood between the profane and the sacred, the lost and the saved. Conjoined to the newly emerging cult of icons, incense here gained a crucial role in the mechanisms and contents of human-divine interaction.

Again, the prominence of incense piety in the stylites' cult was part of a deepening engagement of a Christian sensorium. Sacred image, pilgrimage to the living stylite or to the saint's shrine, living encounter or dreamed visions, the offering of incense in prayer: all these aspects of devotional piety brought an encounter with the divine through the holy person of the saint. They involved touch, sight, hearing, and smell as distinct and critical elements of the experience; and each sensation was also granted its full meaning in what the taste of the Eucharist represented. Sensory experience carried with it the conceptual structures of sacred ritual: the whole body was engaged, just as the whole person, soul and body, was redeemed in Christ's saving work as reenacted in every liturgy.

Scholarship has emphasized the importance of incense use as a ritual activity in the stories and veneration of the early stylite saints. But certain of the hagiographical texts specifically dwell on smells, with that of incense as a frequent example. In other words, unlike modern scholars, the ancient texts highlight olfactory experience more than ritual activity, or at least grant it a separate significance. The shift here can be seen in the contrast between the Life of Simeon the Elder and that of Simeon the Younger. In the olfactory imagery of the hagiographical texts, it is a shift from true sacrifice by the individual believer, enacted with the body of the saint (Simeon the Elder, a layman), to the perfect sacrifice offered by the ecclesial body, made known through the body of the saint (Simeon the Younger, a priest). I will consider the texts in turn.

The vocation of stylitism was a controversial one in its own time: many, including ascetics, found it gratuitously excessive or exhibitionist. The three hagiographers of the first stylite, Simeon the Elder, had to explain and justify this curious ascetic choice in the absence of any (surviving) direct explanation by the saint himself. Each of the three vitae offers a different perspective from which to view the saint.

Theodoret

In his preface Theodoret frames his situation as one in which sight succeeds where the sound of words fails: "I have the whole world . . . as witnesses to Simeon's indescribable struggles."[131] The world sees what cannot be adequately heard: the sight is Simeon, fulfilling a vocation he received through hearing the gospel,[132] hearing a divine voice, and seeing a vision that portrayed what he must do. Theodoret presents a story in which seeing and hearing drive the narrative just as they have driven the saint's actions from the beginning.

In Theodoret's view, the sights tell the story. As a zealous novice early in his monastic career, Simeon once wrapped a thick, rough rope around his waist so tightly that he bound it into his skin. After some days of enduring this mortification, Simeon in his excess was found out when "someone on seeing him asked the cause of the blood."[133] Unable to convince Simeon to mitigate his practice, "when the monks saw him doing other things of this kind,"[134] they cast him out from their community. Simeon moved on. His next monastic setting again pitted him against firm orders that he lessen the severity of his efforts, this time in relation to fasting. Finally Simeon conceded, "If I see that my body needs nourishment, I will partake of food."[135] But his sight was not directed toward himself. Rather, "keeping heaven always before his eye,"[136] Simeon next chained himself to a mountaintop as he disciplined himself toward unceasing contemplation. Others, however, watched Simeon: "it is said one could see more than twenty large bugs hiding [in the wound caused by the chain rubbing Simeon's leg]. The excellent Meletius also said that he saw it."[137]

Pilgrims came in droves for the sight of Simeon at prayer. "As they all come from every quarter, each road is like a river: one can see collected in that spot a human sea receiving rivers from every side."[138] Yet these pilgrims wanted more than sight, they wanted touch. To escape their devotion, Simeon ascended his pillar. Theodoret recounts the stock *apologia* for Simeon's choice, a listing of Old Testament prophets who underscored their teachings with shocking behavior (Isaiah, Jeremiah, Hosea). Their word had been declared by sight as well as by speech. So, too, had God ordered Simeon to ascend his pillar, "that by the strangeness of the spectacle [God] might gather those who would not be persuaded by speech nor give an ear to prophecy . . . For the novelty of the spectacle is a reliable guarantee of the instruction, and whoever comes to the spectacle departs instructed in divine affairs."[139]

And so Theodoret's story goes: "One could see, as I said, Iberians, Armenians, and Persians coming to gain the benefit of divine baptism;[140] . . . . I myself was an eyewitness;[141] . . . I have not only seen his miracles with my own eyes, but I have also heard his predictions of future events . . . we all saw this clearly[142]. . . . For night and day [Simeon] stands in open view. He had the doors taken away and a good part of the enclosing wall destroyed and so presents to everyone a new and extraordinary spectacle."[143] There were those who would not believe these eyewitness reports. One such sceptic came to the pillar to ask if Simeon were human, because, he said, "I hear everyone talking."[144] It happened at the time when a sore on Simeon's leg had turned gangrenous, a horrific episode lasting many months and attested in every source we have on Simeon. Here is how Theodoret describes the encounter: "[Simeon] ordered that man to climb up and first examine his hands and put his hand inside his garment of skins and see not only his feet but also that extremely painful ulcer. The man saw and marvelled at that worst of ulcers . . . and then came down and told me all."[145]

Theodoret's version of this singular moment of direct encounter clearly owes much to the story of doubting Thomas in the Gospel of John 20:25–29.[146] But note that Theodoret even here characterizes the encounter by what the man saw rather than by what the man touched when he put his hand to Simeon. The conflating of sight and touch is not unusual in ancient sources. Ancient optical theory understood sight to involve an action by the viewer, in which a ray sent forth from the eye physically encountered the object viewed, transmitting information back to the beholder by means of this tactile encounter.[147] Here, Theodoret tells the story so that the emphasis remains on what was seen. Moreover, we should note that this man had come because *hearing* about Simeon was not convincing; *seeing* was. [148]

For Theodoret, vision and sound are the whole story. Simeon is a sight to be seen by all, preaching a word to be heard by all. Still, the picture is puzzling. The sensorium in this account is dramatically incomplete. Touch is conflated into seeing; taste is referenced in the lengthy descriptions of Simeon's notorious fasting. But not once does Theodoret mention smell. The omission might be less abrasive had Theodoret not referred so often to the direct encounters of those who, like himself, climbed the ladder to Simeon's platform. Instead, the blatant absence of olfactory experience in the encounter with Simeon serves to underscore, vehemently, Theodoret's central image that Simeon lived a bodiless, angelic life. It was truly so, as Theodoret described the physical encounter of pilgrim and monk.

Theodoret's silence about smell is heightened by the contrast he presents in this regard to the other two hagiographies. The *vitae* by Antonios and the Syriac disciple share the imagery of sight and hearing in their accounts of Simeon; light and word are the two most common images in Christian tradition.[149] Yet both shift at crucial moments to smell as the definitive experience characterizing the encounter with Simeon. This is a matter of quality, not quantity. In Antonios's *Life of Simeon*, for example, there are only three olfactory episodes. However, these three arguably hold the point of the narrative.

Antonios

First is the notorious rope incident. As told by Antonios, the full weight of the episode is conveyed through its olfactory aspect.[150] In this version, Simeon wore the rope for more than a year; his flesh rotted, and "because of his stench no one could stand near him." Not knowing the problem, the monks complained to the abbot that Simeon's excessive asceticism undermined their morale. The crowning insult, in their view, was the smell. 'Not only [must we put up with] this [behavior], but the stench from his body is so unbearable that no one can stand near him; his bed is full of worms, and we simply cannot bear it.' Investigating, the abbot himself found the stench revolting. The source of the foulness was discovered to everyone's horror. Simeon cried, 'Let me be, my masters and brethren. Let me die a stinking dog, or so I ought to be judged because of what I have done. For all injustice and covetousness are in me, for I am an ocean of sins.' No one, least of all the abbot, could imagine how Simeon could have deserved so cruel a penance.[151]

The extremity of the situation is measured by smell at every point: the perception of the monks and the abbot, the discovery of the mutilation, the denouncement of the mortification, and Simeon's own claim that the repulsive sensory experience was just reward for his spiritual condition. Intensifying Simeon's endurance is the stated horror of these witnesses that the stench was both self-created and self-inflicted. The incident foreshadows the second olfactory episode (rather more reserved), that of the gangrenous sore afflicting Simeon's leg as he stood on his pillar. Antonios describes Simeon's diseased leg as "putrid" and worm-infested, a literal image of decaying mortality.[152] One day when the king of the Arabs approached the pillar for a blessing, a worm fell from Simeon's wound. The king, not knowing what it was, rushed to scoop it up, touching it over his head and heart. Simeon summoned him in horror, 'It is a stinking worm from stinking flesh. Why soil your hand?' But the king refused to give up his prize, answering, 'This will bring blessing and forgiveness of sins to me.' And opening his hand, he found therein not a fetid worm, but a pearl "without price."[153] Thus, according to Antonios, were the fruits of Simeon's labors revealed.

Throughout Antonios's account, interior purity is proportional to exterior suffering. Oppositional themes underlie this *vita*: body and soul are related only antithetically.[154] The saint's body in its foul-smelling corruptibility signifies the fallen human condition. Simeon's labors are the willing endurance of humanity's utter sickness, and through his labors redemption will be achieved. Just as the worm transmutes to the priceless pearl, so, too, will Simeon's stench ultimately transform into the astonishing fragrance of divine incorruptibility. For when Antonios climbs the ladder to find Simeon three days dead, and weeps as he kisses and caresses the corpse, a new smell strikes him. "Throughout [Simeon's] body and his garments was a scented perfume which, from its sweet smell, made one's heart merry."[155] The fragrance was soon enhanced by the rich scent of incense and tapers that surrounded the extraordinary funeral procession carrying Simeon's body to its burial in Antioch's cathedral. Perfumes human and divine thus mingled in an olfactory revelation of what redemption would hold: a beauty surpassing articulation or form, hearing or sight; a beauty revealed when Antonios kissed Simeon's body and breathed in not the stench of death, but the fragrance of life.[156]

Antonios's *vita* of Simeon is a brief text, its message conveyed in stark images. Here it is not the visual encounter with Simeon, but the olfactory one that teaches the divine truth to which the saint's vocation bore witness. That olfactory message drew its force from ancient and enduring pan-Mediterranean traditions, wherein foul odors signified all that was evil, mortal, and corrupt, while sweet scent characterized everything good, divine, and incorrupt.[157]

Antonios employed this olfactory code to underscore his point about penitence and redemption.

The Syriac *Vita*

The most complex picture of the three hagiographies is offered by the Syriac *vita*. In this text, odors fair and foul signify human and divine condition, relation, and interaction. Throughout the narrative, this *vita* presents Simeon's vocation as a life of unceasing worship. Highly liturgical in its imagery and references, the text emphasizes not only liturgical actions but also the sensory experiences that accompany those actions in their liturgical context.

Hence the story of Simeon's career is framed, first and last, by the image of incense. In the beginning we are told that as a young shepherd ignorant of Christianity, Simeon habitually gathered storax and burned it as if in offering.[158] Converted upon hearing the Gospel, he began to gather storax in great earnest, "and, with all reverence, he offered it to our Lord saying, 'Let the sweet smell ascend to God who is in heaven.'"[159] Soon an angel appeared to Simeon, foretelling the career that lay before him and instructing him to build with stones, saying, "This is the sanctuary of that God whom you worship, to whom you burn incense, and to whose writings you paid attention."[160] Simeon began his new work. Towards the end of the *vita*, at the end of Simeon's life, the story is told in retrospect of how Simeon learned to pray by prostration.[161] Early in his career Simeon had lived as a recluse in a cell, with a stone for an altar, and incense and a censer on it. For three nights, an angel came to this stone, prayed by prostration, and then stood upon it. Simeon knew what it meant. Taking the place of the incense on the altar, Simeon mounted the first of his pillars, himself now literally rising like incense heavenward as prayer.[162]

Simeon offers incense; Simeon becomes incense. Within this frame of liturgical reference, every instance of smell in this text will find its signification.[163] Sinners, disease, and death are here marked by the stench they exude far from divine grace.[164] When Simeon's perfect love for his Lord brings him finally into direct combat with Satan, we are told, the monks who served the saint knew the nature of the battle, its greatest intensity, and its conclusion by the olfactory experience that accompanied it. For this is how this text portrays Simeon's near death from gangrene: as hand-to-hand combat with the devil himself even as Job had once endured. One night Satan struck Simeon with a sore on his leg. "Towards morning it burst open and stank; it swarmed with worms and putrid matter was oozing from the saint's foot. . . . The stench was so strong and foul that no one [of the monks] could go even halfway up the ladder without great affliction from the severe rankness of the smell. Even those who served the saint could not go up to him until they had put cedar resin and perfume on their noses. The saint was thus afflicted for nine months until all he could do was breathe." Finally at the point of death, a dazzling angel in a blaze of light rewarded Simeon for his endurance. One morning the disciples climbed the ladder in wonder to find Simeon shining, healed, and radiant, the "unbearably foul stench . . . replaced by a fragrant odor."[165]

Holy stench is a theme that recurs in other hagiographies of the time, not without reason: most common ascetic practices resulted in strong odors.[166] But recall Antonios's treatment of this motif. His most extensive example, Simeon and the rope, set the situation firmly within the human realm: a mortification Simeon created and inflicted. In the Syriac *vita*, the text ascribes particular distress to the disciples during this episode of gangrene because of its olfactory nature, and that distress is exacerbated because here the foulness exceeds human capacity, in their perception. The event seems to transgress religious order to the extreme. Those closest to the saint—the disciples and fellow monks—cannot reconcile sanctity with unbearable stench. In the resolution, the saint is miraculously healed, and the foul odor replaced by the clear fragrance of sanctity. In the grace of the perfected, saved body, Satan's ultimate weapon of mortality is transfigured into health: eternal life.

Finally, this text turns to Simeon's death. Here is how the story is told. It was the height of summer. Heat scorched the land. Simeon fell ill with a burning fever. Then, "a cool, refreshing, and very fragrant wind blew as though a heavenly dew were falling on the saint and were sending forth a fragrant scent from him such as has not been spoken of in the world. There was not just one smell exuding from it, but wave upon wave kept coming. There were multiple scents, each different from the other. To those billowing fragrances none of the sweet spices or excellent and pleasurable herbs of this world can be compared, for they were dispensed by the providence of God."[167] This exquisite odor wafted only about the top half of the pillar. The disciples knew what it meant, but the great crowd gathered at the base of the pillar to pray on Simeon's behalf did not notice it. Surrounded by thick clouds of incense burning in supplication, they did not realize that sacred smells both human and divine now rose up and poured down as earth and heaven joined in witness at the saint's departure. Indeed, when this text, like Antonios's, characterizes the funeral procession and burial by the sumptuous aromas of incense, tapers, "precious spices," and "excellent perfumes,"[168] the reader knows these worldly scents to be mere olfactory icons of the air Simeon now breathes: the 'very fragrance of Paradise.'[169]

Perhaps these observations tell us something about the location of the writers and, by implication, of their audiences. Theodoret's emphasis on spectacle has as one consequence the distancing of the observer from the saint. In a culture of ascetic practices and startling holy lives, if an encounter with Simeon has no olfactory dimension it can only mean that the witness (even the disciple) looks on from afar. In the *vitae* told by Antonios and the Syrian disciple, olfactory imagery brings an intimate proximity with the saint, carrying all the ambiguous qualities that would entail. The witness is positioned close enough to smell the ironic paradox that the holy life produces olfactory results distorting inherited cultural paradigms. Such a location is suitable for an audience of monks rather than of lay pilgrims, for those so close to such a life that they cannot afford to mask completely an ascetic practice of such stark consequences. Yet the texts insist that the ambiguity itself could be revelatory. Certainly in death, no more potent image could be found than that of divine fragrance, opposing and defeating the stench of mortality. Restoration and redemption could be known through the body of the saint, and would be experienced in the life of the worshipping community.

Where Antonios's *Life of Simeon* had used this final scene to balance polarities of corruptibility and incorruptibility, the Syriac *vita* uses it to fulfill the image of the saint's life as the enactment of liturgical process—a process that reestablishes human and divine order, even as it transforms the earthly into heavenly splendor, the fallen into their redeemed condition. In the Syriac *vita*, all that this saint's life accomplished is contained in the single lingering image of incense rising.

Just over a century later, the career of Simeon the Stylite the Younger was at its height. Incense piety was now central to the devotionalism of the cult of saints. The *Life of Simeon the Younger*, written soon after the saint's death in 592, took the motif of stylite as incense and placed it at the core of the saint's very being, at the same time that it prescribed—and described—a piety dominated by incense use. The role of sacred smells in this text is both quantitatively and qualitatively different from the texts relating to Simeon the Elder. And here again it is specifically the smells that matter. More than indicators of ritual meaning, in this text smells are markers and makers of religious knowledge, relation, and power.

In the *Life of Simeon the Younger*, the stylite is not the enactment of incense offering, but the embodiment of it. This is rendered in bluntly literal terms. Simeon's grandparents were perfumers. His birth was foretold in a vision when his mother Martha prayed at the church of John the Baptist for divine guidance regarding her marriage. John himself appeared to her, commanding her to fill the church with perfume. She awoke to find a huge ball of incense in her hand. Burning it as commanded, she filled the church with such fragrance that "those who breathed that sweet odor could not distinguish its nature."[170] And so indeed it would come to pass. Simeon the holy child would climb his first pillar at the age of seven. In a vision he was anointed with sweet-smelling oil and charged to defeat Satan's minions by its very perfume.[171] As he attained perfection in his ascetic discipline, it was fragrance that defined his work. When his spiritual father, the abbot of his monastery, died, Simeon prayed on his pillar with such force that his incense burned and smoked without fire.[172] When marauding Persians swept through the countryside, Simeon was concealed from their sight in a cloud of perfume that left his tunic permanently infused with its scent.[173] In visions, the scents of heaven pour down on him;[174] others perceive Simeon to shed forth the same scents into the world.[175] Simeon's incense offerings fill the monastery with blessings: concretely so, when censing the food supplies enables the monks to cope with feeding the hordes of pilgrims who come in endless numbers.[176] Time and again Simeon heals the sick—himself and others—replacing the stench of mortality with the sweet fragrance of sanctity.[177] Time and again, suppliants who cannot come to the pillar on the Wondrous Mountain offer their urgent prayers to the saint with incense; their prayers answered, they breathe the scent of grace.[178]

This Simeon's practice of prayer on his pillar is notably liturgical long before his ordination to the priesthood. Psalmody, readings from scripture according to the lectionary and from other holy books, hymnody, chanting the creed and the Lord's prayer—such are the components elaborately interwoven to comprise his daily discipline, intensified for occasions of particular solemnity such as the death of the abbot or Simeon's ascension to his great pillar.[179] Eventually Simeon is ordained in ceremonies both ecclesiastical and celestial, with deliberate attention to the eucharistic sacrifice which Simeon celebrates for all who come.[180] In fact, priesthood is the only image by which the text presents the saint before or after his ordination. All his activity is described as ritualized according to liturgical patterns, and all his good works—healings, preachings, ministry to the needy—are presented as hieratically conducted. Simeon is the liturgy. He embodies its process; he performs its transformative, redemptive work.

Various scholars have noted the prevalence of incense references in the Life of Simeon the Younger. But equally striking is the constant attention to the smells that accompany or result from the events described. Incense, oils, clouds, perfumes, visions, wounds, sickness, worship: in the narrative, the circumstances of Simeon's activities are characterized by their smells. To a certain extent this is in contrast to the Lives of Simeon the Elder, where similar situations will be mentioned with no reference to their olfactory dimension. The Life of Simeon the Younger is a text unusually detailed in regard to liturgical practices and other devotional rituals. Yet it is not process alone that matters at each point, but the sensory experience of process as well.

In a chapter of stunning implication, a Syrian nobleman brings Simeon a piece of aloe wood and insists, despite the saint's admonition to the contrary, that Simeon burn it as incense. Simeon calls for a censer, prays, and casts the aloe onto the burner. "Immediately an extraordinary stench spread, to the point that everyone in the monastery was in danger because of it. That stench spread two miles on every side of the monastery . . . [the people] perceived a terrible pestilence which they could not bear."[181] Simeon is not only imaged as incense, he has the power to determine the nature of what constitutes incense.

All these hagiographers present their stories with attention to how the witness, whether pilgrim or monk, would have had contact with the stylite, whether Simeon the Elder or Simeon the Younger. They note the sensory experiences by which the witness would encounter the stylite and know him to be a holy man. In other words, while modern scholars have looked to hagiography to indicate what the stylite might have meant to his world by focusing on the saint himself, ancient hagiographers used their stories also to focus on the witnesses, and in particular on the bodily experiences elicited by the encounter with sanctity—an encounter, after all, between the human and the divine. By stressing this encounter as a sensory one, hagiographers instructed the faithful as to how they, the faithful, should live in, know, and experience their own bodies, as complement to but distinct from the bodily existence of the saint. How the witness—pilgrim or monk—physically experienced the stylite is offered as paradigmatic for how every believer should experience and thereby know and understand God.

There is a subtle but profound epistemological agenda to these texts. Like others of their time, they present sense perception as a crucial instrument for gaining religious knowledge. The saint revealed the divine to the human not only through activity in and with his own body, but also through the sensory experiences he caused within the body of the witness. The believer who read or heard these stories, then, was not a passive spectator as human and divine encountered one another in the locus of the saint's body. Hagiography presented asceticism as a process through which the saint's body was remade and fashioned anew to become the channel for the holy in the physical realm. So, too, did these texts portray the faithful witness to that re-creation as one whose own body was also changed, transformed, and rendered conducive to divine expression in and through human experience. In the case of the witness, that change was indicated through the sensory qualities that accompanied the encounter with the saint. Thus, through the hagiographer's craft, the witness became an active participant in the task of bridging between human and divine, understanding the accomplishment of that bridge not only by the saint's activity, but also by the witness's own physical response to it. Each conveyed an aspect of revelation portrayed as necessary for understanding divine intention. Once again, olfactory cues provide the guidance through a process inclusive of the ecclesial community as a whole.

Olfactory imagery was not the only symbolic mode applied in the *vitae* of Simeon the Elder and Simeon the Younger.[182] But it is noteworthy that it predominates in the *vitae* of the Simeons, all written within a Syrian context (whether in Greek or Syriac), in a way that does not characterize the Byzantine (Greek) hagiographies of subsequent pillar saints.[183] Like the Syriac versions of the *Transitus Mariae*[184] with which they were contemporary, these Simeon texts provide us a vivid measure of the extent and significance reached by incense use in particular, and olfactory piety more generally, in the late antique Christian east. Material evidence supports this picture with its indication of widespread incense practices in association with the cults of Simeon the Elder and Simeon the Younger. Olfactory imagery in late antique texts presumed an intersection with the practices in which the writer and the audience (as well as the saint) were engaged. To omit these ritual associations from our study of late antique asceticism—especially here, in one of its most extreme instances—is to miss a primary resource by which the ancients themselves made sense of ascetic practice whether mild or severe. The intimate identification between Syrian stylitism and incense piety points to a profound reconciliation between the ascetic and liturgical discourses of late antiquity. The anti-sensory rhetoric of asceticism cannot be adequately assessed apart from its larger context within the sensorily engaging experience of the late antique liturgy. Olfactory cues make the point with particular force. The religious significations of smells served to direct the Christian community in their understandings and attitudes towards asceticism as practiced by even the most jarring holy figures of their time.

A Syriac Tradition Continued

At various points in this study, the rich olfactory traditions of Syriac Christianity have been highlighted: the imagery of Ephrem the Syrian; the incense prayers of the Syriac *Transitus Mariae* texts; the Sinful Woman's perfume in Syriac homiletic and hymnographic writings; the *vitae* and the cultic devotion for Simeon the Stylite the Elder and Simeon the Younger; the west Syrian commentaries on holy myron, and the development in the middle ages of the threefold prayer sequence to accompany the incense offering in the Syrian Orthodox liturgy. Most of our earliest evidence for Christian incense use comes from the Syrian Orient; subsequently, Syriac traditions display a deep and lasting pleasure in the olfactory piety cultivated in its Christian communities. As we might expect, then, between the seventh and tenth centuries, when East Syriac Christianity produced an exceptional flourishing of contemplative literature, the poignant evocation of olfactory piety continued. Under Islamic rule and in increasingly unstable social circumstances, the East Syriac mystics sustained the olfactory imagery of late antique asceticism with succinct yet trenchant force.[185] The development is further noteworthy, given the marked impact of Evagrian influence on Syrian traditions of prayer practice.[186] That is, even in a context dominated by an understanding of noetic prayer—culminating in the imageless prayer of the intellect, sharply distinguished from bodily experience—sensory imagery and, indeed, even (physical) sensory experience, could be fruitfully engaged in contemplative instruction.[187]

Thus the seventh-century writer Isaac the Syrian (Isaac of Nineveh) instructed his readers that the highest achievement of ascetic contemplation was the state of constant prayer, and hence of the continual sacrificial offering of praise and thanksgiving to God. This he describes as when the monk, whether awake or asleep, whether eating, drinking, resting, working, or slumbering, attains such a condition that "the perfumes of prayer will breathe in his soul spontaneously."[188] For Isaac, the "senses of the soul"—the spiritual senses—are those which the monk has trained to the point where they can perceive heavenly realities even through their earthly counterparts.[189] Yet the experience of the senses of the soul is one akin to the process of physical sensation: "[I]t is not possible that he whose mind is immersed in earthly case, should perceive with the smell of his soul the clear air of the new world. As the smell of a deadly poison disturbs the constitution of the body, so does pernicious sight disturb the peace of the mind."[190] Nonetheless, physical and spiritual sensation can elide in the presence of sanctity, allowing a tantalizing whiff of the salvation to come. The truly holy monk exudes from his own person the scent of redemption, "the smell which spread from Adam before his transgression . . . the smell which was taken from us and given back to us anew by Christ through His advent, which made the smell of the human race sweet."[191] Indeed, Isaac would pray on behalf of all ascetics, wherever they practiced their discipline of prayer, that God should strengthen them, "that a sweet scent may waft from them at all times giving pleasure to Your will."[192]

Martyrius (Sahdona), in his Book of Perfection, presents prayer as a sacrificial offering which, when the ascetic pursues it fervently and with purity of heart, burns as incense.[193] Following the models of Old Testament sacrifice, to be acceptable to God prayers must be pure, presenting the whole self, and offered as "sacrifices of thanks and praise—the whole burnt offerings of prayer which [God] loves." The activity of prayer requires the ascetic to become, in oneself, embodied sacrifice. In that condition,

> As [God] perceives the pleasing scent of our heart's pure fragrance, He will send the fire of his Spirit to consume our sacrifices and raise up our mind along with them in the flames to heaven. . . . In this way we make our bodies a living and holy and acceptable sacrifice, one that pleases God in our rational service.[194]

Simon of Taibutheh urged his fellow monks to prepare for sleep by throwing "sweet spices of prayers, psalms, and spiritual theory on the censer of your heart," to meditate upon before slumber. "When you wake you will feel the happiness that has wafted through your soul all the night," as the soul has offered its prayer as incense (citing Psalms 141:2).[195] Truly blessed, Simon wrote, was the monk who establishes his heart as a house in which he dwells with his heavenly consort (Christ) in glorious harmony with their children, the thoughts of prayer, and "who has ordered, with joy of heart, his mind, the censer, to go and perfume them and pour upon them the perfumed oil of love, peace, joy, and comfort."[196] Such will be the experience of the ascetic who does not fear to plead for divine assistance when assaulted by the wiles of the Evil One: "mercy will be poured upon him immediately with loving-kindness and pity, and sweet perfume will waft around him; his limbs will expand, and his heart will be renewed."[197] Thus fragrance characterizes the outpourings of the human heart no less than the divine response to them.

For Joseph the Visionary, pure prayer gains its fragrance first from the sacrificial quality with which it is offered, and then from the odor that marks its divine reception. While the true vision of God is beyond the senses, beyond any corporeal likeness or image, yet those ascetics who attain its perception will know the experience by the smell that accompanies it.

> Whenever [those who are worthy] draw nigh unto prayer and unto divine service in order to do the spiritual priestly service in the inward holy of holies, a fiery impulse stretches in their soul, which exhales sweet odor, the perfume of which is ineffable. When the soul which has been found worthy of it smells it, it rises from mortality to life, leaves darkness for light. . . . The mind will also become intoxicated and enraptured, as with strong wine, in the vision of that fiery impulse through which it will undergo a change in the exquisite odor of that holy smell.[198]

As one anonymous Syriac writer explained it, "holy" and "delightful" fragrance was one of the rewards of continual prayer.[199] These writers are clearly drawing on the familiar commonplaces we have seen throughout this study, of experiencing divine presence as marked by sweet scent, and of perceiving that divine indication as one that penetrates and changes (sanctifies) the identity of the one who perceives. Yet within the tradition of asceticism and contemplative prayer, especially as pursued in the Christian east—and above all, in the Syrian Orient—those commonplaces came to be strongly undergirded by the practices of olfactory piety: the burning of incense in private or collective prayer, anointment with holy oil to obtain blessings, the scents of liturgical celebrations, the perfumed cleansings of altars and sacred spaces. Joined to these fragrant devotional activities were the venerated memories of martyrs and saints, their stories recited in feast day celebrations and studied in the context of contemplative reading—holy men and women whose lives and deaths were cherished as embodied examples of liturgical sacrifice. Stylite, wandering grazer, or, less histrionically, the quiet monastic or convent dweller: the ascetic contemplative was one who participated in a religious worldview profoundly permeated by olfactory sensibilities as well as olfactory practices. Guided by smells, the Christian community demarcated the places, activities, and members of its body, granting order and purpose to the whole.

> Remember that you share in the stink of Adam
> and that you too are clothed with his illness.
>
> Isaac the Syrian, Homily 5[1]

Ascetic Stench: Sensation and Dissonance

The career of Simeon the Stylite, discussed in the last chapter, offers a striking example of how incense usage established an intersection between devotional practices, religious images, and ascetic meaning. Yet, as the consideration of Simeon's *vitae* showed, the olfactory dimensions of Simeon's vocation were not confined to the sacrificial or relational associations common to incense traditions of the Mediterranean. Simeon's pursuit of ascetic discipline was further characterized in olfactory terms that clearly unsettled the ancient Christian sensibility of religious order. At each phase of his career, Simeon disturbed his fellow Christians, whether his monastic brethren, his ecclesiastical superiors, his devotees, or his disciples. In each case, the distress he caused was not simply the cognitive discomfort of seeing his self-mortification. It was a physically experienced dismay: Simeon's holy career was repeatedly marred by the stench of his practices. Wounds, sores, filth, infection, illness, and gangrene accompanied the saint's great ascetic feats. If one sign of Simeon's sanctity (or at least of his ascetic self-discipline) was his own apparent immunity to the resulting stink, no one else in his vicinity enjoyed a similar charism. The odors of Simeon's ascetic virtuosity sorely tested the tolerance of others. More than an aesthetic issue, Simeon's stench profoundly challenged the entire system of olfactory codes by which the ancient world was ordered. It was no small comfort to his followers that Simeon's body finally breathed the sweet fragrance of sanctity at his death: but how could they account for the fetid smell surrounding the saint for the many decades of his ascetic life?

The dissonance of Simeon's case was real. However, in the ascetically dominated discourse of late antique Christianity, it raised an alarmingly common problem. The cultural discomfort—even fear—of stench ran deep. Christianity had incorporated the ancient Mediterranean olfactory codes into its customs and expressions, as we have seen, and not only by habit. Christian leaders found these codes useful as paedagogical tools in the instruction and guidance of the larger populace. The liturgical developments of the fourth and fifth centuries utilized incense and perfumes to delineate the processes of human-divine interactions. The scents of worship were understood to exude a beauty worthy of God's pleasure and, ultimately, a beauty of heavenly source. By contrast, whatever disordered the pattern of right relation was marked by its inverse: opposed to the liturgical foretaste of heaven's eternal fragrance was the stench of unredeemed mortality. Because Christians understood mortality to be a situation occasioned by Adam and Eve's sin, they saw it always as a moral condition rather than a physical trait. The physical consequences of mortality—sickness, bodily decay, and disintegration—were the direct results of that sin, and therefore always the indication of sin's presence. To be mortal was to reek of sin. Rottenness and putrefaction were mortality's nature, revolting stink its unmistakable mark.

When Christians looked to nature for revelation of divine activity, they did not find much to contradict the clarity of such a moral paradigm. Origen may have mocked "Egyptians who shiver with fear at the trivial physical experience of flatulence,"[2] but Christians did not question the basic medical perspective that noxious odors caused illness and even death.[3] A learned scholar such as Jerome might cite a host of classical authorities in support of the medicinal value of the dung of various animals and birds.[4] But everyone knew that the basic medical principle in such cases was that of like-treating-like: excrement was the refuse of mortality, irredeemably and inexorably abominable.[5] It was equally well known that rotten matter was the source of venomous reptiles, worms, and lice.[6] Bad odor heralded decay, the creep of putrescence; Christian women frightened off would-be rapists with threats of stench, infections, and wounds.[7] Ancient embalming practices were directly rooted in the effort to control the smell of a disintegrating corpse.[8] Paulinus of Nola cited the visceral aversion people had to the smell of dead bodies as a paradigm for thinking about sin: "Let us avoid not merely committing sin but even thinking of it, as we would hold our noses to avoid the infectious emanation and the foul stench from a rotting corpse."[9] Stench marked human wounds so foul that only the miracle of divine power—mediated through the saints—could bring their healing.

Such healing was made indisputably known when the intolerable odor turned to holy sweetness.[10]

Olfactory order, then, was divine order: divinely ordained and, by common perception, naturally sustained. Saints were perceived to participate in this divine order to the extent that they could display its pattern in their bodies and in their works. Rather than Adam's stink, "the very fragrance of Paradise" (as Ephrem Syrus called it)[11] wafted from their bodies and clung to their garments;[12] the promise of salvation was heralded in the scents exuded by relics. The power to control olfactory sensation was even more striking. Gregory the Wonderworker could purify air that stank of pagan sacrifices;[13] Simeon the Stylite the Younger could burn incense without fire, filling the air with celestial sweetness or lethal stench as he willed.[14] When the clothing of St. Irene, the abbess of Chrysobalanton, accidentally caught fire while she was at prayer, one of her sister nuns smelled the burning flesh and ran to douse the flames. Yet when she pulled the still smoldering cloth from where it stuck to the saint's skin, "a strange fragrance. . .incomparably more fragrant than any perfume and precious scents," began to fill the convent. It lasted many days while Irene healed of her wounds.[15] In Christian ritual and Christian legend, then, fragrance and stench not only symbolized redemption and damnation, but also were active and powerful agents by which those conditions were effected.[16]

Yet, as we have seen repeatedly in this study, the employment of abundant scents in every possible domain of daily life—for medicinal, culinary, hygienic, and social purposes no less than pleasure; for religious, political, and domestic functioning—made it difficult for Christians to apply olfactory paradigms without constant contradiction or exception. A frequent strategy was the rhetorical tainting of sweet scents as perfumes of deceit, with the admonition that Satan was as likely to be found in sweet odors as in foul.[17]

In such a context, it was crucial to separate holy and mundane usages. Preaching on the moral dangers of sweet smells, as discussed in chapter 4, was a patristic commonplace. John Chrysostom, for example, insisted that ornamental perfumes could only conceal (or even engender) foulness of soul; the true Christian should be adorned only with "the fragrance of virtue"—that of moral conduct or of good works.[18] Ephrem provided a more poetic image: the sweet fragrance of scripture could be turned to poison where erroneous exegesis was employed.[19] Cyril of Jerusalem referred to heretical gospels as bearing a "spurious odor of sanctity," through which the unsuspecting could be led astray.[20] Palladius described the duplicitous bishop Theophilus of Alexandria, by his ingratiating behavior, as "exud[ing] sweet fragrance to disguise the bad odor of his jealousy."[21] The Syriac mystic Abdisho Hazzaya warned that Satan hovered close by the Christian at prayer, wafting his perfume drawn from the smells of creation.[22] Such admonitions were frequent in late antique homilies, but allude to a discordant element that emerged in concert with the olfactory intensification of Christian piety. Good smells could mislead; worse still, despite the possibilities of saintly manipulation, good practices might yield bad smells.

Alas, all too often they did. Ancient authors complain that fasting made the breath foul;[23] coarse sackcloth roughened the skin and made it "evil-smelling".[24] Sometimes the "foul odor" of asceticism irritated the Egyptian monks.[25] Isaac the Syrian encouraged his monastic brethren, "Dearer to God are trials for righteousness' sake than all vows and sacrifices. And dearer, too, is the odor of the sweat of the fatigue they cause, than all the drugs of sweet scent and exquisite perfumes."[26] But cultural habits are hard to break. The Ps.-Basilian canons advised that "virgins ought to refrain from using too much perfume."[27] Athanasius, too, found the use of perfume by dedicated virgins a problem.[28] Aphrahat sternly rebuked the consecrated Sons of the Covenant that it did not behoove their holy office if they wore "gorgeous apparel" or adorned and anointed their hair with "sweet-scented unguents".[29] John Chrysostom might urge the people of Antioch, "Only stand near the man who fasts, and you will at once partake of his good odor, for fasting is a spiritual perfume; and through the eyes, the tongue, and every part, it manifests the good disposition of the soul."[30] But Theodore of Sykeon castigated the Christians of Constantinople for going straight to the baths after attending the eucharistic liturgy, evidently to wash off the unsavory smells acquired from just such proximity among the congregation.[31]

Indeed, the nature of Christian ascetic practices required a certain reconfiguration of the categories "good" and "bad" odors. The binary "aroma of Christ" named by Paul in 2 Corinthians 2:14–16, "to one a fragrance from death to death, to the other a fragrance from life to life," provided the crucial biblical model for this process. Paulinus of Nola noted that the "stench" of a loved one is not "stench" to the lover.[32] He further insisted that since the odor of monks was nauseating to pagans, the smells of pagans ought to "stink in our nostrils".[33] Maximus of Turin called for Christians to pursue vigils, fasting, and abstinence, in order that their lives should become as flowers yielding sweet aromas to Christ and to God, no matter their effect on one's neighbors.[34] Prudentius wrote that the odor of St. Lawrence burning to death was "noxious," "vengeful," and "nauseous" to the unredeemed, but "nectar sweet," "soothing," and "delightful" to the faithful who had been present at his martyrdom.[35] To be sure, Christian authors took particular pleasure in describing martyrdoms through reversed olfactory sensations: a favorite topos was the stench of burning flesh transformed into the sweetest of scents, as in the *Martyrdom of St. Polycarp* with which this book began.[36]

In hagiography, a different rhetorical strategy emerged. Holy but unpleasant olfactory experiences are not infrequently cited in the stories of saints, offering at least a nod to real life experiences. But these were often judiciously muted in the hagiographical telling. For example, abstinence from bathing was commonly mentioned as one gruelling aspect of ascetic discipline, without comment on the olfactory aspects of this practice.[37] Instead, we find references to the "smell of asceticism" or even the "sweet smell of asceticism" wafting from the saint's person.[38] As St. Syncletica intensified her ascetic regime, for example, "the sweet fragrance of her most glorious sufferings passed on to many."[39] The monk Pambo reported to his monastic brethren that when he journeyed to visit the holy Abba Pamoun, "I, Pambo, the most unworthy, smelled the sweet fragrance of that brother a mile before I got to his home."[40] The literary portrayal of a saint, then, might affirm the rigors of physical endurance without acknowledging the sensory experience or perception that resulted.

Silence or euphemism on these matters might have been didactic, another strategy to redirect the Christian valuation of smells, as some hagiographical episodes seem to beg for olfactory consideration. For instance, the holy fool Symeon of Emesa tied a dead dog to his waist; shocked the marketplace with his voracious appetite for lupines, a legume notorious in antiquity for producing excessive flatulence; and defecated in public, making plain, among other things, his incontinent consumption of raw meat.[41] But Symeon's hagiographer, Leontios of Neapolis, makes no reference to smell in the course of his narrative of these events. Rather, Leontios indicates here, as with the larger course of Symeon's activities in Emesa, that Symeon's socially offensive behavior was meant didactically, to shake the complacency of Christian urban culture.[42] As if to underscore the point, Leontios also insists that Symeon could burn incense in the palm of his hand without pain or wound.[43] Perhaps the ancient audience would also have imaginatively supplied the malodorous aspects of the episodes, and that, too, would have been edifying: for here was a holy man whose person exuded not the heavenly fragrance of redemption, but the blunt stench of mortality. The Fool's lesson would not have been missed: whatever its earthly successes, Christian society could not deceive itself as to the reality of its fallen condition.

Indeed, the absence of comment by Symeon the Fool's hagiographer cannot be taken to indicate that smell did not matter, nor even that the olfactorily unpleasant aspects of ascetic discipline might not have seemed painfully awkward—recall the anger of Simeon the Stylite's monastic brethren early in his career. By the later fifth century, the motif of sanctity known through stench began to appear in hagiographical literature. While not a dominant motif, it was one that added a profound complexity to the issue of how and what olfactory experience could teach the late antique Christian about humanity, divinity, and salvation. In every instance of its appearance, the effect is jarring—and clearly was so for the ancients no less than ourselves. But to appreciate the problematic conjunction of sanctity and stench, we need to consider how stench was normally (and normatively) employed as imagery in Christian teaching.

Stench and Morality: Mortality and Sin

Recall John Chrysostom's denunciation of perfumes, mentioned above. Perfumes, John says, are used by those who consort with courtesans, actors, and dancers; their use in his view is tantamount to moral depravity. Here is the passage:

> Nothing is more unclean for the soul than when the body has such a fragrance [as perfume]. For the fragrance of the body and the clothes would be a sign of the stench and filthiness of the inner man. When the devil attacks and breaks down the soul with self-indulgence, and fills it with great frivolity, then he (Satan) wipes off the stain of his own corruption on the body also with perfumes. Just as those who are continually afflicted with a nasal discharge and catarrh will stain their clothes, their hands, and their faces as they continually wipe off their discharge from their noses, so also the soul of this wicked man will wipe off the discharge of evil on his body. Who will expect anything noble and good from one who smells of perfumes? . . . Let your soul breathe a spiritual fragrance.[44]

To make clear the moral condition of the perfumed man, Chrysostom employs a simile that begins as an olfactory image (scent and its easy transferability through physical contact); but continues with tactile and visual implications (the matter discharged by a sick nose). He thus moves from olfactory sensation to the bodily organ that enables it, moving at the same time from the exterior to the interior person, from superficial appearance to real condition. Moreover, the actions of the man described—wiping the discharge, dirtying his garments and skin (set in direct parallel to the moral implications of associating with actors, dancers, or harlots)—are equally distressing in terms of their behavioral meanings. Cultural categories of propriety and violation, of cleanliness and filth, of order and depravity are all summoned with a mere rhetorical flourish—the transmutation of an olfactory experience into a moral revelation.[45] The rhetorical force of the passage depends on using a combination of sensory images to evoke feelings of repulsion, horror, and disgust.

The listener is meant to recoil (and does). This is an olfactory variation on the ancient topos of the body as a sack of excrement; or the seductive beauty of the beloved's body belied by the worm-eaten corpse it would become.[46]

The equation of stench with sin, and hence with false religion, was used in exactly this way: to elicit visceral revulsion at both the physical and moral levels. Arnobius of Sicca had scorned pagan statues ("idols") as not merely powerless, but frankly disgusting, desecrated by repeated, witless insults from the natural world.

> Really, do you not see that these statues, so lifelike that they seem to breathe, whose feet and knees you touch and stroke in prayer, sometimes crumble away under dripping rain; that again they disintegrate through decay and rot; how vapors and smoke begrime and discolor them and they grow black. . . . newts, shrews, mice, and light-shunning cockroaches place in them their nests. . .that hither they gather all kinds of filth and other things suited to their needs, hard bits of half-gnawed bread, bones dragged in against the future, rags, wool. . . Do you not see, finally, swallows full of filth flying around within the very domes of the temples, tossing themselves about and bedaubing now the very faces, now the mouths of the divinities, the beard, eyes, noses, and all other parts on which the outpourings of their emptied fundament falls?[47]

Gregory of Nyssa referred to the former life of Christian converts as sordid and licentious, "a foul and odorous memory which disgusts the soul in shame."[48] Chrysostom described unconverted pagans in similar terms as wretchedly deformed and ugly, but ugliest of all for their stench increased by "the smell of burning fat, the filth of blood, and the smoke of sacrifices."[49] Patristic texts are rife with admonitions that "sin is more foul than putrefaction;"[50] that angels cannot smell decaying corpses, but do smell and flee from stinking souls;[51] that the churches are filled with the stench of sin and, even worse, "the foul breath of blasphemy which comes stinking" from the mouth of heresy.[52] Indeed, heretics were punished by putrid deaths: Arius, for one, died in a "disgusting" latrine, drowning in his own excrement.[53]

One holy man fled to the wilderness, sickened by the smell of people.[54] Another rebuked himself for "recoiling from the sweat of others" while ignoring the "foul pus" of his own wounded soul, sick with pride.[55] A vision appeared while a monastic community ate together, revealing that some (the faithful) ate honey and others (the false) ate excrement.[56] Augustine recalled himself in his student days, "putrid" with ambition, wallowing in licentiousness as if in the debauchery of Babylon, "rolling in its dung as if rolling in spices and precious ointments."[57] Gluttony, wrote Philoxenus of Mabbug, "is a noxious form [of sin] . . . the sickness alike of the body and the soul, the vessel of stinkingness, the odor of filth, the fountain of the excrement of the body."[58] Even the thought of fornication could cast "an evil smell" into the soul of a monk, "making a fetid odor arise therefrom."[59] Pachomius instructed his monks to think of the human person, mortal and fallen, as "he who is all stench."[60] In admonitions to penitent self-examination the words of the Psalmist were frequently cited, "For my wounds grow foul and fester / because of my foolishness."[61]

The imagery of stench was used with no restraint to engage the entire panorama of physical decay—understood to be not natural, but the complete violation of nature; of terrifying and helpless disintegration, of the fear and loathing generated by abhorrence. Prudentius described St. Lawrence bringing the lame, the sick, and the blind to the palace of the persecuting prefect, their ulcerated limbs "flow[ing with] the foul corruption of disease." Ensuring his own martyrdom in the process, the saint then warned the prefect that just such a sight awaited him in hell.

> You would behold [the haughty magnates of this world] clothed in rags,
> their nostrils dripping mucus foul,
> their beards with spittle all defiled,
> their purblind eyes made blear with rheum.
> Than sin-stained soul, nought is more vile
> Nought so leprous, nought so sear;
> The wound of crime is ever raw
> And reeks of Hell's ill-smelling cave.[62]

Disgust, as William Miller has pointed out, is invariably an experience with moral dimensions.[63] Its moral impetus, in fact, is drawn precisely from its interconnection with physical experience and process as understood within a given culture. To the ancient mind, smell was the sensation most intimately enmeshed with disgust in the full range of its meanings. Christian writers were adept at manipulating the connection.[64] That demons, heretics, and hell were best characterized by stench, they took to be axiomatic.[65] In monastic writings, women, too, fit this category, filling the monk's thoughts with their lingering and fetid memory.[66]

The moral identification of stench did in fact touch a nerve of profound cultural fear. This could be presented in edifying terms. In late antique Christian legend, Herod of Judea was remembered to have died a wretched death, fully representative of his evil soul and fitting punishment for his reprehensible crime in murdering John the Baptist.

A divine punishment that was pitiless overtook [Herod], and he fell ill of a sickness through which he stank, and his body melted away into a mass of worms, and he suffered most grievous pains, and at length people were unable to come near him because of his putrid smell. . . . His bowels and legs were swollen with running sores, and matter flowed from them, and he was consumed by worms.[67]

Such depiction of death was not only a literary artifice for moral condemnation. It also echoed the poignant repugnance with which epidemic illness was described, as in accounts of the bubonic plague that struck the eastern Roman Empire in 542 and continued in repeated outbreaks for decades thereafter. The texts are frankly grim: the authors rely on descriptions of the odors of the sickness, the infected sores, and the abandoned and decaying corpses to convey the horror of the experience.[68] To the ancients, bad odors were effectively torturous; they were one reason Roman prisons were known for their brutality.[69] Hence in Christian literature, no image was so damning as that of the tyrant (whether political or ecclesiastical) who would use stench as a form of torture and even of terrorism. In Roman tradition, *damnatio memoriae* was demonstrated by effacing and covering the portrait of the disgraced person with foul-smelling substance.[70] During the iconoclastic crisis of the Byzantine Empire, iconoclasts desecrated holy images by rubbing them with cow dung, grease, and other things "with nauseating stench," befouling the fragrances of myron and incense with which they had formerly been redolent.[71] Repulsive stench represented moral status, unequivocally; indeed, it actualized the condition of moral degradation it was believed to represent.

A pointed example is found in John of Ephesus's *Ecclesiastical History*, in his narrative of the sixth-century persecutions against the non-Chalcedonians of north Mesopotamia. John attributes particular savagery to the Chalcedonian bishop of Amida, Abraham bar Kaili, who terrorized the city by leaving the corpses of the executed on public display until people were overcome by the stench. Events culminated, John claims, in Abraham's deployment of lepers to despoil the homes of dissenting Syrian Orthodox laity.

[Abraham] took a band (of lepers) as many as they were in a monastery of lepers located outside the city, called, 'Mar Romanus.' He sent them and let them dwell in the house of a [Syrian Orthodox] believer. The latter was compelled to leave his house and to flee from their hideous appearance full of terror, when he saw their disfigured faces and their body, wholly putrid and rotten, producing an abominable stink, while their hands were putrid and dripping blood and pus, a more hideous sight than that of the dead placed in graves! In addition, their souls were also bitter and impudent, and their thoughts adamant on the destruction of the Christians, as they cast their malice, decay and stink over their beautiful and clean furniture. They rolled in their beds, filling them with stinking pus and turning them abhorrent. . . . they would all soak their hands, while putrid, in all these vessels [of oil, honey or something else] making them abhorrent and filthy until no one would eat from them again.[72]

The passage is a lacerating assault on the moral imagination. John means to convey the enormity of unjust and violent persecution at the hands of "heretics" by tapping powerful cultural prejudices of the time, and he uses intensive engagement of sensory experience to do so. The most pervasive image of the passage, emphasized repeatedly to make the point, is the smell the lepers left behind.[73] John's condemnation of the lepers is extreme, but the real measure he implies is that of Abraham bar Kaili's character.

The image of foul smell provided Christians a powerful instrument of moral suasion. The fact that its usage often followed common rhetorical conventions did not lessen its impact. Stench carried unambiguous associations in late antique Christianity.[74] In the arena of ascetic practice, its presence and even its discussion raised serious issues in the Christian imagination. Given the prevalence of foul odor as a topos for moral condition, how should the ascetic approach the task of fashioning a self, body and soul, that would accomplish and radiate right relation with the divine? How could one train oneself to the point where one exuded that "aroma of Christ" of which Paul had spoken, "spreading the fragrance of the knowledge of God" everywhere (2 Cor 2:14–16)? It was instructive to use images. But it was the consequence of bodily practices that they yielded physical smells. How could the smells of asceticism be used? What should they mean?

Ascetic Senses

Given the wretched state of the human condition as late antique Christians saw it, ascetic practice could not shirk its task. Baptism brought the Christian into a body worthy of God's creation; Eucharist nourished it. But like any fragile substance, this new body, this new self, could only be sustained if its cleanliness and purity were preserved. The ascetic must be fiercely vigilant, as the monk John the Nazirite warned his companions, "lest the whole body be struck with the ulcers of sin, and grow putrid with the tumor of negligence."[75] Pseudo-Macarius did not mince his words. He used the image of rotting meat. The apostles, he instructed, had been salted by the salt of the Holy Spirit, for Christ had called them "the salt of the earth" (Mt 5:13).

For [the apostles] ministered to the souls of men the heavenly salt of the Spirit, seasoning them and keeping them free from decay and from anything harmful, away from the fetid condition they were in. Indeed, it is just as flesh—if it is not salted, it will decay and give off a stench, so that all the bypassers will turn aside from the fetid odor. Worms crawl all over the putrid meat; there they feed, eat, and burrow. But when salt is poured over it, the worms feeding on that meat perish and the fetid odor ceases. It is indeed the nature of salt to kill worms and dispel fetid odors.[76]

Ps.-Macarius goes on to explore this metaphor at length, elaborating the precise manner in which the soul, like meat, grows rancid; just how the worms of corruption burrow in to feed upon its decay; and the exact process by which salt destroys the rottenness, cleanses the wounds, and renders pure and healthy the soul which is the body's very life in its devotion to God. It was a metaphor that Origen, too, had employed (albeit with more restraint), and which is not uncommon in monastic literature.[77]

Ps.-Macarius is an author lavish in his descriptions of the glorious beauty that attends "the new man," whom Christ seeks to make in his devotees and whom the devoted ascetic will surely become if he perseveres in his labors with purity of heart.[78] Yet, in contrast to his shining descriptions of what that "new man" will be, metaphors of filth and stench frequently adorn his homilies. Housekeeping is a favorite image for this author, as for others we have noted: the presentation of the soul as a house or palace that must be adequately prepared if the divine is going to dwell in it.[79] But where some would use the image to elicit the joys of the cleaned and freshened house, Ps.-Macarius dwells upon the filth, dung, foul odors, refuse, and decay that must first be cleared away before fresh perfume can render the air worthy of its divine visitor.[80] The desert mother Syncletica was another who urged that the soul be cleaned and freshened, as a house would be if royalty were coming: vermin must be fumigated, rot and mold swept away, and the air sweetened to make the house of the soul fitting for divine visitation.[81]

To emphasize the filth was to state plainly the difficulty of the task. "Violence and unending pain are the lot of those who aim to ascend to heaven with the body, and this especially at the early stages of the enterprise," John Climacus warned his monks; "The more the putrefaction, the greater the need for treatment."[82] But, he urged, the goal must be held steadily in sight: "The man who renounces the world because of fear [of God] is like burning incense, which begins with fragrance and ends in smoke."[83] In pursuit of complete transformation, utter destruction would need to be part of the process. As exemplars of those who did not flinch from what was required, John Climacus pointed to monks in his community who chose to live apart in the penitence of extreme self-mortification. He described his visit to them: there was "no rest for them in beds, no clean and laundered clothing. They were bedraggled, dirty, and verminous. . . . What a dreadful place they lived in! It was dark, stinking, filthy, and squalid."[84] Do not mistake the ascetic's vocation, he admonished. Asceticism was a life of mourning, not of theologizing: "The difference between a theologian and a mourner is that the one sits in a professorial chair while the other passes his days in rags on a dungheap."[85]

Indeed, the ascetic must face the disciplining of the senses with firm determination. If the laity must be advised to guard their senses against the dangers of the slightest pleasure, how much moreso the ascetic whose life was conducted in grueling austerity?[86] But it was one thing to deal with biblical texts by finding ways to allegorize their sensory images. It was another to urge the ascetic to retrain the body's own sensations. "Let prayer wipe clean the murky thoughts, let faith wipe clean the senses outwardly," wrote Ephrem the Syrian;[87] "Let the path of the ear be cleared; let the sight of the eye be chastened; / let the contemplation of the heart be sanctified."[88] Smell, too, could be guided into a new order. Theodoret reported that the monks of Syria "taught the sense of smell not to hanker after fragrant odors, since by nature they produce flaccidity and limpness."[89] To taste the sweetness of divine goodness, a certain violence to the bodily senses was necessary, Diodochus explained.[90] Purification of the sense of smell would lead to its reward in the divine perfume God would pour down in response, John of Dalyatha urged.[91]

Such guidance became enshrined, for example, in Athonite tradition. In the eighteenth century, Nicodemus of the Holy Mountain devoted his *Handbook of Spiritual Counsel* to the ascetic training of the senses, drawing on the whole history of orthodox monasticism that preceded him.[92] Chapter 5, "Guarding the Sense of Smell," restates the classical theme that sweet smells weaken the body's dispositions and lead to moral dissolution, and cites various biblical admonitions against the use of perfumes. But Nicodemus, too, counsels that ascetic devotion will yield a changed olfactory sensibility.

> If you really want your body, my brother, to be fragrant and to exude a pleasant odor, do not remain idle. Do each day fifty or even one hundred prostrations and as many reverences as you can. Naturally the activity of the body creates heat, which evaporates certain unnecessary liquids of the body and digests others and thereby makes the body thin. It is these liquids of the body that produce the heavy and unpleasant odor of the body. So when the body is dried out and made thin, it becomes more vital, well managed, and consequently pleasant smelling. . . . This is again the reason why the bodies of virtually all the craftsmen

and laborers and especially of the ascetic monks do not exude any heavy odor, but rather exude a pleasant and fragrant odor. St. Isaac [the Syrian] also wrote about this and said: 'The odor of an anchorite is most sweet, and to encounter him brings joy to the heart of those who have discernment.'[93]

But Isaac the Syrian had also warned that habits and dispositions were like smells, lingering a very long time before finally dissipating.[94] How should the odors of asceticism be treated? When was stench the indication of sin, and when did it mark the battle against that very condition? When did it reveal divine disfavor, and when did it demonstrate shared participation in divine combat against evil? The incense and holy oil of the ascetic's prayer devotion or liturgical participation did not mask the odors of ascetic practice. Here was treacherous territory, daunting to negotiate. Nonetheless, there was no path that could avoid the question.

Asceticism: Holy Stench, Holy Weapon

The intentional employment of stench as a means of ascetic devotion, whether as a literary device or in ascetic practice, presented a stark shock to the late antique religious sensibility. Yet, employed it was. The instrumental use of stench pervaded monastic literature. A saint might choose to subject himself or herself to foul stench, intolerable to others, as a penitential practice. Abba Arsenius refused to change the water in which he soaked his palm leaves. When another monk complained, Arsenius explained, "Instead of the perfumes and aromatics which I used in the world I must bear this bad smell."[95] Such activity could be undertaken for disciplinary purposes. The Syrian monk Sabinus deliberately kept his food, "in such a way that it went mouldy and emitted a great stench. The character of such food was intended to blunt his bodily appetites and by the stench of the food extinguish pleasure."[96] Stench could be a form of exercising the monastic virtue of humility. St. Radegunde voluntarily undertook the most repulsive cleaning tasks in her convent despite her royal lineage, with particular devotion to the privy.[97] The occasional descriptions of holy men or women who ate incense ashes with their bread, an allusion to Psalm 102:9, make a similar point.[98]

Ascetics could perceive bad odors as a test of their resolve, or of their obedience to their vows. One desert monk who was ill dutifully ate the food his disciple had prepared for him, although by accident the brother had used the wrong vessel, pouring "linseed oil, with a nasty smell, used for the light," instead of honey into the food. The disciple was horrified to discover his error only after the old monk had eaten in silence, but the elder was not disturbed, "Do not distress yourself, if God had wished me to eat honey, you would have poured honey on it."[99] Simeon the Stylite, prior to his career on top of the pillar, chose to enclose himself for eighteen months, having a supply of grain and a large urn of water with him for survival. After five months a terrible stench began to spread from the water, carrying even well beyond the enclosure. Simeon, "troubled by the reeking smell," perceived this to be a test from Satan and filled the urn with earth and stones to cover the foulness. As the heat of summer blazed, Simeon's life grew endangered from lack of water; praying mightily, he suddenly found a small supply of clear, chilled water to soothe his thirst—the sign of divine aid in response to his steadfast labors.[100]

Deliberate subjection to rank odors could also be a form of instruction in compassion, a poignant paedagogical tool. Radegunde, like the saintly bishops Basil of Caesarea and Rabbula of Edessa, personally participated in the care and feeding of poor, sick, and leprous outcasts. "She herself washed the bodies of the poor. She rubbed thoroughly what was there, without feeling disgust at hard skin, mange, lice or pus. She sometimes even pulled out worms and cleaned up festering skin sores."[101] Even her devoted servant was repulsed by the sight of Radegunde kissing the lepers.[102] Jerome praised the young widow Fabiola for a similar ministry at a hospice she had founded for the sick and poor, where she spent long hours tending the patients herself despite the worms swarming in their gangrenous and foul-smelling flesh.[103] Simeon the Stylite the Younger had to instruct his monks that they must not be ashamed to touch a sick brother despite the fetid odor of illness, but must serve him with all dutiful attention.[104] The Edessan monk Hala ignored the jeers of onlookers and even his fellow monks when he collected rags from dunghills, then cleaned and patched them together to make rugs and blankets for the destitute.[105]

More often, however, the didactic force of such stories carried a darker admonition as well as disciplinary effect. Syncletica admonished her fellow nuns that the most efficient way to fight sexual temptation was to attack the image of the desired one mentally, gouging out the eyes, tearing the cheeks, slashing off the lips, and viewing the object of longing as "nothing but a mixture of blood and phlegm." Then, to complete the exercise, "it is necessary on the whole to represent the body of the beloved as a wound that smells oppressive, and is inclined to putrefy, briefly put, as resembling a corpse."[106] Imagining the body as putrefaction would destroy the temptation. But the same process could be presented in literal rather than hypothetical terms. A devout monk of Scetis became tormented by the memory of a beautiful woman. Hearing of her death, he hastened to her burial site.

> He opened the tomb, gathered the liquid flowing from the cadaver with his coat, and brought it back into his cell. The stench was intolerable, but he stared at this

infection in front of his eyes, fighting his thoughts by saying, 'See here what you desired; well, now you have it, sit down again.' And he subjected himself to this stench until the battle in him had ceased.[107]

The representation of the decaying corpse was meant to reflect the human condition; the evocation of its smell, its texture, its sight was meant to appall the audience's sensibilities—to shock them out of complacency—even as the monk's act represented a fundamental violation of the social order. But in this episode, the monk ultimately turned the tables on Satan's wiles. Penitence, punishment, and discipline forged together in the monk's actions to become a form of spiritual combat. For having fought the demon of fornication within himself, the monk then used Satan's own weapon against him, subjecting himself to the "intolerable stench" and to meditation on the sight of the corpse's "infected" decay until he had conquered his inner turmoil. The very mark of Satan's domain, the stench of mortality, became the means of his defeat at the hands of a monk.[108]

Hence we can appreciate both the cultural dilemma and the ascetic power carried in the (not infrequent) stories of monks whose extreme self-mortifications caused serious, self-inflicted infection. Descriptions of the ulcerated flesh of ascetics, of gangrenous wounds, of worm-eaten limbs, of ugly suppurations, of putrescent sores, were meant to horrify the audience as well as to astound with the measure of ascetic endurance thus offered.[109] And such descriptions did horrify, in reality as well as in audience response. According to Antonios, it had been the stench of Simeon the Stylite's self-inflicted wounds that caused his fellow monks to call for his expulsion from the monastery.[110] In similar episodes, Simeon the Stylite the Younger crouched on his heels for a year until the backs of his legs and thighs congealed together with gangrene and the stench disturbed the entire monastery.[111] Theodore of Sykeon buried himself in a cave for two years until he was carried out covered with sores, pus, and worms, and "a stench such that no one could stand near him."[112]

The radicality of these episodes lay not only in willing subjection to stench as a means of self-mortification. It lay, further, in the fact that these saints had willfully induced the wounds that produced the abhorrent infection.[113] Unlike the monk from Scetis, these saints did not meditate on mortal rot. They enacted it, literally turning into the very experience of putrifying flesh that the rhetorical image of sin as stench was meant to convey. And the crowning achievement (didactically speaking) was that no one within reach could escape the affliction of the resulting smell. The transgressive qualities of smell—its uncontainability, the fact that it spreads invisibly yet tangibly—are traits that render olfactory experience dangerous, terrifying, and powerful. Such self-mortification tortured others no less than the saint involved.

This situation was not simply repulsive to the late antique mind (in the literary or actual evocation of disgust), but frightening. Illness was no game. Its smells were nauseating, offensive, unbearable; they signalled the fragility of life in no uncertain terms.[114] All too often illness was not the saint's choice, nor within the saint's control. And if not self-chosen, the suffering of terminal illness caused a saint to become the very image of all a saint could not be: helpless, rank with foul odors, disfigured; a living image of fallen mortality rather than redeemed glory. Struck by gangrene or cancer, a saint in illness could occasion such putrefaction that even the most devoted of disciples could not bear to approach.[115] The caprice of disease defeated every intention, no matter how virtuous. Whether self-inflicted or randomly caused, illness measured mortality always in tragic terms.

Here, too, the Bible provided models according to which ascetic illness could be set into theological order. The paramount model was Job, righteous and pious in his faith, unjustly struck down by ignominious disease at Satan's mere whim and God's inscrutable acquiescence.[116] Job haunted the Christian imagination no less than the Jewish. The extracanonical *Testament of Job* had elaborated the just man's affliction and its traits, adding sensory details beyond what had been described in the biblical text.[117] Still, a certain sensory reserve prevailed in both the biblical account and the extracanonical version, for despite the discussions of wounds, sores, and the dunghill on which Job lay, olfactory descriptions barely appear in these texts. To the late antique Christian, however, the olfactory aspects of Job's condition were precisely the measure of its horror. The situation carried the irony of the human dilemma: Job's exterior (physical) condition mirrored humanity's interior (moral) state, while Job's moral innocence could not relieve his bodily suffering in any way. The same literary conventions were used to depict Job as those which availed to elicit the moral response of disgust when describing sin. Thus Ambrose of Milan imagined Job's lament: "I am full of pains from evening until morning. My body is corrupted with the putrefaction of worms and I moisten the clods of the earth with scrapings of bloody matter from my sores."[118] Illness as the mark of mortality imaged the reality of human vulnerability and human tragedy.

In cases of ascetic illness, then, hagiographers turn to the language of spiritual warfare. The saint struck down by involuntary infection was another Job. Stench becomes the primary weapon both employed by Satan and used by the saint against him. The resulting presentation of holy combat is even more forceful than in the case of the monk of Scetis meditating on the drippings of a corpse. For the saint's own flesh is the proof of mortality's sovereignty over the human condition at the same time that it is proof of the Christian saint's steadfast devotion to God. In Jacob of Serug's "Homily on Simeon the Stylite," he spoke of the saint's battle with gangrene in just these terms. Simeon was the "second Job," fighting Satan on his pillar of rock instead of a dunghill. And like the first Job, Simeon prevailed. For while the infection raged, Satan grew weary as Simeon persevered, undaunted, in his ceaseless prayer. In Jacob's telling, Simeon finally amputated his foot to survive, continuing his prayer practice unabated, while Satan lay defeated, "wallowing in blood and sprinkled with pus and covered in mucus."[119]

A notable example was St. Syncletica, whose lengthy ascetic career was intensified by lung cancer. At the end of her life, the cancer was complicated by an infection apparently causing gangrene in her jaw.

> Putrefaction and the heaviest stench governed her whole body so that the ones who served her suffered more than she did. Most of the time they withdrew, not bearing the inhuman odor; but when need called, the multitude approached, kindling incense, and again withdrew because of the inhuman stench. The blessed one [Syncletica] clearly saw the adversary, and did not at all agree to have human aid brought to her, demonstrating again in this her own virility [andreia]. But those who came with her exhorted her to anoint the places with unguent for their own weakness, but she was not persuaded. For she believed that through external assistance they would destroy the glorious contest.[120]

Eventually, out of mercy for her attendants, Syncletica allowed a doctor to apply an ointment of aloe, myrrh, and myrtle. But Syncletica agreed to this solace for the nuns because she understood the treatment as tantamount to preparation for burial, for which myrrh was the most common spice employed.[121] Thus by this action she anticipated her own death, which did in fact follow quickly, "for how was she able to take meals, when she was ruled by such putrefaction and stench?"[122]

Here as in other cases of this theme, the intensity of the saint's endurance is heightened by the sensory horror of stench.[123] The event appears to transgress religious order to the extreme. Those closest to the saint—the disciples and fellow monastics—cannot reconcile the holy one's presence with unbearable stench. In each incident of this type, however, the resolution finds the holy body miraculously healed (even if by death), and the foul odor transformed to the clear, exquisite fragrance of sanctity.[124] In the grace of the redeemed body, Satan's ultimate weapon—mortality itself—is transfigured into health: the scent of eternal life.

The theme of the saint unwillingly afflicted with mortal illness only to die with the sweet odor of sanctity was thus patterned on the raising of Lazarus in John 11:1–44. In that gospel episode the fear of stench distressed the bystanders, even as the graphic evocation of a putrefying corpse returned to life foreshadowed the death and resurrection of Christ.[125] Yet the paradox remained: the raising of Lazarus, the resurrection of Christ, the miraculous healing of the afflicted saint—all were as promises, for humanity remained caught in the fallen order. It was in fact Lazarus's decaying corpse, like the repulsive body of the mortally ill saint, that imaged the lingering truth of humanity's present reality. Ps.-Macarius describes it thus:

> For Lazarus also, whom the Lord raised up, exuded so fetid an odor that no one could approach his tomb, as a symbol of Adam whose soul exuded such a great stench and was full of blackness and darkness. But you, when you hear about Adam and the wounded traveller and Lazarus, do not let your mind wander as it were into the mountains, but remain inside with your soul, because you also carry the same wounds, the same smell, the same darkness.[126]

In the experience of stench, as nowhere else, ancient Christians placed the confrontation with humanity's fallen state. It was, necessarily, a confrontation with the mortality that stench revealed: the wounds of sin, the wounds of suffering, were the wounds enacted in the ravaging course of disease. Illness, putrescence, death, and decay had their source in the human act of sin. Their true healing required the divine act of salvation. Romanos Melodos retold the story of Lazarus in just these terms, using smells to depict the processes of disintegration and revivification that caused Hades to cry out to Death in dismay, "the bad odor has disappeared. / Alas, Jesus . . . sending His fragrance towards us, / Has perfumed the ill-smelling corpse." Death's response was a cry of terror as the two watched what followed: "The fragrance of the Son of God permeated His friend [Lazarus], / And made ready his body for the call of the Giver of Life."[127]

Other patristic authors might treat the raising of Lazarus as a depiction of conversion, of life transformed from death (the stench of sin) to salvation (the fragrance of life).[128] Eusebius, writing in the surge of Christian optimism that followed the Peace of Constantine, used it as an historical rather than a moral model, and presented it in medical terms. The measure of a great physician, he wrote, was the determination to treat affliction despite the danger of contagion, and to heal the sick one even though gaining the infection himself. This was the model of Christ's salvific choice to submit not only to incarnation, but to death.

> [So] He by Himself saved from the very abyss of death us, who were not merely sick or oppressed by grievous sores and wounds already putrifying, but even

lying among the dead; for none other in heaven possessed such strength as to minister unscathed for the salvation of so many. He, then, it was who alone laid hold upon the grievous suffering of our corruption, alone endured our sorrows, alone took upon Himself the penalty for our wickednesses; and where we were, I will not say, half dead, but even by this time altogether foul and stinking in tombs and graves, He raised us up.[129]

As the Divine Physician, Christ had done more than treat his human suppliants with compassion. He had gone further, entering into their sickness, taking their very mortality into himself. Late antique writers found the physical ramifications astounding. Ephrem Syrus had marvelled that Christ's method of healing had at each encounter been through the humblest, even the most despicable, matter of his own body:

A worthless body may be adorned
with jewels. Through You, Honorable One,
even worthless [things] become beautiful.
So great is contact with You that even if someone
cast a stone at You, it would be a pearl.
Even Your sweat, for one who is worthy,
is baptism, and the dust of Your garments,
for one who is infirm, is a great fount
of all aids, and even Your spittle,
if it reach the face, would enlighten the eyes.
If upon a stone You should rest Your head,
they would divine and tear it apart, and if You slept
upon a dunghill, it would become a church
for prayers, and if, again, You broke
ordinary bread, for us it would be the medicine of life.[130]

Yet, as Theodoret of Cyrrhus insisted, the incarnation did not, and could not, pollute the divine nature. Rather, Christ was like the sun, which "cannot be polluted when it passes through corpses, putrid mud, and many other evil-smelling substances."[131] Indeed, the sun could dry up the foul odors of dung and slime without itself being tainted.[132] So, too, the physical body of the incarnate Christ had been the source of healing, not of harm; of salvation, not of degradation. Whatever in the human body was foul with disease, must in the body of Christ be sweet with life. Hence Romanos presents the Doubting Thomas as one who begged his risen Lord, "show me Thy wounds / that I may drain and drink them as though they were springs."[133]

Late antique hagiography is filled with accounts of saints who suffered the stench of illness and infection during their careers, but who in death exuded the fragrance of sanctity. The fruits of an ascetic practice devoted to the battle with Satan were a body that could reveal the miracle of salvation even in a suffering death, a scent that could transform a corpse into a holy and life-giving relic. What the ascetic sought in the use of stench was more than the remaking of the human body in its mortal form. It was the remaking of life itself, from a nature ridden with the demise of mortality to one redolent with grace.

For the ascetic, as for every ancient Christian, the scents of ritual practices pierced deeply into the odors of mortal life—scents of the liturgy, of monastic devotion, of individual piety. Syriac priests offered their incense prayers with images that pivoted on a changed order of olfactory sensibility: "The perfume of Your death [O Christ] has become the incense which expiates our debts."[134] When Ephrem Syrus described the fragrances of paradise, he intimated that Christians could catch the hint of that eternal perfume in the healing scents of worship.

> The breath that wafts
>   from some blessed corner of Paradise
> gives sweetness
>   to the bitterness of this region,
> it tempers the curse
>   on this earth of ours.
> That Garden is
>   the life-breath
> of this diseased world
>   that has been so long in sickness;
> that breath proclaims that a saving remedy
>   has been sent to heal our mortality.[135]

In the ancient Christian worldview, sweet scents of religious source—not the perfumes of mundane pleasures, but the fragrances of human-divine interaction and of divine presence or favor—instructed the faithful in relation to the divine, whether employed in ritual, engaged in imagery, or received in grace. Stench, by contrast, instructed on the human domain: the fallen human condition and location. Stench was not about action by God, whether punishment or disfavor. Rather, its source was always the work of Satan, always the result of human sin and the condition that sin effected.

To the ancient Christian mind, stench was ultimately the experience of alienation. Bad odor estranged people from the body itself, and from one another (hence John Chrysostom's concern with good manners). Vile smells indicated a wounded body; but further, stench caused a wounded community, whether social or ecclesial. When monks or nuns complained about foul odors from another's practice, common devotion began to fray. When disciples could not bear to approach their teacher, the imposed distance, like the smell, was agonizing. Stench rendered intimacy impossible, even in the task of devotion to God. Ephrem Syrus lamented, "It is easy to understand how mankind has come to hate creation: / Having become hateful to themselves, they hold creation to be hateful."[136] How poignant, then, was Ephrem's charge to ascetic endurance:

> Bear up, O life of mourning,
>   so that you may attain Paradise;
> its dew will wash off your squalor,
>   while what it exudes will render you fragrant.[137]

Ephrem's words here were not only words of encouragement. They were words of hope. The hope on which they rested was a vision of life to come, the final ordering principle for all ancient Christian thought and practice. The smells of human experience were generated in a physical domain distinct from, yet intertwined with, the domain of divine reality. But the hope of the ancient Christian lay in salvation: a life that would join together all that the Fall had separated into an unnatural and alienated state. The stinking corpse of Lazarus had been suddenly filled with the fragrance of eternal life. So, too, did the ancient Christian olfactory imagination work always with a view to eschatology. The life to come was that which gave meaning to the life the Christian knew here and now, in this present state of mortality. Every smell, every olfactory encounter, experience, or expression—whether known or imagined, whether physical or figurative—had its meaning in relation to this expectation: the resurrected life would be a life sensorily experienced and sensorily known. Whether in the stench of hell or the perfumed sweetness of heaven, the Christian faced an olfactory future.

RESURRECTION, SENSATION, AND KNOWLEDGE

We must eagerly hasten to Christ's fragrant perfume, so that the smell of death may flee far from us.

Paulinus of Nola, *Poem* 31.531–32[1]

Since we no longer gaze upon the Tree of Life, nor glory in that Beauty [of paradise], henceforth butchers and bakers and a variety of pastries and fragrant foods have been given to us for enjoyment, and some such things console us for our fall from that place.

Basil of Caesarea, *On the Origin of the Human Person*, 2.7[2]

Bodily Expectation

Ancient Christianity developed in a world where diverse religious cultures shared certain basic assumptions. One was the notion that human experience extended beyond the confines of the physical, mortal body and the physically finite world. There was another domain, eternal and infinite, where the divine had its natural habitat. At times and under certain conditions the limited and the limitless realms intersected, and the human person might know divine presence or action through the very channels that otherwise served to conceal it. A fragrant scent, a glimpse of radiance, a sweet taste, an echo of song, a delicate sensation: by such sensed encounters, the peoples of the ancient Mediterranean world expected and experienced interaction with their gods.

Basic, too, was the understanding that human life was not limited to that of the mortal body in its temporal duration. Instead, human life took place in multiple times and multiple geographies.[3] Greeks, Romans, Jews, and Christians all knew of an idyllic, protological time when human existence was characterized by beauty, joy, comfort, and close consort with the divine.[4] By the turn of the Common Era, these religions recognized a "fallenness" or imperfection to the present, earthly order of human life, and knew that another life awaited every mortal after death, whether for good or for ill.[5] What is striking about this broad scheme of experiential domains, times, and spaces, however, is the consistency with which each domain was known, and even defined, by sensory characteristics. Whether in a perfect body, a diminished or "fallen" one, a condemned or a redeemed one, the ancient Mediterranean imagination explored human experience as necessarily sensory even when it exceeded the apparent confines of mortal existence. Indeed, by the time Christianity emerged in Mediterranean history, the "afterlife" of Greek and Roman religions, no less than in Judaism, had gained an extensive, thickly detailed geography described in numerous literary works. More than a map of spaces, depictions of the afterlife relied on sensory qualities to evoke what the experience of eternity would be.[6] When the Gospel of Luke ascribed to Jesus the parable of Lazarus and the rich man (Lk 16:19–31), with Lazarus borne by angels to reside in the sweetness of Abraham's bosom and the rich man tormented by thirst in the scorching fires of Hades, it offered a story recognizable in multiple religious traditions across the Mediterranean world.[7]

Christianity, then, developed in a wider religious culture that assumed human experience of the divine to be mediated through the body; that utilized the body further to express human-divine relation; and that understood human expectation of life to come in and through bodily sensations. In each of these areas, it was the body as a sensing and sensory entity that mattered. Often, smell alone was sufficient to identify human-divine engagement as the ordering context. For ancient Christians, this olfactory sensibility was displayed in practice, in teaching, and in perceived experience: in the extensive ritual uses of incense and holy oils in domestic, civic, monastic, and ecclesiastical activities; in the sensed fragrance of divine presence or approval; in the "fragrance" of virtue, the "odor of sanctity," the sweet scent of relics; the stench of immorality, demons, or heresy; the rank odors of hell; the perfumed delights of heaven. Over the course of late antiquity, Christianity developed an olfactory culture it could define as its own, which, by virtue of its sheer pervasiveness in every context of daily life, could carry the task of negotiating the religious significations of human existence as a bodily one.

This book has looked at olfactory practices to consider ancient Christian experience of the divine in the world or in worship; and at ancient Christian expression of human-divine relation in devotional actions, in ethical activity, or in ascetic discipline. But for the ancient Christian, the ordering principle for all experience and expression was the expectation of what would come in "the next life." Whatever healing, beauty, or goodness might be experienced in this world, it offered the barest glimpse—the faintest whiff—of what the redeemed life would be. And every depiction of heaven and hell that ancient Christians knew or put forward relied on olfactory sensation to define, delineate, and describe what awaited in the life to come. Hence, every odor, foul or fair, became a model—or even a foretaste—of a future beyond the limits of mortal time or space; every smell was a reminder that the events of this present life had fullness of meaning only in relation to the next.

Ancient Christian writers shared the Pauline understanding that in the final resurrection "we shall all be changed" (1 Cor 15:51), and the belief that the resurrected body will not be the same as the body now inhabited. In the early Christian centuries, a rich diversity of opinions was displayed in literary debates about the end of time, about resurrection, about afterlife in the current dispensation and in the dispensation to come.[8] Yet Christians were certain there would be a body nonetheless, of some sort; one in which the oneness of the believer, body and soul, would find its true meaning. For, they claimed, the body changed in the life to come would remain the body in which and through which the human person knows God. And in the resurrected life, so these writers said, knowing God would be the sum total of human existence. "There will be one activity," Origen insisted, and that would be "to apprehend God."

> One will see the Father and the things of the Father for oneself, just as the Son does, no longer merely recognizing in the image the reality of the one whose image it is. And I think this will be the end (to telos), when the Son hands over the Kingdom to God his Father, and when God becomes all in all.[9]

Freed of the earthly uses and weaknesses of the body, then, redeemed humanity would find a continuity from mortal to immortal life through the body's continuation as a human instrument of knowledge. Indeed, the body would continue its existential role: it would be the location in which one receives God's revelation. It would continue its expressive role: it would enact and manifest one's relationship with one's Creator. And it would at last fulfill its epistemological role: if, in this life, the body provides limited knowledge of God, there, in the world to come, the body would be unlimited in what it could experience of the divine. Unable to explain the unexplainable—the fullness of God that would be known—ancient Christian writers often relied on olfactory images to suggest the promised end towards which all Christian teaching and ritual pointed. Eschatology was the constant companion of every aspect of Christian life and activity: the end held the key.

For the ancient Christian, smells could mark human-divine interaction and relation precisely because they indicated a certain seepage between the divine and human domains in anticipation of what would come. The salient traits of smells that have repeatedly been highlighted in the course of this study—their invisibility and their uncontainability—made them especially effective "messengers" across the boundary lines separating these realms. In earliest Christianity, attunement to this olfactory seepage was most evident in texts and stories that elaborated the biblical world into a fully fashioned imaginal space—a place of frequent, even continual, exchange between human and divine figures; of constant divine visitations, and of human transport to "other" worlds—all marked by fragrances delectable, thrilling, and unforgettable.[10] This understanding was substantiated in early Christian experience through the occasional but riveting reports that martyrdoms at times were accompanied by just such olfactory signs.[11]

In late antiquity, however, the context for such a sensibility had profoundly altered. No longer "strangers in a strange land," but rather inhabiting a natural, political, and social landscape they now perceived as their own, Christians looked for and expected to find a deep continuity between their religious experience in the world they knew and that which would await them in the life to come. This did not mean they no longer marvelled at the ineffability, the incomprehensibility, of what the resurrected life would be. The sharp urgency of some early Christian apocalyptic expectation had diminished, it was true.[12] But the conviction that this world would pass away and God's kingdom be established in terms that defied human understanding or imagination remained unequivocal; so, too, the conviction that the human body would be changed, as Ambrose said, from putrescence to life.[13]

The late antique Christian expected to experience in the body frequent hints of that future life, and the richness of late antique liturgical life offered repeated sensory windows through which to gain those hints. The concreteness of the ritual context could not but affect the reception of eschatological hope laid before late antique Christian worshippers.[14] As graphically horrifying as depictions of hell could be,[15] just as glorious were the representations of heaven: a place that contained and surpassed all the beauty that had once been Adam and Eve's in that first paradise of God's making, according to late antique preachers. To some, heaven was the place where the saints and martyrs now lived in bliss, awaiting the final resurrection to come. To others, it was the place where all the faithful, or those blessed as such, would arrive once that resurrection had been accomplished. From either perspective, to hear such images in a liturgical setting was to encounter a hint of their evocation in one's own body. Prudentius's "Hymn for the Lighting of the Lamp," for example, extolled the beauty of evening prayers offered amidst flickering candles of sweet-scented wax and gleaming lamps burning perfumed oil. But the hymn's ending turns from the fragrant light of the church at vespers to the scene of the day that awaits in paradise:

There [in paradise] bright roses exhale fragrance from gardens rare,
and where murmuring springs water the earth around,
Modest violets bloom, crocus and marigold,
Lifting radiant flowers, rich in their saffron hues.

There sweet balsams distill perfume from slender tress,
The rare cinnamon breathes spices that fill the air,
And the leaf of the nard floats from the hidden spring
To the mouth of the stream laving the pleasant strand.

Here the souls of the blest wandering in grassy meads
Blend their voices in song, chanting melodious hymns
That devoutly resound throughout the happy glades,
And with radiant feet they tread the lilies fair.[16]

Liturgical practices not only mirrored the celestial life, but also offered a real anticipation of the life one would know. The scents of paradise could and did mingle among the sweetest of earthly fragrances, of this the late antique Christian could be certain. After all, Christian legends of the time described how the first descendents of Adam and Eve had lived outside Eden yet so close by that "they enjoyed the sweet scent and perfume of the breezes which were wafted forth to them from Paradise."[17] Accounts of the Dormition of the Virgin Mary, appearing for the first time in the fifth and sixth centuries, included lavish reports of the paradisical splendor in which the Virgin now rested in promise of the general resurrection of the faithful to come.[18] Hagiography, too, offered the example of saints who had experienced the fragrance of paradise, or who were fed in their remote desert cells with sweet-scented fruits miraculously provided by angelic visitors.[19] Pachomius was reported to have had many trips to paradise, and to have instructed his monks, "No tree or plant growing in paradise is ever deprived of fruits profusely giving out great fragrance. A man cannot bear that fragrance without passing out, unless the Lord gives him grace."[20] In the context of late antique piety, this was not only the working of biblical imagination. The Egyptian monk Patermuthius told his disciples that he had made a physical visit to paradise, where he had seen a great company of saints and eaten of the fruits. To prove the event, he had brought back a large, "deliciously scented" fig which he bequeathed to his disciples as a relic and also a reminder:

> The priest Copres who was telling us the story, being at that time a young man, saw this fig in the hands of Patermuthius' disciples, and kissed it, and admired its scent. 'For many years,' he said, 'it remained with his disciples, being kept as evidence of the father's visit to paradise. It was of enormous size. Indeed a sick man had only to smell it and he was at once cured of his illness.'[21]

Ascetical literature and guidebooks included long discussions on guarding the senses, as we have noted, so that the practicing ascetic would be able to render the body open to experience of the divine—indeed, to experience of paradise—through its sensory activity.[22] It was late antiquity, too, that saw the emergence of cultivating monastic gardens as earthly representations of the heavenly Eden and of the lushly fragrant beauty that awaited the blessed in the life to come.[23] Late antique Christians lived in a context of constant, concrete interaction between notions of the future life and experiences within the present one that found their articulation through bodily, sensory encounters.

This, too, was the interactive context in which relic veneration flourished.[24] As an area of religious devotional practice, relic veneration was already apparent in nascent form in the New Testament era: the story of the woman healed by touching the hem of Jesus' garment (Mk 5:25–34 and parallels), or the related story from Acts 19:11–12 of people healed by pieces of cloth that had touched the apostle Paul, assume the view that sacred power was available through contact with a holy body. The notion that the holy body could be a source of blessing after death was already apparent in Jewish pilgrimage practices common well before the first century, not only in the holy city of Jerusalem but at various shrines and tombs associated with Jewish martyrs and patriarchs.[25] Jewish veneration of bones in their burial and memorial practices laid a foundation for Christian treatment of their own martyrs when, by the late second century, the practice of collecting the bones as well as sand or objects stained with blood from the martyrs' wounds becomes widely attested in Christian sources.[26] What changes with the fourth century is not only the intensity of ritual devotion Christians allocated to veneration of their relics, but further the explicit association of sweet fragrance with the deaths, bodies, and relics of the saints and martyrs. We have already discussed this shift in relic veneration in the context of the developing olfactory piety of late antiquity. But in this chapter, in a consideration of eschatology and resurrection, the cult of relics must again be highlighted, this time for its contribution to a climate of anticipatory interaction between the present and future lives; for it was the smell of relics that established this connection.

Certainly, the "odor of sanctity" that appeared at a saint's death, or that filled the air at the discovery of relics, or that flowed from a saint's corpse, carried as its primary signification the validation of the person's identity *as* holy, *as* a saint, and as divinely blessed.[27] That odor breathed forth the air of the place to which the saint had gone; it wafted the fragrance of the immortal body the saint acquired in the Kingdom of Heaven, as opposed to the stench of the mortal one the saint had had in earthly life.[28] In relics, the late antique Christian could smell—and see, and touch—a portion of the saint's body already radiating its resurrected glory. Relics were literally pieces—promises—of the redeemed body in its glorified state. They heralded in the present life a beauty, a power, from the (divine) life to come. Late antique Christian writers worked out careful theological justification for the cult of relics, seeing in the relation between the body part and the whole saint an analogy to the body of Christ, individual and collective; and to God, whose power could be diffused throughout creation without diminishment or loss to the whole.[29]

The practices that articulated relic veneration established a sensory context that induced a rich aesthetic sensibility for devotees, engaging and directing sensation and meaning so that relics would be granted their proper religious apprehension. The entire scene of devotional activity compelled the participant towards a paradisical—and thus, eschatological—encounter: the beauty of the saint's shrine, its architecture and pictorial adornment; the fragrance of incense offerings, the perfumed holy oil poured through the reliquary; the flowers, linens, and ornaments hung at the tomb.[30] Surrounded by the accoutrements of a holy place, embedded in layers of devotional ritual practices, relics simply could not be experienced as the bones or body parts of a corpse; but rather, and only, as wondrous heralds and guarantors of a new, healed, holy life that would some day come about for the faithful Christian. Relics themselves could transfer infusions of that new life into this sorrowful world: hence their healing power; hence their "odor of sanctity."

Once again, smell was the signifier of the relic's status as well as the means of enacting its powers. Smell marked the relic as a tangible portion of the redeemed body to come; smell was also the vehicle of its power to affect the present life and effect change in the present body. For the odor of the relic was both its own, "new" odor, and that "fragrance of life" wafting from the place where the saint now resided. This "odor of sanctity" permeated and worked within the body of the believer who venerated the saint and sought divine aid or blessing through the saint. In Byzantine tradition, the olfactory piety associated with relics was embellished further through the popular use of carrying ampullae, tiny flasks of holy oil from a saint's tomb or the myrrh that gushed from relics or miracle-working icons. People also prized encolpia—small reliquaries worn as jewelry, that could carry a tiny relic or a piece of cloth soaked in the aromatic oil drawn from a holy tomb or collected from relics. Both flasks and encolpia were decorated with engraved, incised, or enameled images from the Bible or of the saint or the holy place (the particular shrine; or Jerusalem and its pilgrimage sites, for example). Such objects engaged the believer with a concise yet rich array of sensory experiences: visual (through the decoration of the container), tactile (as the object was touched in ritual veneration, or continually knocked against the body as a reminder when worn on a pin or around the neck), auditory (by the prayers chanted in offering to the saint), gustatory (through reverencing by kiss), and, most pervasively, olfactory (by the fragrance from the oil or relic that would permeate all of these other experiences).[31] In the fourteenth century, pieces of cloth from the garment covering the relics of patriarch Athanasios I of Constantinople were burned over a censer and the fumes inhaled as a certain cure for harsh illness.[32] The odor of sanctity pervaded the experience of relic piety, and was its most common element; but that odor was also the means by which a believer's entire sensorium was awakened and engaged.

The odor of sanctity associated with the cult of saints and veneration of relics was another vividly concrete instance of religious encounter carrying eschatological import. Holy smells elicited in the believer's body an experience of the promised life to come. Concern for religious epistemology characterized late antique Christianity in both its practices and its rhetoric: Christians were taught, exhorted, trained, and encouraged to use their senses and their bodies as instruments for gaining knowledge of God. However, while theologians and religious leaders insisted on the limited nature of bodily experience and sensory knowledge, the ancient Christian lived in a discursive context that continually indicated the contrary. Sense perception and bodily sensation could and did cross the boundaries of the spaces, times, and domains that separated human and divine lives, or present and future dispensations.[33] Hence, ancient Christianity shaped its understanding of the end of time and the final resurrection through a constant referencing of bodily sensory experience as the guide for how and what to expect in the life to come. Christian olfactory piety had as its telos the cultivation of revelatory expectation.

Salvific Knowing

The resurrected body was a major point of contention for Christians from their very beginnings.[34] Christians debated the notion heatedly and sometimes with violent discord, amongst themselves and with Jews and pagans. The "body" of the resurrected Christ was one focus for these disputes; the resurrected "body" of the believing Christian in the final dispensation was another. The arguments for both hinged on the seemingly irreconcilable distinctions between human and divine, mortal and immortal, changeable and changeless. Discussion centered on the problems of matter, nature, and identity. Of what would the resurrected body consist? How can that which is necessarily subject to change, be rendered changeless? In what way could the continuity of self be ensured? Because they were so highly contested, the resurrection of Christ and the resurrected human body became classic topics for Christian thinkers to address. Most often, their treatment was argued through presentation of the body as "flesh." Despite the frequency of discussion, however, relatively few writers spoke directly to the issue of the resurrected body as a sensing body.[35] Yet, the religious imagination of ancient Christianity clearly presumed just such an entity, and indeed relied upon its assumed traits in order to cultivate both the practice of religion in the present life and the motivation of its reward in the expected life to come.

Tertullian had argued that in joining body and soul God had created a union so intimate one could not tell whether the soul bears the body, or the body the soul.[36] Perhaps, he decided, one might allow supremacy to the soul, "as more akin to God."[37] But such a division would not hold, he insisted, for without the body, the soul could know little if anything of the created world, and could accomplish nothing of society, culture, learning, or political order. What then could the soul do without the body in the life to come?

> For what enjoyment of nature, what fruition of the world, what savouring of the elements, does the soul feed upon except by means of the flesh? What think you? Through it as intermediary the soul is enriched by the whole apparatus of the senses, sight, hearing, taste, smell, touch. . . . By the flesh are the manual arts, by the flesh are liberal and professional studies, by the flesh are activities, occupations, and services: and to such a degree does the whole of the soul's living belong to the flesh, that to the soul to cease to live is exactly the same thing as to retire from the flesh. . . . Thus the flesh, while it is reckoned the servant and handmaid of the soul, is found to be its consort and coheir: if in things temporal, why not also in things eternal?[38]

Why not, indeed?[39] But the late antique intellectual faced the dilemma of reconciling philosophical categories with a fully expounded incarnational theology. In that situation, it was difficult to apprehend a continuity between the sensory life of the body and the resurrected life to come.[40] Such continuity was especially difficult to imagine on the issue of epistemology. What does intellect teach us, Gregory of Nyssa asked, if not that because this universe is known through our senses, there must be another reality which surpasses the senses?[41] Even the parable of Lazarus and the rich man must teach this, he continued, for with their bodies buried in their graves how could the rich man experience the scorching fires of hell or burning thirst; or how could Lazarus experience "rest" in the bosom of Abraham? "The Scripture must be teaching us that it is some invisible and incorporeal condition of life, in which the soul lives."[42] Did not God reveal knowledge of a good that "eye has not seen nor ear heard, nor thought attained"?[43] What could this be, Gregory asked, except the resurrected life: "This is nothing else, according to my judgment, but to be in God Himself; for the good which is beyond hearing, sight, and heart would be that very thing which surpasses everything." Here, exactly, would be "the blessedness we hope for."[44] For Gregory, to "be in God Himself" would be a state of existence. It would in some way be bodily. But knowledge in that state would be the result of intellect present in that condition; or, it would be the result of the infused "blessedness" that would overwhelm all other modes of awareness.

The notion of bodily resurrection presented conceptual dilemmas for the philosophically disciplined Christian thinker; so, too, did the Bible. In his treatise "Death as a Good," Ambrose of Milan argued for the compatibility of Plato and scripture in understanding the soul. In one instance, as he argues for the insignificance of the body in relation to the soul's lasting worth, he draws from Plato's *Symposium* (as transmitted through Plotinus's *Enneads* 3.5) and the Song of Songs, to discuss the soul as a garden that will flower and bear fruit when nourished by the divine.[45] Further along, he supports his case by pointing to the ease with which the bodily senses are deceived, and more than this, their propensity to deceive the person. One must not be tempted by the senses, he exhorts, for the same impediments distort the operations of all five, sight, hearing, smell, touch, and taste.[46] Nonetheless, mindful that "the just have the reward of seeing the face of God," Ambrose describes how in the life to come the blessed soul will be able to see because it will be freed of the present body's limitations, including bodily sensory operation:

> Then we will be allowed to look upon the glory of God, and His face will be revealed, but now we are enveloped in the thick substance of the body and covered over by the stains and pollutions of the flesh, as it were, and we cannot see with total clarity . . . For . . . how can [a creature] see the dazzling face of his eternal Creator while covered with the clothing that is this body?[47]

Yet the sensing body could not be shifted from the center of Christian practices nor the forms of awareness they generated. An early fifth-century Syriac hymn assures the congregation that their dearly departed did surely profit by the vigils, offerings, and above all the incense offered in their memory.[48] Jacob of Serug, in rather more harrowing terms, described the souls of the dead huddled around the eucharistic offering at the memorial masses offered on their behalf. There they drink the "fragrance of life" (*riha d-hayye*) emanating from the holy oblation, for sustenance until the eschaton when they would be rejoined to their bodies for eternity.[49] The senses were essential even to the interlude between death and resurrection for the souls of the departed, and especially smell: inhaling the scent of the Eucharist was in itself the means of enduring temporal death until the new dispensation.

Ephrem described how at death the soul departs from the body, leaving the former house of the soul as an abominable (corrupt) shell until, at the final resurrection, "The wondrous odor of that treasury of life [Christ] flies into the body," and life returns.[50] The saints prefigured what will happen, Ephrem explains. Recalling the story of Elisha's bones in 2 Kings 13:20–21, a story which in the biblical text locates holy power in touch and makes no mention of odor or breathing, Ephrem writes:

The type [for resurrection] is the buried one [Elisha] whose fragrance gave life
   to the dead man:
The man dead one day breathed life from the one long dead.
The life-giving fragrance wafted from his bones and entered into the corpse,
a symbol of the One who gives life to all.[51]

The olfactory piety of ancient Christianity presumed that fragrance could be depicted as the conveyor of life because it was so often understood to be the vehicle for divine action. Christian practices and rhetorical instruction presumed, further, that fragrance could and must be experienced even in death; and then again, in the life beyond.

At the end of the day, ancient Christian writers had to confess, without the body the soul would not, could not be wholly or knowingly in the presence of God. Though baffled at the thought, Augustine pointed out that Adam and Eve before the Fall had inhabited "a paradise both material and spiritual," to be enjoyed by both their inward and outer senses.[52] As Ephrem put it, God had not placed Adam in paradise until he was fully made, body and soul. Together body and soul had entered paradise, together they had left after the Fall, together they would enter again in the resurrection. Ephrem pictured the souls of the dead encamped at the gates of paradise, awaiting their reunion with their bodies so as to enter therein and together give praise to their Savior.[53] Jacob of Serug's *Homily on Simeon the Stylite* retells the story of Simeon's gangrene as a mighty battle between the saint and Satan, which Simeon won when he finally amputated his diseased foot. The stylite then bid a poignant farewell to his severed limb, which had labored so valiantly in God's service:

Why are you shaken and grieved since your hope is kept (Ps 42:5)? For again onto that tree from which you have been cut off you will be grafted. Go, wait for me until I come and do not grieve. For without you I will not rise up on the last day. Whether to the bridal chamber or to Gehenna I will walk on you. And whether to heaven or to the abyss, our way is one. We will be one when we are resurrected just as we have been, for death or life, for judgment or fire, or for the kingdom.[54]

For the body was also the loyal companion, the steadfast comrade, in the cosmic battle between good and evil. The believer's body was the battleground, as Christ's had been. And just as his body was the place in which Christ defeated hunger, thirst, weariness, and death, so, too, must the believer also defeat Satan by refusing him victory in these assaults on the weaknesses of the mortal body. The body was the means by which a Christian was faithful, just as it was the means by which the faithful Christian knew both Tempter and Creator. Without the body, the activity and knowledge of the soul were insufficient. Hence the sorrow that afflicted where the dead reposed, as the soul yearned for its partner.

Augustine and Ephrem wrote from opposite edges of the late antique Christian world, representing different poles of Christian culture. Yet both gave unusually sustained attention to the question of sense perception in the resurrected body, as they struggled to provide definitive understandings of what the resurrected life would be. It is worth completing our explorations with their respective presentations, Augustine in Book 22 of the City of God, and Ephrem in his Hymns on Paradise. For both writers, the entire reason for human existence is knowledge of God. But how in the life to come would the human person know? And what would be known?

I have already noted Augustine's limited interest in sense perception, and his near complete neglect of smell, in the context of his discussions on religious epistemology.[55] In the City of God, Augustine was brought back to the issue of the senses when he turned to the question of the resurrection. In painstaking detail he considered the form and constitution of the resurrected body. What would be its lifestage: would babies be resurrected as adults? Would the elderly and infirm have their worn and wrinkled bodies, or the glow of youth? What about aborted fetuses? What about those who had been excessively fat or thin?[56] And of what would this body be reconstituted? There was not only the problem of dismemberment of those who had been martyred, but also of other lost bodily traces— hair clippings, toe and fingernails, limbs lost to disease, travellers eaten by wild beasts. Would every bodily organ be revived, and if so why, if some organs were no longer necessary?[57] Augustine scrupulously attended to each and every problem. His primary concern was to ensure a continuity of the self as an individual person with an individual history.[58] Hence he insisted on the continuation of gender; and that martyrs would still have their scars, although their wounds would no longer be able to hurt them—for humanity must never be allowed to forget the particular history that it forged while inhabiting its fallen state.[59]

Bodily integrity ensured, there remained to ask what modes of knowledge the body would have in its redeemed life of glory. In Book 22, Augustine envisions paradise as above all else a place of rest, where knowledge of God will fill our being because of the new kind of body we shall inhabit. Yes, we shall be there bodily, but in bodies that have "a new beauty," "a beauty in the body, and yet not of the body."[60] In this body,

> How complete, how lovely, how certain will be the knowledge of all things, a knowledge without error, entailing no toil! For there we shall drink of God's Wisdom at its very source, with supreme felicity and without any difficulty. How wonderful will be that body which will be completely subdued to the spirit, will receive from the spirit all that it needs for its life, and will need no other nourishment![61]

Augustine admitted that the philosophers raised a serious problem in delimiting the perceptions available to the bodily senses as opposed to those of the mind. But in the resurrected body, he argued, such a distinction could no longer be sustained. Bodily and spiritual perception would be one and the same: perfection was that condition in which all things would be held still, in utter unity. There, too, sight would be the highest sense, its operation fulfilling the requirements of true knowledge. Redemption would be that "rest" which would accompany perfect contemplation of God. For Augustine, in paradise, seeing will be the consummation of the human experience of God.

> [W]e shall then see the physical bodies of the new heaven and the new earth in such a fashion as to observe God in utter clarity and distinctness, seeing him present everywhere and governing the whole material scheme of things by means of the bodies we shall then inhabit . . . in the future life, wherever we turn the spiritual eyes of our bodies we shall discern, by means of our bodies, the incorporeal God directing the whole universe.[62]

There, at last, Augustine says, we will find our rest and behold our Lord.

> There that precept will find fulfillment: 'Be still, and know that I am God,' (Ps 46:11). . . . There we shall have leisure to be still, and we shall see that He is God. . . . restored by Him and perfected by His greater grace we shall be still and at leisure for eternity, seeing that he is God, and being filled by Him when he will be all in all (1 Cor 15:28). . . . This we shall then know perfectly, when we are perfectly at rest, and in stillness see that he is God. . . . There we shall be still and see; we shall see and shall love; we shall love and we shall praise.[63]

Although Augustine concedes a final paradise which is material and embodied, his highest reflection is founded on the vision of the heavenly city in

Revelation 21–22. Remembrance of Eden's garden, that place of God's first creation, is not present in his discussions here, but rather considered earlier, in
Book 14, when he discusses the pre-lapsarian existence of Adam and Eve. The
choice of biblical texts is important, for Augustine's use of Revelation 21–22
allows him to present the resurrected sensorium in essentially mono-sensory
terms: it is the vision of Revelation 21–22, the sight of the heavenly city, that is
the canvas for his depiction of the resurrected life. It is a vision requiring of the
senses only sight for its realization, a privileging of visuality that carries to its
culmination Augustine's Neoplatonic training. Christianity in many ways will
continue to privilege visual culture throughout its history.[64]

Yet, another current flourished as well. For Ephrem, paradise will be all that
Eden was, and more. The nature of the resurrected body, then, must be such as
to enable full awareness of its home. Ephrem's biblical base is both the Garden
of the Genesis creation account, and its poetic echo in the Song of Songs.
Hence Ephrem's *Hymns on Paradise* are an olfactory *tour de force*, a dazzling sensory
encounter, reminiscent of the Song of Songs in their lush imagery.[65] Here
paradise is "that treasure of perfumes, / that storehouse of scents,"[66] "all fragrant;"[67] a place where colors are "full of joy" and "scents [are] most wonder-
ful,"[68] where

a vast censer
    exhaling fragrance
impregnates the air
    with its odoriferous smoke,
imparting to all who are near it
    a whiff from which to benefit.[69]

Indeed,

There too did I see
    the bowers of the just
dripping with unguents
    and fragrant with scents,
garlanded with fruits
    crowned with blossoms.[70]

Nor does Ephrem present these scents as mere adornment. The perfumed air
of paradise is life-giving in the most basic sense: it is food for those who dwell
in its midst. "Instead of bread, it is the very fragrance of Paradise that gives

nourishment / instead of liquid, this life-giving breeze does service."[71] Here, indeed, is the Fragrance of Life:

> for its scent gives nourishment to all
>> at all times,
> and whoever inhales it
>> is overjoyed and forgets his earthly bread;
> this is the table of the Kingdom.[72]

It was so in the beginning:

> The air of Paradise
>> is a fountain of delight
> from which Adam sucked
>> when he was young;
> its very breath, like a mother's breast,
>> gave him nourishment in his childhood.[73]

It is so now, as the fallen world finds itself redeemed. Just as Ephrem names the Eucharist the Medicine of Life, so, too, does he cast the air of paradise accordingly. For,

> More numerous and glorious
>> than the stars
> in the sky that we behold
>> are the blossoms of that land,
> and the fragrance which exhales from it
>> through divine Grace
> is like a physician
>> sent to heal the ills
> of a land under a curse;
>> by its healing breath it cures
> the sickness that entered in
>> through the serpent.[74]

To be in this place requires the means to experience it. Thus, Ephrem explains, in paradise the body, healed and glorified in its resurrected state, will be robed in "garments of glory" that replace its former "garments of shame."[75] In this condition, the body, no longer hindered, will receive utterly the sensory feast that paradise pours forth on every side. "Being unburdened, / the senses stand in awe and delight / before the divine Majesty."[76] In paradise, one's entire being will be permeated by the encounter with the divine. Living there will be the absolute experience of God's presence.

In Ephrem's view, soul and body require each other for existence even in the world to come. Without the body, the soul would not be able to perceive or be conscious of paradise (the root here is *rgsh*, to feel, perceive, be conscious or aware of). In *Hymns on Paradise* 8, he makes his point:

> . . . I considered
> how the soul cannot
>   have perception of Paradise
> without its mate, the body,
>   its instrument and lyre.
> . . .
> That the soul cannot see
>   without the body's frame,
> the body itself persuades,
>   since if the body becomes blind
> the soul is blind in it
>   groping about with it;
> see how each looks
>   and attests to the other,
> how the body has need of the soul
>   in order to live,
> and the soul too requires the body
>   in order to see and to hear.
> . . .
> Though the soul exists
>   of itself and for itself,
> yet without its companion
>   it lacks true existence;
> . . .
> If the soul, while in the body,
>   resembles an embryo
> and is unable to know
>   either itself or its companion,
> how much more feeble will it then be
>   once it has left the body,
> no longer possessing on its own
>   the senses
> which are able to serve
>   as tools for its use.

For it is through the senses of its companion
that it shines forth and becomes evident.[77]

What Ephrem describes is an encounter between subject and object in which
the person will be saturated at every level of awareness and being by the object
sought, to the point where the subjective encounter is swallowed up by the
immensity of presence in the midst of what is divine. Significantly, however, the
human self would not be lost in this event, nor obliterated by the power of God's
Being. Rather, it would be a relationship between creature and Creator of completion, of full realization of self within Self. The resurrected life would be that condition in which nothing separates us from God. Bathed in divinity from without,
we will radiate divinity from within, aglow from our inmost heart to our outer-
most limbs. Those who enter paradise will be astonished at what they become:

> People behold themselves
>   in glory
> and wonder at themselves,
>   discovering where they are.
> The nature of their bodies,
>   once troubled and troublesome,
> is now tranquil and quiet,
>   resplendent
> from without in beauty,
>   and from within with purity,
> the body in evident ways,
>   the soul in hidden ways.[78]

Ephrem insists that sense perception is the foundational experience of the
human-divine encounter both in the present and in the life to come. Yet he
repeatedly admonishes that the senses are insufficient for the task, and will
continue to be so even in their redeemed state. Inadequate at best, the senses
are a feeble medium through which to receive knowledge of God. Nonetheless,
in Ephrem's view it is precisely their inadequacy that renders them crucial.
When open to God, the senses receive God's revelation at every turn; they take
it in, they convey it, they mediate, they actively encounter and transmit. What
the senses do not do is intentionally, willfully, or consciously manipulate what
they receive; they do not function as does the rational mind. For Ephrem,
rationality alone is the seeking of *disembodied* knowledge: therein it fails. God
cannot be known except when allowed to permeate the whole of one's being.
This will be true in the resurrected body as it is true now.

Again for Ephrem, the essential image is that of breathing the fragrant, life-giving air of paradise: it is this fragrance that instills knowledge of God even as it gives and sustains the health which is the essence of life as God intends it to be. The aroma of paradise mingles in the air of worship or the odors of blessing that waft from the saints, hinting of the life to come, preaching God's saving work, proclaiming as a herald the final healing that awaits, and infusing true life into the faithful who inhale and consume it. The air of paradise acts much like the Eucharist, in Ephrem's reckoning. In the end, as Ephrem presents the scene, by this air the faithful will know all that they can know of the divine, in that final life of glory.

For those writers who paused to consider it, the question of the resurrected body as a sensing body presented a serious challenge. But I would argue that these occasional discussions hold together the entire matrix of ancient Christian understanding: Bible, liturgy, devotional activity, social location, political ideology, religious instruction, and individual and collective discipline all stand conjoined where the resurrected body was considered as a sensing body. The ancient Christian valuation of sense perception as a mode of religious knowing yielded a vivid commitment to the human person as an embodied and sensing being, created by God for just that purpose. Here lay the basic core of Christian identity: what the Christian sensed was God, known through every aspect of the believer's existence, body, mind, and soul, here and hereafter.

Once again, I would argue that we see this most clearly in the ancient Christian treatment and understanding of smell. Religious scents—incense, holy oil, relics—continually attended the late antique Christian in the course of daily life. In the hands of Christian writers, these scents could be used to maintain a persistent level of religious awareness, whether employed metaphorically or with reference to actual usage. These smells were tapped to elicit the experience of the believer's body in its mode as a liturgical body; they set the events and activities of daily life into a liturgical frame of reference and pattern of order; they linked the biblical world to the present and future lives. But they served, further, as continual reminders that the present life, the present world, was not the believer's final home. As such, they were reminders not of death, but of life.

Holy fragrance carried the Christian memory of the breath of life received from God by his first creation, and renewed by Christ for the next. To the late antique Christian, every smell found its meaning and value, for good or for ill, in relation to that memory. It was a memory sustained at every turn by the smells of the ancient Christian world. It was a memory redolent with hope.

NOTES

Introduction

1.   John of Damascus, *On the Divine* 1.11; trans. Anderson, 20. John is referring to Gregory of Nazianzus, Homily 28.13.

2.   Isaac the Syrian, Homily 82, "How Much Honour Humility Possesses and How High Its Rank Is," ed. Bedjan, *Mar Isaacus*, 574–81, at p. 577; trans. Wensinck, 384–89, at p. 386 (adapted).

3.   For a highly suggestive profile of western Christianity according to the sensory models of seeing and hearing, see David Chidester, *Word and Light: Seeing, Hearing, and Religious Discourse* (Urbana/Chicago: University of Illinois Press, 1992). The recent study by Georgia Frank, *The Memory of the Eyes: Pilgrimage to Living Saints in Christian Late Antiquity* (Berkeley: University of California Press, 2000) argues powerfully for an approach to visuality and visual piety that engages the sensorium in much fuller terms than has often been the case. See the magisterial study by Elliot R. Wolfson, *Through a Speculum that Shines: Vision and Imagination in Medieval Jewish Mysticism* (Princeton: Princeton University Press, 1994), for the tradition (and dominance) of visuality in Judaism.

4.   An excellent introduction to the issues can be found in Sarah Coakley, ed., *Religion and the Body* (Cambridge: Cambridge University Press, 1997). David Chidester, "Material Terms for the Study of Religion," *JAAR* 68 (2000): 367–80, observes that in recent discussion "[i]n the study of the sensory dynamics of religion, the eye and ear—the hegemony of the gaze, the kingdom of hearing— seem to be replaced by attention to tactility" (p. 375). For a fine example of the

challenge to the standard emphasis on visuality, see Elizabeth D. Harvey, ed., *Sensible Flesh: On Touch in Early Modern Culture* (Philadelphia: University of Pennsylvania Press, 2003).

5. Groundbreaking in this regard were Peter Brown, *The Body and Society: Men, Women, and Sexual Renunciation in Early Christianity* (New York: Columbia University Press, 1988); Aline Rousselle, *Porneia: On Desire and the Body in Antiquity*, trans. Felicia Pheasant (Oxford: Basil Blackwell Ltd., 1988); Elizabeth A. Clark, *Ascetic Piety and Women's Faith: Essays on Late Ancient Christianity* (Lewiston, NY/Toronto: Edwin Mellen Press, 1986). The undercurrent of this reassessment can be traced in no small degree to the work of Michel Foucault, and especially his *History of Sexuality*, vol. 2, *The Use of Pleasure*, trans. Robert Hurley (New York: Pantheon Books, 1985), and vol. 3, *The Care of the Self*, trans. Robert Hurley (New York: Vintage Books, 1988). Foucault's paradigms in these volumes are now being substantially challenged: see Kathy L. Gaca, *The Making of Fornication: Eros, Ethics, and Political Reform in Greek Philosophy and Early Christianity* (Berkeley: University of California Press, 2003).

6. Two of the finest recent studies are Teresa M. Shaw, *The Burden of the Flesh: Fasting and Sexuality in Early Christianity* (Minneapolis: Augsburg Fortress, 1998); and Susanna Elm, *'Virgins of God': The Making of Asceticism in Late Antiquity* (Oxford: Oxford University Press, 1994).

7. E. R. Dodds, *Pagan and Christian in an Age of Anxiety* (Cambridge: Cambridge University Press, 1965), remains a remarkably influential study despite the huge body of scholarship that challenges or substantially qualifies its perspective. Annick LeGuérer, *Scent: The Essential and Mysterious Power of Smell*, trans. Richard Miller (New York: Kodansha International, 1994), takes this view of Christianity as a religion hostile to the body in general and smell in particular.

8. See S. A. Harvey, "St. Ephrem on the Scent of Salvation," *JTS*, n.s., 49 (1998): 109–128; eadem, "Olfactory Knowing: Signs of Smell in the *Lives* of Simeon Stylites," in *After Bardaisan: Studies on Continuity and Change in Syriac Christianity in Honour of Professor Han J. W. Drijvers*, ed. G. J. Reinink and A. C. Klugkist, OLA 89 (Leuven: Peeters Press, 1999) 23–34; eadem, "Incense Offerings in the Syriac *Transitus Mariae*: Ritual and Knowledge in Ancient Christianity," in *The Early Church in its Context: Essays in Honor of Everett Ferguson*, ed. Abraham J. Malherbe, Frederick W. Norris, and James W. Thompson (Leiden: Brill, 1998), 175–91; eadem, "Why the Perfume Mattered: The Sinful Woman in Syriac Exegetical Tradition," in *In Dominico Eloquio/In Lordly Eloquence: Essays on Patristic Exegesis in Honor of Robert Louis Wilken*, ed. Paul M. Blowers, Angela Russell Christman, David G. Hunter, and Robin Darling Young (Grand Rapids: Eerdmans Press, 2001), 69–89.

9. I am influenced here most especially by Catherine Bell, *Ritual Theory, Ritual Practice* (New York/Oxford: Oxford University Press, 1992).

10. Most prominently in Constance Classen, David Howes, and Anthony Synnott, *Aroma: The Cultural History of Smell* (London/New York: Routledge, 1994).

11. Classen, Howes, and Synnott, *Aroma*; Constance Classen, *The Color of Angels: Cosmology, Gender and the Aesthetic Imagination* (New York: Routledge, 1998); Constance Classen, *Worlds of Sense: Exploring the Senses in History and Across Cultures* (New York/London: Routledge, 1993); David Howes, ed., *The Varieties of Sensory Experience: A Sourcebook in the Anthropology of the Senses* (Toronto: University of Toronto Press, 1991); Anthony Synnott, *The Body Social: Symbolism, Self and Society* (New York/London: Routledge, 1993).

12. Marcel Detienne, *The Gardens of Adonis: Spices in Greek Mythology*, trans. Janet Lloyd, 2nd ed. (Princeton: Princeton University Press, 1994). The importance of Detienne's study of spices is carried further in the same book in the introduction by Jean-Pierre Vernant and the afterword by Froma Zeitlin, pp. vii–xli and 133–45, respectively; and then in the volume which Detienne and Vernant edited together, *The Cuisine of Sacrifice Among the Greeks*, trans. Paula Wissing (Chicago: University of Chicago Press, 1989).

13. Alain Corbin, *The Foul and the Fragrant: Odor and the French Social Imagination*, trans. Miriam L. Kochan, Roy Porter, and Christopher Prendergast (Camabridge, MA: Harvard University Press, 1986). While the importance of Corbin's book cannot be overstated, it is interesting that he basically omitted religion from his study. See also Piero Camporesi, *The Incorruptible Flesh: Bodily Mutation and Mortification in Religion and Folklore*, trans. Tania Croft-Murray, Latin texts trans. Helen Elsom, Cambridge Studies in Oral and Literate Culture 17 (Cambridge: Cambridge University Press, 1988); idem, *The Anatomy of the Senses: Natural Symbols in Medieval and Early Modern Italy*, trans. Allan Cameron (Cambridge: Polity Press, 1994).

14. Jean-Pierre Albert, *Odeurs de Sainteté: La mythologie chrétienne des aromates*, 2nd ed., Recherches d'histoire et de sciences sociales 42 (Paris: École des Hautes Études en Sciences Sociales, 1996).

15. Béatrice Caseau, "Euodia. The Use and Meaning of Fragrances in the Ancient World and their Christianization (100–900 A.D.)," (PhD. diss., Princeton University, 1994). See further Caseau, "Christian Bodies: The Senses and Early Byzantine Christianity," in *Desire and Denial in Byzantium*, ed. Liz James (Aldershot, Hampshire: Ashgate Publishing, 1999), 101–109; eadem, "Les usages médicaux de l'encens et des parfums: Un aspect de la medicine populaire antique et de sa christianisation,"in *Air, Miames et Contagion: Les épidémies dans l'Antiquité et au Moyen Age*, ed. Sylvie Bazin-Tacchella, Danielle Quéruel and Évelyne Samama (Langres: Dominique Guéniot, 2001), 74–85.

16. Saara Lilja, *The Treatment of Odours in the Poetry of Antiquity*, Commentationes Humanarum Litterarum 49 (Helsinki: Societas Scientiarum Fennica, 1972). Lilja's discussion of the symbolism of incense follows the interpretations of E. G. F. C. Atchley, *A History of the Use of Incense in Divine Worship*, Alcuin Club Collections 13 (London: Longmans, Green, and Co., 1909), a basic but problematic study and now much outdated.

Chapter 1. The Olfactory Context

1.   Clifford Geertz, *Negara: The Theatre State in Nineteenth Century Bali* (Princeton: Princeton University Press, 1980), 105; cited in Catherine Bell, *Ritual Theory, Ritual Practice* (New York/Oxford: Oxford University Press, 1992), 44.

2.   Exemplified for Christians in texts such as 4 Maccabees with its strongly Stoic character; e.g., Stanley K. Stowers, "4 Maccabees," *Harper's Bible Commentary*, ed. James L. Mays, (San Francisco: Harper and Row, 1988), 922–34.

3.   *Martyrdom of Polycarp* 15.1–16.1; trans. Musurillo, *Acts of the Christian Martyrs*, 2–21, at pp. 14–15.

4.   For an important discussion of Christian martyrdom as a sacrificial system competing with and opposed to that of the pagan Roman Empire, see now Robin Darling Young, *In Procession Before the World: Martyrdom as Public Liturgy in Early Christianity* (Milwaukee: Marquette University Press, 2001). On the vast geographical spread of the ancient frankincense trade, see Gus W. Van Beek, "Frankincense and Myrrh," *The Biblical Archaeologist* 23 (1960): 70–95. Further references are given below.

5.   I have been helped most by Marcel Detienne and Jean-Pierre Vernant, *The Cuisine of Sacrifice Among the Greeks*, trans. Paula Wissing (Chicago: University of Chicago Press, 1989); Nancy Jay, *Throughout Your Generations Forever: Sacrifice, Religion and Paternity* (Chicago: University of Chicago Press, 1992); Stanley K. Stowers, "Greeks Who Sacrifice and Those Who Do Not: Towards an Anthropology of Greek Religion," in *The Social World of the First Christians: Essays in Honor of Wayne A. Meeks*, ed. L. Michael White and Larry A. Yarbrough (Minneapolis: Fortress Press, 1995), 293–333.

6.   See esp. Mary Beard, John North, and Simon Price, eds., *Religions of Rome*, vol. 2, *A Sourcebook* (Cambridge: Cambridge University Press, 1998), 78–115, 148–65; Simon Price, *Religions of the Ancient Greeks* (Cambridge: Cambridge University Press, 1999), 25–46, 97, 177–78; Louise Bruit Zaidman and Pauline Schmitt Pantel, eds., *Religion in the Ancient Greek City*, trans. Paul Cartledge (Cambridge: Cambridge University Press, 1992), 27–45. For a summary listing of the ritual components of Greek sacrifice, see Walter Burkert, *Greek Religion*, trans. John Raffan (Cambridge, MA: Harvard University Press, 1985), 55–118. For some Hellenistic and Roman examples, see, e.g., Ovid, *Fasti* 4.247–348, and Livy, *Annals of Rome* 29.14 , both on the origins of the cult of the Great Mother in Rome; Pausanias, *Description of Greece*, Elis, 1.20.2–3 on worshipping Eileithyia and Sosipolis; Ovid, *Fasti* 4.133–62, on washing the statue of Venus; Theocritus, *Idyll* 15 on the Festival of Adonis; Athenaeus, *Deipnosophists* 11.462 on sacrifice made at sea, 15.674 on wreaths worn to honor specific deities, 15.678b on the bones of the heroine Europa carried in wreaths; Philostratus, *Life of Apollonius* 1.10–11, 31–32 on excessive and moderate sacrifices; Eusebius, *Preparation of the Gospel* 4.9.1–2 on proper animals, birds, grains, and incense for sacrifice (oracle of Apollo), 5.11.1–12.2 on herbs, spices, and resin to mix for purifying statues of Hecate.

7.   Lucian, *Of Sacrifice* 13; trans. Harmon, 1:189. See Saara Lilja, *The Treatment of Odours in the Poetry of Antiquity* (Helsinki: Societas Scientiarum Fennica, 1972), 31–47 for numerous citations.

8.   Although blood sacrifice was not always required, other basic elements such as incense, lamps, and hymns were deemed essential for daily rites in the late antique period. The use of incense appears to have increased during the Hellenistic and Roman periods due to changes in trade (discussed further below). See Martin Nilsson, "Pagan Divine Service in Late Antiquity," HTR 38 (1945): 63–69.

9.   Examples are legion, but see, e.g., the *Homeric Hymn to Demeter*, passim; Plutarch, *On Isis and Osiris*, ch. 15; Apuleius, *Metamorphoses* 11; Louis V. Zabkar, *Hymns to Isis in Her Temple at Philae* (Hanover, NH: Brandeis University Press, 1988); Erik Hornung, *Conceptions of God in Ancient Egypt: The One and the Many*, trans. John Baines (Ithaca, NY: Cornell University Press, 1982), 133–34; Cynthia W. Shelmerdine, "Shining and Fragrant Cloth in Homeric Epic," in *The Ages of Homer: A Tribute to Emily Townsend Vermeule*, ed. Jane B. Carter and Sarah P. Morris (Austin: University of Texas Press, 1995), 99–107; Lilja, *The Treatment of Odours*, 19–30; Marcel Detienne, *The Gardens of Adonis: Spices in Greek Mythology*, trans. Janet Lloyd (Princeton: Princeton University Press, 1994). Saul Levin, "The Etymology of *nectar* and exotic scents in Early Greece," *Studi Micenei ed Egeo-anatolici* 13 (1971): 31–50 has an interesting discussion of etymology, the foods and drinks of the gods as opposed to humans, and the ancient spice trade.

10.   As Libanius extolled in his praise for the region of Daphne on the outskirts of Antioch, in his *Oration* 11: *The Antiochikos*, sec. 235–36: "Of Daphne, there has never yet been a fitting description, nor will there ever be. . .with shady paths, harmonious bird songs, a gentle breeze, and odours sweeter than incense." Trans. Norman, p. 55.

11.   E.g., A. Lallemand, "Le parfum comme signe fabuleux dans les pays mythiques," in *Peuples et pays mythique*, Actes du Ve Colloque du Centre Recherches Mythologiques de l'Université de Paris X, ed. François Jouan et Bernard Deforge, (Paris: Les Belles Lettres, 1988), 73–90; Joël Thomas, "La nourriture d'immortalité en Grèce et à Rome," and Alain Moreau, "Le fabuleux, le divin, le parfum: Aphrodite maîtresse des odeurs," both in *Saveurs, Senteurs: Le Goût de la Méditerranée*, ed. Paul Carmignani, Jean-Yves Laurichesse, and Joël Thomas, Actes du Colloque Université de Perpignan Novembre 1997 (Perpignan: Presses Universitaires, 1998), 13–22 and 41–58, respectively.

12.   Plutarch, *Lives*, "Alexander" 4.2–6; Philostratus, *Life of Apollonius* 1.5.

13.   Athenaeus, *Deipnosophists* 15.674e, 675f–676a.

14.   The theme is prominent in Sophocles' *Philoctetes*. See also Detienne, *Gardens of Adonis*, 10–11, 24–25, 90–91, 92–98.

15.   Eunapius, *Lives of the Sophists* 483; trans. Wright, 467.

16.   Philostratus, *Life of Apollonius* 1.31.

17.   Plutarch, *On Isis and Osiris* 79–80; trans. Gwyn Griffiths, 244–46.

18. Lucian (?), *On the Syrian Goddess* 30; trans. Attridge and Oden, 43. The authorship for this text remains contested, but the dating (second century C.E.) seems solid.

19. To reduce the function of sacrificial incense to the masking of the odor of animal slaughter, as has sometimes been done by scholars, is to miss entirely the complex of aesthetic and ritual issues for which incense was the prime signifier. Yet such a view has been commonplace in scholarly literature.

20. An especially helpful guide may be found in Jacob Milgrom, *Leviticus* 1–16, Anchor Bible (New York: Doubleday, 1991), 54, 236–38, 597, 628–32, 1014–15, 1024–31. For the broader context of ancient near eastern sacrificial practices, see, e.g., J. Quaegebeur, ed., *Ritual and Sacrifice in the Ancient Near East*, OLA 55 (Leuven: Peeters and Departement Oriëntalistiek, 1993).

21. The difficulty of dating the biblical texts and especially of ascertaining the impact of later redactors on earlier sources makes the evidence for the First Temple sacrificial system extremely tenuous. In addition to Milgrom, *Leviticus* 1–16, a helpful study utilizing archaeological evidence is Victor Avigdor Hurowitz, "Solomon's Golden Vessels (1 Kings 7:48–50) and the Cult of the First Temple," in *Pomegranates and Golden Bells: Studies in Biblical, Jewish, and Near Eastern Ritual, Law, and Literature in Honor of Jacob Milgrom*, ed. David P. Wright, David Noel Freedman, and Avi Hurvitz, (Winona Lake, IN: Eisenbrauns, 1995), 151–64. Various implements in this study indicate the use of incense (incense shovels, burners or firepans, altars) and point to other odors that may have marked sacred ritual (floral motifs decorating the menorah, tongs that appear to have been used either with the incense altar or to trim or remove lampwicks—lamp oil made a pungent odor, whether scented or simple—and libation cups).

22. Kjeld Nielsen, *Incense in Ancient Israel*, SVT 38 (Leiden: E. J. Brill, 1986). Paul Heger, *The Development of Incense Cult in Israel* (New York: Walter de Gruyter, 1997). Heger curiously restricts himself to the biblical texts, with no use of archaeological evidence. See also, e.g., Menahem Haran, *Temples and Temple Service in Ancient Israel: An Inquiry into Biblical Cult Phenomena and the Historical Setting of the Priestly School*, 2nd ed. (Winona Lake, IN: Eisenbrauns, 1985); E. P. Sanders, *Judaism, Practice and Belief 63 B.C.E.–60 C.E.* (London: SCM Press, 1992), 77–102, esp. at p. 83 for the casting of lots among the priests to see who would offer incense. Although dated in some respects, the classic study for the development of Christian practice and doctrine remains Robert Daly, *Christian Sacrifice: The Judeo-Christian Background Before Origen* (Washington, DC: Catholic University of America Press, 1978).

23. Lawrence H. Schiffman, "Communal Meals at Qumran," RQ 10 (1979): 45–56.

24. Ex 30:31–38.

25. Lev 16:1–14. See C. Houtman, "On the Function of the Holy Incense (Exodus XXX 34–8) and the Sacred Anointing Oil (Exodus XXX 22–33)," VT 42 (1992): 458–65.

26. Lev 2:1–2, 15–16; 24:7.

27. Gregory Dix, *The Shape of the Liturgy*, 2nd ed. (1945; repr. London: A & C Black, 1993), 425–26.

28. Béatrice Caseau, "Euodia: The Use and Meaning of Fragrances in the Ancient World and their Christianization (100–900 A.D.)" (PhD. diss., Princeton University, 1994), 82–90.

29. Tamid 2.8; trans. Herbert Danby, *The Mishnah* (Oxford: Clarendon Press, 1933), 585.

30. See now William K. Gilders, *Blood Ritual in the Hebrew Bible: Meaning and Power* (Baltimore: Johns Hopkins University Press, 2004).

31. In addition to Gilders, *Blood Ritual in the Hebrew Bible*, see the important discussion comparing Israelite and Greek cultic uses of blood in Stanley K. Stowers, "On the Comparison of Blood in Greek and Israelite Ritual," in *Hesed Ve-Emet: Studies in Honor of Ernest S. Frerichs*, ed. Jodi Magness and Seymour Gitin, (Atlanta: Scholars Press, 1998), 179–94.

32. Clement, *Christ the Educator* 2.8.67; trans. Wood, at p. 151.

33. Origen, *Homilies on Leviticus* 13.5.2; trans. Barkley, at p. 242.

34. Notably Psalm 22.

35. Two recent studies addressing this issue are: Marie E. Isaacs, *Sacred Space: An Approach to the Theology of the Epistle to the Hebrews*, JSNT Supplement Series 73 (Sheffield: JSOT Press, 1992); and John Dunnill, *Covenant and Sacrifice in the Letter to the Hebrews*, SNTS 75 (Cambridge: Cambridge University Press, 1992).

36. Also mentioned in Acts 2:46, 3:1.

37. Phil 4:18.

38. Phil 2:17. Cf. 2 Tim 4:6: "For I am already on the point of being sacrificed; the time of my departure has come."

39. Above all, see the masterful study by Harold W. Attridge, "Making Scents of Paul: The Background and Sense of 2 Cor. 2:14–7," in *Early Christianity and Classical Culture*, ed. John T. Fitzgerald, Thomas H. Olbricht, and L. Michael White (Leiden/Boston: E. J. Brill, 2003), 71–88. Attridge gives both a thorough review of the scholarship, and a strong argument for a coherently interwoven joining of traditions in Paul's choice of terminology.

40. Against such a mechanical reading see Jeffrey John, "Anointing in the New Testament," in *The Oil of Gladness: Anointing in the Christian Tradition*, ed. Martin Dudley and Geoffrey Rowell (London: SPCK, 1993), 46–76 at pp. 69–70. See further discussion in chapter 2.

41. E.g., Sirach 24:1–21, 39:12–16, discussed further below; Ps.-Clem., Homily 13.15–16.

42. E.g., Plutarch, *Lives*, "Alexander" 4.2–6; Philo, *de Som.* 1.49–51. For a late antique example, Paulinus of Nola, *Poem* 27.148–68, 235–45.

43. Ignatius, *To the Ephesians* 17.1; trans. Lake, *Apostolic Fathers* 1:191.

44. Mark Johnson, *The Body in the Mind: The Bodily Basis of Meaning, Imagination, and Reason* (Chicago: University of Chicago Press, 1987), argues that scholars have often ignored the degree to which bodily experience underlies basic metaphorical language.

45. See esp. Ignatius, *To the Ephesians* 8.1, 11.2, 21.1; *To the Romans* 2.2, 3.2, 4.1–3, 5.1–6.3; *To Polycarp* 6.1. On the role of letters in directing Christian perceptions of martyrdom, see Young, *In Procession Before the Word*.

46. As Caroline Bynum has commented, the fact that recent scholarship has shown the actual numbers of martyrs to be fewer than previously thought (or claimed) does not diminish the degree to which the threat of persecution or martyrdom exercised profound fear among early Christian communities. Caroline Walker Bynum, *The Resurrection of the Body in Western Christianity, 200–1336* (New York: Columbia University Press, 1995), 21–58.

47. Pliny, *Letter* 10.96.

48. Caseau, "*Euodia*," 92–98. Consider Cyprian, *On the Lapsed* 8: "Was not that altar, where [the apostate] was going to his death, in fact his funeral pyre? When he saw that altar of the devil, smoking and reeking with its foul stench, should he not have fled in terror, as from the place where his soul must burn?" Trans. Bévenot, 19. Compare Eusebius, HE 4.41.9.

49. So, too, Young, *In Procession Before the World*; and Philip A. Harland, "Christ-Bearers and Fellow-Initiates: Local Cultural Life and Christian Identity in Ignatius' Letters," JECS 11 (2003): 481–99.

50. Irenaeus, *Against Heresies* 4.18.1–2; trans. Sheerin, *The Eucharist*, pp. 246–47.

51. G. E. M. de Ste. Croix, "Why were the early Christians persecuted?" *Past and Present* 26 (1963): 6–38 remains the fundamental study.

52. S. R. F. Price, *Rituals and Power: The Roman Imperial Cult in Asia Minor* (Cambridge: Cambridge University Press, 1984), on the subtle qualifications conveyed by ritual details in the rites of the imperial cult. Price points out that the role of the imperial cult in persecutions against Christians has been greatly exaggerated by historians who have not been attentive to such details.

53. Robert Wilken, *The Christians as the Romans Saw Them*, 2nd ed. (New Haven: Yale University Press, 2003), esp. 48–67.

54. *Acts of the Scillitan Martyrs* 3, 5; trans. Musurillo, *Acts of the Christian Martyrs*, 86–88.

55. Everett Ferguson, "Spiritual Sacrifice in Early Christianity and its Environment," ANRW II.23.2, ed. W. Haase, (Berlin: Walter de Gruyter, 1980) 1151–89; Johannes Quasten, *Music and Worship in Pagan and Christian Antiquity*, trans. Boniface Ramsey (Washington, DC: National Association of Pastoral Musicians, 1983), 59–65; Charles Manning, "Seneca and Roman Religious Practice," in *Religion in the Ancient World: New Themes and Approaches*, ed. Matthew Dillon, (Amsterdam: A. M. Hakkert, 1996), 311–19.

56. E.g., Philostratus, *Life of Apollonius* 1.1, 10–11, 31–32. The philosophical critique of blood sacrifice was older than the Hellenistic era, however. See Plato, *Republic* 2.364b–365a; idem, *Laws* 10.885b, 906b–c.

57. Philo, *Spec.* I.273–77; here as cited in Daly, *Christian Sacrifice*, at pp. 68–69.

58. Philo, *Det.* 17–21; here trans. Winston, *Philo of Alexandria*, at p. 256. Cf. Philo, *Deus* 7–9; *Spec.* I. 269–72; trans. Winston, *Philo of Alexandria*, at pp. 157–59.

59. 1QS, "Rule of the Community," col. 9:4–5; cited in Dennis Green, "To '. . . Send Up, Like the Smoke of Incense, the Works of the Law'—The Similarity of Views on an Alternative to Temple Sacrifice by Three Jewish Sectarian Movements of the Late Second Temple Period," in M. Dillon, ed., *Religion in the Ancient World*, 167–75.

60. Lucretius, *On the Nature of Things* 5.1197–1202; trans. Rouse, 424–25.

61. See Dirk Obbink, "The Origin of Greek Sacrifice: Theophrastus on Religion and Cultural History," in *Theophrastean Studies: On Natural Science, Physics and Metaphysics, Ethics, Religion, and Rhetoric*, ed. William W. Fortenbaugh and Robert W. Sharples (New Brunswick, NJ: Transaction Books, 1988), 272–95.

62. Porphyry, *On Abstinence* 2.7, 9.

63. Porphyry, *On Abstinence* 2.5. Ovid presents a similar representation of religious history in *Fasti* 1.337–53: before the appearance of the spice trade, Romans sacrificed grain with a pinch of salt; the sweet smells came from the wood of juniper and laurel trees, and garlands of violets.

64. Porphyry, *On Abstinence* 2.15; trans. Taylor, 72. Compare Porphyry, *Life of Pythagoras* 36, on the simplicity of offerings that Pythagoras habitually sacrificed.

65. "What to me is the multitude of your sacrifices? says the Lord. I have had enough of burnt offerings of rams and the fat of fed beasts . . . bring no more vain offerings; incense is an abomination to me. . . . Cease to do evil, learn to do good; seek justice, correct oppression; defend the fatherless, plead for the widow" (Isa 1.12–17). Compare, e.g., Am 5.21–27.

66. Eusebius, *Proof of the Gospel*, bk. 1, uses the criticisms from the Hebrew prophets to justify Christian practice and to claim its superiority over pagan and Jewish traditions.

67. Origen, *Contra Celsum* 8.17; trans. Chadwick, 464.

68. Origen, *On Prayer*, 2.2; trans. Greer, *Origen*, 83.

69. Clement, *Stromateis* 7.6; trans. Oulton and Chadwick, *Alexandrian Christianity*, 112.

70. Clement, *Stromateis* 7.6; trans. Oulton and Chadwick, *Alexandrian Christianity*, 112.

71. Arnobius of Sicca, *The Case Against the Pagans* 7.26–30; trans. McCracken, 2:507–13.

72. Eusebius, *Preparation of the Gospel* 4.10.1–2, citing Porphyry, *On Abstinence* 2.34. The whole of book 4 deals with a critique of pagan religion drawing heavily from Greek philosophy. But Eusebius also contrasts Porphyry's *On Oracles* with

the same author's On Abstinence, to claim that self-contradiction is inherent in Greek tradition.

73. E.g., Porphyry, On Abstinence 2.6.

74. Tertullian, Apology 23.5, 39.15. Compare, e.g., Tatian, Discourse to the Greeks 19.

75. Tertullian, On Idolatry 11.7; trans. Waszink and van Winden, 43.

76. Sibylline Oracles 8.485–500; trans. Collins, 428. See also Quasten, Music and Worship, p. 60.

77. Irenaeus, Against Heresies 4.17.4; trans. Sheerin, Eucharist, at p. 245.

78. Clement, Stromateis 7.3; trans. Oulton and Chadwick, Alexandrian Christianity, 101.

79. Athenagoras, Plea 13.2; trans. Sheerin, Eucharist, at p. 37.

80. Clement, Stromateis 7.6; trans. Oulton and Chadwick, Alexandrian Christianity, 114.

81. E.g., Methodius Olympius, Symposium 5.8; Aphrahat, Demonstration 18 "On Celibacy."

82. Apostolic Constitutions 2.26.8; trans. Donaldson, ANF 7: 410.

83. Origen, Hom. Lev. 9.8.1–2; trans. Barkley, 193.

84. Origen, Hom. Lev. 9.9.4; trans. Barkley, 196.

85. Origen, Hom. Lev. 9.9.6; trans. Barkley, 197–98.

86. Origen, Hom. Lev. 9.9.7; trans. Barkley, 198–99.

87. Origen, Hom. Lev. 8.5. For a detailed study of Origen's notion of Christian sacrifice, see Theo Hermans, Origène: Théologie Sacrificielle du Sacerdoce des Chrétiens, TH 102 (Paris: Éditions Beauchesne, 1996).

88. Origen, Hom. Lev. 9.8.3; trans. Barkley, 194.

89. R. J. Forbes, Studies in Ancient Technology, 2nd ed., vol. 3 (Leiden: E. J. Brill, 1965); Nigel Groom, Frankincense and Myrrh: A Study of the Arabian Incense Trade (London/New York: Longman, Libraire du Liban, 1981); J. Innes Miller, The Spice Trade of the Roman Empire (Oxford: Clarendon Press, 1969); P. Fauré, Parfums et aromates de l'antiquité (Paris: Fayard, 1987); Irene and Walter Jacob, eds., The Healing Past: Pharmaceuticals in the Biblical and Rabbinic World (Leiden: E. J. Brill, 1993); Carmignani, Laurichesse, and Thomas, eds., Saveurs, Senteurs: Le Goût de la Méditerranée, 13–195. There is also a wealth of information in Andrew Dalby, Dangerous Tastes: The Story of Spices (Berkeley: University of California Press, 2000).

90. E.g., Musaeus, Hero and Leander 260–71; Marcus Aurelius, Meditations 8.24.

91. See David S. Potter, "Odor and Power in the Roman Empire," in Constructions of the Classical Body, ed. James I. Porter (Ann Arbor: University of Michigan Press, 1999), 169–89.

92. Athenaeus, Deipnosophists 15.486–87.

93. Theophrastus, Concerning Odors 1; trans. Hort, 2:327. Ancient theories of sense perception will be discussed in more depth in chapter 3.

94. Theophrastus, Odors 1; trans. Hort, 2:327.

95. For contrasting views on Theophrastus's cosmology, see Marlien van Raalte, "The Idea of the Cosmos as an Organic Whole in Theophrastus' *Metaphysics*," and John Ellis, "The Aporematic Character of Theophrastus' *Metaphysics*," both in *Theophrastean Studies*, ed. William Fortenbaugh and Robert Sharples (New Brunswick, NJ: Transaction Books, 1988), 189–215 and 216–23, respectively.

96. Theophrastus, *Odors* 1; trans. Hort, 2:329.

97. Brilliantly discussed in Detienne, *Gardens of Adonis*. See also Constance Classen, David Howes, and Anthony Synnot, *Aroma: The Cultural History of Smell* (London/New York: Routledge, 1994).

98. Theophrastus, *Enquiry into Plants* 9.7.

99. The view is ubiquitous in ancient texts. E.g., the two works preserved in the Hippocratic corpus, *Airs, Waters, Places* (probably authentic as a product of the Hippocratic school), and *Breaths* (not a medical text, but preserved in the corpus nonetheless), both ed. and trans. by W.H.S. Jones in Hippocrates, *Works*; for a late antique example, Paulinus of Nola, *Poem* 17.21–44. Plutarch noted the health-giving exhalations of the Nile, and which time of day brought their greatest effect: *Isis and Osiris* 38, 40, 41, 79–80. While it falls outside the bounds of this study, it is interesting to consider the connection between ancient views of smells, and the medical traditions that placed strong emphasis on breath and breathing; see, e.g., Armelle Debru, *Le Corps Respirant: La pensée physiologique chez Galen* (New York: E. J. Brill, 1996).

100. E.g., Thucydides, *History* 2.49.

101. Lesley Dean-Jones, "The Cultural Construct of the Female Body in Classical Greek Science," in *Women's History and Ancient History*, ed. Sarah B. Pomeroy, (Chapel Hill: University of North Carolina Press, 1991), 111–37; Helen King, "The Daughter of Leonides: Reading the Hippocratic Corpus," in *History as Text: The Writing of Ancient History*, ed. Averil Cameron, (London, Duckworth, 1989), 11–32; *Hippocratic Aphorisms* 5.59, in Hippocrates, *Works*, Jones ed.; Soranus, *Gynecology* 9, 153.

102. 3 Maccabees 5.

103. *Acts of Paul and Thecla* 35.

104. A commonplace well known in late antiquity also: Gregory of Nyssa, *Life of Moses* 2.258; Palladius, *Dialogue on the Life of John Chrysostom* 5.86–87; Basil of Caesarea, *Letters* 10.

105. Eusebius, *Eclogae Propheticae* 111:12. Cf. Jean Baudrillard, *Seduction*, trans. Brian Singer (New York: St. Martin's Press, 1990), 76–77.

106. Notably in Theophrastus, *Enquiry into Plants*, bk. 9.

107. Theophrastus, *Enquiry into Plants* 9.7.3; trans. Hort, 2:249–51.

108. In addition to other citations in this chapter, see also Jean-Pierre Brun, "The Production of Perfumes in Antiquity: The Cases of Delos and Paestum," *AJA* 104 (2000): 277–308; Cynthia Wright Shelmerdine, *The Perfume Industry of*

Mycenaean Pylos, SMAP 34 (Göteborg: Paul Aströms Förlag, 1985); Pierre Grimal, *Les jardins romains*, 2nd ed. (Paris: Presses Universitaires de France, 1969); Edmund Launert, *Perfume and Pomanders: Scent and Scent Bottles* (London: Potterton Books, 1987); Renate Smollich, *Der Bisamapfel in Kunst undWissenschaft* (Stuttgart: Deutscher Apotheker Verlag, 1983); Dieter Martinetz, Karlheinz Lohs, Jörg Janzen, *Weihrauch und Myrrhe: Kulturgeschichte undWirtschaftliche Bedeutung, Botanik, Chemie, Medizin* (Stuttgart: Wissenschaftliche Verlagsgesellschaft mbH, 1988).

109. Forbes, *Ancient Technology*, 1–24; Lise Manniche, *Sacred Luxuries: Fragrance, Aromatherapy, and Cosmetics in Ancient Egypt* (Ithaca, NY: Cornell University Press, 1999); A. Lucas, "Cosmetics, Perfumes, and Incense in Ancient Egypt," *JEA* 16 (1930): 41–53. A further problem is that the ancients were not consistent in their use of names for spices, and sometimes followed different criteria for classification than modern botanists would, hence applying the same name to different plants. See Wilfred H. Schoff, "Cinnamon, Cassia, and Somaliland," *JAOS* 40 (1920): 260–70; idem, "Aloes," *JAOS* 42 (1922): 171–85.

110. K. Nielsen, *Incense in Ancient Israel*. The Song of Songs is a central text in this consideration; its exegesis will be discussed in chapter 3, pp. 123–25. But for an example on this point, see Jill M. Munro, *Spikenard and Saffron:The Imagery of the Song of Songs* (Sheffield: Sheffield Academic Press, 1995).

111. Jdt 10:1–5; Prov 7.17–18; Song of Songs.

112. G. Ryckmans, "De l'or, de l'encens, et de la myrrhe," *RB* 58 (1951): 372–76.

113. Jerry Stannard, "Alimentary and Medicinal Uses of Plants," in *Medieval Gardens*, ed. Elisabeth MacDougall (Washington, DC: Dumbarton Oaks Publications, 1986), 69–91.

114. E.g., Van Beek, "Frankincense and Myrrh;" Yehuda Feliks, "The Incense of the Tabernacle," in Wright, Freedman, and Hurvitz, *Pomegranates and Golden Bells*, 125–49; Robert Houston Smith, "'Bloom ofYouth': A Labelled Syro-Palestinian Unguent Jar," *JHS* 112 (1992): 163–67; Giuseppe Donato and Monique Seefried, *The Fragrant Past: Perfumes of Cleopatra and Julius Caesar* (Rome: Instituto Poligrafico e Zecca dello Stato/Emory University, Museum of Art and Architecture, 1989); Soranus's *Gynecology*, esp. "Materia Medica," Temkin, trans., 214–44; Guido Majno, *The Healing Hand: Man and Wound in the AncientWorld* (Cambridge, MA: Harvard University Press, 1975); Martinetz, Lohs, Janzen, *Weihrauch und Myrrhe*; Dalby, *DangerousTastes*.

115. Groom, *Frankincense and Myrrh*; Miller, *SpiceTrade*.

116. Pliny, *Natural History* (hereafter NH). OnTheophrastus and Pliny, and the tradition they represent, see Roger French, *Ancient Natural History* (London/New York: Routledge, 1994); Mary Beagan, *Roman Nature:The Thought of Pliny the Elder* (Oxford: Clarendon Press, 1992).

117. Pliny, NH 12.7.15.

118. Pliny, NH 13.11.

119. Pliny, NH 13.27.

120. Pliny, NH 14.27.

121. Pliny, NH 13.22.

122. Pliny, NH 12.40.

123. See above, n. 6.

124. Soranus, *Gynecology* 224 (frankincense), 231 (myrrh). Harald Nielsen, *Ancient Ophthalmological Agents* (Odense: Odense University Press, 1974), 57–58. See also Majno, *Healing Hand;* Lilja, *Treatment of Odors,* 163–72.

125. Béatrice Caseau, "Les usages médicaux de l'encens et des parfums: Un aspect de la medicine populaire antique et de sa christianisation," in *Air, Miames et Contagion: Les épidémies dans l'Antiquité et au Moyen Age,* ed. Sylvie Bazin-Tacchella, Danielle Quéruel, and Évelyne Samama (Langres: Dominique Guéniot, 2001), 74–85; eadem, "Euodia," 194–226. Consider Plutarch's discussion of the three daily incense offerings to the sun, where the type of incense was chosen by consideration of air quality at each time of day, and the maximum health benefit to the body at each time: Plutarch, *Isis and Osiris* 79–80.

126. Athenaeus cites Chrysippus for the etymology that *myra* (perfumes) "took their name from the great toil (*moros*)and foolish labor with which they were obtained." Athenaeus, *Deipnosophists* 15.686; trans. Gulick, 7:177.

127. Pliny, NH 13.2.18.

128. Pliny, NH 13.1.

129. Pliny, NH 13.4. For different perfumes used on different body parts, see also Athenaeus, *Deipnosophists* 15.689.

130. Pliny, NH 13.5. For perfume in wine, see Athenaeus, *Deipnosophists* 166c–d, Gulick, ed., 1:288. Athenaeus also indicates that particular spice combinations could lessen the intoxicating qualities of wine, or diminish the chance of a headache afterwards: *Deipnosophists* 11.464.

131. Pliny, NH 13.2; trans. Hort, 4:101.

132. Pliny, NH 13.4; trans. Hort, 4:111.

133. Pliny, NH 12.41.84; trans. Hort, 4: 62. Here Pliny speaks of the trade with India, China, and the Arabian peninsula. Elsewhere he comments, "in no year does India absorb less than 50 million sesterces of our empire's wealth, sending back merchandise to be sold with us at a hundred times its prime cost." NH 6.26.101; Hort, 2:417. Compare Athenaeus, *Deipnosophists* 15.686–92, on perfumes, their production, and properties.

134. Pliny, NH 12.40.81; trans. Hort, 4:61.

135. NH 12.30–40. See Caseau, "Euodia," 29–47; Groom, *Frankincense and Myrrh;* Miller, *Spice Trade.*

136. Tertullian, *The Chaplet* 10.4–5; trans. Quain, 253.

137. Tertullian, *Apology* 42.7; trans. Daly, 107.

138. Tertullian, *Apology* 42.7; trans. Daly, 107. Consider, too, the universal patristic exegesis of the gifts of the Magi in Mt 2:11, that gold signified Christ's kingship, frankincense his divinity (for incense is offered to divinity), and myrrh his humanity (for myrrh anoints the dead). E.g., Irenaeus, *Against Heresies* 3.9; Gregory of Nazianzus, *ad Julianum Tributorum Exaequatorem*, Migne PG 35: 1057.34. Basil of Caesarea also expounded at length on the image of myrrh for the dead in his *Homily on Psalm* 44 9.

139. Tertullian, *On Idolatry* 11.2; trans. Waszink and Van Winden, 43.

140. Tertullian, *On Idolatry* 12.5; trans. Waszink and Van Winden, 47.

141. Tertullian, *On Idolatry* 16.1; trans. Waszink and Van Winden, 55.

142. Tertullian, *On Idolatry* 17.

143. E.g., Canons of Elvira (c. 305), 2, 3; Canons of Ancyra (c. 314–19), 1–9; Charles Joseph Hefele and Henri Leclerq, eds., *Histoire des conciles* (Paris: Letouzet et Ane, 1907; repr. Hildesheim: Georg Olms Verlag, 1973), 1.1.

144. *To His Wife* 2.5; trans. Le Saint, 30. On the adornment of entrances with lamps and wreaths to honor the imperial cult, see also Tertullian, *On Idolatry* 15.

145. Tertullian, *To His Wife* 2.8; trans. Le Saint, here at p. 35.

146. Tertullian, *On Idolatry* 11.

147. Origen, *Exhortation to Martyrdom* 45; trans. Greer, *Origen*, 74–75. See also Origen, *Contra Celsum* 7.6, citing the support of the Pythagorean Numenius of Apamea for this view, and 8.60 for Celsus's agreement. Compare Justin Martyr, *2 Apology* 5.4, combining this view of demons with the story of the Nephilim in Genesis 6:4; Clement, *Stromateis* 7.3; Porphyry, *On Abstinence* 2.58; Eusebius, *Preparation of the Gospel* 5.2.1.

148. Aristides, *Apology* 15, 16; *Letter to Diognetus* 5, 6; Tertullian, *Apology* 42.

149. Clement, *Christ the Educator* 2.8.66–67; trans. Wood, 150–51. Compare Plutarch, *Moralia: Table-Talk*, bk. 7, question 5.3.

150. Clement, *Christ the Educator* 2.1.4; trans. Wood, 96–97.

151. Clement, *Christ the Educator* 2.1.5–7.

152. There is a marvelous treatment on this point in Blake Leyerle, "Clement of Alexandria on the Importance of Table Etiquette," JECS 3 (1995): 123–41.

153. Athanaeus, *Deipnosophists* 1.28a–34e (on fragrance as crucial to the quality of the wine), 11.464 (on the perfumed cups).

154. Clement, *Christ the Educator* 2.2.30; trans. Wood, 120.

155. Quasten argued that it was just this tradition of dining that led Christians to ban music at meals, except for the singing of Psalms or other hymnody: *Music in Pagan and Christian Antiquity*, 128–32.

156. There is no better description of the aesthetic richness of the Roman dinner party than Athenaeus, *Deipnosophists*. On the proper use of scents during dinner, see esp. 11.462–63; 15.665–66, 685, 692.

157. Clement, *Christ the Educator* 2.1.15; trans. Wood, 107.

158. Clement, *Christ the Educator* 2.1.11; trans. Wood, 102–103.

159. Clement, *Christ the Educator* 2.1.14; trans. Wood, 106.

160. Clement, *Christ the Educator* 2.8.61.

161. Clement, *Christ the Educator* 2.8.65; trans. Wood, 150. Compare the Pseudo-Clementine Homily 13, where "the chaste woman" is described as one who "perfumes the church with her good reputation, and glorifies it by her purity." Indeed, here moral virtues are the complete adornment of such a good Christian woman: "The chaste woman is adorned with the Son of God as with a bridegroom. She is clothed with holy light. Her beauty lies in a well-regulated soul; she is fragrant with ointment, even with a good reputation. She is arrayed in beautiful vesture, even in modesty. She wears about her precious pearls, even chaste words. And she is radiant, for her mind has been brilliantly lighted up. Into a beautiful mirror does she look, for she looks into God. Beautiful cosmetics does she use, namely, the fear of God, with which she admonishes her soul. Beautiful is the woman, not because she has chains of gold on her, but because she has been set free from transient lusts." Homily 13.15–16; trans. Smith, ANF 8: 220.

162. Clement, *Christ the Educator* 2.8.66–68; trans. Wood, 151.

163. Clement, *Christ the Educator* 2.8.64; trans. Wood, 149.

164. Clement, *Christ the Educator* 2.8.66. Compare Athenaeus, *Deipnosophists* 15.686–92, on the medicinal values of perfumes and how these contribute to a happy banquet.

165. Clement, *Christ the Educator* 2.8.66, 68; trans. Wood, 150, 151.

166. Clement, *Christ the Educator* 2.8.69, 76.

167. Tertullian, *The Apparel of Women*; Clement, *Christ the Educator* 3.

168. Maria Wyke, "Woman in the Mirror: The Rhetoric of Adornment in the Roman World," in *Women in Ancient Societies: 'An illusion of the night,'* ed. Léonie Archer, Susan Fischler, and Maria Wyke (New York: Routledge, 1994), 134–51; Marcia Colish, "Cosmetic Theology: The Transformation of a Stoic Theme," *Assays* 1 (1984): 3–14.

169. Clement, *Christ the Educator* 2.8.70–76; Tertullian, *The Chaplet*.

170. Tertullian, *The Chaplet* 13.8; trans. Quain, 264. See Germaine Guillaume-Coirier, "Les Couronnes militaires végétales à Rome: Vestiges indo-européens et croyances archaïques," RHR 210 (1993): 387–411. Athenaeus, *Deipnosophists* 15.665–86, presents a magnificent discussion of wreaths, their types, uses, and medicinal as well as ornamental effects.

171. Tertullian, *The Chaplet* 5; cf. idem, *Apology* 42.6.

172. Clement, *Christ the Educator* 2.8.76.

173. Clement, *Stromateis* 7.7.36; trans. Chadwick and Oulton, *Alexandrian Christianity*, 115.

174. *Letter to Diognetus* 5.8–9; trans. Lake, *Apostolic Fathers*, 361.

175. Methodius, *Symposium* 6.3; trans. Musurillo, 92–93.

176. Origen, *Hom. Gen.* 3.5; trans. Heine, 96.

177. Origen, *Hom. Gen.* 3.6; trans. Heine, 98–99. Origen here cites 2 Cor 2:15, Am 6:6, and Song 4:14 to support his interpretation.

178. Origen, *Hom. Gen.* 11.1–2; trans. Heine, 169–70.

179. Origen, *Hom. Lev.* 3.7.2; trans. Barkley, 65.

180. The *Letter of the Churches of Lyons and Vienne* is preserved in Eusebius, HE 5.1. 3–63; here at 5.1.35; trans. Lake, 1:423. See the important article by Annick Lallemand, "Le Parfum des martyrs dans les Actes des martyrs de Lyon et le Martyre de Polycarpe," in SP 16.2, ed. E.A. Livingstone, TU 129 (Berlin: Akademie Verlag, 1985), 186–92. For a wider ranging survey of the theme, including intriguing Islamic examples, see also Suzanne Evans, "The Scent of a Martyr," *Numen* 49 (2002): 193–211.

181. See chapter 2, p. 71–72.

182. *Odes of Solomon* 11.15.

183. The bibliography is vast. See, for example, James L. Kuegel, *In Potiphar's House: The Interpretive Life of Biblical Texts*, 2nd ed. (Cambridge, MA: Harvard University Press, 1994); Michael Stone and Theodore A. Bergren, eds., *Biblical Figures Outside the Bible* (Harrisburg, PA: Trinity Press International, 1998); and Gary A. Anderson, *The Genesis of Perfection: Adam and Eve in Jewish and Christian Imagination* (Louisville, KY: Westerminster John Knox, 2001).

184. 1 Enoch 24.3–5; trans. E. Isaac, in *Old Testament Pseudepigrapha*, ed. Charlesworth, 1:26. For discussion on the textual versions of the geographical passages as they indicate ancient conceptions of the earthly location of paradise, see J. T. Milik, "Hénoch au pays des aromates," *RB* 65 (1958): 70–77.

185. 1 Enoch 25.4–6; trans. Isaac, in *Old Testament Pseudepigrapha*, ed. Charlesworth, 1:26.

186. The odd conjoining of stench and fragrance in a paradisical context is also found in Herodotus, *Histories* 3.107–12, where he cites the extraordinary marvel that laudanum, sweetest of perfume spices, becomes entangled while growing in the horridly stinking beards of he-goats. In both cases, the extremes are juxtaposed to heighten the sense of strangeness and wonder. See the interesting discussion in François Hartog, *The Mirror of Herodotus: The Representation of the Other in the Writing of History*, trans. Janet Lloyd (Berkeley: University of California Press, 1988), 232–33.

187. 1 Enoch 32.3–6; trans. Isaac, in *Old Testament Pseudepigrapha*, ed. Charlesworth, 1:28.

188. I follow the translations by M. D. Johnson in *Old Testament Pseudepigrapha*, ed. Charlesworth, 2:249–95. Johnson has conveniently set the Greek Apocalypse and the Latin *vita* in parallel columns. See also the important evidence from the

Armenian and Georgian versions included in Gary A. Anderson and Michael E. Stone, eds., *A Synopsis of the Books of Adam and Eve*, 2nd ed. (Atlanta, GA: Scholars Press, 1999).

189. *Life of Adam and Eve* 36:1–2; trans. Johnson, in *Old Testament Pseudepigrapha*, ed. Charlesworth, 2:272.

190. *Life of Adam and Eve* 40–43.

191. *Apoc.* 22–29; trans. Johnson, in *Old Testament Pseudepigrapha*, ed. Charlesworth, 2:285.

192. *Apoc.* 33.3–5; trans. Johnson, in *Old Testament Pseudepigrapha*, ed. Charlesworth, 2:289. The speakers in this passage switch without identification, but this portion seems to be written as though Eve were speaking.

193. *Apoc.* 38:1–4; trans. Johnson, in *Old Testament Pseudepigrapha*, ed. Charlesworth, 2:291.

194. *Apoc.* 40; trans. Johnson, in *Old Testament Pseudepigrapha*, ed. Charlesworth, 2:291–93.

195. *Martyrdom of Perpetua and Felicitas*, sec. 13; ed. and trans. Musurillo, *Acts of the Christian Martyrs*, 106–31, at p. 123.

196. For the intertextuality of these traditions, see Frithiof Rundgren, "*Odor Suavitatis*: On the Phenomenon of Intertextuality," *OS* 36–37 (1987–88): 85–97.

197. *Ode* 11:14–15; trans. Charlesworth, *Odes of Solomon*, 49–59.

198. The story of Joseph and Aseneth has received a major reassessment in the recent study by Ross Shepard Kraemer, *When Aseneth Met Joseph: A Late Antique Tale of the Biblical Patriarch and His Egyptian Wife, Reconsidered* (New York: Oxford University Press, 1998). Where previous scholarship tended to favor a first century C.E. dating and a Jewish origin, Kraemer argues here for a fourth-century C.E. date and a Christian origin. I follow the translation Kraemer provided in her collection, *Women's Religions in the Greco-Roman Worlds: A Sourcebook* (New York: Oxford University Press, 2004), 308–27.

199. *Aseneth*, 8.4; trans. Kraemer, 315.

200. *Aseneth*, 15.4–17.3; trans. Kraemer, 321–24.

201. Detienne, *Gardens of Adonis*, 29–36. The legend appears in Egyptian and Sanskrit texts, and from the time of Herodotus (*Histories* 2.73) in various Greek and Latin authors.

202. Lactantius, *The Phoenix*, trans. McDonald, *Lactantius: Minor Works*, 207–20, at p. 216. The authorship is disputed although the ascription to Lactantius is found in ancient texts; there is no overt allusion of any kind in the poem to Christianity.

203. E.g., *1 Clement* 25.2, trans. Lake, *Apostolic Fathers* 1:1–122, at 52–53; Lactantius, *The Phoenix*; Ambrose of Milan, *On the Decease of his Brother Satyrus*, bk. 2, *On Belief in the Resurrection*, 59, trans. de Romestin, NPNF, 2nd ser., 10:183.

Chapter 2. The Christian Body

1. Romanos, "On the Nativity (2) (Adam and Eve)," *Kontakion* 2.6; trans. Carpenter, 1:17.

2. To take two of the most important examples: Averil Cameron, *Christianity and the Rhetoric of Empire: The Development of Christian Discourse* (Berkeley: University of California Press, 1991); Paul Bradshaw, *The Search for the Origins of Christian Worship: Sources and Methods for the Study of Early Liturgy*, 2nd ed. (New York: Oxford University Press, 2002).

3. The earliest law against pagan sacrifice dated from Constantine's reign, on Dec. 17, 321. A comprehensive law of Theodosius I, Arcadius, and Honorius from Nov. 8, 392, forbid not only public sacrifice, but domestic cult as well, specifying prohibitions on candles, incense, and wreaths: *Theodosian Code*, 16.10.12. The sequence of imperial legislation against paganism from 321 through 435 is collected in Book 16 of the Theodosian Code. This legislation is discussed with scrupulous care in Frank Trombley, *Hellenic Religion and Christianization, c. 370–529*, 2nd ed. (Boston/Leiden: Brill Academic Publishers, 2001), 1:1–97. For further helpful discussion on the problems of tracking "Christianization" through the legal evidence, see David Hunt, "Christianizing the Roman Empire: The Evidence of the Code," in *The Theodosian Code*, ed. Jill Harries and Ian Wood, (Ithaca, NY: Cornell University Press, 1993), 143–58. On the Christianization of civic time, similarly, see Angelo Di Berardino, "Liturgical Celebrations and Imperial Legislation in the Fourth Century," in *Prayer and Spirituality in the Early Church*, vol. 3, *Liturgy and Life*, ed. Bronwen Neil, Geoffrey D. Dunn, and Lawrence Cross (Sydney: St. Paul's Publications, 2003), 211–32.

4. The brief reign of the emperor Julian "the Apostate," for nineteen months in 360–62, was the momentary reversal of fortune in this process. The bitter fear of the Christian response to Julian and what he represented continued well into the fifth century; Cyril of Alexandria, for one, wrote a defense against Julian's critique of Christianity, more than seventy years after the emperor's untimely death. Although at the time people could not have understood the finality of Julian's place as the "last pagan emperor," circumstances had already changed sufficiently that Julian was limited in the anti-Christian measures he could take. See now the discussion of religious identity in Vasiliki Limberis, "'Religion' as the Cipher for Identity: The Cases of Emperor Julian, Libanius, and Gregory of Nazianzus," *HTR* 93 (2000): 373–400; on Julian's critique of Christianity, see esp. Robert Wilken, *The Christians as the Romans Saw Them*, 2nd ed. (New Haven: Yale University Press, 2003), 164–96.

5. Cameron, *Christianity and the Rhetoric of Empire*.

6. See now the fine study by Michael Gaddis, *'There is no Crime for Those Who Have Christ': Religious Violence in the Christian Roman Empire* (Berkeley: University of California Press, 2005).

7.   The shift in sensibility is discussed with considerable insight in Béatrice Caseau, "Christian Bodies: The Senses and Early Byzantine Christianity," in *Desire and Denial in Byzantium*, ed. Liz James (Aldershot, Hampshire: Ashgate Publishing, 1999), 101–109.

8.   As in the *Odes of Solomon*, an especially beautiful example.

9.   As discussed in chapter 1, pp. 42–44.

10. Basil, *On the Hexaemeron*, Hom. 1; trans. Way, *Saint Basil, Exegetical Homilies*, at pp. 12, 19. Basil's *On the Hexaemeron* became paradigmatic for Byzantine attitudes towards the created order. See Cyril Mango, *Byzantium: The Empire of New Rome* (London: Weidenfeld and Nicolson, 1980), 166–76.

11. Gregory of Nyssa, *On the Making of Man* 2.1; trans. Moore and Wilson, NPNF, 2nd ser., 5:390.

12. Ephrem, *Hymns on Virginity* 20.12; trans. McVey, *Ephrem the Syrian, Hymns*, 348–49.

13. Ephrem often speaks of scripture and the natural world as the two witnesses to God; or of scripture, nature, and incarnation as the three forms by which knowledge of God is revealed. Summaries may be found in Sebastian P. Brock, *The Luminous Eye: The Spiritual World Vision of Saint Ephrem the Syrian* (Kalamazoo: Cistercian Publications, 1992), 40–43, 53–84; and idem, *St. Ephrem the Syrian, Hymns on Paradise* (Crestwood, NY: St. Vladimir's Seminary Press, 1990) 41–45.

14. Ephrem, *Hymns on Virginity* 27–30.

15. A favorite image of Ephrem's, as in *Hymns on Virginity* 20.12, cited above. See Sidney H. Griffith, "The Image of the Image Maker in the Poetry of St. Ephrem the Syrian," SP 25, ed. Elizabeth A. Livingstone (Leuven: Peeters Press, 1993) 258–69.

16. Ephrem, *Hymns on Virginity* 6.7–8; trans. McVey, *Ephrem the Syrian, Hymns*, 290.

17. Ephrem, *Hymns on Faith* 18 is a particularly well-known example. See P. Yousif, "St. Ephrem on Symbols in Nature: Faith, the Trinity, and the Cross (Hymns on Faith, No. 18)," ECR 10 (1978): 52–60; idem, "Le Symbolisme de la croix dans la nature chez Saint Éphrem de Nisibe," in *Symposium Syriacum 1976*, ed. René Lavenant, OCA 205 (Rome: Pontificum Institutum Studiorum Orientalium, 1978), 207–27.

18. Basil, *On the Hexaemeron*, Hom. 5.2; trans. Way, *Saint Basil, Exegetical Homilies*, 69.

19. Ephrem, *Hymns on Virginity* 29.

20. Prudentius, *Hymn* 11.61–76; trans. Eagan, *The Poems of Prudentius*, at pp. 80–81. Compare Maximus of Turin in his *Sermon* 56, "On Pentecost": "Indeed, as the result of Christ's resurrection the air is healthier, the sun warmer, and the earth more fertile. As a result of it the young branch comes into leaf, the green stalks grow into fruit, and the vine ripens into vine sprouts. If all things, then, are clothed in flowers when the flesh of Christ blossoms anew, then it must be the

case that when it bears fruit, everything else must bear fruit as well." Trans. Ramsey, 234–37.

21. Ephrem, *Hymns on Faith* 81.9. See now Edward G. Mathews, Jr., "St. Ephrem, Madrashe on Faith, 81–5: Hymns on the Pearl, I–V," *SVTQ* 38 (1994): 45–72.

22. Ephrem, *Hymns on Faith* 14.5 (my trans.). In his *Baptismal Instructions*, John Chrysostom presents a similar notion of baptism creating the body anew, but his imagery dwells on the sense of sight. See especially his 4th *Instruction*, sec. 14.

23. Ephrem, *Hymns on Virginity* 31.16; trans. McVey, *Ephrem the Syrian, Hymns*, 401. For Ephrem's presentation of the senses and theory of their modes of perception, see now Ute Possekel, *Evidence of Greek Philosophical Concepts in the Writings of Ephrem the Syrian*, CSCO 580/Sub. 102 (Louvain: Peeters Press, 1999), 186–229. Possekel focuses most closely on Ephrem's treatment of sight and hearing, as being his dominant concern in terms of the senses; however, she also primarily draws on his *Prose Refutations*, which in this matter would appear to differ from the full sensory imagination employed in his hymns. See further in the present chapter; chapter 3, pp. 132–34; and chapter 6, pp. 235–39.

24. Cyril of Jerusalem, *Catechetical Homilies*; trans. McCauley and Stephenson, *The Works of Saint Cyril of Jerusalem*. This point is discussed at length in chapter 3.

25. Cyril, *Cat. Hom.* 4.22; trans. McCauley and Stephenson, 1:130.

26. Cyril, *Cat. Hom.* 18.19–20; trans. McCauley and Stephenson, 2:131.

27. Ephrem, *Hymns on Virginity* 35:12; trans. McVey, *Ephrem the Syrian, Hymns*, 419.

28. Ephrem, *Hymns on Virginity* 37.2. Cf. Gregory of Nyssa on the digestion of the sacramental bread and wine in his *Catechetical Oration*, ch. 37; trans. Srawley, 107–12. For a thorough treatment of Ephrem on the Eucharist, see Pierre Yousif, *L'Eucharistie chez Saint Éphrem de Nisibe*, OCA 224 (Rome: Pontificum Institutum Studiorum Orientalum, 1984).

29. Ephrem, *Hymns on Nativity* 28.7; trans. McVey, *Ephrem the Syrian, Hymns*, 216. The "garment" here is the garment of flesh, the body, Christ took from Mary.

30. Augustine's *Confessions*, of course, are an extended exposition on this theme.

31. Cyril, *Cat. Hom.* 4.23; trans. McCauley and Stephenson, 1:130–31.

32. Ephrem, *Hymns on Nisibis* 69.3, 5. Trans. Brock, *Harp of the Spirit*, 77.

33. Augustine, *Confessions* 10.27.38; trans. Chadwick, 201.

34. As they are elsewhere in early Christian literature, for example, in the *Martyrdom of Polycarp* 15.2.

35. Ephrem, *Hymns on Nativity* 16:15.

36. Ephrem, *Hymns on Virginity* 19.1; trans. McVey, *Ephrem the Syrian, Hymns*, 341.

37. Thus the terminology of Genesis 2:7 follows a different set of lexical roots. The Peshitta reads *nshamta d-haye*, "breath of life," the same reading Ephrem knew. See Ephrem's *Commentary on Genesis*, sec. 2.4.

38. Ephrem, *Hymns on Paradise* 11.14, on Acts 2:1–4; trans. Brock, 159.

39. Ephrem, *Hymns on Nativity* 15.11.

40. Syriac writers knew a tradition that the Apostles experienced the presence of a fragrance at Pentecost. Modern scholars are not agreed on the tradition's source: cf. Witold Witakowski, "The Origin of the 'Teaching of the Apostles,'" *IV Symposium Syriacum*, ed. H. J. W. Drijvers, R. Lavenant, C. Molenberg, and G. J. Reinink, OCA 229 (Rome: Pontificum Institutum Studiorum Orientalium, 1987), 161–71; Frithiof Rundgren, "*Odor Suavitatis*: On the Phenomenon of Intertextuality," OS 36–37 (1987–1988): 85–97.

41. Han J. W. Drijvers and Jan Willem Drijvers, *The Finding of the True Cross: The Judas Kyriakos Legend in Syriac*, CSCO 565/Sub. 93 (Louvain: Peeters Press, 1997), 64–67.

42. *Life of Melania the Younger* 6; trans. Clark, 30.

43. Gregory the Great, *Dialogues* 3.30 (rededication of a formerly Arian church), 4.17 (holy death); Jerome, *Life of Hilarion* 46 (relics); Lucian, *On the Revelation of St. Stephen* (relics); Evagrius Scholasticus, *Eccl. Hist.* 2.3 (relics).

44. *Acts of Thomas* 55; trans. Drijvers in *New Testament Apocrypha*, ed. Schneemelcher, 2:362.

45. *Life of Daniel the Stylite* ch. 33.

46. John Moschus, *Spiritual Meadow* 106: Abba Theodulos and the Syrian monk.

47. The predominance of these two sensory images in Christian tradition has long been recognized. A fresh evaluation of these images as specifically sensory ones may be found in David Chidester, *Word and Light: Seeing, Hearing, and Religious Discourse* (Urbana/Chicago: University of Illinois Press, 1992).

48. Basil, *On the Hexaemeron*, Homily 6.11; trans. Way, *Saint Basil, Exegetical Homilies*, 103.

49. Late antique Christian writers constantly allude to the liturgy when writing about the senses and sensory experience. Extremely helpful for understanding the pervasive presence of "the ritual body" in a religious culture is Catherine Bell, *Ritual Theory, Ritual Practice* (New York/Oxford: Oxford University Press, 1992), 94–117. There is also a very interesting discussion in Theodore W. Jennings, "On Ritual Knowledge," JR 62 (1982): 111–27.

50. A useful summary may be found in Jeffrey John, "Anointing in the New Testament," in *The Oil of Gladness: Anointing in the Christian Tradition*, ed. Martin Dudley and Geoffrey Rowell (London: SPCK, 1993), 46–76. Also helpful are the two following chapters of the same volume, "Anointing in the Early Church" by John Halliburton, pp. 77–91; and "Anointing in the Syriac Tradition," by Sebastian P. Brock, pp. 92–100.

51. However, the Sinful Woman and her perfume become a favorite theme in late antique hymns and homilies, and a rich expansion of the olfactory imagery ensues. The material will be treated in chapter 3, pp. 148–55.

52. Edward Yarnold, *The Awe-Inspiring Rites of Initiation: The Origins of the RCIA*, 2nd ed. (Collegeville, MN: Liturgical Press, 1994), provides a lucid overview.

53. Paul Bradshaw, *The Search for the Origins of Christian Worship*, is an indispensable guide to the primary sources and the scholarly debates surrounding them.

54. Hippolytus, *Apostolic Tradition* 5. The Blessing of the Oil is immediately followed by the Blessing of Cheese and Olives. The sequence makes it hard to assess the status of the oil in relation to the eucharistic bread and wine, for it is not the only additional substance to be blessed.

55. Hippolytus, *Apostolic Tradition* 21.6–8.

56. Hippolytus, *Apostolic Tradition* 21.10.

57. Hippolytus, *Apostolic Tradition* 21.19–22.3.

58. Tertullian, On Baptism 7.

59. *Gospel of Philip* 22, 41, 58, 59, 60, 67, 72, 80, 83, 84, 94, 106; trans. Layton, Gnostic Scriptures, 325–53.

60. *Gospel of Philip* 67, 83; trans. Layton, Gnostic Scriptures, 343, 346.

61. *Gospel of Philip* 94; trans. Layton, Gnostic Scriptures, 348–49.

62. The understanding of chrism and its "spiritual perfume" in the *Gospel of Philip* echoes the theme of God's fragrance as the means by which he and his believers are known in the related *Gospel of Truth*, sections 5 and 7; trans. Layton, Gnostic Scriptures, 250–64. These passages will be discussed further in chapter 3. The *Gospel of Truth* may be Valentinus's most brilliant rhetorical achievement; the *Gospel of Philip* was produced later from his school. It is interesting that the *Gospel of Philip* (22, 58) associates chrism and fire, a combination appearing also in the fourth- or fifth-century Syriac *Acts of John*. See A. F. J. Klijn, "An Ancient Syriac Baptismal Liturgy in the Syriac Acts of John," NT 6 (1963): 216–28 and in Charis kai Sophia, Festschrift Karl Heinrich Rengstorf, ed. Ulrich Luck (Leiden: Brill, 1964), 216–28. For a related tradition on the holy fire motif, see Sebastian P. Brock, "Fire from Heaven: From Abel's Sacrifice to the Eucharist. A Theme in Syriac Christianity," SP 25, ed. Elizabeth A. Livingstone (Leuven: Peeters Press, 1993): 229–43.

63. *Acts of Thomas*, ch. 27, 51.

64. *Acts of Thomas*, ch. 5; trans. Drijvers in New Testament Apocrypha, ed. Schneemelcher, 2:341.

65. The Coptic insertion is a notorious bone of contention for scholars of the Didache. The problems and debates are laid out in Kurt Niederwimmer, *The Didache: A Commentary*, ed. Harold W. Attridge, trans. Linda M. Maloney (Minneapolis: Fortress Press, 1998), esp. 165–67. See also Arthur Vööbus, Liturgical Traditions in the Didache, PETSE 16 (Stockholm: ETSE, 1968) 41–60. An interesting hypothesis for the insertion was offered in Stephen Gero, "The So-Called Ointment Prayer in the Coptic Version of the Didache: A Re-Evaluation," HTR 70 (1977): 67–84, where the author argues that the Coptic term for myron in this text—itself an unstable reading—in fact refers to incense. I will return to this thesis. Gero's hypothesis has not received general acceptance by scholars, although it has received extensive scholarly discussion and appreciation.

66. Even in the fourth century, it is difficult to tell from liturgical texts whether oil is being consecrated for baptism or for the sick. For an example, see G.J. Cuming, "Thmuis Revisited: Another Look at the Prayers of Bishop Sarapion," TS 41 (1980): 568–75.

67. *Apostolic Constitutions* 7.27.1–2 and 44.2. See the discussion in Vööbus, *Liturgical Traditions*, 46–50.

68. In addition to Yarnold, *Awe-Inspiring Rites*, see Aidan Kavanaugh, *The Shape of Baptism: The Rite of Christian Initiation* (New York: Pueblo Press, 1978), 3–78; and Hugh M. Riley, *Christian Initiation: A Comparative Study of the Interpretation of the Baptismal Liturgy in the Mystagogical Writings of Cyril of Jerusalem, John Chrysostom, Theodore of Mopsuestia, and Ambrose of Milan* (Washington, DC: Catholic University of America Press, 1974). For the notably contrasting traditions of the Syriac sources, see, e.g., A. F. J. Klijn, "An Ancient Syriac Baptismal Liturgy;" Sebastian P. Brock, *The Holy Spirit in the Syrian Baptismal Tradition*, Syrian Churches Series 9, 2nd ed. (Poona: Anita Printers, 1998); idem, "Some Early Syriac Baptismal Commentaries," OCP 46 (1980): 20–61; Charles Munier, "Initiation Chrétienne et Rites d'Onction (II–IIIe Siècles)," and "Rites d'Onction Baptême Chrétien et Baptême de Jésus," both in RSR 4 (1990): 115–25 and 217–34 respectively; B. Varghese, *Les onctions baptismales dans la tradition syrienne*, CSCO 512/Subs. 82 (Louvain: Peeters Press, 1989).

69. Although the use of blessed oil to anoint the sick was commonplace throughout late antique Christianity, no official "rite" for anointing the sick was established. See, e.g., Halliburton, "Anointing in the Early Church;" and Lizette Larson-Miller, "Women and the Anointing of the Sick," CCR 12 (1991): 37–48.

70. Once again, a very helpful survey of methods and schools of thought can be found in Bradshaw, *The Search for the Origins of Christian Worship*, 144–70.

71. Cyril, *Mystagogical Lectures* 2.3; trans. McCauley and Stephenson, 2:163. Debate on the authorship of this work has been fierce. The evidence in favor of Cyril's authorship seems now definitively argued in Alexis James Doval, *Cyril of Jerusalem, Mystagogue: The Authorship of the Mystagogic Catecheses*, Patristic Monograph Series 17 (Washington, DC: Catholic University of America Press, 2001).

72. John Chrysostom, *Baptismal Instructions* 2.24; trans. Harkins, 52. See also 11.27: "The devil will not dare to look upon such a sight. . . . you will be able to hold the serpent in check." Trans. Harkins, at p. 169.

73. Theodore, *Cat. Hom.* 13.18. (Note that the edition of Tonneau and Devreesse follows a different numbering of the homilies than the translation by Mingana. I have followed the numbering in Tonneau and Devreesse in my citations.) The imagery is shared in the three anonymous Syriac commentaries from the fifth–seventh centuries edited and translated in Sebastian P. Brock, "Some Early Syriac Baptismal Commentaries," OCP 46 (1980): 20–61, at pp. 36–39; these also have the imagery of the imprint (= tattoo) on the imperial soldier, as found in Theodore. See below, n. 77.

74. Gregory of Nazianzus, Or. 40, *On Holy Baptism*; trans. Browne and Swallow, NPNF, 2nd ser., 7:360–77.

75. Ambrose, *Sacraments* 2.(4); trans. Deferrari, *Saint Ambrose*, 270.

76. Brock, "Some Early Syriac Baptismal Commentaries," 40–41.

77. Theodore, *Cat. Hom.* 13.17–19. Gregory of Nazianzus also likens it to the brand on a sheep: Or. 40.15.

78. Brock, *Holy Spirit*, 44–46. See Yarnold, *Awe-Inspiring Rites*, 178.

79. Ephrem, *Hymns on Virginity* 7.6; Brock, *Holy Spirit*, 149–51.

80. Theodore, *Cat. Hom.* 14.8; trans. Mingana, Woodbrooke Studies 6:54.

81. E.g., John Chrysostom, *Baptismal Instructions* 4; Theodore, *Cat. Hom.* 15; Brock, "Some Early Syriac Baptismal Commentaries," 44–45.

82. This aspect is discussed with great insight by Jean Daniélou, *The Bible and the Liturgy* (Notre Dame, IN: University of Notre Dame Press, 1956), 114–26. In western rites, then, the myron is specifically associated with confirmation. Significantly, post-baptismal anointment seems to have been unknown in Syriac tradition prior to the very end of the fourth century. Eventually the west Syrians also took up the use of myron (scented in their case with a single spice, balsam) for the post-baptismal anointing, but East Syriac tradition used only olive oil. Only from the thirteenth century onwards did the west Syrians adopt the practice from the Copts of adding multiple spices to the myron. See Brock, *Holy Spirit*, 47; idem, "Anointing in the Syriac Tradition." For an argument that some Syrian groups practiced a post-baptismal anointing from a very early date, see Alistair Logan, "Post-Baptismal Chrismation in Syria: The Evidence of Ignatius, the Didache, and the Apostolic Constitutions," JTS, n.s., 49 (1998): 92–108.

83. Ambrose, *Sacraments* 1; Cyril, *Mystagogical Lectures* 3. Compare the anonymous Syriac commentaries that explain the post-baptismal anointing with myron: "because [the initiate] receives a sweet and spiritual scent by means of the imprint." Brock, "Some Early Syriac Baptismal Commentaries," 42–43.

84. Ambrose, *Sacraments* 1.(3); trans. Deferrari, *St. Ambrose*, 270.

85. Cyril, *Mystagogical Lectures* 3.4; trans. McCauley and Stephenson, 2:171–72.

86. John Chrysostom, *Baptismal Instructions* 11.27; trans. Harkins, 169.

87. Dionysius, *Ecclesiastical Hierarchy* 3.404C–D.

88. Dionysius, *Ecclesiastical Hierarchy* 4.477C.

89. A formidable challenge to the standard scholarly treatment of Dionysius's thought has been mounted for some time now in the publications of Alexander Golitzin, who has argued forcefully to contextualize the Neoplatonism of Dionysius's system within the native Syrian traditions in which he lived and wrote. See especially Golitzin, *Et Introibo ad Altare Dei: The Mystagogy of Dionysius Areopagita, with special reference to its predecessors in the eastern Christian tradition*, Analecta Vlatadon 59 (Thessalonika: Patriarchikon Idryma Paterikon Meleton, 1994);

and, e.g., idem, "A Contemplative and a Liturgist: Father Georges Florovsky on the Corpus Dionysiacum," *SVTQ* 43 (1999): 131–61.

90. Cyril of Jerusalem, *Procatechesis* 1; trans. McCauley and Stephenson, 1:69–70.

91. Cyril of Jerusalem, *Catechetical Homilies* 13, 14; trans. McCauley and Stephenson, 2:4–52. The conjunction of marital and sacrificial imagery was a familiar one in Christian homiletics. See also, e.g., Ambrose, *Sacraments* 6, 7, 9.

92. Cyril, *Mystagogical Lectures* 3; Cyril seems to use the terms *chrisma* and *myron* interchangeably here, as does Chrysostom in his *Baptismal Instructions*.

93. Cyril, *Mystagogical Lectures*, 3.(3); trans. McCauley and Stephenson, 2:170–71. Compare an anonymous baptismal address, perhaps of the late fifth century, preserved in Syriac: "Do you, therefore, receive the sweet scent of the myron, leaving nothing that smells foul in yourself. It is not physical (lit. bodily) myron that (the minister) is anointing you with, made with costly preparation like the (myron) that anointed Aaron; nor is it with myrrh, cinnamon, iris and sweet scented cane, compounded by cosmetic skill, that they are going to anoint you for 'a sweet scent' as is fitting. No, it is with myron that he is going to anoint you, that heavenly and divine myron, whose anointing the Lord himself received on his body." "A Baptismal Address Attributed to Athanasius," ed. and trans. Sebastian P. Brock, OC 61 (1977): 92–102, sec. 10–11, at p. 101.

94. Cyril, *Mystagogical Lectures* 3.(7); trans. McCauley and Stephenson, 2:173.

95. John Chrysostom, *Baptismal Instructions* 6.22–3; trans. Harkins, 101–102.

96. John Chrysostom, *Baptismal Instructions* 10.17; trans. Harkins, 155.

97. Ephrem, *Hymns on Virginity* 4–7.

98. *Hymns on Virginity* 4.5–6.

99. *Hymns on Virginity* 4.11. Ephrem here seems to conflate the anointing by the Sinful Woman with that by Mary of Bethany.

100. John Chrysostom, "Homily on the Martyrs," trans. Mayer and Allen, *John Chrysostom*, 93–97, at p. 96.

101. See L. Petit, "Du pouvoir de consacrer le Saint Chrême," and "Composition et consécration du Saint Chrême," *Échoes d'Orient* 3 (1899): 1–7, 129–42. For the significance in the later Byzantine Empire, see D.M. Nichol, "*Kaiseralbung*. The Unction of Emperors in Late Byzantine Coronation Ritual," *BMGS* 2 (1976): 37–52; and Christopher Walter, "The Significance of Unction in Byzantine Iconography," *BMGS* 2 (1976): 53–74. Present-day Greek Orthodox practice has the Holy Myrrh prepared approximately once every ten years, under the direction of the Ecumenical Patriarch of Constantinople and with the participation of numerous church hierarchs. In this manner, Holy Myrrh was prepared and consecrated in May 2002, at the Phanar in Constantinople (*Orthodox Observer*, April 2002, 6).

102. Paulinus of Nola, *Poem* 33; trans. Walsh, 340–41.

103. Gregory of Nazianzus, Or. 40.38; trans. Browne and Swallow, NPNF, 2nd ser., 7:374.

104. E. G. F. C. Atchley, *History of the Use of Incense in Divine Worship*, Alcuin Club Collections 13 (London: Longmans, Green, and Co., 1909), 97. Tertullian, *Apology* 42, and *On Idolatry* 11, had noted the commonality of Christian use of myrrh and frankincense in burial practices, as discussed above, chapter 1, p. 36.

105. A sixth-century Syriac liturgical guide for a bishop's entry into a city may be seen in E. Khouri-Sarkis, "Réception d'un évêque syrien au VIe siècle," *L'Orient Syrien* 2 (1957): 137–84. Incense was offered at several points during the rite.

106. Sozomen, *Eccl. Hist.* 2.4, 5.17; Philostorgius, *Eccl. Hist.* 1.17 (epitome of Photius).

107. The importance of processions as a feature of late antique city life has been studied by a number of scholars. For liturgy, however, the issues are treated with great insight by Robert Taft, "Toward the Origins of the Offertory Procession in the Syro-Byzantine East," *OCP* 36 (1970): 73–107; idem, "The Liturgy of the Great Church: An Initial Synthesis of Structure and Interpretation on the Eve of Iconoclasm," *DOP* 34–35 (1980–81): 45–75; idem, *A History of the Liturgy of St. John Chrysostom*, vol. 2, *The Great Entrance: A History of the Transfer of Gifts and Other Pre-anaphoral Rites*, 2nd ed., OCA 200 (Rome: Pontificum Institutum Studiorum Orientalium, 1978); Thomas F. Mathews, *The Early Churches of Constantinople: Architecture and Liturgy* (University Park, PA: Pennsylvania State University Press, 1971); idem, "'Private' Liturgy in Byzantine Architecture: Toward a Reappraisal," *CA* 30 (1982): 125–38 [= idem, *Art and Architecture in Byzantium and Armenia: Liturgical and Exegetical Approaches* (Brookfield, VT: Variorum, 1995), ch. 3]. Thomas Mathews has offered trenchant critique of the standard art-historical interpretation of Christian procession in liturgy and art as a prime example of borrowing from imperial ceremonial; Mathews looks instead to anti-imperial themes in the depiction of Christ's Entry into Jerusalem—a favorite scene of late antique Christian artists—and to important gospel and liturgical emphases that procession expressed both in ritual and in art. See Thomas Mathews, *The Clash of the Gods: A Reinterpretation of Early Christian Art*, rev. ed. (Princeton: Princeton University Press, 1999), 3–53. For the imperial traditions in their late antique context, see esp. Sabine MacCormack, *Art and Ceremony in Late Antiquity* (Berkeley: University of California Press, 1981); Michael MacCormick, *Eternal Victory* (Cambridge: Cambridge University Press, 1986).

108. The indispensible study remains John F. Baldovin, *The Urban Character of Christian Worship: The Origins, Development, and Meaning of Stational Liturgy*, OCA 228 (Rome: Pontificum Institutum Studiorum Orientalium, 1987).

109. On processions as an organizing principal of early Christian church iconography, and common pagan practices (including candles and incense)

providing models for early Christian icon veneration, see Mathews, *Clash of the Gods,* 150–90.

110. For a treatment of the shift to a public Christian presence as it affected urban topography and architecture, see the interesting discussion in Annabel Wharton, *Refiguring the Post Classical City: Dura Europos, Jerash, and Ravenna* (Cambridge: Cambridge University Press, 1995).

111. *The Book of Pontiffs (Liber Pontificalis)* 34. There is an excellent discussion in Caseau, "Euodia," 109–16.

112. Caseau, "Euodia," 109–16; Gero, "The So-Called Ointment Prayer." It is in fact the ubiquity of incense use for this purpose that underlies Gero's argument concerning the Coptic ointment prayer added to the *Didache.*

113. Eusbius, *Eccl. Hist.* 10.3–4.

114. Eusebius, *Eccl. Hist.* 10.4.68; trans. Oulton and Lawlor, 2:441.

115. The point is well argued in Paul Bradshaw, *Daily Prayer in the Early Church* (New York: Oxford University Press, 1982), 76–77, 112–13.

116. Egeria, *Travels* 24.10.

117. Ephrem, *Hymns on Nisibis* 17.4.4–6.

118. Ephrem, *Hymns on Julian Saba* 1–4.

119. *Apostolic Constitutions* 8.47.3. See the discussion in Gero, "The So-Called Ointment Prayer," at pp. 76–77.

120. *Syriac Life,* sec. 1, 2, 4, 112. See Doran, *Lives of Simeon Stylites.* The particular case of Simeon's associations with incense is discussed in detail in chapter 4, pp. 186–97.

121. Theodoret, *Questions on Exodus* 28.

122. E.g., G. Dix, *The Shape of the Liturgy* (London: A & C Black, 1945; repr. 1993), 425–30; R. Taft, *The Great Entrance,* 149–62; J. Mateos, *La célébration de la Parole dans la Liturgie byzantine: Étude historique,* OCA 191 (Rome: Pontificium Institutum Studiorum Orientalium, 1971), 135–39.

123. As discussed above, chapter 1, pp. 11–22.

124. Ephrem, *Hymns on Fasting* 9.7; *Hymns on Virginity* 42.31–33; *Hymns on Nisibis* 1.1, 9.5; *Hymns on Nativity* 2.18; *Commentary on Genesis* 3.2.2., 6.13.2.

125. *Hymns on Nisibis* 17.4 (my trans.).

126. *Hymns on Nativity* 22.27–28.

127. *Hymns on Virginity* 31.3–5; trans. McVey, *Ephrem the Syrian, Hymns,* 399. Cf. *Hymns on Nativity* 22.28.

128. For Ephrem's rendering of this classic Christian theme, see P. Yousif, "Le sacrifice et l'offrande chez Saint Éphrem de Nisibe," *Parole de l'Orient* 15 (1988/9): 21–40.

129. *Homily on Our Lord* 8.3; trans. Amar and Mathews, *St. Ephrem the Syrian: Selected Prose Works,* 285.

130. For discussion of the different positions on authorship, see J. Melki, "S. Ephrem le Syrien, un bilan de l'édition critique," *Parole de l'Orient* 11 (1983): at pp. 58–60. In his critical edition and translation of the *Hymns on Julian Saba*, Beck is inclined against Ephremian authorship, though he would place the collection as a whole in the first or second generation after Ephrem's death; CSCO 323/Scr. Syr. 141, p. xv. A reasoned and sustained argument for the authenticity of the first four hymns of the cycle will be found in Sidney H. Griffith, "Julian Saba, 'Father of the Monks' of Syria," JECS 2 (1994), at pp. 198–203.

131. Again, this would be one of our earliest references to Christian incense piety.

132. *Hymns on Julian Saba* 1.5 (my trans.).

133. *Hymns on Julian Saba* 4.2 (my trans.). Compare the related imagery in 7.18.

134. In a parallel passage, Ephrem speaks of writing his hymns on the three great bishops of Nisibis (Jacob, Babu, and Vologeses) as like unto the weaving of flowers into a crown: *Hymns on Nisibis* 17.2. Again, the image is of fragrance carrying and conveying the essence of truth.

135. *Hymns on Virginity* 11.14; trans. McVey, *Ephrem the Syrian, Hymns*, 309 (altered from "exhaled the scent of His vitality" for *riha d-hayuteh*).

136. *Riha d-hayuta. Hymns on Fasting* 4.6 (my trans.).

137. *Riha d-haye. Hymns on Nisibis* 39.19.

138. Basil, Homilies on Psalms 1.1; *Sayings of the Desert Fathers*, Anon. Ser., 1441; Regnault, *Les Sentences des pères du désert*, 146.

139. Augustine, *On Nature and Grace* 41; trans. Holmes, Wallis, and Warfield, NPNF 5:135; *Confessions*. 10.4.5; trans. Chadwick, 181.

140. Ephrem, *Hymns on Virginity* 42.31–32; trans. McVey, *Saint Ephrem, Hymns*, 440.

141. Ephrem, *Hymns on Paradise* 3.16; trans. Brock, 96.

142. John of Ephesus, *Lives of the Eastern Saints* 31, PO 18: 579 ('etra d-besme)(my trans.).

143. For incense as an accompaniment of pilgrimage piety, see Gary Vikan, *Byzantine Pilgrimage Art*, Dumbarton Oaks Byzantine Collection Publications 5 (Washington, DC: Dumbarton Oaks, 1982).

144. E.g., the *Life of Daniel the Stylite*, ch. 96; John of Ephesus, *Lives of the Eastern Saints* 55, at PO 19:196; John Moschus, *Spiritual Meadow* 57; Anahid of Persia, trans. Brock and Harvey, *Holy Women of the Syrian Orient*, at pp. 97–98. Antonius, *Life of Simeon the Stylite*, sec. 29, 31; *Syriac Life of Simeon*, sec. 116, 125, 126. (For the *Lives of Simeon the Stylite*, see Doran, *Lives of Simeon Stylites*.) For further discussion of Simeon the Stylite the Elder and Simeon the Stylite the Younger, see chapter 4.

145. E.g., the *Life of Theodore of Sykeon*, ch. 27, 36, 43, 45, 51, 52, 66, 72, 101, 114, 115; the *Chronicle of Zuqnin*, pt. 3, trans. Harrak, at p. 87. The case of Simeon the Sylite is discussed in chapter 4. Thus incense burned to a saint was not only

honorific, but also marked efficacy. Consider the Greek adage, "No one burns incense/for a saint who doesn't work miracles." Cited in Laurie Kain Hart, *Time, Religion and Social Experience in Rural Greece* (Landham, MD: Rowman and Littlefield, 1992), 194.

146. John Moschus, *Spiritual Meadow* 235.

147. *Chronicle of Zuqnin* 4 (720–21). Describing the Bishop Habib's prayer which would elicit an urgently needed speech from a corpse, the author writes: "[the bishop] kneeled down, prayed, stood up, and using incense, made fragrant the sweet odour of his heart's tears before the Saviour." Trans. Harrak, p. 154.

148. Gregory of Tours, *Book of Miracles of Saint Martin* 2.38.

149. E.g., *Papyri Graecae Magicae* 4.475–86, trans. Beard, North, and Price, *Religions of Rome*, 2:269–70; Marvin W. Meyer and Richard Smith, *Ancient Christian Magic: Coptic Texts of Ritual Power* (Princeton: Princeton University Press, 1999), 259–73, 275–92; J. G. Gager, ed., *Curse Tablets and Binding Spells from the Ancient World* (New York; Oxford University Press, 1992); Fritz Graf, *Magic in the Ancient World*, trans. Franklin Philip (Cambridge, MA: Harvard University Press, 1997), 106, 109–11; Jean-Louis Olive, "Parfums magiques et rites de fumigations en Catalogne (de l'ethnobotanique à la hantise de l'environnement)," in *Saveurs, Senteurs: Le Goût de la Méditerranée*, ed. Paul Carmignani, Jean-Yves Laurichesse, and Joël Thomas (Perpignon: Presses Universitaires, 1998), 145–95; Gary Vikan, "Art, Medicine, and Magic in Early Byzantium," DOP 38 (1984): 65–86, idem, "Art and Marriage in Early Byzantium," DOP 44 (1990): 145–63 [= idem, *Sacred Images and Sacred Power in Byzantium* (Aldershot, Hampshire: Ashgate Publishing, 2003), chs. 9 and 10, respectively]; Eunice Dauterman Maguire, Henry P. Maguire, and Maggie J. Duncan-Flowers, *Art and Holy Powers in the Early Christian House* (Urbana, IL: University of Illinois Press, 1989), 202; Christine Kondoleon, *Antioch: The Lost Ancient City* (Princeton: Princeton University Press, 2000), 162 (cat. item 49).

150. Compare the examples still in use in the nineteenth century amongst Assyrians: G. P. Badger, *The Nestorians and their Rituals* (London, 1852; repr. London: Darf Publishers, 1987), 1:24, 39.

151. Catherine Bell, *Ritual Theory, Ritual Practice*, forcefully articulates how the process of "ritualization" is a matter of differentiating some acts from others, and, in the context of religious ritual, of distinguishing sacred from profane. I will argue that the use of incense described in Christian narratives is a literary mechanism that enables "ritualization," which for these writers is a process specifically effected through identification with liturgical ritual.

152. Cyril of Alexandria, Letter 24, ACO 1, 1, 1, pp. 117–18.

153. For an excellent overview of how liturgical practices developed through late antiquity and into the Middle Ages, in both eastern and western Christianity, see Béatrice Caseau, "L'eucharistie au centre de la vie religieuse des communautés chrétiennes (fin du Ie—Xe siècle)," in *Encyclopedia eucharistia*, ed. Maurice Brouard (Paris: Édition du Cerf, 2001), 117–36.

154. Egeria, *Travels* 24–25.

155. Prudentius, *Hymns*, 5.13–24, 154–60; trans. Eagan, 29–38. Scholars debate the exact context of this hymn, whether it was written for evening vespers, or for the lighting of the Paschal candle on Easter night.

156. Gregory of Tours makes a similar point when he writes that miraculous substances appearing at the tombs of saints or martyrs, or plants and flowers blooming at the shrines, signify by their own paucity or abundance, frailty or lushness, whether or not a given harvest will be thin or plentiful. E.g., Gregory of Tours, *Glory of the Martyrs* 30, 90.

157. Gregory of Nazianzus, *Oration on his Brother, St. Caesarius* 16; John Chrysostom, *Commentary on John*, Homily 5.

158. Cf., e.g., the funeral descriptions for the Edessan martyrs: Shmona and Guria, sec. 66; Habib, sec. 38, 38A; ed. and trans. Burkitt, *Euphemia and the Goth with the Acts of Martyrdom of the Confessors of Edessa*. Compare the funeral for the Persian martyr Anahid, trans. Brock and Harvey, *Holy Women of the Syrian Orient*, at pp. 97–98. The funeral of St. Radegund is another case in point: Gregory of Tours, *Glory of the Confessors* 104.

159. *Acts of Thomas* 6–7; trans. Klijn, 67–68 (adapted).

160. Ephrem, *Hymns on the Nativity* 25.

161. Basil, *On the Hexaemeron*, Homily 2.1; trans. Way, *Saint Basil, Exegetical Homilies*, 21.

162. Gregory of Nyssa, *Commentary on the Song of Songs*, Hom. 1; trans. McCambley, 54.

163. Jerome, *Against Vigilantius* 4–7; trans. Fremantle, NPNF, 2nd ser., 6:418–20.

164. Andrew Palmer and Lyn Rodley, "The Inauguration anthem of Hagia Sophia in Edessa: A new edition and translation with historical and architectural notes and a comparison with a contemporary Constantinopolitan Kontakion," BMGS 12 (1988): 117–68. See at p. 143, verse 16: "Here sacrifices of the mind in spirit and in truth,/not in reeking smoke and streams of blood, are/offered untiringly as an odor of sweetness unto God."

165. Jacob of Serug, *Festal Homily* 6, "On the Baptism of our Redeemer in the Jordan," lines 1–13; trans. Kollamparampil, 162–63.

166. Paulinus of Nola, *Poem* 14; trans. Walsh, 77–81.

167. See especially Dennis Trout, "Christianizing the Nolan Countryside: Animal Sacrifice at the Tomb of St. Felix," JECS 3 (1995): 281–98. For further discussion, idem, *Paulinus of Nola: Life, Letters, and Poems* (Berkeley: University of California Press, 1999), 160–97.

168. Paulinus of Nola, *Poem* 25: "Our joy must be sober and our prayers unimpassioned . . . There must be no mob dancing in decorated streets. None must strew the ground with leaves or the threshold with foliage. There must be no crazed procession through a city where Christ dwells. I would have no secular display befoul devoted Christians. No wind must waft the scent of foreign ritual, for our entire proceedings must be redolent of the elegance of chastity.

Saintly people recognize as their sole perfume that sprinkled in Christ's name, which breathes forth the chaste fragrance of God." Trans. Walsh, 246. See also Paulinus, *Poems* 14, 18, 21, 33.

169. Prudentius, *Hymn* 10, "For the Burial of the Dead," and *The Martyrs' Crowns*, passim.

170. Consider the devoted widow of Lyons, who prided herself on her exemplary conduct at her husband's tomb: "I have always offered the most fragrant wine from Gaza in the sanctuary of my God on behalf of your [the husband's] repose." Gregory of Tours, *Glory of the Confessors* 64; trans. van Dam, 71.

171. Joshua the Stylite, *Chronicle* 30–31. For an excellent description of the events and rituals surrounding martyrs' festivals, see now Johan Leemans, Wendy Mayer, Pauline Allen, and Boudewijn Dehandschutter, ed. and trans., *'Let Us Die that We May Live': Greek Homilies on Christian Martyrs from Asia Minor, Palestine, and Syria* (c. A.D. 350–A.D. 450) (London: Routledge, 2003), 5–22 and passim.

172. John of Damascus, *On the Divine Images* 1.24; trans. Louth, 38.

173. John of Damascus, *On the Divine Images* 1.36; trans. Louth, 42–43.

174. John of Damascus, *On the Divine Images* 3.35; trans. Louth, 108–109.

175. *The Synodicon in the West Syrian Tradition*, ed. and trans. Arthur Vööbus, CSCO 367–68/Scr. Syr. 161–62 (Louvain: Secretariat du CorpusSCO, 1975): [XL] Resolutions of Johannon to Sargis, 15, 45; [XLVIII] Resolutions of Ja'qob of Urhai to Johannon, 1–5.

176. See chapter 1, pp. 50–52, especially on the *Life of Adam*.

177. E.g., Hesychius of Jerusalem, *Homily* 11, on Lazarus, 1.

178. Ambrose, *Sacraments* 1.3; trans. Deferrari, *Saint Ambrose*, 6.

179. Cyril of Jerusalem, *Cat. Hom.* 16.16; trans. McCauley and Stephenson, 2:85. The image remains classic for Christian tradition: Jonathan Edwards attributed "beauty and sweetness" to the Holy Spirit, following the type of the holy oil mandated in Exodus 30:25. See Jonathan Edwards, *Religious Affections*, ed. John E. Smith (New Haven: Yale University Press, 1959) 3.2, p. 201. An especially beautiful rendering is given by the twentieth-century Romanian theologian Dumitru Staniloae: "The chrism symbolizes in the most adequate way possible the fluidity of the Holy Spirit extending into all the parts of the ecclesial organism. He spreads out like an oil, but more especially like a perfume. Whoever receives the Holy Spirit in the Church receives him in the form of a fluid or a fragrance, a breath of life spreading out from him into all the other members of the Church, binding him to them and thereby sustaining the whole organism and its sobornicity." Dumitru Staniloae, *Theology and the Church*, trans. Robert Barringer (Crestwood, NY: St. Vladimir's Seminary Press, 1980), 69.

180. Gregory of Tours, *Book of Miracles* 1.9; trans. van Dam, *Saints and Their Miracles in Late Antique Gaul*, 210.

181. Piacenza Pilgrim, *Travels*, sec. 7 (incubation of lepers), sec. 18, sec. 20, sec. 25, sec. 30 (incense use by Jews at the Oak of Mamre), sec. 42 (miraculous oil from a rock in the Red Sea, smelling like sulphur).

182. Piacenza Pilgrim, *Travels* 11; trans. Wilkinson, *Jerusalem Pilgrims Before the Crusades*, 82.

183. Paulinus, *Poem* 27, tr. 285; *Poem* 18, tr. 120; *Poem* 19, tr. 144. Compare, e.g., Ephrem, *Hymns on Virginity* 17–19; Romanos the Melodist, *Kontakion* 59, "On All Martyrs." The identification of relics with the "odor of sanctity" becomes a commonplace from this point on; see W. Deonna, "EUWDIA: Croyances antiques et modernes: L'Odeur suave des dieux et des élus," *Genava* 17 (1939): 167–263.

184. Paulinus, *Poems* 18, 19, 21, 27. Compare Gregory of Tours, *Glory of the Martyrs* 50; *Glory of the Martyrs* 9. The practice was common at saints' shrines east and west; compare John Chrysostom, "Homily on the Martyrs." For an example of a reliquary designed for just this purpose, see Christine Kondoleon, *Antioch: The Lost Ancient City*, at p. 224: item 114, Reliquary Lid (late 5th–6th century).

185. Paulinus, *Poem* 21; trans. Walsh, 192.

186. Compare, e.g., exorcism and healing by holy oil in Cyril of Scythopolis, *Lives: Saba* 27, 45, 63; *Euthymius* 47, 52; *Cyriacus* 9.

187. Evagrius, *Eccl. Hist.* 2.3; trans. Whitby, 65.

188. Paulinus, *Poem* 10; trans. Walsh, 59.

189. Paulinus, *Poem* 31; trans. Walsh, 326.

190. Atchley, *Incense in Divine Worship*, was one of the first to make serious use of the full array of early Christian literature, including hagiography, for the study of incense practices. In a review of Atchley's book, Hippolyte Delehaye stressed exactly this point: that saints' *Lives* not only provide important data for the introduction and persistance of incense usage, but further "fournissent souvent de précieux indices sur la signification." *AB* 30 (1911) 93–95, at p. 94.

191. The studies gathered in Michel van Esbroeck, *Aux origines de la Dormition de la Vierge: Études historiques sur les traditions orientales*, Variorum Collected Studies Series CS 472 (Brookfield, VT/Aldershot, Hampshire: Ashgate Publishing, 1995) are indispensable for any work now done on the Transitus. Stephen J. Shoemaker, *Ancient Traditions of the Virgin Mary's Dormition and Assumption* (Oxford: Oxford University Press, 2002), offers a fresh and, indeed, vigorously bold reassessment of both the broader scholarship and the ancient manuscript traditions. See also S. Mimouni, *Dormition et Assomption de Marie. Histoire des traditions anciennes*, TH 98 (Paris: Éditions Beauchesne, 1995). M. Jugie, *La Mort et l'Assomption de la Sainte Vierge: Étude Historico-Doctrinale*, Studi e Testi 114 (Città del Vaticano: Biblioteca Apostolica Vaticana, 1944) remains classic. Also useful for the liturgical connection discussed here is J. Ledit, *Marie dans la Liturgie de Byzance*, TH 39 (Paris: Éditions Beauchesne, 1976).

192. See above all Shoemaker, *Ancient Traditions*, 32–77; and Michel van Esbroeck, "Les textes littéraires sur l'Assomption avant le Xe siècle," in *Les actes apocryphes des apôtres: christianisme et monde païen*, ed. François Bovon et al. (Geneva: Labor et Fides, 1981), 265–85 [= van Esbroeck, *Aux origines de la Dormition de la Vierge*, ch. 1]. Primary Greek and Latin texts were edited in Constantinus Tischendorf, *Apocalypses Apocryphae Mosis, Esdrae, Pauli, Iohannis, item Mariae Dormitio, additis Evangeliorum et Actuum apocryphorum supplementis* (Leipzig: Herm. Mendelssohn, 1866), 95–136; these were substantially supplemented by the work of Antoine Wenger, *L'Assomption de la T. S. Vierge dans la Tradition Byzantine du VIe au Xe Siècle: Études et Documents*, Archives de l'Orient Chrétien 5 (Paris: Insitut Français d'Études Byzantines, 1955). Victor Arras, *De Transitu Mariae Apocrypha Aethiopice, II*, CSCO 352/Scrip. Aeth. 69 (Louvain: Secretariat du CorpusSCO, 1974), 72–74, also lists helpful bibliography.

193. Ed. and trans. in William Wright, *Contributions to the Apocryphal Literature of the New Testament* (London: Williams and Norgate, 1865).

194. Ed. and trans. William Wright, "The Departure of My Lady Mary from this World," *JSL*, n.s., 6–7 (1865): vol. 6, pp. 417–48; vol. 7, pp. 110–60.

195. Ed. and trans. in Agnes Smith Lewis, *Apocrypha Syriaca: The Protevangelium Jacobi and Transitus Mariae*, Studia Sinaitica 11 (London: E. J. Clay and Sons, 1902).

196. In addition to the works by Shoemaker, Jugie, van Esbroeck, and Mimouni noted above n. 191, see also S. C. Mimouni, "La tradition littéraire syriaque de l'histoire de la dormition et de l'assomption de Marie," *Parole de l'Orient* 15 (1988–9): 143–68. The Syriac Transitus plays a key role in tracking the evolution of the feast day of the Assumption: see Alphonse Raes, "Aux origines de la fête de l'Assomption en Orient," *OCP* 12 (1946): 262–74; Athanase Renoux, "Le Codex Arménien Jérusalem 121, II: édition comparée du texte et de deux autres manuscrits," *PO* 36 (Turnhout: Brepols, 1971), 141–388, esp. 189–92; B. Capelle, "La Fête de la Vierge à Jérusalem au Ve siècle," *Le Muséon* 56 (1943): 1–33; Michel van Esbroeck, "Étude comparée des notices byzantines et caucasiennes pour la fête de la Dormition," *Aux origines de la Dormition de la Vierge*, ch. 2; idem, "Le culte de la Vierge de Jérusalem à Constantinople aux 6e–7e siècles," *REB* 46 (1988): 181–90 [= van Esbroeck, *Aux origines de la Dormition de la Vierge*, ch. 10]; S. C. Mimouni, "La Fête de la Dormition de Marie en Syrie à l'époque Byzantine," *The Harp* 5 (Kottayam, Kerala: SEERI, 1992): 157–74.

197. van Esbroeck, "Les textes littéraires sur l'Assomption avant le Xe siècle," at pp. 265–75, proposes a system to classify the huge body of manuscripts surviving in ancient Christian languages for the *Transitus Mariae*. He establishes two basic families signified by their primary Marian images, the first by "The palm of the Tree of Life" and the second by "Bethlehem and incense offerings." Syriac texts are among the very earliest witnesses to both and, for the second family, provide the oldest extant forms. van Esbroeck points out, p. 269, that while the first family does not lack instances of sacred odors, in the second family incense offerings (as well as divine scents) are continually featured. van

Esbroeck rightly stresses that the second family is a development out of the first, rather than representing a separate Marian tradition, and it is with this sense of continuum that I set up these three recensions for consideration. Although van Esbroeck places all three of these Syriac recensions in the second family, from the olfactory perspective this classification does not hold up. The fifth-century Syriac Dormition edited by Wright (van Esbroeck's S2) is much closer to the first family, with significantly less incense imagery; the primary Greek text here (Vat. Grec. 1982, van Esbroeck's G1) is that edited in Wenger, L'Assomption de la T. S.Vierge dans la Tradition Byzantine, 209–41. The sixth-century Syriac History in Six Books, also edited by Wright, is clearly close to the Greek tradition of the second family (van Esbrock's G2), represented by the text edited in Tischendorf, Apocalypses Apocryphae, 95–112. The later sixth-century Syriac History in Five Books, edited by Smith Lewis, is notably different in the quality and intensity of its olfactory imagery, as will be seen below. The perfume imagery in Vat. Grec. 1982 is discussed in Frédéric Manns, Le récit de la Dormition de Marie (Vatican grec 1982): Contribution à l'étude des origines de l'exégèse chrétienne, Studium Biblicum Franciscanum Collectio Maior 33 (Jerusalem: Franciscan Printing Press, 1989), at pp. 144–53, in terms of the schematic poles of incense (sacrificial) imagery and divine presence (perfume). Shoemaker, Ancient Traditions, 32–57, reviews this classification system, and expands the types of evidence involved.

198. By "instance of holy fragrance" I mean any mention of smell, fair or foul, granted religious meaning by the text.

199. One more Syriac recension is related to Wright's History in Six Books and Smith Lewis' History in Five Books, found incorporated into another Syriac History of the Blessed Virgin Mary, edited and translated by E. A. Wallis Budge in his collection The History of the Blessed Virgin Mary and the History of the Likeness of Christ which the Jews of Tiberias Made to Mock at, Luzac's Semitic Text and Translation Series, vols. 4 and 5 (London: Luzac and Co., 1899). These three Histories are closely interrelated; van Esbroeck, "Les textes littéraires sur l'Assomption avant le Xe siècle," in his chart on p. 266 and thereafter, essentially treats them as their own group (S 3). When analyzed for olfactory imagery, however, the three show prominent differences. Budge's text (like Wright's History in Six Books) has fifteen instances of holy fragrance, and in these instances contains elements of both the Histories edited by Wright and Smith Lewis. Nonetheless, Smith Lewis's recension stands alone for the quality of its olfactory imagery, as will be seen below. I will cite the most important correspondences with Budge in the notes that follow. Both Raes, "Aux origines de la fête de l'Assomption en Orient," and van Esbroeck, "Étude comparée des notices byzantines et caucasiennes pour la fête de la Dormition," at pp. 9–10, have indicated the antiquity and/or liturgical significance of Smith Lewis's recension over that of Budge.

200. One of van Esbroeck's most interesting points is that the second manuscript family for the Transitus, characterized by its incessant incense offerings,

flourished largely in the miaphysite Syrian Orthodox domain of the Christian Orient. He sees its development, along with the celebration of the Feast of the Dormition on August 15, as part of the imperial politics under successive Byzantine regimes of the fifth and sixth centuries that engaged the cult of the Virgin Mary in the efforts to resolve the Christological divisions following from the Council of Chalcedon in 451. In addition to "Les textes littéraires sur l'Assomption avant le Xe siècle," see his studies "Étude comparée des notices byzantines et caucasiennes pour la fête de la Dormition," and "Le culte de la Vierge de Jérusalem à Constantinople aux 6e–7e siècles." For the imperial involvements in—and manipulations of—the cult of Mary in the fifth and sixth centuries, see Kenneth G. Holum, *Theodosian Empresses:Women and Imperial Dominion in Late Antiquity* (Berkeley: University of California Press, 1982); and Vasiliki Limberis, *Divine Heiress: The Virgin Mary and the Creation of Christian Constantinople* (New York/London: Routledge, 1994). Shoemaker, *Ancient Traditions*, 256–79, trenchantly critiques the argument regarding an anti-Chalcedonian milieu for the flourishing of particular *Transitus* traditions. Having argued extensively for much earlier origins to the materials that grew into the *Transitus* legends, as well as for significant diversity in the forms of Marian understanding these denote, Shoemaker insists that the Dormition narratives remained basically disinterested in the particular debates fought at Chalcedon and subsequently over its Christological definition.

201. Syriac Dormition, Wright, *Contributions to the Apocryphal Literature of the New Testament*, p. 19.

202. Ibid., p. 31.

203. Ibid., p. 36.

204. Ibid., p. 24.

205. Ibid., p. 36.

206. Ibid., p. 34. As so often, there are interesting pre-Christian parallels. Compare, e.g., the Egyptian Queen Ahmose's conception of Hatshepsut by the god Amun, as discussed in Erik Hornung, *Conceptions of God in Ancient Egypt: The One and the Many*, trans. John Baines (Ithaca, NY: Cornell University Press, 1982), 133–35.

207. Syriac Dormition, Wright, *Contributions to the Apocryphal Literature of the New Testament*, p. 40.

208. The three feasts of the Syriac *Transitus* were January 6 (although van Esbroeck thinks December 24 rather than January 6), May 15, and August 13, and were tied to the agrarian cycle. See the discussions in van Esbroeck, "Les textes littéraires sur l'Assomption avant le Xe siècle," p. 274; Raes, "Aux origines de la fête de l'Assomption en Orient;" and Mimouni, "La Fête de la Dormition de Marie en Syrie à l'époque Byzantine."

209. But here the Holy Spirit rather than Mary tells the story of the Annunciation; the olfactory aspect may not have seemed important or appropriate from the

changed narrative view. The story is not included in the *Transitus* portion of Budge's edition of the *History of the Virgin Mary*.

210. *History in Six Books*, Wright, "The Departure of My Lady Mary from this World," p. 136.

211. Ibid., pp. 131–32, 148.

212. Ibid., p. 129.

213. Its usage is mandated for the Marian feasts instituted in this text. *History in Six Books*, Wright, "The Departure of My Lady Mary from this World," p. 153.

214. *History in Six Books*, Wright, "The Departure of My Lady Mary from this World," pp. 136, 146.

215. Ibid., pp. 136, 140–41, 153, 155.

216. Ibid., pp. 129, 150–51.

217. Ibid., pp. 156, 158.

218. van Esbroeck, as noted above n. 197, sees these recensions as closely inter-related. In Smith Lewis's edition, for example, the Annunciation is again an olfactory event.

219. The situation is discussed in Shoemaker, *Ancient Traditions*, 46–57; and Mimouni,"La tradition littéraire syriaque de l'histoire de la dormition et de l'assomption de Marie," 165–66. In editing her text, which she claimed to be based on the oldest manuscripts of the Syriac, Smith Lewis filled in the lacunae of her primary manuscript by using Wright's 1865 edition of the *History in Six Books*, as well as a manuscript of Rendel Harris's, copied in 1857, but which she was certain represented a text as ancient as her own. She claimed that the version included in the *History of the Virgin* edited and translated by Budge was based on later manuscripts, and therefore chose not to consult his edition, which was edited at the same time that her own work was under way. It is noteworthy that scholarly discussions of the Syriac *Transitus* are generally restricted to the fifth-century *Dormition* edited by Wright in 1865; occasionally, scholars will also mention Wright's sixth-century *History in Six Books*. The Smith Lewis edition of the *History in Five Books* is rarely utilized, although both Raes and van Esbroeck have noted its importance concerning the establishment of the feast of the Dormition on August 15; see above, n. 196. In part this neglect is due to the prob-lems of her edition as cited here, but the omission seems also due to the agenda of scholars to establish the oldest version of a text, as close to an "original" as possible. This "quest for origins" is unfortunate when it obscures the fluid nature of ancient texts. As seen with the Syriac *Transitus*, textual evolution itself may have important historical information to convey. The notable exception is Shoemaker, *Ancient Traditions*, who repeatedly utilizes Smith Lewis's edition for establishing early and varied forms of the Dormition narrative.

220. van Esbroeck, "Étude comparée des notices byzantines et caucasiennes pour la fête de la Dormition," 9–10; Raes, "Aux origines de la fête de l'Assomption en Orient."

221. E.g., *History in Five Books*, Smith Lewis, *Apocrypha Syriaca*, pp. 20, 36, 37, 47, 59, 62, 65, 68. While Budge's *History of the Virgin* contains far fewer incidences of holy fragrance than Smith Lewis's *History in Five Books* (fifteen, as opposed to forty-two in the latter), a similar perspective on the path of sacred smells can be seen. For example, "Mary went and offered up incense, and prayed, and she saw that the sweet smell ascended into heaven, and that it went in through the door thereof." Budge, pp. 98–99.

222. *History in Five Books*, Smith Lewis, *Apocrypha Syriaca*, p. 20.

223. Ibid., pp. 37, 52.

224. Ibid., p. 68.

225. Ibid., p. 63.

226. One passage from Budge's *History of the Virgin* is quite different from its counterparts in Wright's and Smith Lewis's recensions, and demonstrates exactly this point. As the apostles performed their liturgical service at the house where Mary's body lay in state, the odors of their worship, of her sanctified body, and of the heavenly hosts in attendance were perceived to be commingled in this way: "the people of Bethlehem saw the clouds coming and sprinkling sweet dew over all the house. . . . And the people of Bethlehem saw as it were [the appearance of] the waves of the sea when they break upon the shore, for even thus were the waves of sweet smells and odours which came forth from the upper chamber. And like the rushing water which a full and overflowing spring poureth out in torrents, even so did the odour of sweet scents go forth from the foundations of the upper chamber." Trans. Budge, pp. 134–35.

227. Ephrem, *Hymns on Nisibis* 17.4.4–6; *Hymns on Julian Saba* 1–4; *Apostolic Constitutions* 8.47.3; Theodoret, *Questions on Exodus* 28.

228. As discussed in chapter 4, pp. 186–97. Cf. S. A. Harvey, "The Sense of a Stylite: Perspectives on Simeon the Elder," *VC* 42 (1988): 376–94. See below for the motif in the Greek *Vita* of Simeon the Younger.

229. Ps.-Ephrem, "On Hermits and Desert Dwellers," lines 97–108, 485–96.

230. The controversy over the title "Theotokos" was a central issue in the clash between Cyril of Alexandria and Nestorius, and their respective supporters. For discussion of the public turmoil (as distinct from the theological debates *per se*), see Limberis, *Divine Heiress*; Cameron, *Rhetoric of Empire*, esp. at pp. 165–70; Averil Cameron, "The Theotokos in Sixth Century Constantinople: A City Finds its Symbol," *JTS*, n.s., 29 (1978): 79–108; Timothy Gregory, *Vox Populi: Popular Opinion and Violence in the Religious Controversies of the Fifth Century A.D.* (Columbus: Ohio State University Press, 1979). Crucial now is the extensive commentary in Nicholas Constas, *Proclus of Constantinople and the Cult of the Virgin in Late Antiquity: Homilies 1–5, Texts and Translations*, SVC 66 (Leiden: E. J. Brill 2003).

231. Here trans. Mother Mary and Archimandrite Kallistos Ware, *The Lenten Triodion* (London: Faber and Faber, 1977), 428. See Joseph, *Mariale*, Migne, *PG*

105: cols. 984–1414, esp. Canon 1, Ode 8 at cols. 989–90; Canon 6, Ode 1 at cols. 1019–1020; and for February at cols. 1957–58.

232. Cf. Sebastian P. Brock, "The priesthood of the baptised: Some Syriac perspectives," *Sobornost/ECR* 9 (1987): 14–22, stressing both the priestly nature of baptized personhood, as well as its distinction from ordained priesthood.

Chapter 3. Olfaction and Christian Knowing

1.   See Stanley Stowers' critique of social theories that attempt to reconcile disparate cultural aspects into an essentially metaphysical totality: "the idea of a totally integrated umbrella of a culture's ideas and symbols greatly exaggerates the unity and integration possible for any culture. A better description would be of a hodgepodge of often loosely linked, often conflicting and changing local domains and practices of symbolization that sometimes have a set of symbols and concepts widely perceived as highest or hegemonic. Even these latter are often contested." Stanley K. Stowers, "Paul and Slavery: A Response," *Semeia* 83/84 (1998): 295–311, at pp. 300–301.

2.   Roger French, *Ancient Natural History: Histories of Nature* (New York: Routledge, 1994). Of course, in the Greek and Roman periods dissection was largely confined to animals, so that animals provided most of the information by which ancient scientists considered the workings of the human body. See Margaret Tallmadge May, *Galen, On the Usefulness of the Parts of the Body* (Ithaca, NY: Cornell University Press, 1968) 1:13–43 ("Anatomy before Galen").

3.   A Christian example would be Basil of Caesarea's *Homilies on the Hexaemeron*, which present numerous moral exempla taken from ancient animal science.

4.   The point was consistently made by ancient authors: cf. Aristotle, *On the Soul*, 2.9; and Theophrastus, *Concerning Odors*, 2.4, where the latter comments, "one might almost say, our sense of smell is inferior to that of all other animals." Trans. Hort, 2:331. Cicero, *On the Nature of the Gods*, bk. 2, declared the human person superior to animals in all of the five senses, but his context is a deliberately flawed representation of the Stoic position, which he will then refute in book 3; it is difficult to know whether this particular point was part of his misrepresentation. The relative weakness of human olfaction compared with that of other mammals is well established in modern scientific research, although humans do have the capacity to recognize approximately 10,000 scents. Other mammals rely on smell for basic survival, utilizing it as a principal source of information for food, danger (detecting or repelling predators), and mates. E.g., Harvey Richard Schiffman, *Sensation and Perception: An Integrated Approach*, 2nd ed. (New York: John Wiley and Sons, 1982), 158–76; or more generally, Richard Axel, "The Molecular Logic of Smell," *Scientific American* (October 1995): 154–59. For an overall perspective, including how the scientific understanding of olfaction is changing in contemporary research, see M. J. Serby and K. L. Chobor, eds., *Science of Olfaction* (New York: Springer-Verlag, 1992).

5. In general, the study of John I. Beare, *Greek Theories of Elementary Cognition from Alcmaeon to Aristotle* (Oxford: Clarendon Press, 1906), remains a very useful starting point.

6. For excellent discussions on the ancient understanding of "matter" and "body", see Dale Martin, *The Corinthian Body* (New Haven: Yale University Press, 1995), 3–37; and Teresa M. Shaw, *The Burden of the Flesh: Fasting and Sexuality in Early Christianity* (Minneapolis: Fortress Press, 1998), 27–78; similarly, on the notion of "physicalism," see Julia Annas, *Hellenistic Philosophy of Mind* (Berkeley: University of California Press, 1992), 37–70, 123–56.

7. E.g., Plato, *Timaeus* 44d–47e; Plotinus, *Enneads* 4.5–6.

8. Lucretius, *On the Nature of Things* 4.478–79; trans. Rouse, 283.

9. This crucial aspect of ancient understanding is sometimes missing in scholarly debate. See, e.g., Carl W. Griffin and David L. Paulsen, "Augustine and the Corporeality of God," HTR 95 (2002): 97–118.

10. See the discussion in chapter 1, pp. 31–33.

11. The text is edited with translation and commentary in George M. Stratton, *Theophrastus and the Greek Physiological Psychology before Aristotle* (New York: MacMillan, 1917).

12. An insightful analysis of how Theophrastus differed from his teacher Aristotle, and critiqued him by implication, is given in French, *Ancient Natural History*, 83–103. See also two further (and opposing) considerations of Theophrastus's cosmology: Marlein van Raalte, "The Idea of the Cosmos as an Organic Whole in Theophrastus' *Metaphysics*," and John Ellis, "The Aporematic Character of Theophrastus' *Metaphysics*," both in *Theophrastean Studies: On Natural Science, Physics and Metaphysics, Ethics, Religion, and Rhetoric*, ed. William W. Fortenbaugh and Robert W. Sharples (New Brunswick, NJ: Transaction Books, 1988), 188–215 and 216–23, respectively.

13. Annas, *Hellenistic Philosophy of Mind*, 17–33, sets up the changes in medical thinking as a framing context in which to consider how Hellenistic philosophy develops; A. A. Long, *Hellenistic Philosophy: Stoics, Epicureans, Sceptics*, 2nd ed. (Berkeley: University of California Press, 1986), also provides lucid treatment of the prominence given to theories of sense perception in these thought systems. See further David E. Hahm, "Early Hellenistic Theories of Vision and the Perception of Color," in *Studies in Perception: Interrelations in the History of Philosophy and Science*, ed. Peter Machamer and Robert G. Turnbull (Columbus: Ohio State University Press, 1978), 60–95.

14. An excellent collection of texts on Epicurean and Stoic epistemology, including discussion of sense perception, is found in A. A. Long and D. N. Sedley, *The Hellenistic Philosophers*, vol. 1 (Cambridge: Cambridge University Press, 1987), 78–97 (Epicureans), 236–66 (Stoics and Academics). See also Edward N. Lee, "The Sense of an Object: Epicurus on Seeing and Hearing," and Heinrich von Staden, "The Stoic Theory of Perception and its 'Platonic' Critics," both in

Machamer and Turnbull, *Studies in Perception*, 27–59 and 96–136, respectively; David Furley, "Democritus and Epicurus on Sensible Qualities," in *Passions and Perceptions: Studies in Hellenistic Philosophy of Mind, Proceedings of the Fifth Symposium Hellenisticum*, ed. Jacques Brunschwig and Martha C. Nussbaum (Cambridge: Cambridge University Press, 1993), 72–94.

15. Plato, *Timaeus* 66d–67a.

16. Plato, *Timaeus* 65a, 66d–67a. Compare his comments in *Republic* 9.9; *Philebus* 50e–52b.

17. Aristotle, *On the Soul*, 2.9; trans. Hett, 119. On the problems of human odor identification still baffling modern scientists see, e.g., R. A. de Wijk, F. R. Schab, and W. S. Cain, "Odor Identification," in *Memory for Odors*, ed. Frank R. Schab and Robert G. Crowder (Mahwah, NJ: Lawrence Erlbaum Associates, 1995), 21–37.

18. Aristotle, *On the Soul* 2. 9; *On the Senses* 5. See the helpful discussion of smell in T. K. Johansen, *Aristotle on the Sense-Organs* (Cambridge: Cambridge University Press, 1997), 226–51.

19. Theophrastus, *On the Senses*; *Concerning Odors*; and *Inquiry into Plants*. For a summary, see Stratton, *Theophrastus*, 36–42. It is worth noting that scientists continue to have problems with the categorization of smells; e.g., Schiffman, *Sensation and Perception*, 159–63. In fact, olfaction is still the sense we know the least about: see Trygg Engen, *The Perception of Odors* (New York: Academic Press, 1982), 1–15, and passim; Schiffman, *Sensation and Perception*, 163–65; Gary K. Beauchamp, "The Chemical Senses and Pleasure," in *Pleasure: The Politics and the Reality*, ed. David M. Warburton (New York: John Wiley and Sons, 1994), 29–37. Rachel Herz, "Verbal Coding in Olfactory versus Nonolfactory Cognition," *Memory and Cognition* 28.6 (2000): 957–64, argues that olfaction is unique among the five senses in part because it is less connected to the brain's system of linguistic processing than are the other senses: "it appears that odors are more experientially and neurologically distant from language than perception through the other senses is" (p. 957). This neurological situation may well account for the historical difficulty of defining and categorizing smells. I am grateful to Professor Herz for helpful discussion on this and other issues.

20. There is an interesting collection of fragments of Theophrastus gleaned from later citations in William W. Fortenbaugh, Pamela M. Huby, Robert W. Sharples, and Dimitri Gutas, *Theophrastus of Eresus: Sources for His Life, Writings, Thought and Influence, Part Two, Psychology, Human Physiology, Living Creatures, Botany, Ethics, Religion, Politics, Rhetoric and Poetics, Music, Misc.* (New York: E. J. Brill, 1992), esp. passages 276, 277 A–C, 303, 338, 430, 431, 432, 433. For the continuing tradition among sixth-century Neoplatonists, see Priscian, *On Theophrastus On Sense-Perception with 'Simplicius' On Aristotle's On the Soul* 2.5–12, trans. Pamela Huby, Carlos Steele, and J. O. Urmson, notes by Peter Lautner (Ithaca, NY: Cornell University Press, 1997).

21. E.g., Plato, *Timaeus*, 47a–c. See the discussions in Johansen, *Aristotle on the Sense-Organs*, 21–115; Robert G. Turnbull, "The Role of the 'Special Sensibles' in

the Perception Theories of Plato and Aristotle," in Machamer and Turnbull, *Studies in Perception*, 3–26.

22. Beare, *Greek Theories of Elementary Cognition*, 87–89, 123.

23. It is interesting to note that scientists still classify the senses into two basic categories, which follow the mode of stimulation: the physical senses (sight and sound: those senses stimulated by a physical quantity), and the chemical senses (smell, taste, and trigeminal or common chemical sense; for these, the stimulus is a molecule of a specific chemical). The chemical senses are the oldest in human evolution, and have their functions oriented towards survival. See C. Van Toller, G. H. Dodd, and Anne Billing, eds., *Ageing and the Sense of Smell* (Springfield, IL: Charles C. Thomas, 1985), at p. 4; D. M. Stoddart, "The Senses: Meeting Biological Needs," in *Tastes and Aromas: The Chemical Senses in Science and Industry*, ed. Graham A. Bell and Annesley J. Watson (Oxford/Sydney: Blackwell Science Ltd. and University of New South Wales Press, 1999), 1–11; Beauchamp, "The Chemical Senses and Pleasure."

24. Galen, *On the Usefulness of the Parts of the Body*, 8.6–7. See the important discussions in Rudolph E. Siegel, *Galen on Sense Perception* (New York: S. Karger, 1970), 140–57; Michael Frede, "On Galen's Epistemology," in *Galen: Problems and Prospects*, ed. Vivan Nutton (London: Wellcome Institute for the History of Medicine, 1981), 65–84. Galen was not entirely wrong: "Olfactory receptors are more directly connected to the brain than those of any other sense, being only one synapse away from the olfactory bulb. They also have the most direct access to the environment of any modality and are the only receptors located outside the blood barrier." Trygg Engen, *Odor Sensation and Memory* (New York: Praeger, 1991), 110. See also Herz, "Verbal Coding;" Steven Van Toller, "The Enjoyment of Smells: Central, Autonomic and Trigeminal Interactions in Odour Perception," in Warburton, *Pleasure*, 15–21; Gerd Kobal, "Pleasure Responses of the Brain: Olfactory Evoked Potential Activity and Hedonics," in Warburton, *Pleasure*, 22–28.

25. Cicero, *On The Nature of the Gods* 2.140–41; trans. Walsh, 98. Cicero here represents the Stoics through the character of Balbus, whose overall position he will then refute through Cotta's presentation of the Sceptic critique.

26. Lucretius, *On the Nature of Things* 4.225–29; trans. Rouse, 265.

27. There is some parallelism between Lucretius's understanding and that of modern scientists who work on the chemical process of smell. See Schiffman, *Sensation and Perception*, 159; Engen, *The Perception of Odors*, 6–7, 17–34; Van Toller, Dodd, and Billing, *Ageing and the Sense of Smell*, 19–21.

28. Lucretius, *On the Nature of Things* 4.692–704; trans. Rouse, 297–99. Compare Kobal, "Pleasure Responses."

29. Compare Philo, who at one moment could describe sense perception, including smell, as operating independently of the will and, at another, could dismiss smell as the mere servant of the sense of taste, providing no substance of its own. Philo, *Allegorical Interpretation* 3.56; *On the Sacrifice of Cain and Abel* 6.43–44.

Compare, e.g., S.L. Youngentob, "Introduction to the Sense of Smell: Understanding Odours from the Study of Human and Animal Behaviour," in Bell and Watson, *Tastes and Aromas*, 23–37.

30. Scholars are still reassessing the terms on which this was the case. See, e.g., Stanley K. Stowers, *A Re-Reading of Romans: Justice, Jews, and Gentiles* (New Haven: Yale University Press, 1994); Troels Engberg-Pedersen, *Paul and the Stoics: An Essay in Interpretation* (Edinburgh: T & T Clark, 2000). For an example of context for New Testament literature, see, e.g., Abraham Malherbe, *Moral Exhortation, A Greco-Roman Sourcebook* (Philadelphia: Westminster Press, 1986).

31. Tertullian, *On the Prescription Against Heretics* 7.

32. Robert M. Grant, *Theophilus of Antioch: Ad Autolycum* (Oxford: Oxford University Press, 1970).

33. Robert Wilken, *The Christians as the Romans Saw Them*, 2nd ed. (New Haven: Yale University Press, 2003), 94–125, is especially helpful on this issue.

34. Robert Hauk, "'They Saw What They Said They Saw': Sense Knowledge in Early Christian Polemic," HTR 81 (1988): 239–49, offers a lively discussion of the problem through consideration of Origen and the pseudo-Clementine Homilies. However, the article states as the ancient context, "a thought world dominated by Platonic thinking" (p. 239), without acknowledging (a) the extent to which "Platonic thinking" by the Common Era had been qualified through the impact of Peripatetic, Stoic, and Epicurean discussions—it was not until Origen's time, in fact, with the impact of Plotinus, that Platonic thought began to rise in prominence; or (b) the fact that paganism traditionally expressed human-divine interaction through reliance on sensory experience. On the latter point, see, e.g., Robin Lane Fox, *Pagans and Christians* (San Francisco: Harper and Row, 1987), 102–67.

35. E.g., Origen, *Contra Celsum* 7.37–38. The theme is pervasive in Origen's works, of course, but in *Contra Celsum* bk. 7 he specifically replies to the question of sense perception as a basis for knowledge.

36. *Contra Celsum* 7.34; trans. Chadwick, 421.

37. Augustine, *Trinity*, 9.6–7, 15.12. The discussion of sight occupies book 11. Margaret Miles and Sabine MacCormack are two scholars whose treatments of Augustine on the senses are exceptionally nuanced. See Margaret Miles, "Vision: The Eye of the Body and the Eye of the Mind in Saint Augustine's *De trinitate* and *Confessions*," JR 63 (1983): 125–42; eadem, *Augustine on the Body* (Missoula, MT: Scholars Press, 1979); Sabine MacCormack, *The Shadows of Poetry: Vergil in the Mind of Augustine* (Berkeley: University of California Press, 1998), esp. ch. 2 ("The Scent of a Rose").

38. Augustine, *Confessions* 10.32.48: "The allurement of perfumes is not a matter of great concern to me. When they are absent, I do not look for them. When they are present, I do not reject them. I am ready to go without them all the time." Trans. Chadwick, 207.

39. Cf. Augustine, *On Nature and Grace* 55, where Augustine argues against Pelagius that the sense of smell is involuntary and cannot be controlled by the will, since one must inhale smells whenever one breathes. Ancient philosophers and medical writers had long noted that smell was not necessarily contingent on breathing.

40. I follow the translation by Henry Chadwick, *Saint Augustine: Confessions* (Oxford: Oxford University Press, 1991).

41. *Confessions* 2.3.8; trans. Chadwick, 28. Augustine evokes the imagery of Song of Songs 4–5. Compare, e.g., *Confessions,* 3.1.1.

42. *Confessions* 7.17.23; trans. Chadwick, 127–28.

43. E.g., *Confessions* 1.20.31; 2.5.10; 4.10.15; 4.11.17; 7.17.23; 10.7.11; 10.8.13; 10.9.16; 10.21.30.

44. *Confessions* 9.10.24; trans. Chadwick, 171.

45. *Confessions* 4.7.12; trans. Chadwick, 59.

46. *Confessions* 10.6.8; trans. Chadwick, 183.

47. *Confessions* 10.27.38; trans. Chadwick, 201.

48. E.g., Frede, "On Galen's Epistemology."

49. Ute Possekel, *Evidence of Greek Philosophical Concepts in the Writings of Ephrem the Syrian*, CSCO 580/Sub. 102 (Louvain: Peeters Press, 1999), presents just such an analysis of the senses in the works of Ephrem, drawing primarily (but not exclusively) on his *Prose Refutations*. Possekel teases out various elements of Platonic, Aristotelian, and Stoic doctrines of epistemology that contribute at different points to Ephrem's presentation of the senses. Most often Ephrem seems to follow Stoic teachings, which Possekel speculates he may have gained from handbooks or other such means common to "the hellenized culture in which he lived and thought" (p. 221). Possekel devotes her primary attention in discussion of the senses to Ephrem's understanding of vision and hearing, claiming that Ephrem does this also (p. 203). Yet as has been shown already in the present study, Ephrem had a great deal to say about smell; one must look to his poetry, and especially to the intensely sensory language of his poetic imagery and metaphors, to tease out his thoughts on smell.

50. Lactantius, "The Workmanship of God," trans. McDonald in *Lactantius: Minor Works,* 3–56; Gregory of Nyssa, "On the Making of Man," trans. Moore and Wilson, NPNF, 2nd ser., 5:386–427; Theodoret of Cyrus, *On Divine Providence,* trans. Halton; Nemesius, "On the Nature of Man," trans. Telfer, *Cyril of Jerusalem and Nemesius of Emesa,* 203–453. For a sense of the pervasive place of such discussion in patristic literature, see D. S. Wallace-Hadrill, *The Greek Patristic View of Nature* (New York: Barnes and Noble, 1968), esp. 40–65. For a more focused treatment, see Thomas Halton, "The Five Senses in Nemesius, *De Natura Hominis* and Theodoret, *De Providentia,*" *SP* 20, ed. E. A. Livingstone (Leuven: Peeters Press, 1989): 94–101.

51. As discussed in chapter 1, esp. with regard to Clement's *Christ the Educator*.

52. Chapter 2, pp. 59–65.

53. Lactanius, *Workmanship of God* 16.

54. Nemesius, *Nature of Man* 1.2; trans. Telfer, 229.

55. Nemesius, *Nature of Man* 1.4; trans. Telfer, 235–36.

56. Gregory, *On the Making of Man* 30.2–3; NPNF, 2nd ser., 5:422.

57. Theodoret, *On Divine Providence* 6.18–19; trans. Halton, 79. Each of these four treatises expounds this theme, as do the pre-Christian discussions of the senses cited above.

58. Nemesius, *Nature of Man* 6.27; trans. Telfer, 322.

59. Lactantius, *Workmanship of God* 10.

60. Theodoret, *On Divine Providence* 3.35–36.

61. Nemesius, *Nature of Man* 11; 9.31; 16.39. Nemesius was the one out of these authors who seems to have studied Galen directly and extensively, and to have been in a position to critique him on his own terms. His treatment of smell, in *Nature of Man* ch. 11, follows Galen's work *On the Organ of Smell*. See Telfer's introduction to the translation, 206–11, and the commentary at pp. 337–38; and Wallace-Hadrill, *Greek Patristic View of Nature*, 40–65.

62. E.g., Plato, *Timaeus*; Cicero, *On the Nature of the Gods*, bk. 2; Lucretius, *On the Nature of Things*; Plotinus, *Enneads* 2.9. The late antique Christian treatises on nature and divine providence may also be an indication of Christianity's increased reconciliation with, and appropriation of, the conventions of learned discourse as transmitted through classical *paideia*. See George Kennedy, *A New History of Classical Rhetoric* (Princeton: Princeton University Press, 1994), 257–70; Robert A. Kaster, *Guardians of Language: The Grammarian and Society in Late Antiquity* (Berkeley: University of California Press, 1988), 70–95.

63. So, for example, D. S. Wallace-Hadrill wrote his volume *The Greek Patristic View of Nature* in direct response to the negative position put forth by E. R. Dodds, *Pagan and Christian in an Age of Anxiety* (Cambridge: Cambridge University Press, 1965).

64. Basil, *Letters*, 233–36; see also *Letter* 8.

65. Gregory of Nazianzus, *Oration* 28.13 (Second Theological Oration); trans. Wickham and Williams, 232.

66. John Chrysostom, *Homily 5 on Second Corinthians*, esp. sec. 2–3; trans. Chambers, NPNF 12:300–305. I have followed this translation, but altered it slightly to render the passage more clearly.

67. See above, pp. 100–105.

68. John Chrysotom, *Hom. 5 on 2 Cor.* 2; NPNF 12:301.

69. John Chrysostom, *Hom. 5 on 2 Cor.* 2–3; NPNF 12:302.

70. Justin, *Dialogue with Trypho* 128; Tertullian, *Apology* 21.12–13. Although the Nicene Creed was not in fact finalized until the Council of Constantinople in 381, the phrase "light from light" had been part of the original version presented at Nicea in 325: see J. N. D. Kelly, *Early Christian Creeds*, 3rd ed. (London: Longman's, 1972), 205–62, 297–98. See also John of Damascus, *On the Divine Images* 1.11.

71. Gregory of Nyssa, *Against Eunomius* 2.9; trans. Moore and Wilson, NPNF, 2nd ser., 5:114.

72. Gregory, *Against Eunomius* 2.9; trans. Moore and Wilson, NPNF, 2nd ser., 5:115.

73. Eusebius, *Proof of the Gospel* 5.1.19.7–24. 8. See also Athanasius, in his *Letter to Serapion*, sec. 23, where he explores the nature of perfumed scent in treating the Holy Spirit as the unction that anointed Christ, and with which the baptized Christian is anointed by Christ.

74. Plotinus, *Enneads* 5.1; trans. Armstrong, 5:30–33.

75. Lactantius, *Workmanship of God* 10; trans. McDonald, 33.

76. *Gospel of Truth* 7.33.39–34.32; trans. Layton, *Gnostic Scriptures*, 260–61.

77. See the fine discussions by Marie-Odile Boulnois, *Le Paradoxe Trinitaire chez Cyrille d'Alexandrie: Herméneutique, analyses philosophiques et argumentation théologique* (Paris: Institut d'Études Augustiniennes, 1994), 159–77; and Lionel R. Wickham, "Symbols of the Incarnation in Cyril of Alexandria," in *Typus, Symbol, Allegorie bei den östlichen Vätern und ihren Parallelen im Mittelalter*, ed. Margot Schmidt (Regensburg: Friedrich Pustet, 1982), 41–53.

78. John of Damascus, *On the Divine Images* 1.11; trans. Anderson, 20.

79. Ex 30:22–33; discussed in chapter 1, pp. 15–16.

80. The Septuagint wording was especially suggestive: "The scent of your ointments is better than all spices." This wording was followed constantly in Greek patristic texts.

81. Ambrose, *The Holy Spirit*; trans. Deferrari, *Saint Ambrose: Theological and Dogmatic Works*, 31–214.

82. Ambrose, *Holy Spirit* 9.100–104; trans. Deferrari, 72–73.

83. Ambrose, *Holy Spirit* 9.100; trans. Deferrari, 72.

84. Ambrose, *Holy Spirit* 9.102; trans. Deferrari, 72–73.

85. Ambrose, *Holy Spirit* 9.102A–103; trans. Deferrari, 73.

86. Gregory of Nyssa, *On the Holy Spirit*; trans. Moore and Wilson, NPNF, 2nd ser., 5:315–25.

87. Gregory of Nyssa, *On the Holy Spirit*; trans. Moore and Wilson, NPNF, 2nd ser., 5:321.

88. Benoît Gain, *L'Église de Cappadoce au IVe siècle d'après la correspondence de Basile de Césarée (330–379)*, OCA 225 (Rome: Pontificium Institutum Orientale, 1985),

191–200; Jean Daniélou, "Onction et baptême chez Grégoire de Nysse," *Ephemerides Liturgicae* 90 (1976): 440–45; Jean Daniélou, "Chrismation prébaptismale et divinité de l'Ésprit chez Grégoire de Nysse," *RSR* 56 (1968): 177–98.

89. Ambrose, *The Holy Spirit* 1.8.95–96; trans. Deferrari, 70–71.

90. Ambrose, *The Holy Spirit* 2.5.38–40; trans. Deferrari, 110. As with the other images here discussed, this one was no doubt a trope in Christian texts of the time. Compare, e.g., Maximus of Turin, *Sermon* 55, "On the Holy Pasch," trans. Ramsey, *The Sermons of Saint Maximus of Turin*, at p. 134.

91. Cutting, bruising, tearing, and crushing were common methods of perfume production, as described in Theophrastus's treatise *On Odors*, or Pliny's *Natural History*. Discussed in chapter 1, pp. 31–36.

92. The monumental Anchor Bible commentary by Marvin Pope, *Song of Songs: A New Translation with Introduction and Commentary* (New York: Doubleday, 1977), contains encyclopedic surveys of the history of Jewish and Christian exegesis on this text. While Jewish and Christian commentators established distinctive traditions in their religious readings of the Song, there was near universal agreement among ancient and medieval writers that the Song's subject was divine-human relation, whether for Judaism or for Christianity. The fairly recent scholarly convention of reading the Song as an example of ancient near eastern love poetry has by no means eclipsed the Song's traditional interpretation for either of these two religions. Among patristic commentators, Theodore of Mopsuestia was perhaps the best known but not the only one to take the position that the Song represented a human love story, although he nonetheless attempted a "spiritual" reading of it: Pope, *Song*, 119–20; and see now, Robert C. Hill, *Theodoret of Cyrhus: Commentary on the Song of Songs* (Brisbane: Centre for Early Christian Studies/Australian Catholic University, 2001). For an especially fine treatment of the medieval Christian outworking of the patristic models, see E. Ann Matter, *The Voice of My Beloved: The Song of Songs in Western Medieval Christianity* (Philadelphia: University of Pennsylvania Press, 1990).

93. The role of the Song in late antique rhetoric of the body and sexuality has received important scholarly discussion. See especially Averil Cameron, "Early Christianity and the Discourse of Female Desire," in *Women in Ancient Societies: 'An Illusion of the Night'*, ed. Léonie Archer, Susan Fischler, and Maria Wyke, (New York: Routledge, 1994), 152–68; Elizabeth A. Clark, "The Uses of the Song of Songs: Origen and the Later Latin Fathers," in *Ascetic Piety and Women's Faith: Essays on Late Ancient Christianity*, ed. eadem, (Lewiston, NY: Edwin Mellen Press, 1986), 386–427. Jerome's use of the Song in his *Letter* 22 to Eustochium has received particular scholarly attention.

94. A splendid anthology of patristic exegesis on the Song is now available: Richard A. Norris, Jr., *The Song of Songs: Interpreted by Early Christian and Medieval Commentators* (Grand Rapids, MI: Eerdman's, 2003). See chapter 4, pp. 172–78, for Origen and Gregory of Nyssa on the Song.

95. E.g., Ambrose, *Mysteries*, chs. 7 and 9.

96. Ambrose, *Mysteries* 6.29; trans. Deferrari, 15–16.

97. Theophrastus, *Concerning Odors* 2, 13; trans. Hort, 329, 381.

98. Basil, *Letter* 8; trans. Deferrari, LCL 1:46–93, at 66–67; Gregory of Nyssa, *On the Soul and the Resurrection* 2. In the late 1990s, scientists at the Imperial College of Science, Technology and Medicine in London, England, announced their initiative to develop a diagnostic breathalyzer "that will tell a doctor what is wrong and which drugs to prescribe from the smell of a patient's breath" (*Manchester Guardian Weekly*, September 20, 1998).

99. E. A. Wallis Budge, ed. and trans., *The Syriac Book of Medicines* (London: Oxford University Press, 1913; repr. St. Helier: Armorica Book Co., 1976) 2:618–19.

100. This skill of Hilarion's was revealed when a suspect monk brought a gift of green pulse to Hilarion and his fellow monk Hesychius. "When Hesychius served it in the evening, Hilarion exclaimed that he was not able to bear its foul odor and asked him where it had come from. Hesychius answered that a certain monk, wishing to give the first fruits of his little field to the brothers, had brought it. 'Don't you notice a most loathsome stench, the stench of avarice in the foul pulse? Give it to the cattle, give it to the brute animals and see if they will eat it.' No sooner did he place it in the stalls as he had been bidden than the cattle bellowed in fear and, bursting their bonds, fled in all directions." Jerome, *Life of St. Hilarion* 28; trans. Ewald, 266. According to Rabbinic tradition, the critical sign that Bar Khokba was not the Messiah was his inability to judge or discern through smell: *Tract Sanhedrin* 11, trans. Michael Rodkinson, *Babylonian Talmud*, vol. 7 (New York: New Talmud Publishing Co., 1902), 283–84. The discussion here focuses on Isaiah 11:3: "[The Messiah] shall not judge by what his eyes see,/or decide by what his ears hear."

101. So the Syriac version of the *Life of Mary, Niece of Abraham of Qidun*, here trans. Brock and Harvey, *Holy Women of the Syrian Orient*, 33. The Syriac has *riha d-'abiluta* (Bedjan, *AMS* 6:490), literally "the scent of mourning," with *riha* as always an ambiguous term; *'abiluta* is a technical term for ascetic practice. By contrast, the Latin version removes any ambiguity: "odorata ejus corpusculum suavissimo odore abstinentiae fragrare," PL 73:655. The Latin is translated in Ward, *Harlots of the Desert: A Study of Repentance in Early Monastic Sources* (Kalamazoo: Cistercian Publications, 1987), 92–101, at p. 96.

102. *Life of Malkha of Klysma*, ed. Bedjan, *AMS* 5:440.

103. Gregory the Great, *Letters* 8.35, to the ex-consul Leontius; trans. J. Barmby, NPNF, second ser., 12b:243. Compare the topos as found in Gregory of Nazianzus, *Letter* 6 to Basil: "I would rather breathe you than the air, and only live while I am with you, either actually in your presence, or virtually by your likeness in your absence." Trans. Browne and Swallow, NPNF, second ser., 7:448.

104. Chronicle of Zuqnin, Pt. 4 (769–70), trans. Harrak, 324–25. The chronicler cites Isaiah 3:24, "Instead of perfume there will be rottenness."

105. Ephrem, Hymns on Nativity 16.14–15; trans. McVey, Ephrem the Syrian, Hymns, 151.

106. Anonymous Memra 2.112–22; ed. and trans. Sebastian P. Brock, "Two Syriac Verse Homilies on the Binding of Isaac," Le Muséon 99 (1986): 61–129, at p. 125. On p. 90, Brock cites an intriguing Jewish parallel for Isaac's smell as a comfort for Sarah, from a sixteenth-century Hebrew narrative poem by Rabbi Yehudah ibn 'Abbas: Isaac lying on the pyre awaiting his death urges Abraham, "Take a little of my ashes and tell Sarah, 'This is a smell (to remind you) of Isaac.'"

107. Paulinus, Poem 25, trans. Walsh, 248.

108. Acts of John, ch. 84; trans. Knut Schäferdiek, in New Testament Apocrypha, ed. Schneemelcher, 2:200. The Acts of John is a work of immensely complex transmission. I quote from Schäferdiek's reconstruction of the Greek text. See his commentary in New Testament Apocrypha, 2:152–71.

109. Ephrem, Homily on Our Lord 20.5; trans. Amar and Mathews, 297.

110. Gospel of Truth 5.30:23–32; trans. Layton, Gnostic Scriptures, 259.

111. Ephrem, "Third Discourse to Hypatius," trans. Mitchell, Prose Refutations 1:liv.

112. Anonymous Hymn 15, vv. 8, 13, 20–21; trans. Brock, Bride of Light, 48–56, at pp. 51, 53, 55. Note the allusions to Song 4:11 and 5:5 in v. 13.

113. Insightful discussion on this point is offered in Kathleen Corrigan, "The Witness of John the Baptist on an Early Byzantine Icon in Kiev," DOP 42 (1988): 1–11; and on a larger scale in Averil Cameron, "The Language of Images: The Rise of Icons and Christian Representation," in The Church and the Arts, ed. Diana Wood, SCH 28 (Oxford: Blackwell Publishers, 1992), 1–42. See also William Loerke, "'Real Presence' in Early Christian Art," in Monasticism and the Arts, ed. Timothy Gregory Verdon (Syracuse: Syracuse University Press, 1984), 29–51.

114. Paulinus of Nola, Poem 25, trans. Walsh, 251 (the archangel Gabriel at the Annunciation); Poem 6.84, trans. Walsh, 42 (Gabriel's appearance to Zechariah, the father of John the Baptist).

115. Armenian Infancy Gospel 7, 17; Arabic Gospel 30; both in Évangiles Apocryphes 2: L'Évangile de l'enfance, ed. and trans. Paul Peeters (Paris: Auguste Picard, 1914).

116. François Nau, Les Récits inédits du Moine Anastase (Paris: Picard et Fils, 1902) 1:8–9.

117. Augustine, Confessions 6.13.23; trans. Chadwick, 108.

118. Cyril of Scythopolis, Life of Euthymius 60.

119. John Cassian, Conferences 4.5; trans. Ramsey, 157.

120. Ammonas, Letter 13, trans. Chitty, at p. 18.

121. Paulinus, Poem 21, trans. Walsh, 175.

122. Life of Antony (Syriac version) 12.4; trans. Draguet, La vie primitive de S. Antoine conservée en Syriaque,.

123. *Life of St. Ioannikios* 60; trans. Denis F. Sullivan, in *Byzantine Defenders of Images*, ed. Alice-Mary Talbot, 243–352, at 326.

124. Ps.-Ephrem, *Hymns on Epiphany* 3.10–14; trans. Brock, *The Holy Spirit in the Syrian Baptismal Tradition*, 99. The Syriac text of these pseudonymous *Hymns on Epiphany* is included in Beck's edition of Ephrem's *Hymns on Nativity*, CSCO 186–87/Scr. Syr. 82–83 (Louvain: Secrétariat du Corpus SCO, 1959).

125. Prudentius, *Hymn* 4:16–24, "A Hymn After the Repast." Trans. Eagan, 25.

126. *The Martyrdom of Abo the Perfumer from Baghdad*, trans. Lang, *Lives and Legends of the Georgian Saints*, 115–33, at p. 127.

127. Severus of Minorca, *Letter on the Conversion of the Jews*, ed. and trans. Scott Bradbury (Oxford: Clarendon Press, 1996).

128. Severus of Minorca, *Letter on the Conversion of the Jews* 20–26, pp. 110–21.

129. E.g., S. A. Harvey, "St. Ephrem on the Scent of Salvation," *JTS*, n.s., 49 (1998): 109–28.

130. Grosdidier de Matons, ed., *Romanos le Mélode*, 2:79–111 (Hymn 11). Trans. Carpenter, *Kontakia of Romanos*, 1:13–21 (Nativity 2).

131. Romanos, *Nativity* 2, strophe 6.1–6; trans. Carpenter, 1:17.

132. Romanos, *Nativity* 2, strophe 7.1–11; trans. Carpenter, 1:17.

133. Isaac, *Treatise* 43, Bedjan, p. 317; trans. Wensinck, p. 211 (adapted).

134. Ephrem, *Hymns on Paradise* 4.4, trans. Brock, 98.

135. Ephrem, *Hymns on Nisibis* 39.19.

136. Paul Féghali, "La descente aux enfers dans la tradition syriaque," *Parole de l'Orient* 15 (1988/9): 127–42, treats related themes and images.

137. Ephrem, *Hymns on Nisibis* 50.10 (my trans.); "living fragrance who gives life to all": *riha haya mahe kol*.

138. Ephrem, *Homily on Our Lord* 3.

139. Ephrem, *Hymns on Virginity* 37.2; trans. McVey, *Ephrem*, 425.

140. Ephrem, *Homily on Our Lord* 5.2; trans. Amar and Mathews, *Ephrem*, at p. 281. Compare Symeon the New Theologian, Hymn 2.11–29:

> This my defiled tabernacle, subject to corruption,
> Has been united to your all-pure body
> And my blood has been mixed with your blood.
> I know that I have been united also to your Godhead
> And have become your most pure body,
> A member shining with light, holy, glorious, transparent.

As cited by Kallistos Ware, "'My helper and my enemy': The Body in Greek Christianity," in *Religion and the Body*, ed. Sarah Coakley (Cambridge: Cambridge University Press, 1997), at p. 103.

141. *Hymns on Epiphany* 3.20 (my trans.). See the discussion and commentary in J. Obied, "L'onction baptismale dans HdE III de Saint Éphrem, Traduction et analyse," *Parole de l'Orient* 17 (1992): 7–36. I do not accept Prof. Obied's argument that this hymn, unlike the rest of this collection, was in fact authored by Ephrem. But the olfactory themes in this hymn are very rich. Especially compelling is the image of the "odor of the heart" in *Hymns on Epiphany* 3.14–15, necessary to make the odor of the holy chrism effective in the sacrament of anointing. In *Hymns on Fasting* 7.8, Ephrem speaks of Daniel's friends protected from fire by their scent, pure from their fasting.

142. Jacob of Serug, Homily 22; Bedjan, *Homiliae Selectae*, 1:546 (my trans.).

143. Jacob, Homily 16; Bedjan, *Homiliae Selectae*, 1:423 (my trans.). For discussion of these passages by Jacob, see Michael Guinan, "The Eschatology of James of Sarug" (PhD. diss., Catholic University of America, 1972), ch. 1, "Death," 12–71, esp. pp. 51–52, 62–63.

144. Quoted in Joseph P. Amar, "Perspectives on the Eucharist in Ephrem the Syrian," *Worship* 61 (1987): 449. The entire hymn is translated by Amar in *Praise and Thanksgiving: Liturgical Music of the Maronite Church* (Brooklyn: Diocese of St. Maron, 1986) 1:2. I am grateful to Professor Amar for discussing this hymn with me. See also the comparative context suggested in Paul Krüger, "Le sommeil des âmes dans l'oeuvre de Narsaï," *L'Orient Syrien* 4 (1959): 193–210.

145. Compare the broader discussion in Tanios Bou Mansour, "L'Eucharistie chez Jacques de Saroug," *Parole de l'Orient* 17 (1992): 37–60.

146. As general introductions, see René Bornert, *Les Commentaires byzantins de la divine liturgie du 7e au 15e siècle* (Paris: Institut français d'études byzantines, 1966); Paul Meyendorff, *St. Germanus of Constantinople, On the Divine Liturgy* (Crestwood, NY: St. Vladimir's Seminary Press, 1984), 23–54; and Hans-Joachim Schultz, *The Byzantine Liturgy: Symbolic Structure and Faith Expression*, trans. Matthew J. O'Connell (New York: Pueblo Publishing, 1986), 14–20 (John Chrysostom and Theodore of Mopsuestia), 25–28 (Dionysius the Areopagite), 43–49 (Maximus Confessor), 67–76 (Germanus of Constantinople), 114–32 (Symeon the New Theologian and Nicholas Cabasilas).

147. See, e.g., Gregory Dix, *The Shape of the Liturgy* (repr. 2nd ed. 1945, London: A & C Black, 1993), 434–526. Compare the related example of imperial coronations, Janet L. Nelson, "Symbols in Context," in *The Orthodox Churches and the West*, ed. Derek Baker, SCH 13 (Oxford: Basil Blackwell, 1976), 97–119.

148. A useful introduction may be found in Andrew Louth, *Denys the Areopagite* (Wilton, CT: Morehouse-Barlow, 1989).

149. Louth, *Denys*, provides an overview. But the traditional debates are also well represented, for example, in Bernard McGinn, *The Presence of God: A History of Western Christian Mysticism*, vol. 1, *The Foundations of Mysticism: Origins to the Fifth Century* (New York: Crossroad, 1992), 157–82; John Meyendorff, *Christ in Eastern Christian*

Thought (Crestwood, NY: St. Vladimir's Seminary Press, 1975), 91–112. In recent years, the works of Paul Rorem have been especially influential but have continued this reading, e.g., Biblical and Liturgical Symbols with the Pseudo-Dionysian Synthesis (Toronto: Pontifical Institute for Medieval Studies, 1984); idem, Pseudo-Dionysius: A Commentary on the Texts and an Introduction to their Influence (New York: Oxford University Press, 1993).

150. Important critiques have been done by Alexander Golitzin, "The Mysticism of Dionysius Areopagita: Platonist or Christian?" Mystics Quarterly 19 (1993): 98–114; idem, "Hierarchy vs. Anarchy? Dionysius Areopagita, Symeon the New Theologian, Nicetas Stethatos, and their Common Roots in Ascetical Tradition," SVTQ 38 (1994): 131–79.

151. Louth, Denys, makes the effort in this direction. But the real ground-breaking work has been done by Alexander Golitzin, Et Introibo ad Altare Dei:The Mystagogy of Dionysius Areopagita, with special reference to its predecessors in the eastern Christian tradition, Analekta Vlatadon 59 (Thessalonika: Patriarchikon Idryma Paterikon Meleton, 1994), esp. 349–92; idem, "'A Contemplative and a Liturgist': Father Georges Florovsky on the Corpus Dionysiacum," SVTQ 43 (1999): 131–61. For an insightful discussion that sets Dionysius within the shifting domains of late antique/early Byzantine sociology of knowledge, see Averil Cameron, "The Language of Images."

152. Dionysius, Celestial Hierarchy 1.3; trans. Luibheid, Pseudo-Dionysius, 146.

153. Dionysius, Celestial Hierarchy 2.4; trans. Luibheid, Pseudo-Dionysius, 151.

154. E.g., the fine analysis of Golitzin, "Contemplative and Liturgist," at pp. 143–52. The pattern will be discussed further in chapter 4, at pp. 181–86.

155. Golitzin, Et Introibo ad Altare Dei, 148–54.

156. Dionysius, Celestial Hierarchy 2.5; trans. Luibheid, Pseudo-Dionysius, 152.

157. Dionysius, Ecclesiastical Hierarchy 1.4.

158. Dionysius, Ecclesiastical Heirarchy 2.3.8; trans. Luibheid, Pseudo-Dionysius, 208.

159. Dionysius, Ecclesiastical Hierarchy 3.3.3; trans. Luibheid, Pseudo-Dionysius, 212.

160. Above all, see W. Strothmann, Das Sakrament der Myron-Weihe in der Schrift De ecclesiastica hierarchia des Pseudo-Dionysius Areopagita, Göttinger Orientforschungen, Reihe I, Band 15 (Wiesbaden: Otto Harrassowitz, 1977–78); and also Golitzin, Et Introibo ad Altare Dei, 203–208; Louth, Denys, 63–65.

161. Dionysius, Ecclesiastical Hierarchy 4.2; trans. Luibheid, Pseudo-Dionysius, 224–25. See the discussion in Golitzin, Et Introibo ad Altare Dei, 203–204.

162. Dionysius, Ecclesiastical Hierarchy 4.3.1; trans. Luibheid, Pseudo-Dionysius, 225.

163. Dionysius, Ecclesiastical Hierarchy 4.3.2; trans. Luibheid, Pseudo-Dionysius, 226–27.

164. Dionysius, Ecclesiastical Hierarchy 4.3.12; trans. Luibheid, Pseudo-Dionysius, 232.

165. Dionysius, Ecclesiastical Hierarchy 4.3.4.; trans. Luibheid, Pseudo-Dionysius, 289.

166. Maximus Confessor, *The Church's Mystagogy: In which are explained the symbolism of certain rites performed in the divine synaxis*, trans. Berthold, *Maximus Confessor*, 181–225.

167. Scholars have often presented Maximus as succeeding in this endeavor far more than Dionysius, and thereby achieving a greater accomplishment for Christian intellectual history. The reassessment of Dionysius that Golitzin demonstrates may well challenge such a view. But see esp. Andrew Louth, *Maximus the Confessor* (New York: Routledge, 1996); and idem, *Wisdom of the Byzantine Church: Evagrius of Pontos and Maximos the Confessor*, 1997 Paine Lectures in Religion (Columbia: University of Missouri, 1998), where, at pp. 34–35, he presents Maximus in a scheme of three churches exactly like that posited earlier by Golitzin for Dionysius.

168. Maximus, *Mystagogy* 2; trans. Berthold, *Maximus Confessor*, 189.

169. R. Allers, "Microcosmus, from Anaximandros to Paracelsus," *Traditio* 2 (1944): 319–407; Lars Thunberg, *Microcosm and Mediator* (Lund: C. W. K. Gleerup, 1965). As George Berthold, *Maximus Confessor*, points out at p. 219 n. 67, there is a humorous critique of the religious value of this tradition in Gregory of Nyssa, *On the Making of the Man* 16.1.

170. Maximus, *Mystagogy* 24 (at Berthold, *Maximus Confessor*, 212–13) takes an example using eye, ear, and tongue.

171. On the importance of visual piety, see the classic expositions of John of Damascus, *On the Divine Images*, and Theodore the Studite, *On the Holy Icons*. For the cultural and socio-political shifts that presaged a Byzantine iconophile piety, see, e.g., Averil Cameron, "The Language of Images;" Corrigan, "The Witness of John the Baptist;" Loerke, "'Real Presence;'" and now the groundbreaking study of Georgia Frank, *The Memory of the Eyes: Pilgrimage to Living Saints in Christian Late Antiquity* (Berkeley: University of California Press, 2000); eadem, "The Pilgrim's Gaze in the Age Before Icons," in *Visuality Before and Beyond the Renaissance: Seeing as Others Saw*, ed. Robert S. Nelson (Cambridge: Cambridge University Press, 2000), 98–115. Cf. also Gary Vikan, "Icons and Icon Piety in Early Byzantium," in *Byzantine East, Latin West: Art-Historical Studies in Honor of Kurt Weitzmann*, ed. Christopher Moss and Katherine Kiefer (Princeton: Dept. of Art and Archaeology, Princeton University, 1995); and Liz James, "Color and Meaning in Byzantium," *JECS* 11 (2003): 223–33.

172. Germanus, *On the Divine Liturgy*.

173. Germanus, *On the Divine Liturgy* 1; trans. Meyendorff, 57. The passage cites Song 1:3, 1:4, and Psalm 133 (132):2, all in their LXX versions.

174. Germanus, *On the Divine Liturgy* 30; trans. Meyendorff, 79.

175. Germanus, *On the Divine Liturgy* 30; trans. Meyendorff, 81.

176. Germanus, *On the Divine Liturgy* 37; trans. Meyendorff, 87.

177. The shift from Dionysius to Germanus as one from an "ahistorical" to "historical" understanding of the liturgy as a process of memory has been

much discussed by scholars. E.g., Robert Taft, "The Liturgy of the Great Church: An Initial Synthesis of Structure and Interpretation on the Eve of Iconoclasm," DOP 34–35 (1980–81): 45–75; Schultz, The Byzantine Liturgy, 4–135.

178. Symeon, 14th Ethical Discourse; trans. Golitzin, St. Symeon the New Theologian, 1:171–81.

179. See Golitzin's comments, St. Symeon the New Theologian, 1:175 n. 1; and idem, "Hierarchy vs. Anarchy?"

180. Symeon, 14th Ethical Discourse; trans. Golitzin, St. Symeon the New Theologian, 1:174.

181. Symeon, 14th Ethical Discourse; trans. Golitizin, St. Symeon the New Theologian 1:176.

182. For a list of the primary texts and their features, see Sebastian P. Brock, "Jacob of Edessa's Discourse on the Myron," OC 63 (1979): 20–36, at pp. 20–22. The first such discourse is that by the seventh-century patriarch John of the Sedre, now edited and translated in Jouko Martikainen, Johannes I. Sedra. Einleitung, Syrische Texte, Übersetzung, und vollständiges Wörterverzeichnis, Göttinger Orientforschungen 1/34 (Wiesbaden: Otto Harrassowitz, 1991), 171–210. Later examples by George of the Arabs and Moshe bar Kepha may be found in R. H. Connolly and H. W. Codrington, Two Commentaries on the Jacobite Liturgy by George Bishop of the Arab Tribes and Moses bar Kepha, Together with the Syriac Anaphora of St. James and a Document entitled the Book of Life (London: Williams and Norgate, 1913).

183. See the discussion in chapter 2, pp. 73–74. On the consecration of the myron in Byzantine tradition, see L. Petit, "Du pouvoir de consacrer le Saint Chrême," and "Composition et consécration du Saint Chrême," Échos d'Orient 3 (1899): 1–7, 129–42.

184. Strothmann, Das Sakrament der Myron-Weihe, provides editions of the Syriac versions of Dionysius's Ecclesiastical Hierarchy 4.

185. Critical edition with translation in Brock, "Jacob of Edessa's Discourse on the Myron." The citations are from Brock's text.

186. Jacob of Edessa, Discourse 7; trans. Brock, 31.

187. Jacob of Edessa, Discourse 8; trans. Brock, 32.

188. Jacob of Edessa, Discourse 7; trans. Brock, 31.

189. Jacob of Edessa, Discourse 17; trans. Brock, 34.

190. For the continuing Syriac tradition of the relationship between the myron and the experience of divine presence, especially of the Holy Spirit, see Emmanuel-Pataq Siman, L'Expérience de l'Ésprit par l'église d'après la tradition syrienne d'Antioche, TH 15 (Paris: Éditions Beauchesne, 1971), esp. 92–104.

191. See esp. Juan Mateos, "'Sedre' et prières connexes dans quelque anciennes collections," OCP 28 (1962): 239–87; Jacob Thekeparampil, "Weihrauchsymbolik in den syrischen gebeten des mittelalters und bei pseudo-Dionysius," in Typus,

Symbol, Allegorie, ed. Margot Schmidt and C. Geyer (Regensburg: Friedrich Pustet, 1982), 131–45; Jacob Thekeparampil, "Prayers After Incense," *Parole de l'Orient* 6/7 (1975–76): 325–40; Joseph P. Amar, "The Syriac *Hoosoyo*: A Consideration of Narrative Techniques," *Diakonia* 22 (1988–89): 153–68.

192. Discussed in chapter 2, p. 77.

193. The Church of the East had always had its autonomous existence in the Persian Empire, developing quite independently from the churches of the Roman Empire although with occasional, and important, interaction. But the arrival into Persia of the exiled dyophysites following the closing of the theological school of Edessa in 489 precipitated a deliberate parting of the ways for the Church of the East. For the Syrian Orthodox, such a move came later, in the second half of the sixth century, in the context of imperial persecutions against those who rejected the Council of Chalcedon. I do not in any way wish to imply that the different Syriac-speaking churches were united historically, for they were often at bitter odds with one another; but they did share certain fundamental dispositions, and the strength of incense imagery and piety is one place where there is consistency across Syrian Orthodox, Church of the East, and Maronite traditions. For the autonomous development of Christianity in Persia, see J.-M. Fiey, *Jalons pour une histoire de l'église en Iraq,* CSCO 310/Sub. 36 (Louvain, 1970); Samuel Hugh Moffett, *A History of Christianity in Asia,* vol. 1, *Beginnings to 1500* (San Franciso: Harper SanFrancisco, 1992).

194. On the development of this sequence, see Mateos, "Sedre;" and especially Amar, "The Syriac *Hoosoyo,*" 156–62.

195. Amar, "The Syriac *Hoosoyo;*" Thekeparampil, "Prayers After Incense."

196. Thekeparampil, "Prayers After Incense."

197. Trans. Thekeparampil, "Prayers After Incense," 332–33 (Prayer 16). Thekeparampil focuses on the prayers after incense, while Mateos, "Sedre," focuses on those during the incense offering. For an example of a fuller ritual context, see the service for the anointing of the sick edited and translated by Y. Moubarac, *Pentalogie Maronite, antiochienne/domaine,* vol. 4, *Livre du Pain et du Vin, de L'eau, de L'huile et du Baume* (Beirut: Cénacle Libanais, 1984), 359–75.

198. Thekeparampil, "Prayers After Incense," 336.

199. A point particularly well made by Amar, "The Syriac *Hoosoyo,*" 162–64.

200. The following is adapted from select portions of Susan Ashbrook Harvey, "Why the Perfume Mattered: The Sinful Woman in Syriac Exegetical Tradition," in *In Dominico Eloquio/In Lordly Eloquence: Essays on Patristic Exegesis in Honor of Robert Wilken,* ed. Paul M. Blowers, Angela Russell Christman, David Hunter, and Robin Darling Young (Grand Rapids: Eerdmans Press, 2001), 69–89, where the major texts are cited with their editions and, if possible, translations. Though Syriac scholars have occasionally remarked upon the sizable body of surviving texts on the Sinful Woman, these texts have seen little scholarly attention apart from the publication of critical editions and translations. For an exception see

Hannah Hunt, "The Tears of the Sinful Woman: A Theology of Redemption in the Homilies of St. Ephraim and his Followers," *Hugoye: Journal of Syriac Studies* 1:2 (1998): http://www.acad.cua.edu/syrcom/Hugoye.

201. The Pharisee is not named as Simon until Lk 7:40 when Jesus addresses him by that name.

202. Victor Saxer, "Les Saintes Marie Madeleine et Marie de Béthanie dans la tradition liturgique et homilétique orientale," *RSR* 32 (1958): 1–37. Eastern Christianity in general did not associate Mary Magdalene with the Sinful Woman, venerating her instead as one of the myrrh-bearing women who came to Christ's tomb and found he had risen. However, later copyists and editors of the printed editions often added subtitles to the homilies or hymns on the Sinful Woman, identifying her as Mary Magdalene (there is an allusion to "seven demons" having followed the Woman in Jacob of Serug's homily, although the name 'Mary Magdalene' is not mentioned: Jacob, *Homily* 51, at Bedjan, *Homiliae Selectae*, 2:408, line 20; see n. 210 below for full citation). The tremendously influential tradition of Mary Magdalene as penitent harlot was a western development, receiving its first real impetus in the sixth century from Gregory the Great. For an overview, see Susan Haskins, *Mary Magdalene: Myth and Metaphor* (New York: Harcourt, Brace, 1994).

203. Sermon 4, ed. Beck, CSCO 311/Scr. Syr. 134, 79–81, with German trans. CSCO 312/Scr. Syr. 135, 99–109. English trans. by Gwynn, NPNF, 2nd ser., 13:336–41. The authenticity of these sermons in general, and this one in particular, remains very doubtful. Beck's discussion of this sermon, CSCO 312/Scr. Syr. 135, at pp. x–xii, demonstrates the uncertainty. Cf. Sebastian P. Brock, "Dramatic Dialogue Poems," *Symposium Syriacum IV*, ed. H. J. W. Drijvers, R. Lavenant, C. Molenberg, and G. J. Reinink, OCA 229 (1987): 135–47, at 142. For the extant Greek version, which has important differences in content, see CPG III, 3952; F. Halkin, *Novum Auctarium bibliothecae hagiographicae graecae*, SH 65 (Brussels: Société des Bollandistes, 1984), 1162d–e. On the medieval influence of this text, see A. C. Mahr, *Relations of Passion Plays to St. Ephrem the Syrian* (Columbus, OH: The Wartburg Press, 1942); idem, *The Cyprus Passion Cycle* (Notre Dame, IN: University of Notre Dame Press, 1947) 36–38, 50–52. An abbreviated version of this homily, "On the Sinful Woman," is still sung today by Syrian Orthodox Christians in the daily prayers (following the *Shehimo*) at the Soutoro ("Protection," or the office at the end of the day) for Monday.

204. "On the Sinful Woman," lines 79–96 (my trans.); Beck, CSCO 311/Scr. Syr. 134, at p. 80 (cf. NPNF, 2nd ser., 13:337).

205. John Chrysostom, *Homilies on Matthew* 80.

206. Y. 'Abd Al-Masih, "A Discourse by St. John Chrysostom on the Sinful Woman in the Sa'idic Dialect," *BSAC* 15 (1958–60): 11–39. Severus of Antioch's *Homily* 118, "On the Woman written about in Luke, that is, the Prostitute or the Sinful Woman," is extant only in Syriac; ed. and trans. Maurice Brière, "Les

Homiliae Cathédrales de Sévère d'Antioche: Hom. 118," PO 26 (Paris: Firmin-Didot, 1948): 357–74. For the Sinful Woman's perfume interpreted as the perfume of virtues in earlier patristic tradition, see Clement of Alexandria, *Christ the Teacher* 2.8; and Origen, *Fragments on Luke* 113, trans. Lienhard, 173. Severus, *Homily* 118, at Brière, pp. 372–74, also interprets the incense of Exodus 30:23–25 and 31 as a compound of virtues; so, too, Origen on sacrificial incense, *Homilies on Leviticus* 9.8. For the paradigmatic allegorical treatments of perfumes, see Origen's and Gregory of Nyssa's commentaries on the Song of Songs, discussed in chapter 4, pp. 172–79.

207. Ephrem, *Homily on Our Lord*. Ephrem also has important discussion of the Sinful Woman elsewhere: see especially *Hymns on Nisibis* 60, and the *Commentary on the Diatessaron* VII.18, X.8–9. For contrast, see Ephrem's treatments on Mary of Bethany in *Hymns on Virginity* 4.11 and 6.7.

208. *Homily on Our Lord* 44.1; trans. Amar and Matthews, 219.

209. *Homily on Our Lord* 46.1; trans. Amar and Matthews, 322.

210. Jacob of Serug, Homily 51, "On the Sinful Woman whose Sins Our Lord forgave," ed. Bedjan, *Homiliae Selectae* 2:402–28.

211. Jacob of Serug, Homily 51, at Bedjan, *Homiliae Selectae* 2:411, lines 20–21 (my trans.).

212. Jacob of Serug, Homily 51, at Bedjan, *Homiliae Selectae*, 2:410, lines 12–15 (my trans.).

213. Jacob of Serug, Homily 51, at Bedjan, *Homiliae Selectae*, 2:414–15.

214. Jacob of Serug, Homily 51, at Bedjan, *Homiliae Selectae*, 2:415, lines 10–14, (my trans.).

215. The classic work by Jean Daniélou, *The Bible and the Liturgy* (Notre Dame, IN: University of Notre Dame Press, 1956), remains an excellent starting point.

216. See also the sacrificial stress in the anonymous Syriac homilies I and III, ed. and trans. F. Graffin, "Homélies anonymes du VIe siècle: Homélies sur la pécheresse I, II, III," PO 41 (Turnhout: Brepols, 1984), 449–527.

217. Ed. and trans. Grosdidier de Matons, *Romanos le Mélode: Hymnes* 3:13–43, *Kontakion* 21. The 'Ephremic' homily circulated in Greek, as cited above; but Romanos would also have been familiar with the Syriac themes from his upbringing in Emesa. There continues to be considerable debate about the relationship between Ephrem and Romanos, with polarized views about how much Syriac influence on the great Greek hymnographer there may have been. The most conservative arguments, strictly limiting Syriac influence, have been made by José Grosdidier de Matons, *Romanos le Mélode et les origines de la poésie religieuse à Byzance* (Paris: Éditions Beauchesne, 1977); the strongest case in support of such influence by William Petersen, *The Diatessaron and Ephrem Syrus as Sources of Romanos the Melodist*, CSCO 475/Sub. 74 (Louvain: Peeters Press, 1985), and idem, "The Dependence of Romanos the Melodist upon the Syriac Ephrem: Its

Importance for the Origin of the Kontakion," *VC* 39 (1985): 171–87. In contrast to both positions, Sebastian Brock stresses the fluidity of cultural interaction in the deeply bilingual late antique Syrian Orient; see his "From Ephrem to Romanos," *SP* 20, ed. Elizabeth A. Livingstone (Leuven: Peeters Press, 1989), 139–51; and idem, "Syriac and Greek Hymnography: Problems of Origin," *SP* 16, ed. Elizabeth A. Livingstone (Berlin: Akademie-Verlag, 1985), 77–81. Romanos was not the only Greek writer to draw upon the 'Ephremic' homily; see ps.-Chrysostom, PG 59:531–36. R. J. Schork, *Sacred Song from the Byzantine Pulpit: Romanos the Melodist* (Gainesville: University Press of Florida, 1995), provides a fine treatment of the dramatic mode in Romanos's kontakia. However, his discussion and translation of "The Sinful Woman," pp. 20–21, 77–85, do not mention the 'Ephremic' homily on which Romanos drew for the scene at the Perfume Seller's shop.

218. Romanos, "On the Sinful Woman," strophe 1; trans. Carpenter, *Kontakia of Romanos*, 1: 97–107, at p. 101. I follow the translation of Carpenter because hers renders the olfactory imagery most graphically, but two other fine translations of this homily into English are available: Schork, *Sacred Song from the Byzantine Pulpit*, 77–85; and Ephrem Lash, *St. Romanos the Melodist, Kontakia On the Life of Christ* (San Francisco: HarperCollins, 1995), 75–84.

219. Strophe 2; trans. Carpenter, *Kontakia of Romanos*, 1:102.

220. Discussed by Carpenter at *Kontakia of Romanos*, 1:103, n. 6.

221. Strophe 6; trans. Carpenter, *Kontakia of Romanos*, 1:103.

222. Strophe 17; trans. Carpenter, *Kontakia of Romanos*, 1:107.

223. Greek Orthodox Christians sing the Troparion of the Sinful Woman at the Bridegroom Matins for Holy Wednesday during the week preceeding Easter. The hymn is not the one by Romanos, but that of the ninth-century hymnographer, Kassia. For an edition, translation, and commentary see Antonia Tripolitis, *Kassia: The Legend, the Woman, and her Work* (New York: Garland Publishing, 1992), 76–79 (where the editor mistakenly names the Sinful Woman as Mary Magdalene, although the troparion and the standard service books leave her nameless). This troparion is generally referred to as the Kassiani. Kassia shares with the homilies considered here the tradition of having the Woman speak in her own voice, but does not include any reference to the Perfume Seller or his shop.

224. Anonymous Homily III, sec. 16–17; ed. Graffin, PO 41:496–99 (my trans.).

Chapter 4. Redeeming Scents

1. Lucretius, *De Rerum Natura* (On the Nature of Things), 3. 327–30; trans. Rouse, 193.

2. The scholarship is massive, and has been especially sparked by the models proposed in Michel Foucault's landmark work, *The History of Sexuality*, especially vol. 2, *The Use of Pleasure*, trans. Robert Hurley (New York: Pantheon Books, 1985)

and vol. 3, *The Care of the Self*, trans. Robert Hurley (New York: Vintage Books, 1986). A recent and very readable discussion is James Davidson, *Courtesans and Fishcakes: The Consuming Passions of Classical Athens* (London: HarperCollins, 1997). Other important studies that have helped to define the territory are: David Halperin, John J. Winkler, Froma Zeitlin, eds., *Before Sexuality: The Construction of Erotic Experience in the Ancient Greek World* (Princeton: Princeton University Press, 1990); John J. Winkler, *The Constraints of Desire: The Anthropology of Sex and Gender in Ancient Greece* (New York: Routledge, 1990); David M. Halperin, *One Hundred Years of Homosexuality and Other Essays on Greek Love* (New York: Routledge, 1990). For an important new challenge to Foucault's paradigm, see now Kathy L. Gaca, *The Making of Fornication: Eros, Ethics, and Political Reform in Greek Philosophy and Early Christianity* (Berkeley: University of California Press, 2003).

3. The two pivotal works have been Aline Rousselle, *Porneia: On Desire and the Body in Antiquity*, trans. Felicia Pheasant (Oxford: Basil Blackwell, 1988); Peter Brown, *The Body and Society: Men, Women, and Sexual Renunciation in Early Christianity* (New York: Columbia University Press, 1988). More recently, two important studies have brought fresh reconsideration of earliest and late antique Christianity, respectively: Dale B. Martin, *The Corinthian Body* (New Haven: Yale University Press, 1995); and Teresa M. Shaw, *The Burden of the Flesh: Fasting and Sexuality in Early Christianity* (Minneapolis: Fortress Press, 1998).

4. The range and fruitfulness of this discussion may be sampled in the useful volume edited by Vincent L. Wimbush and Richard Valantasis, *Asceticism* (New York: Oxford University Press, 1995).

5. Consider Béatrice Caseau, "Christian Bodies: The Senses and Early Byzantine Christianity," in *Desire and Denial in Byzantium*, ed. Liz James (Aldershot, Hampshire: Ashgate Publishing, 1999), 101–109.

6. Marcus Aurelius, *Meditations* 5.28; trans. Kirk, 57 (adapted).

7. An excellent discussion of the philosophical base into which Christianity emerged will be found in Stanley K. Stowers, "Self-Mastery in Greco-Roman Culture and Earliest Christian Literature," in *Paul in the Greco-Roman World: a Handbook*, J. Paul Sampley, ed. (Harrisburg, PA: Trinity Press International, 2003), 524–50.

8. Discussed in chapter 1, pp. 39–42.

9. See the discussion in chapter 2, p. 59.

10. Basil, *Address to Young Men on Reading Greek Literature* 9; trans. Deferrari and McGuire, 415.

11. Basil, *Address to Young Men* 9; trans. Deferrari and McGuire, 421.

12. Discussed in chapter 3, pp. 110–14.

13. Gregory of Nyssa, *The Lord's Prayer*, Sermon 4; trans. Graef, 64.

14. Gregory of Nyssa, *The Lord's Prayer*, Sermon 4; trans. Graef, 66.

15. Gregory of Nyssa, *The Lord's Prayer*, Sermon 5; trans. Graef, 78.

16. Gregory of Nyssa, *The Beatitudes*, Sermon 8; trans. Graef, 171.

17. John Chrysostom, *Address on Vainglory and the Right Way for Parents to Bring Up Their Children* 1; trans. Laistner, 85.

18. Chrysostom, *On Vainglory* 27; trans. Laistner, 98.

19. Chrysostom, *On Vainglory* 54; trans. Laistner, 110. Compare Chrysostom on the continual attacks of Satan against Christians living in the world: "That which seems the slightest of all these attacks, the scent of perfume falling from courtesans as they pass somewhere nearby has captured and taken us away as prisoners by a mere accident." *Sermon 3 on Lazarus and the Rich Man*; trans. Roth, *St. John Chrysostom on Wealth and Poverty*, 59.

20. Discussed in chapter 1, p. 39–44. Clement, *Christ the Educator*, book 2, contains much positive assessment of the use of scents for therapeutic purposes; but book 3, treating smells in a context of cosmetic use and moral irresponsibility, is every bit as castigating about perfumes as Chrysostom here.

21. Preaching on the feast day of the martyr St. Pelagia of Antioch, Chrysostom exhorted his congregation: "Let us fill the highway with incense. For the road wouldn't seem as venerable, if someone waved a censer along its entire length and perfumed the air with the sweet smell, as it would now, if everyone passing along it today were to relate to themselves the martyrs' struggles and so walk home, each making their tongue a censer." Chrysostom, "A Homily on Pelagia, Virgin and Martyr," 3; trans. Mayer in *'Let Us Die that We May Live'*, ed. Leemans, Mayer, Allen and Dehandschutter, 148–61, at 154. Chrysostom here shifts from the ritual use of incense in the public ceremonial to the image of incense as the herald spreading good news, an image embodied by the congregation spreading the stories of the martyrs' witness throughout their communities (and hence evocative of 2 Cor 2:14–16).

22. Chapter 2, pp. 69–74; and chapter 3, p. 114–16.

23. Ambrose, *Flight from the World* 1.3; trans. McHugh, 282.

24. Ambrose, *Flight from the World* 4.21; trans. McHugh, 298.

25. Augustine, *Confessions* 10.35.54–55; trans. Chadwick, 210–11.

26. Ambrose, *Jacob and the Happy Life* 2.(1.3–4); trans. McHugh, 147–48. Jewish exegesis of Genesis 27:27 is interesting in its olfactory aspects as well: rabbinic tradition plays upon the "smell of treachery," while the (fetid) goatskins of Jacob's disguise are fragrant with the air of paradise. See Avivah Gottlieb Zornberg, *Genesis: The Beginning of Desire* (Philadelphia: Jewish Publication Society, 1995), 177 and citations.

27. I am helped above all by David Dawson, *Allegorical Readers and Cultural Revision in Ancient Alexandria* (Berkeley: University of California Press, 1992); and Frances M. Young, *Biblical Exegesis and the Formation of Christian Culture* (Cambridge: Cambridge University Press, 1997).

28. Ambrose, *Joseph* 3.14; trans. McHugh, 198 (adapted).

29. It was the allusion to liturgical practice that was the primary difference from earlier uses of this trope. Compare Clement of Alexandria, *Christ the Educator* 2.8: "It is highly requisite for the men who belong to us to give forth the odor not of ointments but of nobleness and goodness. And let women breathe the odor of the true royal ointment, that of Christ, not of unguents and scented powders; and let her always be anointed with the ambrosial chrism of modesty, and find delight in the holy unguent, the Spirit." Trans. Wood, 233.

30. John Chrysostom, *Hom. on Timothy* 2; trans. Schaff, NPNF 13:415.

31. Two recent studies on Athanasius of Alexandria emphasize the importance of "the body" in Athanasius's thinking in exactly these terms—as the location of human-divine relation, and as a crucial source of religious knowledge: Alvyn Pettersen, *Athanasius and the Human Body* (Bristol: The Bristol Press, 1990); and David Brakke, *Athanasius and the Politics of Asceticism* (Oxford: Clarendon Press, 1995). Neither approaches the body through the category of sensory experience in any major way, but Brakke, in particular, provides significant discussion of ascetic and ecclesiastical practices as critical for understanding Athanasius's incarnational theology.

32. E.g., Augustine, *Confessions* 8.6.15; Paulinus of Nola, *Poems* 25 and 27.

33. Aphrahat, *Demonstration* 6.1; trans. Gwynn, NPNF, 2nd ser., 12:363.

34. Ephrem, *Hymns on Faith* 20.11; trans. Brock, *Syriac Fathers on Prayer and the Spiritual Life*, 33–35, here at pp. 34–35.

35. Jonah 3. Ephrem, *Hymns on Virginity* 50. 2–6; trans. McVey, *Ephrem*, 458.

36. Paphnutius, *Life of Onnophrius* 21; trans. Vivian, 158–59.

37. Paphnutius, *Life of Onnophrius* 20; trans. Vivian, 158.

38. E.g., *On St. Coluthus*, sec. 6, sec. 92 (trans. S. E. Thompson); *On St. Victor*, sec. 26 (trans. A. B. Scott); both in DePuydt, *Encomiastica*.

39. Cited in Mark Sheridan, "The Development of the Interior Life of Certain Early Monastic Writings in Egypt," in *The Spirituality of Ancient Monasticism*, Acts of the International Colloquium, Cracow-Tyniec 16–19 Nov. 1994, ed. Marek Starowieyski (Cracow-Tyniec: Wydawnictwo Benedyktynów, 1995), 91–104, at p. 101.

40. Theodoret, *History of the Monks of Syria* 13.19; trans. Price, 107.

41. On this as a literary motif, see G. J. M. Bartelink, "Les oxymores Desertum civitas et Desertum floribus vernans," *SM* 15 (1973): 7–15.

42. John Cassian, *Conferences* 1.1; trans. Ramsey, 41. In his commentary on this passage (pp. 67–68, at 68), Ramsey notes other patristic examples as well as other references in the *Conferences* to the fragrance of virtue: 9.19, 10.10.9, 17.19.2, 20.19.1, 20.12.14, 24.25.6; and to the fragrance of spiritual knowledge: 14. 16. 7. In turn, Cassian follows the convention of sin (or demon possession) as indicated by intolerable stench. Cassian, *Conferences* 2.11.5, with Ramsey's commentary on pp. 108–109.

43. John Moschos, *Spiritual Meadow*, Prologue; trans. Wortley, 3. For the same motif, see the Prologue to the *Miracles of St. Artemios*, in Crisafulli and Nesbitt, 77; or the Prologue to bk. 1, ch. 2, of Thomas of Marga's *Historia Monastica*, where the image of gathering choice scents from the fields is extended to include the scents of the threshing, grinding, kneading, and baking of the sacrificial offering. The motif is used for St. Antony the Great in the canon still sung for his feast day, at Ode 7: "(Holy Father Antony,) Your hands are cups of fragrance, spreading as from a flowery meadow the sweet smell of virtue and salvation to those who cry with love: 'Blessed are you forevermore!'" See "January 17: Commemoration of our Holy and God-bearing Father Anthony the Great," in the *January Menaion, Service Books of the Byzantine Churches*, vol. 5 (Newton Centre, MA: Sophia Press, 1992), pp. 247–48. For the Greek text, see http://www.qub.ac .uk/ibs/glt/texts/Jan/17.htm.

44. Leontius of Neopolis, *Life of Simeon Salos* 4; trans. Krueger, 163. To this day there is a saying amongst the monks of Mt. Athos, "When a hermit's mouth opens, it will fill you with fragrance." See Hierotheos Vlachos, *A Night in the Desert of the Holy Mountain: Discussion With a Hermit on the Jesus Prayer*, trans. Effie Mavromichali (Levadia, Greece: Birth of Theotokos Monastery, 1991), 20; the theme of asceticism, prayer, and fragrance recurs often in this book.

45. Ps.-Chrysostom, *On the Holy Cross* 3; trans. Browne, 32.

46. Romanos, *Kontakion* 46. 3; trans. Carpenter, *Kontakia* 2:136.

47. Ambrose, "Concerning Virgins," trans. de Romestin, NPNF, 2nd ser., 10:361–87.

48. Ambrose, "Concerning Virgins" 1.7.39; trans. de Romestin, NPNF, 2nd ser., 10:369.

49. Ambrose, "Concerning Virgins" 2.2.18; trans. de Romestin, NPNF, 2nd ser., 10:376.

50. On the models for this understanding of biblical exegesis, see especially Young, *Biblical Exegesis and the Formation of Christian Culture*. Recently, the role of biblical interpretation specifically as an impetus for ascetic activity has been thoroughly reconsidered in Elizabeth A. Clark, *Reading Renunciation* (Princeton: Princeton University Press, 1999). See also eadem, "The Uses of the Song of Songs: Origen and the Later Latin Fathers," in *Ascetic Piety and Women's Faith: Essays on Late Ancient Christianity*, ed. Elizabeth Clark (Lewiston, NY: Edwin Mellen Press, 1986), 386–427.

51. *Apocalypse of Paul* 9; trans. Duensing and de Santos Otero, in *New Testament Apocrypha*, ed. Wilhelm Schneemelcher, 718.

52. Gregory of Nyssa, *The Beatitudes*, Sermon 8.

53. The most influential passages were: Ex 24:9–18, 34:29–35; Num 12:8; 1 Kings 19:8–13; Isa 6:1–7; Ezek 1:1–28; Dan 7:1–28; Mk 9:2–8; Mt 17:1–8; Lk

9:28–36; 2 Cor 12:2–4. Passages such as Mt 5:8 held out the promise for every believer.

54. For examples of exegetical discussion, see, e.g., Gretchen Kreahling McKay, "The Eastern Christian Exegetical Tradition of Daniel's Vision of the Ancient of Days," *JECS* 7 (1999): 139–61; and Angela Russell Christman, "What did Ezekiel See?: Patristic Exegesis of Ezekiel 1 and Debates about God's Incomprehensibility," *Pro Ecclesia* 8 (1999): 338–63. For the treatment of such passages within contemplative and liturgical contexts, see Alexander Golitzin, "Liturgy and Mysticism: The Experience of God in Eastern Orthodox Christianity," *Pro Ecclesia* 8 (1999): 159–86; idem, "The Image and Glory of God in Jacob of Serug's Homily, 'On that Chariot that Ezekiel the Prophet Saw,'" *SVTQ* 47 (2003): 323–64.

55. Plato, *Symposium*, 220c; Porphyry, *Life of Plotinus*, sec. 23.

56. To sense the breadth of this tradition especially in eastern monasticism, see, e.g., B. Fraigneau-Julien, *Les Sens Spirituels et la Vision de Dieu selon Syméon le Nouveau Théologien*, TH 67 (Paris: Éditions Beauchesne, 1985); Harry Austryn Wolfson, "The Internal Senses in Latin, Arabic, and Hebrew Philosophic Texts," *HTR* 28 (1935): 69–133. An example from the west may be found in Wolfgang Riehle, *The Middle English Mystics*, trans. Bernard Standring (London: Routledge, 1981), 104–25.

57. E.g., 2 Cor 4:16; Rom 7:22; Eph 3:16.

58. E.g., the excerpts in *Philo, Selections*, trans. Winston, at pp. 157–74.

59. Most important are the studies by Karl Rahner, "Le début d'une doctrine des cinq sens spirituels chez Origène," *RAM* 13 (1932): 113–45; and John M. Dillon, "*Aisthésis Noêtê*: A Doctrine of Spiritual Senses in Origen and in Plotinus," in *Hellenica et Judaica: Hommage à Valentin Nikiprowetzky*, ed. A. Caquot, M. Hadas-Lebel, and J. Riaud (Leuven: Peeters Press, 1986), 443–55.

60. Excellent expositions on this point can be found in Martin, *The Corinthian Body*, 3–37; Stowers, "Self-Mastery."

61. Even in the extreme positions that viewed matter as evil, the body could be seen as crucial for the process of human salvation. See, e.g., Jason David BeDuhn, *The Manichaean Body: In discipline and ritual* (Baltimore, MD: Johns Hopkins University Press, 2000).

62. E.g., Origen, *Contra Celsum* 1.48, 7.38; idem, *Homilies on Leviticus* 3.2; idem, *Commentary on the Song of Songs*, Pro. 2, 1.4; idem, *Dialogue with Heraclides*, trans. Chadwick, 448–50; Gregory of Nyssa, *Commentary on the Song of Songs*, Hom. 1, Hom. 11, Hom. 15; Ambrose, *Holy Spirit* 2.7. (67); Augustine, *On Free Will* 2.3.27–37; idem, *Trinity* 9.6–7, 11, 15.12.

63. Evagrius has very few references to smell; they are brief and unoriginal when they appear, referring to the stench of demons, prayer as incense, the compound fragrance of virtues, or the fragrance of divine grace: e.g., *Praktikos*

39; *Chapters on Prayer* 1, 76, 77, 141, 147. The *Kephalaia Gnostica* contains more extensive discussion of sense perception both physical and spiritual, and several references to spiritual (or sacramental) anointment: 1.33, 34, 36; 2.35; 3.29, 43, 76, 85; 4.18, 21, 22, 25, 29, 68; 5.53, 58, 59, 78. In his *Sentences to a Virgin*, Evagrius includes an epithalamium closely modelled on the Song of Songs, including the image of the Bridegroom's sweet-smelling perfume: Susanna Elm, "Evagrius Ponticus' *Sententiae ad Virginem*," DOP 45 (1991): 97–120, at p. 106. For an especially illuminating treatment of Evagrius on the senses and imageless prayer, see Columba Stewart, "Imageless Prayer and the Theological Vision of Evagrius Ponticus," JECS 9 (2001): 151–71. In this article Stewart also emphasizes the critical problem of how the ascetic could make use of key biblical texts that present human encounter with the divine as a sensory one.

64. Columba Stewart has an insightful discussion contrasting Evagrius and ps-Macarius on just this point: see Stewart, *'Working the Earth of the Heart':The Messalian Controversy in History, Texts, and Language to A.D. 431* (Oxford: Clarendon Press, 1991), 116–38.

65. Ps.-Macarius, Homily 33.1; trans. Maloney, 201.

66. The epistemological agenda is often missed when scholars discuss the spiritual senses; the problem seems to lie in the way that modern scholars have approached "mysticism" as a category of religious experience. For an important corrective, see John Peter Kenney, "The Presence of Truth in the *'Confessions*,'" SP 27, ed. E. A. Livingstone (Leuven: Peeters Press, 1993), 329–36.

67. Compare Origen, *Dialogue with Heraclides*, trans. Chadwick, 448–53.

68. The reading conflates Song 1:3b and 4ab; or in the Vulgate, 1:2b and 3ab. I follow the translation of Lawson, *Origen, The Song of Songs: Commentary and Homilies*, here at Comm. 1.4, p. 74.

69. Origen, Comm. 1.4; trans. Lawson, 77–79.

70. Song 1:12b; Vulgate Song 1:11b; Origen, Comm. 2.9; trans. Lawson, 159.

71. Origen, Comm. 2.9; trans. Lawson, 159–60.

72. Origen, Comm. 2.9; trans. Lawson, 160.

73. Origen, Comm. 3 [4]:14; trans. Lawson, 244.

74. Origen, Comm. 3 [4]:14; trans. Lawson, 246.

75. E.g., Gregory of Nyssa, Comm. SS., Hom. 15.

76. I follow the translations in Gregory of Nyssa, *The Life of Moses*, trans. Malherbe and Ferguson; and Gregory of Nyssa, *Commentary on the Song of Songs*, trans. McCambley. One awaits eagerly the forthcoming translation of Gregory's *Commentary on the Song* by Richard A. Norris.

77. Mariette Canevet, *Grégoire de Nysse et l'herméneutique biblique. Étude des rapports entre le langage et la connaissance de Dieu* (Paris: Études Augustiniennes, 1983), esp. at 327–28 (her discussion of perfume imagery); and Verna E. F. Harrison, *Grace and*

Human Freedom According to St. Gregory of Nyssa (Lewiston, NY: Edwin Mellen Press, 1992), esp. 88–131, where the discussion of perfume imagery is found in a longer chapter treating epistemology and human participation in the divine.

78. A point stressed by Harrision, *Grace and Human Freedom*, 61–131.

79. Gregory of Nyssa, *Life of Moses* 1.49–55; 2.68, 79, 182, 258, 286.

80. Gregory of Nyssa, *Life of Moses* 1.5; 2.156, 217, 239.

81. Gregory of Nyssa, *Life of Moses* 2.239.

82. Gregory of Nyssa, *Comm. SS, Hom.* 1; trans. McCambley, 53.

83. Gregory of Nyssa, *Comm. SS, Hom.* 3; trans. McCambley, 83.

84. Gregory of Nyssa, *Comm. SS, Hom.* 3; trans. McCambley, 84.

85. Gregory of Nyssa, *Comm. SS, Hom.* 3; trans. McCambley, 86.

86. Gregory of Nyssa, *Comm. SS, Hom.* 3; trans. McCambley, 87.

87. Gregory of Nyssa, *Comm. SS, Hom.* 4; trans. McCambley, 96.

88. Gregory of Nyssa, *Comm. SS, Hom.* 4; trans. McCambley, 98.

89. Gregory of Nyssa, *Comm. SS, Hom.* 6; trans. McCambley, 134.

90. Gregory of Nyssa, *Comm. SS, Hom.* 9; trans. McCambley, 180–81.

91. Gregory of Nyssa, *Comm. SS, Hom.* 15; trans. McCambley, 269.

92. Cyril of Scythopolis, *Life of Euthymius* 19.

93. Cyril of Scythopolis, *Life of Euthymius* 22, 29.

94. Cyril of Scythopolis, *Life of Euthymius* 24, 29.

95. Cyril of Scythopolis, *Life of Euthymius* 29.

96. John Climacus, *Ladder*, Step 15; trans. Luibheid and Russell, 176.

97. John Climacus, *Ladder*, Step 25; trans. Luibheid and Russell, 222, 225.

98. John Climacus, *Ladder* , Step 26; trans. Luibheid and Russell, 240.

99. John Climacus, *Ladder*, Step 4; trans. Luibheid and Russell, 102.

100. In addition to the passage just cited from John Climacus, *Ladder*, Step 4, see, e.g., the *Life of Theodore of Sykeon*, ch. 108; the report of the fragrant oil collected from the relics of John the Baptist and the martyr Lawrence in the *Life of Matrona of Perge*, sec. 12 and 38; the myrrh-gushing relics of St. Theodora of Thessalonike described in the account of the *Translation* of her relics, sec. 3, 8, and 9; this same Theodora's myrrh-gushing icon, recounted at the end of her *Life*, sec. 59 and 61. The account of Theodora precedes by a little (she died in 892) the title *myroblytes* ("giving forth perfumed oil") given to St. Demetrios in the tenth century, as noted by Talbot, *Holy Women of Byzantium* (Washington, DC: Dumbarton Oaks Publications, 1996), at p. 217, n. 271.

101. The mature expression of this monastic goal is found in Gregory Palamas, *The Triads*. But Gregory is building on profound Byzantine traditions. See the superb discussion on Symeon the New Theologian and his experience of Divine Light in Alexander Golitzin, *St. Symeon the New Theologian, On the Mystical Life: The*

Ethical Discourses, vol. 3, *Life, Times, and Theology* (Crestwood, NY: St. Vladimir's Seminary Press, 1997), 81–120.

102. E.g., Vlachos, *A Night in the Desert of the Holy Mountain.*

103. Compare Alexander Golitzin, "A Testimony to Christianity as Transfiguration: The Macarian Homilies and Orthodox Spirituality," in *Orthodox and Wesleyan Spirituality,* ed. S. T. Kimbrough, Jr. (Crestwood, NY: St. Vladimir's Seminary Press, 2002), 129–56.

104. On asceticism as a characteristic of earliest Syriac Christianity, see Robert Murray, "The Characteristics of the Earliest Syriac Christianity," in *East of Byzantium: Syria and Armenia in the Formative Period,* ed. Nina Garsoian, Thomas Mathews, and Robert Thomson (Washington, DC: Dumbarton Oaks Publications, 1982), 3–16; Susan Ashbrook Harvey, *Asceticism and Society in Crisis: John of Ephesus and the "Lives of the Eastern Saints,"* (Berkeley: University of California Press, 1990), 1–21. See especially the magisterial overview now offered by Sidney H. Griffith, "Asceticism in the Church of Syria: The Hermeneutics of Early Syrian Monasticism," in *Asceticism,* ed. Vincent Wimbush and Richard Valantasis, (New York: Oxford University Press, 1995), 220–45.

105. As Griffith, "Asceticism in the Church of Syria" has noted, the reputation among modern scholars was indelibly set by Peter Brown in his groundbreaking article, "The Rise and Function of the Holy Man in Late Antiquity," first published in *JRS* 61 (1971): 80–101, and then with revised footnotes in Brown's collection *Society and the Holy in Late Antiquity* (Berkeley: University of California Press, 1982), 103–52. See esp. the latter at pp. 109–10: "Syria was the great province for ascetic stars. . . . [Syrian holy men] were virtuoso cadenzas on the sober score first written by the 'Great Men' of Egypt." For a critique of this image precisely from the perspective of liturgical activity, see Susan Ashbrook Harvey, "The Stylite's Liturgy: Ritual and Religious Identity in Late Antiquity," *JECS* 6 (1998): 523–39. A telling example of the notoriety engendered by the first stylite, Simeon, may be seen in the hagiography of his successor: *Life of Daniel the Stylite,* ch. 6.

106. Sebastian P. Brock, *The Syriac Fathers on Prayer and the Spiritual Life* (Kalamazoo: Cistercian Publications, 1987), x–xli, contains an excellent discussion of Syrian ascetic tradition in this regard, including the profoundly biblical basis of a great deal of Syriac ascetic and contemplative developments.

107. E.g., Philo, *On the Cherubim,* 98–105; trans. Winston, 204–205.

108. E.g., Origen, *On Exodus, Homily* 9; *Life of Syncletica,* ch. 80; Ps-Macarius, *Homilies,* 1.2, 1.7, 5.7, 10.4, 15.45; John Chrysostom, *Baptismal Instructions* 2.12 (on the need of catechumens for daily exorcism, to prepare their "palace" for its Royal Visitor). See also the image and its larger associations in Alexander Golitzin, "The Place of the Presence of God: Aphrahat of Persia's Portrait of the Christian Holy Man," in *Synaxis Eucharistiae: Charisteria eis Timen tou Gerontos Aimilianou,* ed. Simonas Petras Monastery (Athens: Indiktos Press, 2003), 391–447.

109. Chapter 1, at critiques of traditional religions, pp. 21–29.

110. Origen, *On Exodus, Homily* 9.3–4; trans. Heine, 338–45.

111. Aphrahat, *Demonstration* 1. 2–5. See the helpful discussion in Robert Murray, *Symbols of Church and Kingdom: A Study in Early Syriac Tradition* (Cambridge: Cambridge University Press, 1975; rev. ed. Piscataway, NJ: Gorgias Press, 2004), 218–36.

112. Ephrem, *Verse Homily* 2.93–123 (my trans.). On the housekeeping theme, see S. A. Harvey, "Housekeeping: An Ascetic Theme in Late Antiquity," in *'To Train His Spirit with Books': Studies in Syrian Asceticism in honor of Sidney H. Griffith*, ed. Robin A. Darling Young and Monica Blanchard (Washington, DC: Catholic University of America Press, forthcoming).

113. Jacob of Serug, Festal Homily 1: *On the Nativity* 1. 391–410; trans. Kollamparampil, 59–60. On this passage of Jacob's, see further S. A. Harvey, "Interior Decorating: Jacob of Serug on Mary's Preparation for the Incarnation," *SP* (forthcoming).

114. *Book of Steps*, Discourse 12. 1–2; trans. Brock, *The Syriac Fathers on Prayer*, 45, 46–48.

115. Sebastian P. Brock, "The Prayer of the Heart in Syriac Tradition," *Sobornost* 4 (1982): 131–42; idem, "Fire from Heaven: From Abel's Sacrifice to the Eucharist. A Theme in Syriac Christianity," *SP* 25, ed. Elizabeth A. Livingstone (Leuven: Peeters Press, 1993), 229–43.

116. The Syriac was edited by Edmund Beck as Verse Homily 2 among the spurious homilies of Ephrem in CSCO 334/Scr. Syr. 148 (Louvain: Secrétariat du Corpus SCO, 1973), 16–28. I use the English translation by Joseph Amar, "On Hermits and Desert Dwellers," in *Ascetic Behavior in Greco-Roman Antiquity: A Sourcebook*, ed. Vincent Wimbush (Minneapolis: Fortress Press, 1990), 66–80.

117. Evagrius Scholasticus, *Ecclesiastical History* 1. 21.

118. 1 Kings 17:1–7; Mt 3:1–4, 4.1–11, and parallels.

119. For the Syriac exegetical tradition on this passage, see the fine study of Matthias Henze, *The Madness of King Nebuchadnezzar: The Ancient Near Eastern Origins and Early History of Interpretation of Daniel 4* (Leiden: E. J. Brill, 1999), 143–79, 251–69; and further, Gary Anderson, *The Genesis of Perfection: Adam and Eve in Jewish and Christian Imagination* (Louisville, KY: Westminster John Knox, 2001), 135–54.

120. See the discussion in Harvey, *Asceticism and Society in Crisis*, 4–13.

121. The Syriac term here translated "service" is *teshmeshta*, meaning the Divine Liturgy.

122. "On Hermits and Desert Dwellers," lines 97–106, 485–97; trans. Amar, 70, 79.

123. See also "On Hermits and Desert Dwellers," lines 281–92.

124. For convenience, I will refer to the hagiographies related to Simeon the Elder as they are translated by Robert Doran, *The Lives of Simeon Stylites* (Kalamazoo: Cistercian Publications, 1992). The reference to Simeon burning storax as a young shepherd is found in the Syriac *Life*, sec. 1–2. The critical

studies on the evidence for Simeon the Elder are Hans Lietzmann, ed., *Das Leben des Heiligen Symeon Stylites*, TU 32.4 (Leipzig: Hinrichs, 1908); Hippolyte Delehaye, *Les Saints Stylites*, SH 14 (Brussels: Société des Bollandistes, 1923); Paul Peeters, "Un Saint Hellénisé par Annexion: Syméon Stylite," in idem, *Orient et Byzance: Le Tréfonds Oriental de l'Hagiographie Byzantine*, SH 26 (Brussels: Société des Bollandistes, 1950) 93–136; A.-J. Festugière, *Antioche paienne et chrétienne. Libanius, Chrysostome et les moines de Syrie* (Paris: de Boccard, 1959), 347–406, 493–506; Alice Leroy-Molinghen, "À propos de la Vie de Syméon Stylite," *Byzantion* 34 (1964): 375–84.

For the Syriac *Life*, Doran followed the earlier recension (A), Vat. Syr. 117, edited by Assemani, *Acta Sanctorum Martyrum Orientalium*, 2:273–394. A slightly later recension (B), Brit. Mus. Add. 14484, was edited in Bedjan, *AMS* 4:507–644; and translated by Frederick Lent, "The Life of St. Simeon Stylites," *JAOS* 35 (1915–17): 103–98. The relationship between the two recensions is problematic; while B has seemed the superior text for literary quality, A has been perhaps underestimated. See Robert Doran, "Comments on the Syriac Versions of the Life of Simeon Stylites," *AB* 102 (1984): 35–48.

125. Syriac *Life*, sec. 116–126; Antonios's *Life*, sec. 28–32.

126. *Life of Daniel the Stylite*, ch. 96.

127. Ed. and trans. by Paul Van Den Ven, *La Vie Ancienne de S. Syméon Stylite le Jeune (521–592)*, 2 vols., SH 32 (Brussels: Société des Bollandistes, 1962–70). In both his introduction and commentary on the *Life of Simeon the Younger*, Van Den Ven discusses the incense references at length; see esp. 1:151*; 2:127 n. 5.

128. Above all, see George Tchalenko, *Villages Antiques de la Syrie du Nord*, vol. 1 (Paris: Geunther, 1953) 227–76; and Jacqueline Lafontaine-Dosogne, *Itinéraires archéologiques dans la région d'Antioche: recherches sur le monastère et sur l'iconographie de S. Syméon Stylite le Jeune*, Bibliothèque de Byzantion 4 (Brussels: Éditions de Byzantion, 1967).

129. See esp. Gary Vikan, *Byzantine Pilgrimage Art* (Washington, DC: Dumbarton Oaks Publications, 1982); idem, "Art, Medicine, and Magic in Early Byzantium," *DOP* 38 (1984): 65–86.

130. The censer reappears in later depictions of Simeon the Elder, for example in Russian iconography. See, e.g, Anna Trifonova, *The Russian Icon of the Novgorod Museum Collection* (St. Petersberg: Madoc, 1992), pl. 79–80; N.V. Rozanova, *Rostov-Suzdal Painting of the 12th-16th Centuries* (Moscow: "Izobrazit. Iskussto," 1970), pl. 117.

131. Theodoret, *History of the Monks of Syria* 26.1; Doran, p. 69.

132. In Athanasius's *Life of Antony*, ch. 2, Antony converted when he heard Jesus' words to the rich man from Matthew 19:21. Simeon heard the beatitudes in a conflation of Luke 6:21, 25 and Matthew 5:4, 8; Theodoret, *History of the Monks of Syria*, 26.2.

133. Theodoret, *History of the Monks of Syria* 26.5; Doran, 72.

134. Ibid.

135. Theodoret, *History of the Monks of Syria* 26.7; Doran, 73.

136. Theodoret, *History of the Monks of Syria* 26.10; Doran, 74.

137. Theodoret, *History of the Monks of Syria* 26.10; Doran, 74.

138. Theodoret, *History of the Monks of Syria* 26.11; Doran, 75.

139. Theodoret, *History of the Monks of Syria* 26.12; Doran, 76.

140. Theodoret, *History of the Monks of Syria* 26.13; Doran, 77.

141. Theodoret, *History of the Monks of Syria* 26.14; Doran, 77.

142. Theodoret, *History of the Monks of Syria* 26.19; Doran, 79.

143. Theodoret, *History of the Monks of Syria* 26.22; Doran, 81.

144. Theodoret, *History of the Monks of Syria* 26.23; Doran, 82.

145. Ibid.

146. As Han J. W. Drijvers, "Spätantike Parallelen zur altchristlichen Heiligenverehrung unter besonderer Berücksichtigung des syrischen Stylitenkultus," *Göttingen Orientforschungen* 1, Reihe: *Syriaca* 17 (1978): 77–113, at 100.

147. Beare, *Greek Theories of Elementary Cognition from Alcmaeon to Aristotle* (Oxford: Clarendon Press, 1906), 86–92.

148. Theodoret repeatedly stresses that it was the sight of Simeon that drove home the message he proclaimed. In addition to passages already cited, see Theodoret, *History of the Monks of Syria* 26.25; 26.26.

149. Chidester, *Word and Light: Seeing, Hearing, and Religious Discourse* (Urbana/Chicago: University of Illinois Press, 1992), adds the important element of physiological process to the consideration of how this imagery has functioned in Christian tradition.

150. Antonios, *Life of Simeon the Stylite*, ch. 5–8.

151. Antonios, *Life of Simeon the Stylite*; trans. Doran, 89–90.

152. Antonios, *Life of Simeon the Stylite*, ch. 17.

153. Antonios, *Life of Simeon the Stylite*, ch. 18; Doran, 95.

154. Harvey, "Sense of a Stylite."

155. Antonios, *Life of Simeon the Stylite*, ch. 28; Doran, 98.

156. The phrase is not infrequent in patristic tradition. Cf. Harvey, "St. Ephrem on the Scent of Salvation."

157. Constance Classen, David Howes, and Anthony Synnott, *Aroma: The Cultural History of Smell* (London/New York: Routledge, 1994); Béatrice Caseau, "Euodia: The Use and Meaning of Fragrances in the Ancient World and their Christianization (100–900 A.D.)" (PhD. diss., Princeton University, 1994); Deonna, "*EUWDIA*: Croyances antiques et modernes: L'Odeur suave des dieux et des élus," *Genava* 17 (1939): 167–263.

158. Syriac Life, ch. 1.

159. Syriac Life, ch. 2; trans. Doran, 104–105.

160. Syriac Life, ch. 4; trans. Doran, 106.

161. This is in fact the second time this vision is reported, but its earlier telling in ch. 98 omits the incense.

162. Syriac Life, ch. 112; Doran, 181.

163. Incense is not the only liturgical marker in this text. The Syriac Life, like the chapter by Theodoret, puts great stress on the ecclesiastical and liturgical context of Simeon's career as stylite. Both vitae establish this in contrast to the disorder and danger (both spiritual and physical) that seemed to characterize his early years in monasteries, when his ascetic practices proved impossible for his superiors to regulate, leading to his expulsion from the monasteries he had joined. In his solitary vocation, however, he came under the watchful guidance of the periodeutes Mar Bassus, who succeeded in bringing order (and health) to Simeon's practices by bringing them into accord with the ecclesiastical calendar (e.g., his most difficult fasts now coincided with Lent), and with eucharistic piety (Simeon now received the Eucharist at the beginning and end of his great ascetic feats). Simeon's pillar stood on land owned by the local parish priest. Local priests, the regional periodeutes, and the bishop of Antioch all celebrated the liturgy at Simeon's pillar and administered the Eucharist to him. The good works for which Simeon was renowned—his impact on imperial and regional politics; or in civic, domestic, and environmental concerns— all emerged during this post-monastic period of his life, and thus in the context of ecclesiastical order. See my discussion in Harvey, "Stylite's Liturgy." See also Golitzin, Et Introibo ad Altare Dei, 385–90.

164. Syriac Life, chs. 39, 69, 83, 97.

165. Syriac Life, chs. 52–53; Doran, 134.

166. See the discussion of sanctity and stench in chapter 5.

167. Syriac Life, ch. 116; Doran, 185–86.

168. Syriac Life, ch. 126.

169. Ephrem Syrus, Hymns on Paradise 9.17. Olfactory sensation is the most prevalent image by which Ephrem characterizes paradise in this cycle of Hymns.

170. Life of Simeon the Younger, ch. 2 (my trans.).

171. Life of Simeon the Younger, ch. 19.

172. Life of Simeon the Younger, ch. 37.

173. Life of Simeon the Younger, ch. 59–60.

174. Life of Simeon the Younger, ch. 29, 35.

175. Life of Simeon the Younger, ch. 215, 243.

176. Life of Simeon the Younger, ch. 113, 122.

177. Life of Simeon the Younger, ch. 26, 27, 31, 153, 212, 227, 234.

178. Life of Simeon the Younger, ch. 53, 70, 198, 231, 235.

179. Life of Simeon the Younger, ch. 37, 113.

180. *Life of Simeon the Younger*, ch. 134–35.

181. *Life of Simeon the Younger*, ch. 222 (my trans.).

182. For discussion of other symbolic schemes present in the Simeon hagiographies, see, e.g., Drijvers, "Spätantike Parallelen;" Harvey, "Sense of a Stylite;" David Frankfurter, "Stylites and *Phallobates*: Pillar Religions in Late Antique Syria," *VC* 44 (1990): 168–98; Antony Eastmond, "Body vs. Column: The Cults of St. Symeon Stylites," in *Desire and Denial in Byzantium*, ed. Liz James (Aldershot, Hampshire: Ashgate Publishing, 1999), 87–100.

183. The *Life of Daniel the Stylite*, whose career came in between those of the two Simeons but was played out in Constantinople, is interesting in this regard: Daniel himself is a Syrian whose proclamations are often obscure to the Constantinopolitans because he speaks Syriac (e.g., *Life of Daniel the Stylite*, ch. 10, 14, 17, and 28, where the landlord speaks to Daniel in Syriac so that others will not understand what he says). Yet the only reference in the *vita* to incense is the perfunctory summons to the disciples to burn incense at this stylite's death, *Life of Daniel the Stylite*, ch. 96. For *vitae* of other Byzantine stylites, see Delehaye, *Les Saints Stylites*.

184. See above, chapter 2, Excursus, p. 90–98.

185. For the social and political context, see Cynthia Villagomez, "The Fields, Flocks, and Finances of Monks: Economic Life at Nestorian Monasteries, 500–850" (PhD diss., University of California Los Angeles, 1998). It is interesting that in the early ninth century, the learned Syriac scientist Job of Edessa included a sophisticated treatment of smells and olfaction in his *Book of Treasures*, Discourse 3. 6–7. Job of Edessa also wrote a work on the five senses that has not survived. Deeply familiar with the works of Aristotle and Galen, Job was a lively and original thinker in his own right. See the discussion in Mingana's introduction to the *Book of Treasures*, xv–xlviii.

186. The discussion in Brock, *Syriac Fathers on Prayer*, is helpful, esp. at pp. xxi–xxxiv.

187. The contrast to these East Syrian writers may be seen in the late fifth-, early sixth-century west Syrian theologian and monastic leader, Philoxenus of Mabbug, himself strongly influenced by Evagrian writings on the contemplative life. In his thirteen *Ascetic Discourses*, for example, Philoxenus devotes much of the first three discourses to the cultivation of the spiritual senses and the overcoming of the physical senses. In his presentation, both sets of senses involve five sensory modes; the five physical senses, however, are only capable of perceiving elements of the physical domain, and therefore are incapable of experiencing anything "spiritual" or "divine". In the Second and Third Discourses, Philoxenus elaborates on sight and hearing, describing what the spiritual eye and ear can experience that the bodily ones cannot; he gives no discussion of the other three senses except in the most general terms. In the Tenth and Eleventh Discourses, on gluttony ("lust of the belly"), and the

Twelfth and Thirteenth, on fornication, he refers a number of times to smells, invariably as morally dangerous and usually as markers of moral dissolution. He does not employ liturgical olfactory imagery. See the edition and translation of E. A. Wallis Budge, *The Discourses of Philoxenus*. There is an interesting if rather problematic discussion on Philoxenus and the experience of sensation in Kilian McDonnell and George T. Montague, *Christian Initiation and Baptism in the Holy Spirit: Evidence from the First Eight Centuries*, 2nd ed. (Collegeville, MN: Liturgical Press, 1994), 299–338.

188. Isaac the Syrian, Homily 35; trans. Wensinck, 174.

189. E.g., Isaac, Homily 3; trans. Wensinck, 14–28.

190. Isaac, Homily 74; trans. Wensinck, 362.

191. Isaac, Homily 82; trans. Wensinck, 382 (adapted).

192. Isaac, *The 'Second Part,'* 5.26; trans. Brock, CSCO 555/Scr. Syr. 225, 18.

193. Martyrius, *Book of Perfection*, 2.8; trans. Brock, *Syriac Fathers on Prayer*, 198–239.

194. Martyrius, *Book of Perfection*, 2.8. 19–20; trans. Brock, *Syriac Fathers on Prayer*, 210–11. In these two sections (2.8.19–20), Martyrius alludes to the sacrificial images from Psalms 141:2, Genesis 8:21, 1 Kings 18:38, 2 Chronicles 7:1, and Romans 12:1.

195. Simon of Taibutheh, *Medico-Mystical Work*; trans. Mingana, 26. Compare Thomas of Marga, *Book of Governors*, 1. 4: ". . . eventide, when a solitary should be diligent in casting choice aromas into the censer of his heart, to make from them a sweet-smelling savor for the whole night;" trans. Budge, 2: 53–54.

196. Simon of Taibutheh, *Medico-Mystico Work*; trans. Mingana, 29–30.

197. Simon of Taibutheh, *Medico-Mystico Work*; trans. Mingana, 35–36. Compare the Syriac mystic John of Dalyatha, *Letter* 13.2: "Sanctify your couch by the hovering of the Spirit over you, let the fragrance of your limbs waft like spices from the place where you lie by (means of) the *maggnanuta* [overshadowing] of the All-Holy." Cited in Sebastian P. Brock, "*Maggnanuta*: A Technical Term in East Syrian Spirituality and its Background," in *Mélanges Antoine Guillaumont: Contributions à l'étude des christianismes orientaux*, Cahiers d'Orientalisme 20 (Geneva 1988), 121–29, at p. 124.

198. Joseph's works have sometimes circulated under the name of his brother, Abdisho, and under that attribution they were translated by Mingana. I cite here Mingana's translations, and therefore as Mingana presents them: 'Abdisho' Hazzaya, "On Spiritual Theory"; trans. Mingana, *Woodbrooke Studies* 7, 148–49. On the vision of God as an experience beyond and above all corporeal senses, see 'Abdisho' Hazzaya, "On the prayer which comes to the mind in the sphere of serenity," trans. Mingana, 151–62. But Joseph's understanding of this highest level of contemplation is a particularly subtle one in its sensory qualities. See the texts by him translated in Brock, *Syriac Fathers on Prayer*, 314–25.

199. Anonymous 2, "On Prayer, from the teaching of the Solitaries," trans. Brock, *Syriac Fathers on Prayer*, 180–85.

Chapter 5. Sanctity and Stench

1. Isaac, Homily 5, ed. Bedjan, *Mar Isaacus*, 60–80, at p. 79; trans. Wensinck, 42–55, at p. 54 (adapted).

2. Origen, *Contra Celsum* 5.35; trans. Chadwick, 292. The Pythagorean aversion to beans was a commonplace noted among educated authors of antiquity. For its medical context, see Mirko D. Grmek, *Diseases in the Ancient Greek World*, trans. Mireille Muellner and Leonard Muellner (Baltimore: Johns Hopkins University Press, 1989), 210–44.

3. E.g., Paulinus of Nola, Poem 17.22–44; Leontius, *Life of Simeon the Fool*, trans. Krueger, 167.

4. Jerome, *Against Jovinian* 2.6, citing Aristotle, Theophrastus, Marcellus of Side, Flavius the Grammarian, Pliny the Younger, and Dioscorides.

5. Basil of Caesarea was embarrassed when he cited Philippians 3:4–8, where Paul likens the benefits of the Mosaic Law to dung, because "excrement of the body. . .we abominate and dispose of as quickly as possible." Basil, *Long Rules*, Q/R 8; trans. Wagner, 255. Cicero had praised divine wisdom for the construction of the human body by noting that the functions of eliminating inevitably offensive bodily waste were located as far as possible from the organs of sight and smell: *On the Nature of the Gods*, 2.141.

6. E.g., Philo, Prov. 2.104 (51–61), and Prob. 72–81; trans. Winston, 182, 249.

7. E.g., Palladius, *Lausiac History* 65.3; *Sayings of the Desert Fathers*, Anon. Ser.; trans. Stewart, *World of the Desert Fathers*, 3.2.(52), at pp. 14–15. See the discussion in Liz Wilson, *Charming Cadavers: Horrific Figurations of the Feminine in Indian Buddhist Hagiographic Literature* (Chicago: University of Chicago Press, 1996), 169–74. It is interesting to recall how frequently dung and other foul-smelling applications or fumigations were used as gynecological treatments in Greek and Roman medicine. See Ann Ellis Hanson, "The Medical Writers' Woman," in *Before Sexuality: The Construction of Erotic Experience in the Ancient Greek World*, ed. David Halperin, John J. Winkler, and Froma Zeitlin (Princeton: Princeton University Press, 1990), 309–38; and Lesley Dean-Jones, "The Cultural Construct of the Female Body in Classical Greek Science," in *Women's History and Ancient History*, ed. Sarah B. Pomeroy (Chapel Hill: University of North Carolina Press, 1991), 111–37.

8. For an epigraphic example from Egypt, see Richmond Lattimore, *Themes in Greek and Latin Epitaphs* (Urbana, IL: University of Illinois Press, 1962), 232. In general, see Dominic Montserrat, ed., *Changing Bodies, Changing Meanings: Studies on the Human Body in Antiquity* (New York: Routledge, 1998), esp. chapters 7 (Terry Wilfong, "Reading the Disjointed Body in Coptic: From Physical Modification to Textual Fragmentation," pp. 116–36), and 9 (Dominic Monserrat, "Unidentified Human Remains: Mummies and the Erotics of Biography," pp. 162–97).

9. Paulinus, *Poem* 28; trans. Walsh, 302.

10. *Miracles of St. Artemios*, especially miracles 3, 13, 22.

11. Ephrem, *Hymns on Paradise* 9.17; see S. A. Harvey, "St. Ephrem on the Scent of Salvation," JTS, n.s., 49 (1998): 109–28.

12. Again, the imagery is pervasive. E.g., Melania the Younger or Simeon the Stylite the Younger at prayer: Gerontius, *Life of Melania the Younger* 6; *Life of Simeon the Younger* 59–60, 215, 243.

13. Gregory of Nyssa, *Life of Gregory the Wonderworker* 35.

14. *Life of Simeon the Younger* 37, 222.

15. The *Life of St. Irene, Abbess of Chrysobalanton* 11; trans. Rosenqvist, 49. St. Irene lived in the later tenth century; the vita dates from c. 1000.

16. Caseau, "*Euodia*. The Use and Meaning of Fragrances in the Ancient World and their Christianization (100–900 A.D.)" (PhD. diss., Princeton University, 1994), passim, emphasizes the ancient conviction concerning the medicinal and hygienic efficacy of odors as critical to understanding why they were accorded such religious powers. See also eadem, "Les usages médicaux de l'encens et des parfums: Un aspect de la medicine populaire antique et de sa christianisation," in *Air, Miames et Contagion: Les épidémies dans l'Antiquité et au Moyen Age*, ed. Sylvie Bazin-Tacchella, Danielle Quéruel and Évelyne Samama (Langres: Dominique Guéniot, 2001), 74–85.

17. E.g., Shenute, Fragment Vienna K 913, in Dwight Wayne Young, *Coptic Manuscripts from the White Monastery: Works of Shenute*, MPER, n.s., 22 (Vienna: Österreichische Nationalbibliothek/Verlag Brüder Hollinek, 1993), 31.

18. E.g., John Chrysostom, *On Wealth and Poverty*, Sermon 1, at p. 26; Sermon 6, at pp. 105–6. Cf. Chrysostom, "Homily on the Holy Martyrs," sec. 4, trans. Mayer, 125.

19. Ephrem, *Hymns on the Nativity* 28.8–10.

20. Cyril of Jerusalem, *Cat. Hom.* 4.36; trans. McCauley and Stephenson, 1:137.

21. Palladius, *Dialogue on the Life of St. John Chrysostom*; trans. Meyer, 50.

22. Abdisho Hazzaya (Joseph the Visionary), "The Letter to One of His Friends, On the Workings of the Grace," trans. Mingana, *Woodbrooke Studies* 7:173.

23. Martial, *Epigrams* 4.4; Paulinus of Nola, *Letters* 22.

24. Jerome, *Letters* 24.

25. Serapion of Thmuis, *Letter to the Monks*, sec. 2, sec. 15.

26. Isaac, *Homily* 6; Bedjan, *Mar Isaacus*, 81–99 at p. 94; trans. Wensinck, 55–67, at p. 64.

27. Cited in S. Elm, *'Virgins of God': The Making of Asceticism in Late Antiquity* (Oxford: Oxford University Press, 1994), 230–31.

28. Athanasius, *Second Letter to Virgins* 15–18, 29–31. Athanasius, as might be expected, cites the Song of Songs repeatedly in this discussion, urging the virgins to remain faithful to their true spouse, Christ.

29. Aphrahat, *Demonstration* 6.8.

30. John Chrysostom, *On the Statues*, Hom. 4; trans. Stephens, NPNF 9:406 (adapted).

31. *Life of Theodore of Sykeon* 137: "For no one who has anointed himself with myrrh and perfumes washes off the pleasant scent thereof and no one who has lunched with the Emperor straightaway runs to the baths." Trans. Baynes and Dawes, 178.

32. Paulinus, *Poem* 18; trans. at p. 248, when the faithful Christian weeps with joy at the recovery of his stolen cows.

33. Paulinus, *Letter* 22; trans. Walsh, 197–99, at p. 198.

34. Maximus of Turin, *Sermon* 66; trans. Ramsey, 162.

35. Prudentius, *Book of the Martyrs' Crown* 2.385–92; trans. Eagan, 120. The imagery is based on the complex of olfactory symbolism utilized in 2 Corinthians 2:14–16.

36. The model here was the *Martyrdom of Polycarp*, 15.1–16.1, as discussed in chapter 1, pp. 11–13. See also, e.g., Jacob of Serug, "On the martyr Habib," Bedjan, *AMS* 1: 160–72, at 172; Simeon of Beth Arsham, *Second Letter on the Martyrs of Najran*, trans. in Brock and Harvey, *Holy Women of the Syrian Orient*, at 105, 107. The same motif is used more literarily by Romanos in his *Kontakion* 46, on the Three Children in the Furnance, strophe 21–22; trans. Carpenter, 2:145.

37. Examples are legion, but see, e.g., Cyril of Scythopolis, *Life of John the Hesychast* 3; Palladius, *Lausiac History* 55.2.

38. E.g., Gregory of Nazianzus, *ad Hellen.*, PG 37.1451; the *Life of Abraham of Qidunaya*, Syriac version ("smell of asceticism," "*riha d'abilutha*," trans. Brock and Harvey, *Holy Women of the Syrian Orient*, 27–36 at p. 33) and Latin version ("sweet smell of asceticism," "*suavissimo odore abstinentiae*," trans. Ward, *Harlots of the Desert*, 92–101 at p. 96); the Syriac *Life of Malkha of Klysma*, ed. Bedjan, *AMS* 5: 421–69, at p. 440.

39. Ps.-Athanasius, *Life of Syncletica* 21; trans. Castelli, 275.

40. "The Story of Abba Pambo," trans. Vivian, *Journeying into God*, 31.

41. Leontius, *Life of Simeon the Fool*, ed. Rydén and Festugière, p. 145 (dead dog), pp. 146, 153 (lupines), p. 148 (defecation); trans. Krueger, 151, 153, 157.

42. On the didactic aspects of these episodes and their literary tradition, see Krueger, *Symeon the Holy Fool: Leontius' Life and the Late Antique City* (Berkeley: University of California Press, 1996), esp. chs. 5 and 6.

43. Leontius, *Life of Simeon the Fool*, trans. Krueger, 151–52.

44. John Chrysostom, *On Wealth and Poverty*, Sermon 1; trans. Roth, 26. Even those who sold perfumes were held to be morally suspect in Byzantine society. See Judith Herrin, "'Femina Byzantina': The Council in Trullo on Women," *DOP* 46 (1992): 97–105, at 104.

45. For another example of smells as morally revelatory, see Ephrem, *Hymns on Virginity* 4.11, where Ephrem describes the perfume with which Mary of Bethany anointed Christ's head, "waft[ing] its scent" and "test[ing] the reclining as in a furnace," exposing the disciples' greed while revealing the true faith of Mary. Trans. McVey, 279.

46. W. Miller, *The Anatomy of Disgust* (Cambridge, MA: Harvard University Press, 1997); A. Corbin, *The Foul and the Fragrant: Odor and the French Social Imagination*, trans. Miriam L. Kochan, Roy Porter, and Christopher Prendergast (Cambridge, MA: Harvard University Press, 1986).

47. Arnobius, *Against the Pagans* 6.16; trans. McCracken, 469.

48. Gregory of Nyssa, *Life of Moses* 2.68–79, discussing the plague of frogs on the Egyptians.

49. John Chrysostom, *Baptismal Instructions* 1.5; trans. Harkins, 24.

50. John Chrysostom, Homily 2 on 1 Tim., trans. Schaff, NPNF 13:415; John of Ephesus, *Lives of the Eastern Saints* 3; ed. and trans. Brooks, PO 17:54–55; Romanos Melodos, *Kontakion* 9, "On the Woman of Samaria;" trans. Carpenter 1:87–96.

51. *Sayings of the Desert Fathers*, Anon. Ser.; trans. Stewart, *World of the Desert Fathers*, 7.2.19, at p. 25; *A Panegyric on Macarios, Bishop of Tkôw, Attributed to Dioscorus of Alexandria*, ed. and trans. D. Johnson (CSCO 416/Scr. Cop. 42, Louvain: 1980) 17; *Apocalypse of Paul* 16.

52. The phrase is Tertullian's, *Scorpiace* 7, ANL 11:393. But the image continues unabated. E.g., John Chrysostom, *Homilies on Matthew* 68 and 88; Callinicos, *Life of Hypatios*, 43.1–8; John Rufus, *Plerophories*, 26, 40, 65. The association of heresy with disease (and hence, in some contexts, with stench), had a long history in philosophical discourse, based in the rhetoric of psychagogy which often employed medical terminology or imagery to describe different therapies for flaws or weaknesses prohibiting the cultivation of virtue. This rhetorical tradition was employed in the New Testament epistles, both by Paul and by others, with respect to handling problems of discord in early Christian communities; through these epistles it entered into early Christian discourse regarding "heresy" and "orthodoxy." See, e.g., Abraham J. Malherbe, "Medical Imagery in the Pastoral Epistles," in *Texts and Testaments: Critical Essays on the Bible and Early Church Fathers in Honor of Stuart Dickson Currie*, ed. W. Eugene March (San Antonio, TX: Trinity University Press, 1980), 19–35; Clarence Glad, *Paul and Philodemus: Adaptability in Epicurean and Early Christian Psychagogy* (Leiden: E. J. Brill, 1995).

53. Theodoret, *History of the Monks of Syria* 1.9. A similar death was reported for Nestorius: Theodore Nissen, *Supplementary Tales to John Moschus's Spiritual Meadow*, 220; trans. Wortley, 197–98. Christian writers here draw upon the classical literary tradition that assigned physically horrifying deaths to morally depraved leaders. See Jacques Schamp, "La Mort en Fleurs: Considérations sur la maladie 'pédiculaire' de Scylla," *L'Antiquité Classique* 60 (1991): 139–70.

54. *Sayings of the Desert Fathers*, Anon. Ser.; trans. Stewart, *World of the Desert Fathers*, 3.4.(132D), at p. 43.

55. Simon of Taibutheh, *Mystico-Medical Work*; trans. Mingana, 68.

56. *Sayings of the Desert Fathers*, Anon. Ser.; trans. Stewart, *World of the Desert Fathers*, 1.11.8, at pp. 5–6.

57. Augustine, *Confessions* 2.1.1, 2.3.8; trans. Chadwick, 24, 28.

58. Philoxenus, 10th *Discourse*; trans. Budge, 349.

59. Philoxenus, 13th *Discourse*; trans. Budge, 534.

60. *Paralipomena* 19; trans. Veilleux, *Pachomian Koinonia* 2:42.

61. Ps 38:5.

62. Prudentius, *Book of the Martyrs' Crown* 2.150–288; trans. Eagan, 105–28, at 112, 116–17.

63. Miller, *Anatomy of Disgust*, passim.

64. On the importance of engaging the senses as a rhetorical strategy of ancient writers, see M. Carruthers, *The Craft of Thought: Meditation, rhetoric, and the making of images, 400–1200* (New York: Cambridge University Press, 1998), 130–33.

65. Examples are ubiquitous. See., e.g., *Acts of Judas Thomas*, 55–57; *Lives of the Desert Fathers* 9.9–10; Cyril of Scythopolis, *Life of Eythymius* 24; Evagrius Ponticus, *Praktikos* 39; *Paralipomena* 7, Veilleux 2: 28; *Life of Daniel the Stylite* 28, 33, 72, 82, 98; John Rufus, *Plerophories* 27. For the Jewish and Christian literary traditions, see Martha Himmelfarb, *Tours of Hell: An Apocaplytic Form in Jewish and Christian Literature* (Philadelphia: University of Pennsylvania Press, 1983), esp. 106–26. The role of smell would continue to terrify Christian traditions of hell: see Thomas H. Seiler, "Filth and Stench as Aspects of the Iconography of Hell," in *The Iconography of Hell*, ed. Clifford Davidson and Thomas H. Seiler (Kalamazoo: Medieval Institute Publications, 1992), 132–40; Piero Camporesi, *The Fear of Hell: Images of Damnation and Salvation in Early Modern Europe*, trans. Lucinda Byatt (University Park, PA: Pennsylvania State University Press, 1991), esp. 69–89.

66. E.g., *Concerning Thoughts*, 24, trans. Tim Vivian, "Words to Live By: *A Conversation that the Elders Had with One Another Concerning Thoughts (Peri Logismon)*," *SVTQ* 39 (1995): 127–41; *Sayings of the Desert Fathers*, Sys. Sayings, trans. Ward, *Wisdom of the Desert Fathers*, 41, at p. 10; Palladius, *Lausiac History* 23.5.

67. *Cave of Treasures*, 47.20–22; trans. Budge, 218–19. The description follows the literary conventions discussed in Schamp, "La Mort en Fleurs."

68. Three contemporary accounts survive: Procopius of Caesarea, *Wars* 2.22–23; Evagrius Scholasticus, *Ecclesiastical History* 4.29; and John of Ephesus, *Ecclesiastical History*, as preserved in the Chronicle of Zuqnin, Part 3, trans. Harrak, 94–113, and also in Witakowski, *Pseudo-Dionysius of Tel-Mahre, Chronicle, Part III*, 74–98. See Pauline Allen, "The 'Justinianic' Plague," *Byzantion* 49 (1979): 5–20.

69. This was a literary topos as well as a characteristic of ancient punishment. See 4 Maccabees 15:19; Tertullian, *To the Martyrs; Martyrdom of Perpetua and Felicitas; Life of Sts. David, Symeon, and George of Lesbos*, trans. Abrahamse and Domingo-Forasté, in *Byzantine Defenders of Images*, ed. Alice-Mary Talbot, 143–241, at p. 200. In the fifth-century epic romance *Euphemia and the Goth*, the young Syrian maiden Euphemia is subjected to excessively cruel punishment by the Goths: beaten nearly to death, she is buried alive in a tomb, in which the stench from the rotting corpses suffocates her. The moment at which she is saved by the intervention of the Edessan martyr saints Shmona, Guria, and Habib is marked by the sudden transformation of the horrible smell into the fragrance of sweet spices. *Euphemia and the Goth*, 24, 27, 41.

70. Hans Belting, *Likeness and Presence*, trans. Edmund Jephcott (Chicago: University of Chicago Press, 1994), 106 fig. 54; see also Karl Anton Neugebauer, "Die Familie Des Septimius Severus," *Die Antike* 12 (1936): 155–72, at 156.

71. *Life of the Patriarch Nikephoros I of Constantinople*, trans. Elizabeth A. Fisher, in *Byzantine Defenders of Images*, ed. Talbot, 25–141, at 125.

72. The account of Abraham's activities is from John of Ephesus's *Ecclesiastical History*, Part II, preserved in the *Chronicle of Zuqnin, Part III* (Ps.-Dionysius of Tell-Mahre). For the Syriac, see Chabot, *Incerti auctoris chronicon anonymum*, at pp. 33–44; English translation in Harrak, *Chronicle of Zuqnin*, 60–64, and also in Witakowski, *Pseudo-Dionysius of Tel-Mahre, Chronicle*, 32–37.

73. *Chronicle of Zuqnin, Part III*, trans. Harrak, pp. 63–64.

74. It is important to remember that physiologically speaking, smells do not in and of themselves mean anything. Whether a smell is perceived to be good or bad, pleasant or nauseous, depends entirely on the associations it carries for the individual (and for the culture). It is, furthermore, very difficult for the body to learn to change its habitual response to a given odor. In this critical role of association for meaning, smell differs from other sense modalities. See Trygg Engen, *Odor Sensation and Memory* (New York: Praeger, 1991); Rachel Herz, "Verbal Coding in Olfactory versus Nonolfactory Cognition," *Memory and Cognition* 28 (6) (2000): 957–64; R. A. De Wijk, F. R. Schab, and W. S. Cain, "Odor Identification," in *Memory for Odors*, ed. Frank R. Schab and Robert G. Crowder (Mahwah, NJ: Lawrence Erlbaum Associates, 1995), 21–37.

75. John of Ephesus, *Lives of the Eastern Saints* 3; trans. Brooks, PO 17:55.

76. Ps.-Macarius, Homily 1.5; trans. Maloney, 39–40.

77. Origen, *Homily 27 on Numbers*, trans. Greer, *Origen*, 245–69, at p. 263; in addition to Ps.-Macarius, Homily 1.5, see idem, Homily 24.4.

78. Ps.-Macarius, Homily 44.1: "Whoever approaches God and truly desires to be a partner of Christ must approach with a view to this goal, namely, to be changed and transformed from his former state . . . A new mind and a new soul and new eyes, new ears, a new spiritual tongue, and, in a word, new

humans—this is what he came to effect in those who believe in him." Trans. Maloney, 223. Ps.-Macarius here uses Paul's image of "the new man" in contrast to "the old man," of 2 Corinthians 5:17.

79. Chapter 4, pp. 182–86.

80. Ps.-Macarius, *Homilies* 15.33, 45; 27.19; 28.1; 33.3; 43.2. Compare John Chrysostom, *Homily on the Holy Martyrs*, sec. 4; trans. Mayer, 125.

81. Ps.-Athanasius, *Life of Syncletica* 80; compare chapters 25, 66.

82. John Climacus, *Ladder of Divine Ascent*, Step 1; trans. Luibheid and Russell, 75, 77–78. Cf. Mt 11:12.

83. John Climacus, *Ladder*, Step 1; trans. Luibheid and Russell, 76.

84. John Climacus, *Ladder*, Step 5; trans. Luibheid and Russell, 125, 127.

85. John Climacus, *Ladder*, Step 7; trans. Luibheid and Russell, 139.

86. See the sermons discussed in chapter 4, pp. 158–62; also the monastic instruction of John Climacus, *Ladder*, Step 15, at Luibheid and Russell, 183.

87. Ephrem, *Hymns on Faith* 20.17; trans. Brock, *Syriac Fathers on Prayer*, 35.

88. Ephrem, *Hymns on the Nativity* 1.83; trans. McVey, 73.

89. Theodoret, *History of the Monks of Syria*, Pro. 7; trans. Price, 6.

90. Diadochus, *Chapters* 23–24; trans. des Places, 95–96; cf. also Diadochus, *Vision*, Response to Question 2; trans. des Places, 169, on the "perfume of the desert" discernible to the one who lives a pure life.

91. Robert Beulay, *L'Enseignement Spirituel de Jean de Dalyatha: Mystique Syro-Oriental du VIIIe Siècle* (Paris: Éditions Beauchesne, 1990), 92.

92. Nicodemus of the Holy Mountain, *A Handbook of Spiritual Counsel*, trans. Peter A. Chamberas (New York: Paulist Press, 1989).

93. Nicodemus, *Handbook* 5; trans. Chamberas, 102–3. It is interesting to note that in this same chapter, Nicodemus rails at length against what he holds to be the worst olfactory temptation confronting the monks of his day: not the abundance of perfumes that were standard in late antique Mediterranean culture, but the habit of smoking tobacco! This he denounces on three grounds: as contrary to virtuous living, as inappropriate to the character of priesthood, and as severely detrimental to one's health. "When the clergy [or monastics] draw into their body both through their mouth and their nose that most foul smelling smoke, that many cannot bear and faint, how can they then be, according to the very nature of their calling, an aroma and a fragrance of Christian life [2 Cor 2:14–16] for those who are around them?" Nicodemus, *Handbook* 5; trans. Chamberas, 104.

94. Isaac, *Homily* 69; trans. Wensinck, 322.

95. *Sayings of the Desert Fathers*, Arsenios, 18; trans. Ward, 11.

96. Theodoret of Cyrrhus, *History of the Monks of Syria* 3.21; trans. Price, 46.

97. Venatius Fortunatus, *Life of Radegunde*; trans. Petersen, *Handmaids of the Lord*, 381–400, at p. 391.

98. E.g., Jerome, Letter 108 "To Eustochium," trans. Petersen, *Handmaids of the Lord*, 150 (referring to Paula); *Sayings of the Desert Fathers*, Isaac, 6, trans. Ward, 100; Cyril of Scythopolis, *Life of John the Hesychast* 19, trans. Price, 235.

99. *Sayings of the Desert Fathers*, Anon. Ser.; trans. Ward, *Wisdom of the Desert Fathers* 19, at p. 5.

100. Syriac *Life of Simeon Stylites* 97; trans. Doran, 171.

101. Fortunatus, *Life of Radegunde*; trans. Petersen, 388. For Basil and the lepers, see Gregory of Nazianzus, *Oration* 43.63; for Rabbula and the lepers, see the Syriac *Life of Rabbula of Edessa*, ed. Bedjan, AMS 4:396–450, at pp. 444–45. While late antique authors clearly employed literary conventions in praising such figures for their ministry to the poor and sick, there is no denying the suffering of victims involved. See now the striking study by Susan R. Holman, *The Hungry are Dying: Beggars and Bishops in Roman Cappadocia* (New York: Oxford University Press, 2001).

102. Fortunatus, *Life of Radegunde*; trans. Petersen, 399.

103. Jerome, *Letter* 77 "To Oceanus, on the death of Fabiola;" trans. Gorce, 2:109–33.

104. *Life of Simeon the Younger* 27.

105. John of Ephesus, *Lives of the Eastern Saints* 33; PO 18:599.

106. Ps.-Athanasius, *Life of Syncletica* 29; trans. Castelli, 280.

107. Trans. Elm, 'Virgins of God,' 257. The story is also translated in Ward, *Wisdom of the Desert Fathers* 10 (*Sayings of the Desert Fathers*, Anon. Ser., 40).

108. Perhaps the same concept of reversal accounts for the curious olfactory elements in the deutero-canonical book of Tobit, wherein a fish liver and heart are burned with incense to exorcize a demon, and gall from the same fish anoints and heals the eyes of Tobit, blinded by sparrow dung after he had been polluted by corpse contact: Tobit 2.7–10, 6.1–8, 15–17, 8.1–3, 11.9–15. The imagery is discussed in Lionel Rothkrug, "The 'Odor of Sanctity,' and the Hebrew Origins of Christian Relic Veneration," HR/RH 8 (1981): 95–134, at pp. 116–17.

109. See the remarks by Robert Browning, "The 'Low-Level' Saint's Life in the Early Byzantine World," in *The Byzantine Saint*, ed. Sergei Hackel, SSS 5 (London: Fellowship of SS Alban and Sergius, 1981; repr. Crestwood, NY: St. Vladimir's Seminary Press, 2001), 117–27, at 126: "The evil-smell resulting from the holy man's self-mortification is mentioned again and again in the lives as evidence that he has passed beyond the normal human state and gained superhuman powers." The frequency of such descriptions led Evelyne Patlagean to utilize hagiography as a source for the study of illness; see her *Pauvreté économique et pauvreté sociale à Byzance 4e–7e siècles* (Paris: Mouton, 1977), esp. 73–112. See also S. A. Harvey, "Physicians and Ascetics: An Expedient Alliance," DOP 38 (1984): 87–93.

110. Antonios, *Life of Simeon the Stylite* 5–8. While all three *vitae* of Simeon the Stylite narrate this episode, only Antonios discusses the role of smell in the

detection and anger of the monks. In Theodoret's account, *History of the Monks of Syria* 26.5, it is the sight of blood on Simeon's tunic that gives the clue; the Syriac *Life*, 21, simply says the abbot found out about it.

111. *Life of Symeon the Younger* 26, 31.

112. *Life of Theodore of Sykeon* 20; trans. Baynes and Dawes, 101.

113. John the Hermit stood motionless under a rock for so long that his feet putrified: *Lives of the Desert Fathers* 13.7; trans. Russell, 93–94. See also *Life of Daniel the Stylite* 28, 72, 82; John Moschus, *Spiritual Meadow* 10.

114. E.g., Syriac *Life of Simeon Stylites* 83, trans. Doran, 163; Cyril of Scythopolis, *Life of Sabas* 62, trans. Price, 173.

115. E.g., Syriac *Life of Simeon Stylites* 48–52; ps.-Athanasius, *Life of Syncletica* 111; *Life of Theodore of Sykeon* 20.

116. Other frequent biblical exemplars were King David as Christian exegetes ascribed the Psalms of lament to him (e.g., Psalms 6, 38, 88); and the sore-ridden begger Lazarus in the parable of Lazarus and the rich man (Lk 16:19–31). In classical tradition the parallel story was that of Philoctetes, hauntingly portrayed in Sophocles' tragedy of the same name. Having offended the gods by inadvertently trespassing on sacred ground, Philoctetes, the most just of men, was struck with a hideous wound in his foot. His agony from the pain and the stench of the gangrenous infection proved intolerable to all other men, who also feared that his cries and the smell would cause the pollution of any sacrifices or libations they might make. For ten years, Philoctetes lived abandoned on the island of Lemnos, suffering piteously. His innocence, the extremity of his condition, and the horror of his smell form the axis round which Sophocles' play revolves.

117. *Testament of Job.* Trans. R. P. Spittler, in Charlesworth, *Old Testament Pseudepigrapha*, 1:829–68. The text probably dates to the first century B.C.E. or the first century C.E..

118. Ambrose, "The Prayer of Job and David," trans. McHugh, *Saint Ambrose: Seven Exegetical Works*, 327–420, at 331.

119. Jacob of Serug, "Homily on Simeon the Stylite," ed. Bedjan, *AMS* 4:655–57; trans. Harvey, in *Ascetic Behavior in Greco-Roman Antiquity*, at pp. 20–22. Jacob is the only authority who mentions amputation as the method by which Simeon survived this episode with gangrene. All three *vitae* of Simeon describe the extremity of suffering he endured through the gangrenous wound in his leg, but all three claim a miraculous cure.

120. Ps.-Athanasius, *Life of Syncletica* 111; trans. Castelli, 309–10.

121. Hence in patristic exegesis of the gifts of the Magi—gold, frankincense, and myrrh—the myrrh was to prefigure the anointing at Christ's death; and the fine oil with which the sinful woman anointed Christ (Mk 14:3–9 and

parallels) prefigured his burial anointment. This passage in the *Life of Syncletica* is probably modelled on the gospel image of Jesus' anointment in anticipation of his passion.

122. Ps.-Athanasius, *Life of Syncletica* 112; trans. Castelli, 310.

123. Cf. the context as discussed in E. A. Castelli, 'Mortifying the Body, Curing the Soul: Beyond Ascetic Dualism in *The Life of Saint Syncletica,"* *Differences* 4 (1992): 134–53.

124. On the hagiographical formula, see Browning, "'Low-Level' Saint's Life."

125. When Jesus approached Lazarus's tomb and asked that the stone be removed, "Martha, the sister of the dead man, said to him, 'Lord, by this time there will be an odor, for he has been dead four days.'" (Jn 11:39). The scene is vividly captured in Byzantine iconography of the incident, which shows the crowd holding their noses or covering their faces against the stench. See, e.g., M. Acheimastou-Potamianou, ed., *Holy Image, Holy Space: Icons and Frescoes from Greece* (Athens: Greek Ministry of Culture, Byzantine Museum of Athens, 1988), 81 (pl. 8).

126. Ps.-Macarius, *Homily* 30.8; trans. Maloney, 193.

127. Romanos, *Kontakion* 14, strophe 12–13; trans. Carpenter, 1:140–48, at 145–46.

128. E.g., Ambrose, *Concerning Repentence* 63: "What, then, we read concerning Lazarus we ought to believe of every sinner who is converted, who though he may have been stinking, nevertheless is cleansed by the precious ointment of faith. For faith has such grace that there where the dead stank the day before, now the whole house is filled with good odor." Trans. de Romestin, NPNF, 2nd ser., 10:353. See further sec. 64 in the same text.

129. Eusebius, *Ecclesiastical History* 10.4.10–15; trans. Oulton and Lawlor, 2:403–5.

130. Ephrem, *Hymns on the Nativity* 19.14; trans. McVey, 189. Compare Ephrem's *Homily on Our Lord,* for the importance of touch with the incarnate body of Christ.

131. Theodoret, *On Divine Providence* 10.16; trans. Halton, 140. Compare Origen, *Contra Celsum* 4.15.

132. So, e.g., the *Testament of Benjamin* 8.1–3, from the *Testaments of the Twelve Patriarchs;* trans. Kee, in Charlesworth, *Old Testament Pseudepigrapha,* 1:775–828, at 828.

133. Romanos, *Kontakion* 30, "On Doubting Thomas," strophe 14; trans. Carpenter, 1:329–36, at p. 334.

134. Thekeparampil, "Incense Prayers," 251.

135. Ephrem, *Hymns on Paradise* 11.10; trans. Brock, 157.

136. Ephrem, *Hymns on Paradise* 15.11; trans. Brock, 185.

137. Ephrem, *Hymns on Paradise* 7.3; trans. Brock, 119.

Chapter 6. Resurrection,
Sensation, and Knowledge

1. Paulinus, *Poem* 31, trans. Walsh, 326 .

2. As cited in Teresa M. Shaw, *The Burden of the Flesh: Fasting and Sexuality in Early Christianity* (Minneapolis: Fortress Press, 1998), 198.

3. There are suggestive models in the studies collected by Jamie Scott and Paul Simpson-Housley, eds., *Sacred Places and Profane Spaces: Essays in the Geographics of Judaism, Christianity, and Islam* (Westport, CT: Greenwood Press, 1991).

4. For Judaism and Christianity, protology was explored in relation to Genesis 1–3 and the life of Adam and Eve in Eden. The Prometheus legends among the Greeks served similarly to identify an ideal time. Greeks and Romans both carried traditions that recalled the "ages" of human life, from an original "Golden Age" to the sorely diminished present (e.g., Ovid, *Metamorphoses*, bk. 15; Porphyry, *On Abstinence*). See Jean Delumeau, *History of Paradise: The Garden of Eden in Myth and Tradition*, trans. Matthew O'Connell (New York: Continuum: 1995), 3–21.

5. For the primary traditions, see Alan E. Bernstein, *The Formation of Hell: Death and Retribution in the Ancient and Early Christian Worlds* (Ithaca, NY: Cornell University Press, 1993). When the notion of a resurrected life first appears in Second Temple Judaism, it seems to have been an understanding that it would only happen for "the righteous." See Bernstein, *Formation of Hell*, 131–202; also Lionel Rothkrug, "The 'Odor of Sanctity,' and the Hebrew Origins of Christian Relic Veneration," *HR/RH* 8 (1981): 95–134.

6. Thus the enigmatic fragment of Heraclitus: "Souls smell in Hades." The verb here is *osmaomai*, probably meaning "to have a sense of smell" rather than "to stink." P. 208 n. 3 in *The Presocratic Philosophers: A critical history with a selection of texts*, ed. G.S. Kirk, J.E. Raven, and M. Schofield, 2nd ed. (Cambridge: Cambridge University Press, 1983). I am grateful to Mary Louise Gill for discussion on this passage.

7. The surveys in Bernstein, *Formation of Hell*, 19–266; and Delumeau, *History of Paradise*, 3–38, are helpful. The classic comparison in scholarship is between Odysseus's interview with denizens of the underworld in *Odyssey*, bk. 12—summoned from their place of pale shadows—and the elaborate tour given to Aeneas in Virgil's *Aeneid*, bk. 6, where a fully fashioned geography is displayed in morally differentiated terms. Similarly, Jewish traditions saw the development from the lifeless shades of Sheol in the oldest parts of the Hebrew Bible to extensive "tours" of heaven and hell that characterize much Jewish literature starting from the second century B.C.E.. See, e.g., Martha Himmelfarb, *Tours of Hell: An Apocalyptic Form in Jewish and Christian Literature* (Philadelphia: University of Pennsylvania Press, 1983); eadem, *Ascent to Heaven in Jewish and Christian Apocalypses* (New York: Oxford University Press, 1993); John J. Collins and Michael

Fishbane, eds., *Death, Ecstasy, and Other Worldly Journeys* (Albany: State University of New York Press, 1995); Christopher Rowland, "The Visions of God in Apocalyptic Literature," *JSJ* 10 (1979): 137–54; Jacques Schwartz, "Les Voyages au Ciel dans la littérature apocalyptique," in *L'Apocalyptique: Études d'histoire des religions* 3, ed. M. Philonenko and M. Simon (Paris: Paul Geuthner, 1977), 91–126. Also useful for the Hebrew Bible background are the studies collected in Gerard P. Luttikhuizen, ed. *Paradise Interpreted: Representations of Biblical Paradise in Judaism and Christianity* (Leiden: E. J. Brill, 1999).

8. Two studies are indispensable to any consideration of these issues: Caroline Walker Bynum's magisterial study *The Resurrection of the Body in Western Christianity, 200–1336* (New York: Columbia University Press, 1995); and the meticulous survey of ancient Christian sources by Brian E. Daley, *The Hope of the Early Church: A Handbook of Patristic Eschatology* (Cambridge: Cambridge University Press, 1991). See also Bernstein, *Formation of Hell;* Delumeau, *History of Paradise.* There is a useful collection and discussion of the primary Greek and Latin early Christian texts in Joanne E. McWilliam Dewart, *Death and Resurrection,* MFC 22 (Wilmington, DE: Michael Glazier, 1986).

9. Origen, *Commentary on John* 1.16.92, 20.7.47; as cited and translated in Daley, *The Hope of the Early Church,* at p. 50. In addition to Daley's nuanced discussion (*Hope of the Early Church,* 47–60), see Lawrence R. Hennessey, "A Philosophical Issue in Origen's Eschatology: The Three Senses of Incorporeality," in *Origeniana Quinta: Papers of the 5th International Origen Congress, Boston College, 14–18 August 1989,* ed. Robert Daly (Leuven: Peeters Press, 1992), 373–80.

10. Discussed in chapter 1, pp. 46–56. See especially Himmelfarb, *Ascent to Heaven.*

11. E.g., the *Martyrdom of Polycarp;* the *Martyrs of Lyons and Vienne.* See the discussion in chapter 1, pp. 11–13, 46–47.

12. On the other hand, expectation of an imminent "end" characterized only some of earliest Christian literature, and even for the earliest Christians there was a range of meanings as to what constituted that expectation. See Daley, *Hope of the Early Church,* 5–32.

13. Ambrose, *On Belief in the Resurrection* ("On the Decease of his Brother Satyrus, Book 2") 55; trans. de Romestin, NPNF, 2nd series, 10:174–97.

14. The presentation of Eden or paradise as a temple or sanctuary was a characteristic of Jewish and early Christian apocalyptic literature from roughly the third century B.C.E.. See Himmelfarb, *Ascent to Heaven;* J. T. A. G. M. van Ruiten, "Eden and the Temple: The Rewriting of Genesis 2:4–3:24 in the *Book of Jubilees,*" in *Paradise Interpreted,* ed. Luttikhuizen, 63–94; Stephen E. Robinson, "The Testament of Adam and the Angelic Liturgy," *RQ* 45.12 (1985): 105–10.

15. Chapter 5, p. 208.

16. Prudentius, *Hymn* 5.113–25; trans. Eagan, 36.

17. *Cave of Treasures* 7.7; trans. Budge, 75. The *Cave of Treasures*, a sixth-century Syriac compilation, thus shares in the tradition of a "double fall," that is, that the expulsion of Adam and Eve from Eden did not for the first generations impose a grim life of suffering and toil—a life that came later, after the death of Seth. See Lucas Van Rompay, "Memories of Paradise: The Greek 'Life of Adam and Eve' and Early Syriac Tradition," *Aram* 5 (1993): 555–70. The notion continued that there remained an earthly paradise, distinct from the heavenly one, to which access had been denied to humans since the expulsion of Adam and Eve; see, e.g., Delumeau, *History of Paradise*, 39–70. Syriac writers, for example, portrayed the access as reopened by the death and resurrection of Christ: see, e.g., Robert Murray, "The Lance which Re-opened Paradise: A Mysterious Reading in the Early Syriac Fathers," *OCP* 39 (1973): 224–34, 491.

Jewish extracanonical literature of the same period shares many of the same themes. Consider, e.g., the fifth- or sixth-century Hebrew text of 3 Enoch, describing the paths of the winds of God. When finally these winds fall upon Eden, "In the midst of the garden they mingle and blow from one side to the other. They become fragrant from the perfumes of the garden and from the spices of Eden until, scattering, saturated with the scent of pure perfume, they bring the scent of the spices of the garden and the perfumes of Eden before the righteous and the godly who shall inherit the garden of Eden and the tree of life in time to come, as it is written,

> Awake, north wind
> Come, wind from the south!
> Breathe over my garden,
> to spread its sweet smell around.
> Let my beloved come into his garden,
> let him taste its rarest fruit. [Song of Songs 4:16]

> 3 Enoch 23.18; trans. Philip Alexander, in Charlesworth,
> *Old Testament Pseudepigrapha* 1:223–315.

18. See the textual discussions in chapter 2, "Excursus: Incense Offerings in the Syriac *Transitus Mariae*," pp. 90–98. Equally rich in olfactory liturgical imagery were the Greek texts on the Dormition: see the discussion and translations in Brian E. Daley, *On the Dormition of Mary: Early Patristic Homilies* (Crestwood, NY: St. Vladimir's Seminary Press, 1998).

19. E.g., Paphnutius, *Histories* 28–35; trans. Vivian, 161–65.

20. *Bohairic Life of Pachomius*; trans. Veilleux, *Pachomian Koinonia*, 1:167–68.

21. *Lives of the Desert Fathers* 10.21–22; trans. Russell, 85.

22. Chapter 4. See also Shaw, *Burden of the Flesh*, 214–19 ("The Body of Paradise").

23. See the studies in Elisabeth B. MacDougall, ed., *Medieval Gardens* (Washington, DC: Dumbarton Oaks Publications, 1986), esp. Paul Meyvaert, "The Medieval Monastic Garden," 23–54 ; Naomi Miller, "Paradise Regained: Medieval Garden Fountains," 135–54 ; Marilyn Stokstad, "The Garden as Art," 175–86; and Brian E. Daley, "The 'Closed Garden' and the 'Sealed Fountain': Song of Songs 4: 12 in the late Medieval Iconography of Mary," 253–78.

24. See above, chapter 2, pp. 83–89, for the context within the developments of liturgical practices.

25. John Wilkinson, "Jewish Holy Places and the Origins of Christian Pilgrimage," in *The Blessings of Pilgrimage*, ed. Robert Ousterhout (Urbana: University of Illinois Press, 1990), 41–53; Rothkrug, " 'Odor of Sanctity.' "

26. E.g., *The Martyrdom of St.Polycarp* 18.2–3; *The Martyrdom of Perpetua and Felicitas* 21; both in Musurillo, *Acts of the Christian Martyrs*, at pp. 16–17 and 128–31, respectively. In addition to the important material brought out in Rothkrug, " 'Odor of Sanctity,' " there remains much that is useful in H. Delehaye, *Les Origines du Culte des Martyrs*, 2nd ed., SH 20 (Brussels: Société des Bollandistes, 1933). The traditions of bone veneration from the hero cults of Greek religions were also very important; see Walter Burkert, *Greek Religion*, trans. John Raffan (Cambridge, MA: Harvard University Press, 1985), 203–8; Robin Lane Fox, *Pagans and Christians* (San Francisco: Harper and Row, 1987), 146–47. Peter Brown's classic study, *The Cult of the Saints: Its Rise and Function in Latin Christianity* (Chicago: University of Chicago Press, 1981), focuses on the third through sixth centuries in the Latin west.

27. E.g., Ephrem, *Hymns on Virginity* 17–19; John Chrysostom, "Homily on the Martyr Babylas" 10; *Bohairic Life of Pachomius* 123 (death of Pachomius) and 207 (death of Theodore), trans. Veilleux, *Pachomian Koinonia* 1:178, 259; *Life of Rabbula*, ed. Bedjan, *AMS* 4:441, 449; *Sayings of the Desert Fathers*, Sisoes, 14, trans. Ward, 180; Philoxenus of Mabbug, *On the Indwelling of the Holy Spirit*, trans. Brock, *Syriac Fathers on Prayer*, 106–27, at 122–23; for Simeon the Stylite, see above, chapter 4, pp. 186–96. See the entries for "euodia" in the Dumbarton Oaks Database of Byzantine Hagiography, http://www.doaks.org/Hagio.html. The classic study for the continuing western Christian tradition remains W. Deonna, "EUWDIA: Croyances antiques et modernes: L'Odeur suave des dieux et des élus," *Genava* 17 (1939): 167–263. For the sweet fragrance of the corpses of Jewish holy men in medieval Jewish legends, see Louis Jacobs, "The Body in Jewish Worship: Three Rituals Examined," in *Religion and the Body*, ed. Sarah Coakley (Cambridge: Cambridge University Press, 1997), 71–89.

28. As in the *Martyrs of Lyons and Vienne*, discussed in chapter 1, pp. 46–47.

29. There is a fine discussion and translation by Gillian Clark, "Victricius of Rouen: Praising the Saints," *JECS* 7 (1999): 365–99. For another example, Nicholas Constas, "An Apology for the Cult of Saints in Late Antiquity: Eustratius Presbyter of Constantinople, 'On the State of Souls after Death (CPG

7522),'" JECS 10 (2002): 267–85. See also the insightful consideration of Bynum, *Resurrection*, 104–14; eadem, "Material Continuity, Personal Survival and the Resurrection of the Body: A Scholastic Discussion in its Medieval and Modern Contexts," in her collection *Fragmentation and Redemption: Essays on Gender and the Human Body in Medieval Religion* (New York: Zone Books, 1992), 239–98, 393–417.

30. Beautifully discussed in Patricia Cox Miller, "'The Little Blue Flower is Red': Relics and the Poeticizing of the Body," JECS 8 (2000): 213–36; eadem, "'Differential Networks': Relics and Other Fragments in Late Antiquity," JECS 6 (1998): 113–38. See, e.g., Paulinus of Nola, *Poems on St. Felix*; Ephrem, *Hymns on Julian Saba*.

31. Some examples may be found in Eunice Dauterman Maguire, Henry P. Maguire, and Maggie J. Duncan-Flowers, eds. *Art and Holy Powers in the Early Christian House* (Urbana, IL/Chicago: University of Illinois Press, 1989), e.g., 24–29; Gary Vikan, *Byzantine Pilgrimage Art* (Washington, DC: Dumbarton Oaks Publications, 1982). Numerous encolpia and pilgrimage ampullae are included in the catalogue *The Glory of Byzantium: Art and Culture of the Middle Byzantine Era, A.D. 843–1261*, Helen C. Evans and William D. Wixom, eds. (New York: Metropolitan Museum of Art, 1997). I am grateful to Jeffrey Anderson, in particular, for helpful discussion on the use of encolpia.

32. *Oration on the Translation of the Relics of Our Holy Father Athanasios Patriarch of Constantinople*, secs. 31–32, 63. See the discussion, edition, and translation by Alice-Mary Talbot, *Faith Healing in Late Byzantium: The Posthumous Miracles of the Patriarch Athanasios I of Constantinople by Theoktistos the Stoudite* (Brookline: MA: Hellenic College Press, 1983), esp. pp. 19, 82–85, 112–15.

33. For example, in his early seventh-century commentary on the liturgy, at *Memra* 5, ch. 2, Gabriel of Qatar noted the different meanings attending the incense offerings during the eucharistic liturgy; these include the signification of different times as well as differences in actions. The designations are located within the liturgy itself with the temporal marker, "at this moment," or "at this point," i.e., of the liturgy. At the Great Entrance, the incense "is a symbol of the delight that is to come," i.e., in the future life (5.2.12); at the Gospel reading, it denotes "the sweetness of our Lord's words" (5.2.30). At the anaphora, incense signifies the aromatic spices used to embalm the crucified Christ at his burial (5.2.64); the incense is removed from the altar after the epiclesis (lit. "hovering"), "because corruptibility, which was the reason for the embalming, is dissolved" with the resurrection (5.2.72). See the edition, translation, and commentary by Sebastian P. Brock, "Gabriel of Qatar's Commentary on the Liturgy," *Hugoye* 6.2 (July 2003), http://syrcom.cua.edu/Hugoye/Vol6no2/HV6N2Brock.html.

34. Indeed, resurrection was an idea much debated amongst Jews prior to and during the time of Jesus' ministry.

35. Again, Bynum, *Resurrection of the Body*, and Daley, *Hope of the Early Church*, are indispensible guides.

36. Tertullian, *On the Resurrection of the Flesh* 7. For a rich discussion of the context of Tertullian's views, as well as a nuanced account of what was at stake in his presentation of resurrection, see Bynum, *Resurrection*, 21–58.

37. Tertullian, *On the Resurrection of the Flesh* 7; trans. Evans, 22–23.

38. Tertullian, *On the Resurrection of the Flesh* 7; trans. Evans, 22–25.

39. So, too, the twentieth-century theologian C. S. Lewis: "What the soul cries out for is the resurrection of the senses. Even in this life [as opposed to eternity] matter would be nothing to us if it were not the source of sensations." C. S. Lewis, *Letters to Malcolm: Chiefly on Prayer* (1963; repr. New York: Harcourt, 1992), *Letter* 22, at p. 121.

40. The conundrum of Greek philosophical tradition and incarnation theology is considered with great insight in Columba Stewart, "Imageless Prayer and the Theological Vision of Evagrius Ponticus," *JECS* 9 (2001): 173–204.

41. Gregory of Nyssa, *On the Soul and the Resurrection* 1; trans. Roth, 34. Cf. Wis 13:5. On the confusing inconsistency—and even incoherence—of Gregory's views on the resurrection, see Bynum, *Resurrection*, 81–86.

42. Gregory of Nyssa, *On the Soul and the Resurrection* 5; trans. Roth, 70–71.

43. Quoting 2 Corinthians 2:9, citing Isaiah 64:4. Gregory of Nyssa, *On the Soul and the Resurrection* 10; trans. Roth, 116.

44. Gregory of Nyssa, *On the Soul and the Resurrection* 10; trans. Roth, 116.

45. Ambrose, *Death as a Good* 5.19–20; trans. McHugh, *Saint Ambrose: Seven Exegetical Works*, 69–113, at 84–87.

46. Ambrose, *Death as a Good* 9.40–41; trans. McHugh, 98–99.

47. Ambrose, *Death as a Good* 11.49; trans. McHugh, 106.

48. "Suffrages of Mar Balai" 6; trans. Hugh Connolly, "Some Early Syriac Hymns," *Downside Review* 35 (1916): 137–46, at p. 143. The attribution to Balai is uncertain, as for all of these hymns.

49. Jacob of Serug, Homily 22, ed. Bedjan, *Homiliae Selectae* 1:546. Cf. Michael Guinan, "The Eschatology of James of Serug" (PhD. diss., Catholic University of America, 1972). On the phrase, "fragrance of life" in Syriac tradition, see S. A. Harvey, "St. Ephrem on the Scent of Salvation," *JTS*, n.s., 49 (1998): 109–128. For the relation between memorial practices for the dead and notions of the resurrected body especially in the Latin west, see Bynum, *Resurrection*, 52–58; and the memorial practices considered in Brown, *The Cult of the Saints*.

50. *Riha tmiha d-haw gaza d-hayye*, Ephrem, *Hymns on Nisibis* 70.19.

51. *Hymns on Nisibis* 50.11 (my trans.).

52. Augustine, *City of God*, 14.11; trans. Bettenson, 569.

53. Ephrem, *Hymns on Paradise* 8.9–10.

54. Jacob of Serug, "Homily on Simeon the Stylite," ed. Bedjan, *AMS* 4:650–65; here trans. S. A. Harvey, in *Asceticism in Greco-Roman Antiquity*, ed. Wimbush, 15–28, at p. 22.

55. Chapter 3, pp. 107–10.

56. Augustine, *City of God* 22.13–17.

57. Augustine, *City of God* 22.12, 20, 24.

58. See Bynum, *Resurrection*, 94–104; eadem, "Material Continuity."

59. Augustine, *City of God* 22.17, 20.

60. Augustine, *City of God* 22.17, 19; trans. Bettensen, 1057, 1062.

61. Augustine, *City of God* 22.24; trans. Bettensen, 1076.

62. Augustine, *City of God* 22.29; trans. Bettensen, 1086–87.

63. Augustine, *City of God* 22.30; trans. Bettensen, 1090–91.

64. This is the central thesis of David Chidester, *Word and Light: Seeing, Hearing, and Religious Discourse* (Urbana IL/Chicago: University of Illinois Press, 1992). Chidester here focuses on western Christianity, and considers sight as the dominant sensory image and mode in Roman Catholic tradition, while arguing for hearing as the dominant aspect in Protestant tradition. In eastern Christianity, the Orthodox churches have been often characterized with reference to their emphasis on the visual piety of icons. None of these branches are monolithic, and all can and should be treated with attunement to their greater complexity. Yet considerable insight into the cultures and histories of these branches can be gained from these sensory characterizations.

65. Jean Daniélou, "Terre et Paradis chez les Pères de l'église," *Eranos Jahrbuch* 22 (1953), 433–72, has a fine discussion of Ephrem's *Hymns on Paradise* in this study on the physicality of the early Christian conception of the afterlife. See also Kathleen McVey, "Images of Joy in Ephrem's Hymns on Paradise: Returning to the Womb and the Breast," *JCSSS* 3 (2003): 59–77; N. Sed, "Les Hymnes sur le Paradis de Saint Ephrem et les traditions Juives," *Le Muséon* 81 (1968): 455–501. It is important to remember that Revelation did not enter the Syriac canon until some centuries after Ephrem's death.

66. *Hymns on Paradise* 11.15; trans. Brock, 159.

67. *Hymns on Paradise* 1.5; trans. Brock, 79.

68. *Hymns on Paradise* 4.7; trans. Brock, 100.

69. *Hymns on Paradise* 11.13; trans. Brock, 158.

70. *Hymns on Paradise* 5.6; trans. Brock, 104.

71. *Hymns on Paradise* 9.17; trans. Brock, 142.

72. *Hymns on Paradise* 11.15; trans. Brock, 159.

73. *Hymns on Paradise* 11.1; trans. Brock, 154.

74. *Hymns on Paradise* 11.9; trans. Brock, 157.

75. See the important discussions in Gary Anderson, *Genesis of Perfection: Adam and Eve in Jewish and Christian Imagination* (Louisville, KY: Westminster John Knox, 2001), 117–34; and Sebastian P. Brock, "Clothing Metaphors as a Means of Theological Expression in Syriac Tradition," in *Typus, Symbol, Allegorie bei den östlichen Vätern und ihren Parallelen im Mittelalter*, ed. Margot Schmidt and C. Geyer (Regensburg: Friedrich Pustet, 1982), 11–40.

76. *Hymns on Paradise* 9.17; trans. Brock, 142.

77. *Hymns on Paradise* 8.2b, 4, 5b, 6. Trans. Brock, 132–33.

78. *Hymns on Paradise* 7.12; trans. Brock, 123.

BIBLIOGRAPHY

Primary Sources

Abdisho Hazzaya (= Joseph the Visionary). "Mystical Treatises."

    Edited and translated by Alphonse Mingana. *Woodbrooke Studies*. Vol. 7, *Early Christian Mystics*, 145–75. Cambridge: W. Heffer and Sons, 1934.

Acta Apostolorum Apocrypha.

    Edited by R. A. Lipsius and M. Bonnet. 3 vols. Leipzig, 1891–1903; repr. Hildesheim: Georg Olms, 1959.

Acta Conciliorum Oecumenicorum.

    Edited by E. Schwartz. Berlin: de Gruyter, 1924–40. Rev. ed. J. Staub, 1971.

Acta Martyrum et Sanctorum.

    Edited by Paul Bedjan. 7 vols. Paris/Leipzig: Otto Harrassowitz, 1890–97; repr. Hildesheim: Georg Olms, 1968.

Acta Sanctorum Martyrum Orientalium. Pars 2.

    Edited by J. S. Assemani. Rome, 1748.

The Acts of the Christian Martyrs.

    Edited and translated by Herbert Musurillo. Oxford: Clarendon Press, 1972.

Acts of John.

    Edited by Eric Junod and Jean-Daniel Kaestli. *Acta Johannis.* CCSA 1–2. Turnhout: Brepols, 1983.

Translation and commentary by Knut Schäferdiek. In *New Testament Apocrypha*, edited by Wilhelm Schneemelcher, 2:152–209.

Acts of Paul and Thecla.

Edited by R. A. Lipsius and M. Bonnet. *Acta Apostolorum Apocrypha* 1:23–44, 104–17, 235–72.

Translation and commentary by Wilhelm Schneemelcher. In *New Testament Apocrypha*, edited by Wilhelm Schneemelcher, 2:220–22, 239–46.

Acts of Thomas.

Greek text edited by R. A. Lipsius and M. Bonnet. *Acta Apostolorum Apocrypha* 2.2:99–288.

Translation and commentary by H. J. W. Drijvers. In *New Testament Apocrypha*, edited by Wilhelm Schneemelcher, 2:322–411.

Syriac text edited by William Wright. *Apocryphal Acts of the Apostles* 1:171–333.

Translation and commentary by A. F. J. Klijn. *The Acts of Thomas*. Supplement 5 to NT. Leiden: E. J. Brill, 1962.

Ambrose. *Concerning Repentence.*

Edited by O. Faller. CSEL 73, 117–206. Vienna: 1955.

Translated by H. de Romestin. NPNF, 2nd ser., 10:327–59.

———. "Concerning Virgins."

Edited by J. P. Migne. PL 16:197–244.

Translated by H. de Romestin. St. *Ambrose, Select Works and Letters*. NPNF, 2nd series, 10:361–87.

———. *Death as a Good.*

Edited by Karl Schenkl. CSEL 32.1, 703–53. Vienna: 1897.

Translated by M. P. McHugh. *Saint Ambrose: Seven Exegetical Works*, 69–113.

———. *Flight from the World.*

Edited by Karl Schenkl. CSEL 32.2. Vienna: 1897.

Translated by M. P. McHugh. *Saint Ambrose, Seven Exegetical Works*, 279–323.

———. *The Holy Spirit.*

Edited by O. Faller. CSEL 79, 15–222. Vienna: 1964.

Translated by R. J. Deferrari. *Saint Ambrose, Theological and Dogmatic Works*, 31–214.

———. *Jacob and the Happy Life.*

Edited by Karl Schenkl. CSEL 32.2. Vienna: 1897.

Translated by M. P. McHugh. *Saint Ambrose, Seven Exegetical Works*, 117–84.

———. *On the Decease of his Brother Satyrus and On the Resurrection.*

Edited by O. Faller. CSEL 73.7, 207–325. Vienna: 1955.

Translated by H. de Romestin. NPNF, 2nd series, 10:159–97.

————. *The Prayer of Job and David.*

Edited by Karl Schenkl. CSEL 32.2. Vienna: 1897.

Translated by M. P. McHugh. *Saint Ambrose, Seven Exegetical Works,* 327–420.

————. *Sacraments.*

Edited and translated by Bernard Botte. *Ambroise de Milan, Des Sacrements: Des Mystères; Explication du symbole.* SC 25 bis. Paris: Éditions du Cerf, 1994.

Translated by R. J. Deferrari. *Saint Ambrose, Theological and Dogmatic Works,* 265–328.

————. *Saint Ambrose, Theological and Dogmatic Works.* Translated by R. J. Deferrari. FC 44. Washington, DC: Catholic University of America Press, 1963.

————. *Seven Exegetical Works.* Translated by Michael P. McHugh. FC 65. Washington, DC: Catholic University of America Press, 1972.

———— and Gregory Nazianzen. *Funeral Orations.* Translated by Leo P. McCauley. FC 22. New York: Fathers of the Church, 1953.

Ammonas. *Letters.*

Edited and translated by Bernard Outtier and Lucien Regnault. In *Lettres des Pères du Désert: Ammonas, Macaire, Arsène, Sérapion de Thmuis,* edited by Bernard Outtier, André Louf, Michel Van Parys, and Claire-Agnès Zirnheld, 1–60. Spiritualité Orientale 42. Bégrolles-en-Mauges: Abbaye de Bellefontaine, 1985.

Anastasius the Monk. *Works.*

Edited and translated by François Nau. *Les Récits inédits du Moine Anastase.* Paris: Picard et Fils, 1902.

Anthony. *Letters.*

Edited and translated by Samuel Rubenson. *The Letters of St. Antony: Monasticism and the Making of a Saint,* 197–232. Minneapolis: Fortress, 1995.

Aphrahat. *Demonstrations.*

Edited and translated by D. I. Parisot. *Aphraatis Sapientis Persae Demonstrationes.* PS 1. Edited by R. Graffin. Paris: Firmin-Didot, 1894.

Demonstrations 1, 5, 6, 8, 10, 17, 21–22 translated by J. Gwynn. NPNF, 2nd series, 13:343–412.

Demonstrations 11–13, 15–19, 21, 23 translated by Jacob Neusner. In idem, *Aphrahat and Judaism: The Jewish-Christian Argument in fourth-century Iran,* 1–119. Leiden: E. J. Brill, 1971.

Apocalypse of Paul.

In *Apocalypses Apocryphae,* edited by C. Tischendorf, xiv-xviii, 34–69.

Translated by Hugo Duensing and Aurelio de Santos Otero. In *New Testament Apocrypha,* edited by Wilhelm Schneemelcher, 2:712–48.

Apocalypses Apocryphae Mosis, Esdrae, Pauli, Iohannis, item Mariae Dormitio, additis Evangeliorum et Actuum apocryphorum supplementis. Edited by Constantinus Tischendorf. Leipzig: Herm. Mendelssohn, 1866.

Apocrypha Syriaca: The Protevangelium Jacobi and Transitus Mariae. Edited and translated by Agnes Smith Lewis. Studia Sinaitica 11. London: E. J. Clay and Sons, 1902.

Apocryphal Acts of the Apostles. Edited and translated by William Wright. 2 vols. London, 1871; repr. Amsterdam: Philo Press, 1968.

Apostolic Constitutions.

Edited and translated by Marcel Metzger. *Les Constitutions Apostoliques.* SC 320, 329, 336. Paris: Éditions du Cerf, 1985–87.

Translated by James Donaldson. *Constitutions of the Holy Apostles.* ANF 7:385–505.

The Apostolic Fathers. Edited and translated by Kirsopp Lake. 2 vols. LCL. New York: G. P. Putnam's Sons, 1924.

Apuleius. *Metamorphoses.*

Edited and translated by J. Arthur Hanson. LCL. Cambridge, MA: Harvard University Press, 1989.

Aristides. *Apology.*

Edited by J. Geffcken. *Zwei griechische Apologeten.* Leipzig: Teubner, 1907.

Translated by D. M. Kay. *The Apology of Aristides the Philosopher.* ANF 10:257–79.

Aristotle. *The Complete Works of Aristotle.* Edited by J. Barnes. Princeton: Princeton University Press, 1984.

———. *On the Soul.* Edited and translated by W. S. Hett. LCL. Cambridge, MA: Harvard University Press, 1935.

Arnobius of Sicca. *The Case Against the Pagans.*

Edited by A. Riefferscheid. CSEL 4. Vienna: 1875.

Translated by George E. McCracken. ACW 8. New York: Newman Press, 1949.

Aseneth.

Edited by M. Philonenko. *Joseph et Aseneth: Introduction, texte critique, traduction, et notes.* Studia Post Biblica. Leiden: E. J. Brill, 1968 (shorter version).

Edited by Cristoph Burchard. *Joseph und Aseneth.* Pseudepigraphica Veteris Testamenti Graece, vol. 5. Leiden: E. J. Brill, 2003 (longer version).

Translated by Ross Kraemer. "Aseneth." In *Women's Religions in the Greco-Roman World: A Sourcebook,* edited by Ross Kraemer, 308–27. New York: Oxford University Press, 2004.

Athanasius. *Letter to Serapion.*

Edited by Joseph Lebon. *Lettres à Sérapion sur la divinité du Saint-Esprit.* SC 15. Paris: Éditions du Cerf, 1947.

Translated by C. R. B. Shapland. In *The Letters of Saint Athanasius Concerning the Holy Spirit,* 58–149. New York: Philosophical Library, 1951.

———. *The Life of Antony.*

Edited and translated by L. Bouyer. *LaVie de S.Antoine.* 2nd ed. Abbaye de Bellefontaine: Fontenelle, 1977.

Translated by Robert C. Gregg. *Athanasius: The Life of Anthony and the Letter to Marcellinus.* NewYork: Paulist Press, 1980.

Syriac version edited and translated by R. Draguet. *La vie primitive de S.Antoine conservée en Syriaque.* CSCO 417/Scr. Syr. 183. Louvain: Peeters Press, 1980.

———. *Second Letter toVirgins.*

Edited by J. Lebon. "Athanasiana Syriaca II: Une letter attribuée à saint Athanase d'Alexandrie." *Le Muséon* 41 (1928): 169–216.

Translated by David Brakke. *Athanasius and the Politics of Asceticism,* 292–302. Oxford: Clarendon Press, 1995.

(Pseudo-Athanasius). "A Baptismal Address Attributed to Athanasius."

Edited and translated by Sebastian P. Brock. *OC* 61 (1977): 92–102.

(Pseudo-Athanasius). "The Life and Activity of the Holy and BlessedTeacher Syncletica."

Edited by J.P. Migne. *PG* 28:1487–1558.

Translated by Elizabeth Castelli. In *Ascetic Behavior in Greco-Roman Antiquity,* edited by VincentWimbush, 265–311. Minneapolis: Fortress Press, 1990.

Athenaeus. *The Deipnosophists.*

Edited and translated by Charles Burton Gulick. LCL. NewYork: G. P. Putnam's Sons, 1933.

Augustine. *City of God.*

Edited and translated by Pierre de Labriolle. *Saint Augustin, La Cité de Dieu.* 2 vols. Paris: Garnier, 1941–46.

Translated by Henry Bettenson. *St. Augustine, Concerning the City of God, against the Pagans.* NewYork: Penguin Books, 1984.

———. *Confessions.*

Edited by Martin Skutella, *Sancti Augustini Confessiones.* Rev. ed. Lucas Verheijen. CCSL 27.Turnhout: Brepols, 1981.

Translated by Henry Chadwick. Oxford/NewYork: Oxford University Press, 1991.

———. *On Nature and Grace.*

Edited by C. F. Urba and J. Zycha. CSEL 60, 233–99.Vienna: 1913.

Translated by P. Holmes, R. E.Wallis, and B. B.Warfield. NPNF, 1st series, 5:121–51.

———. *The Trinity.*

Edited by W.J. Mountain. CCSL 50, 50A.Turnhout: 1968.

Translated by Stephen McKenna. FC 45. Washington, DC: Catholic University of America Press, 1963.

Basil of Caesarea. *Address to Young Men on Reading Greek Literature*.

    Edited and translated by R. J. Deferrari and M. R. P. McGuire. In *Saint Basil: The Letters*, edited by R. J. Deferrari, 4:365–435. LCL. Cambridge MA: Harvard University Press, 1970.

———. *De Hominis Structura*.

    Edited and translated by Alexis Smets and Michel van Esbroek. *Basile de Césarée: Sur l'origine de l'homme*. SC 160. Paris: Éditions du Cerf, 1970.

———. *Exegetical Homilies*. Translated by Agnes Clare Way. FC 46. Washington, DC: Catholic University of America Press, 1963.

———. *Homilies on the Hexaemeron*.

    Edited and translated by S. Giet. *Homélies sur l'Hexaéméron*. SC 26. Paris: Éditions du Cerf, 1968.

    Translated by Agnes Clare Way. *Saint Basil, Exegetical Homilies*, 1–151. FC 46. Washington, DC: Catholic University of America Press, 1963.

———. *Letters*.

    Edited and and translated by R. J. Deferrari. *Saint Basil: The Letters*. LCL. Cambridge MA: Harvard University Press, 1970.

———. *Long Rules*.

    Edited by J. P. Migne. PG 31:889–1052.

    Translated by M. Monica Wagner. *Saint Basil, Ascetical Works*. FC 9. Washington, DC: Catholic University of America Press, 1950.

Baynes, Norman, and Elizabeth Dawes. *Three Byzantine Saints*. London: Mowbrays, 1948; repr. Crestwood, NY: St. Vladimir's Seminary Press, 1977.

Beard, Mary, John North, and Simon Price, eds. *Religions of Rome*. Vol. 2, *A Sourcebook*. Cambridge: Cambridge University Press, 1998.

The Book of Pontiffs.

    Edited by L. Duchesne. *Le Liber Pontificalis*. 2 vols. Paris: 1886–92. Repr. with third volume corrections and additions by C. Vogel. Paris: Boccard, 1955–57.

    Translated by Raymond Davis. Liverpool: Liverpool University Press, 1989.

Brock, Sebastian P. *Bride of Light: Hymns on Mary from the Syriac Churches*. Moran 'Eth'o 6. Kerala: St. Ephrem Ecumenical Research Institute, 1994.

———. *The Syriac Fathers on Prayer and the Spiritual Life*. Kalamazoo: Cistercian Publications, 1987.

———. "Two Syriac Verse Homilies on the Binding of Isaac." *Le Muséon* 99 (1986): 61–129.

——— and Susan Ashbrook Harvey. *Holy Women of the Syrian Orient*. Berkeley: University of California Press, 1987; updated edition with new Preface, 1998.

Burkitt, F. C., *Euphemia and the Goth with the Acts of Martyrdom of the Confessors of Edessa, Shmona, Guria, and Habib*. London: Williams and Norgate, 1913.

Callinicos. *Life of Hypatios.*

Edited and translated by G. J. M. Bartelink. *Callinicos, Vie D'Hypatios: Introduction, texte critique, traduction, et notes.* SC 177. Paris: Éditions du Cerf, 1971.

Cave of Treasures.

Edited and translated by Su-Min Ri. *La Caverne des trésors: les deux recensions syriaques.* CSCO 486–87/Scr. Syr. 207–208. Louvain: Peeters Press, 1987.

Translated by E. A. Wallis Budge. *The Book of the Cave of Treasures: A History of the patriarchs and the kings, their successors, from the Creation to the Crucifixion of Christ, translated from the Syriac text of the British Museum ms. Add. 25875.* London: The Religious Tract Society, 1927.

Cicero. *On the Nature of the Gods.*

Edited and translated by H. Rackham. LCL. Cambridge, MA: Harvard University Press, 1933.

Translation and commentary by P. G. Walsh. *Cicero, The Nature of the Gods.* Oxford: Clarendon Press, 1997.

Clement of Alexandria. *Clément d'Alexandrie, Le Pédagogue.*

Vol. 1 edited and translated by Henri-Irénée Marrou and Marguerite Harl. SC 70. Paris: Éditions du Cerf, 1960.

Vol. 2 edited and translated by Henri-Irénée Marrou and Claude Mondésert. SC 108. Paris: Éditions du Cerf, 1965.

Vol. 3 edited and translated by Henri-Irénée Marrou, Claude Mondésert, and Chantal Matray. SC 158. Paris: Éditions du Cerf, 1970.

Translated by Simon P. Wood. *Christ the Educator.* FC 23. New York: Fathers of the Church, 1954.

———. *Stromateis.*

Edited by Otto Stählin and Ludwig Früchtel. GCS 12, 15, 17, 52. 1905–80.

Books 3 and 7 translated in J. E. L. Oulton and Henry Chadwick. *Alexandrian Christianity.* Philadelphia: Westminster, 1954.

Clement of Rome. *First Epistle to the Corinthians (1 Clement).*

Edited and translated by Kirsopp Lake. In *The Apostolic Fathers* 1:1–122. LCL. New York: MacMillan, 1912.

(Pseudo-)Clementine. *Homilies.*

Edited by B. Rehm, J. Irmscher, and F. Paschke. *Die Pseudoklementinen I: Homilien.* GCS 42. 2nd ed. 1969.

Translated by T. Smith, "Pseudo-Clementine Literature," ANF 8:67–346.

"*Le Codex Arménien Jérusalem 121.* II: Édition comparée du texte et de deux autres manuscripts." Edited and translated by Athanase Renoux. PO 36. Turnhout: Brepols, 1971.

Connolly, Hugh. "Some Early Syriac Hymns." *Downside Review* 35 (1916): 137–46.

Connolly, R.H., and H.W. Codrington, eds. and trans. *Two Commentaries on the Jacobite Liturgy by George Bishop of the Arab Tribes and Moses bar Kepha, Together with the Syriac Anaphora of St. James and a Document entitled the Book of Life*. London: Williams and Norgate, 1913.

Cyprian. *On the Lapsed*.

Edited by G. Hartel. CSEL 3.1. Vienna: 1868.

Translated by Maurice Bévenot. *St. Cyprian, The Lapsed, The Unity of the Church*. ACW 25, 13–42. Westminster, MD: Newman Press, 1957.

Cyril of Alexandria. *Dialogues on the Trinity*.

Edited and translated by G.M. de Durand. *Cyrille d'Alexandrie: dialogues sur La Trinité*. 3 vols. SC 231, 237, 246. Paris: Éditions du Cerf, 1976–78.

———. *Letter 24*.

ACO 1, 1, 1, pp. 117–18.

Translated by J.L. McEnerny. *St. Cyril of Alexandria: Letters*. FC 76–77. Washington, DC: Catholic University of America Press, 1987.

Cyril of Jerusalem. *Mystagogical Lectures*.

Edited and translated by Auguste Piédagnel et Pierre Paris. *Cyrille de Jérusalem, Catéchèses mystagogiques*. SC 126. Paris: Éditions du Cerf, 1966.

———. *Works*.

Edited by W.K. Reischl and J. Rupp. *S. Cyrilli: Opera quae supersunt omnia*. 2 vols. Munich: 1848–60; repr. Hildesheim: Georg Olms, 1967.

Translated by Leo P. McCauley and Anthony Stephenson. *The Works of Saint Cyril of Jerusalem*. Vol. 1, FC 61; vol. 2, FC 64. Washington, DC: Catholic University of America Press, 1969–70.

Cyril of Scythopolis. *Lives*.

Edited by Eduard Schwartz. *Kyrillos von Skythopolis*. TU 49:2. Leipzig, 1939.

Translation and commentary by R.M. Price and John Binns. *Cyril of Scythopolis, The Lives of the Monks of Palestine*. Kalamazoo: Cistercian Publications, 1991.

Daley, Brian E. *On the Dormition of Mary: Early Patristic Homilies*. Crestwood, NY: St. Vladimir's Seminary Press, 1998.

Depuydt, Leo, ed. *Encomiastica from the Pierpont Morgan Library*. CSCO 545/Scr. Cop. 48. Louvain, 1993.

Dewart, Joanne E. McWilliam. *Death and Resurrection*. MFC 22. Wilmington, DE: Michael Glazier, 1986.

Diadochus of Photicus. *Chapters*.

Edited and translated by Édouard des Places. *Diadoque de Photicé, Oeuvres Spirituelles*, "Cent chapitres sur la perfection spirituelle." SC 5, 84–163. Paris: Éditions du Cerf, 1997.

————. *Vision.*

Edited and translated by Édouard des Places. *Diadoque de Photicé, Oeuvres Spirituelles,* "Vision de Saint Diadoque, évêque de Photicé en Épire." SC 5, 168–83. Paris: Éditions du Cerf, 1997.

————. *Works.*

Edited and translated by Édouard des Places. *Diadoque de Photicé, Oeuvres Spirituelles.* SC 5. Paris: Éditions du Cerf, 1997.

(Pseudo)-Dionysius the Areopagite. *Corpus Dionysiacum.*

The Complete Works. Translated by Colm Luibheid with commentary by Paul Rorem. New York: Paulist Press, 1987.

Vol. 1, *de divinis nominibus.* Edited by Beata Regina Suchla. PTS 33. Berlin: Walter de Gruyter, 1990.

Vol. 2, *de coelesti hierarchia, de ecclesiastica hierarchia, de mystica theologia, epistulae.* Edited by Günter Heil and Adolph Martin Ritter. PTS 36. Berlin: Walter de Gruyter, 1991.

————. *Denys L'aréopagite, La Hiérarchie Céleste.* Edited by Günter Heil, translated by Maurice de Gandillac. SC 58. Paris: Éditions du Cerf, 1958.

(Pseudo-)Dionysius of Tel-Mahre. Chronicle (= Chronicle of Zuqnin).

Edited by J.-B. Chabot. *Incerti auctoris chronicon anonymum pseudo-Dionysianum vulgo dictum.* CSCO 104/Scr. Syr. 53. Louvain: Secrétariat du CorpusSCO, 1933.

Translated by Amir Harrak. *The Chronicle of Zuqnin, Parts III and IV, A.D. 488–775.* Toronto: Pontifical Institute of Mediaeval Studies, 1999.

Part 3 is also translated by W. Witakowski. *Pseudo-Dionysius of Tel-Mahre, Chronicle, Part III.* Liverpool: Liverpool University Press, 1996.

Dioscorus of Alexandria. *A Panegyric on Macarios, Bishop of Tkôw, Attributed to Dioscorus of Alexandria.* Edited and translated by D. Johnson. CSCO 415–16/Scr. Cop. 41–42. Louvain: Secrétariat du CorpusSCO, 1980.

Drijvers, Han J. W. and Jan Willem Drijvers. *The Finding of the True Cross: The Judas Kyriakos Legend in Syriac.* CSCO 565/Sub. 93. Louvain: Peeters Press, 1997.

Dumbarton Oaks Database of Byzantine Hagiography. http://www.doaks.org/Hagio.html.

Ephrem. *Commentary on the Diatessaron.*

Translated by Carmel McCarthy. *Saint Ephrem's Commentary on Tatian's Diatessaron.* JSSS 2. Oxford: Oxford University Press, 1993.

————. *Commentary on Genesis.*

Edited by R. M. Tonneau. *Sancti Ephraem Syri in Genesim et in Exodum commentarii.* CSCO 152–53/Scr. Syr. 71–72. Louvain: Secrétariat du CorpusSCO, 1955.

Translated by Joseph P. Amar and Edward G. Mathews. *Ephrem: Selected Prose Works.* FC 91, 59–213. Washington, DC: Catholic University of America Press, 1994.

——. *The Harp of the Spirit: Eighteen Poems of Saint Ephrem.* Translated by Sebastian P. Brock. SSS 4. 2nd ed. London: Fellowship of St. Alban and St. Sergius, 1983.

——. Homily on Our Lord.

Edited and translated by Edmund Beck. *Des heiligen Ephraem des Syrers Sermo de Domino Nostro.* CSCO 270–71/Scr. Syr. 116–17. Louvain: Secrétariat du CorpusSCO, 1966.

Translated by Joseph P. Amar and Edward G. Mathews. *St. Ephrem the Syrian: Selected Prose Works.* FC 91, 269–332. Washington, DC: Catholic University of America Press, 1994.

——. Hymns. Translated by Kathleen McVey. *Ephrem the Syrian, Hymns.* Mahweh, NJ: Paulist Press, 1989.

——. Hymns on Faith.

Edited and translated by Edmund Beck. *Des heiligen Ephraem des Syrers Hymnen de Fide.* CSCO 154–55/Scr. Syr. 74. Louvain: Secrétariat du CorpusSCO, 1955.

——. Hymns on Fasting.

Edited and translated by Edmund Beck. *Des heiligen Ephraem des Syrers Hymnen de Ieiunio.* CSCO 246–47/Scr. Syr. 106–107. Louvain: Secrétariat du CorpusSCO, 1964.

——. Hymns on Julian Saba.

Edited and translated by Edmund Beck. *Des heiligen Ephraem des Syrers Hymnen auf Abraham Kidunaya und Julianos Saba.* CSCO 322–23/Scr. Syr. 140–41. Louvain: Secrétariat du CorpusSCO, 1972.

——. Hymns on the Nativity.

Edited and translated by Edmund Beck. *Des heiligen Ephraem des Syrers Hymnen de Nativitate (Epiphania).* CSCO 186–87/Scr. Syr. 82–83. Louvain: Secrétariat du CorpusSCO, 1959.

Translated by Kathleen McVey. *Ephrem the Syrian, Hymns,* 61–217. Mahweh, NJ: Paulist Press, 1989.

——. Hymns on Nisibis.

Edited and translated by Edmund Beck. *Des heiligen Ephraem des Syrers Carmina Nisibena.* CSCO 218–19/Scr. Syr. 92–93. Louvain: Secrétariat du CorpusSCO, 1961.

——. Hymns on Paradise.

Edited and translated by Edmund Beck. *Des heiligen Ephraem des Syrers Hymnen de Paradiso und Contra Julianum.* CSCO 174–75/Scr. Syr. 78–79. Louvain: Secrétariat du CorpusSCO, 1957.

Translated by Sebastian P. Brock. *St. Ephrem the Syrian, Hymns on Paradise.* Crestwood, NY: St. Vladimir's Seminary Press, 1990.

——. Hymns on Virginity.

Edited and translated by Edmund Beck. *Des heiligen Ephraem des Syrers Hymnen de Virginitate.* CSCO 223–24/Scr. Syr. 94–95. Louvain: Secrétariat du CorpusSCO, 1962.

Translated by Kathleen McVey. *Ephrem the Syrian, Hymns,* 259–468. Mahweh, NJ: Paulist Press, 1989.

————. *Prose Refutations.*

St. Ephrem's *Prose Refutations of Mani, Marcion, and Bardaisan.*

Vol. 1 edited and translated by C. W. Mitchell. Vol. 2 edited and translated by E. A. Bevan and F. C. Burkitt. London: Williams and Northgate, 1921.

————. *Selected Prose Works.* Translated by Joseph P. Amar and Edward G. Mathews, Jr. FC 91. Washington, DC: Catholic University of America Press, 1994.

————. *Verse Homily (Sermon) 2.*

Edited and translated by Edmund Beck. *Des Heiligen Ephraem des Syrers Sermones* 1. CSCO 305–306/Scr. Syr. 130–31. Louvain: Secrétariat du CorpusSCO, 1970.

————. *Verse Homily (Sermon) 4.*

Edited and translated by Edmund Beck. *Des Heiligen Ephraem des Syrers, Sermones* 2, 79–81 (text), 99–109 (German trans.). CSCO 311–12/Scr. Syr. 134–35. Louvain: Secrétariat du CorpusSCO, 1970.

Translated by John Gwynn. NPNF, 2nd series, 13:336–41.

(Pseudo-Ephrem). "On Hermits and Desert Dwellers."

Edited (as Sermon 2) by Edmund Beck. *Des Heiligen Ephraem des Syrers Sermones* 4, 16–28. CSCO 334–35/Scr. Syr. 148–49. Louvain: Sécretariat du CorpusSCO, 1973.

Translated by Joseph P. Amar. In *Ascetic Behavior in Greco-Roman Antiquity: A Sourcebook,* edited by Vincent Wimbush, 66–80. Minneapolis: Fortress Press, 1990.

Eunapius. *Lives of the Sophists.*

Edited and translated by Wilmer Cave Wright. LCL. Cambridge, MA: Harvard University Press, 1968.

Eusebius. *Demonstratio Evangelica.*

Edited by A. Heikel. GCS 23. Leipzig/Berlin: J. C. Hinrichs, 1913.

Translated by W. J. Ferrar. *Eusbeius, The Proof of the Gospel.* Repr. Grand Rapids, MI: Baker Book House, 1981.

————. *Ecclesiastical History.*

Edited and translated by Kirsopp Lake (vol. 1), and J. E. L. Oulton and H. J. Lawlor (vol. 2). 2 vols. LCL. Cambridge, MA: Harvard University Press, 1926–32.

————. *Eclogae Propheticae.*

Edited by T. Gaisford. *Eusebii Pamphili episcopi Caesariensis eclogae propheticae* . Oxford: e Typographeo Academico, 1842.

————. *Preparation of the Gospel.*

Edited by Édouard des Places, translated by Odile Zink. *Eusèbe de Césarée, La Préparation Évangélique.* Vol. 4. SC 262. Paris: Éditions du Cerf, 1979.

Translated by E. H. Gifford. Repr. Grand Rapids: Baker Book House, 1981.

Evagrius Ponticus. *Chapters on Prayer.*

    Ed. J. P. Migne. PG 79:1165–1200 (among the works of Nilus).

    ———. *Kephalaia Gnostica.*

    Edited and translated by Antoine Guillaumont. *Les Six Centuries des "Kephalaia Gnostica" d'Évagre le Pontique.* PO 28. 1958.

    ———. *Praktikos.*

    Edited and translated by Antoine Guillaumont and Claire Guillaumont. *Evagre le Pontique, Traité pratique, ou, Le Moine.* 2 vols. SC 170–71. Paris: Éditions du Cerf, 1971.

    Translated by John Eudes Bamberger. *The Praktikos and Chapters on Prayer,* 3–42. Kalamazoo: Cistercian Publications, 1981.

    ———. *The Praktikos and Chapters on Prayer.* Translated by John Eudes Bamberger. Kalamazoo: Cistercian Publications, 1981.

Evagrius Scholasticus. *Ecclesiastical History (Eccl. Hist).*

    Edited by J. Bidez and L. Parmentier. *The Ecclesiastical History of Evagrius with the Scholia.* London: 1898; repr. Amsterdam: A. M. Hakkert, 1964.

    Translated by Michael Whitby. Liverpool: Liverpool University Press, 2000.

Évangiles Apocryphes 2: *L'Évangile de l'enfance.* Edited and translated by Paul Peeters. Paris: Auguste Picard, 1914.

Fortunatus, Venantius. *Life of Radegund.*

    Edited by Bruno Krusch. MGH AA 4 (2).

    Translated by Joan Petersen. *Handmaids of the Lord,* 381–400. Kalamazoo: Cistercian Publications, 1996.

Gabriel of Qatar. *Commentary on the Liturgy.*

    Edited and translated by Sebastian P. Brock. "Gabriel of Qatar's Commentary on the Liturgy." *Hugoye* 6.2 (July 2003): http://syrcom.cua.edu/Hugoye/Vol6no2/HV6N2Brock.html.

Galen. *On the Usefulness of the Parts of the Body.*

    Edited by Georg Helmreich. *Galen, Peri chreias morion (de usu partium).* 2 vols. Leipzig: Teubner, 1907–1909.

    Translated by Margaret Tallmadge May. Ithaca, NY: Cornell University Press, 1968.

Germanus of Constantinople. *On the Divine Liturgy.*

    Edited and translated by Paul Meyendorff. Crestwood, NY: St. Vladimir's Seminary Press, 1984.

Gerontius. *The Life of Melania the Younger.*

    Edited and translated by Denys Gorce. *Vie de Sainte Mélanie.* SC 90. Paris: Éditions du Cerf, 1962.

    Translated by Elizabeth A. Clark. Lewiston, NY: Edwin Mellen Press, 1984.

Graffin, François. "Homélies anonymes du VIe siècle: Homélies sur la pécheresse I, II, III." PO 41:449–527. 1984.

Gregory the Great. *Dialogues.*

Edited and translated by Adalbert de Vogüé and Paul Antin. *Grégoire le Grand, Dialoges.* 3 vols. SC 251, 260, 265. Paris: Éditions du Cerf, 1978–80.

Translated by Odo John Zimmerman. *St. Gregory the Great: Dialogues.* FC 39. New York: Fathers of the Church, 1959.

———. *Letters.*

Edited by Paul Ewald and Ludo Moritz Hartmann. MGH. *Epistolae* 1–2. 2 vols. Berlin: 1887–1899.

Translated by J. Barmby. "Selected Espistles of Gregory the Great, Bishop of Rome, Books I–XIV." NPNF, 2nd ser., 12b:73–243, 13:1–111.

Gregory of Nazianzus. *Discours 27–31 (Discours théologiques).*

Edited and translated by Paul Gallay with M. Jourjan. SC 250. Paris: Éditions du Cerf, 1978.

Translated by Lionel Wickham and Frederick Williams. In *Faith Gives Fullness to Reasoning: The Five Theological Orations of Gregory of Nazianzus,* edited by Frederick W. Norris. Supplements to *VC* 13. New York: E. J. Brill, 1991.

———. *Letters.*

Edited and translated by Paul Gallay. *Saint Grégoire de Nazianze, Lettres.* 2 vols. Paris: Les Belles Lettres, 1964–67.

Translated by C. G. Browne and J. E. Swallow. NPNF, 2nd series, 7:446–56.

———. *Oration 7. On his Brother St. Caesarius.*

Edited by J. P. Migne. PG 35:756–87.

Translated by Leo P. McCauley. *Ambrose and Gregory of Nazianzus, Funeral Orations,* 5–25. FC 22. New York: Fathers of the Church, 1953.

———. *Oration 40. On Holy Baptism.*

Edited by Claudio Moreschini, translated by Paul Gallay. *Grégoire de Nazianze, Discours 38–41.* SC 358. Paris: Éditions du Cerf, 1990.

Translated by Charles Gordon Browne and James Edward Swallow. NPNF, 2nd series, 7:360–77.

———. *Oration 43. On Basil the Great.*

Edited and translated by Jean Bernardi. *Grégoire de Nazianze, Discours.* SC 384. Paris: Éditions du Cerf, 1992.

Translated by Leo P. McCauley. *Ambrose and Gregory of Nazianzus, Funeral Orations,* 27–99. FC 22. New York: Fathers of the Church, 1953.

Gregory of Nyssa. *Against Eunomius.*

Edited by Werner Jaeger. *Gregorii Nysseni, Opera.* Vol. 1, *Contra Eunomium, Libri I–II.* Leiden: E. J. Brill, 1952.

Translated by W. Moore and H. A. Wilson. NPNF, 2nd series, 5:33–314.

———. *Catechetical Oration.*

Edited and translated by J. H. Srawley. *The Catechetical Oration of St. Gregory of Nyssa.* Cambridge: Cambridge University Press, 1903.

———. *Commentary on the Song of Songs (Comm. SS).*

Edited by Hermann Langerbeck. *Gregorii Nysseni in Canticum Canticorum,* Vol. 6 of *Gregorii Nysseni Opera,* edited by Werner Jaeger. Leiden: E. J. Brill, 1960.

Translated by Casimer McCambley. *St. Gregory of Nyssa, Commentary on the Song of Songs.* Brookline: Hellenic College Press, 1987.

———. *Gregorii Nysseni Opera.* Edited by Werner Jaeger. Leiden: E. J. Brill, 1952–.

———. *Life of Gregory the Wonderworker.*

Edited by J. P. Migne. PG 44:893–958.

Translated by Michael Slusser. In *St. Gregory Thaumaturgos: Life and Works,* edited by Michael Slusser, 41–90. FC 98. Washington, DC: Catholic University of America Press, 1998.

———. *Life of Moses.*

Edited by Herbert Musurillo. *Gregorii Nysseni, De Vita Moysis,* in vol. 7.1 of *Gregorii Nysseni Opera,* edited by W. Jaeger and Hermannus Langerbeck. Leiden: E. J. Brill, 1964.

Translated by Abraham J. Malherbe and Everett Ferguson. New York: Paulist Press, 1978.

———. *The Lord's Prayer.*

Edited by J. P. Migne. PG 44:1120–93.

Translated by Hilda Graef. *St. Gregory of Nyssa, The Lord's Prayer, the Beatitudes,* 21–84. ACW 18. New York: Newman Press, 1954.

———. *On the Holy Spirit.*

Edited by J. P. Migne. PG 45:1304–17.

Translated by W. Moore and H. A. Wilson. NPNF, 2nd series, 5:315–25.

———. *On the Making of Man.*

Edited and translated by J. LaPlace. *Grégoire de Nysse, La création de l'homme.* SC 6. Paris: Éditions du Cerf, 1943.

Translated by W. Moore and H. A. Wilson. NPNF, 2nd series, 5:386–427.

———. *On the Soul and the Resurrection.*

Edited by J. P. Migne. PG 46:11–160.

Translated by Catharine P. Roth. Crestwood, NY: St. Vladimir's Seminary Press, 1993.

Gregory of Tours. *Book of Miracles.*

Edited by J. P. Migne. PL 71.

Translated by Raymond van Dam. *Saints and Their Miracles in Late Antique Gaul.* Princeton: Princeton University Press, 1993.

————. *Glory of the Confessors.*

    Edited by Bruno Krusch. MGH. SRM 1.1. Hannover, 1885.

    Translated by Raymond van Dam. Liverpool: Liverpool University Press, 1988.

————. *Glory of the Martyrs.*

    Edited by Bruno Krusch. MGH. SRM 1.1. Hannover, 1885.

    Translated by Raymond van Dam. Liverpool: Liverpool University Press, 1988.

Hesychius of Jerusalem. *Homilies.*

    Edited and translated by Michel Aubineau. *Les Homélies Festales d'Hésychius de Jérusalem.* SH 59. Brussels: Société des Bollandistes, 1980.

Hippocrates. *Works.*

    Edited and translated by W. H. S. Jones. LCL. Cambridge, MA: Harvard University Press, 1968.

Hippolytus. *Apostolic Tradition.*

    Edited and translated by Gregory Dix. *The Treatise on the Apostolic Tradition of St. Hippolytus of Rome.* London: SPCK, 1937.

    Translation and commentary by Alistair Stewart-Sykes. *Hippolytus, On the Apostolic Tradition.* Crestwood, NY: St. Vladimir's Seminary Press, 2001.

The History of the Blessed Virgin Mary and the History of the Likeness of Christ which the Jews of Tiberias Made to Mock at.

    Edited and translated by E. A. Wallis Budge. Luzac's Semitic Text and Translation Series. London: Luzac and Co., 1899.

Hymn to Demeter.

    Edited and translated by Hugh G. Evelyn White. *Hesiod, The Homeric Hymns and the Homerica,* 288–325. LCL. Cambridge, MA: Harvard University Press, 1914.

    Edited and translated by N. J. Richardson. *The Homeric Hymn to Demeter.* Oxford: Clarendon Press, 1974.

Ignatius of Antioch. *Letters.*

    Edited and translated by Kirsopp Lake. *The Apostolic Fathers,* 1:166–277. LCL. New York: MacMillan, 1912.

    Translation and commentary by William R. Schoedel. *Ignatius of Antioch: A Commentary on the Letters of Ignatius of Antioch.* Philadelphia: Fortress Press, 1985.

Isaac of Nineveh (Isaac the Syrian). *Mystic Treatises.*

    Edited by Paul Bedjan. *Mar Isaacus Ninivita de Perfectione Religiosa.* Paris/Leipzig: Otto Harrassowitz, 1909.

    Translated by A. J. Wensinck. *Mystic Treatises by Isaac of Nineveh, Translated from Bedjan's Syriac Text with an Introduction and Registers.* 1923; repr. Wiesbaden: Dr. Martin Sändig oHG, 1969.

————. The 'Second Part': Chapters IV–XLI.

Edited and translated by Sebastian P. Brock. CSCO 554–55/Scr. Syr. 224–25. Louvain: Secrétariat du CorpusSCO, 1995.

Jacob of Edessa. Discourse on the Myron.

Edited and translated by Sebastian P. Brock. "Jacob of Edessa's Discourse on the Myron." OC 63 (1979): 20–36.

Jacob of Serug. Homilies.

Edited by Paul Bedjan. Homiliae Selectae Mar Jacobi Sarugensis. 5 vols. Paris/Leipzig: Otto Harrasowitz, 1905–10.

————. "Homily on the Martyr Habib." Edited by Paul Bedjan. AMS 1:160–72.

————. "Homily on Simeon the Stylite."

Edited by Paul Bedjan. AMS 4:650–65.

Translated by Susan Ashbrook Harvey. In Ascetic Behavior in Greco-Roman Antiquity, edited by Vincent Wimbush, 15–28. Minneapolis: Fortress Press, 1990.

————. Select Festal Homilies. Translated by Thomas Kollamparampil. Rome: Centre for Indian and Interreligious Studies, 1997.

January Menaion, Service Books of the Byzantine Churches, vol. 5. Newton Centre, MA: Sophia Press, 1992.

Jerome. Against Jovinian.

Edited by J. P. Migne. PL 23:211–338.

Translated by W. H. Fremantle. NPNF, 2nd ser., 6:346–416.

————. Against Vigilantius.

Edited by J. P. Migne. PL 23:339–52.

Edited and translated by W. H. Fremantle. NPNF, 2nd ser., 6:417–23.

————. Letters.

Edited and translated by Denys Gorce. Lettres Spirituelles de Saint Jérome. 2 vols. Paris: Libraire Lecoffre, J. Gabalda, 1932–34.

Letter 127, "To Principia." Translated by Joan Petersen, Handmaids of the Lord, 108–22. Kalamazoo: Cistercian Publications, 1996.

————. Life of St. Hilarion.

Edited by J. P. Migne. PL 23:29–54.

Translated by Marie Ligouri Ewald. In Early Christian Biographies, edited by Roy J. Deferrari, 245–87. FC 15. New York: Fathers of the Church, 1952.

Job of Edessa. Book of Treasures.

Edited and translated by Alphonse Mingana. Encyclopedia of Philosophical and Natural Sciences as taught in Baghdad about A.D. 817, or Book of Treasures by Job of Edessa. Cambridge: W. Heffer and Sons, 1935.

John Cassian. *Conferences.*

    Edited by Michael Petschenig. CSEL 13. Vienna: 1896.

    Translated by Boniface Ramsey. *John Cassian: The Conferences.* ACW 57. New York: Newman Press, 1997.

John Chrysostom. *Address on Vainglory and the Right Way for Parents to Bring Up Their Children.*

    Edited by B. K. Exarchos. *John Chrysostomus, Über Hoffart und Kindererziehung.* Das Wort der Antike 4. Munich: Hueber, 1955.

    Translated by M. L. W. Laistner. *Christianity and Pagan Culture in the Later Roman Empire,* 75–122, 129–40. Ithaca, NY: Cornell University Press, 1951.

———. *Apologist.* Translated by Margart Schatkin and Paul Harkins. FC 73. Washington DC: The Catholic University of America Press, 1985.

———. *Baptismal Instructions.*

    Edited by Antoine Wenger. *Huit catéchéses baptismales inédites.* SC 50. Paris: Éditions du Cerf, 1957.

    Translated by Paul W. Harkins. ACW 31. New York: Newman Press, 1963.

———. *Commentary on John.*

    Edited by J. P. Migne. PG 59.

    Translated by Thomas Aquinas Goggin. *Saint John Chrysostom, Commentary on Saint John the Apostle and Evangelist.* 2 vols. FC 33, 41. New York: Fathers of the Church, 1957, 1960.

———. "Homily on the Holy Martyrs."

    Edited by J. P. Migne. PG 50:645–54.

    Translated by Wendy Mayer. In '*Let Us Die that We May Live,*' edited and translated by Johan Leemans, Wendy Mayer, Pauline Allen, and Boudewijn Dehandschutter, 115–25. London: Routledge, 2003.

———. "Homily on the Martyr Babylas."

    Edited and translated by M. A. Schatkin, C. Blanc, B. Grillet, and J.-N. Guinot. *Jean Chrysostome. Discours sur Babylas suivi de l'Homelie sur Babylas,* 294–312. SC 362. Paris: Éditions du Cerf, 1990.

    Translated by Wendy Mayer. In '*Let Us Die that We May Live,*' edited and translated by Johan Leemans, Wendy Mayer, Pauline Allen, and Boudewijn Dehandschutter, 140–47. London: Routledge, 2003.

———. "Homily on the Martyrs."

    Edited by J. P. Migne. PG 50:661–66.

    Translated by Wendy Mayer and Pauline Allen. *John Chrysostom,* 93–98. New York: Routledge, 2000.

———. "A Homily on Pelagia, Virgin and Martyr."

    Edited by J. P. Migne. PG 50:579–84.

Translated by Wendy Mayer in 'Let Us Die that We May Live,' edited and translated by Johan Leemans, Wendy Mayer, Pauline Allen, and Boudewijn Dehandschutter, 148–61. London: Routledge, 2003.

————. *Homilies on Matthew.*

Edited by J. P. Migne. PG 57–58.

Translated by G. Prevost and M. O. Riddle. NPNF, 2nd series, 10.

————. *Homilies on Second Corinthians.*

Edited by J. P. Migne. PG 61:9–61.

Translated by Talbot W. Chambers. NPNF 12:300–305.

————. *Homilies on the Statues.*

Edited by J. P. Migne. PG 49:15–222.

Translated by W. R. W. Stephens. *Homilies on the Statues to the People of Antioch.* NPNF 9:317–489.

————. *Homilies on Timothy.*

Edited by J. P. Migne. PG 62:663–700.

Translated by Philip Schaff. NPNF 13:519–43.

————. "On the Sinful Woman."

Edited and translated by Y. Abd Al-Masih. "A Discourse by St. John Chrysostom on the Sinful Woman in the Sa'idic Dialect." *BSAC* 15 (1958–60): 11–39.

————. *On Wealth and Poverty.*

Edited by J. P. Migne. PG 48:963–1054.

Translated by C. Roth. *St. John Chrysostom on Wealth and Poverty.* Crestwood, NY: St. Vladimir's Seminary Press, 1984.

(Pseudo-Chrysostom). *On the Holy Cross.*

Edited and translated by Gerald M. Browne. *Chrysostomus Nubianus, An Old Nubian Version of Ps.-Chrysostom, In venerabilem crucem sermo.* Rome: Papyrologica Castroctaviana, 1984.

John Climacus. *The Ladder of Divine Ascent.*

Edited by J. P. Migne. PG 88.

Translated by Colm Luibheid and Norman Russell. New York: Paulist Press, 1982.

John of Damascus. *On the Divine Images.*

Edited by Bonifatius Kotter. *Die Schriften des Johannes von Damaskos,* vol. 3. PTS 17. Berlin: Walter de Gruyter, 1975.

Translated by Andrew Louth. *St. John of Damascus, Three Treatises on the Divine Images.* Crestwood, NY: St. Vladimir's Seminary Press, 2003.

Also translated by David Anderson. *St. John of Damascus: On the Divine Images; Three Apologies Against Those Who Attack the Divine Images.* Crestwood, NY: St. Vladimir's Seminary Press, 1980.

John of Ephesus. *The Lives of the Eastern Saints.*

Edited and translated by E. W. Brooks. PO 17–19. 1923–25.

John Moschus. *Pratum Spirituale.*

Edited by J. P. Migne. PG 87.3:2852A–3112B.

Translated by John Wortley. *The Spiritual Meadow.* Kalamazoo: Cistercian Publications, 1992.

John Rufus. *Plerophories.*

Edited and translated by F. Nau. *Plérophories, témoignages et révélations contre le concile de Chalcédoine,* 5–208. PO 8. 1912.

John of the Sedre. *Discourses.*

Edited and translated by Jouko Martikainen. *Johannes I. Sedra. Einleitung, Syrische Texte, Übersetzung, und vollständiges Wörterverzeichnis.* Göttinger Orientforschungen 1 / 34. Wiesbaden: Otto Harrassowitz, 1991.

Joseph the Hymnographer. *Mariale.*

Edited by J. P. Migne. PG 105:984–1414.

Joseph the Visionary (Abdisho). "On Spiritual Prayer," "On the Stirrings of the Mind during Prayer." Translated by Sebastian P. Brock. *Syriac Fathers on Prayer and the Spiritual Life,* 313–25. Kalamazoo: Cistercian Publications, 1987.

Joshua the Stylite. *Chronicle.*

Edited and translated by William Wright. Cambridge: Cambridge University Press, 1882.

Translation and commentary by Frank R. Trombley and John W. Watt. *The Chronicle of Pseudo-Joshua the Stylite.* Liverpool: Liverpool University Press, 2000.

Justin Martyr. *Dialogue with Trypho.*

Edited by E. J. Goodspeed. *Die ältesten Apologeten.* Göttingen: Vandenhoeck and Ruprecht, 1914.

Translated by A. L. Williams. *The Dialogue with Trypho.* London: SPCK, 1930.

Kraemer, Ross Shephard. *Women's Religions in the Greco-Roman World: A Sourcebook.* New York: Oxford University Press, 2004.

Lactantius. *Minor Works.*

Translated by Mary Francis McDonald. FC 54. Washington, DC: Catholic University of America Press, 1965.

———. *The Phoenix.*

Edited by S. Brandt. CSEL 27, 135–47. Vienna: 1897.

Translated by Mary Francis McDonald. *Lactantius: Minor Works,* 207–20. FC 54. Washington, DC: Catholic University of America Press, 1965.

———. *The Workmanship of God.*

Edited by S. Brandt. CSEL 27, 3–64. Vienna: 1897.

Translated by Mary Francis McDonald. *Lactantius: Minor Works*, 3–56. FC 54. Washington, DC: Catholic University of America Press, 1965.

Layton, Bentley. *The Gnostic Scriptures*. Garden City, NY: Doubleday, 1987.

Das Leben des Heiligen Symeon Stylites. Edited by Hans Lietzmann. TU 32.4. Leipzig: Hinrichs, 1908.

The Lenten Triodion. Translated by Mother Mary and Archimandrite Kallistos Ware. London: Faber and Faber, 1977.

Leontius of Neopolis. *Life of Simeon the Fool*.

Edited and translated by L. Rydén and A. J. Festugière. *Vie de Syméon le Fou et Vie de Jean de Chypre*, 1–222. Bibliothèque archéologique et historique 95. Paris: Geuthner, 1974.

Translated by Derek Krueger. *Symeon the Holy Fool: Leontius' Life and the Late Antique City*, 131–71. Berkeley: University of California Press, 1996.

'*Let Us Die that We May Live*': *Greek Homilies on Christian Martyrs from Asia Minor, Palestine, and Syria* (c. A.D. 350–A.D. 450). Edited and translated by Johan Leemans, Wendy Mayer, Pauline Allen, and Boudewijn Dehandschutter. London: Routledge, 2003.

Letter to Diognetus.

Edited and translated by Kirsopp Lake. *Apostolic Fathers* 2:350–79. LCL. New York: G. P. Putnam's Sons, 1924.

Leviticus 1–16. Translation and commentary by Jacob Milgrom. Anchor Bible. New York: Doubleday, 1991.

Libanius. *Opera*. 12 vols.

Edited by R. Foerster. Leipzig: 1903–27; repr. Hildesheim: Georg Olms, 1963.

————. *Select Orations* (3, 11, 31, 34, 36, 42, 43, 58, 62). Translations in A. F. Norman. *Antioch as a Centre of Hellenic Culture as Observed by Libanius*. Liverpool: Liverpool University Press, 2000.

Life of Daniel the Stylite.

Edited by H. Delehaye. *Les Saints Stylites*, 1–94. SH 14. Brussels: Société des Bollandistes, 1923; repr. 1962.

Translated by Norman Baynes and Elizabeth Dawes. *Three Byzantine Saints*, 1–84. London: Mowbrays, 1948; repr. Crestwood, NY: St. Vladimir's Seminary Press, 1977.

Life of Malkha of Klysma.

Edited by Paul Bedjan. *AMS* 5:421–69.

Life of Matrona of Perge.

Edited in *Acta Sanctorum Novembris* 3:790–813. Brussels: Société des Bollandistes, 1910.

Translated by Jeffrey Featherstone and Cyril Mango. In *Holy Women of Byzantium*, edited by Alice-Mary Talbot, 13–64. Washington, DC: Dumbarton Oaks Publications, 1996.

Life of the Patriarch Nikephoros I of Constantinople.

Edited by C. de Boor. Nicephori archiepiscopi Constantinopolitani opuscula historica, 139–217. Leipzig: Teubner, 1880; repr. 1975.

Translated by Elizabeth A. Fisher. In Byzantine Defenders of Images, edited by Alice-Mary Talbot, 25–141. Washington, DC: Dumbarton Oaks Publications, 1996.

Life of Rabbula of Edessa.

Edited by Paul Bedjan. AMS 4:396–450.

The Life of Simeon the Stylite the Younger.

Edited and translated by Paul Van Den Ven. La Vie Ancienne de S. Syméon Stylite le Jeune (521–592). 2 vols. SH 32. Brussels: Société des Bollandistes, 1962–70.

The Life of St. Irene, Abbess of Chrysobalanton.

Edited and translated by Jan Olof Rosenqvist. Uppsala: Uppsala University, 1986.

The Life of St. Simeon Stylites. (Syriac Life.)

Edited by Paul Bedjan. AMS 4:507–644.

Translated by Frederick Lent. JAOS 35 (1915–17): 103–98.

(See also below, The Lives of Simeon Stylites.)

Life of St. Theodora of Thessalonike, and the Translation of the Relics of St. Theodora of Thessalonike. Translated by Alice-Mary Talbot. In Holy Women of Byzantium, edited by Alice-Mary Talbot, 159–237. Washington, DC: Dumbarton Oaks Publications, 1996.

Life of Sts. David, Symeon, and George of Lesbos.

Edited by J. van den Gheyn. "Acta graeca ss. Davidis, Symeonis et Georgii Mitylenae in insula Lesbo." AB 18 (1899): 209–59.

Translated by Dorothy Abrahamse and Douglas Domingo-Forasté. In Byzantine Defenders of Images, edited by Alice-Mary Talbot, 143–241. Washington, DC: Dumbarton Oaks Publications, 1998.

Life of Theodore of Sykeon.

Edited by Theophilus Joannou. Mnemeia agiologika, 361–495. Venice: 1884.

Translated by Norman Baynes and Elizabeth Dawes. Three Byzantine Saints, 87–192. London: Mowbrays, 1948; repr. Crestwood, NY: St. Vladimir's Seminary Press, 1977.

Lives and Legends of the Georgian Saints. Translated by David Marshall Lang. Crestwood, NY: St. Vladimir's Seminary Press, 1976.

Lives of the Desert Fathers.

Edited by A.-J. Festugière. Historia Monachorum in Aegypto. SH 34. Brussels: Société des Bollandistes, 1961.

Translated by Norman Russell. Kalamazoo: Cistercian Publications, 1980.

The Lives of Simeon Stylites. Translated by Robert Doran. Kalamazoo: Cistercian Publications, 1992.

Livy. *Annals of Rome.*

Edited and translated by B.O. Foster. *Ab Urbe Condita.* 14 vols. LCL. Cambridge, MA: Harvard University Press, 1961–1984.

Lucian. *On the Revelation of St. Stephen.*

Edited by S. Vanderlinden. "Revelatio Sancti Stephani." *REB* 4 (1946): 178–217.

Lucian of Samosata. *Of Sacrifice.*

Edited and translated in Lucian of Samosata, *Works,* vol. 1, by A.M. Harmon. LCL. New York: Cambridge, MA: Harvard University Press, 1968.

——— (attributed). *The Syrian Goddess (De Dea Syria).*

Edited and translated by Harold W. Attridge and Robert A. Oden. Missoula, MT: Scholars Press, 1976.

Lucretius. *On the Nature of Things.*

Edited and translated by W.H.D. Rouse. *Lucretius, De Rerum Natura.* Rev. ed. by Martin Ferguson Smith. LCL. Cambridge, MA: Harvard University Press, 1982.

(Pseudo-)Macarius. *Homilies.*

Edited by Hermann Dorries, Erich Klostermann, and Matthias Kroeger. *Die 50 Geistlichen Homilien des Makarios.* PTS 6. Berlin: De Gruyter, 1964.

Translated by George A. Maloney. *Pseudo-Macarius,* The Fifty Spiritual Homilies and the *"Great Letter."* New York: Paulist Press, 1992.

Marcus Aurelius. *Meditations.*

Edited and translated by C.R. Haines. *The Communings with Himself of Marcus Aurelius Antoninus.* LCL. Cambridge, MA: Harvard University Press, 1979.

Translated by Russell Kirk. *Marcus Aurelius, Meditations/Epictetus, the Encheiridion.* Chicago: Henry Regnery, 1956.

Martial. *Epigrams.*

Edited and translated by Walter Ker. Rev. ed. LCL. Cambridge, MA: Harvard University Press, 1979.

Maximus Confessor. *Mystagogy.*

Edited by J.P. Migne. PG 91:658–718.

Translated by George Berthold. *Maximus Confessor: Selected Writings,* 181–225. New York: Paulist Press, 1985.

Maximus of Turin. *Sermons.*

Edited by A. Mutzenbecher. CCSL 23. Turnhout: 1962.

Translated by Boniface Ramsey. *The Sermons of Saint Maximus of Turin.* ACW 50. New York: Newman Press, 1989.

Methodius. *Symposium.*

Edited by G.N. Bonwetsch. GCS 27. 1917.

Translated by Herbert Musurillo. *St. Methodius, The Symposium: A Treatise on Chastity.*
ACW 27. Westminster, MD: Newman Press, 1958.

Meyer, Marvin W., and Richard Smith. *Ancient Christian Magic: Coptic Texts of Ritual Power.*
Princeton: Princeton University Press, 1999.

Miracles of St. Artemios: A collection of miracle stories by an anonymous author of seventh century
Byzantium. Edited and translated by Virgil S. Crisafulli and John W. Nesbitt. New York:
E. J. Brill, 1997.

Mishnah. Translated by Herbert Danby. Oxford: Clarendon Press, 1933.

Musaeus. *Hero and Leander.*

Edited by Thomas Gelzer, translated by Cedric Whitman. LCL. Cambridge, MA:
Harvard University Press, 1975.

Nemesius. *On the Nature of Man.*

Edited by J. P. Migne. PG 60:503–818.

Translated by William Telfer. *Cyril of Jerusalem and Nemesius of Emesa,* 203–453. LCC 4.
Philadelphia: The Westminster Press, 1955.

New Testament Apocrypha. Rev. ed. by Wilhelm Schneemelcher, translation by R. McL.
Wilson. Louisville, KY: Westminster/John Knox Press, 1991.

Nicodemus of the Holy Mountain. *Handbook of Spiritual Counsel.*

Edited by Soterios N. Schoinas. *Symvoulevtikon Encheiridion.* Volos: 1958.

Translated by Peter A. Chamberas. *Nicodemus of the Holy Mountain, A Handbook of*
Spiritual Counsel. New York: Paulist Press, 1989.

The Odes of Solomon.

Edited and translated by J. H. Charlesworth. 2nd ed. Missoula, MT: The Scholars
Press, 1977.

The Old Testament Pseudepigrapha. Edited by J. H. Charlesworth. 2 vols. Garden City, NY:
Doubleday and Co., 1983.

Origen. *Contra Celsum.*

Edited and translated by Marcel Borret. *Origène, Contre Celse.* SC 132, 136, 147, 150,
227. Paris: Éditions du Cerf, 1967–76.

Translated by Henry Chadwick. Cambridge: Cambridge University Press, 1965.

———. *The Dialogue with Heraclides.*

Edited and translated by Jean Scherer. *Entretien d'Origène avec Héraclide.* SC 67. Paris:
Éditions du Cerf, 1960.

Translated by Henry Chadwick. In *Alexandrian Christianity,* edited by J. E. L. Oulton and
Henry Chadwick, 430–55. Philadelphia: The Westminster Press, 1954.

———. *Exhortation to Martyrdom.*

Edited by P. Koetschau. GCS 2. Berlin: 1899.

Translated by Rowen Greer. *Origen*, 41–79. New York: Paulist Press, 1979.

———. Homilies on *Genesis and Exodus* (Hom. Gen).

Edited by W. A. Baehrens. GCS 29. Berlin: 1920.

Translated by Ronald Heine. FC 71. Washington, DC: Catholic University of America Press, 1981.

———. Homilies on *Leviticus* (Hom. Lev.).

Edited by W. A. Baehrens. GCS 29. Berlin: 1920.

Translated by Gary Wayne Barkley. FC 83. Washington, DC: Catholic University of America Press, 1990.

———. Homilies on *Luke*.

Edited by Max Rauer. GSC, Origenes Werke 9. Berlin: 1959.

Translated by Joseph Lienhard. *Origen: Homilies on Luke, Fragments on Luke*. FC 94. Washington, DC: Catholic University of America Press, 1996.

———. Homily 27 on *Numbers*.

Edited by W. A. Baehrens. GCS 30. Berlin: 1921.

Translated by Rowen Greer. *Origen*, 245–69. New York: Paulist Press, 1979.

———. On *Prayer*.

Edited by P. Koetschau. GCS 3. Berlin: 1899.

Translated by Rowen Greer. *Origen*, 81–170. New York: Paulist Press, 1979.

———. On the *Song of Songs*.

Edited by W. A. Baehrens. GCS 33. Leipzig: 1925.

Translated by R. P. Lawson. *Origen, The Song of Songs: Commentary and Homilies*. ACW 26. New York: Newman Press, 1956.

———. *Origen: An Exhortation to Martyrdom, Prayer, and Select Works*. Translated by Rowen Greer. New York: Paulist Press, 1979.

Ovid. *Fasti*.

Edited and translated by James George Frazer; rev. ed. by G. P. Goold. LCL. Cambridge, MA: Harvard University Press, 1989.

Translated by Betty Rose Nagle. *Ovid's Fasti: Roman Holidays*. Bloomington, IN: University of Indiana Press, 1995.

———. *Metamorphoses*.

Edited and translated by Frank Justus Miller; rev. ed by G. P. Goold. 2 vols. LCL. Cambridge, MA: Harvard University Press, 1977–84.

Pachomian Koinonia. Translated by Armand Veilleux. 3 vols. Kalamazoo: Cistercian Publications, 1981.

Pachomius. *Paralipomena*.

Translated by Armand Veilleux. *Pachomian Koinonia*, 2:19–70. Kalamazoo: Cistercian Publications, 1981.

Palamas, Gregory. *Triads*.

Edited by John Meyendorff. *Grégoire Palamas. Défense des saints hesychastes. Introduction, texte critique, traduction et notes*. 2nd ed. 2 vols. Spicilegium Sacrum Lovaniense 30–31. Louvain: Peeters Press, 1973.

Translated by John Meyendorff and Nicholas Gendle. *Gregory Palamas, The Triads*. New York: Paulist Press, 1983.

Palladius. *Dialogue on the Life of St. John Chrysostom*.

Edited and translated by Anne-Marie Malingrey and Philippe Leclercq. *Palladios, Dialogue sur la vie de Jean Chrysostome*. SC 341. Paris: Éditions du Cerf, 1988.

Translated by Robert T. Meyer. ACW 45. New York: Newman Press, 1985.

Paphnutius. *Histories and Life of Onnophrius*.

Translated by Tim Vivian. *Histories of the Monks of Upper Egypt and the Life of Onnophrius by Paphnutius*, 143–66. Kalamazoo: Cistercian Publications, 1993.

Paulinus of Nola. *Letters*.

Edited by W. Hartel. CSEL 30. Vienna: 1894.

Translated by P. G. Walsh. *The Letters of St. Paulinus of Nola*. ACW 35. New York: Newman Press, 1966.

———. *Poems*.

Edited by W. Hartel. CSEL 30. Vienna: 1894.

Translated by P. G. Walsh. ACW 40. New York: Newman Press, 1975.

Pausanias. *Description of Greece*.

Edited and translated by W. H. S. Jones. LCL. Cambridge, MA: Harvard University Press, 1978.

Pentalogie Maronite, antiochienne/domaine. Vol. 4, *Livre du Pain et du Vin, de L'eau, de L'huile et du Baume*. Edited by Y. Moubarac. Beirut: Cénacle Libanais, 1984.

Petersen, Joan. *Handmaids of the Lord: Holy Women in Late Antiquity and the Early Middle Ages*. Kalamazoo: Cistercian Publications, 1996.

Philo, *Allegorical Interpretation (Legum Allegoriarum)*.

Edited and translated by F. H. Colsun and G. H. Whitaker. Philo 1:140–473. LCL. Cambridge, MA: Harvard University Press, 1968–87.

———. *Every Good Man is Free (Prob: Quod Omnis Probus Liber Sit)*.

Edited and translated by F. H. Colsun and G. H. Whitaker. Philo 9:2–101. LCL. Cambridge, MA: Harvard University Press, 1968–87.

————. On the Cherubim (de Cherubim).

> Edited and translated by F.H. Colsun and G.H.Whitaker. Philo 2:3–85. LCL. Cambridge, MA: Harvard University Press, 1968–87.

————. On Dreams (de somniis).

> Edited and translated by F.H. Colsun and G.H. Whitaker. Philo 5:285–579. LCL. Cambridge, MA: Harvard University Press, 1968–87.

————. On Providence (de Providentia).

> Edited and translated by F.H. Colsun and G.H. Whitaker. Philo 9:447–507. Cambridge, MA: Harvard University Press, 1968–87.

————. On the Sacrifice of Cain and Abel (de Sacrificiis Abelis et Caini).

> Edited and translated by F.H. Colsun and G.H. Whitaker. Philo 2:88–196. LCL. Cambridge, MA: Harvard University Press, 1968–87.

————. On the Unchangeableness of God (Deus: Quod Deus Immutabilis).

> Edited and translated by F.H. Colsun and G.H. Whitaker. Philo 3:3–101. LCL. Cambridge, MA: Harvard University Press, 1968–87.

————. Philo of Alexandria. The Contemplative Life, the Giants, and Selections. Translated by David Winston. Mahwah, NJ: Paulist Press, 1981.

————. The Special Laws. (Spec.: De Specialibus Legibus).

> Edited and translated by F.H. Colsun and G.H. Whitaker. Philo 7:98–607. LCL. Cambridge, MA: Harvard University Press, 1968–87.

————. That the Worse is Wont to Attack the Better (Det.: Quod deterius potiori insidiari soleat). Edited and translated by F.H. Colsun and G.H. Whitaker. Philo 2:198–321. LCL. Cambridge, MA: Harvard University Press, 1968–87.

————. Works. Edited and translated by F.H. Colsun and G.H. Whitaker. 10 vols. + 2 supplements. LCL. Cambridge, MA: Harvard University Press, 1968–87.

Philostorgius. Ecclesiastical History (Eccl. Hist.).

> Edited by J. Bidez. GCS 21, 1–150. 1913.

> Translated by Edward Walford. London: Henry G. Bohn, 1855.

Philostratus. The Life of Apollonius of Tyana.

> Edited and translated by F.C. Conybeare. 2 vols. LCL. New York: MacMillan, 1912.

Philoxenus of Mabbug. The Discourses of Philoxenus, Bishop of Mabbôgh, A.D. 485–519. Edited and translated by E.A. Wallis Budge. 2 vols. London: Asher, 1893.

Piacenza Pilgrim. Travels.

> Translated by John Wilkinson. Jerusalem Pilgrims Before the Crusades, 79–89. Warminster: Aris and Phillips, 1977.

Plato. The Laws.

> Edited with commentary by E.B. England. 2 vols. Manchester: Manchester University Press, 1921.

————. *The Republic.*

Edited and translated by Paul Shorey. 2 vols. LCL. New York: G. P. Putnam's Sons, 1930–35.

————. *Symposium.*

Edited and translated by W. R. M. Lamb. *Plato: Selections. Lysias. Symposium. Gorgias.* LCL. Cambridge, MA: Harvard University Press, 1967.

————. *Timaeus.*

Translated by Francis MacDonald Cornford. *Plato's Cosmology: The Timaeus of Plato translated with a running commentary.* London: Routledge and Keegan Paul, 1966.

Pliny the Elder. *Natural History.* Edited and translated by H. Rackham. LCL. Cambridge, MA: Harvard University Press, 1938.

Pliny the Younger. *Letters.*

Edited and translated by William Melmoth, revised by W. M. L. Hutchinson. LCL. New York: Macmillan , 1952.

Plotinus. *Enneads.*

Edited and translated by A. H. Armstrong. LCL. Cambridge, MA: Harvard University Press, 1984.

Plutarch. *Lives.*

Edited and translated by Bernadotte Perrin. LCL. Cambridge, MA.: Harvard University Press, 1984.

————. *Moralia: Table-talk.*

Edited and translated by E. L. Minar, F. H. Sandbach, and W. C. Helmbold. 9 vols. LCL. Cambridge, MA: Harvard University Press, 1961.

————. *On Isis and Osiris.*

Edited and translated by John Gwyn Griffiths. *Plutarch's De Iside et Osiride.* Cardiff: University of Wales Press, 1970.

Porphyry. *Life of Plotinus.*

Edited and translated by Luc Brisson, Jean-Louis Cherlonneix, Marie-Odile Goulet-Cazé, Richard Goulet, Mirko Grmek, Jean-Marie Flamand, Sylvain Matton, Jean Pépin, Henri Dominique Saffrey, Alain-Ph. Segonds, Michel Tardieu, and Pierre Thillet. *Porphyre, La Vie de Plotin.* Vol. 2: 131–86. Histoire des doctrines de l'Antiquité Classique 6, 16. Paris: J. Vrin, 1982.

————. *On Abstinence.*

Edited by Esme Wynne-Tyson, translated by Thomas Taylor. *Porphyry on Abstinence from Animal Food.* New York: Barnes and Noble, 1965.

The Presocratic Philosophers: A critical history with a selection of texts. Edited by G. S. Kirk, J. E. Raven, and M. Schofield. 2nd ed. Cambridge: Cambridge University Press, 1983.

Priscian. *On Theophrastus On Sense-Perception with 'Simplicius' On Aristotle's On the Soul 2.5–12*. Translated by Pamela Huby, Carlos Steele, and J. O. Urmson, notes by Peter Lautner. Ithaca, NY: Cornell University Press, 1997.

Proclus of Constantinople. *Homilies 1–5*.

Edited and translated by Nicholas Constas. In *Proclus of Constantinople and the Cult of the Virgin in Late Antiquity: Homilies 1–5, Texts and Translations*, Nicholas Constas, 125–272. SVC 66. Leiden: E. J. Brill, 2003.

Procopius. *Works*.

Edited and translated by H. B. Dewing. 7 vols. LCL. Cambridge, MA: Harvard University Press, 1979.

Prudentius. *Book of the Martyrs Crown*.

Edited by M. P. Cunningham. CCSL 126, 251–389. Turnhout, 1966.

Translated by M. Clement Eagan. *Poems of Prudentius*, 95–280. FC 43. Washington, DC: Catholic University of American Press, 1962.

———. *Hymns*.

Edited by M. P. Cunningham. CCSL 126, 3–72. Turnhout, 1966.

Translated by M. Clement Eagan. *The Poems of Prudentius*, 3–92. FC 43. Washington, DC: Catholic University of American Press, 1962.

———. *The Poems of Prudentius*. Translated by M. Clement Eagan. FC 43. Washington, DC: Catholic University of American Press, 1962.

(Pseudo-Athanasius). See subentries under Athanasius.

(Pseudo-Chrysostom). See subentry under John Chrysostom.

(Pseudo-Ephrem). See subentry under Ephrem.

Romanos the Melodist. *Kontakia*.

Edited and translated by José Grosdidier de Matons. *Romanos le Mélode*. 5 vols. SC 99, 110, 114. Paris: Éditions du Cerf, 1965.

Translated by Marjorie Carpenter. *The Kontakia of Romanos, Byzantine Melodist*. 2 vols. Columbia: University of Missouri Press, 1970.

Selected Kontakia translated by Ephrem Lash. *On the Life of Christ: Kontakia by Romanos the Melodist*. San Francisco: HarperCollins, 1995.

Selected Kontakia also translated by R. J. Schork. *Sacred Song from the Byzantine Pulpit: Romanos the Melodist*. Gainesville: University Press of Florida, 1995.

Sayings of the Desert Fathers.

———. Alphabetical Collection.

Edited by J. P. Migne. PG 65:71–440.

Translated by Benedicta Ward. *Sayings of the Desert Fathers*. Rev. ed. Kalamazoo: Cistercian Publications, 1984.

————. Anonymous Series.

    Edited by Lucien Regnault. *Les Sentences des pères du désert série des anonymes.* Spiritualité Orientale 43. Sablé-sur-sarthes: Solesmes-Bellefontaine, 1985.

    Portions are translated in Columba Stewart. *The World of the Desert Fathers: Stories and Sayings.* Oxford: SLG Press, 1986.

————. Systematic Sayings.

    Edited by Jean-Claude Guy. *Les Apophtegmes des pères, Collection Systématique.* SC 387, 484. Paris: Éditions du Cerf, 1993–.

    Portions are translated in Benedicta Ward. *The Wisdom of the Desert Fathers.* Rev. ed. Oxford: SLG Press, 1986.

Serapion of Thmuis. *Letter to the Monks.*

    Edited by J. P. Migne. PG 40:925–41.

    Translated by B. Outtier, A. Louf, M. Van Parys, and Cl.-A. Zirnheld. *Lettres des Pères du Désert: Ammonas, Macaire, Arsene, Serapion de Thmuis,* 117–47. Spiritualité Orientale 42. Begrolle-en-Mauges, Maine-&-Loire: Abbaye de Bellefontaine, 1985.

Severus of Antioch. *Homily 118.*

    Edited and translated by Maurice Brière. "Les Homiliae Cathédrales de Sévère d'Antioche: Hom. 118." PO 26:357–74. 1948.

Severus of Minorca. *Letter on the Conversion of the Jews.*

    Edited and translated by Scott Bradbury. Oxford: Clarendon Press, 1996.

Sheerin, Daniel. *The Eucharist.* MFC 7. Wilmington, DE: Michael Glazier, 1986.

Shenute of Atripe. *Works.*

    Edited and translated by Dwight Wayne Young. *Coptic Manuscripts from the White Monastery: Works of Shenute.* MPER, n.s., 22. Vienna: Österreichische Nationalbibliothek/ Verlag Brüder Hollinek, 1993.

Sibylline Oracles.

    Translated by John J. Collins. In *Old Testament Pseudepigrapha,* edited by J. H. Charlesworth, 1:415–29. Garden City, NY: Doubleday, 1983.

Simeon of Beth Arsham. *Second Letter on the Martyrs of Najran.*

    Edited by Irfan Shahid. *The Martyrs of Najran.* SH 49. Brussels: Société des Bollandistes, 1971.

    Translated by Sebastian P. Brock and Susan Ashbrook Harvey. *Holy Women of the Syrian Orient,* 105–15. Berkeley: University of California Press, 1987; updated ed. with new Preface, 1998.

Simon of Taibutheh. *Medico-Mystical Work.*

    Translated by Alphonse Mingana. *Woodbrooke Studies.* Vol. 7, *Early Christian Mystics,* 1–69. Cambridge: Heffer and Sons, 1934.

The Song of Songs: Interpreted by Early Christian and Medieval Commentators. Translated by Richard A. Norris, Jr. Grand Rapids, MI: Eerdman's, 2003.

Song of Songs: A New Translation with Introduction and Commentary. Translation and commentary by Marvin Pope. New York: Doubleday, 1977.

Sophocles. *Philoctetes.*

    Edited by T. B. L. Webster. Cambridge: Cambridge University Press, 1979.

    Translated by Judith Affleck. Cambridge: Cambridge University Press, 2001.

Soranus. *Gynecology.*

    Edited by Johannes Ilberg. *Sorani Gynaeciorum libri IV, De signis fracturarum, De fasciis, Vita Hippocratis secundum Soranum.* Leipzig: Teubner, 1927.

    Translated by Oswei Temkin. Baltimore: Johns Hopkins University Press, 1956.

Sozomen. *Ecclesiastical History* (*Eccl. Hist.*).

    Edited by J. Bidez, translated by A.-J. Festugière. *Sozomène, Histoire ecclésiastique.* SC 306. Paris: Éditions du Cerf, 1983.

    Translated by Chester D. Hartranft. NPNF, 2nd ser., 2:332–613.

Symeon the New Theologian. *Ethical Discourses.*

    Edited and translated by Jean Darrouzès. *Syméon le nouveau théologien, Traités théologiques et éthiques.* SC 122, 129. Paris: Éditions du Cerf, 1966–67.

    Translated by Alexander Golitzin. *St. Symeon the New Theologian, On the Mystical Life: The Ethical Discourses.* 3 vols. Crestwood, NY: St. Vladimir's Seminary Press, 1995–97.

The Synodicon in the West Syrian Tradition.

    Edited and translated by Arthur Vööbus. CSCO 367–68/Scr. Syr. 161–62. Louvain: Secrétariat du CorpusSCO, 1975.

The Syriac Book of Medicines.

    Edited and translated by E. A. Wallis Budge. London: Oxford University Press, 1913; repr. St. Helier: Armorica Book Co., 1976.

Talbot, Alice-Mary, ed. *Byzantine Defenders of Images: Eight Saints' Lives in English.* Washington, DC: Dumbarton Oaks Publications, 1998.

———, ed. *Holy Women of Byzantium.* Washington, DC: Dumbarton Oaks Publications, 1996.

Tatian. *Oratio Ad Graecos.*

    Edited by Miroslav Marcovich. New York: W. De Gruyter, 1995.

    Translated by Molly Whitaker. *Tatian, Discourse to the Greeks.* New York: Clarendon Press, 1982.

Tertullian. *Apologetical Works, and Minucius Felix, Octavius.* Translated by R. Arbesmann, Emily Joseph Daly, and Edwin Quain. FC 10. New York: Fathers of the Church, 1950.

———. *Apology.*

    Edited by H. Hoppe. CSEL 69. Vienna: 1939.

Translated by Emily Joseph Daly. In *Tertullian, Apologetical Works*, translated by R. Arbesmann, Emily Joseph Daly, and Edwin Quain, 3–126. FC 10. New York: Fathers of the Church, 1950.

———. *The Apparel of Women.*

Edited by Aem. Kroymann. CCSL 1, 341–70. Turnhout: 1954.

Translated by Edwin Quain. In *Tertullian: Disciplinary, Moral and Ascetical Works*, 111–49. FC 40. New York: Fathers of the Church, 1959.

———. *The Chaplet.*

Edited by Aem. Kroymann. CCSL 2, 1037–65. Turnhout: 1954.

Translated by Edwin A. Quain. In *Tertullian: Disciplinary, Moral and Ascetical Works*, 225–70. FC 40. New York: Fathers of the Church, 1959.

———. *Disciplinary, Moral and Ascetical Works.* Translated by Rudolph Arbesmann, Emily Joseph Daly, and Edwin A. Quain. FC 40. New York: Fathers of the Church, 1959.

———. *On Baptism.*

Edited by R. F. Refoulé and M. Drouzy. *Traité du baptême.* SC 35. Paris: Éditions du Cerf, 1952.

Translated by S. Thelwall. ANF 3:669–81.

———. *On Idolatry.* Edited and translated by J. H. Waszink and J. C. M. van Winden. Leiden: E. J. Brill, 1987.

———. *On the Prescription Against Heretics.*

Edited by Aem. Kroymann. CSEL 70, 1–58. Vienna: 1942.

Translated by Peter Holmes. ANF 3:243–65.

———. *On the Resurrection of the Flesh.* Edited and translated by E. E. Evans. *Tertullian's Treatise on the Resurrection.* London: SPCK, 1960.

———. *To His Wife.*

Edited by Aem. Kroymann, CSEL 70, 96–124. Vienna: 1942.

Translated by William P. Le Saint. *Tertullian, Treatises on Marriage and Remarriage.* ACW 13. Westminster, MD: Newman Press, 1951.

———. *To the Martyrs.*

Edited by E. Dekkers. CCSL 1, 1–8. Vienna: 1954. Translated by R. Arbesman. In *Tertullian, Disciplinary, Moral and Ascetical Works*, 13–29. FC 40. New York: Fathers of the Church, 1959.

———. *Treatises on Marriage and Remarriage.* Translated by William P. Le Saint. ACW 13. Westminster, MD: Newman Press, 1951.

Testament of Job.

Translated by R. P. Spittler. In *Old Testament Pseudepigrapha*, edited by J. H. Charlesworth, 1:829–68. Garden City, NY: Doubleday, 1983.

Testaments of the Twelve Patriarchs.

Translated by H. C. Kee. In Old Testament Pseudepigrapha, edited by J. H. Charlesworth, 1:775–828. Garden City, NY: Doubleday, 1983.

Theocritus. Idylls.

Edited and translated by J. M. Edmonds. LCL. Cambridge, MA: Harvard University Press, 1950.

Theodore of Mopsuestia. Catechetical Homilies (Cat. Hom.).

Edited and translated by Raymond Tonneau and Robert Devreesse. Les Homélies Catéchétiques de Théodore de Mopsueste. Studi e Testi 145. Città del Vaticano: Biblioteca Apostolica Vaticana, 1949.

Edited and translated by Alphonse Mingana. Woodbrooke Studies. Vols. 5–6. Cambridge: W. Heffer and Sons, 1933.

Theodore the Studite. On the Holy Icons.

Edited by J. P. Migne. PG 99:327–51.

Translated by Catharine Roth. Crestwood, NY: St. Vladimir's Seminary Press, 1981.

Theodoret of Cyrus. Commentary on the Song of Songs.

Edited by J. P. Migne. PG 81:28–213.

Translated by Robert C. Hill. Theodoret of Cyrhus: Commentary on the Song of Songs. Brisbane: Centre for Early Christian Studies, Australian Catholic University, 2001.

———. History of the Monks of Syria.

Edited and translated by P. Canivet and A. Leroy-Molinghen. Théodoret de Cyr, Histoire des moines de syrie. SC 234, 257. Paris: Éditions du Cerf, 1977–79.

Translated by R. M. Price. Kalamazoo: Cistercian Publications, 1985.

———. On Divine Providence.

Edited by Yvan Azéma. Théodoret de Cyr. Discours sur la Providence. Paris: Les Belles Lettres, 1954.

Translated by Thomas Halton. ACW 49. New York: Newman Press, 1988.

———. Questions on Exodus.

Edited by N. Fernández Marcos and A. Sáenez-Badillos. Theodoreti Cyrensis Quaestiones in Octoteuchum. Madrid: Textos y Estudios "Cardinal Cisneros," 1979.

Theodosian Code.

Edited by Theodor Mommsen and P. M. Meyer. Theodosiani libri XVI cum Constitutinibus Simmondianis et Leges novellae ad Theodosianum pertinentes. Berlin: Weidmann, 1954.

Translated by Clyde Pharr. The Theodosian Code and novels, and the Sirmondian constitutions. Princeton: Princeton University Press, 1952.

Theoktistos the Stoudite. *Miracles of Patriarch Athanasios I of Constantinople.*

Edited and translated by Alice-Mary Talbot. *Faith Healing in Late Byzantium: The Posthumous Miracles of the Patriarch Athanasios I of Constantinople by Theoktistos the Stoudite.* Brookline, MA: Hellenic College Press, 1983.

Theophilus of Antioch. *Ad Autolycum.*

Edited and translated by Robert M. Grant. Oxford: Oxford University Press, 1970.

Theophrastus. *Enquiry into Plants and Minor Works on Odours and Weather Signs.* Edited and translated by Arthur Hort. 2 vols. LCL. New York: G. P. Putnam's Sons, 1916.

———. *Theophrast, de odoribus.*

Edited and translated by Ulrich Eigler, Georg Wöhrle, and Bernhard Herzhoff. Stuttgart: Teubner, 1993.

Theophrastus of Eresus: Sources for His Life, Writings, Thought and Influence. Part Two, Psychology, Human Physiology, Living Creatures, Botany, Ethics, Religion, Politics, Rhetoric and Poetics, Music, Misc.

Edited and translated by William W. Fortenbaugh, Pamela M. Huby, Robert W. Sharples, and Dimitri Gutas. New York: E. J. Brill, 1992.

Thomas of Marga. *Historia Monastica.*

Edited and translated by E. A. Wallis Budge. *The Book of Governors: The Historia Monastica of Thomas Bishop of Marga* A.D. 40. 2 vols. London: Paul, Trench and Trubner, 1893.

Thucydides. *History of the Peloponnesian War.*

Edited and translated by C. Forster Smith. 4 vols. LCL. New York: G. P. Putnam's Sons, 1919–23.

Tract Sanhedrin. Translated by Michael Rodkinson. *Babylonian Talmud.* Vol. 7. New York: New Talmud Publishing Co., 1902.

Transitus Mariae.

(Ethiopic) Edited and translated by Victor Arras. *De Transitu Mariae Apocrypha Aethiopice,* II. CSCO 352/Scrip. Aeth. 69. Louvain: Secrétariat du CorpusSCO, 1974.

(Greek) Edited and translated by Antoine Wenger. *L'Assomption de la T. S. Vierge dans la Tradition Byzantine du VIe au Xe Siècle: Études et Documents.* Archives de l'Orient Chrétien 5. Paris: Insitut Français d'Études Byzantines, 1955.

(Syriac) Edited and translated by William Wright. "The Departure of My Lady Mary from this World." JSL, n.s., 6–7 (1865): vol. 6, 417–48; vol. 7, 110–60.

Vivian, Tim. *Journeying into God: Seven Early Monastic Lives.* Minneapolis: Fortress Press, 1996.

Wright, William. *Contributions to the Apocryphal Literature of the New Testament.* London: Williams and Norgate, 1865.

Zabkar, Louis V. *Hymns to Isis in Her Temple at Philae.* Hanover, NH: Brandeis University Press, 1988.

Secondary Sources

Acheimastou-Potamianou, M., ed. *Holy Image, Holy Space: Icons and Frescoes from Greece.* Athens: Greek Ministry of Culture, Byzantine Museum of Athens, 1988.

Albert, Jean-Pierre. *Odeurs de Sainteté: La mythologie chrétienne des aromates.* 2nd ed. Recherches d'histoire et de sciences sociales 42. Paris: École des Hautes Études en Sciences Sociales, 1996.

Allen, Pauline. "The 'Justinianic' Plague." *Byzantion* 49 (1979): 5–20.

Allers, R. "Microcosmus, from Anaximandros to Paracelsus." *Traditio* 2 (1944): 319–407.

Amar, Joseph P. "Perspectives on the Eucharist in Ephrem the Syrian." *Worship* 61 (1987): 441–54.

———. *Praise and Thanksgiving: Liturgical Music of the Maronite Church.* Brooklyn: Diocese of St. Maron, 1986.

———. "The Syriac Hoosoyo: A Consideration of Narrative Techniques." *Diakonia* 22 (1988–89): 153–68.

Anderson, Gary A. *The Genesis of Perfection: Adam and Eve in Jewish and Christian Imagination.* Louisville, KY: Westminster John Knox, 2001.

——— and Michael E. Stone, eds. *A Synopsis of the Books of Adam and Eve.* 2nd ed. Atlanta, GA: Scholars Press, 1999.

Annas, Julia. *Hellenistic Philosophy of Mind.* Berkeley: University of California Press, 1992.

Atchley, E. G. F. C. *A History of the Use of Incense in Divine Worship.* Alcuin Club Collections 13. London: Longmans, Green, 1909.

Attridge, Harold W. "Making Scents of Paul: The Background and Sense of 2 Cor. 2:14–7." In *Early Christianity and Classical Culture,* edited by John T. Fitzgerald, Thomas H. Olbricht, and L. Michael White, 71–88. Leiden/Boston: E. J. Brill, 2003.

Axel, Richard. "The Molecular Logic of Smell." *Scientific American,* October 1995, 154–59.

Badger, G. P. *The Nestorians and their Rituals.* London: 1852; repr. London: Darf Publishers, 1987.

Baldovin, John. *The Urban Character of Christian Worship: The Origins, Development, and Meaning of Stational Liturgy.* OCA 228. Rome: Pontificum Institutum Studiorum Orientalium, 1987.

Bartelink, G. J. M. "Les oxymores Desertum civitas et Desertum floribus vernans." *Studia Monastica* 15 (1973): 7–15.

Baudrillard, Jean. *Seduction.* Translated by Brian Singer. New York: St. Martin's Press, 1990.

Beagan, Mary. *Roman Nature: The Thought of Pliny the Elder.* Oxford: Clarendon Press, 1992.

Beare, J. I. *Greek Theories of Elementary Cognition from Alcmaeon to Aristotle.* Oxford: Clarendon Press, 1906.

Beauchamp, Gary K. "The Chemical Senses and Pleasure." In *Pleasure: The Politics and the Reality*, edited by David M. Warburton, 29–37. New York: John Wiley and Sons, 1994.

BeDuhn, Jason David. *The Manichaean Body: In discipline and ritual*. Baltimore, MD: Johns Hopkins University Press, 2000.

Bell, Catherine. *Ritual Theory, Ritual Practice*. New York/Oxford: Oxford University Press, 1992.

Bell, Graham A., and Annesley J. Watson, eds. *Tastes and Aromas: The Chemical Senses in Science and Industry*. Oxford/Sydney: Blackwell Science Ltd. and University of South Wales Press, 1999.

Belting, Hans. *Likeness and Presence*. Translated by Edmund Jephcott. Chicago: University of Chicago Press, 1994.

Bernstein, Alan E. *The Formation of Hell: Death and Retribution in the Ancient and Early Christian Worlds*. Ithaca, NY: Cornell University Press, 1993.

Beulay, Robert. *L'Enseignement Spirituel de Jean de Dalyatha: Mystique Syro-Oriental du VIIIe Siècle*. Paris: Éditions Beauchesne, 1990.

Bornert, René. *Les Commentaires byzantins de la divine liturgie du 7e au 15e siècle*. Paris: Institut français d'études byzantines, 1966.

Boulnois, Marie-Odile. *Le Paradoxe Trinitaire chez Cyrille d'Alexandrie: Herméneutique, analyses philosophiques et argumentation théologique*. Paris: Institut d'Études Augustiniennes, 1994.

Bovon, F., M. van Esbroeck, R. Goulet, E. Jounod, J.-D. Kaestli, F. Morard, G. Poupon, J.-M. Prieur, and Y. Tissot, eds. *Les actes apocryphes des apôtres: christianisme et monde païen*. Geneva: Labor et Fides, 1981.

Bradshaw, Paul. *Daily Prayer in the Early Church*. New York: Oxford University Press, 1982.

———. *The Search for the Origins of Christian Worship: Sources and Methods for the Study of Early Liturgy*. 2nd ed. New York: Oxford University Press, 2002.

Brakke, David. *Athanasius and the Politics of Asceticism*. Oxford: Clarendon Press, 1995.

Brock, Sebastian P. "Anointing in the Syriac Tradition." In *The Oil of Gladness*, edited by Martin Dudley and Geoffrey Rowell, 92–100. London: SPCK, 1993.

———. "Clothing Metaphors as a Means of Theological Expression in Syriac Tradition." In *Typus, Symbol, Allegorie bei den östlichen Vätern und ihren Parallelen im Mittelalter*, edited by Margot Schmidt and C. Geyer, 11–40. Regensburg: Friedrich Pustet, 1982.

———. "Dramatic Dialogue Poems." *Symposium Syriacum IV*, edited by H. J. W. Drijvers, R. Lavenant, C. Molenberg, and G. J. Reinink, 135–47. OCA 229. Rome: Pontificum Institutum Studiorum Orientalium, 1987.

———. "Fire from Heaven: From Abel's Sacrifice to the Eucharist. A Theme in Syriac Christianity." *SP 25*, edited by Elizabeth A. Livingstone, 229–43. Leuven: Peeters Press, 1993.

———. "From Ephrem to Romanos." *SP 20*, edited by Elizabeth A. Livingstone, 139–51. Leuven: Peeters Press, 1989.

———. *The Holy Spirit in the Syrian Baptismal Tradition.* Syrian Churches Series 9, edited by Jacob Vellian. 2nd ed. Poona: Anita Printers, 1998.

———. *The Luminous Eye: The Spiritual World Vision of Saint Ephrem the Syrian.* Kalamazoo: Cistercian Publications, 1992.

———. "*Maggnanuta:* A Technical Term in East Syrian Spirituality and its Background." In *Mélanges Antoine Guillaumont: Contributions à l'étude des christianismes orientaux,* 121–29. Cahiers d'Orientalisme 20. Geneva: 1988.

———. "The Prayer of the Heart in Syriac Tradition." *Sobornost* 4 (1982): 131–42.

———. "The priesthood of the baptised: Some Syriac perspectives." *Sobornost/ECR* 9 (1987): 14–22.

———. "Some Early Syriac Baptismal Commentaries." *OCP* 46 (1980): 20–61.

———. "Syriac and Greek Hymnography: Problems of Origin." *SP* 16, edited by Elizabeth A. Livingstone, 77–81. Berlin: Akademie-Verlag, 1985.

Brown, Peter. *The Body and Society: Men, Women, and Sexual Renunciation in Early Christianity.* New York: Columbia University Press, 1988.

———. *The Cult of the Saints: Its Rise and Function in Latin Christianity.* Chicago: University of Chicago Press, 1981.

———. "The Rise and Function of the Holy Man in Late Antiquity." *JRS* 61 (1971): 80–101.

———. *Society and the Holy in Late Antiquity.* Berkeley: University of California Press, 1982.

Browning, Robert. "The 'Low-Level' Saint's Life in the Early Byzantine World." In *The Byzantine Saint,* edited by Sergei Hackel, 117–27. SSS 5. London: Fellowship of SS Alban and Sergius, 1981; repr. Crestwood, NY: St. Vladimir's Seminary Press, 2001.

Brun, Jean-Pierre. "The Production of Perfumes in Antiquity: The Cases of Delos and Paestum." *AJA* 104 (2000): 277–308.

Burkert, Walter. *Greek Religion.* Translated by John Raffan. Cambridge, MA: Harvard University Press, 1985.

Bynum, Caroline Walker. "Material Continuity, Personal Survival and the Resurrection of the Body: A Scholastic Discussion in its Medieval and Modern Contexts." In *Fragmentation and Redemption: Essays on Gender and the Human Body in Medieval Religion,* edited by Caroline Walker Bynum, 239–98, 393–417. New York: Zone Books: 1992.

———. *The Resurrection of the Body in Western Christianity, 200–1336.* New York: Columbia University Press, 1995.

Cameron, Averil. *Christianity and the Rhetoric of Empire: The Development of Christian Discourse.* Berkeley: University of California Press, 1991.

———. "Early Christianity and the Discourse of Female Desire." In *Women in Ancient Societies: 'An Illusion of the Night,'* edited by Léonie Archer, Susan Fischler, and Maria Wyke, 152–68. New York: Routledge, 1994.

———. ed. *History as Text: The Writing of Ancient History.* London: Duckworth, 1989.

———. "The Language of Images: The Rise of Icons and Christian Representation." In *The Church and the Arts*, edited by Diana Wood, 1–42. SCH 28. Oxford: Blackwell Publishers, 1992.

———. "The Theotokos in Sixth-Century Constantinople: A City Finds its Symbol." *JTS*, n.s., 29 (1978): 79–108.

Camporesi, Piero. *The Anatomy of the Senses: Natural Symbols in Medieval and Early Modern Italy*. Translated by Allan Cameron. Cambridge: Polity Press, 1994.

———. *The Fear of Hell: Images of Damnation and Salvation in Early Modern Europe*. Translated by Lucinda Byatt. University Park, PA: Pennsylvania State University Press, 1991.

———. *The Incorruptible Flesh: Bodily Mutation and Mortification in Religion and Folklore*. Translated by Tania Croft-Murray; Latin texts translated by Helen Elsom. Cambridge Studies in Oral and Literate Culture 17. Cambridge: Cambridge University Press, 1988.

Canevet, Mariette. *Grégoire de Nysse et l'herméneutique biblique. Étude des rapports entre le langage et la connaissance de Dieu*. Paris: Études Augustiniennes, 1983.

Capelle, B. "La Fête de la Vierge à Jérusalem au Ve siècle." *Le Muséon* 56 (1943): 1–33.

Carmignani, Paul, Jean-Yves Laurichesse, and Joël Thomas, eds. *Saveurs, Senteurs: Le Goût de la Méditerraneé. Actes du Colloque Université de Perpignan 13–14–15 Novembre 1997*. Perpignan: Presses universitaires de Perpignan, 1998.

Carruthers, M. *The Craft of Thought: Meditation, rhetoric, and the making of images, 400–1200*. New York: Cambridge University Press, 1998.

Caseau, Béatrice. "Christian Bodies: The Senses and Early Byzantine Christianity." In *Desire and Denial in Byzantium*, edited by Liz James, 101–109. Aldershot, Hampshire: Ashgate Publishing, 1999.

———. "L'eucharistie au centre de la vie religieuse des communautés chrétiennes (fin du Ie—Xe siècle)." In *Encyclopedia eucharistia*, edited by Maurice Brouard, 117–36. Paris: Éditions du Cerf, 2001.

———. "Euodia: The Use and Meaning of Fragrances in the Ancient World and their Christianization (100–900 A.D.)." PhD. diss., Princeton University, 1994.

———. "Les usages médicaux de l'encens et des parfums: Un aspect de la medicine populaire antique et de sa christianisation." In *Air, Miames et Contagion: Les épidémies dans l'Antiquité et au Moyen Age*, edited by Sylvie Bazin-Tacchella, Danielle Quéruel, and Évelyne Samama, 74–85. Langres: Dominique Guéniot, 2001.

Castelli, E. "Mortifying the Body, Curing the Soul: Beyond Ascetic Dualism in *The Life of Saint Syncletica*." *Differences* 4 (1992): 134–53.

Chidester, David. "Material Terms for the Study of Religion." *JAAR* 68 (2000): 367–80.

———. *Word and Light: Seeing, Hearing, and Religious Discourse*. Urbana/Chicago: University of Illinois Press, 1992.

Christman, Angela Russell. "What did Ezekiel See?: Patristic Exegesis of Ezekiel 1 and Debates about God's Incomprehensibility." *Pro Ecclesia* 8 (1999): 338–63.

Clark, Elizabeth A. *Ascetic Piety and Women's Faith: Essays on Late Ancient Christianity.* Lewiston, NY/Toronto: Edwin Mellen Press, 1986.

——. *Reading Renunciation.* Princeton: Princeton University Press, 1999.

——. "The Uses of the Song of Songs: Origen and the Later Latin Fathers." In *Ascetic Piety and Women's Faith*, edited by Elizabeth Clark, 386–427. Lewiston, NY/Toronto: Edwin Mellen Press, 1986.

Clark, Gillian. "Victricius of Rouen: Praising the Saints." JECS 7 (1999): 365–99.

Classen, Constance. *The Color of Angels: Cosmology, Gender and the Aesthetic Imagination.* New York: Routledge, 1998.

——. "The Odor of the Other: Olfactory Symbolism and Cultural Categories." *Ethos* 20:2 (June 1992): 133–66.

——. "Sweet Colors, Fragrant Songs: Sensory Models of the Andes and Amazon." *American Ethnologist* 17 (1990): 722–35.

——. *Worlds of Sense: Exploring the Senses in History and Across Cultures.* London/New York: Routledge, 1993.

—— and David Howes. "Sounding Sensory Profiles." In *The Varieties of Sensory Experience*, edited by David Howes, 257–88. Toronto: University of Toronto Press, 1991.

——, David Howes, and Anthony Synnott. *Aroma: The Cultural History of Smell.* London/New York: Routledge, 1994.

Coakley, Sarah, ed. *Religion and the Body.* Cambridge: Cambridge University Press, 1997.

Colish, Marcia. "Cosmetic Theology: The Transformation of a Stoic Theme." *Assays* 1 (1984): 3–14.

Collins, John J., and Michael A. Fishbane, eds. *Death, Ecstasy, and Other Worldly Journeys.* Albany: State University of New York Press, 1995.

Constas, Nicholas. "An Apology for the Cult of Saints in Late Antiquity: Eustratius Presbyter of Constantinople, 'On the State of Souls after Death (CPG 7522).'" JECS 10 (2002): 267–85.

——. *Proclus of Constantinople and the Cult of the Virgin in Late Antiquity: Homilies 1–5, Texts and Translations.* SVC 66. Leiden: E. J. Brill, 2003.

Corbin, Alain. *The Foul and the Fragrant: Odor and the French Social Imagination.* Translated by Miriam L. Kochan, Roy Porter, and Christopher Prendergast. Cambridge, MA: Harvard University Press, 1986.

Corrigan, Kathleen. "The Witness of John the Baptist on an Early Byzantine Icon in Kiev." DOP 42 (1988): 1–11.

Cuming, G. J. "Thmuis Revisited: Another Look at the Prayers of Bishop Sarapion." TS 41 (1980): 568–75.

Dalby, Andrew. *Dangerous Tastes: The Story of Spices.* Berkeley: University of California Press, 2000.

Daley, Brian E. *The Hope of the Early Church: A Handbook of Patristic Eschatology.* Cambridge: Cambridge University Press, 1991.

Daly, Robert. *Christian Sacrifice: The Judeo-Christian Background Before Origen.* Washington, DC: Catholic University of America Press, 1978.

Daniélou, Jean. *The Bible and the Liturgy.* Notre Dame, IN: University of Notre Dame Press, 1956.

———. "Chrismation prébaptismale et divinité de l'Ésprit chez Grégoire de Nysse." *RSR* 56 (1968): 177–98.

———. "Onction et baptême chez Grégoire de Nysse." *Ephemerides Liturgicae* 90 (1976): 440–45.

———. "Terre et Paradis chez les Pères de l'église." *Eranos Jahrbuch* 22 (1953): 433–72.

Davidson, James. *Courtesans and Fishcakes: The Consuming Passions of Classical Athens.* London: HarperCollins, 1997.

Dawson, David. *Allegorical Readers and Cultural Revision in Ancient Alexandria.* Berkeley: University of California Press, 1992.

Dean-Jones, Lesley. "The Cultural Construct of the Female Body in Classical Greek Science." In *Women's History and Ancient History,* edited by Sarah B. Pomeroy, 111–37. Chapel Hill: University of North Carolina Press, 1991.

Debru, Armelle. *Le Corps Respirant: La pensée physiologique chez Galen.* New York: E. J. Brill, 1996.

Delehaye, H. *Les Origines du Culte des Martyrs.* 2nd ed. SH 20. Brussels: Société des Bollandistes, 1933.

———. Review of *Incense in Divine Worship,* by E. G. F. C. Atchley. *AB* 30 (1911): 93–95.

Delumeau, Jean. *History of Paradise: The Garden of Eden in Myth and Tradition.* Translated by Matthew O'Connell. New York: Continuum, 1995.

Deonna, W. "EUWDIA: Croyances antiques et modernes: L'Odeur suave des dieux et des élus." *Genava* 17 (1939): 167–263.

de Ste. Croix, G. E. M. "Why were the early Christians persecuted?" *Past and Present* 26 (1963): 6–38.

Detienne, Marcel. *The Gardens of Adonis: Spices in Greek Mythology.* Introduction by Jean-Pierre Vernant. Translated by Janet Lloyd. New ed. Princeton: Princeton University Press, 1994.

——— and Jean-Pierre Vernant, eds. *The Cuisine of Sacrifice Among the Greeks.* Translated by Paula Wissing. Chicago: University of Chicago Press, 1989.

De Wijk, R. A., F. R. Schab, and W. S. Cain. "Odor Identification." In *Memory for Odors,* edited by F. R. Schab and Robert G. Crowder, 21–37. Mahwah, NJ: Lawrence Erlbaum Associates, 1995.

Di Berardino, Angelo. "Liturgical Celebrations and Imperial Legislation in the Fourth Century." In *Prayer and Spirituality in the Early Church.* Vol. 3, *Liturgy and Life,* edited by Bronwen Neil, Geoffrey D. Dunn, and Lawrence Cross, 211–32. Sydney: St. Paul's Publications, 2003.

Dillon, John. "*Aisthēsis Noētē*: A Doctrine of Spiritual Senses in Origen and in Plotinus." In *Hellenica et Judaica: Hommage à Valentin Nikiprowetzky*, edited by A. Caquot, M. Hadas-Lebel, and J. Riaud, 443–55. Leuven: Peeters Press, 1986.

Dix, Gregory. *The Shape of the Liturgy.* 2nd ed. London: A & C Black, 1945; repr. 1993.

Dodds, E. R. *Pagan and Christian in an Age of Anxiety.* Cambridge: Cambridge University Press, 1965.

Donato, Giuseppe, and Monique Seefried. *The Fragrant Past: Perfumes of Cleopatra and Julius Caesar.* Rome: Instituto Poligrafico e Zecca dello Stato/Emory University, Museum of Art and Architecture, 1989.

Doran, Robert. "Comments on the Syriac Versions of the Life of Simeon Stylites." *AB* 102 (1984): 35–48.

Douglas, Mary. *Natural Symbols: Explorations in Cosmology.* New York: Pantheon Books, 1982. Repr. with new introduction, New York: Routledge, 1996.

Doval, Alexis James. *Cyril of Jerusalem, Mystagogue: The Authorship of the Mystagogic Catacheses.* Patristic Monograph Series 17. Washington, DC: Catholic University of America Press, 2001.

Downey, Glanville. *Antioch in the Age of Theodosius the Great.* Norman, OK: University of Oklahoma Press, 1962.

Drijvers, Han J. W. "Spätantike Parallelen zur altchristlichen Heiligenverehrung unter besonderer Berücksichtigung des syrischen Stylitenkultus." *Göttingen Orientforschungen* 1, Reihe: Syriaca 17 (1978): 77–113.

Dudley, Martin, and Geoffrey Rowell, eds. *The Oil of Gladness: Anointing in the Christian Tradition.* London: SPCK, 1993.

Dunnill, John. *Covenant and Sacrifice in the Letter to the Hebrews.* SNTS 75. Cambridge: Cambridge University Press, 1992.

Eastmond, Antony. "Body vs. Column: The Cults of St. Symeon Stylites." In *Desire and Denial in Byzantium*, edited by Liz James, 87–100. Aldershot, Hampshire: Ashgate Publishing, 1999.

Edwards, Jonathan. *Religious Affections.* Edited by John E. Smith. New Haven: Yale University Press, 1959.

Ellis, John. "The Aporematic Character of Theophrastus' *Metaphysics*." In *Theophrastean Studies*, edited by William W. Fortenbaugh and Robert W. Sharples, 216–23. New Brunswick, NJ: Transaction Books, 1988.

Elm, Susanna. "Evagrius Ponticus' *Sententiae ad Virginem*." *DOP* 45 (1991): 97–120.

———. *'Virgins of God': The Making of Asceticism in Late Antiquity.* Oxford: Oxford University Press, 1994.

Engberg-Pedersen, Troels. *Paul and the Stoics: An Essay in Interpretation.* Edinburgh: T & T Clark, 2000.

Engen, Trygg. *Odor Sensation and Memory.* New York: Praeger, 1991.

————. *The Perception of Odors*. New York: Academic Press, 1982.

Evans, Helen, and William D. Wixom, eds. *The Glory of Byzantium: Art and Culture of the Middle Byzantine Era, A.D. 843–1261*. New York: Metropolitan Museum of Art, 1997.

Evans, Suzanne. "The Scent of a Martyr." *Numen* 49 (2002): 193–211.

Fauré, P. *Parfums et aromates de l'antiquité*. Paris: Fayard, 1987.

Féghali, Paul. "La descente aux enfers dans la tradition syriaque." *Parole de l'Orient* 15 (1988–89): 127–42.

Ferguson, Everett. "Spiritual Sacrifice in Early Christianity and its Environment." In *ANRW* II.23.2, edited by W. Haase, 1151–89. Berlin: Walter de Gruyter, 1980.

Festugière, A.-J. *Antioche païenne et chrétienne. Libanius, Chrysostome et les moines de Syrie*. Paris: de Boccard, 1959.

Fiey, J.-M. *Jalons pour une histoire de l'église en Iraq*. CSCO 310/Sub. 36. Louvain: Secrétariat du CorpusSCO, 1970.

Forbes, R. J. *Studies in Ancient Technology*. Vol. 3. Leiden: E. J. Brill, 1955; 2nd ed., 1965.

Fortenbaugh, William W. and Robert W. Sharples, eds. *Theophrastean Studies: On Natural Science, Physics and Metaphysics, Ethics, Religion, and Rhetoric*. New Brunswick, NJ: Transaction Books, 1988.

Foucault, Michel. *The History of Sexuality*. Vol. 2, *The Use of Pleasure*. Translated by Robert Hurley. New York: Pantheon Books, 1985. Vol. 3, *The Care of the Self*. Translated by Robert Hurley. New York: Vintage Books, 1986.

Fox, Robin Lane. *Pagans and Christians*. San Francisco: Harper and Row, 1987.

Fraigneau-Julien, B. *Les Sens Spirituels et la Vision de Dieu selon Syméon le Nouveau Théologien*. TH 67. Paris: Éditions Beauchesne, 1985.

Frank, Georgia. *The Memory of the Eyes: Pilgrimage to Living Saints in Christian Late Antiquity*. Berkeley: University of California Press, 2000.

————. "The Pilgrim's Gaze in the Age Before Icons." In *Visuality Before and Beyond the Renaissance: Seeing as Others Saw*, edited by Robert S. Nelson, 98–115. Cambridge: Cambridge University Press, 2000.

Frankfurter, David. "Stylites and Phallobates: Pillar Religions in Late Antique Syria." *VC* 44 (1990): 168–98.

Frede, Michael. "On Galen's Epistemology." In *Galen: Problems and Prospects*, edited by Vivan Nutton, 65–84. London: Wellcome Institute for the History of Medicine, 1981.

French, Roger. *Ancient Natural History: Histories of Nature*. London/New York: Routledge, 1994.

Furley, David. "Democritus and Epicurus on Sensible Qualities." In *Passions and Perceptions: Studies in Hellenistic Philosophy of Mind, Proceedings of the Fifth Symposium Hellenisticum*, edited by Jacques Brunschwig and Martha C. Nussbaum, 72–94. Cambridge: Cambridge University Press, 1993.

Gaca, Kathy L. *The Making of Fornication: Eros, Ethics, and Political Reform in Greek Philosophy and Early Christianity.* Berkeley: University of California Press, 2003.

Gaddis, Michael. *'There Is No Crime for Those Who Have Christ': Religious Violence in the Christian Roman Empire.* Berkeley: University of California Press, 2005.

Gager, John G., ed. *Curse Tablets and Binding Spells from the Ancient World.* New York: Oxford University Press, 1992.

Gain, Benoît. *L'Église de Cappadoce au IVe siècle d'après la correspondence de Basile de Césarée (330–379).* OCA 225. Rome: Pontificium Institutum Orientale, 1985.

Geertz, Clifford. *Negara: The Theatre State in Nineteenth Century Bali.* Princeton: Princeton University Press, 1980.

Gero, Stephen. "The So-Called Ointment Prayer in the Coptic Version of the Didache: A Re-Evaluation." *HTR* 70 (1977): 67–84.

Gilders, William K. *Blood Ritual in the Hebrew Bible: Meaning and Power.* Baltimore: Johns Hopkins University Press, 2004.

Glad, Clarence. *Paul and Philodemus: Adaptability in Epicurean and Early Christian Psychagogy.* Leiden: E. J. Brill, 1995.

Golitzin, Alexander. "'A Contemplative and a Liturgist:' Father Georges Florovsky on the Corpus Dionysiacum." *SVTQ* 43 (1999): 131–61.

———. *Et Introibo ad Altare Dei: The Mystagogy of Dionysius Areopagita, with special reference to its predecessors in the eastern Christian tradition.* Analecta Vlatadon 59. Thessalonika: Patriarchikon Idryma Paterikon Meleton, 1994.

———. "Hierarchy vs. Anarchy? Dionysius Areopagita, Symeon the New Theologian, Nicetas Stethatos, and their Common Roots in Ascetical Tradition." *SVTQ* 38 (1994): 131–79.

———. "The Image and Glory of God in Jacob of Serug's Homily, 'On that Chariot that Ezekiel the Prophet Saw.'" *SVTQ* 47 (2003): 323–64.

———. "Liturgy and Mysticism: The Experience of God in Eastern Orthodox Christianity." *Pro Ecclesia* 8 (1999): 159–86.

———. "The Mysticism of Dionysius Areopagita: Platonist or Christian?" *Mystics Quarterly* 19 (1993): 98–114.

———. "The Place of the Presence of God: Aphrahat of Persia's Portrait of the Christian Holy Man." In *Synaxis Eucharistiae: Charisteria eis Timen tou Gerontos Aimilianou,* edited by Simonas Petras Monastery, 391–447. Athens: Indiktos Press, 2003.

———. *St. Symeon the New Theologian, On the Mystical Life: The Ethical Discourses.* Vol. 3, *Life, Times, and Theology.* Crestwood, NY: St. Vladimir's Seminary Press, 1997.

———. "A Testimony to Christianity as Transfiguration: The Macarian Homilies and Orthodox Spirituality." In *Orthodox and Wesleyan Spirituality,* edited by S. T. Kimbrough, Jr., 129–56. Crestwood, NY: St. Vladimir's Seminary Press, 2002.

Graf, Fritz. *Magic in the Ancient World*. Translated by Franklin Philip. Cambridge, MA: Harvard University Press, 1997.

Green, Dennis. "To '. . . Send Up, Like the Smoke of Incense, the Works of the Law'—The Similarity of Views on an Alternative to Temple Sacrifice by Three Jewish Sectarian Movements of the Late Second Temple Period." In *Religion in the Ancient World: New Themes and Approaches*, edited by Matthew Dillon, 167–75. Amsterdam: A.M. Hakkert, 1996.

Gregory, Timothy. *Vox Populi: Popular Opinion and Violence in the Religious Controversies of the Fifth Century A.D.* Columbus: Ohio State University Press, 1979.

Griffin, Carl W., and David L. Paulsen. "Augustine and the Corporeality of God." HTR 95 (2002): 97–118.

Griffith, Sidney. "Asceticism in the Church of Syria: The Hermeneutics of Early Syrian Monasticism." In *Asceticism*, edited by Vincent Wimbush and Richard Valantasis, 220–45. New York: Oxford University Press, 1995.

———. "The Image of the Image Maker in the Poetry of St. Ephrem the Syrian." SP 25, edited by Elizabeth A. Livingstone, 258–69. Leuven: Peeters Press, 1993.

———. "Julian Saba, 'Father of the Monks' of Syria." JECS 2 (1994): 185–216.

Grimal, Pierre. *Les jardins romains*. 2nd ed. Paris: Presses Universitaires de France, 1969.

Grmek, Mirko D. *Diseases in the Ancient Greek World*. Translated by Mireille Muellner and Leonard Muellner. Baltimore: Johns Hopkins University Press, 1989.

Groom, Nigel. *Frankincense and Myrrh: A Study of the Arabian Incense Trade*. London/New York: Longman, Libraire du Liban, 1981.

Grosdidier de Matons, José. *Romanos le Mélode et les origines de la poésie religieuse à Byzance*. Paris: Éditions Beauchesne, 1977.

Guillaume-Coirier, Germaine. "Les Couronnes militaires végétales à Rome: Vestiges indo-européens et croyances archaïques." RHR 210 (1993): 387–411.

Guinan, Michael. "The Eschatology of James of Sarug." PhD. diss., Catholic University of America, 1972.

Hackel, Sergei, ed. *The Byzantine Saint*. SSS 5. London: Fellowship of SS Alban and Sergius, 1981; repr. Crestwood, NY: St. Vladimir's Seminary Press, 2001.

Hahm, David. "Early Hellenistic Theories of Vision and the Perception of Color." In *Studies in Perception: Interrelations in the History of Philosophy and Science*, edited by Peter Machamer and Robert G. Turnbull, 60–95. Columbus: Ohio State University Press, 1978.

Halkin, F. *Novum Auctarium bibliothecae hagiographicae graecae*. SH 65. Brussels: Société des Bollandistes, 1984.

Halliburton, John. "Anointing in the Early Church." In *The Oil of Gladness*, edited by Martin Dudley and Geoffrey Rowell, 77–91. London: SPCK, 1993.

Halperin, David. *One Hundred Years of Homosexuality and Other Essays on Greek Love*. New York: Routledge, 1990.

————, John J. Winkler, and Froma Zeitlin, eds. *Before Sexuality: The Construction of Erotic Experience in the Ancient Greek World*. Princeton: Princeton University Press, 1990.

Halton, Thomas. "The Five Senses in Nemesius, *De Natura Hominis* and Theodoret, *De Providentia*." SP 20, edited by Elizabeth A. Livingstone, 94–101. Leuven: Peeters Press, 1989.

Hanson, Ann Ellis. "The Medical Writers' Woman." In *Before Sexuality*, edited by David Halperin, John J. Winkler, and Froma Zeitlin, 309–38. Princeton: Princeton University Press, 1990.

Haran, Menahem. *Temples and Temple Service in Ancient Israel: An Inquiry into Biblical Cult Phenomena and the Historical Setting of the Priestly School*. 2nd ed. Winona Lake, IN: Eisenbrauns, 1985.

Harland, Philip A. "Christ-Bearers and Fellow-Initiates: Local Cultural Life and Christian Identity in Ignatius' Letters." JECS 11 (2003): 481–99.

Harrison, Verna. *Grace and Human Freedom According to St. Gregory of Nyssa*. Lewiston, NY: Edwin Mellen Press, 1992.

Hart, Laurie Kain. *Time, Religion and Social Experience in Rural Greece*. Landham, MD: Rowman and Littlefield, 1992.

Hartog, François. *The Mirror of Herodotus: The Representation of the Other in the Writing of History*. Translated by Janet Lloyd. Berkeley: University of California Press, 1988.

Harvey, Elizabeth D., ed. *Sensible Flesh: On Touch in Early Modern Culture*. Philadelphia: University of Pennsylvania Press, 2003.

Harvey, Susan Ashbrook. *Asceticism and Society in Crisis: John of Ephesus and the "Lives of the Eastern Saints."* Berkeley: University of California Press, 1990.

————. "Embodiment in Time and Eternity: A Syriac Perspective." *SVTQ* 43 (1999): 105–30.

————. "Housekeeping: An Ascetic Theme in Late Antiquity." In *'To Train His Spirit with Books': Studies in Syrian Asceticism in honor of Sidney H. Griffith*, edited by Robin A. Darling Young and Monica Blanchard. Washington, DC: Catholic University of America Press, forthcoming.

————. "Incense Offerings in the Syriac *Transitus Mariae*: Ritual and Knowledge in Ancient Christianity." In *The Early Church in its Context: Essays in Honor of Everett Ferguson*, edited by Abraham J. Malherbe, Frederick W. Norris, and James W. Thompson, 175–91. Leiden: E. J. Brill, 1998.

————. "Interior Decorating: Jacob of Serug on Mary's Preparation for the Incarnation." *SP* (forthcoming).

————. "Olfactory Knowing: Signs of Smell in the *Lives* of Simeon Stylites." In *After Bardaisan: Studies on Continuity and Change in Syriac Christianity in Honour of Professor Han J. W. Drijvers*, edited by G. J. Reinink and A. C. Klugkist, 23–34. OLA 89. Leuven: Peeters Press, 1999.

———. "On Holy Stench: When the Odor of Sanctity Sickens." *SP* 35, edited by M. F. Wiles and E. J. Yarnold, 90–101. Leuven: Peeters Press, 2001.

———. "Physicians and Ascetics: An Expedient Alliance." *DOP* 38 (1984): 87–93.

———. "The Sense of a Stylite: Perspectives on Simeon the Elder." *VC* 42 (1988): 376–94.

———. "St. Ephrem on the Scent of Salvation." *JTS*, n.s., 49 (1998): 109–28.

———. "The Stylite's Liturgy: Ritual and Religious Identity in Late Antiquity." *JECS* 6 (1998): 523–39.

———. "Why the Perfume Mattered: The Sinful Woman in Syriac Exegetical Tradition." In *In Dominico Eloquio/In Lordly Eloquence: Essays on Patristic Exegesis in Honor of Robert Louis Wilken*, edited by Paul M. Blowers, Angela Russell Christman, David G. Hunter, and Robin Darling Young, 69–89. Grand Rapids, MI: Eerdmans Press, 2002.

Haskins, Susan. *Mary Magdalene: Myth and Metaphor*. New York: Harcourt Brace, 1994.

Hauk, Robert. "'They Saw What They Said They Saw': Sense Knowledge in Early Christian Polemic." *HTR* 81 (1988): 239–49.

Hefele, Carl Joseph, and Henri Leclerq, eds. *Histoire des Conciles*. 11 vols. Paris: Letouzet et Ane, 1907; repr. Hildesheim: Georg Olms Verlag, 1973.

Heger, Paul. *The Development of Incense Cult in Israel*. New York: Walter de Gruyter, 1997.

Hennessey, Lawrence R. "A Philosophical Issue in Origen's Eschatology: The Three Senses of Incorporeality." In *Origeniana Quinta: Papers of the 5th International Origen Congress, Boston College, 14–18 August 1989*, edited by Robert Daly, 373–80. Leuven: Peeters Press, 1992.

Henze, Matthias. *The Madness of King Nebuchadnezzar: The Ancient Near Eastern Origins and Early History of Interpretation of Daniel 4*. Leiden: E. J. Brill, 1999.

Hermans, Theo. *Origène: Théologie Sacrificielle du Sacerdoce des Chrétiens*. TH 102. Paris: Éditions Beauchesne, 1996.

Herrin, Judith. "'Femina Byzantina': The Council in Trullo on Women." *DOP* 46 (1992): 97–105.

Herz, Rachel. "Verbal Coding in Olfactory versus Nonolfactory Cognition." *Memory and Cognition* 28.6 (2000): 957–64.

Himmelfarb, Martha. *Ascent to Heaven in Jewish and Christian Apocalypses*. New York: Oxford University Press, 1993.

———. *Tours of Hell: An Apocaplytic Form in Jewish and Christian Literature*. Philadelphia: University of Pennsylvania Press, 1983.

Holman, Susan R. *The Hungry are Dying: Beggars and Bishops in Roman Cappadocia*. New York: Oxford University Press, 2001.

Holum, Kenneth. *Theodosian Empresses: Women and Imperial Dominion in Late Antiquity*. Berkeley: University of California Press, 1982.

Hornung, Erik. *Conceptions of God in Ancient Egypt: The One and the Many.* Translated by John Baines. Ithaca, NY: Cornell University Press, 1982.

Houtman, C. "On the Function of the Holy Incense (Exodus XXX 34–8) and the Sacred Anointing Oil (Exodus XXX 22–33)." *VT* 42 (1992): 458–65.

Howes, David, ed. *The Varieties of Sensory Experience: A Sourcebook in the Anthropology of the Senses.* Toronto: University of Toronto Press, 1991.

Hunt, David. "Christianizing the Roman Empire: The Evidence of the Code." In *The Theodosian Code*, edited by Jill Harries and Ian Wood, 143–58. Ithaca, NY: Cornell University Press, 1993.

Hunt, Hannah. "The Tears of the Sinful Woman: A Theology of Redemption in the Homilies of St. Ephraim and his Followers." *Hugoye: Journal of Syriac Studies* 1:2 (1998): http://www.acad.cua.edu/syrcom/Hugoye.

Hurowitz, Victor Avigdor. "Solomon's Golden Vessels (1 Kings 7: 48–50) and the Cult of the First Temple." In *Pomegranates and Golden Bells: Studies in Biblical, Jewish, and Near Eastern Ritual, Law, and Literature in Honor of Jacob Milgrom*, edited by David P. Wright, David Noel Freedman, and Avi Hurvitz, 151–64. Winona Lake, IN: Eisenbrauns, 1995.

Isaacs, Marie E. *Sacred Space: An Approach to the Theology of the Epistle to the Hebrews.* JSNT Supplement Series 73. Sheffield: JSOT Press, 1992.

Jacob, Irene, and Walter Jacob, eds. *The Healing Past: Pharmaceuticals in the Biblical and Rabbinic World.* Leiden: E. J. Brill, 1993.

James, Liz. "Color and Meaning in Byzantium." *JECS* 11 (2003): 223–33.

Jay, Nancy. *Throughout Your Generations Forever: Sacrifice, Religion and Paternity.* Chicago: University of Chicago Press, 1992.

Jennings, Theodore W. "On Ritual Knowledge." *JR* 62 (1982): 111–27.

Johansen, T. K. *Aristotle on the Sense-Organs.* Cambridge: Cambridge University Press, 1997.

John, Jeffery. "Anointing in the New Testament." In *The Oil of Gladness*, edited by Martin Dudley and Geoffrey Rowell, 46–76. London: SPCK, 1993.

Johnson, Mark. *The Body in the Mind: The Bodily Basis of Meaning, Imagination, and Reason.* Chicago: University of Chicago Press, 1987.

——— and George Lakoff. *Metaphors We Live By.* Chicago: University of Chicago Press, 1980.

Jugie, M. *La Mort et l'Assomption de la Sainte Vierge: Étude Historico-Doctrinale.* Studi e Testi 114. Città del Vaticano: Biblioteca Apostolica Vaticana, 1944.

Kaster, Robert. *Guardians of Language: The Grammarian and Society in Late Antiquity.* Berkeley: University of California Press, 1988.

Kavanaugh, Aidan. *The Shape of Baptism: The Rite of Christian Initiation.* New York: Pueblo Press, 1978.

Kelly, J. N. D. *Early Christian Creeds.* 3rd ed. London: Longman's, 1972.

Kennedy, George. *A New History of Classical Rhetoric.* Princeton: Princeton University Press, 1994.

Kenney, John Peter. "The Presence of Truth in the 'Confessions.'" SP 27, edited by Elizabeth A. Livingstone, 329–36. Leuven: Peeters Press, 1993.

Khouri-Sarkis, E. "Réception d'un évêque syrien au VIe siècle." L'Orient Syrien 2 (1957): 137–84.

King, Helen. "The Daughter of Leonides: Reading the Hippocratic Corpus." In History as Text, edited by Averil Cameron, 11–32. London: Duckworth, 1989.

Klijn, A. F. J. "An Ancient Syriac Baptismal Liturgy in the Syriac Acts of John." NT 6 (1963): 216–28. Also in Charis kai Sophia, Festschrift Karl Heinrich Rengstorf, edited by Ulrich Luck, 216–28. Leiden: E. J. Brill, 1964.

Kobal, Gerd. "Pleasure Responses of the Brain: Olfactory Evoked Potential Activity and Hedonics." In Pleasure: The Politics and the Reality, edited by David M. Warburton, 22–28. New York: John Wiley and Sons, 1994.

Kondoleon, Christine. Antioch: The Lost Ancient City. Princeton: Princeton University Press, 2000.

Kraemer, Ross Shepard. When Aseneth Met Joseph: A Late Antique Tale of the Biblical Patriarch and His Egyptian Wife, Reconsidered. New York: Oxford University Press, 1998.

Krueger, Derek. Symeon the Holy Fool: Leontius' Life and the Late Antique City. Berkeley: University of California Press, 1996.

Krüger, Paul. "Le sommeil des âmes dans l'oeuvre de Narsaï." L'Orient Syrien 4 (1959): 193–210.

Kuegel, James L. In Potiphar's House: The Interpretive Life of Biblical Texts. 2nd ed. Cambridge, MA: Harvard University Press, 1994.

Lafontaine-Dosogne, Jacqueline. Itinéraires archéologiques dans la région d'Antioche: recherches sur le monastère et sur l'iconographie de S. Syméon Stylite le Jeune. Bibliothèque de Byzantion 4. Brussels: Éditions de Byzantion, 1967.

Laistner, M. L. W. Christianity and Pagan Culture in the Later Roman Empire. Ithaca, NY: Cornell University Press, 1951.

Lallemand, Annick. "Le parfum comme signe fabuleux dans les pays mythiques." In Peuples et pays mythique, Actes du Ve Colloque du Centre Recherches Mythologiques de l'Université de Paris X, edited by François Jouan et Bernard Deforge, 73–90. Paris: Les Belles Lettres, 1988.

———. "Le Parfum des martyrs dans les Actes des martyrs de Lyon et le Martyre de Polycarpe." In SP 16. 2, edited by Elizabeth A. Livingstone, 186–92. TU 129. Berlin: Akademie Verlag, 1985.

Larson-Miller, Lizette. "Women and the Anointing of the Sick." CCR 12 (1991): 37–48.

Lattimore, Richmond. Themes in Greek and Latin Epitaphs. Urbana, IL: University of Illinois Press, 1962.

Launert, Edmund. Perfume and Pomanders: Scent and Scent Bottles. London: Potterton Books, 1987.

Ledit, J. Marie dans la Liturgie de Byzance. TH 39. Paris: Éditions Beauchesne, 1976.

Lee, Edward N. "The Sense of an Object: Epicurus on Seeing and Hearing." In *Studies in Perception*, edited by Peter Machamer and Robert Turnbull, 27–59. Columbus: Ohio University Press, 1978.

LeGuérer, Annick. *Scent: The Essential and Mysterious Power of Smell.* Translated by Richard Miller. New York: Kodansha International, 1994.

Leroy-Molinghen, Alice. "À propos de la Vie de Syméon Stylite." *Byzantion* 34 (1964): 375–84.

Levin, Saul. "The Etymology of *nectar* and exotic scents in Early Greece." *Studi Micenei ed Egeo-anatolici* 13 (1971): 31–50.

Lewis, C. S. *Letters to Malcolm: Chiefly on Prayer.* 1963; repr. New York: Harcourt, 1992.

Leyerle, Blake. "Clement of Alexandria on the Importance of Table Etiquette." *JECS* 3 (1995): 123–41.

Lilja, Saara. *The Treatment of Odours in the Poetry of Antiquity.* Commentationes Humanarum Litterarum 49. Helsinki: Societas Scientiarum Fennica, 1972.

Limberis, Vasiliki. *Divine Heiress: The Virgin Mary and the Creation of Christian Constantinople.* New York/London: Routledge, 1994.

———. "'Religion' as the Cipher for Identity: The Cases of Emperor Julian, Libanius, and Gregory of Nazianzus." *HTR* 93 (2000): 373–400.

Loerke, William. "'Real Presence' in Early Christian Art." In *Monasticism and the Arts*, edited by Timothy Gregory Verdon, 29–51. Syracuse: Syracuse University Press, 1984.

Logan, Alistair. "Post-Baptismal Chrismation in Syria: The Evidence of Ignatius, the Didache, and the Apostolic Constitutions." *JTS*, n.s., 49 (1998): 92–108.

Long, A. A. *Hellenistic Philosophy: Stoics, Epicureans, Sceptics.* 2nd ed. Berkeley: University of California Press, 1986.

——— and D. N. Sedley. *The Hellenistic Philosophers.* Vol. 1. Cambridge: Cambridge University Press, 1987.

Louth, Andrew. *Denys the Areopagite.* Wilton, CT: Morehouse-Barlow, 1989.

———. *Maximus the Confessor.* New York: Routledge, 1996.

———. *Wisdom of the Byzantine Church: Evagrius of Pontos and Maximos the Confessor.* 1997 Paine Lectures in Religion. Columbia: University of Missouri, 1998.

Lucas, A. "Cosmetics, Perfumes, and Incense in Ancient Egypt." *JEA* 16 (1930): 41–53.

Luttikhuizen, Bernard, ed. *Paradise Interpreted: Representations of Biblical Paradise in Judaism and Christianity.* Leiden: E. J. Brill, 1999.

MacCormack, Sabine. *Art and Ceremony in Late Antiquity.* Berkeley: University of California Press, 1981.

———. *The Shadows of Poetry: Vergil in the Mind of Augustine.* Berkeley: University of California Press, 1998.

MacCormick, Michael. *Eternal Victory.* Cambridge: Cambridge University Press, 1986.

MacDougall, Elisabeth B., ed. *Medieval Gardens*. Washington, DC: Dumbarton Oaks Publications, 1986.

Maguire, Eunice Dauterman, Henry P. Maguire, and Maggie J. Duncan-Flowers, eds. *Art and Holy Powers in the Early Christian House*. Urbana/Chicago: University of Illinois Press, 1989.

Mahr, A. C. *The Cyprus Passion Cycle*. Notre Dame, IN: University of Notre Dame Press, 1947.

———. *Relations of Passion Plays to St. Ephrem the Syrian*. Columbus, OH: The Wartburg Press, 1942.

Majno, Guido. *The Healing Hand: Man and Wound in the Ancient World*. Cambridge, MA: Harvard University Press, 1975.

Malherbe, Abraham. "Medical Imagery in the Pastoral Epistles." In *Texts and Testaments: Critical Essays on the Bible and Early Church Fathers in Honor of Stuart Dickson Currie*, edited by W. Eugene March, 19–35. San Antonio, TX: Trinity University Press, 1980.

———. *Moral Exhortation, A Greco-Roman Sourcebook*. Philadelphia: Westminster Press, 1986.

Mango, Cyril. *Byzantium: The Empire of New Rome*. London: Weidenfeld and Nicolson, 1980.

Manniche, Lise. *Sacred Luxuries: Fragrance, Aromatherapy, and Cosmetics in Ancient Egypt*. Ithaca, NY: Cornell University Press, 1999.

Manning, Charles. "Seneca and Roman Religious Practice." In *Religion in the Ancient World: New Themes and Approaches*, edited by Matthew Dillon, 311–19. Amsterdam: A. M. Hakkert, 1996.

Manns, Frédéric. *Le récit de la Dormition de Marie (Vatican grec 1982): Contribution à l'étude des origines de l'exégèse chrétienne*. Studium Biblicum Franciscanum Collectio Maior 33. Jerusalem: Franciscan Printing Press, 1989.

Mansour, Tanios Bou. "L'Eucharistie chez Jacques de Saroug." *Parole de l'Orient* 17 (1992): 37–60.

Martin, Dale B. *The Corinthian Body*. New Haven: Yale University Press, 1995.

Martinetz, Dieter, Karlheinz Lohs, and Jörg Janzen. *Weihrauch und Myrrhe: Kulturgeschichte und Wirtschaftliche Bedeutung, Botanik, Chemie, Medizin*. Stuttgart: Wissenschaftliche Verlagsgesellschaft mbH, 1988.

Mateos, Juan. *La célébration de la Parole dans la Liturgie byzantine: Étude historique*. OCA 191. Rome: Pontificum Institutum Studiorum Orientalium, 1971.

———. "'Sedre' et prières connexes dans quelque anciennes collections." *OCP* 28 (1962): 239–87.

Mathews, Edward G., Jr. "St. Ephrem, Madrashe on Faith, 81–5: Hymns on the Pearl, I–V." *SVTQ* 38 (1994): 45–72.

Mathews, Thomas F. *Art and Architecture in Byzantium and Armenia: Liturgical and Exegetical Approaches*. Collected Studies 510. Brookfield, VT: Variorum, 1995.

———. *The Clash of the Gods: A Reinterpretation of Early Christian Art*. Rev. ed. Princeton: Princeton University Press, 1999.

————. *The Early Churches of Constantinople: Architecture and Liturgy.* University Park, PA: Pennsylvania State University Press, 1971.

————. "'Private' Liturgy in Byzantine Architecture: Toward a Reappraisal." *Cahiers Archéologiques* 30 (1982): 125–38. [= ch. 3 in idem, *Art and Architecture in Byzantium and Armenia: Liturgical and Exegetical Approaches.* Brookfield, VT: Variorum, 1995.]

Matter, E. Ann. *The Voice of My Beloved: The Song of Songs in Western Medieval Christianity.* Philadelphia: University of Pennsylvania Press, 1990.

McDonnell, Kilian, and George T. Montague. *Christian Initiation and Baptism in the Holy Spirit: Evidence from the First Eight Centuries.* 2nd ed. Collegeville, MN: Liturgical Press, 1994.

McGinn, Bernard. *The Presence of God: A History of Western Christian Mysticism.* Vol. 1, *The Foundations of Mysticism: Origins to the Fifth Century.* New York: Crossroad, 1992.

McKay, Gretchen Kreahling. "The Eastern Christian Exegetical Tradition of Daniel's Vision of the Ancient of Days." *JECS* 7 (1999): 139–61.

McVey, Kathleen. "Images of Joy in Ephrem's Hymns on Paradise: Returning to the Womb and the Breast." *JCSSS* 3 (2003): 59–77.

Melki, J. "S. Ephrem le Syrien, un bilan de l'édition critique." *Parole de l'Orient* 11 (1983): 3–88.

Meyendorff, John. *Christ in Eastern Christian Thought.* Crestwood, NY: St. Vladimir's Seminary Press, 1975.

Miles, Margaret. *Augustine on the Body.* Missoula, MT: Scholars Press, 1979.

————. "Vision: The Eye of the Body and the Eye of the Mind in Saint Augustine's *De trinitate* and *Confessions.*" *JR* 63 (1983): 125–42.

Milik, J. T. "Hénoch au pays des aromates." *RB* 65 (1958): 70–77.

Miller, J. Innes. *The Spice Trade of the Roman Empire.* Oxford: Clarendon Press, 1969.

Miller, Patricia Cox. "'Differential Networks': Relics and Other Fragments in Late Antiquity." *JECS* 6 (1998): 113–38.

————. "'The Little Blue Flower is Red': Relics and the Poeticizing of the Body." *JECS* 8 (2000): 213–36.

Miller, William I. *The Anatomy of Disgust.* Cambridge, MA: Harvard University Press, 1997.

Mimouni, Simon C. *Dormition et Assomption de Marie. Histoire des traditions anciennes.* TH 98. Paris: Éditions Beauchesne, 1995.

————. "La Fête de la Dormition de Marie en Syrie à l'époque Byzantine." *The Harp* 5 (Kottayam, Kerala: St. Ephrem Ecumenical Research Institute, 1992): 157–74.

————. "La tradition littéraire syriaque de l'histoire de la dormition et de l'assomption de Marie." *Parole de l'Orient* 15 (1988–89): 143–68.

Moffett, Samuel Hugh. *A History of Christianity in Asia.* Vol. 1, *Beginnings to 1500.* San Franciso: HarperSanFrancisco, 1992.

Montserrat, Dominic, ed. *Changing Bodies, Changing Meanings: Studies on the Human Body in Antiquity.* New York: Routledge, 1998.

Moreau, Alain. "Le fabuleux, le divin, le parfum: Aphrodite maîtresse des odeurs." In *Saveurs, Senteurs: Le Goût de la Méditerranée*, edited by Paul Carmignani, Jean-Yves Laurichesse, and Joël Thomas, 41–58. Actes du Colloque Université de Perpignan Novembre 1997. Perpignan: Presses Universitaires, 1998.

Munier, Charles. "Initiation Chrétienne et Rites d'Onction (II–IIIe Siècles)." *RSR* 4 (1990): 115–25.

———. "Rites d'Onction Baptême Chrétien et Baptême de Jésus." *RSR* 4 (1990): 217–34.

Munro, Jill M. *Spikenard and Saffron: The Imagery of the Song of Songs*. Sheffield: Sheffield Academic Press, 1995.

Murray, Robert. "The Characteristics of the Earliest Syriac Christianity." In *East of Byzantium: Syria and Armenia in the Formative Period*, edited by Nina Garsoian, Thomas Mathews, and Robert Thomson, 3–16. Washington, DC: Dumbarton Oaks Publications, 1982.

———. "The Lance which Re-opened Paradise: A Mysterious Reading in the Early Syriac Fathers." *OCP* 39 (1973): 224–34.

———. *Symbols of Church and Kingdom: A Study in Early Syriac Tradition*. Cambridge: Cambridge University Press, 1975; rev. ed. Piscataway, NJ: Gorgias Press, 2004.

Nelson, Janet L. "Symbols in Context." In *The Orthodox Churches and the West*, edited by Derek Baker, 97–119. SCH 13. Oxford: Basil Blackwell, 1976.

Neugebauer, Karl Anton. "Die Familie Des Septimius Severus." *Die Antike* 12 (1936): 155–72.

Nichol, D. M. "*Kaiseralbung*. The Unction of Emperors in Late Byzantine Coronation Ritual." *BMGS* 2 (1976): 37–52.

Niederwimmer, Kurt. *The Didache: A Commentary*. Edited by Harold W. Attridge, translated by Linda M. Maloney. Minneapolis: Fortress Press, 1998.

Nielsen, Harald. *Ancient Ophthalmological Agents*. Odense: Odense University Press, 1974.

Nielsen, Kjeld. *Incense in Ancient Israel*. SVT 38. Leiden, E. J. Brill, 1986.

Nilsson, Martin. "Pagan Divine Service in Late Antiquity." *HTR* 38 (1945): 63–69.

Obbink, Dirk. "The Origin of Greek Sacrifice: Theophrastus on Religion and Cultural History." In *Theophrastean Studies*, edited by William W. Fortenbaugh and Robert W. Sharples, 272–95. New Brunswick, NJ: Transaction Books, 1988.

Obied, J. "L'onction baptismale dans HdE III de Saint Éphrem, Traduction et analyse." *Parole de l'Orient* 17 (1992): 7–36.

Olive, Jean-Louis. "Parfums magiques et rites de fumigations en Catalogne (de l'ethnobotanique à la hantise de l'environnement)." In *Saveurs, Senteurs: Le Goût de la Méditerranée*, edited by Paul Carmignani, Jean-Yves Laurichesse, and Joël Thomas, 145–95. Actes du Colloque Université de Perpignan Novembre 1997. Perpignan: Presses Universitaires de Perpignan, 1998.

Ouspensky, Leonid, and Vladimir Lossky. *The Meaning of Icons*. Rev. ed. Translated by G. E. H. Palmer and E. Kadloubovsky. Crestwood, NY: St. Vladimir's Seminary Press, 1982.

Palmer, Andrew, and Lyn Rodley. "The Inauguration anthem of Hagia Sophia in Edessa: A new edition and translation with historical and architectural notes and a comparison with a contemporary Constantinopolitan Kontakion." *BMGS* 12 (1988): 117–68.

Patlagean, Evelyne. *Pauvreté économique et pauvreté sociale à Byzance 4e–7e siècles*. Paris/La Haye: Mouton, 1977.

Peeters, Paul. "Un Saint Hellénisé par Annexion: Syméon Stylite." In *Orient et Byzance: Le Tréfonds Oriental de l'Hagiographie Byzantine*, edited by Paul Peeters, 93–136. SH 26. Brussels: Société des Bollandistes, 1950.

Petersen, William. "The Dependence of Romanos the Melodist upon the Syriac Ephrem: Its Importance for the Origin of the Kontakion." *VC* 39 (1985): 171–87.

——. *The Diatessaron and Ephrem Syrus as Sources of Romanos the Melodist*. CSCO 475/Sub. 74. Louvain: Peeters Press, 1985.

Petit, L. "Du pouvoir de consacrer le Saint Chrême" and "Composition et consécration du Saint Chrême." *Échoes d'Orient* 3 (1899): 1–7, 129–42.

Pettersen, Alvyn. *Athanasius and the Human Body*. Bristol: The Bristol Press, 1990.

Porter, James I., ed. *Constructions of the Classical Body*. Ann Arbor: University of Michigan Press, 1999.

Possekel, Ute. *Evidence of Greek Philosophical Concepts in the Writings of Ephrem the Syrian*. CSCO 580/Sub. 102. Louvain: Peeters Press, 1999.

Potter, David S. "Odor and Power in the Roman Empire." In *Constructions of the Classical Body*, edited by James I. Porter, 169–89. Ann Arbor: University of Michigan Press, 1999.

Price, S. R. F. *Religions of the Ancient Greeks*. Cambridge: Cambridge University Press, 1999.

——. *Rituals and Power: The Roman Imperial Cult in Asia Minor*. Cambridge: Cambridge University Press, 1984.

Quaegebeur, J., ed. *Ritual and Sacrifice in the Ancient Near East*. OLA 55. Leuven: Peeters and Departement Oriëntalistiek, 1993.

Quasten, Johannes. *Music and Worship in Pagan and Christian Antiquity*. Translated by Boniface Ramsey. Washington, DC: National Association of Pastoral Musicians, 1983.

Raes, Alphonse. "Aux origines de la fête de l'Assomption en Orient." *OCP* 12 (Rome, 1946): 262–74.

Rahner, Karl. "Le début d'une doctrine des cinq sens spirituels chez Origène." *RAM* 13 (1932): 113–45.

Riehle, Wolfgang. *The Middle English Mystics*. Translated by Bernard Standring. London: Routledge, 1981.

Riley, Hugh M. *Christian Initiation: A Comparative Study of the Interpretation of the Baptismal Liturgy in the Mystagogical Writings of Cyril of Jerusalem, John Chrysostom, Theodore of Mopsuestia, and Ambrose of Milan*. Washington, DC: Catholic University of America Press, 1974.

Robinson, Stephen E. "The Testament of Adam and the Angelic Liturgy." *RQ* 45.12 (1985): 105–10.

Rorem, Paul. *Biblical and Liturgical Symbols with the Pseudo-Dionysian Synthesis.* Toronto: Pontifical Institute for Medieval Studies, 1984.

———. *Pseudo-Dionysius: A Commentary on the Texts and an Introduction to their Influence.* New York: Oxford University Press, 1993.

Rothkrug, Lionel. "The 'Odor of Sanctity,' and the Hebrew Origins of Christian Relic Veneration." *HR/RH* 8 (1981): 95–134.

Rousselle, Aline. *Porneia: On Desire and the Body in Antiquity.* Translated by Felicia Pheasant. Oxford:Basil Blackwell, 1988.

Rowland, Christopher. "The Visions of God in Apocalyptic Literature." *JSJ* 10 (1979): 137–54.

Rozanova, N. V. *Rostov-Suzdal Painting of the 12th–16th Centuries.* Moscow: "Izobrazit. Iskussto," 1970.

Rundgren, Frithiof. "Odor Suavitatis: On the Phenomenon of Intertextuality." *OS* 36–37 (1987–88): 85–97.

Ryckmans, G. "De l'or, de l'encens, et de la myrrhe." *RB* 58 (1951): 372–76.

Sanders, E. P. *Judaism, Practice and Belief 63* B.C.E.*–60* C.E. London: SCM Press, 1992.

Saxer, Victor. "Les Saintes Marie Madeleine et Marie de Béthanie dans la tradition liturgique et homilétique orientale." *RSR* 32 (1958): 1–37.

Schab, Frank R., and Robert G. Crowder, eds. *Memory for Odors.* Mahwah, NJ: Lawrence Erlbaum Associates, 1995.

Schamp, Jacques. "La Mort en Fleurs: Considérations sur la maladie 'pédiculaire' de Scylla." *L'Antiquité Classique* 60 (1991): 139–70.

Schiffman, Harvey Richard. *Sensation and Perception: An Integrated Approach.* 2nd ed. New York: John Wiley and Sons, 1982.

Schiffman, Lawrence H. "Communal Meals at Qumran." *RQ* 10 (1979): 45–56.

Schmidt, Margot, and C. Geyer, eds. *Typus, Symbol, Allegorie bei den östlichen Vätern und ihren Parallelen im Mittelalter.* Regensburg: Friedrich Pustet, 1982.

Schoff, Wilfred H. "Aloes." *JAOS* 42 (1922): 171–85.

———. "Cinnamon, Cassia, and Somaliland." *JAOS* 40 (1920): 260–70.

Schultz, Hans-Joachim. *The Byzantine Liturgy: Symbolic Structure and Faith Expression.* Translated by Matthew J. O'Connell. New York: Pueblo Publishing, 1986.

Schwartz, Jacques. "Les Voyages au Ciel dans la littérature apocalyptique." In *L'Apocalyptique: Études d'histoire des religions 3,* edited by M. Philonenko and M. Simon, 91–126. Paris: Paul Geuthner, 1977.

Scott, Jamie, and Paul Simpson-Housley, eds. *Sacred Places and Profane Spaces: Essays in the Geographics of Judaism, Christianity, and Islam.* Westport, CT: Greenwood Press, 1991.

Sed, N. "Les Hymnes sur le Paradis de Saint Ephrem et les traditions Juives." Le Muséon 81 (1968): 455–501.

Seiler, Thomas H. "Filth and Stench as Aspects of the Iconography of Hell." In The Iconography of Hell, edited by Clifford Davidson and Thomas H. Seiler, 132–40. Kalamazoo: Medieval Institute Publications, 1992.

Serby, M. J., and K. L. Chobor, eds. Science of Olfaction. New York: Springer-Verlag, 1992.

Shaw, Teresa M. The Burden of the Flesh: Fasting and Sexuality in Early Christianity. Minneapolis: Fortress Press, 1998.

Shelmerdine, Cynthia Wright. The Perfume Industry of Mycenaean Pylos. SMAP 34. Göteborg: Paul Aströms Förlag, 1985.

———. "Shining and Fragrant Cloth in Homeric Epic." In The Ages of Homer: A Tribute to Emily Townsend Vermeule, edited by Jane B. Carter and Sarah P. Morris, 99–107. Austin: University of Texas Press, 1995.

Sheridan, Mark. "The Development of the Interior Life of Certain Early Monastic Writings in Egypt." In The Spirituality of Ancient Monasticism, edited by Marek Starowieyski, 79–89. Acts of the International Colloquium, Cracow-Tyniec 16–19 Nov. 1994. Cracow-Tyniec: Wydawnictwo-Benedyktynów, 1995.

Shoemaker, Stephen J. Ancient Traditions of the Virgin Mary's Dormition and Assumption. Oxford: Oxford University Press, 2002.

Siegel, Rudolph E. Galen on Sense Perception. New York: S. Karger, 1970.

Siman, Emmanuel-Pataq. L'Expérience de l'Ésprit par l'église d'après la tradition syrienne d'Antioche. TH 15. Paris: Éditions Beauchesne, 1971.

Smith, G. Elliot. "Incense and Libations." BJRL 4 (1917–18): 191–262.

Smith, Robert Houston. "'Bloom of Youth': a Labelled Syro-Palestinian Unguent Jar." JHS 112 (1992): 163–67.

Smollich, Renate. Der Bisamapfel in Kunst und Wissenschaft. Stuttgart: Deutscher Apotheker Verlag, 1983.

Soskice, Janet Martin. Metaphor and Religious Language. Oxford: Clarendon Press, 1985.

Staniloae, Dumitru. Theology and the Church. Translated by Robert Barringer. Crestwood, NY: St. Vladimir's Seminary Press, 1980.

Stannard, Jerry. "Alimentary and Medicinal Uses of Plants." In Medieval Gardens, edited by Elisabeth MacDougall, 69–91. Washington, DC: Dumbarton Oaks Publications, 1986.

Stewart, Columba. "Imageless Prayer and the Theological Vision of Evagrius Ponticus." JECS 9 (2001): 173–204.

———. 'Working the Earth of the Heart': The Messalian Controversy in History, Texts, and Language to A.D. 431. Oxford: Clarendon Press, 1991.

Stoddart, D. M. "The Senses: Meeting Biological Needs." In Tastes and Aromas: The Chemical Senses in Science and Industry, edited by Graham A. Bell and Annesley J. Watson, 1–11. Oxford/Sydney: Blackwell Science Ltd. and University of New South Wales Press, 1999.

Stone, Michael, and Theodore A. Bergren, eds. *Biblical Figures Outside the Bible.* Harrisburg, PA: Trinity Press International, 1998.

Stowers, Stanley K. "Greeks Who Sacrifice and Those Who Do Not: Towards an Anthropology of Greek Religion." In *The Social World of the First Christians: Essays in Honor of Wayne A. Meeks,* edited by L. Michael White and Larry A. Yarbrough, 293–333. Minneapolis: Fortress Press, 1995.

———. "On the Comparison of Blood in Greek and Israelite Ritual." In *Hesed Ve-Emet: Studies in Honor of Ernest S. Frerichs,* edited by Jodi Magness and Seymour Gitin, 179–94. Atlanta: Scholars Press, 1998.

———. "Paul and Self-Mastery." In *Paul in the Greco-Roman World: A Handbook,* edited by J. Paul Sampley, 524–50. Harrisburg, PA: Trinity Press International, 2003.

———. "Paul and Slavery: A Response." *Semeia* 83/84 (1998): 295–311.

———. *A Re-Reading of Romans: Justice, Jews, and Gentiles.* New Haven: Yale University Press, 1994.

———. "4 Maccabees." In *Harper's Bible Commentary,* edited by James L. Mays, 922–34. San Francisco: Harper and Row, 1988.

Stratton, George M. *Theophrastus and the Greek Physiological Psychology Before Aristotle.* New York: MacMillan, 1917.

Strothmann, W. *Das Sakrament der Myron-Weihe in der Schrift De ecclesiastica hierarchia des Pseudo-Dionysius Areopagita.* Göttinger Orientforschungen, Reihe I, Band 15. Wiesbaden: Otto Harrassowitz, 1977–78.

Synnott, Anthony. *The Body Social: Symbolism, Self and Society.* London/New York: Routledge, 1993.

Taft, Robert. *A History of the Liturgy of St. John Chrysostom.* Vol. 2, *The Great Entrance: A History of the Transfer of Gifts and Other Pre-anaphoral Rites.* 2nd ed. OCA 200. Rome: Pontificum Institutum Studiorum Orientalium, 1978.

———. "The Liturgy of the Great Church: An Initial Synthesis of Structure and Interpretation on the Eve of Iconoclasm." *DOP* 34–35 (1980–81): 45–75.

———. "Toward the Origins of the Offertory Procession in the Syro-Byzantine East." *OCP* 36 (1970): 73–107.

Tchalenko, George. *Villages Antiques de la Syrie du Nord.* Vol. 1. Paris: Geunther, 1953.

Thekeparampil, Jacob. "Prayers After Incense." *Parole de l'Orient* 6/7 (1975–76): 325–40.

———. "Weihrauchsymbolik in den syrischen gebeten des mittelalters und bei pseudo-Dionysius." In *Typus, Symbol, Allegorie,* edited by Margot Schmidt and C. Geyer, 131–45. Regensburg: Friedrich Pustet, 1982.

Thomas, Joël. "La nourriture d'immortalité en Grèce et à Rome." In *Saveurs, Senteurs,* edited by Paul Carmignani, Jean-Yves Laurichesse, and Joël Thomas, 13–22. Perpignan: Presses Universitaires de Perpignan, 1998.

Thunberg, Lars. *Microcosm and Mediator.* Lund: C. W. K. Gleerup, 1965.

Trifonova, Anna. *The Russian Icon of the Novgorod Museum Collection.* St. Petersberg: Madoc, 1992.

Tripolitis, Antonia. *Kassia: The Legend, the Woman, and her Work.* New York: Garland Publishing, 1992.

Trombley, Frank. *Hellenic Religion and Christianization, c. 370–529.* 2nd ed. 2 vols. Boston/Leiden: Brill Academic Publishers, 2001.

Trout, Dennis. "Christianizing the Nolan Countryside: Animal Sacrifice at the Tomb of St. Felix." JECS 3 (1995): 281–98.

———. *Paulinus of Nola: Life, Letters, and Poems.* Berkeley: University of California Press, 1999.

Turnbull, Robert G. "The Role of the 'Special Sensibles' in the Perception Theories of Plato and Aristotle." *Studies in Perception,* edited by Peter Machamer and Robert Turnbull, 3–26. Columbus: Ohio University Press, 1978.

Van Beek, Gus W. "Frankincense and Myrrh." *The Biblical Archaeologist* 23 (1960): 70–95.

van Esbroeck, Michel. *Aux origines de la Dormition de la Vierge: Études historiques sur les traditions orientales.* Variorum Collected Studies Series CS 472. Brookfield, VT/Aldershot, Hampshire: Ashgate Publishing, 1995.

———. "Le culte de la Vierge de Jérusalem à Constantinople aux 6e–7e siècles." REB 46 (1988): 181–90.

van Raalte, Marlien. "The Idea of the Cosmos as an Organic Whole in Theophrastus' *Metaphysics.*" In *Theophrastean Studies,* edited by William W. Fortenbaugh and Robert W. Sharples, 189–215. New Brunswick, NJ: Transaction Books, 1988.

Van Rompay, Lucas. "Memories of Paradise: The Greek 'Life of Adam and Eve' and Early Syriac Tradition." *Aram* 5 (1993): 555–70.

van Ruiten, J. T. A. G. M. "Eden and the Temple: The Rewriting of Genesis 2:4–3:24 in the Book of Jubilees." In *Paradise Interpreted: Representations of Biblical Paradise in Judaism and Christianity,* edited by Bernard Luttikhuizen, 63–94. Leiden: E. J. Brill.

Van Toller, Steven. "The Enjoyment of Smells: Central Autonomic and Trigeminal Interactions in Odour Perception." In *Pleasure: The Politics and the Reality,* edited by David M. Warburton, 15–21. New York: John Wiley and Sons, 1994.

Van Toller, C., G. H. Dodd, and Anne Billing, eds. *Ageing and the Sense of Smell.* Springfield, IL: Charles C. Thomas, 1985.

Varghese, B. *Les onctions baptismales dans la tradition syrienne.* CSCO 512/Subs. 82. Louvain: Peeters Press, 1989.

Vernant, Jean-Pierre. *Myth and Society in Ancient Greece.* Translated by Janet Lloyd. New York: Zone Books, 1990.

Vikan, Gary. "Art and Marriage in Early Byzantium." DOP 44 (1990): 145–63. [= Ch. 10 in idem, *Sacred Images and Sacred Power in Byzantium*].

———. "Art, Medicine, and Magic in Early Byzantium." DOP 38 (1984): 65–86. [= Ch. 9 in idem, *Sacred Images and Sacred Power in Byzantium*].

———. *Byzantine Pilgrimage Art*. Dumbarton Oaks Byzantine Collection Publications 5. Washington, DC: Dumbarton Oaks Publications, 1982.

———. "Icons and Icon Piety in Early Byzantium." In *Byzantine East, Latin West: Art-Historical Studies in Honor of Kurt Weitzmann*, edited by Christopher Moss and Katherine Kiefer, 569–76. Princeton: Dept. of Art and Archaeology, Princeton University, 1995. [= Ch. 2 in idem, *Sacred Images and Sacred Power in Byzantium*].

———. *Sacred Images and Sacred Power in Byzantium*. Variorum Collected Studies Series CS 778. Aldershot, Hampshire: Ashgate Publishing, 2003.

Villagomez, Cynthia. "The Fields, Flocks, and Finances of Monks: Economic Life at Nestorian Monasteries, 500–850." PhD. diss., University of California Los Angeles, 1998.

Vivian, Tim. "Words to Live By: *A Conversation that the Elders Had with One Another Concerning Thoughts (Peri Logismon)*." *SVTQ* 39 (1995): 127–41.

Vlachos, Hierotheos. *A Night in the Desert of the Holy Mountain: Discussion With a Hermit on the Jesus Prayer*. Translated by Effie Mavromichali. Levadia, Greece: Birth of Theotokos Monastery, 1991.

von Staden, Heinrich. "The Stoic Theory of Perception and its 'Platonic' Critics." In *Studies in Perception*, edited by Peter Machamer and Robert Turnbull, 96–136. Columbus: Ohio University Press, 1978.

Vööbus, Arthur. *Liturgical Traditions in the Didache*. PETSE 16. Stockholm: ETSE, 1968.

Wallace-Hadrill, D. S. *The Greek Patristic View of Nature*. New York: Barnes and Noble, 1968.

Walter, Christopher. "The Significance of Unction in Byzantine Iconography." BMGS 2 (1976): 53–74.

Warburton, David M., ed. *Pleasure: The Politics and the Reality*. New York: John Wiley and Sons, 1994.

Ward, Benedicta. *Harlots of the Desert: A Study of Repentance in Early Monastic Sources*. Kalamazoo: Cistercian Publications, 1987.

Ware, Kallistos. "'My helper and my enemy': The Body in Greek Christianity." In *Religion and the Body*, edited by Sarah Coakley, 90–110. Cambridge: Cambridge University Press, 1997.

Wharton, Annabel. *Refiguring the Post Classical City: Dura Europos, Jerash, and Ravenna*. Cambridge: Cambridge University Press, 1995.

Wickham, Lionel. "Symbols of the Incarnation in Cyril of Alexandria." In *Typus, Symbol, Allegorie bei den östlichen Vätern und ihren Parallelen im Mittelalter*, edited by Margot Schmidt and C. Geyer, 41–53. Regensburg: Friedrich Pustet, 1982.

Wilken, Robert. *The Christians as the Romans Saw Them*. 2nd ed. New Haven: Yale University Press, 2003.

Wilkinson, John. "Jewish Holy Places and the Origins of Christian Pilgrimage." In *The Blessings of Pilgrimage*, edited by Robert Ousterhout, 41–53. Urbana, IL: University of Illinois Press, 1990.

Wilson, Liz. *Charming Cadavers: Horrific Figurations of the Feminine in Indian Buddhist Hagiographic Literature*. Chicago: University of Chicago Press, 1996.

Wimbush, Vincent L., and Richard Valantasis, eds. *Asceticism*. New York: Oxford University Press, 1995.

Winkler, John J. *The Constraints of Desire: The Anthropology of Sex and Gender in Ancient Greece*. New York: Routledge, 1990.

Witakowski, Witold. "The Origin of the 'Teaching of the Apostles.'" *IV Symposium Syriacum*, edited by H. J. W. Drijvers, R. Lavenant, C. Molenberg, and G. J. Reinink, 161–71. OCA 229. Rome: Pontificum Institutum Studiorum Orientalium. 1987.

Wolfson, Elliot R. *Through a Speculum that Shines: Vision and Imagination in Medieval Jewish Mysticism*. Princeton: Princeton University Press, 1994.

Wolfson, Harry Austryn. "The Internal Senses in Latin, Arabic, and Hebrew Philosophic Texts." *HTR* 28 (1935): 69–133.

Wyke, Maria. "Woman in the Mirror: The Rhetoric of Adornment in the Roman World." In *Women in Ancient Societies: 'An illusion of the night,'* edited by Léonie Archer, Susan Fischler, and Maria Wyke, 134–51. New York: Routledge, 1994.

Yarnold, Edward. *The Awe-Inspiring Rites of Initiation: The Origins of the RCIA*. 2nd ed. Collegeville, MN: Liturgical Press, 1994.

Young, Frances. *Biblical Exegesis and the Formation of Christian Culture*. Cambridge: Cambridge University Press, 1997.

Young, Robin Darling. *In Procession Before the World: Martyrdom as Public Liturgy in Early Christianity*. Milwaukee: Marquette University Press, 2001.

Youngentob, S. L. "Introduction to the Sense of Smell: Understanding Odours from the Study of Human and Animal Behaviour." In *Tastes and Aromas*, edited by Graham A. Bell and Annesley J. Watson, 23–37. Oxford/Sydney: Blackwell Science Ltd. and University of South Wales Press, 1999.

Yousif, P. *L'Eucharistie chez Saint Éphrem de Nisibe*. OCA 224. Rome: Pontificum Institutum Studiorum Orientalium, 1984.

———. "Le sacrifice et l'offrande chez Saint Éphrem de Nisibe." *Parole de l'Orient* 15 (1988–89): 21–40.

———. "St. Ephrem on Symbols in Nature: Faith, the Trinity, and the Cross (Hymns on Faith, No. 18)." *ECR* 10 (1978): 52–60.

———. "Le Symbolisme de la croix dans la nature chez Saint Éphrem de Nisibe." In *Symposium Syriacum 1976*, edited by René Lavenant, 207–27. OCA 205. Rome: Pontificum Institutum Studiorium Orientalium, 1978.

Zaidman, Louise Bruit, and Pauline Schmitt Pantel, eds. *Religion in the Ancient Greek City*. Translated by Paul Cartledge. Cambridge: Cambridge University Press, 1992.

Zornberg, Avivah Gottlieb. *Genesis: The Beginning of Desire*. Philadelphia: Jewish Publication Society, 1995.

INDEX OF BIBLICAL CITATIONS

Where citations and discussion require both text and back note, the text page is given first, with the related note in parentheses.

Old Testament

Genesis

1–2	50, 111
1–3	322n.4
2:7	260n.37
2:4–3:24	323.n.14
4:3–5	15
6:4	254n.147
8:20–9:1	15
8:21	311n.194
22	127
25:1–2	45
27:27	99, 163, 299n.26
38:13–26	127
39: 41–45	127

Exodus

24:9–18	169–70 (301n.53)
29:7	67

Psalms

6	320n.116
22	247n.34
37:6 (LXX 38:6)	45
38	320n.116
38:5	208 (316n.61)
42:5	232
45:7–8 (LXX 44:7–8)	119
46:11	234
51:17 (LXX 50:17)	24
88	320n.116
102:9	213
133:2 (LXX 132:2)	67, 119, 142 (292n.173)
141:2 (LXX 140:2)	14, 28, 76, 119, 199 (311n.194)

Proverbs

7:17–18	33 (252n.111)

Song of Songs

1:3	117, 119, 285n.80, 122–23, 125, 142 (292n.173),168, 173 (303n.68)
1:4	142 (292n.173), 173 (303n.68)
1:12	173 (303n.70)
1:13	177
2:1	123, 125
2:13	174
4–5	283n.41
4:11	128 (288n.112), 168
4:12	325 n.23
4:14	256n.177
4:16	324n.17
5:5	128 (288n.112)
8:2	163

Isaiah

1:12–17	249n.65
3:24	288n.104
6:1–7	169 (301n.53)
11:3	287n.100
64:4	230 (327n.43)

Ezekiel

1:1–28	169–70 (301n.53)

Daniel

3	167
4:33	185 (306n.119)
7:1–28	169–70 (301n.53)

Amos

5:21–27	249n.65
6:6	256n.177

Jonah

3	165 (300n.35)

Malachi

1:11	21

Apocryphal/Deuterocanonical Books

Tobit

2:7–10	319n.108
6:1–8, 15–17	319n.108
8:1–3	319n.108
11:9–15	319n.108

Judith

10:1–5	33 (252n.111)

Wisdom

7:25	117
13:5	327n.41

Sirach

24:1–21	18 (247n.41), 47
39:12–16	18 (247n.41), 48

3 Maccabees

5	32 (251n.102)

4 Maccabees

15:19	317n.69

New Testament

Matthew

2:1–11	33, 254n.138
3:1–4	185 (306n.118)
3:16	12
4:1–11	185 (306n.118)
5:4	307n.132
5:8	302n.53, 307n.132
5:13	210
11:12	318n.82
17:1–8	169 (301n.53)
19:21	307n.132
25:1–13	84
26:6–7	18
26:6–13	148, 150

Mark

1:3	184
1:10	12
5:24–34	227
6:13	66
9:2–8	169–70 (301n.53)
14:3–9	148, 321n.121

Luke

3:22	12
4:18	66, 67
4:28–30	128
6:21, 25	307n.132

Ephesians

3:16	170 (302n.57)
5:2	18
6:16	30

Philippians

2:17	18 (247n.38)
3:4–8	312n.5
4:18	18 (247n.37)

2 Timothy

1:15	177
4:6	247n.38
4:10	177
4:14	177

Hebrews

1:3	117
11:38	185

James

5:14–15	66

1 John

2:20	66
2:27	66

Revelation

2:10	43
5:8	18
6:2	43
8:3–5	18
10:1	43
21–22	235

Ambrose of Milan (continued)
allegory, 163. Works: "Concerning
Virgins," 167–68; "Death as a Good,"
231; "Flight from the World," 161;
The Holy Spirit, 119–20, 122–25
Ammonas (monk), 129
Ampullae, in pilgrimage, 326n31
Anahid (martyr), 270n158
Angels, scent of, 129
Animals: in ancient science, 278n3; dis-
section of, 278n2; sense perception
in, 101
Animal sacrifice: food from, 14; Lucian
on, 13; odor of, 246n19;
Theophrastus on, 23; in Torah, 17.
See also Blood sacrifice
Annunciation, 183–84; as olfactory
event, 92, 93; in *Transitus Mariae*, 92,
93, 275n209, 276n218
Anointment: apotropaic, 69–70; in baptism, 67–73, 120, 121–22, 133, 164,
285n73; against demons, 69–70; in
early Christian communities, 18;
Germanus on, 142–43; *hatma* (seal)
of, 70; of King David, 130; of nostrils, 71; in Old Testament, 67, 121;
olfactory aspects of, 67; post-baptismal, 264n82; of sick, 294n197. *See
also* Oil, holy
Anthropology, senses in, 5
Antiquity: bad odors of, 209; contemplative life in, 170; modes of
knowledge in, 100; sacrifice in,
13–14; sensory experience in,
100–105; sensory perception in,
4–5; sexuality in, 297n2; view of
corporeality, 102. *See also* Paganism;
Science, ancient
Antony the Great, Saint, 301n43;
Athanasius's *Life* of, 130, 307n132;
conversion of, 307n132
Antonios (monk): *Life of Simeon*, 186,
190–92, 320n110; olfactory tropes
of, 190–92, 194, 215
Aphraphat (Persian sage): bodily
imagery of, 182–83; *Demonstration I*,
182–83; on fragrance, 165, 204

Apocalypse, Christian, 323n12;
ineffability of, 225
Apocalypse of Paul, 169
Apollo, sacrifice to, 244n6
Apollonius of Tyana, 14
Apostates: as incense-burners, 20; odor
of, 126–27
Apostles: at Mary's Dormition, 96;
ministration to soul, 210–11
Apostolic Constitutions, 28; incense in, 77;
myron in, 68–69
Apples, fragrance of, 178
Arabian peninsula, spice manufacture
in, 35
Architecture, church:
post-Constantinian, 58, 76
Aristides, 38
Aristotle, 4; on animal senses, 101; on
epistemology of, 283n49; on olfac-
tion, 103–4; on sense perception,
102, 103, 104, 110; Theoprastus
and, 279n12
Arius, death of, 207
Ark of the covenant, offerings before, 15
Arnobius of Sicca, on idols, 207
Aromatics, ancient: Christian use of,
36–37; in funeral practices, 42, 85;
hygienic, 41; manufacture and
trade, 32–36; Pliny the Elder on,
33–35; in Roman life, 30–31;
Tertullian on, 36–37. *See also* Euodia;
Fragrance
Arsenius, Abba, 213
Art, church: post-Constantinian, 58
Artists' stamps, 60, 259n15
Asceticism: biblical basis of, 167–68,
216, 301n50, 305n108; discourse
of, 8; diversity of, 167; embodiment in liturgy, 164, 181–86;
fragrance of, 129–30, 205,
301n44; hagiography of, 196;
incense use in, 83, 95, 186, 201;
internal senses in, 180; mourning
in, 212; olfactory imagery in, 167–79,
198; and post-Constantinian liturgy,
181; pre-Constantinian, 164;
rhetoric of, 157, 162;

religion, 57; in urban topography, 76, 267n110; violence within, 57; visual culture of, 235

Christianity, Byzantine, 146–47; icons in, 87, 209, 292n171; incense use in, 141; monasticism in, 180; olfactory piety in, 228

Christianity, early: austerity in, 2, 6, 48; biblical imagery in, 181; extra-canononical texts of, 48–56; heresy in, 315n52; holy oil in, 66–69; olfactory experience in, 4, 6, 7, 34, 36; olfactory piety in, 232; orthodoxy in, 315n52; religious imagination of, 230; sacrifice in, 17–21, 79, 181; sense perception in, 99, 106; smells in, 1–5, 239; social milieu of, 21–22, 30, 37

Christianity, post-Constantinian: celibacy in, 157; church architecture of, 58, 76; continuity with early Christianity, 57; epistemology of, 229; incense piety in, 20–21; olfactory practices of, 46, 58, 122, 239; pageantry in, 158; pilgrimage in, 58; public practice of, 57; rituals of, 6–7; sensory engagement of, 2–3, 58, 225; socio-political power of, 57–58; use of classical *paideia*, 284n62; visual piety in, 241n3. *See also* Liturgy, post-Constantinian

Christianity, Syriac: in Dionysius the Areopagite's thought, 264n89; dyophysite, 146; incense in, 5, 77, 146; under Islam, 146; miaphysite, 146–47, 294n193; myron in, 71, 145–46, 197; mystics, 197–98; olfactory experience in, 5, 182, 197–200; olfactory piety in, 182, 197, 199–200; olfactory symbolism in, 95; olive oil in, 73; post-baptismal anointment in, 264n82; prayer in, 198–99; Sinful Woman in, 148–55. *See also* Asceticism, Syriac

Christianity, Western: resurrected body in, 327n49; sensory models of, 241n3

Christians: as aroma of Christ, 115; importance of body for, 111; ritual memory of, 135; Satan's attacks against, 299n19; socio-political power of, 122

Christians, early: marriage with pagans, 37; in Roman society, 21–22, 30, 37; unsuitable professions for, 38

Christians, lay: role of smells for, 97, 98; sensory experiences of, 160

Christology, 59; incense in, 142, 148; odor and source in, 118; Virgin Mary in, 96, 275n200

Church, as Bride, 124, 142. *See also* Song of Songs

Churches, post-Constantinian, 86; architecture of, 58, 76; furnishings of, 84

Church of the East, 146; in Persian Empire, 294n193

Cicero: on human body, 312n5; on senses, 104, 278n4; on skepticism, 280n25; on Stoicism, 280n25

Cinnamon, power of, 178

Circumcision, Origen on, 45

Citron, 33

Civic time, Christianization of, 258n3

Cleansing, rituals of, 16, 200

Clement of Alexandria: *Christ the Educator*, 299n20, 300n29; on divine self-sufficiency, 26; on flowers, 43; on funeral rites, 85; on incense, 31; medical knowledge of, 110; on olfactory danger, 161; on perfumes, 40, 41–42, 100; on physical experience, 59; on sacrifice, 17, 24–25; on self-control, 40, 42; on sensory experience, 39, 43, 46, 150, 158, 159; on table etiquette, 39, 254n152; on wreaths, 42

Communities, Christian: anointings in, 18; discord in, 315n52; effect of stench on, 221; smells in, 97, 196, 200

Community, role of sacrifice in, 13

Constantinople, Council of, 285n70

Consubstantiality, 116–18, 119; in incarnation theology, 156

Coronations, imperial, 290n147

Dualism: Augustine's, 107, 109; Cartesian, 170–71; Platonic, 170
Dung: medicinal use of, 202, 312n7; Mosaic law as, 312n5
Dyophysites: in Persia, 294n193; in Syriac Christianity, 146

Ecclesiology, Gregory of Nyssa's, 177
Eden: expulsion from, 324n17; fragrance of, 50; in Jewish extracanonical literature, 324n17; as temple, 323n14. *See also* Paradise
Edessa: martyrs of, 77, 270n158, 317n69; theological school of, 294n193
Egeria (pilgrim), 77, 84
Egyptians, incense offerings of, 14
Ekstasis, from body, 170
Eleazar b. Diglai, R., 16
Elijah of Amida, 82
Embalming: ancient, 202; of Christ, 326n33
Encolpia (reliquaries), 228, 326n31
Enkrateia (self-mastery), 158
I *Enoch*, olfactory experience in, 49–50, 52
III *Enoch*, 324n17
Ephrem the Syrian, 60–62; bodily imagery of, 182–83; on body and soul, 63–64; on Bread of Life, 64; on Christ's healing, 219; on Eucharist, 132–33, 236, 260n28; on fragrance, 152, 165, 197; on Fragrance of Life, 64–65, 79, 81, 132, 133, 236; on fragrance of paradise, 203, 221, 235–39, 309n169; on Fragrance of scripture, 203; hymns on bishops, 268n134; on incarnation, 128; on incense, 78–81; on Jonah, 82; on Mary of Bethany, 315n45; on Medicine of Life, 236; on natural beauty, 86; olfactory sensation in, 127, 309n169; on resurrection, 232, 236–37; and Romanos, 296n217; on sacrifice, 267n128; on sanctified body, 62–63; on scripture, 259n13; on sense perception, 238, 260n23;

on sensory experience, 83, 212, 282n49; on Sinful Woman, 150–51, 154; on souls of the dead, 232; on stench of mortality, 132. Works: *Homily on Our Lord*, 152; *Hymns on Faith*, 259n17; *Hymns on Fasting*, 290n141; *Hymns on Julian Saba*, 79 (authorship of, 268n130; incense piety in, 79, 268n131); *Hymns on Paradise*, 233, 235–38, 328n65; *Prose Refutations*, 283n49
Epicureans: epistemology of, 279n14; on sense perdeption, 102, 103, 110
Epiphany Hymns (ps.-Ephrem), 289n124; baptismal anointing in, 133; olfactory themes in, 290n141
Epistemology: Aristotelian, 283n49; Epicurean, 279n14; Platonic, 283n49; Stoic, 279n14, 283n49
Epistemology, religious: Augustine's, 233; bodily rewards in, 141; codification of, 135; Gregory of Nyssa's, 230; in liturgical commentaries, 135; olfactory experience in, 99–100, 108; olfactory practice in, 156; perfume in, 154; post-Constantinian, 229; of spiritual senses, 303n66; senses in, 4, 5, 7, 110
Eschatology, 224; olfactory imagination in, 221
Eternity. *See* Afterlife; Paradise
'Etro (incense vapor), 147
Eucharist: apotropaic power of, 133, 134; dead souls at, 231; effect on body, 210; effect on sensory experience, 64; Ephrem on, 132–33, 236, 260n28; fragrance of, 133; Gregory of Nyssa on, 260n28; incense during, 138, 326n33; liturgy of, 72, 138, 139; as "Medicine of Life," 81; olfactory imagery in, 72; sacrifice in, 151; sanctification through, 62–63; Simeon the Stylite the Younger's celebration of, 195
Eunapius, 14
Euodia (aroma), Paul the apostle on, 18, 19. *See also* Fragrance; Scents

Heaven. *See* Paradise

Hecate, statues of, 244n6

Helena (mother of Constantine), 65

Hell: Christian traditions of, 316n65; olfactory definition of, 223

Heraclitus, on olfaction, 322n6

Heresy: association with disease, 315n52; stench of, 207

Heretics: death of, 207; stench of, 65, 208

Herod of Judea, death of, 208–9

Heroes, cults of, 325n26

Herodotus, on laudanum, 256n186

Hesychius (monk), 287n100

Hierapolis, temple of, 14

Hilarion (monk), 126, 287n100

Hippolytus, *Apostolic Tradition*, 67, 70

History of the Blessed Virgin Mary (Budge), 274n199, 276n209, 277nn221,226

History of the Virgin Mary in Five Books (Smith Lewis), 91, 274nn197,199, 276n218–19, 277nn221,226; corruption of, 94

History of the Virgin Mary in Six Books (Wright), 91, 274nn197,199, 276n219, 277n226. *See also Transitus Mariae*

Holocaust (burnt offering), 14, 17; Origen on, 28; smell of, 86. *See also* Sacrifice

Holy Spirit: Ambrose on, 119–20; anointment with, 120, 121; association with myron, 293n184; chrism symbolism of, 271n179; fragrance of, 53, 89, 121, 129, 142, 271n179; as holy oil, 121; in *Transitus Mariae*, 275n209; within Trinity, 119; as unguent, 285n73, 300n29

Homilies: catechetical, 134; incense in, 90; sensory experience in, 7; scents in, 66; Syriac, 149–50

Housekeeping, spiritual, 183, 211, 306n112

Human-divine interaction: in Bible, 107, 225; body in, 182, 223, 300n31; fragrance in, 93, 202; in hagiography, 196; holy oil in, 71–73; incense in, 6, 55, 74, 77, 80–81,

96–97, 187; in Mediterranean world, 222; olfaction in, 173; in paganism, 282n34; perfume in, 55, 152, 304n77; physiological experience of, 173; power in, 77; in ritual, 155; sacrifice in, 52; sense perception in, 238, 282n34, 303n63; smells in, 3, 72, 99, 223, 224; in Song of Songs, 124, 170, 286n92; in *Transitus Mariae*, 91–92

Human relations, smells in, 2

Humility, monastic, 213

Hymnography: sensory imagery in, 4, 7–8; Syriac, 150, 197

Iconoclasts, 87, 209

Icons: in Byzantine Christianity, 87, 209, 292n171; myrrh-gushing, 180

Icon veneration, pagan models for, 267n109

Identity: personal odor in, 127; role of sacrifice in, 13

Identity, Christian: in daily life, 36–38; olfactory experience in, 3, 7, 12, 58, 125–34; Paul on, 105; of resurrected body, 229; in ritual celebrations, 87; sensory danger in, 157

Idolatry, 87; Jerome on, 86

Idols, moral revulsion against, 207

Ignatius of Antioch, 18–19

Illness: association with heresy, 315n52; biblical models of, 216–17; care of, 214; in hagiography, 319n109; incense burning during, 83; of saints, 216–17, 220; salvation following, 220; smells of, 201, 216

Immortality: fragrance of, 168; olfactory codes in, 32; symbolism of, 70

Incarnation, 171; Christ's submission to, 218–19; consubstantiality in, 156; Ephrem the Syrian on, 128; in Greek philosophical tradition, 327n40; knowledge of God through, 259n13; material world in, 87–88; myron imagery in, 145; physical reality of, 106;

sanctification through, 62; sense perception in, 127–28; in Sinful Woman story, 152; Theodoret on, 219; theology of, 113, 156, 230, 327n40

Incense, 75–83; as access to God, 52; ancient market for, 34; in *Apostolic Constitutions*, 77; in asceticism, 83, 95, 186, 201; Assyrian use of, 269n150; ban on, 76, 258n3; biblical texts on, 40, 147; in Byzantine liturgy, 141; Christian imagery of, 29, 82; in Christian ritual, 2, 75–83, 299n21; in Christology, 142, 148; in church sanctuaries, 138, 139; composition of, 27, 28, 30; in Day of Atonement, 15, 17; in death and burial, 75, 82; as dialogic device, 96; Egyptian use of, 14; in Ephrem the Syrian's works, 78–81; during Eucharist, 138, 326n33; in forgiveness of sins, 147; in funerals, 75; good works as, 28; Hellenistic use of, 245n8; in homilies, 66, 90; in human-divine relations, 6, 55, 74, 77, 80–81, 96–97, 187; in human sensorium, 187; during illness, 83; instructional capacity of, 147; in Jerusalem Temple, 15–17; in Judaism, 14, 15–17, 246n22, 272n181; knowledge of God through, 148; in liturgical commentaries, 135–36; liturgical use of, 75, 76–78, 326n33; at martyrs' shrines, 161; in Mediterranean culture, 77; merchants, 26; offerings in prayer, 147–48, 188; offerings to sun, 253n125; olfactory dimensions of, 29; pagan use of, 25, 78; Philo on, 22–23; in pilgrimage, 89, 268n143; post-Constantinian use of, 2, 7, 20–21, 135; as prayer, 14, 17, 27, 31, 81, 92; prayers following, 294n197; in processions, 75, 266n105; psalmody as, 82; in public ceremonies, 75; recipes for, 15; in sacred narratives, 90–91; as

sacrifice, 175; in sacrifice, 6, 13–14, 74, 81, 89, 96; in Simeon the Stylite the Elder's cult, 186–87; Simeon the Stylite the Elder's use of, 77, 192, 201, 267n120; stylites as, 194–96; symbolism of, 243n16; in Syriac Christianity, 5, 77, 146; trade in, 82, 245n8; transformative qualities of, 82; in *Transitus Mariae*, 90–98, 197, 273n197, 274n200, 277nn221,226; in Trinitarian theology, 142, 143; vapor, 147; in *Vita* of Simeon the Stylite, 192. *See also* Frankincense; Piety, incense

Incorruptibility: fragrance of, 191; ointment of, 53

Inhaling, and consuming, 132

Intellectuals, Christian: classical legacy of, 106; incarnation theology of, 230; in non-Christian society, 105–6; perfume imagery of, 122; use of ancient science, 114, 122; use of physical senses, 110

Irenaeus, on sacrifice, 21, 26

Irene of Chrysobalanton, Saint: fragrance of, 203

Isaac (the patriarch), 163; sacrifice of, 127; smell of, 288n106

Isaac the Syrian: on ascetic stench, 204; on prayer, 198; on smells, 1

Isaiah (the prophet), visions of, 169

Islam, Syriac Christianity under, 146

Jacob (bishop of Edessa), on myron, 145, 146

Jacob (bishop of Nisibis), 65, 268n134

Jacob (the patriarch): Ambrose on, 162–63; disguise of, 299n26

Jacob of Serug, 86; Annunciation in, 183–84; on dead souls, 231; on Eucharist, 133, 231; on fragrance, 152; "Homily on Simeon the Stylite," 216–17, 232, 320n119; on Sinful Woman, 151–52, 154, 295n202

Jerome, Saint: on idolatry, 86; on ritual, 86; on Song of Songs, 286n93

Jerusalem: Christian liturgy in, 77, 84; use of incense in, 77

Jerusalem Temple: cult of, 15, 18, 19, 24; destruction of, 16, 19; First, 15, 246n21; incense in, 15–17; sacrifice in, 23

Jesus Christ: and Adam, 131–32; anointment of, 66–67, 73, 86, 120, 121, 148–49, 151, 174; body of, 233; as Bread of Life, 132; breath of, 153, 154; consubstantiality of, 116–18, 119; crucifixion of, 20, 59; descent to Sheol, 132; as Divine Physician, 219; embalming spices of, 326n33; Entry into Jerusalem, 266n107; fragrance of, 45, 64, 71, 90, 123–24, 126, 128–29, 140, 176, 204, 287n103, 300n29; as Fragrance of Life, 132; garment of flesh, 260n29; healing by, 219; as Heavenly Bridegroom, 47, 72, 85, 86, 124, 170; as Levitical High Priest, 30; as Light, 65; olfactory titles of, 147–48; participation in Temple cult, 18; passion narratives of, 11, 12, 18, 72, 168; presence within believer, 133; redemption of body, 61, 88, 233; rejection by Nazarenes, 128; relationship to God, 19; resurrected body of, 229; as sacrifice, 79, 80–81; sacrifices for, 28–29; submission to death, 218–19; Transfiguration of, 169; as Word, 65. *See also* Christology; Incarnation

Job (the patriarch), Ambrose on, 216

Job of Edessa, *Book of Treasures*, 310n184

John (bishop of Ephesus), incense imagery of, 82

John, Deacon, 166

John Cassian, 166; on fragrance, 129; on stench of sin, 300n42

John Chrysostom: on anointment, 69–70; *Baptismal Instructions*, 260n22; catechetical sermons of, 134; fragrance metaphors of, 114–16; on good manners, 221; on holy oil, 74; on incense, 299n20; on

knowledge of God, 114–16, 124, 128; olfactory analogies of, 118; on pagans, 207; on perfume, 114, 203, 206–7; on Satan, 299n19; on sensory experience, 160–61; on Sinful Woman, 150; on spices, 164; on stench, 204; on stench of sin, 73; visual imagery of, 260n22

John Climacus: *The Ladder of Divine Ascent*, 179–80; on putrefaction, 211–12

John Moschus, *Spirtual Meadow*, 166

John of Dalyatha, 311n197

John of Damascus: *On the Divine Images*, 292n171; olfactory imagery of, 118–19; on sensory experience, 1, 3, 87–88

John of Ephesus, *Ecclesiastical History*, 209–10, 317n72

John of Sedre, 293n182

John the Baptist, relics of, 304n100

John the Hermit, 320n113

John the Nazarite, 210

Jonah (prophet), as censer, 82

Joseph and Aseneth, tale of, 257n198; fragrance in, 53–54

Joseph the Hymnographer, 97

Joseph the Visionary, 199, 203–4, 311n198

Joshua the Stylite, 87

Judaism: holy men in, 325n27; incense use in, 14, 15–17, 246n22, 272n181; resurrection in, 322n5, 326n34; under Roman religious policy, 21; sacrifice in, 14, 15–17, 246n21; visuality in, 241n3

Julian of Cappadocia, 14

Julian Saba (martyr), tomb of, 77, 79–80

Julian "the Apostate," 258n4

Justin Martyr, 116

Kassia (hymnographer), 297n223

Kephalaia Gnostica, 303n63

Knowledge: body as instrument of, 224; Byzantine sociology of, 291n151; classical, 106; disembodied, 238; empirical, 140; finite, 175; human capacity for, 128; modes in antiquity, 100; as moral enterprise, 104; through smells, 19

Knowledge, Christian: resurrected body's, 233, 239; ritual scents in, 65–83; salvific, 229–39; telos of, 9; through olfactory experience, 44; through sensory experience, 43

Knowledge of God, 7; body in, 177, 229; fragrance in, 114–15, 124, 153, 239; incomplete, 115; John Chrysostom on, 114–16, 124, 128; knowledge of humanity through, 144; myron in, 145–46; olfactory experience in, 19, 65, 80; Origen on, 107; physical experience of, 141; resurrected body's, 238; sensory experience in, 55, 99, 114, 127, 159, 238; through creation, 83; through incarnation, 259n13; through incense, 148; through liturgy, 143; through scripture, 259n13

Lactantius: on body, 110, 111; on odor and source, 118; on olfaction, 112; *The Phoenix*, 257n202; on sensory experience, 113

Lamps: as adornments, 254n144; scented oil of, 16

Laudanum, Herodotus on, 256n186

Lawrence, Saint: martyrdom of, 204, 208; relics of, 304n100

Lazarus: Ambrose on, 321n128; fragrance of, 221; resurrection of, 217–18, 321n125; and the rich man, 223, 230, 320n116

Leontios of Neapolis, 205

Lepers: desecration by, 209–10; incubation of, 272n181

Letter to Diognetus, 44

Leviticus, incense in, 30

Lewis, C. S., 327n39

Libanius, *Oration II*, 245n10

Libations, in sacrifice, 13

Life of Adam and Eve, olfactory experience in, 50–53

Life of Daniel the Stylite, 187, 310n183

Life of Matrona of Perge, 304n100

Life of Simeon the Stylite the Elder: incense in, 186, 309n163; liturgical context of, 309n163; olfactory imagery in, 188, 197

Life of Simeon the Stylite the Younger: incense in, 187, 194–96; liturgy in, 195; olfactory imagery in, 188, 197; smells in, 195–96

Life of Syncletica, 321n121

Life of Theodore of Sykeon, 304n100

Light: Christ as, 65; source of, 117; Tertullian on, 116; Uncreated, 180

Lilies, fragrance of, 178

Liturgical commentaries, post-Constantinian, 134–48; emergence of, 136; incense in, 135; for monastics, 134–35; purpose of, 135

Liturgy, Byzantine: incense in, 141; myron in, 141, 145, 293n183

Liturgy, Christian: ascetic practice in, 164, 181–86; baptismal, 153; bible in, 181; celestial, 184–85; development of practices, 269n153; divine revelation through, 135; earthly, 137, 184–85; eucharistic, 72, 138, 139; incense in, 75, 76–78, 326n33; instruction through, 148; of interior person, 137; knowledge of God through, 143; in *Life of Simeon the Stylite the Younger*, 195; mirroring of future life, 226; nature in, 84–86; olfactory experience in, 141, 164, 181; as performance, 135; physical sensations in, 66; processions in, 75–76, 266n107; as process of memory, 292n177; purpose of, 137; role of body in, 5; scents of, 2, 75, 76–78, 161, 220; sensory experience of, 83, 84, 87, 137, 143–44, 161, 261n49; of soul, 137; Syriac, 146; in Syriac asceticism, 185; theophoros, 137; threefold, 184–85

Liturgy, post-Constantinian, 134–48; asceticism and, 181; fragrance in, 202; sensory experience in, 225, 261n49

Oil, holy (*continued*)
Testament, 66; olfactory effects of, 73–74; post-Constantinian use of, 7, 69; in reliquaries, 90, 228, 272n184; from saints' tombs, 228; therapeutic use of, 120; for sick, 263nn66,69. *See also* Anointment; Myron

Oil, scented: hygienic, 41; in lamps, 16; paraliturgical use of, 2

Old Testament: anointment in, 67, 121; incense in, 15–16, 295n206

Olfaction, human: Aristotle on, 103–4; biblical references to, 172; chemical process of, 280n27; elusiveness of, 118; Evagrius Ponticus on, 302n63; and free will, 174; Galen on, 104, 280n24; Heraclitus on, 322n6; in human-divine relations, 173; involuntary, 283n39; Lactantius on, 112; as lower sense, 104, 105; Lucretius on, 105, 280n27; moral danger in, 158–62, 215; physiology of, 140; Plato on, 103, 114; purification of, 212; role in other senses, 44; sacred connotations of, 78; scientific understanding of, 278n4, 280n19; spiritual, 172; Theodoret on, 112, 212; Theophrastus on, 104; weakness of, 101, 278n4. *See also* Senses; Smells

Olfactory codes: ambivalent, 100; Mediterranean, 31, 55, 65, 100, 202; violation of, 8

Olfactory experience: of anointment, 67; austerity in, 41–42; of baptism, 71–73; in Christian identity, 3, 7, 12, 58, 125–34; in Christian liturgy, 141, 164, 181; classification of, 31; Dionysius the Areopagite on, 136, 137–41; in divine revelation, 19, 97; in early Christianity, 4, 6, 7, 34, 36; in Enoch I, 49–50, 52; in Ephrem, 127, 309n169; as epistemological tool, 99–100, 108; in extracanonical literature, 53; in hagiography, 193, 197, 205–6; in knowledge of God, 19, 65, 80;

in *Life of Adam and Eve*, 50–53; in martyrdom, 12; moral dimensions of, 206–7; of pagan divinities, 25; Paul the apostle on, 18, 19; religious knowledge through, 44; in resurrection, 9, 125, 132; role in afterlife, 223–24; role in belief, 64–65; role of faith in, 130; in Roman society, 179; in Sinful Woman story, 154; and social class, 30–31; in Syriac Christianity, 5, 182, 197–200; transgressive, 187. *See also* Sensory experience

Olfactory practices: Christian adoption of, 3; constancy of, 169; post-Constantinian, 46, 58, 122, 239; realia of, 6; in religious epistemology, 156

Olive oil: in myron composition, 145; ritual use of, 73

"On Hermits and Desert Dwellers" (verse homily), 185–86

Onnophrius (holy man), 165–66

"On the Sinful Woman" (Ephremic verse homily), 149–50, 153, 295n203

Onyx, 30

Order, divine: accessibility through fragrance, 93

Orient, Syriac: cultural interaction in, 297n217

Origen: on afterlife, 224; on body, 182; on Christ as priest, 30; on circumcision, 45; on holocaust, 28; on incense, 17, 31; on interior senses, 170; on knowledge of God, 107; on physical world, 106; Platonic thought of, 107, 282n34; on sacrifice, 24, 28–29, 38; on sensory experience, 44–45, 106–7, 150, 158; on Sinful Woman, 174; on spiritual senses, 171, 172. Works: *Against Celsus*, 106–7; *Commentary on the Song of Songs*, 172–75, 296n206; *Exhortation to Martyrdom*, 38; *Homilies on Genesis*, 45; *Homilies on Leviticus*, 45–46; *On Sacrifice*, 250n87

Orthodoxy, Greek: myrrh in, 265n101

Pachomius: on paradise, 226; on stench, 208

Paganism: afterlife in, 223; Eusebius on, 249n72; human-divine interaction in, 282n34; icon veneration in, 267n109; incense use in, 25, 78; legislation against, 258n3; revulsion against, 207; underworld in, 322n7. *See also* Antiquity; Deities, pagan; sacrifice, pagan

Pagans: John Chrysostom on, 207; marriage with Christians, 37

Pageantry, post-Constantinian, 58

Paideia, classical: Christian use of, 284n62

Palladius, 203

Palmas, Gregory: *The Triads*, 304n101

Paphnutius, 165

Papyrus flowers, 34

Paradise: Augustine on, 234–35; earthly location of, 256n184; fragrance of, 51, 52, 53, 55, 72, 88, 203, 221, 226, 235–39, 309n169; graphic depictions of, 225; Mary's arrival in, 94; olfactory definition of, 223; sensory experience of, 232

Passion narratives, 11, 12, 72; Ambrose on, 168; sacrifice in, 18

Patermuthius (monk), 226

Patristic theology, analogy in, 121

Paul, Saint: on Christian identity, 105; on fragrance of Christ, 210; on fragrance of knowledge, 114–15; imitation of Bridegroom, 177; on inner and outer person, 170; at Mary's Dormition, 96; on Mosaic law, 312n5; on new man, 318n78; on olfactory experience, 18, 19; relics of, 227; on resurrection, 224; on sacrifice, 18, 20; scent terminology of, 247n39

Paulinus of Nola: on baptism, 74; on Christian celebration, 270n168; on fragrance, 87, 90, 129–30; on odor of death, 202; on personal odor, 127; on relics, 89

Pentecost, fragrance at, 53, 64–65, 261n40

Perception: of divine will, 95; of pagan deities, 102; of resurrected body, 234; and source, 118. *See also* Sense perception

Perfection, Mediterranean belief in, 222

Perfume: ancient industry, 34; Athanasius on, 204, 285n75; Athenaeus on, 253nn126,130; Augustine on, 282n38; biblical, 33; Christian response to, 100; Clement of Alexandria on, 40, 41–42, 100; complexity of, 34; composition of, 32; of courtesans, 299n19; of desert, 318n90; for differing body parts, 34, 253n130; epistemological function of, 154; Greek etymology of, 253n126; in human-divine relations, 55, 152, 304n77; John Chrysostom on, 114, 203, 206–7; medicinal value of, 255n164; moral dangers of, 175; plant, 33; power of, 35; practical aspects of, 123; production methods, 286n91; sellers, 314n44; of virtue, 150, 295n206; in wine, 32; women's use of, 41. *See also* Fragrance

Persecution, as sacrifice, 20

Persia, Christianity in, 294n193

Peter (bishop of Alexandria), 75

Philoctetes, wound of, 13, 320n116

Philo of Alexandria, 170; on body, 182; on incense, 22–23; on sense perception, 280n29

Philosophy, Greco-Roman: Hellenistic, 279n13; sacrifice in, 22–23

Philoxenus of Mabbug: *Ascetic Discourses*, 310–11n187; on gluttony, 207–8; on spiritual senses, 310n187

Phoenix, myth of, 55, 257nn201–2

Physicality, in asceticism, 162

Physical world: Origen on, 106; positive valuation of, 157; post-Constantinian view of, 136

Piacenza Pilgrim, 89

Piety: cultural meanings in, 4; early, 99; material enhancement of, 88; sensory qualities of, 58–59

Piety, devotional, 8; Byzantine, 141–43

Psychagogy, rhetoric of, 315n52
Purity, interior, 191
Putridity: body as, 214–15; John
    Climacus on, 211–12; odor of,
    31, 202
Pythagoras, sacrifices by, 249n64
Pythagoreans, aversion to beans, 312n2

Qal'at Sim'an, 187

Rabbula of Edessa, care of sick, 214
Radegunde, Saint, 213; care of sick, 214
Redemption: of body, 61, 88, 223, 227;
    fragrance as, 203; role of scents in,
    65–66; through saints' bodies, 194
Red Sea, oil from, 272n181
Relics: fragrance of, 228; of martyrs,
    227, 304n100; myrrh-gushing,
    180, 228, 304n100; odor of sanc-
    tity of, 90, 272n183; post-
    Constantinian, 58; of Saint Paul,
    227; transference of, 75; veneration
    of, 86, 227–29
Religion: as embodied activity, 4; sen-
    sory dynamics of, 241n4
Religion, Greco-Roman: incense in, 78,
    245n8; sacrifice in, 21–22. See also
    Paganism
Reliquaries: holy oil in, 90, 228,
    272n184; jewelry, 228
Renunciants, Christian, 169
Repentance, ritual, 149
Resurrection, 171; Augustine on, 233;
    effect on nature, 259n20; Ephrem
    on, 232, 236–37; foreshadowing
    of, 218; in Judaism, 322n5,
    326n34; olfactory experience in, 9,
    125, 132; Paul on, 224; of senses,
    327n39; sensory experience of,
    221, 229; Tertullian on, 327n36. See
    also Body, resurrected
Revelation, book of: in Syriac canon,
    328n65
Revelation, divine: to body, 224; olfac-
    tory experience in, 19, 97; through
    creation, 83; through fragrance, 65,
    178; through liturgy, 135; through

nature, 59–65, 85, 106, 202,
    259n15
Revulsion: moral dimensions of, 208;
    physical and moral, 206–7
Rgsh (to feel), 237
Ritual, Christian: apologists for, 26;
    body in, 6–7; cleansing, 16, 200;
    and cultural imagination, 55;
    enrichment of, 86; holy oil in,
    66–75, 122, 145; human-divine
    encounter in, 155; identity in, 87;
    incense in, 2, 75–83, 299n21;
    Jerome on, 86; memory in, 135;
    olfactory imagery in, 5; paraliturgi-
    cal, 99; penitential, 81; post-
    Constantinian, 6–7; of sacrifice,
    148; sensory experience in, 2, 4,
    81; superiority of, 249n66
Ritual, Jewish: incense in, 14, 15–17;
    ostentation in, 22–23
Ritual, pagan: incense in, 25; Lucretius
    on, 23
Ritual, paraliturgical: scented oils in, 2
Ritualization, through incense use,
    269n151
Roman Empire: bubonic plague epi-
    demic in, 209, 316n68; Christian
    triumph in, 156; coronations in,
    290n147; as God's kingdom, 157;
    imperial cults in, 37, 248n52,
    254n144; incarnation theology in,
    113; polytheism of, 21; spice trade
    of, 33; status of Christianity in, 57.
    See also Society, Roman
Romanos the Melodist: on Doubting
    Thomas, 219; Hymn on the Nativity
    (2), 131–32; Kontakion on the
    Three Holy Children, 167, 314n36;
    on Lazarus, 218; "On the Sinful
    Woman," 152–55, 297n217; Syriac
    influence on, 296n217
Rushma (mark), of anointing, 70

Sabaei (Arabian tribe), 35, 36
Sabas, Saint, 129
Sacraments, transformative power of,
    185

Sacrifice: in ancient near east, 246n20; to
Apollo, 244n6; burned, 14, 17, 28,
29, 86; Christ as, 79, 80–81;
Christianity as, 27; in early
Christianity, 17–21, 79, 181;
Clement of Alexandria on, 17,
24–25; effect on demons, 38;
Ephrem on, 267n128; ethical action
in, 29; excessive, 244n6, 249n64;
eucharist as, 151; fragrance of, 45,
164; frankincense in, 12, 13, 23, 34;
God's rejection of, 24; good works
as, 166; in human-divine relationship, 52; incense as, 175; incense in,
6, 13–14, 74, 81, 89, 96; of Isaac,
127; Jewish influence on, 18; in
Mediterranean culture, 12–14;
necessity of, 27; in New Testament,
19; Origen on, 24, 28–29, 38; in
passion narratives, 18; in patristic
writing, 24–29; Paul the apostle on,
18, 20; persecution as, 20; prayer as,
166, 199; in Psalms, 24; relational
aspects of, 21–30; ritual, 148; role in
social order, 13; in scripture, 14–15;
spiritual, 22–23; at tombs, 271n170;
in Torah, 16–17; true and false, 86,
270n164; virginity as, 27. See also
Animal sacrifice; Blood sacrifice
Sacrifice, Jewish, 14, 15–17; implements
of, 246n21
Sacrifice, pagan: Christian criticisms of,
25–26; in Greco-Roman philoso-
phy, 22–23; justifications for, 25;
legislation against, 258n3; Roman,
21–22
Saffron, fragrance of, 178
Saints: bodies of, 8, 194, 227; cults of,
58, 180, 194, 268n143; fragrance
of, 203; holy stench of, 9; illnesses
of, 216–17, 220; odor of sanctity,
227–29; olfactory veneration of,
180, 200; spiritual senses of, 179;
tombs of, 87, 90, 228
Salvation: following illness, 220; fragrance
of, 218; role of body in, 302n61;
Virgin Mary's role in, 96, 97

Sanctification, 62–63
Sanctity: fragrance of, 193, 195; invisible,
139; and stench, 205–6
Sanctuaries, church: censing of, 138, 139
Sarah (wife of Abraham), 288n106
Satan: attacks against Christians, 299n19;
during prayers, 203–4; in Sinful
Woman story, 149–50; stench of,
220; use of stench, 216
Saturninus (proconsul), 22
Saturus (martyr), 53
Scents: of angels, 129; of asceticism,
126; cleansing, 88, 200; cosmology
of, 55; in diagnosis of moral condition, 126–27; effect on perceiver,
116; of flowers, 32; in homilies, 66;
human-divine relations in, 99;
liturgical, 2, 75, 76–78, 161, 220;
medicinal use of, 161; of mourning, 287n101; in mystagogical
commentaries, 5; in participatory
knowing, 65–83; physiological
nature of, 117; ritual, 5; role in
ritual space, 88–89; sacrificial, 124;
therapeutic use of, 299n20. See also
Fragrance; Odor; Smells
Science, ancient: of animals, 278n3;
Christian use of, 114, 122; matter
in, 279n6. See also Medical science,
ancient
Scillitan martyrs, trial of, 22
Scripture, Christian: fragrance of, 203;
knowledge of God through,
259n13; narrative purpose of, 167;
olfactory imagery in, 167; Plato's
compatibility with, 231; sacrifice
in, 14–15. See also Bible
Self: as censer, 182; cleansing of,
182–84; competing emotions in,
171; continuity of, 233; formation
of, 157; and odor, 175; within
Self, 238
Self-control: Clement on, 42; sensory,
39–40, 158
Self-mortification: in asceticism, 169,
319n109; of monastics, 212, 215;
through stench, 215

Sense perception: active and passive, 102; in antiquity, 4–5, 101–2, 250n93; in animals, 101; Aristotle on, 102, 103, 104, 110; of creation, 114; cultural understanding of, 6; early Christian view of, 106; Ephrem on, 238, 260n23; in Epicureanism, 102, 103, 110; Galen on, 110; Hellenistic view of, 103, 279n13; in human-divine interaction, 238, 282n34, 303n63; in incarnation, 127–28; instability of, 102–3; in martyrdom, 12; in Mediterranean, 156; Philo on, 280n29; power of, 1; as physical encounter, 102; by rational mind, 101; as religious knowledge, 239; of resurrected body, 239; role for soul, 100–101; in Stoicism, 103, 104, 110

Senses, 202; ascetic, 210–13; Augustine on, 107–10, 162; austerity regarding, 54; as body-soul bridge, 100–101; carnal, 171; chemical, 280n23; Cicero on, 104, 278n4; control of, 39; Evagrius Ponticus on, 303n63; Gregory of Nyssa on, 111–12, 159–60; location of, 111; Maximus Confessor on, 292n170; negative discourse on, 157, 160; physical, 280n23; in post-Constantinian era, 44; purpose of, 101; in religious epistemology, 4, 5, 7, 110; resurrection of, 327n39; role in sexual licentiousness, 156–57. See also Olfaction, human

Senses, interior, 45–46, 170; in eastern monasticism, 180

Senses, spiritual, 8, 107, 169–80; epistemology of, 303n66; Gregory of Nyssa on, 171, 172, 179, 180; in monasticism, 171, 179, 302n56; mysticism in, 303n66; Origen on, 171, 172; Philoxenus of Mabbug on, 310n187; practical use of, 172; training of, 198

Sensorium, human: design of, 62; incense in, 187; liturgy in, 84;

resurrected, 235; in Syriac tradition, 95

Sensory experience: in antiquity, 100–105; in asceticism, 226–27; Augustine on, 233; in Christian daily life, 30–46, 169; in Christian ritual, 2, 4, 81; Clement of Alexandria on, 39, 43, 46, 150, 158, 159; curiosity in, 162; Dionysius on, 136–38; early Christian writers on, 105–14; effect of baptism on, 61, 63; effect of Eucharist on, 64; effluence in, 102; Ephrem on, 83, 212, 282n49; of eternity, 223; in extracanonical literature, 49; Fall of man as, 223; in formation of self, 157; of future life, 227; of God, 55, 99, 129; in *Gospel of Truth*, 128; Gregory of Nyssa on, 113, 169; in grief, 108; in hagiography, 7, 196; in homilies, 7; John Chrysostom on, 160–61; in knowledge of God, 55, 99, 114, 127, 159, 238; of lay Christians, 160; of liturgy, 83, 84, 87, 137, 143–44, 161, 261n49; Marcus Aurelius on, 158; of miracles, 106; in monasticism, 143, 160; moral danger in, 158–62; moral dangers of, 8; Origen on, 44–45, 106–7, 150, 158; of paradise, 232; as partial knowledge, 114; Plato on, 102; in post-Constantinian liturgy, 225, 261n49; in religious imagination, 56; religious knowledge through, 43, 96; of resurrection, 221, 229; rhetorical strategy of, 316n64; and self-control, 39–40, 158; in sermons, 7; Tertullian on, 38, 43, 46, 158. See also Olfactory experience

Sermons, civic: sensory experience in, 7

Seth, death of, 324n17

Severus of Antioch, Homily 118, 150, 295n206

Severus of Minorca, *Letter on the Conversion of the Jews*, 130–31

Sexuality: in antiquity, 297n2; in post-Constantinian texts, 157

revulsion at, 208; role for lay persons, 97, 98; Syrian astrologers on, 126; transformative capacity of, 177; transgressive, 7, 97, 215, 224. *See also* Fragrance; Odors; Olfaction, human; Olfactory experience; Stench

Smoke, sacrificial, 38

Smyrna, Christians of, 11–12, 46

Society, Roman: aromatics in, 30–31; Christian comportment in, 21–22, 30, 37–40; olfactory experience in, 179

Song of Songs, 72; Ambrose's use of, 122, 125; Athanasius on, 313n28; bridal imagery of, 145, 163, 167–68, 173, 176, 178, 303n63; Christian exegesis of, 286n92; exegesis of, 125; floral imagery of, 123; fragrance in, 122, 145, 173; fragrance of virtue in, 178; Gregory of Nyssa on, 172, 175, 176–79, 296n206; human-divine relations in, 124, 170, 286n92; Jerome's use of, 286n93; Jewish exegesis of, 286n92; as love poetry, 286n92; olfactory imagery of, 108, 124–25, 172–75, 176–79, 252n110; Origen on, 172–75, 296n206; patristic exegesis of, 286n94; in rhetoric of body, 286n93; spices in, 74; spiritual senses in, 172

Sophocles, *Philoctetes*, 245n10

Soteriology, Gregory of Nyssa's, 177

Souls: body and, 63–64, 100–101, 170, 230; cleansing of, 211; decay metaphors for, 211; fragrance of, 206; as garden, 231; housekeeping metaphors for, 211; liturgy of, 137; Platonic, 110; role of sense perception for, 100–101; supremacy over body, 230

Souls, dead, 233; Ephrem on, 232; at Eucharist, 231

Space, ritual: human-divine interaction in, 89; role of scent in, 88–89

Spices: ancient names for, 252n109; in burial rites, 36, 42, 85; in Byzantine era, 74; in embalming of

Christ, 326n33; God's gift of, 51; John Chrysostom on, 164; of Magi, 129; in phoenix myth, 55; preparation of, 32; in Song of Songs, 74; in wine, 35, 253n130, 254n153

Spice trade, ancient, 33, 245n9; international, 17; Pliny the Elder on, 35–36, 253n133

Spikenard (ointment), 173–74

Staniloae, Dumitru, 271n179

Statues, pagan: purifying of, 244n6

Stench: alienation by, 220–21; of avarice, 287n100; in Christian discourse, 8–9; cultural fear of, 208; of damnation, 203; of decadence, 54; of decay, 215; of demons, 65, 208; effect on community, 221; as Fall of man, 218; of heresy, 207; of heretics, 65, 208; imagery of, 206–10; mixture with fragrance, 256n186; moral quality of, 154, 206–10; of mortality, 13, 32, 51, 54, 63, 132, 194, 206–10; of pride, 179; role in disgrace, 209; of Roman prisons, 209; and sanctity, 205–6; of Satan, 220; Satan's use of, 216; self-mortification through, 215; sensory horror of, 217; of sin, 54, 73, 206–10, 218, 300n42; sin as, 175; subjection to, 214

Stench, ascetic, 201–21; devotion through, 213–21; disciplinary use of, 213–14; in hagiographies, 193; problem of, 9; of Simeon the Stylite the Elder, 190–92, 201, 214, 215, 320n110; of Simeon the Stylite the Younger, 215

Stoicism: Cicero on, 280n25; epistemology of, 279n14, 283n49; sense perception in, 103, 104, 110; vision in, 101

Storax, 34, 35, 192, 306n124

Stylites: cults of, 8, 107, 186–87; hagiography of, 186–97, 197; as incense, 194–96; incense piety concerning, 186–97; pilgrimage to, 187, 189; vocation of, 188

Suffering, exterior, 191

Sun, incense offerings to, 253n125

Symbols: cultural, 278n1; of Holy Spirit, 271n179; of immortality, 70; of incense, 243n16; olfactory, 95

Symeon Salos, 166, 205

Symeon the New Theologian, 166, 289n140; on breath of life, 144; Divine Light experience of, 304n101; "Feasts and Holy Communion," 143–44

Syncletica, Saint, 205; on cleansing of soul, 211; gangrene of, 217; on temptation, 214

Synodicon, fragrance in, 88

Table etiquette, Clement on, 39, 254n152

Tertullian: on aromatics, 36–37; on body and soul, 230; on classical knowledge, 106; on funeral rites, 85; guidelines for daily life, 36–38; on light, 116; on physical experience, 59; on sacrifice, 25–26; on sensory experience, 38, 43, 46, 158; on wreaths, 42. Works: "On Baptism," 67; On the Resurrection, 327n36

Testament of Job, date of, 320n117

Thanksgiving, Oil of, 67

Thekeparampil, Jacob, 147, 148, 294n197

Theodora of Thessalonike, Saint, 304n100

Theodore of Amida, 82

Theodore of Mopsuestia: on anointment, 70; catechetical sermons of, 134; on Song of Songs, 286n92

Theodore of Sykeon, 204; stench of, 215

Theodore the Studite, On the Holy Icons, 292n171

Theodoret of Cyrrhus: on body, 110; on incarnation, 219; on incense, 77; on olfaction, 112, 212; visual tropes of, 190, 193, 308n148. Works: History of the Monks of Syria, 320n110; Life of Simeon the Stylite the Elder, 188–90

Theodosius I (Roman emperor), Christian legislation of, 57

Theophilus (bishop of Alexandria), 203

Theophilus (bishop of Antioch), Ad Autolycum, 106

Theophrastus, 4, 110; on animal sacrifice, 23; cosmology of, 31, 251n95; Enquiry into Plants, 33; fragments of, 280n20; on incense, 27; on olfaction, 104. Works: On Odors, 31, 32–33, 35, 36, 286n91; On the Senses, 102–3

Theoprastus, 252n116; and Aristotle, 279n12

Thomas, Doubting, 189, 219

Thomas of Marga, Book of Governors, 311n195

Tobacco, monastics' use of, 318n93

Tobit, book of, 319n108

Tombs: of martyrs, 77, 79–80, 161, 227; miracles at, 270n156; sacrifices at, 271n170; of saints, 87, 90, 228

Torah, sacrifice in, 16–17

Transitus Mariae: Annunciation in, 92, 93, 275n209, 276n218; anti-Chalcedonian milieu of, 275n200; Holy Spirit in, 275n209; human-divine interaction in, 91–92; incense offerings in, 90–98, 197, 273n197, 274n200, 277nn221,226; olfactory imagery in, 274n199; prayer in, 92, 94; Syriac recensions of, 91–98, 197, 274n197; textual history of, 273n197, 274nn199–200, 276n219. See also Mary, Virgin

Treachery, smell of, 299n26

Tree of Judgment, 49–50

Tree of Life, 49

Trees: cedar, 34; cypress, 178; fragrant, 49–50

Trinity, Holy: controversies concerning, 59; fragrance of, 124; Holy Spirit within, 119; incense in, 142, 143; olfactory analogies for, 116–17, 119

True Cross, discovery of, 65

Underworld, pagan, 322n7

Valentinus, Gospel of Truth, 118, 128, 262n62

Vergil, Eclogues, 61

Vestments, priestly: signification of, 135

Vienne, martyrs of, 47, 53
Violence, within Christianity, 57
Virginity: Ambrose on, 167–68; as
    sacrificial offering, 27
Virtue: fragrance of, 162–69, 176, 178,
    300n42; perfume of, 150, 295n206
Vision: ancient theories of, 101–2,
    189–90; in atomistic tradition,
    101–2; Augustine on, 234, 282n37;
    in Byzantine monasticism, 180; in
    Christian culture, 235, 308n149;
    Plato on, 104
Visuality: in Judaism, 241n3; in martyr-
    dom, 12; in post-Constantinian
    Christianity, 241n3

Vologeses (bishop of Nisibis),
    268n134

Wanderers, Syriac, 186
Warfare, spiritual, 216
Will, divine: perception through fra-
    grance, 95
Wine: perfumed, 32; spiced, 35,
    253n130, 254n153; storage of, 34
Women, use of perfume, 41
Wondrous Mountain (Antakya), 187,
    195
Wreaths, 244n6, 255n170; fragrant,
    42–43; in imperial cult, 254n144;
    legislation against, 258n3

Text	10/13 Joanna
Display	Joanna, Syntax
Compositor	International Typesetting and Composition
Printer and binder	Maple-Vail Manufacturing Group